HONDA | ACCORD
2003-11 REPAIR MANUAL

CHILTON'S

**Covers U.S. and Canadian models of Honda Accord
2003 through 2011**

Does not include information specific to hybrid models

by Robert Maddox

CHILTON *Automotive Books*
PUBLISHED BY **HAYNES NORTH AMERICA, Inc.**

AUTOMOTIVE PARTS & ACCESSORIES ASSOCIATION MEMBER

Manufactured in USA
©2011, 2012 Haynes North America, Inc.
ISBN-13: 978-1-62092-006-0
Library of Congress Control Number 2012946873

Haynes Publishing Group
Sparkford Nr Yeovil
Somerset BA22 7JJ England

Haynes North America, Inc
861 Lawrence Drive
Newbury Park
California 91320 USA

ABCDE
FGHIJ
KLMNO
PQRS

8Q1

Contents

Mechanic and photographer with a 2003 Honda Accord

ACKNOWLEDGEMENTS

Technical writers who contributed to this project include Tim Imhoff, Joe L. Hamilton, John Wegmann and Mike Stubblefield. We are grateful to Solution Builders for the origination of wiring diagrams.

About this manual

ITS PURPOSE

The purpose of this manual is to help you get the best value from your vehicle. It can do so in several ways. It can help you decide what work must be done, even if you choose to have it done by a dealer service department or a repair shop; it provides information and procedures for routine maintenance and servicing; and it offers diagnostic and repair procedures to follow when trouble occurs.

We hope you use the manual to tackle the work yourself. For many simpler jobs, doing it yourself may be quicker than arranging an appointment to get the vehicle into a shop and making the trips to leave it and pick it up. More importantly, a lot of money can be saved by avoiding the expense the shop must pass on to you to cover its labor and overhead costs. An added benefit is the sense of satisfaction and accomplishment that you feel after doing the job yourself.

USING THE MANUAL

The manual is divided into Chapters. Each Chapter is divided into numbered Sections. Each Section consists of consecutively numbered paragraphs.

At the beginning of each numbered Section you will be referred to any illustrations which apply to the procedures in that Section. The reference numbers used in illustration captions pinpoint the pertinent Section and the Step within that Section. That is, illustration 3.2 means the illustration refers to Section 3 and Step (or paragraph) 2 within that Section.

Procedures, once described in the text, are not normally repeated. When it's necessary to refer to another Chapter, the reference will be given as Chapter and Section number. Cross references given without use of the word "Chapter" apply to Sections and/or paragraphs in the same Chapter. For example, "see Section 8" means in the same Chapter.

References to the left or right side of the vehicle assume you are sitting in the driver's seat, facing forward.

Even though we have prepared this manual with extreme care, neither the publisher nor the author can accept responsibility for any errors in, or omissions from, the information given.

➡ NOTE

A *Note* provides information necessary to properly complete a procedure or information which will make the procedure easier to understand.

✳ CAUTION

A *Caution* provides a special procedure or special steps which must be taken while completing the procedure where the Caution is found. Not heeding a Caution can result in damage to the assembly being worked on.

✳ WARNING

A *Warning* provides a special procedure or special steps which must be taken while completing the procedure where the Warning is found. Not heeding a Warning can result in personal injury.

Introduction

These models are available in two-door coupe and four-door sedan body styles.

The transversely mounted inline four-cylinder or V6 engines used in these models are equipped with electronic fuel injection.

The engine drives the front wheels through either a five-speed manual or a four-speed automatic transaxle via independent driveaxles.

Independent suspension, featuring coil spring/shock absorber units, is used on all four wheels. The power-assisted rack-and-pinion steering unit is mounted behind the engine.

The brakes are disc at the front and either disc or drum at the rear, with power assist standard. Some models are equipped with Anti-lock Braking Systems (ABS).

Vehicle identification numbers

Modifications are a continuing and unpublicized process in vehicle manufacturing. Since spare parts manuals and lists are compiled on a numerical basis, the individual vehicle numbers are essential to correctly identify the component required.

VEHICLE IDENTIFICATION NUMBER (VIN)

This very important number is stamped on the firewall in the engine compartment and on a plate attached to the dashboard inside the windshield on the driver's side of the vehicle. The VIN also appears on the Vehicle Certificate of Title and Registration. It contains information such as where and when the vehicle was manufactured, the model year and the body style (see illustration).

VIN Engine and model year codes

Two particularly important pieces of information found in the VIN are the engine code and model year code. Counting from the left, the engine code designation is the sixth digit, and the model year code is the first digit after the star symbol at the center of the VIN.

Model year codes

3	2003
4	2004
5	2005
6	2006
7	2007
8	2008
9	2009
A	2010
B	2011

Engine codes

5 = K24A4 (2005 and earlier), 4-door model
5 = K24A8 (2006 and 2007), 4-door model
6 = J30A4 (2005 and earlier), 4-door model
6 = J30A5 (2006 and 2007), 4-door model
7 = K24A4 (2005 and earlier), 2-door model
7 = K24A8 (2006 and 2007), 2-door model
8 = J30A4 (2005 and earlier), 2-door model
8 = J30A5 (2006 and 2007), 2-door model
1 = K24Z3 (2008 and later), 2-door model
2 = K24Z2 (2008 and later), 4-door model
2 = K24Z3 (2008 and later), 4-door model
2 = J35Z2 (2008 and later), 2-door model
2 = J35Z3 (2008 and later), 2-door model
3 = J35Z2 (2008 and later), 4-door model

The Vehicle Safety Certification label is affixed to the bottom of the driver's door pillar

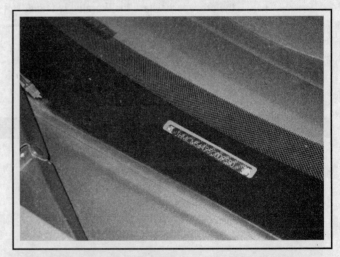

The Vehicle Identification Number (VIN) is stamped into a metal plate fastened to the dashboard on the driver's side - it is visible through the windshield

The engine code number is commonly needed when ordering engine parts. Besides being a component of the VIN, this code can also be found near the right (passenger side) end of the engine, near the exhaust manifold on four-cylinder models (see illustration) or on a pad near the left end of the front cylinder head on V6 models. The engine code is the first five digits of the number. The engines covered by this manual are:

K24A4, K24A8.........2.4L DOHC i-VTEC four-cylinder
J30A4, J30A5..........3.0L SOHC VTEC V6
K24Z2, K24Z3..........i-VTEC four-cylinder
J35Z2............. i-VTEC, Variable Cylinder Management V6
J35Z3.............. i-VTEC V6

TRANSAXLE NUMBER

The transaxle number is commonly needed when ordering transaxle parts. On manual transaxles it's located on the bellhousing, near the starter motor. On automatic transaxles, it's located on the front of the transaxle case, above the dipstick.

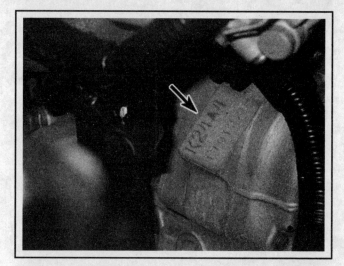

The four-cylinder engine code number (arrow) is located near the exhaust manifold

Buying parts

Replacement parts are available from many sources, which generally fall into one of two categories - authorized dealer parts departments and independent retail auto parts stores. Our advice concerning these parts is as follows:

Retail auto parts stores: Good auto parts stores will stock frequently needed components which wear out relatively fast, such as clutch components, exhaust systems, brake parts, tune-up parts, etc. These stores often supply new or reconditioned parts on an exchange basis, which can save a considerable amount of money. Discount auto parts stores are often very good places to buy materials and parts needed for general vehicle maintenance such as oil, grease, filters, spark plugs, belts, touch-up paint, bulbs, etc. They also usually sell

tools and general accessories, have convenient hours, charge lower prices and can often be found not far from home.

Authorized dealer parts department: This is the best source for parts which are unique to the vehicle and not generally available elsewhere (such as major engine parts, transmission parts, trim pieces, etc.).

Warranty information: If the vehicle is still covered under warranty, be sure that any replacement parts purchased - regardless of the source - do not invalidate the warranty!

To be sure of obtaining the correct parts, have engine and chassis numbers available and, if possible, take the old parts along for positive identification.

MAINTENANCE TECHNIQUES

There are a number of techniques involved in maintenance and repair that will be referred to throughout this manual. Application of these techniques will enable the home mechanic to be more efficient, better organized and capable of performing the various tasks properly, which will ensure that the repair job is thorough and complete.

Fasteners

Fasteners are nuts, bolts, studs and screws used to hold two or more parts together. There are a few things to keep in mind when working with fasteners. Almost all of them use a locking device of some type, either a lockwasher, locknut, locking tab or thread adhesive. All threaded fasteners should be clean and straight, with undamaged threads and undamaged corners on the hex head where the wrench fits. Develop the habit of replacing all damaged nuts and bolts with new ones. Special locknuts with nylon or fiber inserts can only be used once. If they are removed, they lose their locking ability and must be replaced with new ones.

Rusted nuts and bolts should be treated with a penetrating fluid to ease removal and prevent breakage. Some mechanics use turpentine in a spout-type oil can, which works quite well. After applying the rust penetrant, let it work for a few minutes before trying to loosen the nut or bolt. Badly rusted fasteners may have to be chiseled or sawed off or removed with a special nut breaker, available at tool stores.

If a bolt or stud breaks off in an assembly, it can be drilled and removed with a special tool commonly available for this purpose. Most automotive machine shops can perform this task, as well as other repair procedures, such as the repair of threaded holes that have been stripped out.

Flat washers and lockwashers, when removed from an assembly, should always be replaced exactly as removed. Replace any damaged washers with new ones. Never use a lockwasher on any soft metal surface (such as aluminum), thin sheet metal or plastic.

Fastener sizes

For a number of reasons, automobile manufacturers are making wider and wider use of metric fasteners. Therefore, it is important to be able to tell the difference between standard (sometimes called U.S. or SAE) and metric hardware, since they cannot be interchanged.

All bolts, whether standard or metric, are sized according to diameter, thread pitch and length. For example, a standard 1/2 - 13 x 1 bolt is 1/2 inch in diameter, has 13 threads per inch and is 1 inch long. An M12 - 1.75 x 25 metric bolt is 12 mm in diameter, has a thread pitch of 1.75 mm (the distance between threads) and is 25 mm long. The two bolts are nearly identical, and easily confused, but they are not interchangeable.

In addition to the differences in diameter, thread pitch and length, metric and standard bolts can also be distinguished by examining the bolt heads. To begin with, the distance across the flats on a standard bolt head is measured in inches, while the same dimension on a metric bolt is sized in millimeters (the same is true for nuts). As a result, a standard wrench should not be used on a metric bolt and a metric wrench should not be used on a standard bolt. Also, most standard bolts have slashes radiating out from the center of the head to denote the grade or strength of the bolt, which is an indication of the amount of torque that can be applied to it. The greater the number of slashes, the greater the strength of the bolt. Grades 0 through 5 are commonly used on automobiles. Metric bolts have a property class (grade) number, rather than a slash, molded into their heads to indicate bolt strength. In this case, the higher the number, the stronger the bolt. Property class numbers 8.8, 9.8 and 10.9 are commonly used on automobiles.

Strength markings can also be used to distinguish standard hex nuts from metric hex nuts. Many standard nuts have dots stamped into one side, while metric nuts are marked with a number. The greater the number of dots, or the higher the number, the greater the strength of the nut.

Metric studs are also marked on their ends according to property class (grade). Larger studs are numbered (the same as metric bolts), while smaller studs carry a geometric code to denote grade.

It should be noted that many fasteners, especially Grades 0 through 2, have no distinguishing marks on them. When such is the case, the only way to determine whether it is standard or metric is to measure the thread pitch or compare it to a known fastener of the same size.

Standard fasteners are often referred to as SAE, as opposed to metric. However, it should be noted that SAE technically refers to a non-metric fine thread fastener only. Coarse thread non-metric fasteners are referred to as USS sizes.

Since fasteners of the same size (both standard and metric) may have different strength ratings, be sure to reinstall any bolts, studs or nuts removed from your vehicle in their original locations. Also, when replacing a fastener with a new one, make sure that the new one has a strength rating equal to or greater than the original.

Tightening sequences and procedures

Most threaded fasteners should be tightened to a specific torque value (torque is the twisting force applied to a threaded component such as a nut or bolt). Overtightening the fastener can weaken it and cause it to break, while undertightening can cause it to eventually come loose. Bolts, screws and studs, depending on the material they are made of and their thread diameters, have specific torque values, many of which are noted in the Specifications at the end of each Chapter. Be sure to follow the torque recommendations closely. For fasteners not assigned a specific torque, a general torque value chart is presented here as a guide. These torque values are for dry (unlubricated) fasteners threaded into steel or cast iron (not aluminum). As was previously mentioned, the size and grade of a fastener determine the amount of torque that can safely be applied to it. The figures listed here are approximate for Grade 2 and Grade 3 fasteners. Higher grades can tolerate higher torque values.

Fasteners laid out in a pattern, such as cylinder head bolts, oil pan bolts, differential cover bolts, etc., must be loosened or tightened in sequence to avoid warping the component. This sequence will normally be shown in the appropriate Chapter. If a specific pattern is not given, the following procedures can be used to prevent warping.

Initially, the bolts or nuts should be assembled finger-tight only. Next, they should be tightened one full turn each, in a criss-cross or diagonal pattern. After each one has been tightened one full turn, return to the first one and tighten them all one-half turn, following the same

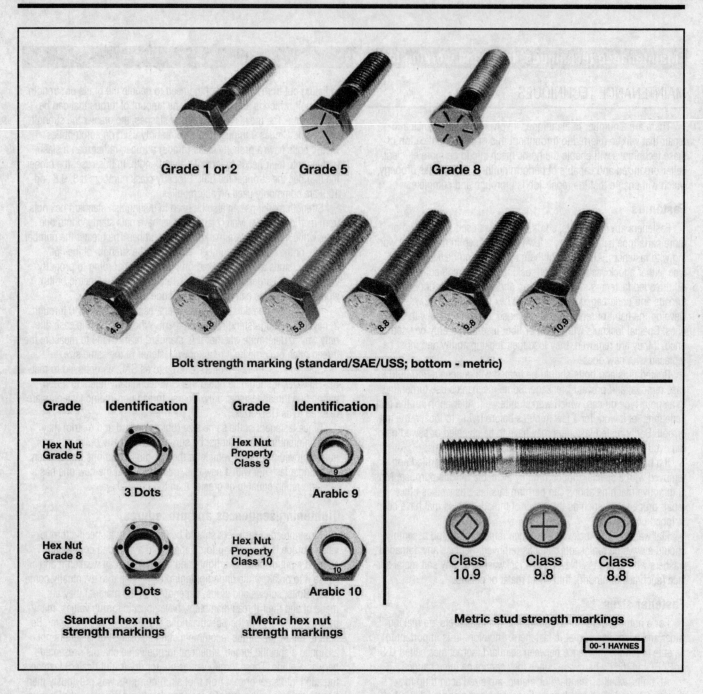

Grade 1 or 2   Grade 5   Grade 8

Bolt strength marking (standard/SAE/USS; bottom - metric)

Grade	Identification
Hex Nut Grade 5	3 Dots
Hex Nut Grade 8	6 Dots

Standard hex nut strength markings

Grade	Identification
Hex Nut Property Class 9	Arabic 9
Hex Nut Property Class 10	Arabic 10

Metric hex nut strength markings

Class 10.9   Class 9.8   Class 8.8

Metric stud strength markings

00-1 HAYNES

pattern. Finally, tighten each of them one-quarter turn at a time until each fastener has been tightened to the proper torque. To loosen and remove the fasteners, the procedure would be reversed.

Component disassembly

Component disassembly should be done with care and purpose to help ensure that the parts go back together properly. Always keep track of the sequence in which parts are removed. Make note of special characteristics or marks on parts that can be installed more than one way, such as a grooved thrust washer on a shaft. It is a good idea to lay the disassembled parts out on a clean surface in the order that they were removed. It may also be helpful to make sketches or take instant photos of components before removal.

When removing fasteners from a component, keep track of their locations. Sometimes threading a bolt back in a part, or putting the washers and nut back on a stud, can prevent mix-ups later. If nuts and bolts cannot be returned to their original locations, they should be kept in a compartmented box or a series of small boxes. A cupcake or muffin tin is ideal for this purpose, since each cavity can hold the bolts and nuts from a particular area (i.e. oil pan bolts, valve cover bolts, engine

Metric thread sizes

	Ft-lbs	Nm
M-6	6 to 9	9 to 12
M-8	14 to 21	19 to 28
M-10	28 to 40	38 to 54
M-12	50 to 71	68 to 96
M-14	80 to 140	109 to 154

Pipe thread sizes

1/8	5 to 8	7 to 10
1/4	12 to 18	17 to 24
3/8	22 to 33	30 to 44
1/2	25 to 35	34 to 47

U.S. thread sizes

1/4 - 20	6 to 9	9 to 12
5/16 - 18	12 to 18	17 to 24
5/16 - 24	14 to 20	19 to 27
3/8 - 16	22 to 32	30 to 43
3/8 - 24	27 to 38	37 to 51
7/16 - 14	40 to 55	55 to 74
7/16 - 20	40 to 60	55 to 81
1/2 - 13	55 to 80	75 to 108

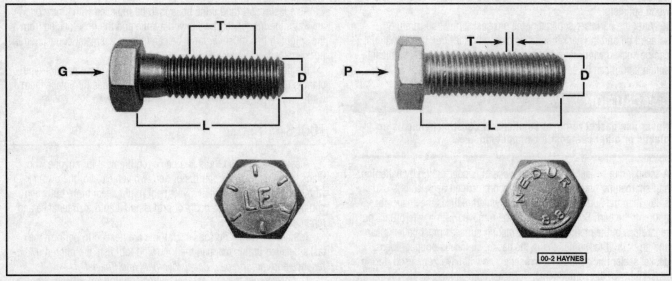

00-2 HAYNES

Standard (SAE and USS) bolt dimensions/grade marks

G   Grade marks (bolt strength)
L   Length (in inches)
T   Thread pitch (number of threads per inch)
D   Nominal diameter (in inches)

Metric bolt dimensions/grade marks

P   Property class (bolt strength)
L   Length (in millimeters)
T   Thread pitch (distance between threads in millimeters)
D   Diameter

mount bolts, etc.). A pan of this type is especially helpful when working on assemblies with very small parts, such as the carburetor, alternator, valve train or interior dash and trim pieces. The cavities can be marked with paint or tape to identify the contents.

Whenever wiring looms, harnesses or connectors are separated, it is a good idea to identify the two halves with numbered pieces of masking tape so they can be easily reconnected.

Gasket sealing surfaces

Throughout any vehicle, gaskets are used to seal the mating surfaces between two parts and keep lubricants, fluids, vacuum or pressure contained in an assembly.

Many times these gaskets are coated with a liquid or paste-type gasket sealing compound before assembly. Age, heat and pressure can sometimes cause the two parts to stick together so tightly that they are very difficult to separate. Often, the assembly can be loosened by striking it with a soft-face hammer near the mating surfaces. A regular hammer can be used if a block of wood is placed between the hammer and the part. Do not hammer on cast parts or parts that could be easily damaged. With any particularly stubborn part, always recheck to make sure that every fastener has been removed.

Avoid using a screwdriver or bar to pry apart an assembly, as they

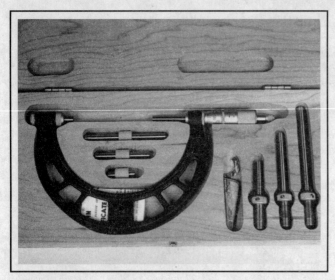

Micrometer set

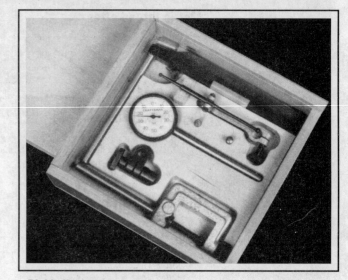

Dial indicator set

can easily mar the gasket sealing surfaces of the parts, which must remain smooth. If prying is absolutely necessary, use an old broom handle, but keep in mind that extra clean up will be necessary if the wood splinters.

After the parts are separated, the old gasket must be carefully scraped off and the gasket surfaces cleaned. Stubborn gasket material can be soaked with rust penetrant or treated with a special chemical to soften it so it can be easily scraped off.

✳✳ CAUTION:

Never use gasket removal solutions or caustic chemicals on plastic or other composite components.

A scraper can be fashioned from a piece of copper tubing by flattening and sharpening one end. Copper is recommended because it is usually softer than the surfaces to be scraped, which reduces the chance of gouging the part. Some gaskets can be removed with a wire brush, but regardless of the method used, the mating surfaces must be left clean and smooth. If for some reason the gasket surface is gouged, then a gasket sealer thick enough to fill scratches will have to be used during reassembly of the components. For most applications, a non-drying (or semi-drying) gasket sealer should be used.

Hose removal tips

✳✳ WARNING:

If the vehicle is equipped with air conditioning, do not disconnect any of the A/C hoses without first having the system depressurized by a dealer service department or a service station.

Hose removal precautions closely parallel gasket removal precautions. Avoid scratching or gouging the surface that the hose mates against or the connection may leak. This is especially true for radiator hoses. Because of various chemical reactions, the rubber in hoses can bond itself to the metal spigot that the hose fits over. To remove a hose, first loosen the hose clamps that secure it to the spigot. Then, with slip-joint pliers, grab the hose at the clamp and rotate it around the spigot. Work it back and forth until it is completely free, then pull it off. Silicone or other lubricants will ease removal if they can be applied

between the hose and the outside of the spigot. Apply the same lubricant to the inside of the hose and the outside of the spigot to simplify installation.

As a last resort (and if the hose is to be replaced with a new one anyway), the rubber can be slit with a knife and the hose peeled from the spigot. If this must be done, be careful that the metal connection is not damaged.

If a hose clamp is broken or damaged, do not reuse it. Wire-type clamps usually weaken with age, so it is a good idea to replace them with screw-type clamps whenever a hose is removed.

TOOLS

A selection of good tools is a basic requirement for anyone who plans to maintain and repair his or her own vehicle. For the owner who has few tools, the initial investment might seem high, but when compared to the spiraling costs of professional auto maintenance and repair, it is a wise one.

To help the owner decide which tools are needed to perform the tasks detailed in this manual, the following tool lists are offered: *Maintenance and minor repair, Repair/overhaul and Special.*

The newcomer to practical mechanics should start off with the *maintenance and minor repair* tool kit, which is adequate for the simpler jobs performed on a vehicle. Then, as confidence and experience grow, the owner can tackle more difficult tasks, buying additional tools as they are needed. Eventually the basic kit will be expanded into the *repair and overhaul* tool set. Over a period of time, the experienced do-it-yourselfer will assemble a tool set complete enough for most repair and overhaul procedures and will add tools from the special category when it is felt that the expense is justified by the frequency of use.

Maintenance and minor repair tool kit

The tools in this list should be considered the minimum required for performance of routine maintenance, servicing and minor repair work. We recommend the purchase of combination wrenches (box-end and open-end combined in one wrench). While more expensive than open end wrenches, they offer the advantages of both types of wrench.

Combination wrench set (1/4-inch to 1 inch or 6 mm to 19 mm)
Adjustable wrench, 8 inch
Spark plug wrench with rubber insert

Spark plug gap adjusting tool
Feeler gauge set
Brake bleeder wrench
Standard screwdriver (5/16-inch x 6 inch)
Phillips screwdriver (No. 2 x 6 inch)
Combination pliers - 6 inch
Hacksaw and assortment of blades
Tire pressure gauge
Grease gun

Oil can
Fine emery cloth
Wire brush
Battery post and cable cleaning tool
Oil filter wrench
Funnel (medium size)
Safety goggles
Jackstands (2)
Drain pan

Dial caliper

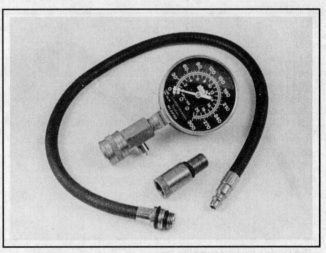

Hand-operated vacuum pump

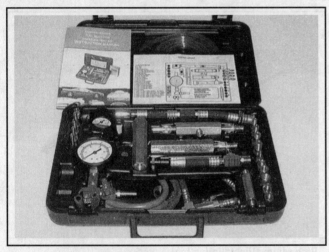

Fuel pressure gauge set

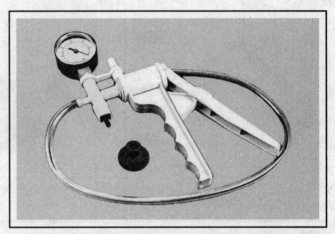

Compression gauge with spark plug hole adapter

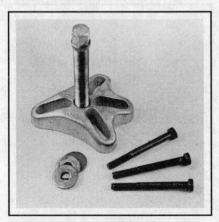

Damper/steering wheel puller

General purpose puller

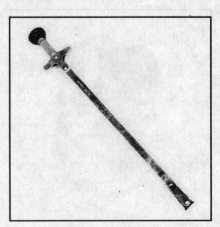

Hydraulic lifter removal tool

➡Note: If basic tune-ups are going to be part of routine maintenance, it will be necessary to purchase a good quality stroboscopic timing light and combination tachometer/dwell meter. Although they are included in the list of special tools, it is mentioned here because they are absolutely necessary for tuning most vehicles properly.

Repair and overhaul tool set

These tools are essential for anyone who plans to perform major repairs and are in addition to those in the maintenance and minor repair tool kit. Included is a comprehensive set of sockets which, though expensive, are invaluable because of their versatility, especially when various extensions and drives are available. We recommend the 1/2-inch drive over the 3/8-inch drive. Although the larger drive is bulky and more expensive, it has the capacity of accepting a very wide range of large sockets. Ideally, however, the mechanic should have a 3/8-inch drive set and a 1/2-inch drive set.

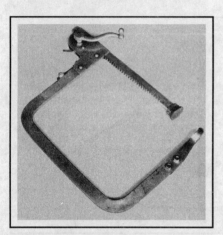

Valve spring compressor

Valve spring compressor

Ridge reamer

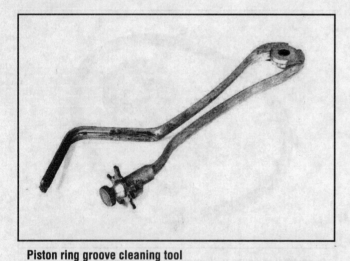

Piston ring groove cleaning tool

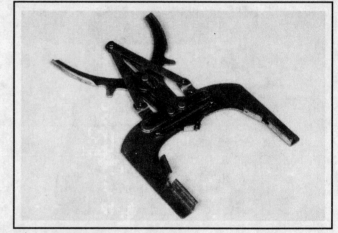

Ring removal/installation tool

Ring compressor

Cylinder hone

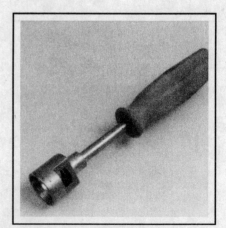

Brake hold-down spring tool

Torque angle gauge

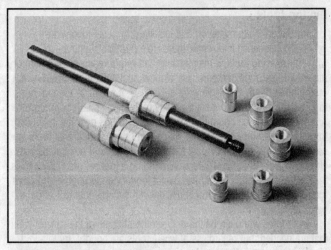

Clutch plate alignment tool

Socket set(s)
Reversible ratchet
Extension - 10 inch
Universal joint
Torque wrench (same size drive as sockets)
Ball peen hammer - 8 ounce
Soft-face hammer (plastic/rubber)
Standard screwdriver (1/4-inch x 6 inch)
Standard screwdriver (stubby - 5/16-inch)
Phillips screwdriver (No. 3 x 8 inch)
Phillips screwdriver (stubby - No. 2)
Pliers - vise grip
Pliers - lineman's
Pliers - needle nose
Pliers - snap-ring (internal and external)
Cold chisel - 1/2-inch
Scribe
Scraper (made from flattened copper tubing)
Centerpunch
Pin punches (1/16, 1/8, 3/16-inch)
Steel rule/straightedge - 12 inch
Allen wrench set (1/8 to 3/8-inch or 4 mm to 10 mm)
A selection of files
Wire brush (large)
Jackstands (second set)
Jack (scissor or hydraulic type)

➡**Note: Another tool which is often useful is an electric drill with a chuck capacity of 3/8-inch and a set of good quality drill bits.**

Special tools

The tools in this list include those which are not used regularly, are expensive to buy, or which need to be used in accordance with their manufacturer's instructions. Unless these tools will be used frequently, it is not very economical to purchase many of them. A consideration would be to split the cost and use between yourself and a friend or friends. In addition, most of these tools can be obtained from a tool rental shop on a temporary basis.

This list primarily contains only those tools and instruments widely available to the public, and not those special tools produced by the vehicle manufacturer for distribution to dealer service departments. Occasionally, references to the manufacturer's special tools are included in the text of this manual. Generally, an alternative method of doing the job without the special tool is offered. However, sometimes there is no alternative to their use. Where this is the case, and the tool cannot be purchased or borrowed, the work should be turned over to the dealer service department or an automotive repair shop.

Valve spring compressor
Piston ring groove cleaning tool
Piston ring compressor
Piston ring installation tool
Cylinder compression gauge
Cylinder ridge reamer
Cylinder surfacing hone
Cylinder bore gauge
Micrometers and/or dial calipers
Hydraulic lifter removal tool
Balljoint separator
Universal-type puller
Impact screwdriver
Dial indicator set
Stroboscopic timing light (inductive pick-up)
Hand operated vacuum/pressure pump
Tachometer/dwell meter
Universal electrical multimeter
Cable hoist
Brake spring removal and installation tools
Floor jack

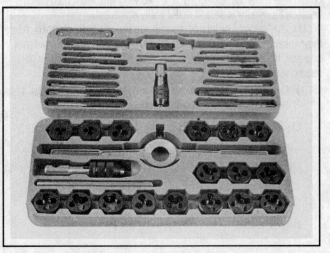

Tap and die set

Buying tools

For the do-it-yourselfer who is just starting to get involved in vehicle maintenance and repair, there are a number of options available when purchasing tools. If maintenance and minor repair is the extent of the work to be done, the purchase of individual tools is satisfactory. If, on the other hand, extensive work is planned, it would be a good idea to purchase a modest tool set from one of the large retail chain stores. A set can usually be bought at a substantial savings over the individual tool prices, and they often come with a tool box. As additional tools are needed, add-on sets, individual tools and a larger tool box can be purchased to expand the tool selection. Building a tool set gradually allows the cost of the tools to be spread over a longer period of time and gives the mechanic the freedom to choose only those tools that will actually be used.

Tool stores will often be the only source of some of the special tools that are needed, but regardless of where tools are bought, try to avoid cheap ones, especially when buying screwdrivers and sockets, because they won't last very long. The expense involved in replacing cheap tools will eventually be greater than the initial cost of quality tools.

Care and maintenance of tools

Good tools are expensive, so it makes sense to treat them with respect. Keep them clean and in usable condition and store them properly when not in use. Always wipe off any dirt, grease or metal chips before putting them away. Never leave tools lying around in the work area. Upon completion of a job, always check closely under the hood for tools that may have been left there so they won't get lost during a test drive.

Some tools, such as screwdrivers, pliers, wrenches and sockets, can be hung on a panel mounted on the garage or workshop wall, while others should be kept in a tool box or tray. Measuring instruments, gauges, meters, etc. must be carefully stored where they cannot be damaged by weather or impact from other tools.

When tools are used with care and stored properly, they will last a very long time. Even with the best of care, though, tools will wear out if used frequently. When a tool is damaged or worn out, replace it. Subsequent jobs will be safer and more enjoyable if you do.

HOW TO REPAIR DAMAGED THREADS

Sometimes, the internal threads of a nut or bolt hole can become stripped, usually from overtightening. Stripping threads is an all-too-common occurrence, especially when working with aluminum parts, because aluminum is so soft that it easily strips out.

Usually, external or internal threads are only partially stripped. After they've been cleaned up with a tap or die, they'll still work. Sometimes, however, threads are badly damaged. When this happens, you've got three choices:

1) *Drill and tap the hole to the next suitable oversize and install a larger diameter bolt, screw or stud.*

2) *Drill and tap the hole to accept a threaded plug, then drill and tap the plug to the original screw size. You can also buy a plug already threaded to the original size. Then you simply drill a hole to the specified size, then run the threaded plug into the hole with a bolt and jam nut. Once the plug is fully seated, remove the jam nut and bolt.*

3) *The third method uses a patented thread repair kit like Heli-Coil or Slimsert. These easy-to-use kits are designed to repair damaged threads in straight-through holes and blind holes. Both are available as kits which can handle a variety of sizes and thread patterns. Drill the hole, then tap it with the special included tap. Install the Heli-Coil and the hole is back to its original diameter and thread pitch.*

Regardless of which method you use, be sure to proceed calmly and carefully. A little impatience or carelessness during one of these relatively simple procedures can ruin your whole day's work and cost you a bundle if you wreck an expensive part.

WORKING FACILITIES

Not to be overlooked when discussing tools is the workshop. If anything more than routine maintenance is to be carried out, some sort of suitable work area is essential.

It is understood, and appreciated, that many home mechanics do not have a good workshop or garage available, and end up removing an engine or doing major repairs outside. It is recommended, however, that the overhaul or repair be completed under the cover of a roof.

A clean, flat workbench or table of comfortable working height is an absolute necessity. The workbench should be equipped with a vise that has a jaw opening of at least four inches.

As mentioned previously, some clean, dry storage space is also required for tools, as well as the lubricants, fluids, cleaning solvents, etc. which soon become necessary.

Sometimes waste oil and fluids, drained from the engine or cooling system during normal maintenance or repairs, present a disposal problem. To avoid pouring them on the ground or into a sewage system, pour the used fluids into large containers, seal them with caps and take them to an authorized disposal site or recycling center. Plastic jugs, such as old antifreeze containers, are ideal for this purpose.

Always keep a supply of old newspapers and clean rags available. Old towels are excellent for mopping up spills. Many mechanics use rolls of paper towels for most work because they are readily available and disposable. To help keep the area under the vehicle clean, a large cardboard box can be cut open and flattened to protect the garage or shop floor.

Whenever working over a painted surface, such as when leaning over a fender to service something under the hood, always cover it with an old blanket or bedspread to protect the finish. Vinyl covered pads, made especially for this purpose, are available at auto parts stores.

acking and towing

> ✳✳ **WARNING:**
>
> **The jack supplied with the vehicle should only be used for changing a tire or placing jackstands under the frame. Never work under the vehicle or start the engine while this jack is being used as the only means of support.**

The vehicle should be on level ground. Place the shift lever in Park, if you have an automatic, or Reverse if you have a manual transaxle. Block the wheel diagonally opposite the wheel being changed. Set the parking brake.

Remove the spare tire and jack from stowage. Remove the wheel cover and trim ring (if so equipped) with the tapered end of the lug nut wrench by inserting and twisting the handle and then prying against the back of the wheel cover.

> ✳ **CAUTION:**
>
> **On some models, the wheel cover can't be removed by prying; the wheel nuts must be removed first. Loosen, but do not remove, the lug nuts (one-half turn is sufficient).**

Place the scissors-type jack under the side of the vehicle and adjust the jack height until the slot in the jack head engages with the raised portion of the ridge on the vertical rocker panel flange nearest the wheel to be changed. There is a front and rear jacking point on each side of the vehicle (see illustration).

The jacking points are located near the front and rear wheel on each side of the vehicle

Turn the jack handle clockwise until the tire clears the ground. Remove the lug nuts and pull the wheel off. Replace it with the spare.

Install the lug nuts with the beveled edges facing in. Tighten them snugly. Don't attempt to tighten them completely until the vehicle is lowered or it could slip off the jack. Turn the jack handle counterclockwise to lower the vehicle. Remove the jack and tighten the lug nuts in a criss-cross pattern.

Install the cover (and trim ring, if used) and be sure it's snapped into place all the way around.

Stow the tire, jack and wrench. Unblock the wheels.

TOWING

As a general rule, the vehicle should be towed with the front (drive) wheels off the ground (the best method is to have the vehicle placed on a flat-bed tow truck). If they can't be raised, place them on a dolly. The ignition key must be in the OFF position, since the steering lock mechanism isn't strong enough to hold the front wheels straight while towing.

Vehicles equipped with an automatic transaxle can be towed from the front with all four wheels on the ground, provided that speeds don't exceed 35 mph and the distance is not over 50 miles. Before towing, check the transmission fluid level (see Chapter 1). If the level is below the HOT line on the dipstick, add fluid or use a towing dolly. Additionally, perform the following steps:

a) *Release the parking brake*
b) *Start the engine*
c) *Move the transaxle gear selector into D, then to Neutral*
d) *Turn off the engine*
e) *Place the ignition key in the OFF (not the LOCK position).*

> ✳✳ **CAUTION:**
>
> **Never tow a vehicle with an automatic transaxle from the rear with the front wheels on the ground.**

When towing a vehicle equipped with a manual transaxle with all four wheels on the ground, be sure to place the shift lever in neutral and release the parking brake.

Equipment specifically designed for towing should be used. It should be attached to the main structural members of the vehicle, not the bumpers or brackets.

Safety is a major consideration when towing and all applicable state and local laws must be obeyed. A safety chain system must be used at all times. Remember that power steering and power brakes will not work with the engine off.

Booster battery (jump) starting

Observe these precautions when using a booster battery to start a vehicle:

a) *Before connecting the booster battery, make sure the ignition switch is in the Off position.*
b) *Turn off the lights, heater and other electrical loads.*
c) *Your eyes should be shielded. Safety goggles are a good idea.*
d) *Make sure the booster battery is the same voltage as the dead one in the vehicle.*
e) *The two vehicles MUST NOT TOUCH each other!*
f) *Make sure the transaxle is in Neutral (manual) or Park (automatic).*
g) *If the booster battery is not a maintenance-free type, remove the vent caps and lay a cloth over the vent holes.*

Connect the red jumper cable to the positive (+) terminals of each battery (see illustration).

Connect one end of the black jumper cable to the negative (-) terminal of the booster battery. The other end of this cable should be connected to a good ground on the vehicle to be started, such as a bolt or bracket on the body.

Start the engine using the booster battery, then, with the engine running at idle speed, disconnect the jumper cables in the reverse order of connection.

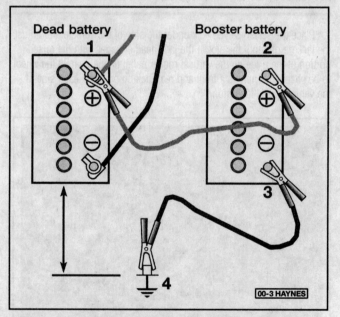

Make the booster battery cable connections in the numerical order shown (note that the negative cable of the booster battery is NOT attached to the negative terminal of the dead battery)

Automotive chemicals and lubricants

A number of automotive chemicals and lubricants are available for use during vehicle maintenance and repair. They include a wide variety of products ranging from cleaning solvents and degreasers to lubricants and protective sprays for rubber, plastic and vinyl.

CLEANERS

Carburetor cleaner and choke cleaner is a strong solvent for gum, varnish and carbon. Most carburetor cleaners leave a dry-type lubricant film which will not harden or gum up. Because of this film it is not recommended for use on electrical components.

Brake system cleaner is used to remove brake dust, grease and brake fluid from the brake system, where clean surfaces are absolutely necessary. It leaves no residue and often eliminates brake squeal caused by contaminants.

Electrical cleaner removes oxidation, corrosion and carbon deposits from electrical contacts, restoring full current flow. It can also be used to clean spark plugs, carburetor jets, voltage regulators and other parts where an oil-free surface is desired.

Demoisturants remove water and moisture from electrical components such as alternators, voltage regulators, electrical connectors and fuse blocks. They are non-conductive and non-corrosive.

Degreasers are heavy-duty solvents used to remove grease from the outside of the engine and from chassis components. They can be sprayed or brushed on and, depending on the type, are rinsed off either with water or solvent.

LUBRICANTS

Motor oil is the lubricant formulated for use in engines. It normally contains a wide variety of additives to prevent corrosion and reduce foaming and wear. Motor oil comes in various weights (viscosity ratings) from 0 to 50. The recommended weight of the oil depends on the season, temperature and the demands on the engine. Light oil is used in cold climates and under light load conditions. Heavy oil is used in hot climates and where high loads are encountered. Multi-viscosity oils are designed to have characteristics of both light and heavy oils and are available in a number of weights from 0W-20 to 20W-50.

Gear oil is designed to be used in differentials, manual transmissions and other areas where high-temperature lubrication is required.

Chassis and wheel bearing grease is a heavy grease used where increased loads and friction are encountered, such as for wheel bearings, ball-joints, tie-rod ends and universal joints.

High-temperature wheel bearing grease is designed to withstand the extreme temperatures encountered by wheel bearings in disc brake equipped vehicles. It usually contains molybdenum disulfide (moly), which is a dry-type lubricant.

White grease is a heavy grease for metal-to-metal applications where water is a problem. White grease stays soft under both low and high temperatures (usually from -100 to +190-degrees F), and will not wash off or dilute in the presence of water.

Assembly lube is a special extreme pressure lubricant, usually containing moly, used to lubricate high-load parts (such as main and rod bearings and cam lobes) for initial start-up of a new engine. The assembly lube lubricates the parts without being squeezed out or washed away until the engine oiling system begins to function.

Silicone lubricants are used to protect rubber, plastic, vinyl and nylon parts.

Graphite lubricants are used where oils cannot be used due to contamination problems, such as in locks. The dry graphite will lubricate metal parts while remaining uncontaminated by dirt, water, oil or acids. It is electrically conductive and will not foul electrical contacts in locks such as the ignition switch.

Moly penetrants loosen and lubricate frozen, rusted and corroded fasteners and prevent future rusting or freezing.

Heat-sink grease is a special electrically non-conductive grease that is used for mounting electronic ignition modules where it is essential that heat is transferred away from the module.

SEALANTS

RTV sealant is one of the most widely used gasket compounds. Made from silicone, RTV is air curing, it seals, bonds, waterproofs, fills surface irregularities, remains flexible, doesn't shrink, is relatively easy to remove, and is used as a supplementary sealer with almost all low and medium temperature gaskets.

Anaerobic sealant is much like RTV in that it can be used either to seal gaskets or to form gaskets by itself. It remains flexible, is solvent resistant and fills surface imperfections. The difference between an anaerobic sealant and an RTV-type sealant is in the curing. RTV cures when exposed to air, while an anaerobic sealant cures only in the absence of air. This means that an anaerobic sealant cures only after the assembly of parts, sealing them together.

Thread and pipe sealant is used for sealing hydraulic and pneumatic fittings and vacuum lines. It is usually made from a Teflon compound, and comes in a spray, a paint-on liquid and as a wrap-around tape.

CHEMICALS

Anti-seize compound prevents seizing, galling, cold welding, rust and corrosion in fasteners. High-temperature anti-seize, usually made with copper and graphite lubricants, is used for exhaust system and exhaust manifold bolts.

Anaerobic locking compounds are used to keep fasteners from vibrating or working loose and cure only after installation, in the absence of air. Medium strength locking compound is used for small nuts, bolts and screws that may be removed later. High-strength locking compound is for large nuts, bolts and studs which aren't removed on a regular basis.

Oil additives range from viscosity index improvers to chemical treatments that claim to reduce internal engine friction. It should be noted that most oil manufacturers caution against using additives with their oils.

Gas additives perform several functions, depending on their chemical makeup. They usually contain solvents that help dissolve gum and varnish that build up on carburetor, fuel injection and intake parts. They also serve to break down carbon deposits that form on the inside surfaces of the combustion chambers. Some additives contain upper cylinder lubricants for valves and piston rings, and others contain chemicals to remove condensation from the gas tank.

MISCELLANEOUS

Brake fluid is specially formulated hydraulic fluid that can withstand the heat and pressure encountered in brake systems. Care must be taken so this fluid does not come in contact with painted surfaces or plastics. An opened container should always be resealed to prevent contamination by water or dirt.

Weatherstrip adhesive is used to bond weatherstripping around doors, windows and trunk lids. It is sometimes used to attach trim pieces.

Undercoating is a petroleum-based, tar-like substance that is designed to protect metal surfaces on the underside of the vehicle from corrosion. It also acts as a sound-deadening agent by insulating the bottom of the vehicle.

Waxes and polishes are used to help protect painted and plated surfaces from the weather. Different types of paint may require the use of different types of wax and polish. Some polishes utilize a chemical or abrasive cleaner to help remove the top layer of oxidized (dull) paint on older vehicles. In recent years many non-wax polishes that contain a wide variety of chemicals such as polymers and silicones have been introduced. These non-wax polishes are usually easier to apply and last longer than conventional waxes and polishes.

CONVERSION FACTORS

LENGTH (distance)

Inches (in)	X 25.4	= Millimeters (mm)	X 0.0394	= Inches (in)
Feet (ft)	X 0.305	= Meters (m)	X 3.281	= Feet (ft)
Miles	X 1.609	= Kilometers (km)	X 0.621	= Miles

VOLUME (capacity)

Cubic inches (cu in; in³)	X 16.387	= Cubic centimeters (cc; cm³)	X 0.061	= Cubic inches (cu in; in³)
Imperial pints (Imp pt)	X 0.568	= Liters (l)	X 1.76	= Imperial pints (Imp pt)
Imperial quarts (Imp qt)	X 1.137	= Liters (l)	X 0.88	= Imperial quarts (Imp qt)
Imperial quarts (Imp qt)	X 1.201	= US quarts (US qt)	X 0.833	= Imperial quarts (Imp qt)
US quarts (US qt)	X 0.946	= Liters (l)	X 1.057	= US quarts (US qt)
Imperial gallons (Imp gal)	X 4.546	= Liters (l)	X 0.22	= Imperial gallons (Imp gal)
Imperial gallons (Imp gal)	X 1.201	= US gallons (US gal)	X 0.833	= Imperial gallons (Imp gal)
US gallons (US gal)	X 3.785	= Liters (l)	X 0.264	= US gallons (US gal)

MASS (weight)

Ounces (oz)	X 28.35	= Grams (g)	X 0.035	= Ounces (oz)
Pounds (lb)	X 0.454	= Kilograms (kg)	X 2.205	= Pounds (lb)

FORCE

Ounces-force (ozf; oz)	X 0.278	= Newtons (N)	X 3.6	= Ounces-force (ozf; oz)
Pounds-force (lbf; lb)	X 4.448	= Newtons (N)	X 0.225	= Pounds-force (lbf; lb)
Newtons (N)	X 0.1	= Kilograms-force (kgf; kg)	X 9.81	= Newtons (N)

PRESSURE

Pounds-force per square inch (psi; lbf/in²; lb/in²)	X 0.070	= Kilograms-force per square centimeter (kgf/cm²; kg/cm²)	X 14.223	= Pounds-force per square inch (psi; lbf/in²; lb/in²)
Pounds-force per square inch (psi; lbf/in²; lb/in²)	X 0.068	= Atmospheres (atm)	X 14.696	= Pounds-force per square inch (psi; lbf/in²; lb/in²)
Pounds-force per square inch (psi; lbf/in²; lb/in²)	X 0.069	= Bars	X 14.5	= Pounds-force per square inch (psi; lbf/in²; lb/in²)
Pounds-force per square inch (psi; lbf/in²; lb/in²)	X 6.895	= Kilopascals (kPa)	X 0.145	= Pounds-force per square inch (psi; lbf/in²; lb/in²)
Kilopascals (kPa)	X 0.01	= Kilograms-force per square centimeter (kgf/cm²; kg/cm²)	X 98.1	= Kilopascals (kPa)

TORQUE (moment of force)

Pounds-force inches (lbf in; lb in)	X 1.152	= Kilograms-force centimeter (kgf cm; kg cm)	X 0.868	= Pounds-force inches (lbf in; lb in)
Pounds-force inches (lbf in; lb in)	X 0.113	= Newton meters (Nm)	X 8.85	= Pounds-force inches (lbf in; lb in)
Pounds-force inches (lbf in; lb in)	X 0.083	= Pounds-force feet (lbf ft; lb ft)	X 12	= Pounds-force inches (lbf in; lb in)
Pounds-force feet (lbf ft; lb ft)	X 0.138	= Kilograms-force meters (kgf m; kg m)	X 7.233	= Pounds-force feet (lbf ft; lb ft)
Pounds-force feet (lbf ft; lb ft)	X 1.356	= Newton meters (Nm)	X 0.738	= Pounds-force feet (lbf ft; lb ft)
Newton meters (Nm)	X 0.102	= Kilograms-force meters (kgf m; kg m)	X 9.804	= Newton meters (Nm)

VACUUM

Inches mercury (in. Hg)	X 3.377	= Kilopascals (kPa)	X 0.2961	= Inches mercury
Inches mercury (in. Hg)	X 25.4	= Millimeters mercury (mm Hg)	X 0.0394	= Inches mercury

POWER

Horsepower (hp)	X 745.7	= Watts (W)	X 0.0013	= Horsepower (hp)

VELOCITY (speed)

Miles per hour (miles/hr; mph)	X 1.609	= Kilometers per hour (km/hr; kph)	X 0.621	= Miles per hour (miles/hr; mph)

FUEL CONSUMPTION *

Miles per gallon, Imperial (mpg)	X 0.354	= Kilometers per liter (km/l)	X 2.825	= Miles per gallon, Imperial (mpg)
Miles per gallon, US (mpg)	X 0.425	= Kilometers per liter (km/l)	X 2.352	= Miles per gallon, US (mpg)

TEMPERATURE

Degrees Fahrenheit = (°C x 1.8) + 32   Degrees Celsius (Degrees Centigrade; °C) = (°F - 32) x 0.56

*It is common practice to convert from miles per gallon (mpg) to liters/100 kilometers (l/100km), where mpg (Imperial) x l/100 km = 282 and mpg (US) x l/100 km = 235

FRACTION/DECIMAL/MILLIMETER EQUIVALENTS

DECIMALS TO MILLIMETERS

Decimal	mm	Decimal	mm
0.001	0.0254	0.500	12.7000
0.002	0.0508	0.510	12.9540
0.003	0.0762	0.520	13.2080
0.004	0.1016	0.530	13.4620
0.005	0.1270	0.540	13.7160
0.006	0.1524	0.550	13.9700
0.007	0.1778	0.560	14.2240
0.008	0.2032	0.570	14.4780
0.009	0.2286	0.580	14.7320
		0.590	14.9860
0.010	0.2540		
0.020	0.5080		
0.030	0.7620		
0.040	1.0160	0.600	15.2400
0.050	1.2700	0.610	15.4940
0.060	1.5240	0.620	15.7480
0.070	1.7780	0.630	16.0020
0.080	2.0320	0.640	16.2560
0.090	2.2860	0.650	16.5100
		0.660	16.7640
0.100	2.5400	0.670	17.0180
0.110	2.7940	0.680	17.2720
0.120	3.0480	0.690	17.5260
0.130	3.3020		
0.140	3.5560		
0.150	3.8100		
0.160	4.0640	0.700	17.7800
0.170	4.3180	0.710	18.0340
0.180	4.5720	0.720	18.2880
0.190	4.8260	0.730	18.5420
		0.740	18.7960
0.200	5.0800	0.750	19.0500
0.210	5.3340	0.760	19.3040
0.220	5.5880	0.770	19.5580
0.230	5.8420	0.780	19.8120
0.240	6.0960	0.790	20.0660
0.250	6.3500		
0.260	6.6040		
0.270	6.8580	0.800	20.3200
0.280	7.1120	0.810	20.5740
0.290	7.3660	0.820	21.8280
		0.830	21.0820
0.300	7.6200	0.840	21.3360
0.310	7.8740	0.850	21.5900
0.320	8.1280	0.860	21.8440
0.330	8.3820	0.870	22.0980
0.340	8.6360	0.880	22.3520
0.350	8.8900	0.890	22.6060
0.360	9.1440		
0.370	9.3980		
0.380	9.6520		
0.390	9.9060	0.900	22.8600
0.400	10.1600	0.910	23.1140
0.410	10.4140	0.920	23.3680
0.420	10.6680	0.930	23.6220
0.430	10.9220	0.940	23.8760
0.440	11.1760	0.950	24.1300
0.450	11.4300	0.960	24.3840
0.460	11.6840	0.970	24.6380
0.470	11.9380	0.980	24.8920
0.480	12.1920	0.990	25.1460
0.490	12.4460	1.000	25.4000

FRACTIONS TO DECIMALS TO MILLIMETERS

Fraction	Decimal	mm	Fraction	Decimal	mm
1/64	0.0156	0.3969	33/64	0.5156	13.0969
1/32	0.0312	0.7938	17/32	0.5312	13.4938
3/64	0.0469	1.1906	35/64	0.5469	13.8906
1/16	0.0625	1.5875	9/16	0.5625	14.2875
5/64	0.0781	1.9844	37/64	0.5781	14.6844
3/32	0.0938	2.3812	19/32	0.5938	15.0812
7/64	0.1094	2.7781	39/64	0.6094	15.4781
1/8	0.1250	3.1750	5/8	0.6250	15.8750
9/64	0.1406	3.5719	41/64	0.6406	16.2719
5/32	0.1562	3.9688	21/32	0.6562	16.6688
11/64	0.1719	4.3656	43/64	0.6719	17.0656
3/16	0.1875	4.7625	11/16	0.6875	17.4625
13/64	0.2031	5.1594	45/64	0.7031	17.8594
7/32	0.2188	5.5562	23/32	0.7188	18.2562
15/64	0.2344	5.9531	47/64	0.7344	18.6531
1/4	0.2500	6.3500	3/4	0.7500	19.0500
17/64	0.2656	6.7469	49/64	0.7656	19.4469
9/32	0.2812	7.1438	25/32	0.7812	19.8438
19/64	0.2969	7.5406	51/64	0.7969	20.2406
5/16	0.3125	7.9375	13/16	0.8125	20.6375
21/64	0.3281	8.3344	53/64	0.8281	21.0344
11/32	0.3438	8.7312	27/32	0.8438	21.4312
23/64	0.3594	9.1281	55/64	0.8594	21.8281
3/8	0.3750	9.5250	7/8	0.8750	22.2250
25/64	0.3906	9.9219	57/64	0.8906	22.6219
13/32	0.4062	10.3188	29/32	0.9062	23.0188
27/64	0.4219	10.7156	59/64	0.9219	23.4156
7/16	0.4375	11.1125	15/16	0.9375	23.8125
29/64	0.4531	11.5094	61/64	0.9531	24.2094
15/32	0.4688	11.9062	31/32	0.9688	24.6062
31/64	0.4844	12.3031	63/64	0.9844	25.0031
1/2	0.5000	12.7000	1	1.0000	25.4000

Safety first!

Regardless of how enthusiastic you may be about getting on with the job at hand, take the time to ensure that your safety is not jeopardized. A moment's lack of attention can result in an accident, as can failure to observe certain simple safety precautions. The possibility of an accident will always exist, and the following points should not be considered a comprehensive list of all dangers. Rather, they are intended to make you aware of the risks and to encourage a safety conscious approach to all work you carry out on your vehicle.

ESSENTIAL DOS AND DON'TS

DON'T rely on a jack when working under the vehicle. Always use approved jackstands to support the weight of the vehicle and place them under the recommended lift or support points.

DON'T attempt to loosen extremely tight fasteners (i.e. wheel lug nuts) while the vehicle is on a jack - it may fall.

DON'T start the engine without first making sure that the transmission is in Neutral (or Park where applicable) and the parking brake is set.

DON'T remove the radiator cap from a hot cooling system - let it cool or cover it with a cloth and release the pressure gradually.

DON'T attempt to drain the engine oil until you are sure it has cooled to the point that it will not burn you.

DON'T touch any part of the engine or exhaust system until it has cooled sufficiently to avoid burns.

DON'T siphon toxic liquids such as gasoline, antifreeze and brake fluid by mouth, or allow them to remain on your skin.

DON'T inhale brake lining dust - it is potentially hazardous (see Asbestos below).

DON'T allow spilled oil or grease to remain on the floor - wipe it up before someone slips on it.

DON'T use loose fitting wrenches or other tools which may slip and cause injury.

DON'T push on wrenches when loosening or tightening nuts or bolts. Always try to pull the wrench toward you. If the situation calls for pushing the wrench away, push with an open hand to avoid scraped knuckles if the wrench should slip.

DON'T attempt to lift a heavy component alone - get someone to help you.

DON'T rush or take unsafe shortcuts to finish a job.

DON'T allow children or animals in or around the vehicle while you are working on it.

DO wear eye protection when using power tools such as a drill, sander, bench grinder, etc. and when working under a vehicle.

DO keep loose clothing and long hair well out of the way of moving parts.

DO make sure that any hoist used has a safe working load rating adequate for the job.

DO get someone to check on you periodically when working alone on a vehicle.

DO carry out work in a logical sequence and make sure that everything is correctly assembled and tightened.

DO keep chemicals and fluids tightly capped and out of the reach of children and pets.

DO remember that your vehicle's safety affects that of yourself and others. If in doubt on any point, get professional advice.

STEERING, SUSPENSION AND BRAKES

These systems are essential to driving safety, so make sure you have a qualified shop or individual check your work. Also, compressed suspension springs can cause injury if released suddenly - be sure to use a spring compressor.

AIRBAGS

Airbags are explosive devices that can CAUSE injury if they deploy while you're working on the vehicle. Follow the manufacturer's instructions to disable the airbag whenever you're working in the vicinity of airbag components.

ASBESTOS

Certain friction, insulating, sealing, and other products - such as brake linings, brake bands, clutch linings, torque converters, gaskets, etc. - may contain asbestos or other hazardous friction material. Extreme care must be taken to avoid inhalation of dust from such products, since it is hazardous to health. If in doubt, assume that they do contain asbestos.

FIRE

Remember at all times that gasoline is highly flammable. Never smoke or have any kind of open flame around when working on a vehicle. But the risk does not end there. A spark caused by an electrical short circuit, by two metal surfaces contacting each other, or even by static electricity built up in your body under certain conditions, can ignite gasoline vapors, which in a confined space are highly explosive. Do not, under any circumstances, use gasoline for cleaning parts. Use an approved safety solvent.

Always disconnect the battery ground (-) cable at the battery before working on any part of the fuel system or electrical system. Never risk spilling fuel on a hot engine or exhaust component. It is strongly recommended that a fire extinguisher suitable for use on fuel and electrical fires be kept handy in the garage or workshop at all times. Never try to extinguish a fuel or electrical fire with water.

FUMES

Certain fumes are highly toxic and can quickly cause unconsciousness and even death if inhaled to any extent. Gasoline vapor falls into this category, as do the vapors from some cleaning solvents. Any draining or pouring of such volatile fluids should be done in a well ventilated area.

When using cleaning fluids and solvents, read the instructions on the container carefully. Never use materials from unmarked containers.

Never run the engine in an enclosed space, such as a garage. Exhaust fumes contain carbon monoxide, which is extremely poisonous. If you need to run the engine, always do so in the open air, or at least have the rear of the vehicle outside the work area.

THE BATTERY

Never create a spark or allow a bare light bulb near a battery. They normally give off a certain amount of hydrogen gas, which is highly explosive.

Always disconnect the battery ground (-) cable at the battery before working on the fuel or electrical systems.

If possible, loosen the filler caps or cover when charging the battery from an external source (this does not apply to sealed or maintenance-free batteries). Do not charge at an excessive rate or the battery may burst.

Take care when adding water to a non maintenance-free battery and when carrying a battery. The electrolyte, even when diluted, is very corrosive and should not be allowed to contact clothing or skin.

Always wear eye protection when cleaning the battery to prevent the caustic deposits from entering your eyes.

HOUSEHOLD CURRENT

When using an electric power tool, inspection light, etc., which operates on household current, always make sure that the tool is correctly connected to its plug and that, where necessary, it is properly grounded. Do not use such items in damp conditions and, again, do not create a spark or apply excessive heat in the vicinity of fuel or fuel vapor.

SECONDARY IGNITION SYSTEM VOLTAGE

A severe electric shock can result from touching certain parts of the ignition system (such as the spark plug wires) when the engine is running or being cranked, particularly if components are damp or the insulation is defective. In the case of an electronic ignition system, the secondary system voltage is much higher and could prove fatal.

HYDROFLUORIC ACID

This extremely corrosive acid is formed when certain types of synthetic rubber, found in some O-rings, oil seals, fuel hoses, etc. are exposed to temperatures above 750-degrees F (400-degrees C). The rubber changes into a charred or sticky substance containing the acid. *Once formed, the acid remains dangerous for years. If it gets onto the skin, it may be necessary to amputate the limb concerned.*

When dealing with a vehicle which has suffered a fire, or with components salvaged from such a vehicle, wear protective gloves and discard them after use.

Troubleshooting

CONTENTS

This section provides an easy reference guide to the more common problems which may occur during the operation of your vehicle. These problems and their possible causes are grouped under headings denoting various components or systems, such as Engine, Cooling system, etc. They also refer you to the chapter and/or section which deals with the problem.

Remember that successful troubleshooting is not a mysterious black art practiced only by professional mechanics. It is simply the result of the right knowledge combined with an intelligent, systematic approach to the problem. Always work by a process of elimination, starting with the simplest solution and working through to the most complex - and never overlook the obvious. Anyone can run the gas tank dry or leave the lights on overnight, so don't assume that you are exempt from such oversights.

Finally, always establish a clear idea of why a problem has occurred and take steps to ensure that it doesn't happen again. If the electrical system fails because of a poor connection, check the other connections in the system to make sure that they don't fail as well. If a particular fuse continues to blow, find out why - don't just replace one fuse after another. Remember, failure of a small component can often be indicative of potential failure or incorrect functioning of a more important component or system.

ENGINE

1   Engine will not rotate when attempting to start

1   Battery terminal connections loose or corroded (Chapter 1).
2   Battery discharged or faulty (Chapter 1).
3   Automatic transmission not completely engaged in Park (Chapter 7) or clutch not completely depressed (Chapter 8).
4   Broken, loose or disconnected wiring in the starting circuit (Chapters 5 and 12).
5   Starter motor pinion jammed in flywheel ring gear (Chapter 5).
6   Starter solenoid faulty (Chapter 5).
7   Starter motor faulty (Chapter 5).
8   Ignition switch faulty (Chapter 12).
9   Starter pinion or flywheel teeth worn or broken (Chapter 5).

2   Engine rotates but will not start

1   Fuel tank empty.
2   Battery discharged (engine rotates slowly) (Chapter 5).
3   Battery terminal connections loose or corroded (Chapter 1).
4   Leaking fuel injector(s), faulty fuel pump, pressure regulator, etc. (Chapter 4).
5   Fuel not reaching fuel rail (Chapter 4).
6   Ignition components damp or damaged (Chapter 5).
7   Worn, faulty or incorrectly gapped spark plugs (Chapter 1).
8   Broken, loose or disconnected wiring in the starting circuit (Chapter 5).
9   Broken or stripped timing belt (Chapter 2).
10   Defective fuel pump relay and/or harness at relay (Chapter 4)

3   Engine hard to start when cold

1   Battery discharged or low (Chapter 1).
2   Malfunctioning fuel system (Chapter 4).
3   Injector(s) leaking (Chapter 4).

4   Engine hard to start when hot

1   Air filter clogged (Chapter 1).
2   Fuel not reaching the fuel injection system (Chapter 4).
3   Corroded battery connections, especially ground (Chapter 1).
4   Malfunctioning EVAP system (Chapter 6)

5   Starter motor noisy or excessively rough in engagement

1   Pinion or flywheel gear teeth worn or broken (Chapter 5).
2   Starter motor mounting bolts loose or missing (Chapter 5).

6   Engine starts but stops immediately

1   Loose or faulty electrical connections at coil or alternator (Chapter 5).
2   Insufficient fuel reaching the fuel injector(s) (Chapters 1 and 4).
3   Vacuum leak at the gasket between the intake manifold and throttle body (Chapters 1 and 4).

7   Oil puddle under engine

1   Oil pan gasket and/or oil pan drain bolt washer leaking (Chapter 2).
2   Oil pressure sending unit leaking (Chapter 2).
3   Valve head cover(s) leaking (Chapter 2).
4   Engine oil seals leaking (Chapter 2).

8   Engine lopes while idling or idles erratically

1   Vacuum leakage (Chapters 2 and 4).
2   Defective EGR valve (Chapter 6).
3   Air filter clogged (Chapter 1).
4   Fuel pump not delivering sufficient fuel to the fuel injection system (Chapter 4).
5   Fuel pulsation damper faulty (Chapter 4)
6   Leaking head gasket (Chapter 2).
7   Timing belt and/or sprockets worn (Chapter 2).
8   Camshaft lobes worn (Chapter 2).
9   Problem in Engine Mount Control System (Chapter 2).

9   Engine misses at idle speed

1   Spark plugs worn or not gapped properly (Chapter 1).
2   Vacuum leaks (Chapter 1).
3   Uneven or low compression (Chapter 2).

10   Engine misses throughout driving speed range

1   Fuel filter clogged and/or impurities in the fuel system (Chapter 1).
2   Low fuel pressure (Chapter 4).

3   Faulty or incorrectly gapped spark plugs (Chapter 1).
4   Faulty emission system components (Chapter 6).
5   Low or uneven cylinder compression pressures (Chapter 2).
6   Weak or faulty ignition system (Chapter 5).
7   Vacuum leak in fuel injection system (Chapter 4), intake manifold (Chapters 2A/2B), fuel injection air control valve (Chapter 6) or vacuum hoses.

11   Engine stumbles on acceleration

1   Spark plugs fouled (Chapter 1).
2   Fuel injection system faulty (Chapter 4).
3   Fuel filter clogged (Chapters 1 and 4).
4   Incorrect ignition timing (Chapter 5).
5   Intake air leak (Chapters 2 and 4).

12   Engine surges while holding accelerator steady

1   Intake air leak (Chapter 4).
2   Fuel pump faulty (Chapter 4).
3   Loose fuel injector wire harness connectors (Chapter 4).
4   Defective ECU or information sensor (Chapter 6).

13   Engine stalls

1   Fuel filter clogged and/or water and impurities in the fuel system (Chapters 1 and 4).
2   Faulty emissions system components (Chapter 6).
3   Faulty or incorrectly gapped spark plugs (Chapter 1).
4   Vacuum leak in the intake manifold or vacuum hoses (Chapters 2 and 4).
5   Valve clearances incorrectly set (Chapters 1 and 2).

14   Engine lacks power

1   Faulty or incorrectly gapped spark plugs (Chapter 1).
2   Fuel injection system malfunction (Chapter 4).
3   Faulty coil(s) (Chapter 5).
4   Brakes binding (Chapter 9).
5   Automatic transaxle fluid level incorrect (Chapter 1).
6   Clutch slipping (Chapter 8).
7   Fuel filter clogged and/or impurities in the fuel system (Chapters 1 and 4).
8   Emission control system not functioning properly (Chapter 6).
9   Low or uneven cylinder compression pressures (Chapter 2).
10 Obstructed exhaust system (Chapter 4).

15   Engine backfires

1   Emission control system not functioning properly (Chapter 6).
2   Fuel injection system malfunctioning (Chapter 4).
3   Vacuum leak at fuel injector(s), intake manifold, air control valve or vacuum hoses (Chapters 2 and 4).
4   Valve clearances incorrectly set and/or valves sticking (Chapters 1 and 2).

16   Pinging or knocking engine sounds during acceleration or uphill

1   Incorrect grade of fuel.

2   Fuel injection system faulty (Chapter 4).
3   Improper or damaged spark plugs (Chapter 1).
4   EGR valve not functioning (Chapter 6).
5   Vacuum leak (Chapters 2 and 4).

17   Engine runs with oil pressure light on

1   Low oil level (Chapter 1).
2   Short in wiring circuit (Chapter 12).
3   Faulty oil pressure sender (Chapter 2).
4   Worn engine bearings and/or oil pump (Chapter 2).

18   Engine diesels (continues to run) after switching off

1   Leaking fuel injector (Chapter 4).
2   Faulty Powertrain Control Module (Chapter 6).
3   Faulty Body Control Module.
4   Faulty ignition switch.

ENGINE ELECTRICAL SYSTEM

19   Battery will not hold a charge

1   Drivebelt defective (Chapter 1).
2   Battery electrolyte level low (Chapter 1).
3   Battery terminals loose or corroded (Chapter 1).
4   Alternator not charging properly (Chapter 5).
5   Loose, broken or faulty wiring in the charging circuit (Chapter 5).
6   Short in vehicle wiring (Chapter 12).
7   Internally defective battery (Chapters 1 and 5).

20   Alternator light fails to go out

1   Faulty alternator or charging circuit (Chapter 5).
2   Drivebelt defective (Chapter 1).
3   Alternator voltage regulator inoperative (Chapter 5).

21   Alternator light fails to come on when key is turned on

1   Warning light bulb defective (Chapter 5).
2   Fault in the printed circuit, dash wiring or bulb holder (Chapter 12).

FUEL SYSTEM

22   Excessive fuel consumption

Dirty or clogged air filter element (Chapter 1).

23   Fuel leakage and/or fuel odor

1   Leaking fuel feed or return line (Chapters 1 and 4).
2   Tank overfilled.
3   Evaporative canister filter clogged (Chapters 1 and 6).
4   Fuel injector internal parts excessively worn (Chapter 4).

COOLING SYSTEM

24 Overheating

1 Insufficient coolant in system (Chapter 1).
2 Radiator core blocked or grille restricted (Chapter 3).
3 Thermostat faulty (Chapter 3).
4 Electric coolant fan circuit problem (Chapter 3).
5 Radiator cap not maintaining proper pressure (Chapter 3).

25 Overcooling

1 Faulty thermostat (Chapter 3).
2 Inaccurate temperature gauge sending unit (Chapter 3).
3 Electric coolant fan circuit problem (Chapter 3).

26 External coolant leakage

1 Deteriorated/damaged hoses; loose clamps (Chapters 1 and 3).
2 Water pump defective (Chapter 3).
3 Leakage from radiator core or coolant reservoir bottle (Chapter 3).
4 Engine drain or water jacket core plugs leaking (Chapter 2).

27 Internal coolant leakage

1 Leaking cylinder head gasket (Chapter 2).
2 Cracked cylinder bore or cylinder head (Chapter 2).

28 Coolant loss

1 Too much coolant in system (Chapter 1).
2 Coolant boiling away because of overheating (Chapter 3).
3 Internal or external leakage (Chapter 3).
4 Faulty radiator cap (Chapter 3).

29 Poor coolant circulation

1 Inoperative water pump (Chapter 3).
2 Restriction in cooling system (Chapters 1 and 3).
3 Thermostat sticking (Chapter 3).

CLUTCH

30 Pedal travels to floor - no pressure or very little resistance

1 No fluid in reservoir (Chapter 1)
2 Faulty clutch master cylinder, release cylinder or hydraulic line (Chapter 8).
3 Broken release bearing or fork (Chapter 8).

31 Unable to select gears

1 Faulty transaxle (Chapter 7).
2 Faulty clutch disc (Chapter 8).

3 Release lever and bearing not assembled properly (Chapter 8).
4 Faulty pressure plate (Chapter 8).
5 Pressure plate-to-flywheel bolts loose (Chapter 8).

32 Clutch slips (engine speed increases with no increase in vehicle speed)

1 Clutch plate worn (Chapter 8).
2 Clutch plate is oil soaked by leaking rear main seal (Chapter 8).
3 Clutch plate not seated. It may take 30 or 40 normal starts for a new one to seat.
4 Warped pressure plate or flywheel (Chapter 8).
5 Weak diaphragm spring (Chapter 8).
6 Clutch plate overheated. Allow to cool.

33 Grabbing (chattering) as clutch is engaged

1 Oil on clutch plate lining, burned or glazed facings (Chapter 8).
2 Worn or loose engine or transaxle mounts (Chapters 2 and 7).
3 Worn splines on clutch plate hub (Chapter 8).
4 Warped pressure plate or flywheel (Chapter 8).
5 Burned or smeared resin on flywheel or pressure plate (Chapter 8).

34 Transaxle rattling (clicking)

1 Release lever loose (Chapter 8).
2 Clutch plate damper spring failure (Chapter 8).
3 Low engine idle speed (Chapter 1).

35 Noise in clutch area

1 Fork shaft improperly installed (Chapter 8).
2 Faulty bearing (Chapter 8).

36 Clutch pedal stays on floor

1 Faulty clutch master or release cylinder (Chapter 8).
2 Broken release bearing or fork (Chapter 8).

37 High pedal effort

1 Piston binding in bore of clutch master or release cylinder (Chapter 8).
2 Pressure plate faulty (Chapter 8).

MANUAL TRANSAXLE

38 Knocking noise at low speeds

1 Worn driveaxle constant velocity (CV) joints (Chapter 8).
2 Worn driveaxle bore in differential case (Chapter 7A).*

39 Noise most pronounced when turning

Differential gear noise (Chapter 7A).*

40 Clunk on acceleration or deceleration

1 Loose engine or transaxle mounts (Chapters 2 and 7A).
2 Worn differential pinion shaft in case.*
3 Worn driveaxle bore in differential case (Chapter 7A).*
4 Worn or damaged driveaxle inboard CV joints (Chapter 8).

41 Clicking noise in turns

Worn or damaged outboard CV joint (Chapter 8).

42 Vibration

1 Rough wheel bearing (Chapters 1 and 10).
2 Damaged driveaxle (Chapter 8).
3 Out of round tires (Chapter 1).
4 Tire out of balance (Chapters 1 and 10).
5 Worn CV joint (Chapter 8).

43 Noisy in neutral with engine running

1 Damaged input gear bearing (Chapter 7A).*
2 Damaged clutch release bearing (Chapter 8).

44 Noisy in one particular gear

1 Damaged or worn constant mesh gears (Chapter 7A).*
2 Damaged or worn synchronizers (Chapter 7A).*
3 Bent reverse fork (Chapter 7A).*
4 Damaged fourth speed gear or output gear (Chapter 7A).*
5 Worn or damaged reverse idler gear or idler bushing (Chapter 7A).*

45 Noisy in all gears

1 Insufficient lubricant (Chapter 7A).
2 Damaged or worn bearings (Chapter 7A).*
3 Worn or damaged input gear shaft and/or output gear shaft (Chapter 7A).*

46 Slips out of gear

1 Worn or improperly adjusted linkage (Chapter 7A).
2 Transaxle loose on engine (Chapter 7A).
3 Shift linkage does not work freely, binds (Chapter 7A).
4 Input gear bearing retainer broken or loose (Chapter 7A).*
5 Dirt between clutch cover and engine block (Chapter 7A).
6 Worn shift fork (Chapter 7A).*

47 Leaks lubricant

1 Driveaxle oil seals worn (Chapter 7).
2 Excessive amount of lubricant in transaxle (Chapters 1 and 7A).
3 Loose or broken input gear shaft bearing retainer (Chapter 7A).*
4 Input gear bearing retainer O-ring and/or lip seal damaged (Chapter 7A).*

48 Locked in gear

Lock pin or interlock pin missing (Chapter 7A).*
* Although the corrective action necessary to remedy the symptoms described is beyond the scope of the home mechanic, the above information should be helpful in isolating the cause of the condition so that the owner can communicate clearly with a professional mechanic.

AUTOMATIC TRANSAXLE

➡Note: Due to the complexity of the automatic transaxle, it is difficult for the home mechanic to properly diagnose and service this component. For problems other than the following, the vehicle should be taken to a dealer or transmission shop.

49 Fluid leakage

1 Automatic transmission fluid is a deep red color. Fluid leaks should not be confused with engine oil, which can easily be blown onto the transaxle by air flow.
2 To pinpoint a leak, first remove all built-up dirt and grime from the transaxle housing with degreasing agents and/or steam cleaning. Then drive the vehicle at low speeds so air flow will not blow the leak far from its source. Raise the vehicle and determine where the leak is coming from. Common areas of leakage are:
   a) Pan (Chapters 1 and 7)
   b) Dipstick tube (Chapters 1 and 7)
   c) Transaxle oil lines (Chapter 7)
   d) Speed sensor (Chapter 7)

50 Transaxle fluid brown or has a burned smell

Transaxle fluid burned (Chapter 1).

51 General shift mechanism problems

1 Chapter 7, Part B, deals with checking and adjusting the shift linkage on automatic transaxles. Common problems which may be attributed to poorly adjusted linkage are:
   a) Engine starting in gears other than Park or Neutral.
   b) Indicator on shifter pointing to a gear other than the one actually being used.
   c) Vehicle moves when in Park.
2 Refer to Chapter 7B for the shift linkage adjustment procedure.

52 Transaxle will not downshift with accelerator pedal pressed to the floor

Throttle valve cable out of adjustment (Chapter 7B).

53 Engine will start in gears other than Park or Neutral

Neutral start switch malfunctioning (Chapter 7B).

54 Transaxle slips, shifts roughly, is noisy or has no drive in forward or reverse gears

There are many probable causes for the above problems, but the home mechanic should be concerned with only one possibility - fluid level. Before taking the vehicle to a repair shop, check the level and condition of the fluid as described in Chapter 1. Correct the fluid level as necessary or change the fluid and filter if needed. If the problem persists, have a professional diagnose the cause.

DRIVEAXLES

55 Clicking noise in turns

Worn or damaged outboard CV joint (Chapter 8).

56 Shudder or vibration during acceleration

1 Excessive toe-in (Chapter 10).
2 Incorrect spring heights (Chapter 10).
3 Worn or damaged inboard or outboard CV joints (Chapter 8).
4 Sticking inboard CV joint assembly (Chapter 8).

57 Vibration at highway speeds

1 Out of balance front wheels and/or tires (Chapters 1 and 10).
2 Out of round front tires (Chapters 1 and 10).
3 Worn CV joint(s) (Chapter 8).

BRAKES

➡Note: Before assuming that a brake problem exists, make sure that:

a) *The tires are in good condition and properly inflated (Chapter 1).*
b) *The front end alignment is correct (Chapter 10).*
c) *The vehicle is not loaded with weight in an unequal manner.*

58 Vehicle pulls to one side during braking

1 Incorrect tire pressures (Chapter 1).
2 Front end out of line (have the front end aligned).
3 Front, or rear, tires not matched to one another.
4 Restricted brake lines or hoses (Chapter 9).
5 Malfunctioning drum brake or caliper assembly (Chapter 9).
6 Loose suspension parts (Chapter 10).
7 Loose calipers (Chapter 9).
8 Excessive wear of brake shoe or pad material or disc/drum on one side.

59 Noise (high-pitched squeal when the brakes are applied)

Front disc brake pads worn out. The noise comes from the wear sensor rubbing against the disc (does not apply to all vehicles). Replace pads with new ones immediately (Chapter 9).

60 Brake roughness or chatter (pedal pulsates)

1 Excessive lateral runout (Chapter 9).
2 Uneven pad wear (Chapter 9).
3 Defective disc (Chapter 9).

61 Excessive brake pedal effort required to stop vehicle

1 Malfunctioning power brake booster (Chapter 9).
2 Partial system failure (Chapter 9).
3 Excessively worn pads or shoes (Chapter 9).
4 Piston in caliper or wheel cylinder stuck or sluggish (Chapter 9).
5 Brake pads or shoes contaminated with oil or grease (Chapter 9).
6 New pads or shoes installed and not yet seated. It will take a while for the new material to seat against the disc or drum.

62 Excessive brake pedal travel

1 Partial brake system failure (Chapter 9).
2 Insufficient fluid in master cylinder (Chapters 1 and 9).
3 Air trapped in system (Chapters 1 and 9).

63 Dragging brakes

1 Incorrect adjustment of brake light switch (Chapter 9).
2 Master cylinder pistons not returning correctly (Chapter 9).
3 Restricted brakes lines or hoses (Chapters 1 and 9).
4 Incorrect parking brake adjustment (Chapter 9).

64 Grabbing or uneven braking action

1 Malfunction of proportioning valve (Chapter 9).
2 Malfunction of power brake booster unit (Chapter 9).
3 Binding brake pedal mechanism (Chapter 9).

65 Brake pedal feels spongy when depressed

1 Air in hydraulic lines (Chapter 9).
2 Master cylinder mounting bolts loose (Chapter 9).
3 Master cylinder defective (Chapter 9).

66 Brake pedal travels to the floor with little resistance

1 Little or no fluid in the master cylinder reservoir caused by leaking caliper piston(s) (Chapter 9).
2 Loose, damaged or disconnected brake lines (Chapter 9).

67 Parking brake does not hold

Parking brake linkage improperly adjusted (Chapters 1 and 9).

SUSPENSION AND STEERING SYSTEMS

➡Note: Before attempting to diagnose the suspension and steering systems, perform the following preliminary checks:

a) *Tires for wrong pressure and uneven wear.*
b) *Steering universal joints from the column to the steering gear for loose connectors or wear.*

c) Front and rear suspension and the steering gear assembly for loose or damaged parts.
d) Out-of-round or out-of-balance tires, bent rims and loose and/or rough wheel bearings.

68 Vehicle pulls to one side

1 Mismatched or uneven tires (Chapter 10).
2 Broken or sagging springs (Chapter 10).
3 Wheel alignment (Chapter 10).
4 Front brake dragging (Chapter 9).

69 Abnormal or excessive tire wear

1 Wheel alignment (Chapter 10).
2 Sagging or broken springs (Chapter 10).
3 Tire out of balance (Chapter 10).
4 Worn shock absorber (Chapter 10).
5 Overloaded vehicle.
6 Tires not rotated regularly.

70 Wheel makes a thumping noise

1 Blister or bump on tire (Chapter 10).
2 Worn shock absorber (Chapter 10).

71 Shimmy, shake or vibration

1 Tire or wheel out-of-balance or out-of-round (Chapter 10).
2 Loose or worn front hub or wheel bearings (Chapters 1, 8 and 10).
3 Worn tie-rod ends (Chapter 10).
4 Worn lower balljoints (Chapters 1 and 10).
5 Excessive wheel runout (Chapter 10).
6 Blister or bump on tire (Chapter 10).

72 Hard steering

1 Lack of lubrication at balljoints and tie-rod ends (Chapters 1 and 10).
2 Front wheel alignment (Chapter 10).
3 Low tire pressure(s) (Chapters 1 and 10).

73 Poor returnability of steering to center

1 Lack of lubrication at balljoints and tie-rod ends (Chapters 1 and 10).
2 Binding in balljoints (Chapter 10).
3 Binding in steering column (Chapter 10).
4 Lack of lubricant in steering gear assembly (Chapter 10).
5 Front wheel alignment (Chapter 10).

74 Abnormal noise at the front end

1 Lack of lubrication at balljoints and tie-rod ends (Chapters 1 and 10).
2 Damaged shock absorber mount (Chapter 10).
3 Worn control arm bushings or tie-rod ends (Chapter 10).
4 Loose stabilizer bar (Chapter 10).

5 Loose wheel nuts (Chapters 1 and 10).
6 Loose suspension bolts (Chapter 10)

75 Wander or poor steering stability

1 Mismatched or uneven tires (Chapter 10).
2 Lack of lubrication at balljoints and tie-rod ends (Chapters 1 and 10).
3 Worn shock absorber/coil spring assemblies (Chapter 10).
4 Loose stabilizer bar (Chapter 10).
5 Broken or sagging springs (Chapter 10).
6 Wheels out of alignment (Chapter 10).

76 Erratic steering when braking

1 Front hub bearings worn (Chapter 10).
2 Broken or sagging springs (Chapter 10).
3 Leaking wheel cylinder or caliper (Chapter 10).
4 Warped discs or drums (Chapter 10).

77 Excessive pitching and/or rolling around corners or during braking

1 Loose stabilizer bar (Chapter 10).
2 Worn shock absorber/coil spring assemblies or mountings (Chapter 10).
3 Broken or sagging springs (Chapter 10).
4 Overloaded vehicle.

78 Suspension bottoms

1 Overloaded vehicle.
2 Worn shock absorber/coil spring assemblies (Chapter 10).
3 Incorrect, broken or sagging springs (Chapter 10).

79 Cupped tires

1 Front wheel or rear wheel alignment (Chapter 10).
2 Worn shock absorber/coil spring assemblies (Chapter 10).
3 Wheel bearings worn (Chapter 10).
4 Excessive tire or wheel runout (Chapter 10).
5 Worn balljoints (Chapter 10).

80 Excessive tire wear on outside edge

1 Inflation pressures incorrect (Chapter 1).
2 Excessive speed in turns.
3 Front end alignment incorrect (excessive toe-in). Have professionally aligned.
4 Suspension arm bent or twisted (Chapter 10).

81 Excessive tire wear on inside edge

1 Inflation pressures incorrect (Chapter 1).
2 Front end alignment incorrect (toe-out). Have professionally aligned.
3 Loose or damaged steering or suspension components (Chapter 10).

82 Tire tread worn in one place

1 Tires out of balance.
2 Damaged or buckled wheel. Inspect and replace if necessary.
3 Defective tire (Chapter 1).

83 Excessive play or looseness in steering system

1 Front hub bearing(s) worn (Chapter 10).
2 Tie-rod end loose (Chapter 10).
3 Steering gear loose or worn (Chapter 10).
4 Worn or loose steering intermediate shaft (Chapter 10).

84 Rattling or clicking noise in steering gear

1 Steering gear loose (Chapter 10).
2 Steering gear defective.

Section

1

TUNE-UP AND ROUTINE MAINTENANCE

1 Maintenance schedule

The maintenance intervals in this manual are provided with the assumption that you, not the dealer, will be doing the work. These are the minimum maintenance intervals recommended by the factory for vehicles that are driven daily. If you wish to keep your vehicle in peak condition at all times, you may wish to perform some of these procedures even more often. Because frequent maintenance enhances the efficiency, performance and resale value of your car, we encourage you to do so. If you drive in dusty areas, tow a trailer, idle or drive at low speeds for extended periods or drive for short distances (less than four miles) in below freezing temperatures, shorter intervals are also recommended.

When your vehicle is new, follow the maintenance schedule to the letter, record the maintenance performed in your owners manual and keep all receipts to protect the new vehicle warranty. In many cases, the initial maintenance check is done at no cost to the owner.

Later models are equipped with a Maintenance Minder located in the instrument panel. Honda recommends oil changes and other maintenance chores through the onboard computer display located between the speedometer and tachometer. Check the display by turning the ignition key to the ON position, then press and release the SELECT/RESET button until the Oil Life Indicator displays. This number is the estimated percentage of oil life remaining. Continued pressing of the SELECT/RESET button will list any other maintenance procedures to be performed. Refer to the corresponding Tune-up and routine maintenance sections for additional information.

For those vehicles not fitted with a Maintenance Minder, the following service intervals are recommended.

EVERY 250 MILES (400 KM) OR WEEKLY, WHICHEVER COMES FIRST

Check the engine oil level (Section 4)
Check the engine coolant level (Section 4)
Check the windshield washer fluid level (Section 4)
Check the brake fluid level (Section 4)
Check the power steering fluid level (Section 4)
Check the automatic transaxle fluid level (Section 4)
Check the tires and tire pressures (Section 5)
Check the operation of all lights
Check the horn operation

EVERY 5000 MILES (8000 KM) OR ONCE A YEAR, WHICHEVER COMES FIRST

All items listed above plus:
Change the engine oil and oil filter (Section 6).

➡**Note: 2006 and later models are equipped with a "Maintenance Minder" system. This calculates maintenance intervals based on operating conditions. The instrument panel displays the percentage of oil life remaining and informs the owner when main maintenance procedures are required. It also displays various maintenance sub-items. Consult your owner's manual for detailed information on these maintenance procedure lists. No matter the conditions, you must change the engine oil at least every 12 months. To keep the maintenance minder system reading properly, it must be reset when - and only when - the necessary service is done (see Section 6).**

EVERY 7500 MILES (12,000 KM) OR 6 MONTHS, WHICHEVER COMES FIRST

All items listed above plus:
Inspect (and replace, if necessary) the windshield wiper blades (Section 7)
Check and service the battery (Section 8)
Check the cooling system (Section 9)
Rotate the tires (Section 10)
Check the seat belts (Section 11)

EVERY 15,000 MILES (24,000 KM) OR 12 MONTHS, WHICHEVER COMES FIRST

All items listed above plus:
Inspect the brake system (Section 12)
Inspect the suspension, steering components and driveaxle boots (Section 13)*
Inspect and replace, if necessary, all underhood hoses (Section 14)
Inspect the fuel system (Section 15)
Check the exhaust system (Section 16)

EVERY 30,000 (48,000 KM) MILES OR 24 MONTHS, WHICHEVER COMES FIRST

All items listed above plus:
Replace the air filter (Section 17)*
Replace the interior ventilation filter (Section 18)*
Check and replace, if necessary, the engine drivebelt (Section 19)
Replace the brake fluid (Section 20)

EVERY 60,000 MILES (96,000 KM) OR 60 MONTHS, WHICHEVER COMES FIRST

Service the cooling system (drain, flush and refill) (Section 21)

EVERY 90,000 MILES (144,000 KM) OR 60 MONTHS, WHICHEVER COMES FIRST

Change the automatic transaxle fluid (Section 22)**

EVERY 105,000 MILES (168,000 KM)

Replace the spark plugs (platinum or iridium type) (Section 23)
Valve clearance check and adjustment (only if noisy) (see Chapter 2A or 2B)
Replace the timing belt, and inspect the water pump (see Chapter 2A or 2B and Chapter 3)*

* Replace every 60,000 miles (100,000 km) and inspect the water pump (V6) if you drive regularly in very high temperatures (over 110-degrees F [43-degrees C]), or in very low temperatures (under -20-degrees F [-29-degrees C]).

EVERY 120,000 MILES (192,000 KM) OR 72 MONTHS, WHICHEVER COMES FIRST

Change the manual transaxle fluid (Section 24)***
*This item is affected by "severe" operating conditions as described below. If your vehicle is operated under "severe" conditions, perform all maintenance indicated with a * at 5000 mile/6 month intervals.
Severe conditions are indicated if you mainly operate your vehicle under one or more of the following conditions:
Operating in dusty areas

Towing a trailer
Idling for extended periods and/or low speed operation
Operating when outside temperatures remain below freezing and when most trips are less than five miles
**If operated under one or more of the folowing conditions, change the automatic transaxle fluid every 30,000 miles.
***If operated under one or more of the following conditions, change the manual transaxle fluid every 60,000 miles.
In heavy city traffic where the outside temperature regularly reaches 90-degrees F (32-degrees C) or higher
In hilly or mountainous terrain

Typical four-cylinder engine compartment layout

1	Engine oil dipstick	5	Air filter housing	8	Radiator cap
2	Engine oil filler cap	6	Battery	9	Power steering fluid reservoir
3	Brake fluid reservoir	7	Coolant reservoir	10	Windshield washer fluid reservoir
4	Underhood fuse/relay block				

Typical V6 engine compartment layout

1	Windshield washer fluid reservoir	5	Radiator cap	8	Air filter housing
2	Power steering fluid reservoir	6	Engine oil filler cap	9	Underhood fuse/relay block
3	Engine oil dipstick	7	Battery	10	Brake fluid reservoir
4	Coolant reservoir				

Typical front underside components (four-cylinder model shown)

1	Automatic transaxle drain plug	3	Engine oil drain plug	5	Catalytic converter
2	Brake caliper	4	Exhaust pipe		

Typical rear underside components

1	Muffler	3	Shock absorber	5	Parking brake cable
2	Exhaust system hanger	4	Drum brake assembly		

2   Introduction

This Chapter is designed to help the home mechanic maintain the Accord with the goals of maximum performance, economy, safety and reliability in mind.

Included is a master maintenance schedule, followed by procedures dealing specifically with each item on the schedule. Visual checks, adjustments, component replacement and other helpful items are included. Refer to the accompanying illustrations of the engine compartment and the underside of the vehicle for the locations of various components.

Servicing the vehicle, in accordance with the mileage/time maintenance schedule and the step-by-step procedures will result in a planned maintenance program that should produce a long and reliable service life. Keep in mind that it is a comprehensive plan, so maintaining some items but not others at the specified intervals will not produce the same results.

As you service the vehicle, you will discover that many of the procedures can - and should - be grouped together because of the nature of the particular procedure you're performing or because of the close proximity of two otherwise unrelated components to one another.

For example, if the vehicle is raised for chassis lubrication, you should inspect the exhaust, suspension, steering and fuel systems while you're under the vehicle. When you're rotating the tires, it makes good sense to check the brakes since the wheels are already removed. Finally, let's suppose you have to borrow or rent a torque wrench. Even if you only need it to tighten the spark plugs, you might as well check the torque of as many critical fasteners as time allows.

The first step in this maintenance program is to prepare yourself before the actual work begins. Read through all the procedures you're planning to do, then gather up all the parts and tools needed. If it looks like you might run into problems during a particular job, seek advice from a mechanic or an experienced do-it-yourselfer.

OWNER'S MANUAL AND VECI LABEL INFORMATION

Your vehicle owner's manual was written for your year and model and contains very specific information on component locations, specifications, fuse ratings, part numbers, etc. The Owner's Manual is an important resource for the do-it-yourselfer to have; if one was not supplied with your vehicle, it can generally be ordered from a dealer parts department.

Among other important information, the Vehicle Emissions Control Information (VECI) label contains specifications and procedures for applicable tune-up adjustments and, in some instances, spark plugs (see Chapter 6 for more information on the VECI label). The information on this label is the exact maintenance data recommended by the manufacturer. This data often varies by intended operating altitude, local emissions regulations, month of manufacture, etc.

This Chapter contains procedural details, safety information and more ambitious maintenance intervals than you might find in manufacturer's literature. However, you may also find procedures or specifications in your Owner's Manual or VECI label that differ with what's printed here. In these cases, the Owner's Manual or VECI label can be considered correct, since it is specific to your particular vehicle.

3   Tune-up general information

The term tune-up is used in this manual to represent a combination of individual operations rather than one specific procedure.

If, from the time the vehicle is new, the routine maintenance schedule is followed closely and frequent checks are made of fluid levels and high wear items, as suggested throughout this manual, the engine will be kept in relatively good running condition and the need for additional work will be minimized.

More likely than not, however, there will be times when the engine is running poorly due to lack of regular maintenance. This is even more likely if a used vehicle, which has not received regular and frequent maintenance checks, is purchased. In such cases, an engine tune-up will be needed outside of the regular routine maintenance intervals.

The first step in any tune-up or diagnostic procedure to help correct a poor running engine is a cylinder compression check. A compression check (see Chapter 2C) will help determine the condition of internal engine components and should be used as a guide for tune-up and repair procedures. If, for instance, a compression check indicates serious internal engine wear, a conventional tune-up will not improve the performance of the engine and would be a waste of time and money. Because of its importance, the compression check should be done by someone with the right equipment and the knowledge to use it properly.

The following procedures are those most often needed to bring a generally poor running engine back into a proper state of tune.

MINOR TUNE-UP

Check all engine related fluids (Section 4)
Clean, inspect and test the battery (Section 8)
Check the cooling system (Section 9)
Check all underhood hoses (Section 14)
Check the air filter (Section 17)
Check and the drivebelt (Section 19)

MAJOR TUNE-UP

All items listed under minor tune-up, plus . . .
Check the fuel system (Section 15)
Replace the air filter (Section 17)
Replace the spark plugs (Section 23)

4 Fluid level checks (every 250 miles [400km] or weekly)

1   Fluids are an essential part of the lubrication, cooling, brake, clutch and other systems. Because these fluids gradually become depleted and/or contaminated during normal operation of the vehicle, they must be periodically replenished. See *Recommended lubricants and fluids* and *Capacities* in this Chapter's Specifications before adding fluid to any of the following components.

→Note: The vehicle must be on level ground before fluid levels can be checked.

ENGINE OIL

▶ Refer to illustrations 4.2 and 4.4

2   The engine oil level is checked with a dipstick located on top of the valve cover (see illustration). The dipstick extends through a metal tube from which it protrudes down into the engine oil pan.

3   The oil level should be checked before the vehicle has been driven, or about 5 minutes after the engine has been shut off. If the oil is checked immediately after driving the vehicle, some of the oil will remain in the upper engine components, producing an inaccurate reading on the dipstick.

4   Pull the dipstick from the tube and wipe all the oil from the end with a clean rag or paper towel. Insert the clean dipstick all the way back into its metal tube and pull it out again. Observe the oil at the end of the dipstick. At its highest point, the level should be between the upper and lower holes (see illustration).

5   It takes one quart of oil to raise the level from the lower hole to the upper hole on the dipstick. Do not allow the level to drop below the lower hole or oil starvation may cause engine damage. Conversely, overfilling the engine (adding oil above the upper hole) may cause oil fouled spark plugs, oil leaks or oil seal failures.

6   Remove the threaded cap from the valve cover to add oil. Use a funnel to prevent spills. After adding the oil, install the filler cap hand tight. Start the engine and look carefully for any small leaks around the oil filter or drain plug. Stop the engine and check the oil level again after it has had sufficient time to drain from the upper block and cylinder head galleys.

7   Checking the oil level is an important preventive maintenance step. A continually dropping oil level indicates oil leakage through damaged seals, from loose connections, or past worn rings or valve guides. If the oil looks milky in color or has water droplets in it, the most likely cause would be a blown cylinder head gasket. The engine should be checked immediately. The condition of the oil should also be checked. Each time you check the oil level, slide your thumb and index finger up the dipstick before wiping off the oil. If you see small dirt or metal particles clinging to the dipstick, the oil should be changed (see Section 6).

ENGINE COOLANT

▶ Refer to illustration 4.9

※ WARNING:

Do not allow antifreeze to come in contact with your skin or painted surfaces of the vehicle. Flush contaminated areas immediately with plenty of water. Don't store new coolant or leave old coolant lying around where it's accessible to children or pets - they're attracted by its sweet smell. Ingestion of even a small amount of coolant can be fatal! Wipe up garage floor and drip pan spills immediately. Keep antifreeze containers covered and repair cooling system leaks as soon as they're noticed.

8   All vehicles covered by this manual are equipped with a pressurized coolant recovery system. A coolant reservoir, located at the front of the engine compartment, is connected by a hose to the base of the radiator filler neck. If the coolant overheats, it can escape through the pressurized filler cap, then through the connecting hose into the reservoir. As the engine cools, the coolant is automatically drawn back into the cooling system to maintain the correct level.

4.2 The engine oil dipstick is located on top of the valve cover

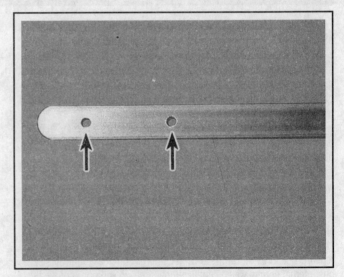

4.4 The oil level should be between the two holes in the dipstick

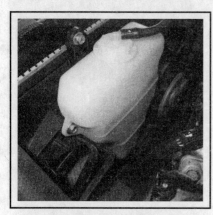

4.9 The cooling system reservoir is located at the front of the engine compartment

4.14 Fluid for the windshield washer system is stored in this plastic reservoir

4.16 The brake fluid level should be near the MAX mark on the translucent plastic reservoir

9 The coolant level in the reservoir should be checked regularly. It must be between the MAX and MIN lines on the tank. The level will vary with the temperature of the engine. When the engine is cold, the coolant level should be at or slightly above the MIN mark on the tank. Once the engine has warmed up, the level should be at or near the MAX mark. If it isn't, allow the fluid in the tank to cool, then remove the cap from the reservoir (see illustration) and add coolant to bring the level up to the MAX line.

❋❋ WARNING:

Do not remove the radiator cap to check the coolant level when the engine is warm!

Use only the recommended coolant listed in this Chapter's Specifications. Do not use supplemental inhibitors or additives. If only a small amount of coolant is required to bring the system up to the proper level, water can be used. However, repeated additions of water will dilute the recommended antifreeze and water solution. In order to maintain the proper ratio of antifreeze and water, it is advisable to top up the coolant level with the correct mixture.

10 If the coolant level drops within a short time after replenishment, there may be a leak in the system. Inspect the radiator, hoses, engine coolant filler cap, drain plugs and water pump. If no leak is evident, have the radiator cap pressure tested.

❋❋ WARNING:

Never remove the radiator cap or the coolant reservoir cap when the engine is running or has just been shut down, because the cooling system is hot. Escaping steam and scalding liquid could cause serious injury.

11 If it is necessary to open the radiator cap, wait until the system has cooled completely, then wrap a thick cloth around the cap and turn it to the first stop. If any steam escapes, wait until the system has cooled further, then remove the cap.

12 When checking the coolant level, always note its condition. It should be relatively clear. If it is brown or rust colored, the system should be drained, flushed and refilled. Even if the coolant appears to be normal, the corrosion inhibitors wear out with use, so it must be replaced at the specified intervals.

13 Do not allow antifreeze to come in contact with your skin or painted surfaces of the vehicle. Flush contacted areas immediately with plenty of water.

WINDSHIELD WASHER FLUID

▸ **Refer to illustration 4.14**

14 Fluid for the windshield washer system is stored in a plastic reservoir which is located at the right front corner of the engine compartment (see illustration). In milder climates, plain water can be used to top up the reservoir, but the reservoir should be kept no more than 2/3 full to allow for expansion should the water freeze. In colder climates, the use of a specially designed windshield washer fluid, available at your dealer and any auto parts store, will help lower the freezing point of the fluid. Mix the solution with water in accordance with the manufacturer's directions on the container. Do not use regular antifreeze. It will damage the vehicle's paint (and smear the windshield).

BRAKE AND CLUTCH FLUID

▸ **Refer to illustration 4.16**

15 The brake master cylinder is located on the driver's side of the engine compartment firewall. The clutch master cylinder fluid reservoir is located right next to it on the firewall, behind the left shock tower. They both use the same type of fluid.

16 The level should be maintained between the MIN and MAX marks on the reservoir (see illustration).

17 If additional fluid is necessary to bring the level up, use a rag to clean all dirt off the top of the reservoir. If any foreign matter enters the master cylinder when the cap is removed, blockage in the brake or clutch release system lines can occur. Also, make sure all painted surfaces around the master cylinder are covered, since brake fluid will ruin paint. Carefully pour new, clean brake fluid into the master cylinder. Be careful not to spill the fluid on painted surfaces. Be sure the specified fluid is used; mixing different types of brake fluid can cause damage to the system. See *Recommended lubricants and fluids* in this Chapter's Specifications or your owner's manual.

18 At this time the fluid and the master cylinder can be inspected for contamination. If deposits, dirt particles or water droplets are seen in the fluid, the system should be drained and refilled with fresh fluid (see Section 20).

4.26 The power steering fluid reservoir is translucent so the fluid level can be checked without removing the cap - keep the fluid between the two lines

4.32 The automatic transaxle dipstick is located on the left side of the engine compartment, near the battery

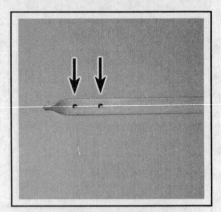

4.34 The automatic transaxle fluid level should be between the two holes in the dipstick

19 Reinstall the master cylinder cap.

20 The brake fluid in the master cylinder will drop slightly as the brake shoes or pads at each wheel wear down during normal operation. If the master cylinder requires repeated replenishing to keep the level up, it's an indication of leaks in the brake system, which should be corrected immediately. Check all brake lines and connections, along with the wheel cylinders, if equipped, and booster (see Chapter 9 for more information). As the clutch wears, the fluid level in the clutch master cylinder reservoir will rise. Unless there is a leak in either system, fluid additions shouldn't be necessary.

21 If you discover that the reservoir is empty or nearly empty, the brake (or clutch) system should be filled, bled (see Chapter 9) and checked for leaks.

POWER STEERING FLUID

♦ **Refer to illustration 4.26**

22 Check the power steering fluid level periodically to avoid steering system problems, such as damage to the pump.

✳✳ CAUTION:

DO NOT hold the steering wheel against either stop (extreme left or right turn) for more than five seconds. If you do, the power steering pump could be damaged.

23 The power steering reservoir is located at the right side of the engine compartment. The reservoir has LOWER LEVEL and UPPER LEVEL fluid level marks on the side. The fluid level can be seen without removing the reservoir cap.

24 Park the vehicle on level ground and apply the parking brake.

25 Run the engine until it has reached normal operating temperature. With the engine at idle, turn the steering wheel back and forth about 10 times to get any air out of the steering system. Shut the engine off with the wheels in the straight-ahead position.

26 Note the fluid level on the side of the reservoir. It should be between the two marks (see illustration).

27 Add small amounts of fluid until the level is correct.

✳✳ CAUTION:

Do not overfill the reservoir. If too much fluid is added, remove the excess with a clean syringe or suction pump.

28 Check the power steering hoses and connections for leaks and wear.

AUTOMATIC TRANSAXLE FLUID

♦ **Refer to illustrations 4.32 and 4.34**

29 The level of the automatic transaxle fluid should be carefully maintained. Low fluid level can lead to slipping or loss of drive, while overfilling can cause foaming, loss of fluid and transaxle damage.

30 The transaxle fluid level should only be checked when the transaxle is hot (at its normal operating temperature). If the vehicle has just been driven over 10 miles (15 miles in a frigid climate), and the fluid temperature is 160 to 175-degrees F, the transaxle is hot.

✳✳ CAUTION:

If the vehicle has just been driven for a long time at high speed or in city traffic in hot weather, or if it has been pulling a trailer, an accurate fluid level reading cannot be obtained. Allow the fluid to cool down for about 30 minutes.

31 If the vehicle has not just been driven, park the vehicle on level ground, set the parking brake and start the engine. While the engine is idling, depress the brake pedal and move the selector lever through all the gear ranges, beginning and ending in Park.

32 Turn the engine off, then remove the dipstick from its tube (see illustration).

33 Wipe the fluid from the dipstick with a clean rag and reinsert it back into the filler tube until the cap seats.

34 Pull the dipstick out again and note the fluid level. The fluid level should be in the operating temperature range (between the upper and lower mark) (see illustration). If the level is at the low side of either range, add the specified automatic transmission fluid through the dipstick tube with a funnel.

35 Add just enough of the recommended fluid to fill the transaxle to the proper level. It takes about one pint to raise the level from the low mark to the high mark when the fluid is hot, so add the fluid a little at a time and keep checking the level until it is correct.

36 The condition of the fluid should also be checked along with the level. If the fluid at the end of the dipstick is black or a dark reddish brown color, or if it emits a burned smell, the fluid should be changed (see Section 22). If you are in doubt about the condition of the fluid, purchase some new fluid and compare the two for color and smell.

MANUAL TRANSAXLE FLUID

➡Note: It isn't necessary to check this lubricant weekly; every 3000 miles (4800 km) or 3 months will be adequate.

37 The manual transaxle does not have a dipstick. To check the fluid level, raise the vehicle and support it securely on jackstands.

➡Note: Be sure the vehicle is level.

On the left side of the transaxle housing, remove the fluid fill plug (it's the upper of the two plugs; the lower one is the drain plug). If the lubricant level is correct, it should be up to the lower edge of the hole.

38 If the transaxle needs more lubricant (if the level is not up to the hole), use a syringe or a gear oil pump to add more. Stop filling the transaxle when the lubricant begins to run out the hole.

39 Install the plug and tighten it securely. Drive the vehicle a short distance, then check for leaks.

5 Tire and tire pressure checks (every 250 miles [400 km] or weekly)

▶ Refer to illustrations 5.2, 5.3, 5.4a, 5.4b and 5.8

1 Periodic inspection of the tires may spare you from the inconvenience of being stranded with a flat tire. It can also provide you with vital information regarding possible problems in the steering and suspension systems before major damage occurs.

2 Normal tread wear can be monitored with a simple, inexpensive device known as a tread depth indicator (see illustration). When the tread depth reaches approximately 1/16-inch (1.6mm), replace the tire(s).

3 Note any abnormal tread wear (see illustration). Tread pattern irregularities such as cupping, flat spots and more wear on one side than the other are indications of front end alignment and/or balance problems. If any of these conditions are noted, take the vehicle to a tire shop or service station to correct the problem.

5.2 A tire tread depth indicator should be used to monitor tire wear - they are available at auto parts stores and service stations and cost very little

5.3 This chart will help you determine the condition of your tires, the probable cause(s) of abnormal wear and the corrective action necessary

UNDERINFLATION

OVERINFLATION

CUPPING

Cupping may be caused by:
• Underinflation and/or mechanical irregularities such as out-of-balance condition of wheel and/or tire, and bent or damaged wheel.
• Loose or worn steering tie-rod or steering idler arm.
• Loose, damaged or worn front suspension parts.

INCORRECT TOE-IN OR EXTREME CAMBER

FEATHERING DUE TO MISALIGNMENT

5.4a If a tire loses air on a steady basis, check the valve core first to make sure it's snug (special inexpensive wrenches are commonly available at auto parts stores

5.4b If the valve core is tight, raise the corner of the vehicle with the low tire and spray a soapy water solution onto the tread as the tire is turned slowly - slow leaks will cause small bubbles to appear

5.8 To extend the life of your tires, check the air pressure at least once a week with an accurate gauge (don't forget the spare!)

4   Look closely for cuts, punctures and embedded nails or tacks. Sometimes a tire will hold its air pressure for a short time or leak down very slowly even after a nail has embedded itself into the tread. If a slow leak persists, check the valve core to make sure it is tight (see illustration). Examine the tread for an object that may have embedded itself into the tire or for a "plug" that may have begun to leak (radial tire punctures are repaired with a plug that is installed in a puncture). If a puncture is suspected, it can be easily verified by spraying a solution of soapy water onto the puncture area (see illustration). The soapy solution will bubble if there is a leak. Unless the puncture is inordinately large, a tire shop or gas station can usually repair the punctured tire.

5   Carefully inspect the inner side of each tire for evidence of brake fluid leakage. If you see any, inspect the brakes immediately.

6   Correct tire air pressure adds miles to the lifespan of the tires, improves mileage and enhances overall ride quality. Tire pressure cannot be accurately estimated by looking at a tire, particularly if it is a radial. A tire pressure gauge is therefore essential. Keep an accurate

gauge in the glove box. The pressure gauges fitted to the nozzles of air hoses at gas stations are often inaccurate.

7   Always check tire pressure when the tires are cold. "Cold," in this case, means the vehicle has not been driven over a mile in the three hours preceding a tire pressure check. A pressure rise of four to eight pounds is not uncommon once the tires are warm.

8   Unscrew the valve cap protruding from the wheel or hubcap and push the gauge firmly onto the valve (see illustration). Note the reading on the gauge and compare this figure to the recommended tire pressure shown on the tire placard on the left door jamb. Be sure to reinstall the valve cap to keep dirt and moisture out of the valve stem mechanism. Check all four tires and, if necessary, add enough air to bring them up to the recommended pressure levels.

9   Don't forget to keep the spare tire inflated to the specified pressure (consult your owner's manual). Note that the air pressure specified for the compact spare is significantly higher than the pressure of the regular tires.

6   Engine oil and oil filter change (every 3000 miles [4800 km] or 3 months)

♦ **Refer to illustrations 6.2, 6.7, 6.12 and 6.14**

1   Frequent oil changes are the best preventive maintenance the home mechanic can give the engine, because aging oil becomes diluted and contaminated, which leads to premature engine wear.

2   Make sure you have all the necessary tools before you begin this procedure (see illustration). You should also have plenty of rags or newspapers handy for mopping up any spills.

3   Access to the underside of the vehicle is greatly improved if the vehicle can be lifted on a hoist, driven onto ramps or supported by jackstands.

❊❊ **WARNING:**

Do not work under a vehicle which is supported only by a bumper, hydraulic or scissors-type jack.

4   If this is your first oil change, get under the vehicle and familiar-

ize yourself with the locations of the oil drain plug and the oil filter. The engine and exhaust components will be warm during the actual work, so try to anticipate any potential problems before the engine and accessories are hot.

5   Park the vehicle on a level spot. Start the engine and allow it to reach its normal operating temperature. Warm oil and sludge will flow out more easily. Turn off the engine when it's warmed up. Remove the filler cap from the valve cover.

6   Raise the vehicle and support it securely on jackstands.

❊❊ **WARNING:**

Never get beneath the vehicle when it is supported only by a jack. The jack provided with your vehicle is designed solely for raising the vehicle to remove and replace the wheels. Always use jackstands to support the vehicle when it becomes necessary to place your body underneath the vehicle.

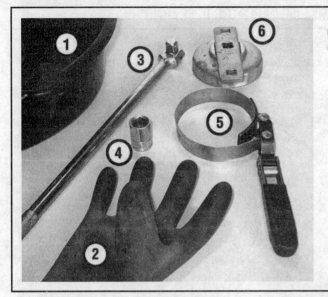

6.2 These tools are required when changing the engine oil and filter

1 **Drain pan** - It should be fairly shallow in depth, but wide in order to prevent spills
2 **Rubber gloves** - When removing the drain plug and filter, it is inevitable that you will get oil on your hands (the gloves will prevent burns)
3 **Breaker bar** - Sometimes the oil drain plug is pretty tight and a long breaker bar is needed to loosen it
4 **Socket** - To be used with the breaker bar or a ratchet (must be the correct size to fit the drain plug)
5 **Filter wrench** - This is a metal band-type wrench, which requires clearance around the filter to be effective
6 **Filter wrench** - This type fits on the bottom of the filter and can be turned with a ratchet or beaker bar (different size wrenches are available for different types of filters)

6.7 Use a proper size box-end wrench or socket to remove the oil drain plug and avoid rounding it off

6.12 Use an oil filter wrench to remove the filter

6.14 Lubricate the oil filter gasket with clean engine oil before installing the filter on the engine

7 Being careful not to touch the hot exhaust components, place the drain pan under the drain plug in the bottom of the pan and remove the plug (see illustration). You may want to wear gloves while unscrewing the plug the final few turns if the engine is hot.

8 Allow the old oil to drain into the pan. It may be necessary to move the pan farther under the engine as the oil flow slows to a trickle. Inspect the old oil for the presence of metal shavings and chips.

9 After all the oil has drained, wipe off the drain plug with a clean rag. Even minute metal particles clinging to the plug would immediately contaminate the new oil.

10 Clean the area around the drain plug opening, reinstall the plug and tighten it securely, but do not strip the threads.

11 Move the drain pan into position under the oil filter.

12 Loosen the oil filter (see illustration) by turning it counterclockwise with an oil filter wrench. Once the filter is loose, use your hands to unscrew it from the block. Keep the open end pointing up to prevent the oil inside the filter from spilling out.

✳✳ WARNING:

The exhaust system may still be hot, so be careful.

13 With a clean rag, wipe off the mounting surface on the block. If a residue of old oil is allowed to remain, it will smoke when the block is heated up. Also make sure that none of the old gasket remains stuck to the mounting surface. It can be removed with a scraper if necessary.

14 Compare the old filter with the new one to make sure they are the same type. Smear some clean engine oil on the rubber gasket of the new filter (see illustration).

15 Attach the new filter to the engine, following the tightening directions printed on the filter canister or packing box. Most filter manufacturers recommend against using a filter wrench due to the possibility of overtightening and damaging the seal.

16 Remove all tools, rags, etc. from under the vehicle, being careful not to spill the oil in the drain pan, then lower the vehicle.

17 Add new oil to the engine through the oil filler cap in the valve cover. Use a funnel, if necessary, to prevent oil from spilling onto the top of the engine. Pour three quarts of fresh oil into the engine. Wait a few minutes to allow the oil to drain into the pan, then check the level on the oil dipstick (see Section 4). If the oil level is at or near the upper hole on the dipstick, install the filler cap hand tight, start the engine and allow the new oil to circulate.

18 Allow the engine to run for about a minute. While the engine is

running, look under the vehicle and check for leaks at the oil pan drain plug and around the oil filter. If either is leaking, stop the engine and tighten the plug or filter.

19 Wait a few minutes to allow the oil to trickle down into the pan, then recheck the level on the dipstick and, if necessary, add enough oil to bring the level to the upper hole.

20 During the first few trips after an oil change, make it a point to check frequently for leaks and proper oil level.

21 The old oil drained from the engine cannot be reused in its present state and should be disposed of. Check with your local auto parts store, disposal facility or environmental agency to see if they will accept the oil for recycling. After the oil has cooled it can be drained into a container (capped plastic jugs, topped bottles, milk cartons, etc.) for transport to one of these disposal sites. Don't dispose of the oil by pouring it on the ground or down a drain!

OIL LIFE INDICATOR RESETTING

22 On 2006 and later models with the Maintenance Minder system, the oil life indicator should be reset after changing the oil. To do this:

a) *Turn the ignition key to the ON (II) position.*
b) *Depress the Select/Reset button until the engine oil life indicator appears on the display.*
c) *Depress and hold the Select/Reset knob for at least 10 seconds (the oil life indicator and the maintenance item code(s) will blink)*
d) *Release the Select/Reset knob then depress it again, this time for at least 5 seconds. The maintenance item code(s) will disappear, and the engine oil life will reset to 100%.*

---

7 Windshield wiper blade inspection and replacement (every 7500 miles [12,000 km] or 6 months)

▶ **Refer to illustrations 7.5a and 7.5b**

1 The windshield wiper and blade assembly should be inspected periodically for damage, loose components and cracked or worn blade elements.

2 Road film can build up on the wiper blades and affect their efficiency, so they should be washed regularly with a mild detergent solution.

3 The action of the wiping mechanism can loosen bolts, nuts and fasteners, so they should be checked and tightened, as necessary, at the same time the wiper blades are checked.

4 If the wiper blade elements are cracked, worn or warped, or no longer clean adequately, they should be replaced with new ones.

5 Lift the arm assembly away from the glass for clearance, press on the release lever, then slide the wiper blade assembly out of the hook at the end of the arm (see illustrations).

6 Attach the new wiper to the arm. Connection can be confirmed by an audible click.

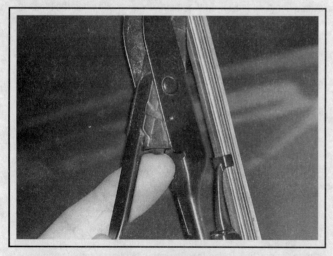

7.5a To release the blade holder, pull up on the release tab . . .

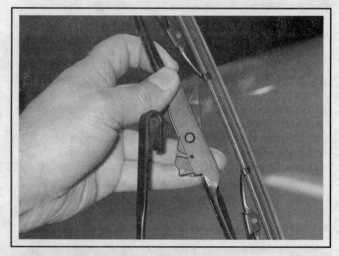

7.5b . . . and pull the wiper blade in the direction of the windshield to separate it from the arm

8   Battery check, maintenance and charging (every 7500 miles [12,000 km] or 6 months)

▶ Refer to illustrations 8.1, 8.6a, 8.6b, 8.7a, 8.7b and 8.8

❊❊ WARNING:

Certain precautions must be followed when checking and servicing the battery. Hydrogen gas, which is highly flammable, is always present in the battery cells, so keep lighted tobacco and all other open flames and sparks away from the battery. The electrolyte inside the battery is actually diluted sulfuric acid, which will cause injury if splashed on your skin or in your eyes. It will also ruin clothes and painted surfaces. When removing the battery cables, always detach the negative cable first and hook it up last!

1   A routine preventive maintenance program for the battery in your vehicle is the only way to ensure quick and reliable starts. But before performing any battery maintenance, make sure that you have the proper equipment necessary to work safely around the battery (see illustration).

2   There are also several precautions that should be taken whenever battery maintenance is performed. Before servicing the battery, always turn the engine and all accessories off and disconnect the cable from the negative terminal of the battery (see Chapter 5, Section 1).

3   The battery produces hydrogen gas, which is both flammable and explosive. Never create a spark, smoke or light a match around the battery. Always charge the battery in a ventilated area.

4   Electrolyte contains poisonous and corrosive sulfuric acid. Do not allow it to get in your eyes, on your skin on your clothes. Never ingest it. Wear protective safety glasses when working near the battery. Keep children away from the battery.

5   Note the external condition of the battery. If the positive terminal and cable clamp on your vehicle's battery is equipped with a rubber or plastic protector, make sure that it's not torn or damaged. It should completely cover the terminal. Look for any corroded or loose connections, cracks in the case or cover or loose hold-down clamps. Also check the entire length of each cable for cracks and frayed conductors.

6   If corrosion, which looks like white, fluffy deposits (see illustration) is evident, particularly around the terminals, the battery should be removed for cleaning. Loosen the cable clamp bolts with a wrench, being careful to remove the ground cable first, and slide them off the terminals (see illustration). Then disconnect the hold-down clamp bolt and nut, remove the clamp and lift the battery from the engine compartment.

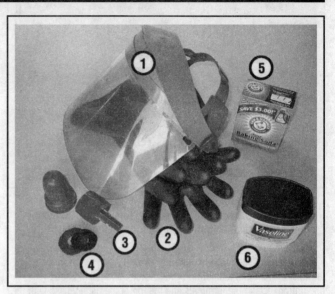

8.1 Tools and materials required for battery maintenance

1   *Face shield/safety goggles* - When removing corrosion with a brush, the acidic particles can easily fly up into your eyes

2   *Rubber gloves* - Another safety item to consider when servicing the battery; remember that's acid inside the battery

3   *Battery post/cable cleaner* - This wire brush cleaning tool will remove all traces of corrosion from the battery posts and cable clamps

4   *Treated felt washers* - Placing one of these on each post, directly under the cable clamps, will help prevent corrosion

5   *Baking soda* - A solution of baking soda and water can be used to neutralize corrosion

6   *Petroleum jelly* - A layer of this on the battery posts will help prevent corrosion

8.6b Removing a cable from the battery post with a wrench - sometimes a pair of special battery pliers is required for this procedure if corrosion has caused deterioration of the nut hex (always remove the ground (-) cable first and hook it up last!)

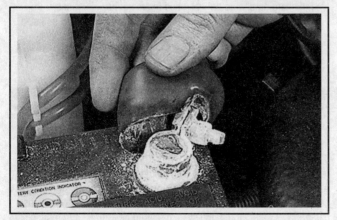

8.6a Battery terminal corrosion usually appears as light, fluffy powder

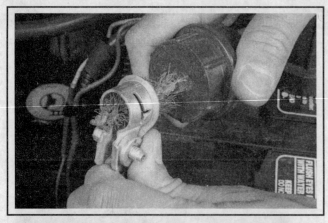

8.7a When cleaning the cable clamps, all corrosion must be removed (the inside of the clamp is tapered to match the taper on the post, so don't remove too much material)

8.7b Regardless of the type of tool used to clean the battery posts, a clean, shiny surface should be the result

7 Clean the cable clamps thoroughly with a battery brush or a terminal cleaner and a solution of warm water and baking soda (see illustration). Wash the terminals and the top of the battery case with the same solution but make sure that the solution doesn't get into the battery. When cleaning the cables, terminals and battery top, wear safety goggles and rubber gloves to prevent any solution from coming in contact with your eyes or hands. Wear old clothes too - even diluted, sulfuric acid splashed onto clothes will burn holes in them. If the terminals have been extensively corroded, clean them up with a terminal cleaner (see illustration). Thoroughly wash all cleaned areas with plain water.

8 Make sure that the battery tray is in good condition and the hold-down clamp fasteners are tight. If the battery is removed from the tray, make sure no parts remain in the bottom of the tray when the battery is reinstalled. When reinstalling the hold-down clamp bolts, do not over-tighten them.

9 Information on removing and installing the battery can be found in Chapter 5. If you disconnected the cable(s) from the negative and/or positive battery terminals, see Chapter 5, Section 1. Information on jump starting can be found at the front of this manual.

10 Corrosion on the hold-down components, battery case and surrounding areas can be removed with a solution of water and baking soda. Thoroughly rinse all cleaned areas with plain water.

11 Any metal parts of the vehicle damaged by corrosion should be covered with a zinc-based primer, then painted.

CHARGING

✳✳ WARNING:

When batteries are being charged, hydrogen gas, which is very explosive and flammable, is produced. Do not smoke or allow open flames near a charging or a recently charged battery. Wear eye protection when near the battery during charging. Also, make sure the charger is unplugged before connecting or disconnecting the battery from the charger.

12 Slow-rate charging is the best way to restore a battery that's discharged to the point where it will not start the engine. It's also a good way to maintain the battery charge in a vehicle that's only driven a few miles between starts. Maintaining the battery charge is particularly important in the winter when the battery must work harder to start the engine and electrical accessories that drain the battery are in greater use.

13 It's best to use a one or two-amp battery charger (sometimes called a "trickle" charger). They are the safest and put the least strain on the battery. They are also the least expensive. For a faster charge, you can use a higher amperage charger, but don't use one rated more than 1/10th the amp/hour rating of the battery. Rapid boost charges that claim to restore the power of the battery in one to two hours are hardest on the battery and can damage batteries not in good condition. This type of charging should only be used in emergency situations.

14 The average time necessary to charge a battery should be listed in the instructions that come with the charger. As a general rule, a trickle charger will charge a battery in 12 to 16 hours.

9 Cooling system check (every 7500 miles [12,000 km] or 6 months)

♦ **Refer to illustration 9.4**

1 Many major engine failures can be attributed to a faulty cooling system. The cooling system also cools the transaxle fluid and thus plays an important role in prolonging transaxle life.

2 The cooling system should be checked with the engine cold. Do this before the vehicle is driven for the day or after the engine has been shut off for at least three hours.

3 Remove the radiator cap by turning it to the left until it reaches a stop. If you hear a hissing sound (indicating there is still pressure in the system), wait until it stops. Now press down on the cap with the palm of your hand and continue turning to the left until the cap can be removed. Thoroughly clean the cap, inside and out, with clean water. Also clean the filler neck on the radiator. All traces of corrosion should be removed. The coolant inside the radiator should be relatively transparent. If it's rust colored, the system should be drained and refilled (see Section 21). If the coolant level isn't up to the top, add additional antifreeze/coolant mixture (see Section 4).

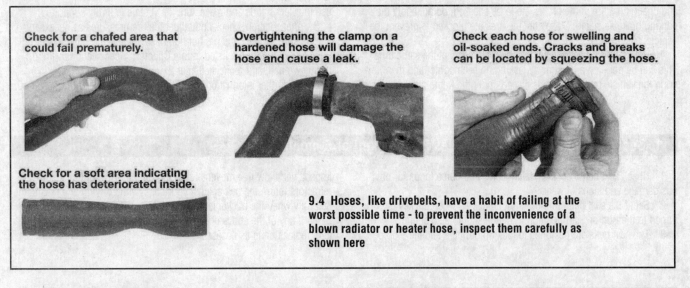

Check for a chafed area that could fail prematurely.

Overtightening the clamp on a hardened hose will damage the hose and cause a leak.

Check each hose for swelling and oil-soaked ends. Cracks and breaks can be located by squeezing the hose.

Check for a soft area indicating the hose has deteriorated inside.

9.4 Hoses, like drivebelts, have a habit of failing at the worst possible time - to prevent the inconvenience of a blown radiator or heater hose, inspect them carefully as shown here

4   Carefully check the large upper and lower radiator hoses along with the smaller diameter heater hoses which run from the engine to the firewall. Inspect each hose along its entire length, replacing any hose which is cracked, swollen or shows signs of deterioration. Cracks may become more apparent if the hose is squeezed (see illustration). Regardless of condition, it's a good idea to replace hoses with new ones every two years.

5   Make sure that all hose connections are tight. A leak in the cooling system will usually show up as white or rust colored deposits on the areas adjoining the leak. If wire-type clamps are used at the ends of the hoses, it may be a good idea to replace them with more secure screw-type clamps.

6   Use compressed air or a soft brush to remove bugs, leaves, etc. from the front of the radiator or air conditioning condenser. Be careful not to damage the delicate cooling fins or cut yourself on them.

7   Every other inspection, or at the first indication of cooling system problems, have the cap and system pressure tested. If you don't have a pressure tester, most gas stations and repair shops will do this for a minimal charge.

10 Tire rotation (every 7500 miles [12,000 km] or 6 months)

▶ **Refer to illustrations 10.2a and 10.2b**

1   The tires should be rotated at the specified intervals and whenever uneven wear is noticed. Since the vehicle will be raised and the tires removed anyway, check the brakes (see Section 12) at this time.

2   Radial tires must be rotated in a specific pattern (see illustrations). Most models are equipped with non-directional tires, but some models may have directional tires, which have a different rotation pattern. When rotating tires, examine the sidewalls. Directional tires have arrows on the sidewall that indicate the direction they must turn, and a set of these tires includes two left-side tires and two right-side tires. The left and right side tires must not be rotated to the other side.

3   Refer to the information in *Jacking and towing* at the front of this manual for the proper procedures to follow when raising the vehicle

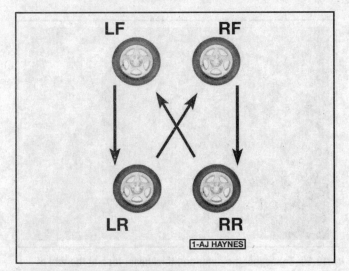

10.2a The recommended rotation pattern for non-directional radial tires

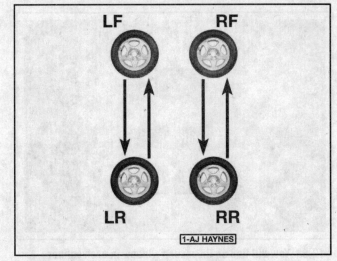

10.2b The recommended rotation pattern for directional radial tires

and changing a tire. If the brakes are to be checked, do not apply the parking brake as stated. Make sure the tires are blocked to prevent the vehicle from rolling.

4 Preferably, the entire vehicle should be raised at the same time. This can be done on a hoist or by jacking up each corner and then lowering the vehicle onto jackstands placed under the frame rails. Always use four jackstands and make sure the vehicle is firmly supported.

5 After rotation, check and adjust the tire pressures as necessary and be sure to check the lug nut tightness. Ideally, lug nuts should be tightened to the torque listed in this Chapter's Specifications with a torque wrench, and rechecked after 25 miles of driving.

6 For further information on the wheels and tires, refer to Chapter 10.

11 Seat belt check (every 7500 miles [12,000 km] or 6 months)

1 Check seat belts, buckles, latch plates and guide loops for obvious damage and signs of wear.

2 See if the seat belt reminder light comes on when the key is turned to the Run or Start position. A chime should also sound.

3 The seat belts are designed to lock up during a sudden stop or impact, yet allow free movement during normal driving. Make sure the retractors return the belt against your chest while driving and rewind the belt fully when the buckle is unlatched.

4 If any of the above checks reveal problems with the seat belt system, replace parts as necessary.

12 Brake system check (every 15,000 miles [24,000 km] or 12 months)

❈❈ WARNING:

The dust created by the brake system is harmful to your health. Never blow it out with compressed air and don't inhale any of it. An approved filtering mask should be worn when working on the brakes. Do not, under any circumstances, use petroleum-based solvents to clean brake parts. Use brake system cleaner only!

➥Note: For detailed photographs of the brake system, refer to Chapter 9.

1 In addition to the specified intervals, the brakes should be inspected every time the wheels are removed or whenever a defect is suspected.

2 Any of the following symptoms could indicate a potential brake system defect: The vehicle pulls to one side when the brake pedal is depressed; the brakes make squealing or dragging noises when applied; brake pedal travel is excessive; the pedal pulsates; or brake fluid leaks, usually onto the inside of the tire or wheel.

DISC BRAKES

▶ Refer to illustrations 12.6a and 12.6b

3 Disc brakes can be visually checked without removing any parts except the wheels. Remove the hub caps (if applicable) and loosen the wheel lug nuts a quarter turn each.

4 Raise the vehicle and place it securely on jackstands.

❈❈ WARNING:

Never work under a vehicle that is supported only by a jack!

5 Remove the wheels. Now visible is the disc brake caliper which contains the pads. There is an outer brake pad and an inner pad. Both must be checked for wear.

6 Measure the thickness of the outer pad at each end of the caliper and the inner pad through the inspection hole in the caliper body (see illustrations). Compare the measurement with the limit given in this

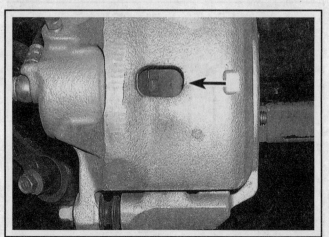

12.6a You will find an inspection window in each caliper - the inner brake pad lining thickness can be determined by looking through this window

12.6b To inspect the outer pad thickness, look at the end of the pad

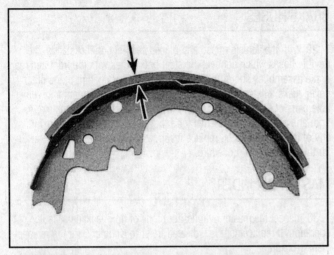

12.14 If the lining is bonded to the brake shoe, measure the lining thickness from the outer surface to the metal shoe, as shown here; if the lining is riveted to the shoe, measure from the lining outer surface to the rivet head

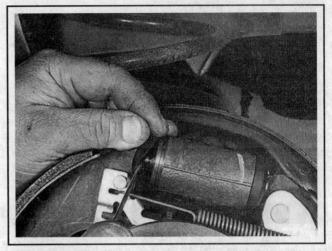

12.16 Check the wheel cylinder boots for leaking fluid indicating that the cylinder must be replaced or rebuilt

Chapter's Specifications; if any brake pad thickness is less than specified, then all brake pads must be replaced (see Chapter 9).

7   If you're in doubt as to the exact pad thickness or quality, remove them for measurement and further inspection (see Chapter 9).

8   Check the disc for score marks, wear and burned spots. If any of these conditions exist, the disc should be removed for servicing or replacement (see Chapter 9).

9   Before installing the wheels, check all the brake lines and hoses for damage, wear, deformation, cracks, corrosion, leakage, bends and twists, particularly in the vicinity of the rubber hoses and calipers.

10 Install the wheels, lower the vehicle and tighten the wheel lug nuts to the torque given in this Chapter's Specifications.

DRUM BRAKES

▶ **Refer to illustrations 12.14 and 12.16**

11 On models with rear drum brakes, make sure the parking brake is off then tap on the outside of the drum with a rubber mallet to loosen it.

12 Remove the brake drums. If the drum still won't come off, refer to Chapter 9.

13 With the drums removed, carefully clean the brake assembly with brake system cleaner.

❋❋ WARNING:

Don't blow the dust out with compressed air and don't inhale any of it (it is harmful to your health).

14 Note the thickness of the lining material on both front and rear brake shoes (see illustration). Compare the measurement with the limit given in this Chapter's Specifications; if any lining thickness is less than specified, then all of the brake shoes must be replaced (see Chapter 9). The shoes should also be replaced if they're cracked, glazed (shiny areas), or covered with brake fluid.

15 Make sure all the brake assembly springs are connected and in good condition.

16 Check the brake components for signs of fluid leakage. With your finger or a small screwdriver, carefully pry back the rubber cups on the

wheel cylinder located at the top of the brake shoes (see illustration). Any leakage here is an indication that the wheel cylinders should be replaced immediately (see Chapter 9). Also, check all hoses and connections for signs of leakage.

17 Wipe the inside of the drum with a clean rag and denatured alcohol or brake cleaner. Again, be careful not to breathe the dangerous brake dust.

18 Check the inside of the drum for cracks, score marks, deep scratches and hard spots which will appear as small discolored areas. If imperfections cannot be removed with fine emery cloth, the drum must be taken to an automotive machine shop for resurfacing.

19 Repeat the procedure for the remaining wheel. If the inspection reveals that all parts are in good condition, reinstall the brake drums, install the wheels and lower the vehicle to the ground.

BRAKE BOOSTER CHECK

20 Sit in the driver's seat and perform the following sequence of tests.

21 With the brake fully depressed, start the engine - the pedal should move down a little when the engine starts.

22 With the engine running, depress the brake pedal several times - the travel distance should not change.

23 Depress the brake, stop the engine and hold the pedal in for about 30 seconds - the pedal should neither sink nor rise.

24 Restart the engine, run it for about a minute and turn it off. Then firmly depress the brake several times - the pedal travel should decrease with each application.

25 If your brakes do not operate as described, the brake booster has failed. Refer to Chapter 9 for the replacement procedure.

PARKING BRAKE

26 Slowly pull up on the parking brake and count the number of clicks you hear until the handle is up as far as it will go. The adjustment is correct if you hear the specified number of clicks (see this Chapter's Specifications). If you hear more or fewer clicks, it's time to adjust the parking brake (see Chapter 9).

27 An alternative method of checking the parking brake is to park the vehicle on a steep hill with the parking brake set and the transmission in Neutral. If the parking brake cannot prevent the vehicle from rolling, it is in need of adjustment (see Chapter 9).

ANTI-LOCK BRAKE SYSTEM (ABS)

28 Carefully inspect the ABS wiring harness. Pay particularly close attention to the harness and connections near each wheel. Look for signs of chafing and other damage caused by incorrectly routed wires. If a wheel sensor harness is damaged, the sensor must be replaced (see Chapter 9).

❊❊ WARNING:

Do NOT try to repair an ABS wiring harness. The ABS system is sensitive to even the smallest changes in resistance. Repairing the harness could alter resistance values and cause the system to malfunction. If the ABS wiring harness is damaged in any way, it must be replaced.

BRAKE HOSES

29 With the vehicle raised and placed securely on jackstands, the flexible hoses which connect the steel brake lines with the front and rear brake assemblies should be inspected for cracks, chafing of the outer cover, leaks, blisters and other damage. These are important and vulnerable parts of the brake system and inspection should be complete. A light and mirror will be needed for a thorough check. If a hose exhibits any of the above defects, replace it with a new one. Refer to Chapter 9 for the replacement procedure.

MASTER CYLINDER

30 Inspect the master cylinder for signs of fluid leakage or faulty operation. If replacement is indicated, refer to Chapter 9 for the replacement procedure.

13 Steering, suspension and driveaxle boot check (every 15,000 miles [24,000 km] or 12 months)

➡Note: For detailed illustrations of the steering and suspension components, refer to Chapter 10.

WITH THE WHEELS ON THE GROUND

▶ **Refer to illustration 13.4**

1 With the vehicle stopped and the front wheels pointed straight ahead, rock the steering wheel gently back and forth. If freeplay is excessive, a front wheel bearing, steering shaft universal joint or lower arm balljoint is worn or the steering gear is out of adjustment or broken. Refer to Chapter 10 for the appropriate repair procedure.

2 Other symptoms, such as excessive vehicle body movement over rough roads, swaying (leaning) around corners and binding as the steering wheel is turned, may indicate faulty steering and/or suspension components.

3 Check the shock absorbers by pushing down and releasing the vehicle several times at each corner. If the vehicle does not come back to a level position within one or two bounces, the shocks/struts are worn and must be replaced. When bouncing the vehicle up and down, listen for squeaks and noises from the suspension components.

4 Check the struts and shock absorbers for evidence of fluid leakage (see illustration). A light film of fluid is no cause for concern. Make sure that any fluid noted is from the shocks and not from some other source. If leakage is noted, replace the shocks as a set.

5 Check the shocks to be sure they are securely mounted and undamaged. Check the upper mounts for damage and wear. If damage or wear is noted, replace the shocks as a set (front and rear).

6 If the shocks must be replaced, refer to Chapter 10 for the procedure.

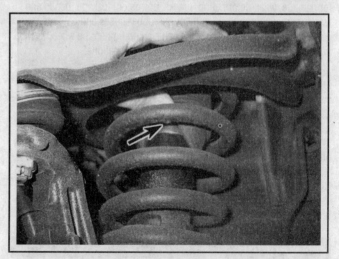

13.4 Check the shocks for leakage at the indicated area

UNDER THE VEHICLE

▶ **Refer to illustrations 13.10 and 13.11**

7 Raise the vehicle with a floor jack and support it securely on jackstands. See *Jacking and towing* at the front of this book for the proper jacking points.

8 Check the tires for irregular wear patterns and proper inflation. See Section 5 in this Chapter for information regarding tire wear and Chapter 10 for information on hub bearing replacement.

13.10 To check the balljoint for wear, try to pry the control arm up and down to make sure there is no play in the balljoint (if there is, replace it)

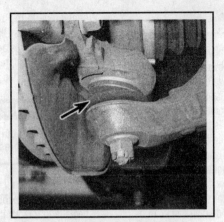

13.11 Check the balljoint boots for damage

13.14 Flex the driveaxle boots by hand to check for cracks and/or leaking grease

9   Inspect the universal joint between the steering shaft and the steering gear housing. Check the steering gear housing for lubricant leakage. Make sure that the dust seals and boots are not damaged and that the boot clamps are not loose. Check the steering linkage for looseness or damage. Check the tie-rod ends for excessive play. Look for loose bolts, broken or disconnected parts and deteriorated rubber bushings on all suspension and steering components. While an assistant turns the steering wheel from side to side, check the steering components for free movement, chafing and binding. If the steering components do not seem to be reacting with the movement of the steering wheel, try to determine where the slack is located.

10 Check the balljoints for wear by trying to move each control arm up and down with a pry bar (see illustration) to ensure that its balljoint has no play. If any balljoint does have play, replace it. See Chapter 10 for the balljoint replacement procedure.

11 Inspect the balljoint boots for damage and leaking grease (see illustration). Replace the balljoints with new ones if they are damaged (see Chapter 10).

12 At the rear of the vehicle, inspect the suspension arm bushings for deterioration. Additional information on suspension components can be found in Chapter 10.

DRIVEAXLE BOOT CHECK

▶ **Refer to illustration 13.14**

➡ **Note: For detailed illustrations of the driveaxles, refer to Chapter 8.**

13 The driveaxle boots are very important because they prevent dirt, water and foreign material from entering and damaging the constant velocity (CV) joints. Oil and grease can cause the boot material to deteriorate prematurely, so it's a good idea to wash the boots with soap and water. Because it constantly pivots back and forth following the steering action of the front hub, the outer CV boot wears out sooner and should be inspected regularly.

14 Inspect the boots for tears and cracks as well as loose clamps (see illustration). If there is any evidence of cracks or leaking lubricant, they must be replaced as described in Chapter 8.

14 Underhood hose check and replacement (every 15,000 miles [24,000 km] or 12 months)

✳✳ WARNING:

Replacement of air conditioning hoses must be left to a dealer service department or air conditioning shop that has the equipment to depressurize the system safely. Never remove air conditioning components or hoses until the system has been depressurized.

GENERAL

1   High temperatures under the hood can cause deterioration of the rubber and plastic hoses used for engine, accessory and emission systems operation. Periodic inspection should be made for cracks, loose clamps, material hardening and leaks.

2   Information specific to the cooling system hoses can be found in Section 9.

3   Most (but not all) hoses are secured to the fittings with clamps. Where clamps are used, check to be sure they haven't lost their tension, allowing the hose to leak. If clamps aren't used, make sure the hose has not expanded and/or hardened where it slips over the fitting, allowing it to leak.

PCV SYSTEM HOSE

4   To reduce hydrocarbon emissions, crankcase blow-by gas is vented through the PCV valve in the water passage on four-cylinder models or the valve cover on V6 models to the intake manifold via a rubber hose. The blow-by gases mix with incoming air in the intake manifold before being burned in the combustion chambers.

5   Check the PCV hose for cracks, leaks and other damage. Disconnect it from the PCV valve and the intake manifold and check the inside for obstructions. If it's clogged, clean it out with solvent. See Chapter 6 for check and replacement.

VACUUM HOSES

6 It's quite common for vacuum hoses, especially those in the emissions system, to be color coded or identified by colored stripes molded into them. Various systems require hoses with different wall thickness, collapse resistance and temperature resistance. When replacing hoses, be sure the new ones are made of the same material.

7 Often the only effective way to check a hose is to remove it completely from the vehicle. If more than one hose is removed, be sure to label the hoses and fittings to ensure correct installation.

8 When checking vacuum hoses, be sure to include any plastic T-fittings in the check. Inspect the fittings for cracks and the hose where it fits over each fitting for distortion, which could cause leakage.

9 A small piece of vacuum hose (1/4-inch inside diameter) can be used as a stethoscope to detect vacuum leaks. Hold one end of the hose to your ear and probe around vacuum hoses and fittings, listening for the hissing sound characteristic of a vacuum leak.

✳✳ WARNING:

When probing with the vacuum hose stethoscope, be careful not to come into contact with moving engine components such as drivebelts, the cooling fan, etc.

FUEL HOSE

✳✳ WARNING:

Gasoline is flammable, so take extra precautions when you work on any part of the fuel system. Don't smoke or allow open flames or bare light bulbs near the work area, and don't work in a garage where a gas-type appliance (such as a water heater or clothes dryer) is present. Since fuel is carcinogenic, wear latex gloves when there's a possibility of being exposed to fuel, and, if you spill any fuel on your skin, rinse it off immediately with soap and water. Mop up any spills immediately and do not store fuel-soaked rags where they could ignite. The fuel system is under constant pressure, so, if any fuel lines are to be disconnected, the fuel pressure in the system must be relieved first (see Chapter 4 for more information).

When you perform any kind of work on the fuel system, wear safety glasses and have a Class B type fire extinguisher on hand.

10 The fuel lines are usually under pressure, so if any fuel lines are to be disconnected, relieve the fuel system pressure first and be prepared to catch spilled fuel.

✳✳ WARNING:

Your vehicle is equipped with fuel injection and you must relieve the fuel system pressure before servicing the fuel lines.

Refer to Chapter 4 for the fuel system pressure relief procedure.

11 Check all flexible fuel lines for deterioration and chafing. Check especially for cracks in areas where the hose bends and just before fittings, such as where a hose attaches to the fuel pump, fuel filter and fuel rail.

12 When replacing a hose, use only hose that is specifically designed for your fuel injection system.

13 Spring-type clamps are sometimes used on fuel return or vapor lines. These clamps often lose their tension over a period of time, and can be sprung during removal. Replace all spring-type clamps with screw clamps whenever a hose is replaced. Some fuel lines use spring-lock type couplings, which require a special tool to disconnect. See Chapter 4 for more information on this type of coupling.

METAL LINES

14 Sections of metal line are often used for fuel line between the fuel pump and the fuel injection unit. Check carefully to make sure the line isn't bent, crimped or cracked.

15 If a section of metal fuel line must be replaced, use seamless steel tubing only, since copper and aluminum tubing do not have the strength necessary to withstand vibration caused by the engine.

16 Check the metal brake lines where they enter the master cylinder and brake proportioning unit (if used) for cracks in the lines and loose fittings. Any sign of brake fluid leakage calls for an immediate thorough inspection of the brake system.

15 Fuel system check (every 15,000 miles [24,000 km] or 12 months)

✳✳ WARNING:

Gasoline is flammable, so take extra precautions when you work on any part of the fuel system. Don't smoke or allow open flames or bare light bulbs near the work area, and don't work in a garage where a gas-type appliance (such as a water heater or clothes dryer) is present. Since fuel is carcinogenic, wear latex gloves when there's a possibility of being exposed to fuel, and, if you spill any fuel on your skin, rinse it off immediately with soap and water. Mop up any spills immediately and do not store fuel-soaked rags where they could ignite. When you perform any kind of work on the fuel system, wear safety glasses and have a Class B type fire extinguisher on hand. The fuel system is under constant pressure, so, before any lines are disconnected, the fuel system pressure must be relieved (see Chapter 4).

1 If you smell gasoline while driving or after the vehicle has been sitting in the sun, inspect the fuel system immediately.

2 Remove the fuel filler cap and inspect if for damage and corrosion. The gasket should have an unbroken sealing imprint. If the gasket is damaged or corroded, install a new cap.

3 Inspect the fuel feed line for cracks. Make sure that the connections between the fuel lines and the fuel injection system are secure and dry.

✳✳ WARNING:

Your vehicle is fuel injected, so you must relieve the fuel system pressure before servicing fuel system components. The fuel system pressure relief procedure is outlined in Chapter 4.

4   Since some components of the fuel system - the fuel tank and the fuel lines, for example - are underneath the vehicle, they can be inspected more easily with the vehicle raised on a hoist. If that's not possible, raise the vehicle and support it on jackstands.

5   With the vehicle raised and safely supported, inspect the gas tank and filler neck for punctures, cracks and other damage. The connection between the filler neck and the tank is particularly critical. Sometimes a rubber filler neck will leak because of loose clamps or deteriorated rubber. Inspect all fuel tank mounting brackets and straps to be sure that the tank is securely attached to the vehicle.

✳✳ WARNING:

Do not, under any circumstances, try to repair a fuel tank (except rubber components).

6   Carefully check all hoses and lines leading away from the fuel tank. Check for loose connections, deteriorated hoses, crimped lines and other damage. Repair or replace damaged sections as necessary (see Chapter 4).

16 Exhaust system check (every 15,000 miles [24,000 km] or 12 months)

▶ Refer to illustration 16.2

1   With the engine cold (at least three hours after the vehicle has been driven), check the complete exhaust system from the engine to the end of the tailpipe. Ideally, the inspection should be done with the vehicle on a hoist to permit unrestricted access. If a hoist isn't available, raise the vehicle and support it securely on jackstands.

2   Check the exhaust pipes and connections for evidence of leaks, severe corrosion and damage. Make sure that all brackets and hangers are in good condition and tight (see illustration).

3   At the same time, inspect the underside of the body for holes, corrosion, open seams, etc. which may allow exhaust gases to enter the passenger compartment. Seal all body openings with silicone or body putty.

4   Rattles and other noises can often be traced to the exhaust system, especially the mounts and hangers. Try to move the pipes, muffler and catalytic converter. If the components can come in contact with the body or suspension parts, secure the exhaust system with new mounts.

5   Check the running condition of the engine by inspecting inside the end of the tailpipe. The exhaust deposits here are an indication of engine state-of-tune. If the pipe is black and sooty or coated with white deposits, the engine may need a tune-up, including a thorough fuel system inspection and adjustment.

16.2 Be sure to check each exhaust system rubber hanger for damage

17 Air filter replacement (every 30,000 miles [48,000 km] or 24 months)

▶ Refer to illustration 17.1

1   The air filter is located inside a housing inside of the engine compartment. To remove the air filter, remove the screws securing the two halves of the air filter housing together, then separate the cover halves and remove the air filter element (see illustration).

2   Inspect the surface of the filter element. If it is dirty, replace it. If it is only moderately dusty, it can be reused by blowing it clean from the back to the front surface with compressed air. Because it is a pleated paper type filter, it cannot be washed or oiled. If it cannot be cleaned satisfactorily with compressed air, discard and replace it. While the cover is off, be careful not to drop anything down into the housing.

✳✳ CAUTION:

Never drive the vehicle with the air filter removed. Excessive engine wear could result and backfiring could even cause a fire under the hood.

17.1 Pull the cover out of the way and remove the element

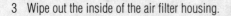

3   Wipe out the inside of the air filter housing.

4   Place the new filter into the air filter housing, making sure it seats properly.

5   Installation of the housing is the reverse of removal.

18 Interior ventilation filter replacement (every 30,000 miles [48,000 km] or 24 months)

▶ **Refer to illustrations 18.2, 18.3 and 18.4**

1   These models are equipped with an air filtering element in the ventilation system, located in a housing above the blower fan, under the right side of the instrument panel.

2   Release the glove box stop, then lower the glove box and let it hang (see illustration).

3   Release the tabs to free the filter from the housing (see illustration).

4   Remove the filter from the housing (see illustration).

5   Installation is the reverse of the removal procedure.

18.2 Release the glove box stops and lower the box

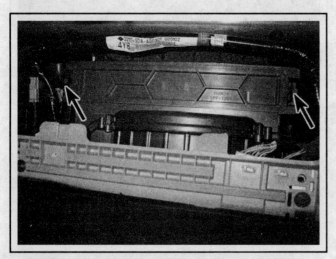

18.3 Release the filter by releasing these tabs . . .

18.4 . . . then pull the filter element from the housing

19 Drivebelt check and replacement (every 30,000 miles [48,000 km] or 24 months)

ACCESSORY DRIVEBELT

1   A single serpentine drivebelt is located at the front of the engine and plays an important role in the overall operation of the engine and its components. Due to its function and material make up, the belt is prone to wear and should be periodically inspected. The serpentine belt drives the alternator, power steering pump, water pump and air conditioning compressor.

Check

▶ **Refer to illustrations 19.3 and 19.4**

2   With the engine stopped, inspect the full length of the drivebelt for cracks and separation of the belt plies. It will be necessary to turn the engine (using a wrench or socket and bar on the crankshaft pulley bolt) in order to move the belt from the pulleys so that the belt can be inspected thoroughly. Twist the belt between the pulleys so that both sides can be viewed. Also check for fraying, and glazing which gives the belt a shiny appearance. Check the pulleys for nicks, cracks, distortion and corrosion.

3   Note that it is not unusual for a ribbed belt to exhibit small cracks in the edges of the belt ribs, and unless these are extensive or very deep, belt replacement is not essential (see illustration).

4   The drivebelt tension is adjusted by an automatic tensioner. Look at the wear indicator on the tensioner (see illustration). The marks should be within the specified range; if not, the belt will have to be replaced.

Replacement

5   Note how the drivebelt is routed, then remove the belt from the pulleys. If you're working on a four-cylinder engine, use a wrench on the tensioner pulley center bolt and turn the tensioner clockwise to release the drivebelt tension. If you're working on a V6 engine, use a wrench on the tensioner pulley center bolt and turn the tensioner counterclockwise to release the drivebelt tension.

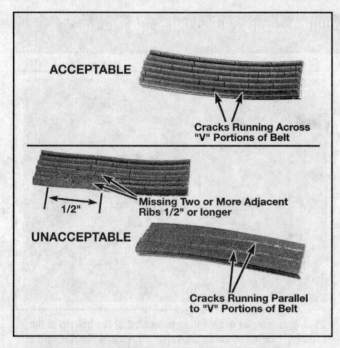

19.3 **Here are some of the more common problems associated with drivebelts (check the belts very carefully to prevent an untimely breakdown)**

6   Fit the new drivebelt onto the crankshaft, alternator, power steering pump, water pump and air conditioning compressor pulleys, as applicable, then turn the tensioner and locate the drivebelt on the pulley. Make sure that the drivebelt is correctly seated in all of the pulley grooves, then release the tensioner.

19.4 **Details of the drivebelt tensioner (4-cylinder model shown)**

1	*Maximum length (belt worn out)*	2	*Belt length indicator*

TENSIONER REPLACEMENT

7   Remove the drivebelt as described previously.
8   If you're working on a four-cylinder model, remove the power steering pump (see Chapter 10).
9   On four-cylinder models, remove the three bolts securing the tensioner to the engine block. On V6 models, remove the two bolts securing the tensioner to the engine block, then detach the tensioner from the engine.
➡**Note: The tensioner pulley can be replaced separately, if necessary.**

10 Installation is the reverse of removal. Be sure to tighten the tensioner (and pulley, if replaced) bolts to the torque listed in this Chapter's Specifications.

20 Brake fluid change (every 30,000 miles [48,000 km] or 24 months)

✳✳ WARNING:

Brake fluid can harm your eyes and damage painted surfaces, so use extreme caution when handling or pouring it. Do not use brake fluid that has been standing open or is more than one year old. Brake fluid absorbs moisture from the air. Excess moisture can cause a dangerous loss of braking effectiveness.

1   At the specified intervals, the brake fluid should be drained and replaced. Since the brake fluid may drip or splash when pouring it, place plenty of rags around the master cylinder to protect any surrounding painted surfaces.
2   Before beginning work, purchase the specified brake fluid (see *Recommended lubricants and fluids* in this Chapter's Specifications).
3   Remove the cap from the master cylinder reservoir.
4   Using a hand suction pump or similar device, withdraw the fluid from the master cylinder reservoir.

5   Add new fluid to the master cylinder until it rises to the base of the filler neck.
6   Bleed the brake system as described in Chapter 9 at all four brakes until new and uncontaminated fluid is expelled from the bleeder screw. Be sure to maintain the fluid level in the master cylinder as you perform the bleeding process. If you allow the master cylinder to run dry, air will enter the system.
7   Refill the master cylinder with fluid and check the operation of the brakes. The pedal should feel solid when depressed, with no sponginess.

✳✳ WARNING:

Do not operate the vehicle if you are in doubt about the effectiveness of the brake system.

21 Cooling system servicing (draining, flushing and refilling) (every 60,000 miles [96,000 km] or 60 months)

❊❊ WARNING:

Do not allow antifreeze to come in contact with your skin or painted surfaces of the vehicle. Rinse off spills immediately with plenty of water. Antifreeze is highly toxic if ingested. Never leave antifreeze lying around in an open container or in puddles on the floor; children and pets are attracted by its sweet smell and may drink it. Check with local authorities about disposing of used antifreeze. Many communities have collection centers which will see that antifreeze is disposed of safely. Never dump used antifreeze on the ground or pour it into drains.

1 Periodically, the cooling system should be drained, flushed and refilled to replenish the antifreeze mixture and prevent formation of rust and corrosion, which can impair the performance of the cooling system and cause engine damage. When the cooling system is serviced, all hoses and the radiator cap should be checked and replaced if necessary.

DRAINING

◆ **Refer to illustration 21.3**

2 Apply the parking brake and block the wheels.

❊❊ WARNING:

If the vehicle has just been driven, wait several hours to allow the engine to cool down before beginning this procedure. Turn the heater control to maximum heat.

3 Move a large container under the radiator drain to catch the coolant. The radiator drain plug is located on the right side lower corner of the radiator (see illustration). Unscrew the drain plug until coolant starts flowing from the drain hole (a pair of pliers may be required to turn it).
4 Remove the radiator cap and allow the radiator to drain.
5 While the coolant is draining, check the condition of the radiator hoses, heater hoses and clamps (refer to Section 9 if necessary).
6 Replace any damaged clamps or hoses. Close the drain plugs.

FLUSHING

7 Fill the cooling system with clean water, following the Refilling procedure.
8 Start the engine and allow it to reach normal operating temperature, then rev up the engine a few times.
9 Turn the engine off and allow it to cool completely, then drain the system as described earlier.
10 Repeat Steps 7 through 9 until the water being drained is free of contaminants.
11 In severe cases of contamination or clogging of the radiator, remove the radiator (see Chapter 3) and have a radiator repair facility clean and repair it if necessary.

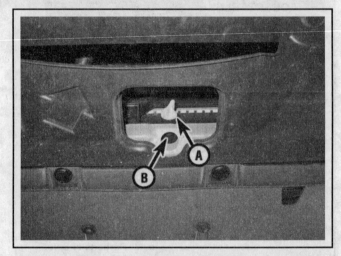

21.3 The radiator drain fitting is located at the bottom of the radiator - before opening the valve (A), push a short length of rubber hose onto the plastic fitting (B) to prevent the coolant from splashing

12 Many deposits can be removed by the chemical action of a cleaner available at auto parts stores. Follow the procedure outlined in the manufacturer's instructions.

➡ **Note: When the coolant is regularly drained and the system refilled with the correct antifreeze/water mixture, there should be no need to use chemical cleaners or descalers.**

13 Remove the coolant recovery reservoir. Drain the reservoir and flush it with clean water, then reconnect the hose.

REFILLING

14 Fill the cooling system with the proper type and mixture of antifreeze (see this Chapter's Specifications), up to the base of the radiator cap filler neck. Loosely install the radiator cap.
15 Place the heater control to maximum heat. Start the engine and run it at approximately 1500 rpm until the radiator fan comes on two times. Feel the upper radiator hose - it should be warm, indicating the thermostat has opened.
16 Turn off the engine and let it cool down. Slowly remove the radiator cap and check the coolant level, adding as necessary.

❊❊ WARNING:

If you hear a hissing sound as you unscrew the cap, STOP. Let the engine cool down longer. Fill the coolant reservoir up to the MIN mark, if necessary.

17 Start the engine, allow it to reach normal operating temperature once again and check for leaks.

22 Automatic transaxle fluid change (every 90,000 miles [144,000 km] or 60 months)

▶ **Refer to illustration 22.6**

1   The automatic transaxle fluid should be changed at the recommended intervals.

2   Before beginning work, purchase the specified transmission fluid (see *Recommended lubricants and fluids* in this Chapter's Specifications).

3   Other tools necessary for this job include jackstands to support the vehicle in a raised position, wrenches, drain pan capable of holding at least four quarts, newspapers and clean rags.

4   The fluid should be drained immediately after the vehicle has been driven. Hot fluid is more effective than cold fluid at removing built up sediment.

❈❈ WARNING:

Fluid temperature can exceed 350-degrees F in a hot transaxle. Wear protective gloves.

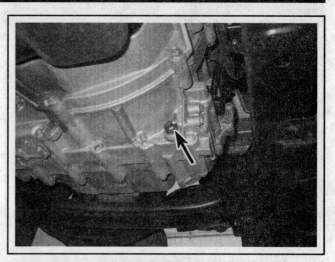

22.6 Location of the transaxle fluid drain plug

5   After the vehicle has been driven to warm up the fluid, raise the front of the vehicle and support it securely on jackstands.

❈❈ WARNING:

Never work under a vehicle that is supported only by a jack!

6   Place the drain pan under the drain plug and remove the drain plug (see illustration). Be sure the drain pan is in position, as fluid will come out with some force. Once the fluid is drained, reinstall the drain plug securely. Measure the amount of fluid drained and write down this figure for reference when refilling.

7   Lower the vehicle.

8   With the engine off, add new fluid to the transaxle through the dipstick tube (see *Recommended lubricants and fluids* for the recommended fluid type). Begin the refill procedure by initially adding 1/3 of the amount drained. Then, with the engine running, add 1/2-pint at a time (cycling the shifter through each gear position between additions) until the level is correct on the dipstick.

9   If desired, repeat Steps 5 through 8 once to flush any contaminated fluid from the torque converter.

10 The old oil drained from the transaxle cannot be reused in its present state and should be disposed of. Check with your local auto parts store, disposal facility or environmental agency to see if they will accept the oil for recycling. After the oil has cooled it can be drained into a container (capped plastic jugs, topped bottles, milk cartons, etc.) for transport to one of these disposal sites. Don't dispose of the oil by pouring it on the ground or down a drain!

23 Spark plug check and replacement (every 105,000 miles [169,000 km] or 84 months, whichever comes first)

▶ **Refer to illustrations 23.2, 23.5, 23.9, 23.10, 23.11a and 23.11b**

1   The spark plugs are located in the center of each cylinder head.

2   In most cases the tools necessary for spark plug replacement include a spark plug socket which fits onto a ratchet (this special socket is padded inside to protect the porcelain insulators on the new plugs and hold them in place), various extensions and a feeler gauge to check the spark plug gap (see illustration). Since these engines are equipped with an aluminum cylinder head(s), a torque wrench should be used when tightening the spark plugs.

3   The best approach when replacing the spark plugs is to purchase the new spark plugs beforehand, check the gaps and then replace each plug one at a time. When buying the new spark plugs, be sure to obtain the correct plug for your specific engine. This information can be found in the Specification Section at the end of this Chapter, in your owner's manual or on the Vehicle Emissions Control Information (VECI) label located under the hood. If differences exist between the sources, purchase the spark plug type specified on the VECI label as it was printed for your specific engine.

4   Allow the engine to cool completely before attempting to remove

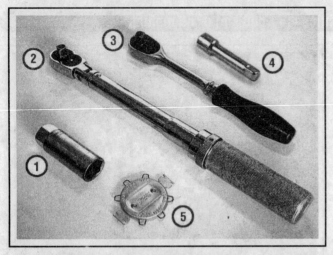

23.2 Tools required for changing spark plugs

1   **Spark plug socket** - This will have special padding inside to protect the spark plug porcelain insulator
2   **Torque wrench** - Although not mandatory, use of this tool is the best way to ensure that the plugs are tightened properly
3   **Ratchet** - Standard hand tool to fit the plug socket
4   **Extension** - Depending on model and accessories, you may need special extensions and universal joints to reach one or more of the plugs
5   **Spark plug gap gauge** - This gauge for checking the gap comes in a variety of styles. Make sure the gap for your engine is included

23.9 Use a ratchet and extension to remove the spark plugs

any of the plugs. During this cooling off time, each of the new spark plugs can be inspected for defects and the gaps can be checked.

5   The gap is checked by inserting the proper thickness gauge between the electrodes at the tip of the plug (see illustration). The gap between the electrodes should be as listed in this Chapter's Specifications or in your owner's manual.

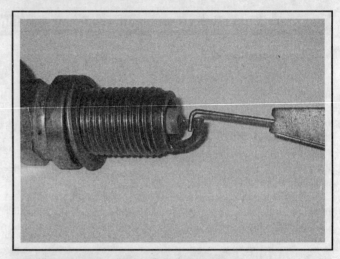

23.5 Spark plug manufacturers recommend using a wire-type gauge when checking the gap - the wire should slide between the electrodes with a slight drag

❋❋ CAUTION:

The manufacturer recommends against adjusting the gap on platinum- or iridium-tipped spark plugs; if the gap is out of specification, replace the plug.

Also, at this time check for cracks in the spark plug body (if any are found, the plug must not be used).

6   Cover the fender to prevent damage to the paint. Fender covers are available from auto parts stores but an old blanket will work just fine.

7   Remove the ignition coils (see Chapter 5).

8   If compressed air is available, use it to blow any dirt or foreign material away from the spark plug area.

❋❋ WARNING:

Wear eye protection!

The idea here is to eliminate the possibility of material falling into the cylinder through the spark plug hole as the spark plug is removed.

9   Place the spark plug socket over the plug and remove it from the engine by turning it in a counterclockwise direction (see illustration).

10 Whether you are replacing the plugs at this time or intend to reuse the old plugs, compare the spark plug to those shown in this chart to get an indication of the general running condition of the engine. (see illustration)

11 Apply a small amount of anti-seize compound to the spark plug threads (see illustration). Install one of the new plugs into the hole until you can no longer turn it with your fingers, then tighten it with a torque wrench (if available) or the ratchet. It is a good idea to slip a short length of rubber hose over the end of the plug to use as a tool to thread it into place (see illustration). The hose will grip the plug well enough to turn it, but will start to slip if the plug begins to cross-thread in the hole - this will prevent damaged threads and the accompanying repair costs.

12 Attach the coil to the new spark plug using a twisting motion until it is firmly seated on the end of the spark plug. Tighten the mounting bolts securely.

13 Repeat the procedure for the remaining spark plugs.

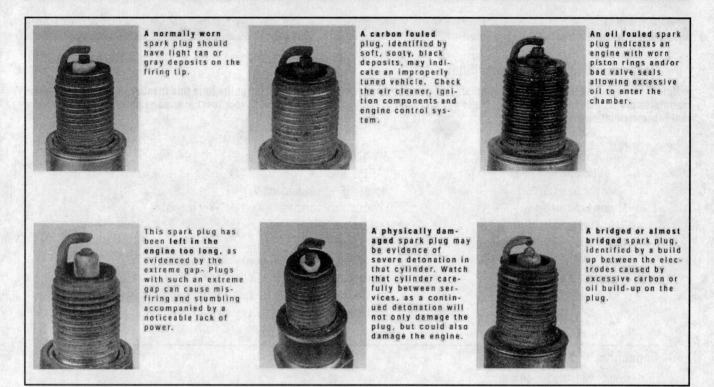

A normally worn spark plug should have light tan or gray deposits on the firing tip.

A carbon fouled plug, identified by soft, sooty, black deposits, may indicate an improperly tuned vehicle. Check the air cleaner, ignition components and engine control system.

An oil fouled spark plug indicates an engine with worn piston rings and/or bad valve seals allowing excessive oil to enter the chamber.

This spark plug has been **left in the engine too long,** as evidenced by the extreme gap- Plugs with such an extreme gap can cause misfiring and stumbling accompanied by a noticeable lack of power.

A physically damaged spark plug may be evidence of severe detonation in that cylinder. Watch that cylinder carefully between services, as a continued detonation will not only damage the plug, but could also damage the engine.

A bridged or almost bridged spark plug, identified by a build up between the electrodes caused by excessive carbon or oil build-up on the plug.

23.10 Inspect the spark plug to determine engine running conditions

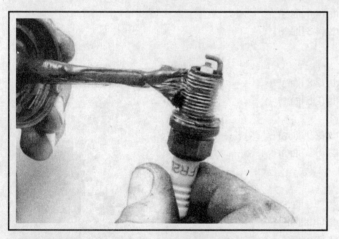

23.11a Apply a thin coat of anti-seize compound to the spark plug threads

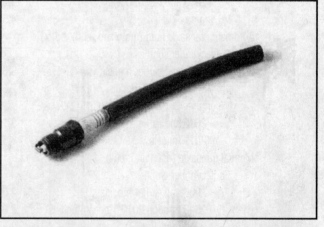

23.11b A length of snug-fitting rubber hose will save time and prevent damaged threads when installing the spark plugs

24 Manual transaxle fluid change (every 120,000 miles [192,000 km] or 72 months)

1   Raise the vehicle and support it securely on jackstands in a level position.

❊❊ WARNING:

Never work under a vehicle that is supported only by a jack!

2   Remove the fill plug, followed by the drain plug. Drain the fluid into a suitable container capable of holding at least four quarts.

3   After the fluid has completely drained, install the drain plug and tighten it to the torque given in this Chapter's Specifications.

4   Fill the transaxle with the recommended lubricant (see *Recommended lubricants and fluids* in this Chapter's Specifications).

5   The old oil drained from the transaxle cannot be reused in its present state and should be disposed of. Check with your local auto parts store, disposal facility or environmental agency to see if they will accept the oil for recycling. After the oil has cooled it can be drained into a container (capped plastic jugs, topped bottles, milk cartons, etc.) for transport to one of these disposal sites. Don't dispose of the oil by pouring it on the ground or down a drain!

Specifications

Recommended lubricants and fluids

➡**Note: The fluids and lubricants listed here are those recommended by the manufacturer at the time this manual was written. Vehicle manufacturers occasionally upgrade their fluid and lubricant specifications, so check with your local auto parts store for the most current recommendations.**

Engine oil
    Type   API "Certified for gasoline engines"
    Viscosity   SAE 5W-20
Automatic transaxle fluid   Honda ATF-Z1 or equivalent
Manual transaxle fluid   Honda manual transmission fluid (MTF) or equivalent
Brake fluid type   DOT 3 brake fluid
Clutch fluid type   DOT 3 brake fluid
Power steering system fluid   Honda power steering fluid or equivalent
Engine coolant   Honda All Season Antifreeze/Coolant Type 2 or equivalent 50/50 mixture of non-silicate antifreeze and water (the genuine Honda antifreeze is a pre-mixed solution - don't add water to it)

Capacities*

Engine oil (including oil filter)	
Four-cylinder engine	
2009 and earlier models	4.4 quarts (4.2 liters)
2010 and later models	4.2 quarts (4.0 liters)
V6 engine	4.5 quarts (4.3 liters)
Automatic transaxle fluid (drain and refill)**	
Four-cylinder engine	
2007 and earlier models	3.0 quarts (2.8 liters)
2008 and later models	2.6 quarts (2.5 liters)
V6 engine	
2010 and earlier models	3.1 quarts (2.9 liters)
2011 models	3.5 quarts (3.3 liters)
Manual transaxle (drain and refill)	
Four-cylinder engine	
2007 and earlier models	2.0 quarts (1.9 liters)
2008 through 2010 5-speed models	2.0 quarts (1.9 liters)
2011 models	2.6 quarts (2.5 liters)
V6 engine	
2010 and earlier models	2.3 quarts (2.2 liters)
2011 models	2.2 quarts (2.1 liters)
Cooling system	
Four-cylinder engine	
Manual transaxle models	
2007 and earlier	1.9 gallons (7.2 liters)
2008 and later models	1.59 to 1.61 gallons (6.0 to 6.1 liters)
Automatic transaxle models	
2007 and earlier	1.87 gallons (7.1 liters)
2008 and later models	1.56 gallons (5.0 liters)

V6 engine
    2007 and earlier models
        Manual transaxle   2.2 gallons (8.2 liters)
        Automatic transaxle   2.23 gallons (8.4 liters)
    2008 and later models   1.74 gallons (6.6 liters)

* All capacities approximate. Add as necessary to bring to appropriate level.
** If you want to flush the converter during a fluid change, purchase twice the amount of fluid listed here.

Ignition system

Spark plug type
    2007 and earlier models
        Four-cylinder engine
            LX-SULEV, EX-SULEV,
                EX-L-SULEV models   NGK: IZFR6K13 or DENSO: SKJ20DR-M13
            All other four-cylinder models   NGK: IZFR6K11 or DENSO: SKJ20DR-M11
        V6 engine   NGK: IZFR6K11 or DENSO: SKJ20DR-M11
    2008 and later models
        Four-cylinder engine
            2008 and later ULEV   NGK: ILZKR7B11S or DENSO: SXU22HCR11S
            2008 and later PZEV   NGK: DILZKR7A11GS
        V6 engine
            2008 and later ULEV   NGK: ILZKR7B11 or DENSO: SXY22HCR11
            2008 and later PZEV   NGK: DILZKR7B11
Spark plug gap
    2007 and earlier models
        Four-cylinder engine
            LX-SULEV, EX-SULEV,
                 EX-L-SULEV models   0.047 to 0.051-inch (1.2 to 1.3 mm)
            All other four-cylinder models   0.039 to 0.043-inch (1.0 to 1.1 mm)
        V6 engine   0.039 to 0.043-inch (1.0 to 1.1 mm)
    2008 and later models   0.039 to 0.043-inch (1.0 to 1.1 mm)
Engine firing order
    Four-cylinder engine   1-3-4-2
    V6 engine   1-4-2-5-3-6

Cylinder locations - four-cylinder engine

Cylinder locations - V6 engine

Cooling system

Thermostat rating	
Starts to open	169 to 176-degrees F (76 to 80-degrees C)
Fully open	194-degrees F (90-degrees C)

Brakes

Disc brake pad lining thickness (minimum)	1/16-inch (1.6 mm)
Drum brake shoe lining thickness (minimum)	1/16-inch (1.6 mm)
Parking brake adjustment	
2007 and earlier models	
Disc brakes	6 to 9 clicks
Drum brakes	4 to 7 clicks
2008 and later models	7 to 9 clicks

Torque specifications	Ft-lbs (unless otherwise indicated)	Nm

➡**Note: One foot-pound (ft-lb) of torque is equivalent to 12 inch-pounds (in-lbs) of torque. Torque values below approximately 15 ft-lbs are expressed in inch-pounds, since most foot-pound torque wrenches are not accurate at these smaller values.**

Engine oil drain plug (use a new sealing washer)		
2007 and earlier models		
Four-cylinder engine	33	44
V6 engine	29	39
2008 and later models	29	39
Automatic transaxle drain plug	36	49
Manual transaxle		
Four-cylinder engine		
Check/fill plug	33	44
Drain plug	29	39
V6 engine		
Fill plug (top of transaxle)	33	44
Check plug (side of transaxle)	106 in-lbs	12
Drain plug	29	39
Drivebelt tensioner mounting bolts		
Four-cylinder engine	16	22
V6 engine		
Long bolt		
J35Z3 engine	33	44
J35Z2 engine	54	74
Short bolt	16	22
Drivebelt tensioner pulley bolt		
Four-cylinder models	41	56
V6 models		
3.0L and 3.5L J35Z3 engines	59	80
3.5L J35Z2 engine	48	65
Spark plugs		
2007 and earlier models	156 in-lbs	18
2008 and later models		
Four-cylinder engine	156 in-lbs	18
V6 engine	16	22
Wheel lug nuts	80	108

Section

Reference to other Chapters

2A

FOUR-CYLINDER ENGINE

1 General information

This Part of Chapter 2 is devoted to in-vehicle repair procedures for the 2.4L DOHC (Double Overhead Camshaft), engine as well as procedures such as timing chain and sprocket(s), balance shaft chain and balance shafts and oil pan removal. All information concerning engine removal and installation can be found in Part C of this Chapter.

All versions of this engine utilize a Double Overhead Camshaft (DOHC), with 4 valves per cylinder (16V). This engine incorporates the i-VTEC (intelligent Variable Valve Timing and lift Electronic Control)

system, which electronically alters valve timing to enhance engine performance. For more information on the i-VTEC system, see Section 11 of this Chapter.

The Specifications included in this Part of Chapter 2 apply only to the procedures contained in this Part. Part C of Chapter 2 contains the Specifications necessary for certain procedures concerning engine rebuilding.

2 Repair operations possible with the engine in the vehicle

Many major repair operations can be accomplished without removing the engine from the vehicle.

Clean the engine compartment and the exterior of the engine with some type of degreaser before any work is done. It will make the job easier and help keep dirt out of the internal areas of the engine.

Depending on the components involved, it may be helpful to remove the hood to improve access to the engine as repairs are performed (refer to Chapter 11 if necessary). Cover the fenders to prevent damage to the paint. Special pads are available, but an old bedspread or blanket will also work.

If vacuum, exhaust, oil or coolant leaks develop, indicating a need for gasket or seal replacement, the repairs can generally be made with the engine in the vehicle. The intake and exhaust manifold gaskets, oil pan gasket, crankshaft oil seals and cylinder head gasket are all accessible with the engine in place.

Exterior engine components, such as the intake and exhaust manifolds, the oil pan, the oil pump, the water pump, the starter motor, the alternator and the fuel system components can be removed for repair with the engine in place.

Since the cylinder head can be removed without pulling the engine, camshaft and valve component servicing can also be accomplished with the engine in the vehicle. Replacement of the timing chain and sprockets is also possible with the engine in the vehicle.

In extreme cases caused by a lack of necessary equipment, repair or replacement of piston rings, pistons, connecting rods and rod bearings is possible with the engine in the vehicle. However, this practice is not recommended because of the cleaning and preparation work that must be done to the components involved.

3 Top Dead Center (TDC) for number 1 piston - locating

▶ **Refer to illustration 3.3**

1   Disable the fuel system (see Chapter 4, Section 2).

2   Remove the spark plugs (see Chapter 1) and install a compression gauge in the number 1 cylinder. Turn the crankshaft clockwise with a socket and breaker bar.

3   When the piston approaches TDC, compression will be noted on the compression gauge. Continue turning the crankshaft until the notch in the crankshaft pulley is aligned with the TDC mark on the front cover (see illustration). At this point, number 1 cylinder is at TDC on the compression stroke.

4   After the number 1 piston has been positioned at TDC on the compression stroke, TDC for any of the remaining pistons can be located by turning the crankshaft clockwise, 180-degrees at a time, and following the firing order.

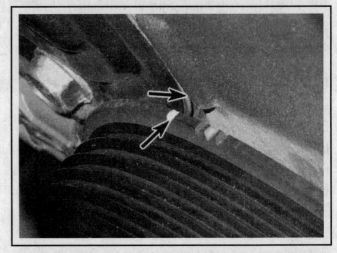

3.3 Align the notch (white) in the crankshaft pulley with the alignment pointer on the engine front cover to obtain TDC

4 Valve cover - removal and installation

REMOVAL

▶ **Refer to illustration 4.2**

1   Disconnect the cable from the negative battery terminal (see Chapter 5, Section 1).

2   Remove the intake manifold cover (see illustration).

3   Remove the ignition coils (see Chapter 5).

4   Remove the bolt attaching the power steering hose bracket to the valve cover.

5   Remove the dipstick and the valve cover breather hose (see Chapter 1).

6   Remove the valve cover nuts (see illustration 4.11). Lift the valve cover off. Tap gently with a soft-face hammer if necessary to break the gasket seal.

INSTALLATION

▶ **Refer to illustrations 4.8 and 4.11**

7   Clean the gasket surfaces on the intake manifold, cylinder head and valve cover. Use a shop rag, lacquer thinner or acetone to wipe off all residue and gasket material from the sealing surfaces.

8   Insert a new valve cover gasket into the grooved recess in the valve cover. Make sure the gasket is positioned properly in the groove (see illustration).

9   Install new spark plug tube seals.

10   Apply a slight amount of RTV sealant to the timing chain cover grooves and the number 5 rocker shaft holder mating areas.

11   Tighten the valve cover nuts in the correct sequence to the torque listed in this Chapter's Specifications (see illustration).

12   The remainder of installation is the reverse of removal.

13   Reconnect the battery (see Chapter 5, Section 1).

4.2 Intake manifold cover nuts

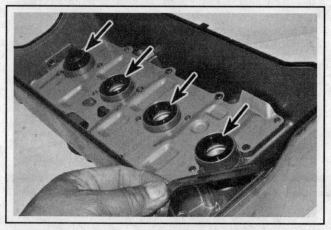

4.8 Install a new valve cover gasket and spark plug tube seals

4.11 Valve cover nut tightening sequence

5 Valve clearance check and adjustment

CHECK

1   Valve clearances generally do not need adjustment unless valvetrain components have been replaced, or a valve job has been performed.

2   The simplest check for proper valve adjustment is to listen carefully to the engine running with the hood open. If the valvetrain is noisy, adjustment is necessary.

ADJUSTMENT

▶ **Refer to illustrations 5.6 and 5.8**

3   The valve clearance must be checked and adjusted with the engine cold.

4   Remove the valve cover (see Section 4).

5   Place the number 1 piston at Top Dead Center (TDC) on the compression stroke (see Section 3).

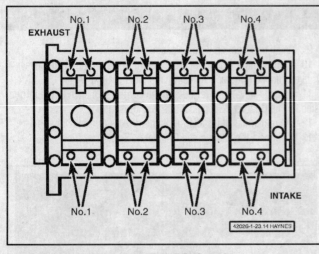

5.6 Valve locations on the 2.4L DOHC engine

5.8 Hold the adjuster screw with a screwdriver to keep it from turning and tighten the locknut using a box-end wrench

6   With the engine in this position, the number 1 cylinder valve clearances can be checked and adjusted (see illustration).

7   Start with the intake valve clearance. Insert a feeler gauge of the correct thickness (see this Chapter's Specifications) between the valve stem tip and the adjusting screw on the rocker arm. Withdraw it; you should feel a slight drag. If there's no drag or a heavy drag, loosen the adjuster nut and back off the adjuster screw. Carefully tighten the adjuster screw until you can feel a slight drag on the feeler gauge as you withdraw it.

8   Hold the adjuster screw with a screwdriver to keep it from turning and tighten the locknut (see illustration). Recheck the clearance to make sure it hasn't changed. Repeat the procedure in this Step and the previ-

ous Step on the other intake valve, then on the two exhaust valves.

9   Rotate the crankshaft pulley 180-degrees clockwise to bring the number 3 cylinder to TDC. Check and adjust the number three cylinder valves.

10 Rotate the crankshaft pulley 180-degrees clockwise to bring the number 4 cylinder to TDC. Check and adjust the number 4 cylinder valves.

11 Rotate the crankshaft pulley 180-degrees clockwise to bring the number 2 cylinder to TDC. Check and adjust the number two cylinder valves.

12 Install the valve cover (see Section 4).

6   Intake manifold and injector base - removal and installation

✳✳ WARNING:

Wait until the engine is completely cool before beginning this procedure.

➡**Note: The intake manifold is actually made up of two pieces. The outer portion, or intake runners, will be referred to as the "intake manifold." The inner portion (the part that mates to the cylinder head) will be referred to as the "injector base."**

REMOVAL

1   Relieve the fuel system pressure (see Chapter 4).

➡**Note: If you're just removing the intake manifold (and not the injector base), skip this Step.**

2   Disconnect the cable from the negative terminal of the battery (see Chapter 5, Section 1).

3   If you are going to remove the injector base, drain the engine coolant (see Chapter 1).

Intake manifold

▸ **Refer to illustrations 6.8, 6.9 and 6.12**

4   Remove the intake manifold cover (see illustration 4.2).

5   Remove the intake duct between the throttle body and the air filter housing (see Chapter 4).

6   Disconnect the accelerator cable and, if equipped, the cruise control cable from the throttle body (see Chapter 4). Position the cables off to the side.

7   Clamp off the coolant hoses attached to the throttle body, then detach the hoses from the throttle body. Be prepared for a little coolant spillage.

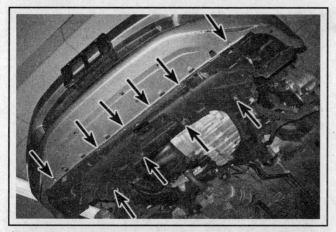

6.8 Retainer locations on the engine splash shield - three retainers on the fenderwells not shown

6.9 Remove the intake manifold brace (upper nut not visible in this photo)

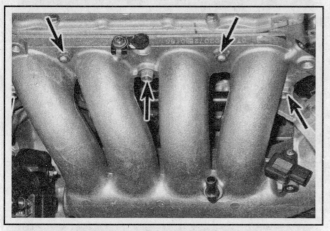

6.12 Intake manifold bolt/nut locations

6.17 Using a pair of pliers, squeeze the hose clamp and slide it down the hose, then twist the hose to break the seal and detach it from the pipe

8   Remove the splash shield from below the engine compartment (see illustration).

9   Disconnect the wiring harness clamps and position the harness off to the side. Remove the intake manifold brace from below the intake manifold (see illustration).

10 Disconnect the power brake booster vacuum hose from the intake manifold and the EVAP hose from the throttle body. If you're working on a model with an automatic transaxle, also remove the small vacuum hose from the rear side of the intake manifold.

11 Disconnect the IAC valve, the TPS, and any other electrical connectors that may interfere with manifold removal. Remove the bolt and detach the wiring harness from the front of the manifold.

12 Remove the intake manifold mounting bolts and nuts (see illustration).

13 Separate the intake manifold from the injector base and remove it.

Injector base

▶ **Refer to illustration 6.17**

14 Remove the intake manifold.

15 Detach the PCV hose from the pipe on top of the injector base.

16 Remove the fuel rail and injectors (see Chapter 4).

17 Detach the coolant hose from the pipe on the underside of the injector base (see illustration).

18 Remove the injector base mounting bolts and nuts, then detach it from the cylinder head.

INSTALLATION

19 Installation is the reverse of removal, noting the following points:

a) *Clean away all traces of old gasket material. Remove oil and dirt with a cloth and solvent, such as brake system cleaner.*

b) *Install new gaskets.*

c) *Tighten the fasteners to the torque listed in this Chapter's Specifications, starting with the center bolts and working towards the ends.*

d) *If the injector base was removed, refill the cooling system (see Chapter 1).*

e) *If only the intake manifold was removed, check the coolant level and add some, if necessary, to bring it to the appropriate level (see Chapter 1).*

f) *After reconnecting the accelerator and (if equipped) cruise control cable(s), adjust if necessary (see Chapter 4).*

g) *Reconnect the battery (see Chapter 5, Section 1).*

h) *Run the engine and check for leaks.*

7 Exhaust manifolds - removal and installation

⁂ WARNING:

The engine must be completely cool before beginning this procedure.

REMOVAL

▶ **Refer to illustrations 7.2, 7.5 and 7.6**

1   Disconnect the cable from the negative battery terminal (see Chapter 5, Section 1).

2   Remove the exhaust manifold heat shield (see illustration).

3   Raise the vehicle and support it securely on jackstands.

4   Remove the splash shield from below the engine compartment (see illustration 6.8). If you're working on a model with an automatic transaxle, remove the driveaxle heat shield.

5   Remove the exhaust manifold brace bolts and the pipe-to-manifold bolts (see illustration). Detach the exhaust pipe from the manifold.

6   Remove the fasteners and detach the exhaust manifold from the cylinder head (see illustration).

INSTALLATION

7   Using a scraper, thoroughly clean the mating surfaces on the cylinder head, manifold and exhaust pipe. Remove the residue with a solvent such as brake system cleaner.

8   Check that the mating surfaces are perfectly flat and not damaged in any way. Warped or damaged manifolds may require machining. Install the new gasket on the studs and place the manifold on the cylinder head. Tighten the nuts and bolts evenly to the torque listed in this Chapter's Specifications.

9   Connect the exhaust pipe to the manifold and tighten the bolts evenly to the torque listed in this Chapter's Specifications.

10   The remainder of installation is the reverse of the removal steps.

11   Reconnect the battery (see Chapter 5, Section 1).

12   Run the engine and check for exhaust leaks.

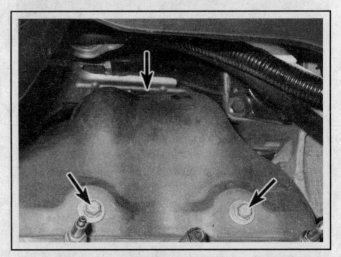

7.2 Exhaust manifold heat shield bolts

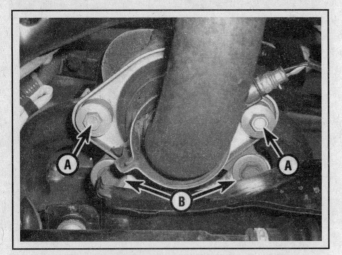

7.5 Location of the exhaust pipe flange bolts (A) and the exhaust manifold brace bolts (B)

7.6 Exhaust manifold mounting nuts and bolts

8 Engine front cover - removal and installation

REMOVAL

1 Disconnect the cable from the negative battery terminal (see Chapter 5, Section 1).

2 Remove the VTC oil control solenoid valve (see Chapter 6).

3 Remove the valve cover (see Section 4).

4 Loosen the right front wheel lug nuts. Raise the front of the vehicle and support it securely on jackstands. Remove the right front wheel.

5 Remove the splash shield from below the engine compartment (see illustration 6.8).

6 Remove the drivebelt (see Chapter 1).

7 Remove the crankshaft pulley (see Section 10).

8 Disconnect the crankshaft position (CKP) sensor harness and other electrical connectors that may interfere with the front cover removal.

9 Drain the engine oil (see Chapter 1).

10 Support the engine with a floor jack. Place a wood block between the jack pad and the oil pan to avoid damaging the pan.

11 Remove the ground cable, the upper engine mount bracket and side engine mount bracket (see Section 20).

12 Remove the mounting bolts and the front cover.

13 Remove the engine cover-to-block gasket.

INSTALLATION

14 Inspect and clean all sealing surfaces of the engine front cover and the block.

15 If necessary, replace the crankshaft seal in the front cover (see Section 9).

16 Apply RTV sealant to the mating surfaces on the front cover, the upper surface contact areas and to the oil pan mating surfaces. Also, apply a small amount of RTV sealant to the inner thread holes.

17 Install a new engine front cover O-ring.

18 Install the front cover and fasteners. Make sure the fasteners are in their original locations. Tighten the fasteners by hand until the cover is contacting the block around its entire periphery.

19 Tighten the bolts to the torque listed in this Chapter's Specifications.

20 Install the crankshaft pulley (see Section 9).

21 Connect the wiring harness connectors. Secure the wiring harnesses with the clamps.

22 Reinstall the remaining parts in the reverse order of removal.

23 Fill the crankcase with the recommended oil (see Chapter 1).

24 Reconnect the battery (see Chapter 5, Section 1).

25 Start the engine and check for leaks. Check all fluid levels.

9 Timing chain and sprockets - removal, inspection and installation

REMOVAL

▸ **Refer to illustration 9.5**

1 Disconnect the cable from the negative battery terminal (see Chapter 5, Section 1).

2 Set the engine to TDC for cylinder number 1 (see Section 3).

3 Remove the valve cover (see Section 4).

4 Remove the engine front cover (see Section 8).

5 Rotate the crankshaft counterclockwise slightly to compress the chain tensioner. Install a 0.05 inch (1.2 mm) pin into the alignment holes (see illustration) and rotate the crankshaft slightly clockwise to secure the pin.

6 Remove the mounting bolts and the timing chain tensioner.

7 Remove the upper timing chain guide from between the camshaft sprockets.

8 Remove the camshaft timing chain guide and the tensioner arm (chain guide).

9 Remove the timing chain.

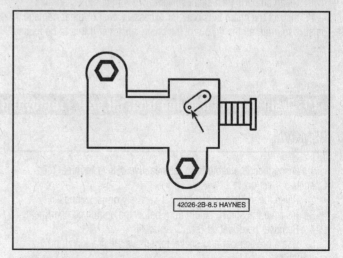

9.5 Align the hole on the lock with the hole in the tensioner, then insert a 0.06 inch (1.5 mm) pin or drill bit through both components to lock the tensioner

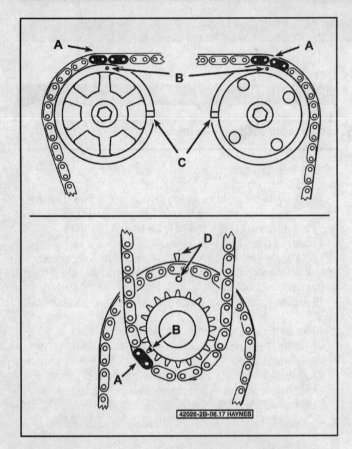

9.16 When the engine is at TDC compression for cylinder no. 1, the bright links (A) on the timing chain must align with the dots (B) on the sprockets. Also check the location of the camshaft sprocket TDC marks (C) and the crankshaft sprocket TDC marks (D)

INSPECTION

10 Clean all parts with clean solvent. Dry with compressed air.

11 Inspect the chain tensioner for excessive wear or other damage. Be sure to drain all the oil out of the chain tensioner if it is to be reused.

12 Inspect the timing chain guides for deep grooves, excessive wear, or other damage.

13 Inspect the timing chain for excessive wear or damage.

14 Inspect the crankshaft and camshaft sprockets for chipped or broken teeth, excessive wear, or damage. Replace any component that is in questionable condition.

INSTALLATION

Refer to illustration 9.16

15 If the crankshaft has been rotated during this procedure, make sure the number one piston is at the top of its stroke (TDC) (see Section 3). The timing mark (round dot) must align with the pointer on the crankshaft sprocket (see illustration 9.16).

16 Set the alignment marks on the camshaft sprockets. Rotate the sprocket until the chain alignment dot (circular indentation) on the variable valve timing control actuator (VTC) is approximately at the 12 o'clock position. Rotate the sprocket until the exhaust camshaft sprocket chain alignment dot is in the same position. Position the TDC alignment marks on the sprockets opposite each other at the 9 and 3 o'clock positions (see illustration).

17 Install the timing chain around the crankshaft sprocket with the colored link on the chain aligned with the dot (circular indentation) on the crankshaft sprocket (see illustration 9.16).

18 Install the timing chain over the exhaust camshaft sprocket and the VTC actuator (intake camshaft sprocket) with the dots (circular indentations) aligned with each pair of colored chain links. The camshaft sprocket alignment links will be positioned in pairs on the timing chain.

19 Install the camshaft timing chain guide and the tensioner arm. Tighten the bolts to the torque listed in this Chapter's Specifications.

20 Install the timing chain tensioner. Tighten the bolts to the torque listed in this Chapter's Specifications.

21 Install the upper timing chain guide. Tighten the bolts to the torque listed in this Chapter's Specifications.

22 Remove the pin from the timing chain tensioner.

23 Install the valve cover (see Section 4).

24 Install the engine front cover (see Section 8).

25 The remainder of installation is the reverse of the removal Steps.

26 Reconnect the battery (see Chapter 5, Section 1).

27 Run the engine and check for oil or coolant leaks.

10 Crankshaft pulley and front oil seal - removal and installation

REMOVAL

1 Disconnect the cable from the negative battery terminal (see Chapter 5, Section 1).

2 Raise the vehicle and support it securely on jackstands.

3 Remove the splash shield from below the engine compartment.

4 Remove the drivebelt (see Chapter 1).

5 Use a breaker bar and socket to remove the crankshaft pulley center bolt.

➡**Note: It will be necessary to lock the pulley in position using a strap wrench or special tool. Be sure to wrap a shop rag around the pulley before installing the strap wrench.**

6 Slide the pulley off the crankshaft.

7 Use a seal puller to remove the crankshaft front oil seal. A screwdriver may be used instead, if the tip is wrapped with tape to avoid scratching the crankshaft.

8 Clean the seal bore and check it for nicks or gouges. Also examine the area of the hub that rides in the seal for signs of abnormal wear or scoring. For many popular engines, a repair sleeve is available to restore a smooth finish to the sealing surface. Check with your auto parts store.

INSTALLATION

9 Coat the lip of the new seal with clean engine oil and drive it into the bore with a seal driver or a socket slightly smaller in diameter than

the seal. The open side of the seal faces into the engine.

10 Using clean engine oil, lubricate the sealing surface of the hub. Install the crankshaft pulley and tighten the bolt to the torque listed in this Chapter's Specifications.

11 The remainder of the installation is the reverse of the removal procedure.

12 Reconnect the battery (see Chapter 5, Section 1).

11 i-VTEC system - description and component checks

GENERAL DESCRIPTION

1 The i-VTEC system is designed to continuously change the intake cam timing over all engine speeds. i-VTEC system combines VTEC technology with VTC technology. Not only does the intake camshaft have two different lobe profiles (VTEC system), it is also equipped with a Variable valve Timing Control (VTC) actuator, which alters the phasing of the camshaft to yield maximum potential power output for any given engine speed. For more information on the i-VTEC system, see Chapter 6.

COMPONENT CHECKS

➥**Note: The VTEC and VTC systems will require specialized diagnostic equipment to access the on-board computer to test the electrical circuits, actuators and sensors. However, there are some mechanical tests of the VTEC and VTC systems that the home mechanic can perform to check for obvious and simple problems within the system. Have the VTEC and VTC systems diagnosed by a dealer service department or other qualified automotive repair facility. Also, some checks and inspections of the VTEC components require removal of the rocker arm assembly (see Section 11).**

VTEC solenoid valve

➥**Note: Most common problems in the VTEC system are associated with the solenoid valve and its filter. Regular engine oil and filter changes are necessary for trouble-free operation of the valve.**

2 The VTEC solenoid valve is located on the rear of the cylinder head. The VTEC solenoid valve filter is mounted directly behind the VTEC solenoid valve (see Chapter 6).

3 Remove the VTEC solenoid valve (see Chapter 6) and check the filter for clogging. Clean and reinstall. A clogged filter screen is often the cause of system problems.

VTC oil control solenoid valve and strainer

Refer to illustration 11.5

➥**Note: Most common problems in the VTC system are associated with the oil control solenoid valve and its strainer. Regular engine oil and filter changes are necessary for trouble-free operation of the valve.**

4 The VTC oil control solenoid valve is located in the cylinder head on the timing chain end of the engine. The VTC oil strainer is located on the right front corner of the cylinder head, near the intake manifold. The strainer cover is retained by two bolts; remove the bolts and cover and check the strainer for clogging, cleaning it as necessary.

5 Remove the VTC oil control solenoid valve (see Chapter 6) and check the strainer for clogging, cleaning it as necessary (if it's too dirty to clean, replace the valve). Look at the position of the valve through

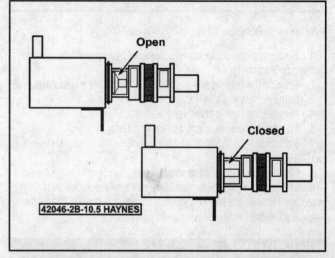

11.5 Check the position of the VTC solenoid valve - if it's stuck open, replace the valve. Be sure to check the condition of the O-ring

the drain port (the port closest to the solenoid portion of the valve); it should be closed. If it's open (see illustration), the solenoid valve must be replaced.

Rocker arms

6 Position the number one piston at Top Dead Center (see Section 3). Remove the valve cover (see Section 4).

7 Press on the primary intake rocker arm for cylinder number 1 to see that it moves independently of the secondary intake rockers. Check the rockers for the other cylinders at their own TDC positions.

VTEC synchronizing assembly

8 Once the rocker arm assemblies have been removed and disassembled (see Section 11), separate the rocker arms and synchronizing components.

VTEC components:

a) *Primary rocker arm*
b) *Secondary rocker arm*
c) *Synchronizing pistons*

9 Inspect the timing spring, making sure it's not broken or collapsed. Replace it if necessary.

10 Inspect all other parts (rocker arms and synchronizing pistons) for wear, galling, scoring or signs of overheating (bluish in color). Use your finger to push on the rocker arm pistons to check for smooth movement. Replace any parts, if necessary.

11 Reassemble each cylinder's components and wrap a rubber band around the rocker arms before trying to assemble them on the rocker shaft (see Section 12).

12 Camshafts and rocker arms - removal, inspection and installation

➡Note: The camshaft holders, the camshafts and the rocker arm assembly are bolted to the cylinder head as one complete assembly. After the assembly is removed from the cylinder head, the different components can be separated on the workbench.

REMOVAL

◆ Refer to illustration 12.6

1 Disconnect the cable from the negative battery terminal (see Chapter 5, Section 1).
2 Position the number one piston at Top Dead Center (see Section 3).
3 Remove the valve cover (see Section 4).
4 Remove the timing chain (see Section 8).
5 Loosen all the rocker arm adjusting screws.
6 Remove the camshaft holder bolts. Follow the correct sequence (see illustration).
7 Remove the upper timing chain guide.
8 Lift the camshaft holders and camshafts off the rocker arm assembly. Remove the rocker arm assembly. Install each bolt into the original camshaft holder for correct reassembly.

※※ CAUTION:

If the intake camshaft sprocket (VTC actuator) is removed from the camshaft and reused later, be sure to store the intake sprocket properly. First seal the advance holes and the retard hole on the number 1 camshaft journal with tape. Next, punch a hole in the tape over one of the advance holes and blow compressed air through the opening to release the lock. Double-check that the sprocket moves freely in the advance and retard positions.

INSPECTION

Rocker arm assembly

9 If you wish to disassemble and inspect the rocker arm assembly, (a good idea as long as you have them off), remove the retaining bolts and slip the rocker arms, springs, collars and bearing caps off the shafts. Mark the relationship of the shafts to the bearing caps and keep the components in order. They must be reassembled in the same posi-

tions from which they were removed.

※※ CAUTION:

It is a good idea to bundle the intake rocker arms together with rubber bands.

10 Thoroughly clean the components and inspect them for wear and damage. Check the rocker arm faces that contact the camshaft and the rocker arm tips. Check the surfaces of the shafts that the rocker arms ride on, as well as the bearing surfaces inside the rocker arms, for scoring and excessive wear. Replace any parts that are damaged or excessively worn. Also, make sure the oil holes in the shafts are not plugged.

Camshaft endplay and runout

11 To check camshaft endplay:
   a) *Install the rocker arm assembly, the camshafts and the camshaft holders and follow the correct torque sequence (see Step 20).*
   b) *Mount a dial indicator on the cylinder head with the pointer resting on the camshaft nose.*
   c) *Using a large screwdriver as a lever at the opposite end, move the camshaft forward-and-backward and note the dial indicator reading.*
   d) *Compare the reading with the endplay listed in this Chapter's Specifications.*
   e) *If the indicated reading is excessive, either the camshaft or the cylinder head is worn. Replace parts as necessary.*

12 To check camshaft runout:
   a) *With the camshafts on the workbench, support the camshaft with a pair of V-blocks and set up a dial indicator with the plunger resting against the center bearing journal on the camshaft.*
   b) *Rotate the camshaft and note the indicated runout.*
   c) *Compare the results to the camshaft runout listed in this Chapter's Specifications.*
   d) *If the indicated runout exceeds the specified runout limit, replace the camshaft.*

Camshaft lobe height

◆ Refer to illustration 12.14

13 Check the camshaft bearing journals and caps for scoring and signs of wear. If they are worn, replace the camshaft holders and rocker arm assembly with a new or rebuilt assembly.
14 Check the cam lobes for wear:
   a) *Check the toe and ramp areas of each cam lobe for score marks and uneven wear. Also check for flaking and pitting.*
   b) *If there's wear on the toe or the ramp, replace the camshaft, but first try to find the cause of the wear. Look for abrasive substances in the oil and inspect the oil pump and oil passages for blockage. Lobe wear is usually caused by inadequate lubrication or dirty oil.*
   c) *Using a micrometer, measure the cam lobe height (see illustration). If the lobe wear is indicated, replace the camshaft.*

15 If any of the conditions described above are noted, the cylinder head is probably getting insufficient lubrication or dirty oil. Make sure you track down the cause of this problem (low oil level, low oil pump capacity, clogged oil passage, etc.) before installing a new cylinder head, camshaft or rocker arm assembly.

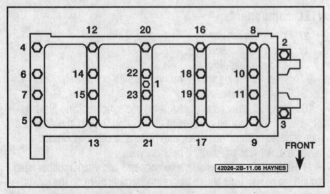

12.6 Camshaft holder bolt loosening sequence

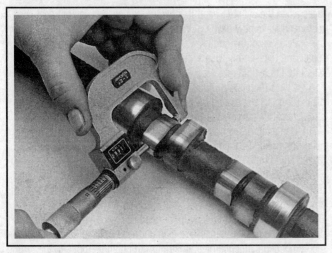

12.14 Measure the camshaft lobe height with a micrometer

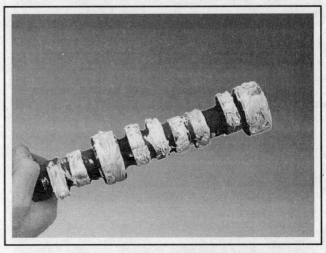

12.18 Be sure to apply camshaft installation lubricant to the lobes and bearing journals before installing the camshaft

INSTALLATION

♦ **Refer to illustrations 12.18 and 12.20**

16 Lubricate all components with engine assembly lubricant or engine oil and reassemble rocker arms on to the shafts.

17 When installing the rocker arms, shafts and springs, note the markings and the difference between the left and right side components.

18 Coat the camshaft lobes and journals with camshaft installation lubricant (see illustration).

19 Make sure the camshaft sprocket timing marks face up and set the camshafts in the rocker shaft holders.

20 Tighten the camshaft holder bolts a little at a time, in the proper sequence (see illustration) to the torque listed in this Chapter's Specifications.

21 The remainder of installation is the reverse of removal. Adjust the valve clearances (see Section 5).

22 Run the engine and check for oil leaks and proper operation.

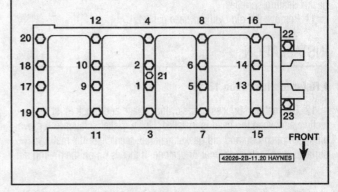

12.20 Camshaft holder bolt tightening sequence

---

13 Cylinder head - removal and installation

※※ **WARNING:**

Wait until the engine is completely cool before beginning this procedure.

REMOVAL

1 Relieve the fuel system pressure (see Chapter 4), then disconnect the cable from the negative battery terminal (see Chapter 5, Section 1).

2 Drain the cooling system (see Chapter 1). Remove the strut brace, if equipped.

3 Remove the drivebelt (see Chapter 1) and the drivebelt tensioner.

4 Remove the exhaust manifold (see Section 7).

5 Remove the intake manifold and injector base (see Section 6).

6 Remove the timing chain (see Section 9), and the camshafts and rocker arm assembly (see Section 12).

7 Label and disconnect the electrical connectors from the cylinder head that will interfere with removal. Use tape and mark each connector to insure correct reassembly. Also detach any coolant hoses that would interfere with removal.

8 Remove the cylinder head bolts and discard them, following the reverse of the tightening sequence (see illustration 13.16). Loosen the bolts in sequence 1/4-turn at a time.

9 Lift the cylinder head off the engine. If resistance is felt, place a wood block against the end and strike the wood block with a hammer. If the cylinder head is still stuck, carefully pry on a casting protrusion to break the gasket seal.

※※ **CAUTION:**

Do not pry between the cylinder head and block mating surfaces!

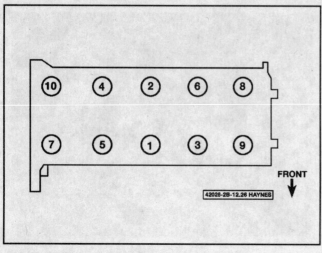

13.16 Cylinder head bolt tightening sequence

10 Store the cylinder head on wood blocks to prevent damage to the gasket sealing surfaces.
11 Remove the old cylinder head gasket.

INSTALLATION

▶ **Refer to illustration 13.16**

12 The mating surfaces of the cylinder head and block must be perfectly clean when the head is installed. Use a gasket scraper to remove all traces of carbon and old gasket material, then clean the mating surfaces with lacquer thinner or acetone. If there's oil on the mating sur-faces when the cylinder head is installed, the gasket may not seal correctly and leaks may develop. When working on the engine block, cover the open areas of the engine with shop rags to keep debris out during repair and reassembly. Use a vacuum cleaner to remove any debris that falls into the cylinders.

13 Check the engine block and cylinder head mating surfaces for nicks, deep scratches and other damage. Have an automotive machine shop check the cylinder head for warpage.

14 Use a tap of the correct size to chase the threads in the cylinder head bolt holes. Dirt, corrosion, sealant and damaged threads will affect torque readings.

15 Install the new gasket on the cylinder block. Make sure the dowel pins are in place and the gasket is installed right-side up (make note of any markings).

16 Carefully position the cylinder head on the engine block without disturbing the gasket. Install new cylinder head bolts and following the recommended sequence (see illustration), tighten the bolts to the torque listed in this Chapter's Specifications.

➡**Note: The method used for the head bolt tightening procedure is referred to as "torque-angle" or "torque-to-yield" method. A special torque angle gauge (available at most auto parts stores) is available to attach to a breaker bar and socket for better accuracy during the tightening procedure.**

17 Install the rocker arm assembly and camshafts (see Section 12).
18 Install the timing chain (see Section 9).
19 Install the exhaust manifold (see Section 7).
20 Install the intake manifold (see Section 6).
21 The remaining installation steps are the reverse of removal. Be sure to adjust the valve clearances (see Section 5).
22 Reconnect the battery (see Chapter 5, Section 1).
23 Change the engine oil and filter (see Chapter 1), refill the cooling system, then start the engine and check carefully for oil and coolant leaks.

14 Oil pan - removal and installation

REMOVAL

▶ **Refer to illustrations 14.14 and 14.16**

1 Disconnect the cable from the negative battery terminal (see Chapter 5, Section 1).
2 Remove the air filter housing (see Chapter 4).
3 On manual transaxles, remove the clutch release cylinder and the hydraulic line bracket mounting bolts (see Chapter 8).
4 Remove the battery and battery tray (see Chapter 5) and the harness connector clamp. Position the harness off to the side.
5 Loosen the front wheel lug nuts. Raise the vehicle and support it securely on jackstands. Remove the front wheels.

6 Drain the engine oil (see Chapter 1).
7 Remove the ground cable and the upper transaxle mount bracket from the transaxle and the engine compartment (see Section 20).
8 Remove the front engine mount stop (brace) and the upper mount bolt (see Section 20).
9 Remove the rear engine mount stop (brace) and the rear mount bolt (see Section 20).
10 Detach the stabilizer bar links from the lower control arms (see Chapter 10).
11 Remove the damper fork from the left shock absorber assembly (see Chapter 10).
12 Separate the left lower control arm from the steering knuckle (see Chapter 10).

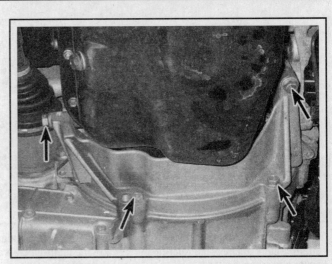

14.14 Location of the transaxle mount nuts

14.16 Location of the transaxle brace mounting bolts

13 Remove the left driveaxle (see Chapter 8).

14 Remove the nuts from the transaxle lower mount (see illustration).

15 Position a floor jack under the transaxle. Place a block of wood between the jack head and the transaxle to prevent damage. Raise the transaxle approximately two inches.

16 Remove the transaxle brace (see illustration).

17 Remove the oil pan bolts.

18 Carefully remove the oil pan from the engine block.

❋❋ CAUTION:

If the oil pan is difficult to separate from the lower crankcase, use a rubber mallet or a block of wood and a hammer to jar it loose. If that doesn't work, an oil pan gasket cutter may be available from your local auto parts store.

INSTALLATION

19 Using a gasket scraper, thoroughly clean all old gasket material from the lower crankcase and oil pan. Remove residue and oil film with a solvent such as acetone or lacquer thinner.

20 Apply a 2 mm bead of RTV sealant to the perimeter of the oil pan, inboard of the bolt holes.

21 Install the oil pan and bolts. Tighten the bolts a little at a time, in a criss-cross pattern beginning with the center bolts and working outward, to the torque listed in this Chapter's Specifications. Allow the RTV to set up no more than 5 minutes (or refer to the instructions on the bottle/tube of sealant).

22 The remaining installation is the reverse of removal. Be sure to tighten the transaxle brace to the torque listed in this Chapter's Specifications.

23 Tighten the driveaxle/hub nuts to the torque listed in the Chapter 8 Specifications. Tighten the wheel lug nuts to the torque listed in the Chapter 1 Specifications.

24 Wait at least three hours before filling the crankcase with oil and running the engine.

25 Change the oil filter and fill the crankcase with the specified engine oil (see Chapter 1).

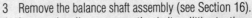

15 Oil pump - removal, inspection and installation

REMOVAL

1 Set the engine to TDC for cylinder number 1 (see Section 3).

2 Remove the oil pan (see Section 14).

3 Remove the balance shaft assembly (see Section 16).

4 Loosen the oil pump mounting bolts a little at a time.

5 When all bolts are loose, remove the bolts and oil pump.

15.6a Use a feeler gauge and straight-edge to check the rotor-to-cover clearance (typical)

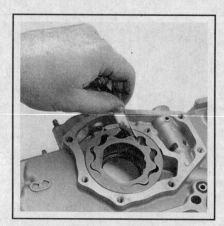

15.6b Use a feeler gauge to check the tooth-tip clearance between the inner and outer rotors (typical)

15.6c Use a feeler gauge to check the outer rotor-to-pump body clearance (typical)

INSPECTION

♦ **Refer to illustrations 15.6a, 15.6b and 15.6c**

6 Check the oil pump rotor-to-cover clearance, tooth tip clearance and outer rotor-to-body clearance (see illustrations). Compare your measurements to the figures listed in this Chapter's Specifications. Replace the pump if any of the measurements exceed the specified limits.

7 Remove the pressure relief valve plug and extract the spring and pressure relief valve plunger from the pump housing. Check the spring for distortion and the relief valve plunger for scoring. Replace parts as necessary.

8 Install the pump rotors. Pack the spaces between the rotors with petroleum jelly (this will prime the pump).

9 Apply clean engine oil to the pump housing bolts, install the housing and tighten the bolts to the torque listed in this Chapter's Specifications. Install the oil pressure relief valve and spring assembly.

Use a new sealing washer on the plug and tighten the plug to the torque listed in this Chapter's Specifications.

INSTALLATION

10 Install the oil pump housing bolts and tighten by hand until snug. Tighten the bolts gradually and evenly to the torque listed in this Chapter's Specifications.

11 Make sure the engine is still set to TDC number 1 (see Section 3).

12 Install the balance shaft assembly (see Section 16) and the oil pan (see Section 14).

13 Refer to Chapter 1 and fill the engine with fresh engine oil. Install a new oil filter.

14 Reconnect the battery (See Chapter 5, Section 1).

15 Run the engine and make sure oil pressure comes up to normal quickly. If it doesn't, stop the engine and find out the cause. Severe engine damage can result from running an engine with insufficient oil pressure!

16 Balance shaft assembly and balance shafts - removal, inspection and installation

REMOVAL

1 Remove the oil pan (see Section 14).

2 Remove the oil pump chain tensioner. Discard the tensioner and obtain a new one for reassembly.

3 Remove the oil pump sprocket bolt. To prevent the sprocket from turning, insert a 6 mm guide pin into the maintenance hole directly behind the oil pump housing below the balance shaft assembly.

4 Remove the oil pump sprocket.

5 Remove the balance shaft assembly mounting bolts and separate the assembly from the lower engine block.

INSPECTION

6 Remove the balance shaft assembly mounting bolts and separate the upper and lower cases.

7 Clean all parts with clean solvent. Dry with compressed air.

8 Inspect the balance shaft chain for excessive wear or damage.

9 Inspect the balance shaft chain sprocket for chipped or broken teeth, excessive wear, or damage.

10 Inspect the balance shaft gears for chipping, scoring or missing teeth. Replace the assembly if necessary.

INSTALLATION

♦ **Refer to illustration 16.11 and 16.14**

11 Working on the two balance shafts, align the center punch mark on the rear (drive) balance shaft with the two marks on the front balance shaft (driven) (see illustration).

12 Apply engine oil to the threads and install the balance shaft case mounting bolts. Torque the bolts to the Specifications listed in this Chapter.

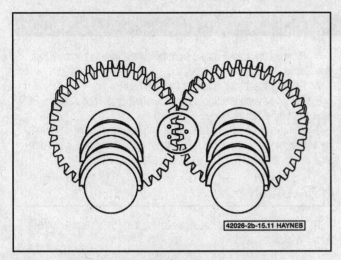

42026-2b-15.11 HAYNES

16.11 Align the center punch mark on the rear (drive) balance shaft with the two marks on the front balance shaft (driven)

42026-2B-15.16 HAYNES

16.14 Align the dowel pin on the rear balance shaft (A) with the mark on the oil pump housing (B)

13 Install the oil pump housing (see Section 15).

14 Align the dowel pin on the rear balance shaft with the mark on the oil pump housing (see illustration).

15 Install the balance shaft assembly onto the lower engine block and install the bolts finger tight

16 Insert a 6 mm guide pin into the maintenance hole directly behind the oil pump housing (see Step 3).

17 Engage the oil pump sprocket with the chain, then with the balance shaft. Install the oil pump sprocket bolt. Tighten the bolt to the torque listed in this Chapter's Specifications.

18 Remove the guide pin.

19 Tighten the balancer assembly mounting bolts to the torque listed in this Chapter's Specifications.

20 Working with a new balance shaft chain tensioner, make sure

the tensioner holder clip is installed onto the tensioner and install the tensioner onto the lower engine block.

21 Tighten the balance shaft chain tensioner bolts to the torque listed in this Chapter's Specifications.

22 Remove the holder clip from the tensioner to apply tension to the chain.

23 Install the oil pan (see Section 14).

24 Refer to Chapter 1 and fill the engine with fresh engine oil. Install a new oil filter.

25 Reconnect the battery (see Chapter 5, Section 1).

26 Run the engine and make sure oil pressure comes up to normal quickly. If it doesn't, stop the engine and find out the cause. Severe engine damage can result from running an engine with insufficient oil pressure!

17 Flywheel/driveplate - removal and installation

1   Remove the transaxle (see Chapter 7).

2   Remove the bolts that secure the flywheel/driveplate to the crankshaft.

3   Clean the flywheel/driveplate and inspect the surface for cracks. Check for worn, cracked or broken ring-gear teeth. Lay the flywheel/driveplate on a flat surface and use a straightedge to check for warpage.

4   Clean and inspect the mating surfaces of the flywheel/driveplate and the crankshaft. If the crankshaft oil seal is leaking, replace it before

reinstalling the flywheel/driveplate (see Section 18).

5   Position the flywheel/driveplate against the crankshaft. Note that offset bolt holes ensure correct installation.

6   Follow a criss-cross pattern and tighten the bolts in several stages to the torque listed in this Chapter's Specifications.

7   The remainder of installation is the reverse of the removal procedure.

18 Rear main oil seal - replacement

1   The transaxle must be removed from the vehicle for this procedure and the flywheel/driveplate must be removed from the engine. Refer to Chapter 7 and Section 17 as necessary.

2   Pry out the old seal with a screwdriver or a seal removal tool.

3   Apply multi-purpose grease to the crankshaft seal journal and the lip of the new seal and install the seal with the spring side in. The lip is

stiff so carefully work it onto the seal journal of the crankshaft.

4   Carefully drive the new seal into place with a seal installation tool to the depth (distance from the edge of the bore to the seal) listed in this Chapter's Specifications. Don't rush it or you may damage the seal.

5   The remaining steps are the reverse of removal.

19 Water passage - removal and installation

✻✻ WARNING:

The engine must be completely cool before beginning this procedure.

➡**Note:** The water passage is a multi-purpose assembly designed to mount the thermostat housing, the water pump, the drivebelt tensioner, the air conditioning compressor, the alternator and PCV hose. The water passage is sealed against the engine block and must not be removed unless a leak develops.

REMOVAL

1 Disconnect the cable from the negative battery terminal (see Chapter 5, Section 1).
2 Drain the cooling system (see Chapter 1).
3 Remove the thermostat from the thermostat housing (see Chapter 3).
4 Remove the alternator (see Chapter 5).
5 Remove the air conditioning compressor without disconnecting the lines (see Chapter 3). Secure the compressor out of the way with wire or rope.
6 Remove the splash shield from below the engine compartment (see Section 6).
7 Remove the intake manifold (see Section 6).
8 Remove the connecting pipe, the water bypass hose and the PCV valve from the water passage.
9 Remove the water passage mounting bolts and separate it from the engine block. Remove the thermostat housing from the water passage.

INSTALLATION

10 Make sure the water passage sealing surface is clean and free from old gasket material.
11 Install a new O-ring into the groove in the water passage.
12 Use RTV sealant to seal the surface between the engine block and the water passage. Apply a small amount of RTV sealer to the inner threads of the bolt holes.
13 Install the water passage and tighten the bolts to the torque listed in this Chapter's Specifications.
14 The remainder of installation is the reverse of removal. Allow at least three hours for the RTV sealant to set-up and dry before refilling the cooling system.
15 Refill the cooling system (see Chapter 1).

20 Powertrain mounts - check and replacement

CHECK

1 There are four engine/transaxle mounts on these models; the front engine mount is computer-controlled. Refer to Section 21 for general information and checks. The following powertrain mount checks apply only to the three non-computer controlled mounts.
2 During the check, the engine must be raised slightly to remove the weight from the mounts.
3 Raise the vehicle and support it securely on jackstands, then position a jack under the engine oil pan. Place a large block of wood between the jack head and the oil pan, then carefully raise the engine just enough to take the weight off the mounts.

✻✻ WARNING:

DO NOT place any part of your body under the engine when it's supported only by a jack!

4 Check the mounts to see if the rubber is cracked, hardened or separated from the casing.
5 Check for relative movement between the mount plates and the engine or frame. Use a large screwdriver or prybar to attempt to move the mounts.
6 If movement is noted, lower the engine and tighten the mount fasteners.
7 Apply the parking brake, block the rear wheels, raise the front of the vehicle and support it securely on jackstands (if not already done).

REPLACEMENT

▶ **Refer to illustrations 20.9, 20.11, 20.16, 20.21 and 20.22**

Right (passenger-side) mount

8 Use a floor jack under the engine to take the weight from the mount.
9 Remove the side-bolt from the mount (see illustration), then remove the bolts holding the engine bracket in place. Remove the mount-to-body bolts and the powertrain mount from the engine compartment.
10 Installation is the reverse of removal. Proceed to Step 26.

Left (driver's-side) mount

11 The driver's-side mount is between the bottom of the transaxle and the subframe (see illustration 14.14). The upper transaxle bracket mounts the top of the transaxle to the engine compartment (see illustration).
12 With the engine/transaxle supported, remove the two nuts from below the subframe, the two bolts at the transaxle, and remove the mount.
13 Remove the upper transaxle bracket bolts and lift the bracket from the engine compartment (see illustration 20.11).
14 Installation is the reverse of removal. Proceed to Step 26.

Front mount

15 The front mount is located between the engine and radiator.

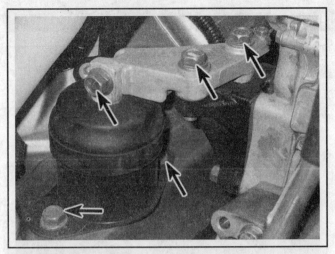

20.9 Location of the right-side mount and bracket mounting bolts

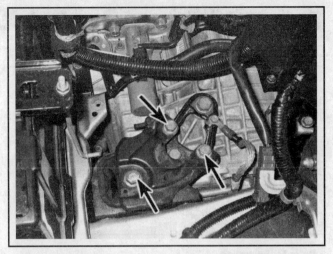

20.11 Location of the upper transaxle mount bracket and mounting bolts

20.16 Location of the front mount stop (brace) bolts (A) and side mounting bolt (B)

20.21 First, remove the rear mount stop (brace) mounting bolts . . .

16 Remove the upper mount stop (brace) bolts and the large side bolt (see illustration).

17 Remove the four bolts holding the mount to the chassis, then disconnect the vacuum hose from the bottom of the mount.

18 Raise the engine enough for the stud to clear the upper bracket and remove the mount.

19 Installation is the reverse of removal. Proceed to Step 26.

Rear mount

20 The rear mount is positioned between the extension bracket and the subframe above the catalytic converter.

21 Remove the rear mount stop (brace) nuts (see illustration).

22 Remove the side-bolt from the rear mount assembly (see illustration).

23 Remove the bolts holding the mount to the subframe.

24 Raise the engine enough for the stud to clear the upper bracket and remove the mount.

25 Installation is the reverse of removal. Proceed to Step 26.

Final tightening, all mounts

26 To ensure maximum bushing life and prevent excessive noise and vibration, the vehicle should be level and the engine weight should be on the mounts during the final tightening stage.

20.22 . . . next, remove the rear mount bolt

➡**Note: Use non-hardening thread locking compound on the nuts/bolts.**

Ensure that the bushings are not twisted or offset. If you have replaced more than one mount, or when you are installing the engine, tighten the mounts in the following order: front, rear, passenger-side and driver's-side.

21 Engine Mount Control System - description and check

DESCRIPTION

1   These models have a special front engine mount that is computer-controlled to reduce idle speed vibrations. The interior of the liquid-filled mount has two chambers. When the engine is idling, the Powertrain Control Module (PCM) signals a control solenoid valve, which allows manifold vacuum to the mount. There, a diaphragm changes the flow of liquid between the two chambers, to cancel vibrations at idle speeds. At engine speeds over 1000 rpm, the vacuum is shut off and the motor mount changes to its normal mode.

CHECK

♦ **Refer to illustration 21.2**

2   If abnormal vibration is noticed at idle, check the vacuum hose (see illustration) to the engine mount control solenoid for signs of damage or leakage.

3   With the vehicle idling warm (less than 800 rpm), have an assistant put the car in gear with their foot on the brake and the parking brake on, while you connect and disconnect the connector on the solenoid valve. There should be a noticeable change in smoothness.

21.2 Location of the vacuum line at the front engine mount

4   Any further diagnostic procedures should be performed by a dealer service department or other qualified automotive repair facility.

Specifications

General

Firing order	1-3-4-2
Bore	3.43 inches (87 mm)
Stroke	3.90 inches (99 mm)
Displacement	144 cubic inches (2.4 liters)
Oil pressure	See Chapter 2C

Front

42026-2B-specs HAYNES

Cylinder locations

Valve adjustment

Intake	0.008 to 0.010 inch (0.21 to 0.25 mm)
Exhaust	
2007 and earlier models	0.011 to 0.013 inch (0.28 to 0.32 mm)
2008 and later models	0.010 to 0.011 inch (0.25 to 0.29 mm)

Camshafts

Lobe height	
2007 and earlier models	
Intake	
Primary	1.3356 inches (33.925 mm)
Secondary	1.1668 inches (29.638 mm)
Exhaust	1.3422 inches (34.092 mm)
All 2008 and later models except PZEV	
Intake	
Primary	1.3285 inches (33.744 mm)
Mid	1.3955 inches (35.456 mm)
Secondary	1.3285 inches (33.744 mm)
Exhaust	1.3500 inches (34.291 mm)
2008 and later PZEV models	
Intake	
Primary	1.3285 inches (33.744 mm)
Mid	1.3959 inches (35.456 mm)
Secondary	1.3285 inches (33.744 mm)
Exhaust	1.3477 inches (34.232 mm)
Endplay	0.002 to 0.008 inch (0.05 to 0.20 mm)
Runout	0.001 inch (0.03 mm)
Journal-to-bearing (oil) clearance	
Journal number 1	0.001 to 0.003 inch (0.030 to 0.069 mm)
Journal number 2, 3, 4, 5	0.002 to 0.004 inch (0.060 to 0.099 mm)

Oil pump

Rotor-to-cover clearance	
2007 and earlier models	
Standard	0.0014 to 0.003 inch (0.035 to 0.070 mm)
Service limit	0.005 inch maximum (0.12 mm)
2008 and later models	
Standard	0.002 to 0.006 inch (0.05 to 0.152 mm)
Service limit	0.0075 inch maximum (0.19 mm)
Tooth tip clearance	
Standard	0.002 to 0.006 inch (0.05 to 0.152 mm)
Service limit	0.008 inch maximum (0.20 mm)

Oil pump (continued)

Outer rotor-to-pump body clearance

Standard	0.006 to 0.008 inch (0.152 to 0.21 mm)
Service limit	0.009 inch maximum (0.23 mm)

Torque specifications	Ft-lbs (unless otherwise indicated)	Nm

➡ **Note: One foot-pound (ft-lb) of torque is equivalent to 12 inch-pounds (in-lbs) of torque. Torque values below approximately 15 ft-lbs are expressed in inch-pounds, since most foot-pound torque wrenches are not accurate at these smaller values.**

Balance shaft sprocket bolt	33	44
Balance shaft case bolts		
Short bolts	104 in-lbs	12
Long bolts	20	27
Balance shaft assembly-to-engine block bolts		
Short bolts	16	22
Long bolts	33	44
Camshaft sprocket bolts		
Intake camshaft sprocket (VTC actuator)	83	113
Exhaust camshaft sprocket	53	72
Camshaft holder bolts		
6 mm bolts	104 in-lbs	12
8 mm bolts	16	22
Crankshaft pulley bolt		
Step 1	36	49
Step 2	Tighten an additional 90-degrees	
Cylinder head bolts*		
Step 1	29	39
Step 2	Tighten an additional 90-degrees	
Step 3	Tighten an additional 90-degrees	
Step 4	Tighten an additional 90-degrees	
Driveplate bolts	54	74
Exhaust manifold bolts/nuts	33	44
Exhaust manifold heat shield bolts	16	22
Exhaust pipe-to-manifold bolts	16	22
Engine front cover bolts	104 in-lbs	12
Flywheel bolts	76	103
Intake manifold cover bolts	104 in-lbs	12
Intake manifold/injector base bolts/nuts	16	22
Oil pump housing bolts	104 in-lbs	12
Oil pump pressure relief valve plug	29	39
Oil pan bolts	104 in-lbs	12
Thermostat housing-to-water passage bolts	104 in-lbs	12
Timing chain tensioner bolts	104 in-lbs	12
Timing chain guides		
Camshaft chain guide bolts	104 in-lbs	12
Tensioner arm bolt	16	22
Upper timing chain guide bolts	16	22
Transaxle brace bolts	33	44
Valve cover nuts	104 in-lbs	12
Water passage mounting bolts	33	44

Bolt(s) must be replaced.

2B

V6 ENGINES

Section

Reference to other Chapters

1 General information

This Part of Chapter 2 is devoted to in-vehicle repair procedures for the 3.0L V6 VTEC engine. Since these procedures are based on the assumption that the engine is installed in the vehicle, many of the steps outlined in this Part of Chapter 2 will not apply if the engine has been removed.

All versions of this engine utilize a Single Overhead Camshaft (SOHC), with 4 valves per cylinder (24V). This engine incorporates the VTEC (Variable valve Timing and lift Electronic Control) system, which electronically alters valve lobe height to enhance engine performance. For more information on the VTEC system, see Section 10 of this Chapter.

The Specifications included in this Part of Chapter 2 apply only to the procedures contained in this Part. Information concerning engine/transaxle removal and engine overhaul or replacement can be found in Part C of this Chapter.

2 Repair operations possible with the engine in the vehicle

Many major repair operations can be accomplished without removing the engine from the vehicle.

Clean the engine compartment and the exterior of the engine with some type of degreaser before any work is done. It will make the job easier and help keep dirt out of the internal areas of the engine.

Depending on the components involved, it may be helpful to remove the hood to improve access to the engine as repairs are performed (refer to Chapter 11 if necessary). Cover the fenders to prevent damage to the paint. Special pads are available, but an old bedspread or blanket will also work.

If vacuum, exhaust, oil or coolant leaks develop, indicating a need for gasket or seal replacement, the repairs can generally be made with the engine in the vehicle. The intake manifold and warm-up catalysts gaskets, oil pan gasket, crankshaft front oil seal and cylinder head gaskets are all accessible with the engine in place.

Exterior engine components, such as the intake manifolds and warm-up catalysts, the oil pan, the oil pump, the water pump (see Chapter 3), the starter motor, the alternator, the ignition coils (see Chapter 5) and the fuel system components (see Chapter 4) can be removed for repair with the engine in place.

Since the cylinder heads can be removed without pulling the engine, valve component servicing can also be accomplished with the engine in the vehicle. Replacement of the camshafts, timing belt and sprockets is also possible with the engine in the vehicle.

In extreme cases caused by a lack of necessary equipment, repair or replacement of piston rings, pistons, connecting rods and rod bearings is possible with the engine in the vehicle. However, this practice is not recommended because of the cleaning and preparation work that must be done to the components involved.

3 Top Dead Center (TDC) for number 1 piston - locating

▸ **Refer to illustrations 3.5 and 3.6**

1   Top Dead Center (TDC) is the highest point in the cylinder that each piston reaches as it travels up-and-down during crankshaft rotation. Each piston reaches TDC on the compression stroke and again on the exhaust stroke, but TDC generally refers to piston position on the compression stroke.

2   Positioning the piston(s) at TDC is an essential part of many other repair procedures discussed in this manual.

3   Before beginning this procedure, be sure to place the transaxle in Neutral and apply the parking brake or block the rear wheels. Remove the spark plugs, as this will make the crankshaft much easier to turn (see Chapter 1).

4   In order to bring any piston to TDC, the crankshaft must be turned using one of the methods outlined below. When looking at the front of the engine, normal crankshaft rotation is clockwise.

a) *The preferred method is to turn the crankshaft with a socket and ratchet attached to the bolt threaded into the front of the crankshaft.*

b) *A remote starter switch, which may save some time, can also be used. Follow the instructions included with the switch. Once the piston is close to TDC, use a socket and ratchet as described in the previous paragraph.*

c) *If an assistant is available to turn the ignition switch to the Start position in short bursts, you can get the piston close to TDC without a remote starter switch. Make sure your assistant is out of the vehicle, away from the ignition switch, then use a socket and ratchet as described in Paragraph a) to complete the procedure.*

5   Turn the crankshaft until the TDC notch on the crankshaft pulley is aligned with the pointer on the timing belt lower cover (see illustration).

6   Locate the camshaft sprocket timing mark on the front cylinder bank. Look through the hole in the timing belt cover to check that the camshaft sprocket timing mark is aligned with the mark on the rear cover (see illustration). If no mark is present, rotate the crankshaft clockwise one revolution and realign the marks.

7   When the crankshaft pulley timing marks are aligned, and the camshaft sprocket timing marks are aligned, the number one piston is at TDC on the compression stroke.

8   After the number one piston has been positioned at TDC on the compression stroke, TDC for any of the remaining pistons can be located by turning the crankshaft 120-degrees at a time and following the firing order, aligning the cylinder number on the camshaft sprocket with the pointer on the timing belt cover (they're arranged in the firing order).

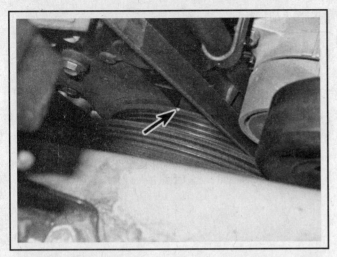

3.5 Align the TDC mark (white) on the crankshaft pulley with the pointer

3.6 Position the inspection hole cover aside and check the alignment of the camshaft sprocket timing mark with the mark on the timing belt cover (there is an inspection hole on each cylinder bank) - the numeral 1 is visible when the number 1 piston is at TDC

4 Valve covers - removal and installation

REMOVAL

♦ **Refer to illustrations 4.6a and 4.6b**

1 Disconnect the cable from the negative battery terminal (see Chapter 5, Section 1).

2 Remove the ignition coil assemblies (see Chapter 5). Remove the harness holders and lift the ignition coil wiring harnesses from the valve covers.

3 Remove the upper intake manifold (see Section 6).

4 At the front valve cover, pull the PCV hose from the left side of the valve cover (see Chapter 6).

5 At the rear valve cover, remove the bolt retaining the power steering hose bracket and move the hose aside.

6 Remove the retaining bolts (see illustrations), then detach the valve cover. If the cover is stuck to the head, bump the end with a block of wood and a hammer to jar it loose.

✳✳ CAUTION:

Don't pry at the cover-to-head joint or damage to the sealing surfaces may occur, leading to oil leaks after the cover is reinstalled.

7 Remove the original gasket and seal washers and clean the mating surfaces of the cylinder head and valve cover. If you removed the rear valve cover, inspect the PCV valve (see Chapter 1) before reattaching it to the valve cover.

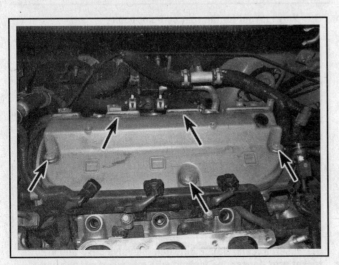

4.6a Valve cover retaining bolts (rear valve cover)

4.6b Valve cover retaining bolts (front valve cover)

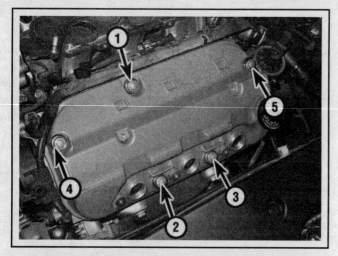

4.9 Valve cover tightening sequence - front shown, rear valve cover tightening sequence is identical

INSTALLATION

▶ **Refer to illustration 4.9**

8   Position a new gasket in the groove and install new seal washers on the bolts.

9   Install the cover and tighten the bolts to the torque listed in this Chapter's Specifications in three equal steps. Follow the correct torque sequence (see illustration).

10 Reinstall the remaining components.

11 Reconnect the battery. Refer to Chapter 5, Section 1.

12 Run the engine and check for oil leaks.

5   Valve clearance - check and adjustment

CHECK

1   The valve clearance generally does not need adjustment unless valvetrain components have been replaced or a valve job has been performed, or if the valves are noisy.

2   The simplest check for proper valve adjustment is to listen carefully to the engine running with the hood open. If the valvetrain is noisy, adjustment is necessary.

3   The valve clearance must be checked and adjusted with the engine cold.

ADJUSTMENT

▶ **Refer to illustrations 5.6, 5.7 and 5.9**

4   Remove the valve covers (see Section 4).

5   Rotate the crankshaft clockwise and position the number 1 piston at TDC (see Section 3).

6   In this position, check and, if necessary, adjust the valves for cylinder number 1 (see illustration). There are four valves for each cylinder.

7   Starting with the intake valve, insert a feeler gauge of the correct thickness (see this Chapter's Specifications) between the valve stem and the rocker arm (see illustration). Withdraw it; you should feel a slight drag. If there's no drag or a heavy drag, loosen the adjuster nut and back off the adjuster screw. Carefully tighten the adjuster screw until you can feel a slight drag on the feeler gauge as you withdraw it.

8   Hold the adjuster screw with a screwdriver to keep it from turning, then tighten the locknut. Recheck the clearance to make sure it hasn't changed. Repeat the procedure in this Step and the previous Step on the other intake valve, then on the two exhaust valves.

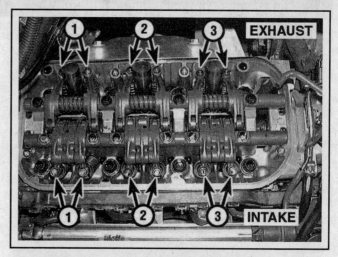

5.6 Valve layout for the rear cylinder bank

5.7 Insert a feeler gauge between the valve stem and the rocker arm, loosen the locknut with a box end wrench and adjust the clearance with a screwdriver

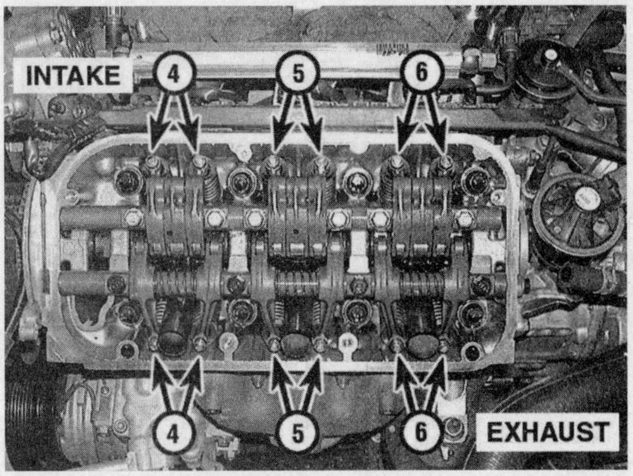

5.9 Valve layout for the front cylinder bank

9 Rotate the crankshaft pulley clockwise until the number 4 on the camshaft sprocket is aligned with the pointer on the timing belt cover (see illustration 3.6). Check and adjust the number 4 cylinder valves (see illustration).

10 Rotate the crankshaft pulley 120-degrees clockwise until the number 2 cylinder is at TDC. Check and adjust the number 2 cylinder valves.

11 Rotate the crankshaft pulley clockwise, follow the firing order listed in this Chapter's Specifications and adjust the remaining valves.

12 Refer to Section 4 and install the valve covers.

6 Intake manifold - removal and installation

WARNING:

Wait until the engine is completely cool before beginning this procedure.

UPPER INTAKE MANIFOLD

Refer to illustrations 6.6a, 6.6b, 6.9a and 6.9b

1 Relieve the fuel pressure (see Chapter 4).

2 Disconnect the cable from the negative battery terminal (see Chapter 5, Section 1).

3 Refer to Chapter 1 and drain the coolant. Remove the coolant hoses from the throttle body and the intake manifold. Plug the coolant hoses.

4 Refer to Chapter 4 and remove the air intake duct, then disconnect the APP sensor connector (see Chapter 4), hoses and other connections from the throttle body.

5 Remove the intake manifold cover.

Note: Follow the reverse order of the tightening sequence on the intake manifold cover (see illustration 6.9b).

6 Disconnect the vacuum hoses from the rear side of the intake manifold (see illustrations). Be sure to mark each hose with tape to insure correct reassembly.

7 Remove the engine harness connectors (IAT, IAC, MAP, EVAP canister, IMRC [see Chapter 6]) from their respective components. Label each connector with tape to insure correct reassembly.

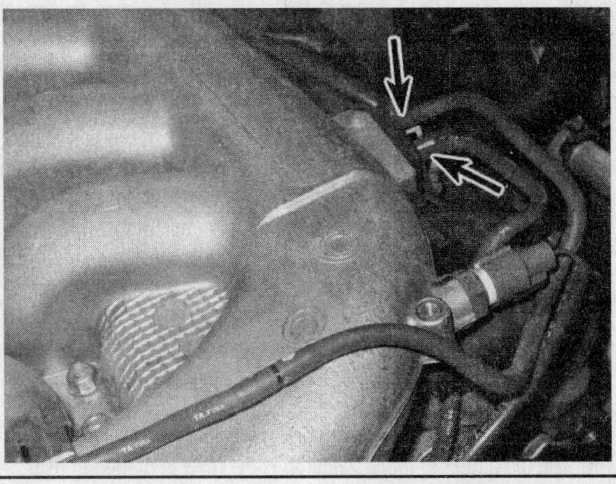

6.6a Vacuum line locations on the rear side of the upper intake manifold

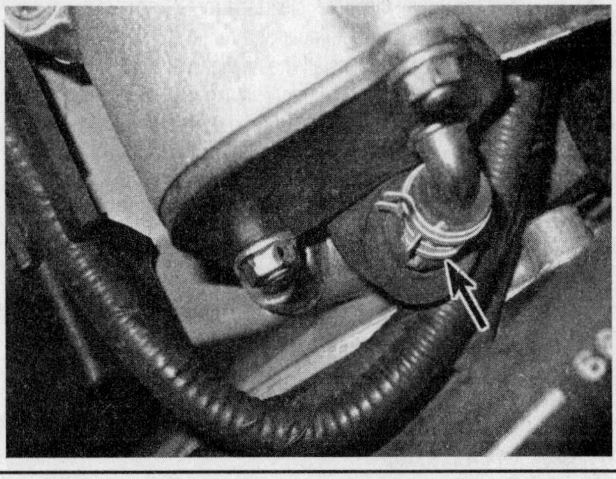

6.6b Vacuum hose location for the PCV valve

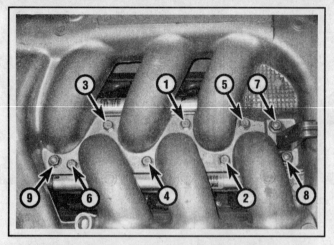

6.9a Upper intake manifold bolt tightening sequence

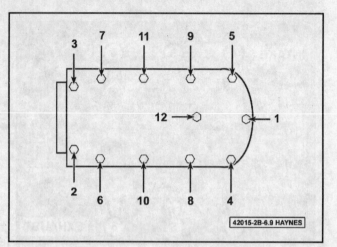

6.9b Intake manifold cover bolt tightening sequence

6.13 Location of the lower intake manifold mounting nuts - the four corner nuts are hidden from view

6.15 Position the gasket over the dowels in the cylinder head and install the lower intake manifold(s)

8 Following the reverse of the tightening sequence (see illustration 6.9a), remove the bolts and nuts and remove the manifold with the throttle body attached.

9 To install the upper manifold, clean the mounting surfaces of the lower manifold with lacquer thinner and remove all traces of the old gasket material or sealant. Install the new gasket over the studs on the lower manifold, then install the upper intake manifold. Tighten the nuts and bolts in sequence (see illustrations) to the torque listed in this Chapter's Specifications.

10 Reconnect the battery (see Chapter 5, Section 1). Refill the cooling system (see Chapter 1).

LOWER INTAKE MANIFOLD

♦ **Refer to illustrations 6.13 and 6.15**

11 Remove the upper intake manifold, if not already done. Remove the power steering pump and position it aside, without disconnecting the hoses (see Chapter 10).

12 Disconnect the electrical connectors at the fuel injectors (label all connectors first) and remove the fuel rails from the lower intake mani-

fold (see Chapter 4).

13 Remove the mounting nuts and bolts, then detach the two lower intake manifold sections from the cylinder heads (see illustration). If they are stuck, don't pry between the gasket mating surfaces or damage may result.

➡**Note: The fuel injectors may be left installed in the lower intake manifolds during removal.**

14 Carefully use a scraper to remove all traces of old gasket material and sealant from the manifold and cylinder heads, then clean the mating surfaces with lacquer thinner or acetone.

15 Install new gaskets (see illustration), then position the lower manifolds on the cylinder heads. Make sure the gaskets and manifolds are aligned over the dowels in the cylinder heads and install the nuts/bolts.

16 Tighten the fasteners, in three equal steps, to the torque listed in this Chapter's Specifications. Work from the center out towards the ends to avoid warping the manifolds.

17 Install the upper intake manifold (see Step 9).

18 The remainder of the installation is the reverse of the removal procedure. Refill the cooling system (see Chapter 1). Run the engine and check for fuel, vacuum and coolant leaks.

7 Exhaust manifolds - removal and installation

This engine does not have exhaust manifolds, per se; the exhaust ports empty into a collector integral with each cylinder head. The upstream (warm-up) catalytic converters bolt to the cylinder heads in place of traditional exhaust manifolds. Refer to Chapter 6 for the removal and installation procedure.

8 Timing belt and sprockets - removal, inspection and installation

REMOVAL

▶ Refer to illustrations 8.10a, 8.10b, 8.11, 8.12a, 8.12b, 8.13, 8.14, 8.15, 8.16, 8.17, 8.18 and 8.19

1 Disconnect the cable from the negative battery terminal (see Chapter 5, Section 1).
2 Place the transaxle in Park or neutral, apply the parking brake and block the rear wheels.
3 Remove the drivebelts (see Chapter 1).
4 Remove the power steering pump (see Chapter 10).

➡Note: Do not disconnect the power steering lines from the pump and position the assembly off to the side.

5 Remove the spark plugs to make it easier to turn the crankshaft (see Chapter 1), then position the number 1 piston at TDC (see Section 3).

6 Loosen the lug nuts on the right front wheel. Raise the front of the vehicle and support it securely on jackstands. Remove the right, front wheel.
7 Remove the right front inner fender splash guard (see Chapter 11).
8 Support the engine by placing a floor jack under the oil pan with a block of wood on the jack to protect the pan. Remove the splash shield under the radiator (see Chapter 3).
9 Remove the two bolts and the wiring harness retainer holding the passenger-side engine mount to the block, remove the through-bolt, and remove the mount (see Section 18). Remove the engine-mount bracket. Remove the engine oil dipstick tube.
10 Remove the upper timing belt covers (see illustrations).
11 If you intend to re-use the belt, mark the belt to indicate the direction of rotation (see illustration).
12 Make sure the timing marks are properly aligned (see illustrations).

8.10a Detach the wiring harness from the retainer (A) and remove the bolts (B) from the upper timing belt cover (front cylinder bank)

8.10b Remove the upper timing belt cover (arrows indicate two of the four bolts) from the rear cylinder bank

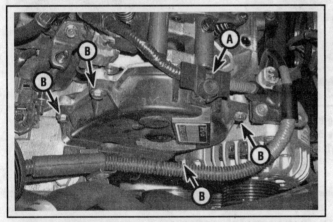
8.11 Mark the direction of rotation on the timing belt

8.12a Camshaft timing marks (front cylinder bank) - align the mark on the sprocket with the mark on the rear cover

8.12b Camshaft sprocket timing marks - rear cylinder bank

8.13 Remove the crankshaft pulley bolt using a strap or chain wrench to hold the pulley (if you use a chain wrench, be sure to wrap the crankshaft pulley with an old piece of drivebelt to protect it)

8.14 Remove the bolts and the lower timing belt cover

8.15 Crankshaft sprocket timing marks

8.16 Thread the long battery hold-down bolt (A) into the boss as shown to hold the timing belt adjuster (B) in position

8.17 Loosen the timing belt idler bolt about six turns

13 Using a strap wrench or equivalent tool to hold the crankshaft, loosen the crankshaft pulley bolt (see illustration). Remove the crankshaft pulley.

➡**Note: When the crankshaft pulley bolt is loosened, the position of the timing marks on the crankshaft pulley and the camshafts may be disturbed. Check and align them again. Temporarily reinstall the crankshaft pulley bolt to turn the crankshaft.**

14 Remove the lower timing belt cover (see illustration).

15 Slip the timing belt guide off the crankshaft sprocket, noting how it's installed. Also note the alignment of the crankshaft sprocket timing marks (see illustration).

16 Remove one of the long hold-down bolts from the battery tray and bevel the threaded end somewhat with a file or grinder. Thread the bolt into the boss so that it pushes against the timing belt adjuster - the bolt is used to hold the adjuster in position (see illustration). Tighten it hand-tight only.

17 Remove the engine mount bracket and loosen the idler pulley bolt six turns, then remove the timing belt (see illustration).

18 The camshaft sprockets can be removed at this point, if they are damaged or to replace the oil seals (see illustration). Remove the keys from the shafts so they don't fall out and get lost.

❊❊ **CAUTION:**

Don't allow the camshaft(s) to turn.

19 If it's worn or damaged, or if you're replacing the crankshaft front oil seal, the crankshaft sprocket can now be removed (see illustration). If it won't come off by hand, carefully pry it off. Also, remove the timing belt guide, noting how it's installed.

INSPECTION

20 Inspect the sprocket teeth for wear and damage. Check the timing belt for any cracks or oil residue. Also check the camshaft for excessive endplay (see Section 12). Check the timing belt tensioner for smooth operation. Replace any worn parts with new ones.

21 Now that the timing belt is removed, inspect the water pump (see Chapter 3).

➡**Note: Because of the work involved in getting at the water pump, it is advisable you replace the water pump anytime the timing belt is removed.**

8.18 Prevent the camshaft from turning by inserting a two-pin spanner through the holes in the sprocket while you loosen the bolt

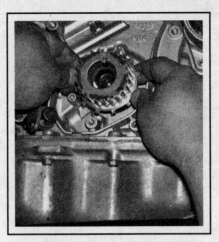

8.19 Carefully remove the crankshaft sprocket

8.26 Install the outer timing belt guide as shown

INSTALLATION

Refer to illustration 8.26

22 Remove all dirt and oil from the timing belt area. Clean the teeth of the sprockets with lacquer thinner.

23 If any of the timing belt sprockets were removed, install them now with their keys and tighten the bolts to the torque listed in this Chapter's Specifications.

24 If removed, install the timing belt guide over the crankshaft sprocket with the chamfered edge facing away from the belt.

25 Recheck the position of the timing marks (see illustrations 8.12a, 8.12b and 8.15). Install the timing belt in a clockwise direction, starting at the crankshaft sprocket and tensioner pulley, then rear camshaft sprocket, water pump, front camshaft sprocket, and idler pulley. If you're re-using the original belt, the arrow you made in Step 11 should point in the normal direction of rotation.

➡Note: If the tensioner piston has extended and you're unable to install the timing belt, remove the tensioner and compress the piston as described below.

26 Install the outer timing belt guide over the crankshaft sprocket with the chamfered edge facing away from the belt (see illustration).

27 Tighten the idler pulley bolt to the torque listed in this Chapter's Specifications. Remove the battery hold-down bolt that was holding the tensioner pulley in position (see illustration 8.16).

28 Turn the crankshaft slowly six revolutions clockwise using a socket and breaker bar on the crankshaft pulley bolt to seat the belt, then return to TDC. Recheck the alignment of cam and crank timing marks.

✳✳ CAUTION:

If you feel any resistance, back up and recheck the belt timing. Do not force the crankshaft to turn or engine damage will occur!

29 Install the lower timing belt cover.
30 Install the crankshaft pulley, aligning the pulley keyway with the crankshaft key. Install the bolt and tighten it to the torque listed in this Chapter's Specifications. Use the method described in Step 13 to keep the crankshaft from turning.

31 Recheck the timing marks (see illustrations 8.12a and 8.12b and 8.15).

✳✳ CAUTION:

If the timing marks are not aligned exactly as shown, repeat the timing belt installation procedure. DO NOT start the engine until you're absolutely certain that the timing belt is installed correctly. Serious and costly engine damage could occur if the belt is installed wrong.

32 Reinstall the remaining parts in the reverse order of removal.
33 Reconnect the battery. Refer to Chapter 5, Section 1.

TENSIONER ADJUSTMENT

♦ **Refer to illustrations 8.37 and 8.38**

➡Note: These models use a tensioner pin with a ring handle to keep the tensioner retracted. If this special tool is not available, it is possible to compress the tensioner and keep it retracted using a plastic wire tie (see Step 37).

34 The belt tensioner does not normally need to be removed or adjusted for a timing belt replacement procedure (unless the tensioner piston has extended), but there other engine procedures (water pump replacement, etc.) that require the tensioner be removed. Once removed, the tensioner piston will extend in length. The following Steps apply only if the tensioner has been removed from the engine.

35 To remove the tensioner, remove the long bolt used in Step 16, and unbolt the tensioner from the block.

36 Retract the tensioner. Align the holes on the rod and the tensioner body with a pin 0.08 inch (2.0 mm) in diameter. Compress the tensioner until the holes align and insert the pin, locking the tensioner in a retracted position.

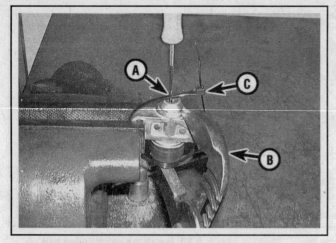

8.37 Retract the piston with a small screwdriver (A) and hold it in with pliers (B) while an assistant tightens the wire-tie (C)

8.38 When timing belt installation is complete, release the tensioner by cutting the wire-tie - pull out the wire-tie with pliers

37 The manufacturer uses a special tool (pin) to retain the piston in the retracted position. If the tool is not available, hold the piston in the retracted position with a pair of adjustable pliers while an assistant tightens a strong plastic wire-tie around the tensioner body and piston (see illustration).

➡ **Note: Set-up the tensioner with the wire-tie in position between the jaws of the pliers and the end of the piston before retracting the piston. This is a very delicate procedure and may require several attempts.**

38 Reinstall the service bolt in the tensioner. Install the tensioner, being careful not to dislodge the wire-tie, and tighten the mounting bolts to the torque listed in this Chapter's Specifications. After completing the remainder of the timing belt installation procedure, cut the wire-tie and pull it out with pliers (see illustration).

9 Crankshaft front oil seal - replacement

▸ **Refer to illustrations 9.2 and 9.4**

1 Remove the timing belt and crankshaft sprocket (see Section 8).
2 Carefully pry the seal out of the engine with a screwdriver or seal removal tool (see illustration). If you use a screwdriver, don't scratch the housing bore or damage the crankshaft (if the crankshaft is damaged, the new seal will end up leaking).
3 Clean the oil seal bore and coat the outer edge of the new seal with a small amount of engine oil to ease installation. Apply multi-purpose grease to the seal lip.
4 Using a seal-driver or a socket with an outside diameter slightly smaller than the outside diameter of the seal, carefully drive the new seal into place with a hammer (see illustration). Make sure it's installed squarely and driven in to the same depth as the original. Check the seal after installation to make sure the garter spring didn't pop out of place.
5 Reinstall the crankshaft sprocket and timing belt (see Section 8).
6 Run the engine and check for oil leaks at the front seal.

9.2 Carefully pry out the oil seal

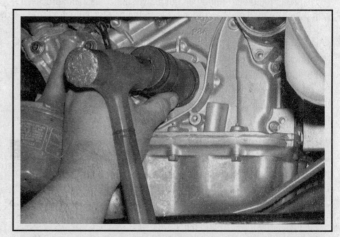

9.4 Lubricate the seal lip and tap the new crankshaft seal into place with a seal driver or a large socket and a hammer

10 VTEC system - general description and component checks

GENERAL DESCRIPTION

1   The VTEC system is Honda's design for Variable Valve Timing and Lift Electronic Control. All engines in the models covered in this manual are equipped with the VTEC system.

2   The differences between conventional engines and the VTEC system is strictly in the components and operation of the valve train.

3   The engine management computer has the ability to physically change which camshaft intake lobes are being used to operate the intake valves. The computer turns the system ON or OFF, depending on sensor input.

4   The following are used to determine VTEC operation:
   a) *Engine speed (rpm)*
   b) *Vehicle speed (mph)*
   c) *Throttle position*
   d) *Engine load measured by Manifold Absolute Pressure (MAP) sensor*
   e) *Coolant temperature*

5   The camshaft has three different intake valve lobe profiles (lift and duration specifications).

6   At low speeds, the secondary intake valve operates on its own camshaft lobe, which has lift and duration profiles designed specifically for increasing torque. The opening is intended to be just enough to keep atomized fuel from puddling at the valve head. This limited valve operation is designed to provide good low end torque and responsiveness, by inducing swirl in the combustion chamber from the primary intake valve, which operates with a normal profile.

7   When performance is needed, the primary and secondary rocker arms are locked together through the use of an electrically controlled hydraulic system. Hydraulically operated synchronizing pistons lock the rocker arms together. When activated, the intake valves open to the higher lift and duration of the rocker arm selected, which has its own camshaft lobe designed with the higher lift profile.

➡**Note: Refer to this Chapter's Specifications for the exact camshaft lobe lift profiles.**

COMPONENT CHECKS

➡**Note: The VTEC system will require specialized diagnostic equipment to access the on-board computer to test the associated electrical circuits, actuators and sensors. However, there are some mechanical tests of the VTEC system that the home mechanic can perform to check for obvious and simple problems within the system. If these simple checks don't reveal any problems, have the VTEC system diagnosed by a dealer service department or other qualified automotive repair facility. Also, some checks and inspections of the VTEC components requires removal of the rocker arm assembly (see Section 11).**

VTEC lock-up control solenoid valve

⬧ **Refer to illustrations 10.8 and 10.9**

➡**Note: Most common problems in the VTEC system are associated with the solenoid valve and its filter. Regular engine oil and filter changes are necessary for trouble-free operation of the valve.**

8   The lock-up VTEC solenoid valve and switch are located on the oil filter housing at the right-rear side of the engine, best viewed through the right fenderwell (see illustration).

9   Remove the oil filter adapter housing from the engine and check the filter/O-ring for clogging (see illustration). Clean and reinstall with a new O-ring. A clogged filter screen is often the cause of system problems.

Rocker arms

⬧ **Refer to illustration 10.11**

10 Position the number one piston at Top Dead Center (see Section 3). Remove the valve cover (see Section 4).

11 Press on the mid intake rocker arm for cylinder number 1 to see that it moves independently of the primary and secondary intake rockers (see illustration). Check the rockers for the other cylinders at their own TDC positions.

10.8 The VTEC solenoid is located on top of the oil filter housing

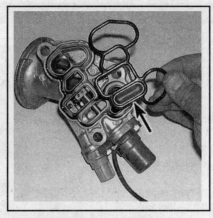

10.9 Whenever problems are suspected in the VTEC system, check the O-ring and filter behind the oil filter adapter housing

10.11 Push down on the mid-rocker of cylinder number 1 to check the action of the VTEC rocker assembly - it should move independently of the primary and secondary intake rockers

10.13 Push down on the plunger of each lost motion assembly - they should move smoothly

10.16 Check for smooth movement of the piston in each VTEC rocker arm

Lost motion assembly

▶ **Refer to illustration 10.13**

12 The lost motion assemblies sit in three pockets in each cylinder head. The rocker arms/shafts must be removed for access to the lost motion assemblies (see Section 11).

13 Test each lost motion assembly by pushing the plunger with your finger (see illustration). A light pressure should move the plunger slightly, and firmer pressure will move it further. If the assembly doesn't move smoothly, replace it.

Synchronizing assembly

▶ **Refer to illustration 10.16**

14 Once the rocker arm assemblies have been removed and disassembled (see Section 11), separate the rocker arms and synchronizing components.

VTEC components:

a) *Primary rocker arm*
b) *Secondary rocker arm*
c) *Mid rocker arm*
d) *Synchronizing piston A*
e) *Synchronizing piston B*
f) *Timing piston*

15 Inspect the timing spring, making sure it's not broken or collapsed. Replace it if necessary.

16 Inspect all other parts (rocker arms and synchronizing pistons) for wear, galling, scoring or signs of overheating (bluish in color). Use your finger to push on the rocker arm pistons to check for smooth movement (see illustration). Replace any parts necessary.

17 Reassemble each cylinder's components and wrap a rubber band around the rocker arms before trying to assemble them on the rocker shaft (see Section 11).

11 Rocker arm assembly - removal, inspection and installation

REMOVAL

▶ **Refer to illustration 11.4**

1   Remove the valve cover (see Section 4).

2   Position the engine at TDC for number 1 piston (see Section 3) and remove the timing belt (see Section 8).

3   Loosen the rocker shaft mounting bolts 1/4-turn at a time, in the reverse of the tightening sequence, until the spring pressure is relieved (see illustration 11.11).

4   Lift the rocker arms and shaft assembly from the cylinder head (see illustration). Do not remove the shaft mounting bolts - they will keep the rocker arm assembly components together.

11.4 Leave the rocker assembly mounting bolts in place as you remove the assembly (this will keep the components in order on the shafts)

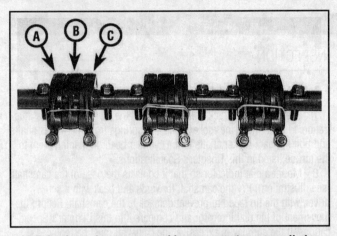

11.5 Intake rocker arm assembly components - rear cylinder bank (on the front cylinder bank A and C are reversed) (note the rubber bands installed to hold the components together)

A   Primary intake rocker arm
B   Mid intake rocker arm
C   Secondary intake rocker arm

INSPECTION

◆ **Refer to illustrations 11.5 and 11.6**

5   If you wish to disassemble and inspect the rocker arm assembly - a good idea as long as you have them off - remove the mounting bolts and slip the rocker arms and springs off the shafts (see illustration). Mark the relationship of the shafts to the bearing caps and keep the parts in order so you can reassemble them in the same positions.

➡**Note: Keep the three intake rockers for each cylinder together by wrapping them with a heavy rubber band.**

6   Thoroughly clean the parts and inspect them for wear and damage. Check the rocker arm faces that contact the camshaft and the rocker arm tips (see illustration). Check the surfaces of the shafts that the rocker arms ride on, as well as the bearing surfaces inside the rocker arms, for scoring and excessive wear. Replace any parts that are damaged or excessively worn. Also, make sure the oil holes in the shafts are not plugged. Check the roller tips for wear and smoothness of operation.

7   Remove the lost motion assemblies from the cylinder head (see illustration 10.13), and clean them. Check for smoothness of plunger operation by pushing down gently with your finger.

8   Check the smoothness of operation of the VTEC pistons in each intake rocker arm (see illustration 10.16).

INSTALLATION

◆ **Refer to illustration 11.11**

9   Lubricate all components with engine oil and reassemble the shafts. When installing the rocker arms, shafts and springs, note the

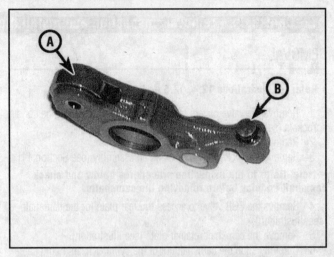

11.6 Inspect the rockers arms for wear and damage at the roller (A) and the valve stem end of the adjusters (B)

11.11 Rocker arm/shaft mounting bolt TIGHTENING sequence

markings and the difference between the left and right side parts.

10 Coat the wear surfaces of the rocker arms with camshaft installation lubricant and install the rocker arm assembly.

11 Tighten the rocker shaft mounting bolts a little at a time, following the recommended tightening sequence (see illustration) to the torque listed in this Chapter's Specifications.

12 The remainder of installation is the reverse of removal.

13 Check the valve clearance and adjust to Specifications (see Section 5).

14 Run the engine and check for oil leaks and proper operation.

12 Camshafts - removal, inspection and installation

REMOVAL

◆ **Refer to illustrations 12.4, 12.5 and 12.6**

1   Remove the valve covers (see Section 4) and the timing belt and sprockets (see Section 8).

2   Remove the ignition coils (see Chapter 5).

3   Remove the rocker arms/shafts as an assembly (see Section 11).

➡**Note: Refer to the Inspection procedures below and check camshaft endplay before removing the camshafts.**

4   Remove the EGR valve to access the rear plate for the camshaft (see illustration).

5   Remove the camshaft retainer plate (see illustration).

6   Carefully slide the camshaft out of the cylinder head, being careful not to nick the lobes or journals as you withdraw it (see illustration).

INSPECTION

◆ **Refer to illustrations 12.8, 12.9a and 12.9b**

7   Keeping careful track of the location of the components (see illustration 11.5), remove the rocker arms and springs from the rocker shafts and bolt the bare rocker shafts to the cylinder head, tightening them to the torque listed in this Chapter's Specifications.

8   Mount a dial indicator so that it contacts the nose of the camshaft (see illustration). Pry the camshaft forwards and back with a screwdriver, with the tip taped to prevent damage to the camshaft. Record the movement of the dial indicator and compare it to this Chapter's Specifications. If the endplay is excessive, the camshaft must be replaced.

9   After the endplay check, remove the rocker shafts and withdraw the camshaft. Measure the journal diameters and lobe heights on each

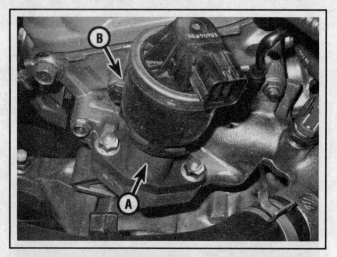

12.4 To access the camshaft plate for the front camshaft, remove the EGR valve (A), then the two bolts on the plate (B) located behind the EGR valve

12.5 Remove the bolts and the camshaft retainer plate

12.6 Pull the camshaft straight out of the cylinder head, taking care not to nick the journals or bearings

12.8 Check the camshaft endplay with a dial indicator

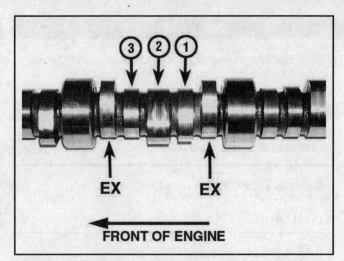

12.9a Arrangement of camshaft lobes on the left cylinder bank (front) camshaft

1   Primary intake lobe   3   Secondary intake lobe
2   Mid intake lobe

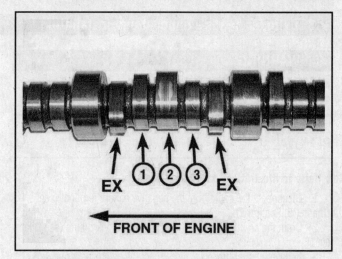

12.9b Arrangement of camshaft lobes on the right cylinder bank (rear) camshaft

1   Primary intake lobe   3   Secondary intake lobe
2   Mid intake lobe

12.10 Remove the two bolts and the timing belt rear cover from each cylinder head

12.11 Pry out the old camshaft oil seal with a screwdriver

12.12 If a seal driver is not available, use a hammer and a large socket to drive the new seal into place

camshaft (see this Chapter's Specifications). Check also for visual signs of wear, scoring, pitting or overheating.

➡Note: The arrangement of lobes is different between the front and rear camshafts (see illustrations).

INSTALLATION

▸ Refer to illustrations 12.10, 12.11 and 12.12

10 Remove the timing belt rear covers from each cylinder head to access the camshaft oil seals (see illustration).

11 The camshaft oil seal should be replaced whenever the camshaft is removed or replaced. Pry the old seal out with a screwdriver or seal removal tool (see illustration).

12 Lubricate the lips with engine oil, then install a new camshaft oil seal by driving it in squarely with a seal installation tool to the same depth as the original seal (see illustration). A socket of the appropriate size will also work.

13 Clean the camshaft thoroughly with solvent, then lubricate the journals and lobes with camshaft installation lubricant and carefully install the camshaft into the cylinder head.

14 Lubricate and install a new O-ring at the end of the camshaft retainer plate and bolt the retainer plates in place.

15 Install the other camshaft in the same manner.

16 Reinstall the remaining components in the reverse order of removal. Refer to Section 5 for the valve adjustment procedure.

17 Run the engine and check for oil leaks at the camshaft seals. Run the engine at low speed for five minutes to allow the air to bleed from the lost motion assemblies, then check for leaks and proper operation.

➡Note: There will be some tappet noise during the first few minutes of operation. If the noise continues, it may indicate a problem with one of the lost motion assemblies.

13 Cylinder heads - removal and installation

Allow the engine to cool completely before beginning this procedure.

REMOVAL

▶ **Refer to illustrations 13.12 and 13.15**

1 Disconnect the cable from the negative battery terminal (see Chapter 5, Section 1).

2 Drain the cooling system, including both block drains (see Chapter 1).

3 Relieve the fuel pressure, disconnect the electrical connectors from the fuel injectors, disconnect the fuel lines, and remove the fuel rails (see Chapter 4).

4 Remove the alternator (see Chapter 5).

5 Remove the ignition coils from the valve covers (see Chapter 5).

6 Remove the power steering pump and set it aside without disconnecting the hoses (see Chapter 10).

7 Remove the upper intake manifold (see Section 6).

8 Remove the warm-up catalysts (see Section 7).

9 Remove the timing belt covers (see Section 8).

10 Remove the timing belt and the camshaft sprockets from the camshafts (see Section 8).

11 Correctly label and remove all the electrical connectors at the lower intake manifold.

12 Remove the water passage assembly from the cylinder head (see illustration).

13 Refer to Section 11 and remove the rocker arms/shafts assembly.

14 Using a socket and breaker bar, loosen the cylinder head bolts in 1/4-turn increments until they can be removed by hand. Loosen them in a sequence opposite that of the tightening sequence (see illustration 13.23).

❋❋ **CAUTION:**

Obtain new cylinder head bolts. The old ones should not be reused.

13.12 Remove the water passage mounting bolts from both cylinder heads - lightly tap the passage with a soft-faced hammer to break the gasket seal and remove the water passage

15 Lift the cylinder head off the engine block. If the head is stuck, pry against an external casting protrusion (see illustration).

❋❋ **CAUTION:**

Don't pry between the head and block. The gasket surfaces may be damaged and leaks could result.

16 Repeat Steps 13 through 15 for the other head.

INSTALLATION

▶ **Refer to illustration 13.23**

17 The mating surfaces of the cylinder heads and block must be perfectly clean when the heads are installed. Use a gasket scraper to remove all traces of carbon and old gasket material. Be careful not to gouge the delicate aluminum. Clean the mating surfaces with lacquer thinner or acetone. If there's oil on the mating surfaces when the head is installed, the gasket may not seal correctly and leaks could develop.

18 When working on the block, stuff the cylinders with clean shop rags to keep out debris. Use a vacuum cleaner to remove material that falls into the cylinders.

19 Check the block and head mating surfaces for nicks, deep scratches and other damage. If damage is slight, it can be removed with a file; if it's excessive, machining may be the only alternative.

20 Use a tap of the correct size to chase the threads in the head bolt holes, then clean the holes with compressed air - make sure that nothing remains in the holes.

❋❋ **WARNING:**

Wear eye protection when using compressed air!

21 Clean the oil-control jets thoroughly and reinstall them with new O-rings. Position the new gaskets over the oil-control jets and locating dowels in the block.

13.15 Pry up carefully on a casting protrusion

22 Carefully set the head on the block without disturbing the gasket.

23 Before installing the new head bolts, apply a small amount of clean engine oil to the threads and under the bolt heads. Install the bolts and special washers and tighten them finger tight. Following the recommended sequence (see illustration), tighten the bolts to the torque listed in this Chapter's Specifications. Repeat the entire procedure to install the other cylinder head, if necessary.

24 The remaining installation steps are the reverse of removal.

25 Reconnect the battery. Refer to Chapter 5, Section 1.

26 Refill the cooling system, change the oil and filter (see Chapter 1), run the engine and check for leaks. Run the engine at low speed for five minutes to allow the air to bleed from the lost motion assemblies, then check for leaks and proper operation.

➡Note: There will be some tappet noise during the first few minutes of operation. If the noise continues, it may indicate a problem with one of the lost motion assemblies.

13.23 Cylinder head bolt TIGHTENING sequence

14 Oil pan - removal and installation

REMOVAL

♦ **Refer to illustrations 14.6a and 14.6b**

1 Disconnect the cable from the negative battery terminal (see Chapter 5, Section 1).

2 Block the rear wheels and set the parking brake. Raise the front of the vehicle and support it securely on jackstands.

3 Remove the engine splash shield.

4 Drain the engine oil and remove the oil filter (see Chapter 1).

5 Unbolt the exhaust crossover pipe from the warm-up catalytic converters (see Chapter 6). Remove the pipe.

6 Remove the bolts/nuts (see illustration) and lower the oil pan. The bolts at the timing belt end of the engine can be removed with a 1/4-inch drive flex-socket, extension and ratchet. If the pan is stuck, use a dull pry tool at the tabs on the casting corners (see illustration). Don't damage the mating surfaces of the pan and block or oil leaks could develop.

INSTALLATION

♦ **Refer to illustration 14.11**

7 Use a scraper to remove all traces of old sealant from the block and oil pan. Be careful not to gouge the delicate aluminum block. Clean the mating surfaces with lacquer thinner or acetone.

8 Make sure the threaded bolt holes in the block are clean.

9 Inspect the oil pump pick-up screen assembly for damage and a blocked strainer (see Section 15).

10 Position a new gasket on the oil pan.

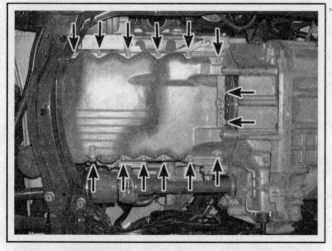

14.6a Remove the bolts from around the perimeter of the oil pan and the oil pan-to-transaxle case bolts (four bolts hidden from view behind the subframe)

14.6b Use a large screwdriver or prybar to pry the pan loose at the cast tabs - DO NOT pry on the gasket surface

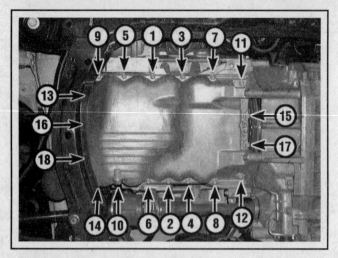

14.11 Oil pan bolt tightening sequence

11 Carefully position the oil pan on the engine block and install the bolts. Follow the correct torque sequence (see illustration) and tighten them to the torque listed in this Chapter's Specifications in three steps.

12 The remainder of installation is the reverse of removal. Be sure to add oil and install a new oil filter.

➡**Note: If the oil pump has been replaced, wait 20 minutes (to allow the sealant to cure) before adding oil.**

13 Reconnect the battery (see Chapter 5, Section 1).

14 Run the engine and check for oil pressure and leaks.

15 Oil pump - removal, inspection and installation

REMOVAL

▶ **Refer to illustrations 15.3 and 15.5**

1 Remove the timing belt, crankshaft sprocket and idler pulley (see Section 8).

2 Refer to Chapter 6 and remove the crankshaft position sensor.

3 Remove the oil pan (see Section 14) and oil pick-up screen (see illustration). If equipped, remove the oil level sensor.

4 Remove the oil filter adapter housing/VTEC solenoid assembly from the front of the oil pump (see Section 10).

5 Remove the bolts and detach the oil pump housing from the engine (see illustration). You may have to pry carefully between the main bearing cap and the pump housing with a screwdriver.

15.3 Oil pick-up screen bolt locations

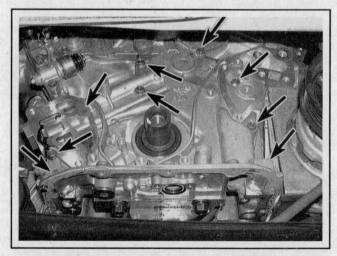

15.5 Oil pump housing bolt locations

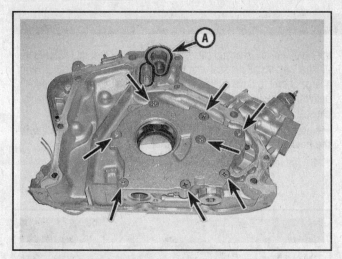

15.6 Remove the screws from the pump cover. Be sure to replace the O-ring seal (A)

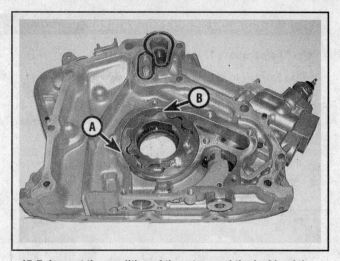

15.7 Inspect the condition of the rotors and the inside of the cover - with feeler gauges, measure the clearances at (A) (outer rotor-to-housing) and (B) (inner rotor-to-outer rotor), lay a straightedge across the face of the pump housing and measure the housing-to-rotor axial clearance and compare to Specifications

INSPECTION

▶ **Refer to illustrations 15.6 and 15.7**

6 Use a large Phillips screwdriver to remove the screws holding the pump cover to the rear of the housing (see illustration).

7 Lift the cover off and inspect the pump rotors (see illustration). If any wear or damage is evident, replace the pump. Check the rotor clearance with a feeler gauge and compare it to this Chapter's Specifications.

8 Use a scraper to remove any traces of old sealant from the pump body and engine block, being careful not to damage the delicate aluminum.

INSTALLATION

9 Replace the old crankshaft oil seal (see Section 9). Apply multipurpose grease to the seal lip.

10 Pack the pump cavity with petroleum jelly and install the cover (this is to prime the pump). Apply thread-locking compound to the threads and tighten the screws securely following a criss-cross pattern.

11 Use acetone or lacquer thinner and a clean rag to remove all traces of oil from the gasket surfaces.

12 Apply a bead of anaerobic sealant to the oil pump flange and the threads of the mounting bolts. Avoid using an excessive amount of sealant, especially around oil passages and bolt holes. Parts must be assembled within five minutes of sealant application, otherwise the material must be removed and reapplied. Wherever O-rings are employed, use new ones.

13 Engage the flat surfaces on the oil pump drive rotor with the matching flats on the crankshaft and slide the pump into place.

14 Install the pump mounting bolts in their original locations and tighten them to the torque listed in this Chapter's Specifications in a criss-cross pattern.

15 Using a new O-ring, install the oil pick-up screen and tighten the fasteners to the torque listed in this Chapter's Specifications.

16 Reinstall the remaining parts in the reverse order of removal.

17 Wait 20 minutes to allow the sealant to cure, then add oil, start the engine and check for oil leaks and pressure.

18 Recheck the engine oil level after operating the engine.

16 Flywheel/driveplate - removal and installation

This procedure is essentially the same as the four cylinder engine. Refer to Part A and follow the procedure outlined there. However, use the bolt torques listed in this Chapter's Specifications.

17 Rear main oil seal - replacement

▶ **Refer to illustrations 17.2 and 17.3**

1   The transaxle must be removed from the vehicle for this procedure and the flywheel/driveplate must be removed from the engine. Refer to Chapter 7 and Section 16 as necessary.

2   The seal can be replaced without removing the oil pan or removing the seal retainer. However, the lip of the seal is quite stiff and it's possible to cock the seal in the retainer bore or damage it during installation. Pry out the old seal with a screwdriver (see illustration).

3   Apply multi-purpose grease to the crankshaft seal journal and the lip of the new seal and carefully drive the new seal into place (see illustration). Install the seal with the spring side in. Use a seal driver or a large socket to drive it into place. The lip is stiff so carefully work it onto the seal journal of the crankshaft. Don't rush it or you may damage the seal.

➡**Note: Drive the seal in squarely and only until it is flush with the back of the seal plate, no further.**

4   The remaining steps are the reverse of removal.

17.2 Carefully pry the rear main seal out - don't damage the surface of the crankshaft or the new seal will leak

17.3 Drive the new seal in squarely until flush with the housing

18 Powertrain mounts - check and replacement

This procedure is essentially the same as the four cylinder engine. Refer to Part A and follow the procedure outlined there.

19 Engine Mount Control System - description and check

This system is essentially the same as the four cylinder engine. Refer to Part A and follow the procedure outlined there.

Specifications

General

Cylinder numbers (timing belt end-to-transaxle end)

Rear (firewall) side   1-2-3

Front (radiator) side   4-5-6

Firing order   1-4-2-5-3-6

Bore

2007 and earlier models   3.39 inches (86.0 mm)

2008 and later models   3.50 inches (89.0 mm)

Stroke

2007 and earlier models   3.39 inches (86.0 mm)

2008 and later models   3.66 inches (93.0 mm)

Displacement

2007 and earlier models   183 cubic inches (3.0 liters)

2008 and later models   212 cubic inches (3.5 liters)

42035-B-SPECS HAYNES

Cylinder locations

Valve adjustment

Intake   0.008 to 0.009 inch (0.20 to 0.22 mm)

Exhaust   0.011 to 0.013 inch (0.28 to 0.32 mm)

Camshaft and rocker arms

Camshaft bearing oil clearance

Standard   0.0020 to 0.0035 inch (0.050 to 0.089 mm)

Service limit   0.006 inch (0.15 mm)

Camshaft lobe height

2007 and earlier models

Intake

Primary   1.3796 inches (35.041 mm)

Mid   1.4348 inches (36.445 mm)

Secondary   1.3891 inches (35.284 mm)

Exhaust   1.4302 inches (36.326 mm)

2008 and later J35Z3 models

Intake

Primary   1.35035 inches (34.299 mm)

Secondary   1.40240 inches (35.621 mm)

Exhaust   1.44724 inches (36.760 mm)

2008 and later J35Z2 models

Intake

Cylinders 1, 2, 3, 4   1.39653 inches. (35.472 mm)

Cylinders 5, 6   1.39641 inches (35.469 mm)

Exhaust

Cylinders 1, 2, 3, 4   1.44815 inches (36.783 mm)

Cylinders 5, 6   1.44724 inches (36.760 mm)

Camshaft endplay

Standard   0.002 to 0.008 inch (0.05 to 0.20 mm)

Service limit   0.008 inch (0.20 mm)

Camshaft runout limit (total indicator reading)   0.001 inch (0.03 mm)

Camshaft and rocker arms (continued)

Rocker arm-to-shaft oil clearance
    2007 and earlier models
        Intake
            Standard   0.0010 to 0.0026 inch (0.026 to 0.067 mm)
            Service limit   0.0026 inch (0.067 mm)
        Exhaust
            Standard   0.0010 to 0.0030 inch (0.026 to 0.077 mm)
            Service limit   0.0030 inch (0.077 mm)
    2008 and later J35Z3 models
        Intake
            Standard   0.00059 to 0.00181 inch (0.015 to 0.046 mm)
            Service limit   0.00181 inch (0.046 mm)
        Exhaust
            Standard   0.00071 to 0.00185 inch (0.015 to 0.046 mm)
            Service limit   0.00185 inch (0.047 mm)
    2008 and later J35Z2 models
        Intake
            Cylinders 1, 2, 3, 4
                Standard   0.00059 to 0.00181 inch (0.015 to 0.046 mm)
                Service limit   0.046 inch (0.00181 mm)
            Cylinders 5, 6
                Standard   0.00071 to 0.0020 inch (0.018 to 0.056 mm)
                Service limit   0.00220 inch (0.056 mm)
        Exhaust
            Cylinders 1, 2, 3, 4
                Standard   0.00059 to 0.00181 inch (0.015 to 0.046 mm)
                Service limit   0.00181 inch (0.046 mm)
            Cylinders 5, 6
                Standard   0.00071 to 0.00185 inch (0.018 to 0.047 mm)
                Service limit   0.00185 inch (0.047 mm)

Oil pump

Outer rotor-to-body clearance
    2007 and earlier models   0.004 to 0.007 inch (0.10 to 0.19 mm)
    2008 and later models   0.002 to 0.004 inch (0.050 to 0.10 mm)
Outer rotor-to-inner rotor (tooth tip) clearance   0.002 to 0.006 inch (0.05 to 0.15 mm)
Housing-to-rotor clearance   0.001 to 0.003 inch (0.02 to 0.07 mm)

Torque specifications	Ft-lbs (unless otherwise indicated)	Nm

➡ **Note: One foot-pound (ft-lb) of torque is equivalent to 12 inch-pounds (in-lbs) of torque. Torque values below approximately 15 ft-lbs are expressed in inch-pounds, since most foot-pound torque wrenches are not accurate at these smaller values.**

Camshaft thrust plate bolts	16	22
Camshaft sprocket bolts	67	90
Crankshaft pulley bolt		
Step 1	47	64
Step 2	Tighten an additional 60 degrees	
Cylinder head bolts** (in sequence, see illustration 13.23)		
2007 and earlier models		
Step 1*	29	39
Step 2*	51	69
Step 3*	72	98
2008 and later models		
Step 1	22	29
Step 2	Tighten an additional 90 degrees	
Step 3	Tighten an additional 90 degrees	
Step 4	Tighten an additional 90 degrees	
Driveplate bolts	54	74
Engine mount bracket bolts		
2007 and earlier models (timing belt side)	33	44
2008 and later models	40	54
Flywheel bolts	78	103
Intake manifold upper cover bolts	104 in-lbs	12
Intake manifold bolts		
Upper intake manifold	16	22
Lower intake manifold(s)	16	22
Oil pan bolts	104 in-lbs	12
Oil pan-to-transaxle bolts		
2007 and earlier models	28	38
2008 and later models	54	74
Oil pick-up screen mounting bolts	104 in-lbs	12
Oil pump cover screws	48 in-lbs	6
Oil pump mounting bolts	104 in-lbs	12
Rocker arm shaft bolts	17	24
Timing belt tensioner bolts	104 in-lbs	12
Timing belt idler pulley bolt	33	44
Timing belt cover bolts	104 in-lbs	12
Rear main oil seal retainer bolts	104 in-lbs	12
Valve cover bolts	104 in-lbs	12
Water passage mounting bolts/nuts	16	22

Perform each Step twice
Caution: *Use new bolts.*

Notes

2C

GENERAL ENGINE OVERHAUL PROCEDURES

1   General information - engine overhaul

▶ **Refer to illustrations 1.1, 1.2, 1.3, 1.4, 1.5 and 1.6**

Included in this portion of Chapter 2 are general information and diagnostic testing procedures for determining the overall mechanical condition of your engine.

The information ranges from advice concerning preparation for an overhaul and the purchase of replacement parts and/or components to detailed, step-by-step procedures covering removal and installation.

The following Sections have been written to help you determine whether your engine needs to be overhauled and how to remove and install it once you've determined it needs to be rebuilt. For information concerning in-vehicle engine repair, see Chapter 2A or 2B.

It's not always easy to determine when, or if, an engine should be completely overhauled, because a number of factors must be considered.

High mileage is not necessarily an indication that an overhaul is needed, while low mileage doesn't preclude the need for an overhaul. Frequency of servicing is probably the most important consideration. An engine that's had regular and frequent oil and filter changes, as well as other required maintenance, will most likely give many thousands of miles of reliable service. Conversely, a neglected engine may require an overhaul very early in its service life.

Excessive oil consumption is an indication that piston rings, valve seals and/or valve guides are in need of attention. Make sure that oil leaks aren't responsible before deciding that the rings and/or guides are bad. Perform a cylinder compression check to determine the extent of the work required (see Section 3). Also check the vacuum readings under various conditions (see Section 4).

Check the oil pressure with a gauge installed in place of the oil pressure sending unit and compare it to this Chapter's Specifications (see Section 2). If it's extremely low, the bearings and/or oil pump are probably worn out.

Loss of power, rough running, knocking or metallic engine noises, excessive valve train noise and high fuel consumption rates may also point to the need for an overhaul, especially if they're all present at the same time. If a complete tune-up doesn't remedy the situation, major mechanical work is the only solution.

An engine overhaul involves restoring the internal parts to the specifications of a new engine. During an overhaul, the piston rings are replaced and the cylinder walls are reconditioned (rebored and/or honed) (see illustrations 1.1 and 1.2). If a rebore is done by an automotive machine shop, new oversize pistons will also be installed. The main

1.1 An engine block being bored - an engine rebuilder will use special machinery to recondition the cylinder bores

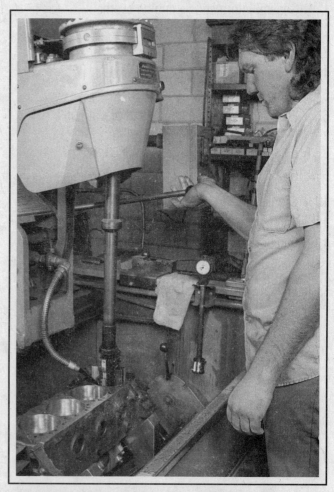

1.2 If the cylinders are bored, the machine shop will normally hone the engine on a machine like this

1.3 A crankshaft having a main bearing journal ground

1.4 A machinist checks for a bent connecting rod, using specialized equipment

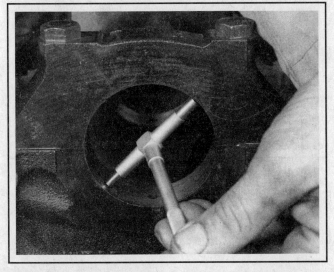

1.5 A bore gauge being used to check the main bearing bore

1.6 Uneven piston wear like this indicates a bent connecting rod

bearings and connecting rod bearings are generally replaced with new ones and, if necessary, the crankshaft may be reground to restore the journals (see illustration 1.3). Generally, the valves are serviced as well, since they're usually in less-than-perfect condition at this point. While the engine is being overhauled, other components, such as the starter and alternator, can be rebuilt as well. The end result should be a like-new engine that will give many trouble-free miles.

→Note: Critical cooling system components such as the hoses, drivebelts, thermostat and water pump should be replaced with new parts when an engine is overhauled. The radiator should be checked carefully to ensure that it isn't clogged or leaking (see Chapter 3). If you purchase a rebuilt engine or short block, some rebuilders will not warranty their engines unless the radiator has been professionally flushed. Also, we don't recommend overhauling the oil pump - always install a new one when an engine is rebuilt.

Overhauling the internal components on today's engines is a difficult and time-consuming task that requires a significant amount of specialty tools and is best left to a professional engine rebuilder (see illustrations 1.4, 1.5 and 1.6). A competent engine rebuilder will handle the inspection of your old parts and offer advice concerning the reconditioning or replacement of the original engine. Never purchase parts or have machine work done on other components until the block has been thoroughly inspected by a professional machine shop. As a general rule, time is the primary cost of an overhaul, especially since the vehicle may be tied up for a minimum of two weeks or more. Be aware that some engine builders only have the capability to rebuild the engine you bring them while other rebuilders have a large inventory of rebuilt exchange engines in stock. Also be aware that many machine shops could take as much as two weeks time to completely rebuild your engine depending on shop workload. Sometimes it makes more sense to simply exchange your engine for another engine that's already rebuilt to save time.

2 Oil pressure check

▶ **Refer to illustrations 2.2a and 2.2b**

1   Low engine oil pressure can be a sign of an engine in need of rebuilding. A "low oil pressure" indicator (often called an "idiot light") is not a test of the oiling system. Such indicators only come on when the oil pressure is dangerously low. Even a factory oil pressure gauge in the instrument panel is only a relative indication, although much better for driver information than a warning light. A better test is with a mechanical (not electrical) oil pressure gauge.

2   Locate the oil pressure sending unit on the engine block:

  a) *On four-cylinder engines, the oil pressure sending unit is located above the oil filter on the rear of the engine block (see illustration).*

  b) *On V6 engines, the oil pressure sending unit is located above the oil filter on the filter adapter (see illustration).*

3   Unscrew and remove the oil pressure sending unit and screw in the hose for your oil pressure gauge. If necessary, install an adapter fitting. Use Teflon tape or thread sealant on the threads of the adapter and/or the fitting on the end of your gauge's hose.

4   Connect an accurate tachometer to the engine, according to the tachometer manufacturer's instructions.

5   Check the oil pressure with the engine running (normal operating temperature) at the specified engine speed, and compare it to this Chapter's Specifications. If it's extremely low, the bearings and/or oil pump are probably worn out.

2.2a Location of the oil pressure sending unit on four-cylinder models - it is most easily accessed through the right front wheelwell

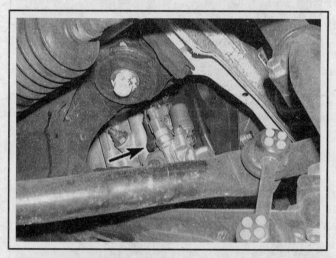

2.2b Location of the oil pressure sending unit on V6 models

3 Cylinder compression check

▶ **Refer to illustration 3.6**

1   A compression check will tell you what mechanical condition the upper end of your engine (pistons, rings, valves, head gaskets) is in. Specifically, it can tell you if the compression is down due to leakage caused by worn piston rings, defective valves and seats or a blown head gasket.

➡**Note: The engine must be at normal operating temperature and the battery must be fully charged for this check.**

2   Begin by cleaning the area around the spark plugs before you remove them (compressed air should be used, if available). The idea is to prevent dirt from getting into the cylinders as the compression check is being done.

3   Remove all of the spark plugs from the engine (see Chapter 1).

4   Block the throttle wide open.

5   Disable the fuel system by removing the PGM-FI main relay number 2 (see Chapter 4, Section 2).

6   Install a compression gauge in the spark plug hole (see illustration).

7   Crank the engine over at least seven compression strokes and watch the gauge. The compression should build up quickly in a healthy engine. Low compression on the first stroke, followed by gradually increasing pressure on successive strokes, indicates worn piston rings. A low compression reading on the first stroke, which doesn't build up during successive strokes, indicates leaking valves or a blown head gasket (a cracked head could also be the cause). Deposits on the undersides of the valve heads can also cause low compression. Record the highest gauge reading obtained.

8   Repeat the procedure for the remaining cylinders and compare the results to this Chapter's Specifications.

9   Add some engine oil (about three squirts from a plunger-type oil can) to each cylinder, through the spark plug hole, and repeat the test.

10   If the compression increases after the oil is added, the piston rings are definitely worn. If the compression doesn't increase significantly, the leakage is occurring at the valves or head gasket. Leakage past the valves may be caused by burned valve seats and/or faces or warped, cracked or bent valves.

11   If two adjacent cylinders have equally low compression, there's a strong possibility that the head gasket between them is blown. The appearance of coolant in the combustion chambers or the crankcase would verify this condition.

12   If one cylinder is slightly lower than the others, and the engine has a slightly rough idle, a worn lobe on the camshaft could be the cause.

3.6 Use a compression gauge with a threaded fitting for the spark plug hole, not the type that requires hand pressure to maintain the seal - V6 engine shown

13   If the compression is unusually high, the combustion chambers are probably coated with carbon deposits. If that's the case, the cylinder head(s) should be removed and decarbonized.

14   If compression is way down or varies greatly between cylinders, it would be a good idea to have a leak-down test performed by an automotive repair shop. This test will pinpoint exactly where the leakage is occurring and how severe it is.

4   Vacuum gauge diagnostic checks

▶ **Refer to illustrations 4.4 and 4.6**

1   A vacuum gauge provides inexpensive but valuable information about what is going on in the engine. You can check for worn rings or cylinder walls, leaking head or intake manifold gaskets, restricted exhaust, stuck or burned valves, weak valve springs, improper ignition or valve timing and ignition problems.

2   Unfortunately, vacuum gauge readings are easy to misinterpret, so they should be used in conjunction with other tests to confirm the diagnosis.

3   Both the absolute readings and the rate of needle movement are important for accurate interpretation. Most gauges measure vacuum in inches of mercury (in-Hg). The following references to vacuum assume the diagnosis is being performed at sea level. As elevation increases (or atmospheric pressure decreases), the reading will decrease. For every 1,000 foot increase in elevation above approximately 2,000 feet, the gauge readings will decrease about one inch of mercury.

4   Connect the vacuum gauge directly to the intake manifold vacuum, not to ported (throttle body) vacuum (see illustration). Be sure no hoses are left disconnected during the test or false readings will result.

5   Before you begin the test, allow the engine to warm up com-

4.4 A simple vacuum gauge can be handy in diagnosing engine condition and performance - four-cylinder model shown

pletely. Block the wheels and set the parking brake. With the transaxle in Park, start the engine and allow it to run at normal idle speed.

※ WARNING:

Keep your hands and the vacuum gauge clear of the fans.

6   Read the vacuum gauge; an average, healthy engine should normally produce about 17 to 22 in-Hg with a fairly steady needle (see illustration). Refer to the following vacuum gauge readings and what they indicate about the engine's condition:

7   A low steady reading usually indicates a leaking gasket between the intake manifold and cylinder head(s) or throttle body, a leaky vacuum hose, late ignition timing or incorrect camshaft timing. Check ignition timing with a timing light and eliminate all other possible causes, utilizing the tests provided in this Chapter before you remove the timing chain cover to check the timing marks.

8   If the reading is three to eight inches below normal and it fluctuates at that low reading, suspect an intake manifold gasket leak at an intake port or a faulty fuel injector.

9   If the needle has regular drops of about two-to-four inches at a steady rate, the valves are probably leaking. Perform a compression check or leak-down test to confirm this.

10 An irregular drop or down-flick of the needle can be caused by a sticking valve or an ignition misfire. Perform a compression check or leak-down test and read the spark plugs.

11 A rapid vibration of about four in-Hg vibration at idle combined with exhaust smoke indicates worn valve guides. Perform a leak-down test to confirm this. If the rapid vibration occurs with an increase in engine speed, check for a leaking intake manifold gasket or head gasket, weak valve springs, burned valves or ignition misfire.

12 A slight fluctuation, say one inch up and down, may mean ignition problems. Check all the usual tune-up items and, if necessary, run the engine on an ignition analyzer.

13 If there is a large fluctuation, perform a compression or leak-down test to look for a weak or dead cylinder or a blown head gasket.

14 If the needle moves slowly through a wide range, check for a clogged PCV system, incorrect idle fuel mixture, throttle body or intake manifold gasket leaks.

15 Check for a slow return after revving the engine by quickly snapping the throttle open until the engine reaches about 2,500 rpm and let it shut. Normally the reading should drop to near zero, rise above normal idle reading (about 5 in-Hg over) and return to the previous idle reading. If the vacuum returns slowly and doesn't peak when the throttle is snapped shut, the rings may be worn. If there is a long delay, look for a restricted exhaust system (often the muffler or catalytic converter). An easy way to check this is to temporarily disconnect the exhaust ahead of the suspected part and redo the test.

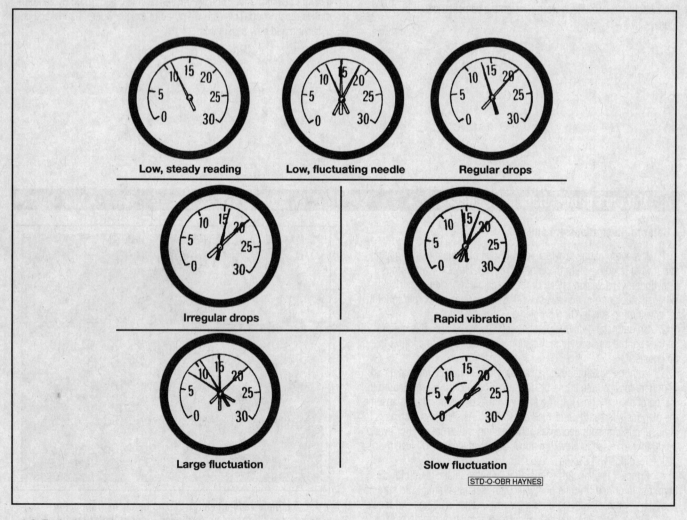

4.6 Typical vacuum gauge readings

5 Engine rebuilding alternatives

The do-it-yourselfer is faced with a number of options when purchasing a rebuilt engine. The major considerations are cost, warranty, parts availability and the time required for the rebuilder to complete the project. The decision to replace the engine block, piston/connecting rod assemblies and crankshaft depends on the final inspection results of your engine. Only then can you make a cost effective decision whether to have your engine overhauled or simply purchase an exchange engine for your vehicle.

Some of the rebuilding alternatives include:

Individual parts - If the inspection procedures reveal that the engine block and most engine components are in reusable condition, purchasing individual parts and having a rebuilder rebuild your engine may be the most economical alternative. The block, crankshaft and piston/connecting rod assemblies should all be inspected carefully by a machine shop first.

Short block - A short block consists of an engine block with a crankshaft and piston/connecting rod assemblies already installed. All new bearings are incorporated and all clearances will be correct. The existing camshafts, valve train components, cylinder head and external

parts can be bolted to the short block with little or no machine shop work necessary.

Long block - A long block consists of a short block plus an oil pump, oil pan, cylinder head, valve cover, camshaft and valve train components, timing sprockets and chain or gears and timing cover. All components are installed with new bearings, seals and gaskets incorporated throughout. The installation of manifolds and external parts is all that's necessary.

Low mileage used engines - Some companies now offer low mileage used engines which is a very cost effective way to get your vehicle up and running again. These engines often come from vehicles which have been in totaled in accidents or come from other countries which have a higher vehicle turn over rate. A low mileage used engine also usually has a similar warranty like the newly remanufactured engines.

Give careful thought to which alternative is best for you and discuss the situation with local automotive machine shops, auto parts dealers and experienced rebuilders before ordering or purchasing replacement parts.

6 Engine removal - methods and precautions

▶ **Refer to illustrations 6.1, 6.2, 6.3 and 6.4**

If you've decided that an engine must be removed for overhaul or major repair work, several preliminary steps should be taken. Read all removal and installation procedures carefully prior to committing to this job.

Locating a suitable place to work is extremely important. Adequate work space, along with storage space for the vehicle, will be needed. If a shop or garage isn't available, at the very least a flat, level, clean work surface made of concrete or asphalt is required.

Cleaning the engine compartment and engine before beginning the

removal procedure will help keep tools clean and organized (see illustrations 6.1 and 6.2).

An engine hoist will also be necessary. Make sure the hoist is rated in excess of the combined weight of the engine and transaxle. Safety is of primary importance, considering the potential hazards involved in removing the engine from the vehicle.

A vehicle hoist will be necessary for engine removal on models equipped with the V6 engine, since on these models the subframe must be removed and the engine/transaxle assembly (powertrain unit) must be lowered from the engine compartment, then the vehicle is raised and the powertrain unit is removed from under the vehicle. If the necessary

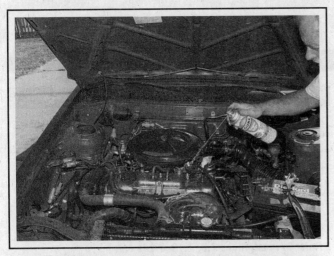

6.1 After tightly wrapping water-vulnerable components, use a spray cleaner on everything, with particular concentration on the greasiest areas, usually around the valve cover and lower edges of the block. If one section dries out, apply more cleaner

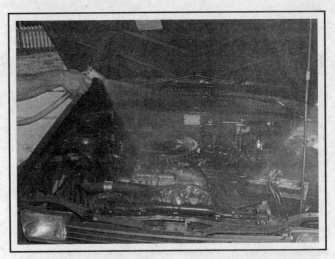

6.2 Depending on how dirty the engine is, let the cleaner soak in according to the directions and hose off the grime and cleaner. Get the rinse water down into every area you can get at; then dry important components with a hair dryer or paper towels

equipment is not available, the engine will have to be removed by a qualified automotive repair facility.

If you're a novice at engine removal, get at least one helper. One person cannot easily do all the things you need to do to remove a big heavy engine and transaxle assembly from the engine compartment. Also helpful is to seek advice and assistance from someone who's experienced in engine removal.

Plan the operation ahead of time. Arrange for or obtain all of the tools and equipment you'll need prior to beginning the job (see illustrations 6.3 and 6.4). Some of the equipment necessary to perform engine removal and installation safely and with relative ease are (in addition to a vehicle hoist and an engine hoist) a heavy duty floor jack (preferably fitted with a transaxle jack head adapter), complete sets of wrenches and sockets as described in the front of this manual, wooden blocks, plenty of rags and cleaning solvent for mopping up spilled oil, coolant and gasoline.

Plan for the vehicle to be out of use for quite a while. A machine shop can do the work that is beyond the scope of the home mechanic. Machine shops often have a busy schedule, so before removing the engine, consult the shop for an estimate of how long it will take to rebuild or repair the components that may need work.

6.3 Get an engine stand sturdy enough to firmly support the engine while you're working on it. Stay away from three-wheeled models: they have a tendency to tip over more easily, so get a four-wheeled unit

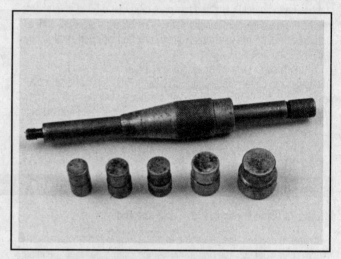

6.4 A clutch alignment tool is necessary if you plan to install a rebuilt engine mated to a manual transaxle

7 Engine - removal and installation

⁕⁕ WARNING 1:

Gasoline is extremely flammable, so take extra precautions when you work on any part of the fuel system. Don't smoke or allow open flames or bare light bulbs near the work area, and don't work in a garage where a gas-type appliance (such as a water heater or clothes dryer) is present. Since gasoline is carcinogenic, wear fuel-resistant gloves when there's a possibility of being exposed to fuel, and, if you spill any fuel on your skin, rinse it off immediately with soap and water. Mop up any spills immediately and do not store fuel-soaked rags where they could ignite. The fuel system is under constant pressure, so, if any fuel lines are to be disconnected, the fuel pressure in the system must be relieved first (see Chapter 4 for more information). When you perform any kind of work on the fuel system, wear safety glasses and have a Class B type fire extinguisher on hand.

⁕⁕ WARNING 2:

The engine must be completely cool before beginning this procedure.

REMOVAL

Four-cylinder models

▸ Refer to illustrations 7.5, 7.19, 7.20a and 7.20b

➡Note: Read through the entire sequence before beginning this procedure.

1 Place protective covers on the fenders and cowl. Place the hood in the fully open position (with the support rod in the lower hole).

2 Relieve the fuel system pressure (see Chapter 4). Disconnect the cable from the negative battery terminal (see Chapter 5, Section 1). Next, disconnect the positive battery cable.

3 Remove the air filter housing and air intake duct (see Chapter 4).

4 Remove the battery and battery tray (see Chapter 5).

5 Remove the battery cables from the fuse/relay center (see Chapter 5). Remove the two mounting bolts from the fuse/relay center and position the fuse/relay center off to the side (see illustration).

6 Disconnect the accelerator cable and cruise control cable, if equipped, from the throttle body (see Chapter 4).

7 Disconnect the fuel line from the fuel rail (see Chapter 4).

8 On manual transaxle models, remove the clutch release cylinder (see Chapter 8).

9 If you're working on a manual transaxle model, detach the shift cables from the transaxle (see Chapter 7A).

10 Unbolt the power steering pump (see Chapter 10). Tie the pump aside without disconnecting the hoses.

11 Remove the alternator (see Chapter 5).

12 On air-conditioned models, unbolt the compressor and set it aside (see Chapter 3).

❊❊ WARNING:

Do not disconnect the refrigerant hoses.

13 Loosen the front wheel lug nuts and the driveaxle/hub nuts. Raise the vehicle and support it securely on jackstands.

➡ **Note: Just raise the vehicle high enough for access to components underneath.**

Drain the cooling system, engine oil and transaxle fluid/lubricant. Also remove the drivebelt (see Chapter 1).

14 Remove the driveaxles (see Chapter 8).

15 Unbolt the exhaust pipe from the exhaust manifold (see Chapter 2A), then remove the front portion of the exhaust pipe.

16 If you're working on an automatic transaxle model, disconnect the shift cable from the transaxle (see Chapter 7B).

17 On automatic transaxle models, detach the torque converter cover from the lower part of the bellhousing, then remove the torque converter-to-driveplate fasteners (see Chapter 7B).

➡ **Note: It's easier to do this now, rather than later when the engine and transaxle have been removed.**

18 Unscrew the nuts holding the transaxle front and rear lower mounts to their crossmember (see Chapter 7).

19 Clearly label and disconnect all vacuum lines, coolant and emissions hoses, electrical connectors and ground straps. Masking tape and/or a touch up paint applicator work well for marking items (see illustration). Take instant photos or sketch the locations of components and brackets, if necessary.

20 Support the engine/transaxle assembly from above with a hoist. Attach the hoist chain to the engine lifting brackets and the transaxle lifting brackets. If no brackets are present, you will have to fasten the chains to some substantial part of the engine and transaxle - one that is strong enough to take the weight, but in a location that will provide good balance (see illustrations). If you're attaching a chain to the stud on the engine, or are using a bolt passing through the chain and into a threaded hole, place a washer between the nut or bolt head and the chain and tighten the nut or bolt securely.

❊❊ WARNING:

Do not place any part of your body under the engine/transaxle when it's supported only by a hoist or other lifting device.

7.5 Remove the two mounting bolts from the fuse/relay center and position the fuse/relay center off to the side

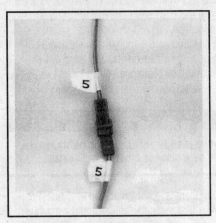

7.19 Label both ends of each wire and hose before disconnecting it

7.20a At the transaxle end, the lifting chain has been bolted to the lifting bracket (a hook would work, too)

7.20b At the engine end, the lifting chain has been bolted to a threaded hole in the belt tensioner

21 Recheck to be sure nothing except the mounts are still connecting the engine/transaxle to the vehicle. Disconnect anything still remaining on the engine and transaxle.

22 Remove the right engine mount, the front engine mount and the transaxle mount (see Chapter 2A).

23 Slowly raise the engine/transaxle assembly out of the vehicle. Be careful not to bang the engine/transaxle assembly into any surrounding components.

24 Move the engine/transaxle assembly away from the vehicle and carefully lower the hoist until the engine/transaxle assembly is on the floor, supported by wood blocks.

25 Remove the transaxle-to-engine mounting bolts and separate the engine from the transaxle. Remove the flywheel or driveplate and mount the engine on an engine stand.

V6 models

→Note 1: Engine removal on V6 models is a difficult job, especially for the do-it-yourself mechanic working at home. Because of the vehicle's design, the manufacturer states that the engine and transaxle have to be removed as a unit from the bottom of the vehicle, not the top. With a floor jack and jackstands, the vehicle can't be raised high enough or supported safely enough for the engine/transaxle assembly to slide out from underneath. The manufacturer recommends that removal of the engine/transaxle assembly only be performed with the use of a frame-contact type vehicle hoist.

→Note 2: Keep in mind that during this procedure you'll have to adjust the height of the vehicle with the vehicle hoist to perform certain operations.

26 Park the vehicle on a frame-contact type vehicle hoist, then engage the arms of the hoist with the jacking points of the vehicle. Raise the hoist arms until they contact the vehicle, but not so much that the wheels come off the ground.

27 Relieve the fuel system pressure (see Chapter 4).

28 Disconnect the cable from the negative battery terminal (see Chapter 5, Section 1). Disconnect the positive battery cable.

29 Unbolt the hood support struts from the hood and reposition the right-side support strut bracket in the lower mounting holes (this will keep the hood in the wide-open position).

30 Disconnect the fuel line from the fuel rail (see Chapter 4).

31 Remove the fender splash shields (see Chapter 11). Cover the fenders and cowl using special pads. An old bedspread or blanket will also work.

32 Remove the accessory drivebelt (see Chapter 1).

33 Remove the air filter housing (see Chapter 4).

34 Disconnect the accelerator cable, the cruise control cable, if equipped, and bracket from the engine and position them aside (see Chapter 4).

35 Remove the battery and the battery tray (see Chapter 5).

36 Remove the battery cables from the fuse/relay center. Remove the two mounting bolts from the fuse/relay center and position the fuse/relay center off to the side (see illustration 7.5).

37 Using a suction gun, remove as much fluid as possible from the power steering fluid reservoir. Detach the power steering feed line from the reservoir and the pressure line from the pump. Plug all of the open fittings to prevent fluid leakage.

38 Remove the retaining clip on the engine compartment firewall and remove the wiring harness.

39 Drain the cooling system (see Chapter 1).

40 Remove the engine cooling fan(s) and the coolant reservoir (see Chapter 3).

41 Detach the heater hoses at the firewall (see Chapter 3).

42 Detach the radiator hoses from the engine.

43 On manual transaxle models, disconnect the shift cable and the select cable from the transaxle (see Chapter 7A). Also disconnect any wiring harness connectors from the transaxle.

44 Clearly label and disconnect all vacuum lines, emissions hoses, wiring harness connectors and fuel lines between the engine and the vehicle. Masking tape and/or a touch up paint applicator work well for marking items (see illustration 7.19). Take instant photos or sketch the locations of components and brackets.

45 Detach the steering shaft from the steering gear input shaft (see Chapter 10).

46 Loosen the front wheel lug nuts, then raise the vehicle. Remove the front wheels.

47 Remove the engine splash shield.

48 Detach the heat shields, exhaust brackets and the exhaust pipes from the warm-up catalysts (see Chapter 6).

49 Remove the exhaust pipe from the warm-up catalysts to the main catalytic converter (see Chapter 6).

50 Drain the engine oil (see Chapter 1).

51 On manual transaxle models, remove the clutch release cylinder and hydraulic line (see Chapter 8).

52 On automatic transaxle models, disconnect the shift cable holder and the shift control cable from the transaxle (see Chapter 7B). Also detach the torque converter cover from the lower part of the bellhousing, then remove the torque converter-to-driveplate fasteners (see Chapter 7B).

→Note: It's easier to do this now, rather than later when the engine and transaxle have been removed.

53 Disconnect the stabilizer bar links (see Chapter 10).

54 Disconnect the balljoints from the lower control arms (see Chapter 10).

55 Remove the shock absorber damper forks from the lower control arms (see Chapter 10).

56 Remove the driveaxles (see Chapter 8).

57 Unplug the downstream oxygen sensor electrical connectors.

58 Remove the air conditioning compressor without disconnecting the hoses (see Chapter 3). Use wire to tie the compressor to a bracket or other components mounted on the uni-body (not the subframe). It is not necessary to discharge the refrigerant from the system.

59 Attach a lifting sling or chain to the engine, using the lifting brackets provided. If not, lifting hooks may be available from your local auto parts store. If not, you will have to fasten the chains to some substantial part of the engine and transaxle - one that is strong enough to take the weight, but in a location that will provide good balance. If you're attaching a chain to the stud on the engine, or are using a bolt passing through the chain and into a threaded hole, place a washer between the nut or bolt head and the chain and tighten the nut or bolt securely.

✳✳ WARNING:

Do not place any part of your body under the engine/transaxle when it's supported only by a hoist or other lifting device.

60 Take up the slack until there is slight tension on the hoist. Position the chain on the hoist so it balances the engine and the transaxle level with the vehicle.

→Note 1: Depending on the design of the engine hoist, it may be helpful to position the hoist from the side of the vehicle, so that when the engine/transaxle assembly is lowered, it will fit between the legs of the hoist.

➡**Note 2: The sling or chain must be long enough to allow the engine hoist to lower the engine/transaxle assembly to the ground, without letting the hoist arm contact the vehicle.**

61 Remove the front and side engine mounts (see Chapter 2B).

62 Remove the rear and side transaxle mounts (see Chapter 2B).

63 Remove the subframe (see Chapter 10).

64 Recheck to be sure nothing is still connecting the engine or transaxle to the vehicle. Disconnect and label anything still remaining.

65 Lower the engine/transaxle assembly. Once the engine/transaxle assembly is on the floor, disconnect the engine lifting hoist and raise the vehicle until it clears the engine/transaxle assembly.

66 Reconnect the chain or sling to support the engine and transaxle.

67 Raise the engine/transaxle assembly, then support the engine with blocks of wood or another floor jack, while leaving the sling or chain attached. Support the transaxle with another floor jack, preferably one with a transaxle jack head adapter. At this point the transaxle can be unbolted and removed from the engine. Be very careful to ensure that the components are supported securely so they won't topple off their supports during disconnection.

68 Reconnect the lifting chain to the engine, then raise the engine and attach it to an engine stand.

INSTALLATION

69 Installation is the reverse of removal, noting the following points:

a) *Check the engine/transaxle mounts. If they're worn or damaged, replace them.*

b) *Attach the transaxle to the engine following the procedure described in Chapter 7.*

c) *When installing the subframe (V6 models), check the subframe alignment and tighten the subframe mounting bolts to the torque listed in Chapter 10 Specifications. Note the locations of the various size bolts (see Chapter 10).*

d) *Tighten the driveaxle/hub nuts to the torque listed in the Chapter 8 Specifications. Tighten the steering shaft to steering gear input shaft to the torque listed in the Chapter 10 Specifications. Tighten the wheel lug nuts to the torque listed in the Chapter 1 Specifications.*

e) *Add coolant, oil, power steering and transaxle fluids as needed (see Chapter 1).*

f) *Reconnect the battery (see Chapter 5, Section 1).*

g) *Run the engine and check for proper operation and leaks. Shut off the engine and recheck fluid levels.*

8   Engine overhaul - disassembly sequence

1 It's much easier to remove the external components if the engine is mounted on a portable engine stand. A stand can often be rented quite cheaply from an equipment rental yard. Before the engine is mounted on a stand, the flywheel/driveplate should be removed from the engine.

2 If a stand isn't available, it's possible to remove the external engine components with it blocked up on the floor. Be extra careful not to tip or drop the engine when working without a stand.

3 If you're going to obtain a rebuilt engine, all external components must come off first, to be transferred to the replacement engine. These components include:

Clutch and flywheel (models with manual transaxle)
Driveplate (models with automatic transaxle)
Ignition system components
Emissions-related components
Engine mounts and mount brackets
Engine rear main seal retainer on V6 models (between flywheel/ driveplate and engine block)

Intake/exhaust manifolds
Fuel injection components
Oil filter
Ignition coils and spark plugs
Thermostat and housing assembly
Water pump

➡**Note: When removing the external components from the engine, pay close attention to details that may be helpful or important during installation. Note the installed position of gaskets, seals, spacers, pins, brackets, washers, bolts and other small items.**

4 If you're going to obtain a short block (assembled engine block, crankshaft, pistons and connecting rods), then remove the timing chain or belt, cylinder head(s), oil pan, oil pump pick-up tube, oil pump and water pump from your engine so that you can turn in your old short block to the rebuilder as a core. See *Engine rebuilding alternatives* for additional information regarding the different possibilities to be considered.

9   Pistons and connecting rods - removal and installation

REMOVAL

▶ **Refer to illustrations 9.1, 9.3 and 9.4**

➡**Note: Prior to removing the piston/connecting rod assemblies, remove the cylinder head and oil pan (see Chapter 2A).**

1   Use your fingernail to feel if a ridge has formed at the upper limit of ring travel (about 1/4-inch down from the top of each cylinder). If carbon deposits or cylinder wear have produced ridges, they must be completely removed with a special tool (see illustration). Follow the manufacturer's instructions provided with the tool. Failure to remove the ridges before attempting to remove the piston/connecting rod assemblies may result in piston breakage.

2   After the cylinder ridges have been removed, turn the engine so the crankshaft is facing up.

3   Before the connecting rods are removed, check the connecting rod endplay with feeler gauges. Slide them between the first connecting rod and the crankshaft throw until the play is removed (see illustration). Repeat this procedure for each connecting rod. The endplay is equal to the thickness of the feeler gauge(s). Check with an automotive machine shop for the endplay service limit (a typical endplay limit should measure between 0.005 to 0.015 inch [0.127 to 0.369 mm]). If the play exceeds the service limit, new connecting rods will be required. If new rods (or a new crankshaft) are installed, the endplay may fall under the minimum allowable. If it does, the rods will have to be machined to restore it. If necessary, consult an automotive machine shop for advice.

4   Check the connecting rods and caps for identification marks. If they aren't plainly marked, use paint or marker to clearly identify each rod and cap (1, 2, 3, etc., depending on the cylinder they're associated with) (see illustration).

5   Remove the connecting rod cap bolts from the number one connecting rod.

➡**Note: The connecting rod bolts must be checked for damaged threads and stretching. The manufacturer specifies that the diameter of a connecting rod bolt must not vary more than 0.004 inch (0.1 mm). Because of the extent of this repair, it is recommended that all new connecting rod bolts be replaced with new ones. Save the old bolts - they'll be required for the bearing oil clearance check during reassembly.**

➡**Note: On four-cylinder models, it will be necessary to remove the main bearing assembly (bedplate) to access the connecting rod bearing caps. Refer to Section 10 and remove the main bearing assembly.**

6   Remove the number one connecting rod cap and bearing insert. Don't drop the bearing insert out of the cap.

7   Remove the bearing insert and push the connecting rod/piston assembly out through the top of the engine. Use a wooden dowel to push on the connecting rod. If resistance is felt, double-check to make sure that all of the ridge was removed from the cylinder.

8   Repeat the procedure for the remaining cylinders.

9   After removal, reassemble the connecting rod caps and bearing inserts in their respective connecting rods and install the cap bolts finger tight. Leaving the old bearing inserts in place until reassembly will help prevent the connecting rod bearing surfaces from being accidentally nicked or gouged.

10   The pistons and connecting rods are now ready for inspection and overhaul at an automotive machine shop.

PISTON RING INSTALLATION

▶ **Refer to illustrations 9.13, 9.14, 9.15, 9.19a, 9.19b and 9.22**

11   Before installing the new piston rings, the ring end gaps must be checked. It's assumed that the piston ring side clearance has been checked and verified correct.

12   Lay out the piston/connecting rod assemblies and the new ring sets so the ring sets will be matched with the same piston and cylinder during the end gap measurement and engine assembly.

13   Insert the top (number one) ring into the first cylinder and square it up with the cylinder walls by pushing it in with the top of the piston (see illustration). The ring should be near the bottom of the cylinder, at the lower limit of ring travel.

9.1 Before you try to remove the pistons, use a ridge reamer to remove the raised material (ridge) from the top of the cylinders

9.3 Checking the connecting rod endplay (side clearance) (typical)

9.4 If the connecting rods and caps are not marked, use permanent ink or paint to mark the caps to the rods by cylinder number (for example, this would be the No. 4 connecting rod)

14 To measure the end gap, slip feeler gauges between the ends of the ring until a gauge equal to the gap width is found (see illustration). The feeler gauge should slide between the ring ends with a slight amount of drag. A typical ring gap should fall between 0.010 and 0.020 inch [0.25 to 0.50 mm] for compression rings and up to 0.030 inch [0.76 mm] for the oil ring steel rails. If the gap is larger or smaller than specified, double-check to make sure you have the correct rings before proceeding.

15 If the gap is too small, it must be enlarged or the ring ends may come in contact with each other during engine operation, which can cause serious damage to the engine. If necessary, increase the end gaps by filing the ring ends very carefully with a fine file. Mount the file in a vise equipped with soft jaws, slip the ring over the file with the ends contacting the file face and slowly move the ring to remove material from the ends. When performing this operation, file only by pushing the ring from the outside end of the file towards the vise (see illustration).

16 Excess end gap isn't critical unless it's greater than 0.040 inch (1.01 mm). Again, double-check to make sure you have the correct ring type.

17 Repeat the procedure for each ring that will be installed in the first cylinder and for each ring in the remaining cylinders. Remember to keep rings, pistons and cylinders matched up.

18 Once the ring end gaps have been checked/corrected, the rings can be installed on the pistons.

19 The oil control ring (lowest one on the piston) is usually installed first. It's composed of three separate components. Slip the spacer/expander into the groove (see illustration). If an anti-rotation tang is used, make sure it's inserted into the drilled hole in the ring groove. Next, install the upper side rail in the same manner (see illustration). Don't use a piston ring installation tool on the oil ring side rails, as they may be damaged. Instead, place one end of the side rail into the groove between the spacer/expander and the ring land, hold it firmly in place and slide a finger around the piston while pushing the rail into the groove. Finally, install the lower side rail.

20 After the three oil ring components have been installed, check to make sure that both the upper and lower side rails can be rotated smoothly inside the ring grooves.

21 The number two (middle) ring is installed next. It's usually stamped with a mark which must face up, toward the top of the piston. Do not mix up the top and middle rings, as they have different cross-sections.

➡Note: Always follow the instructions printed on the ring package or box - different manufacturers may require different approaches.

9.13 Install the piston ring into the cylinder, then push it down into position using a piston so the ring will be square in the cylinder

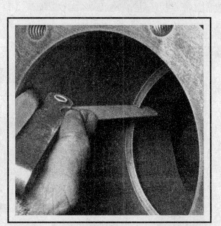

9.14 With the ring square in the cylinder, measure the ring end gap with a feeler gauge

9.15 If the ring end gap is too small, clamp a file in a vise as shown and file the piston ring ends - be sure to remove all raised material

9.19a Installing the spacer/expander in the oil ring groove

9.19b DO NOT use a piston ring installation tool when installing the oil control ring side rails

ENGINE BEARING ANALYSIS

Debris

Babbitt bearing embedded with debris from machinings

Microscopic detail of debris

Microscopic detail of gouges

Overplated copper alloy bearing gouged by cast iron debris

Aluminum bearing embedded with glass beads

Microscopic detail of glass beads

Damaged lining caused by dirt left on the bearing back

Misassembly

Result of a lower half assembled as an upper - blocking the oil flow

Excessive oil clearance is indicated by a short contact arc

Polished and oil-stained backs are a result of a poor fit in the housing bore

Result of a wrong, reversed, or shifted cap

Overloading

Damage from excessive idling which resulted in an oil film unable to support the load imposed

Damaged upper connecting rod bearings caused by engine lugging; the lower main bearings (not shown) were similarly affected

The damage shown in these upper and lower connecting rod bearings was caused by engine operation at a higher-than-rated speed under load

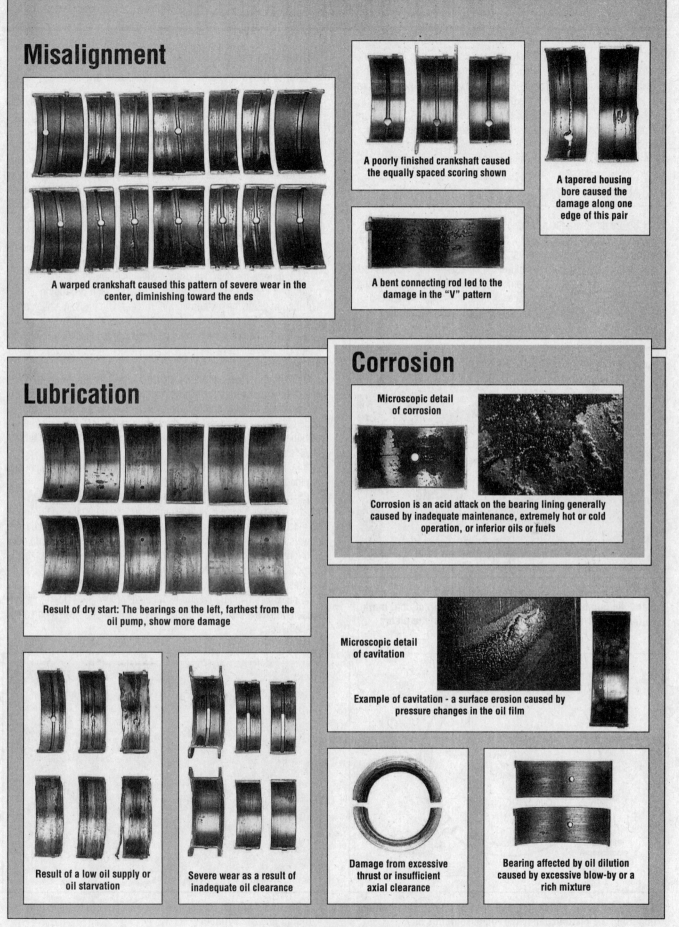

Misalignment

A poorly finished crankshaft caused the equally spaced scoring shown

A tapered housing bore caused the damage along one edge of this pair

A warped crankshaft caused this pattern of severe wear in the center, diminishing toward the ends

A bent connecting rod led to the damage in the "V" pattern

Lubrication

Result of dry start: The bearings on the left, farthest from the oil pump, show more damage

Result of a low oil supply or oil starvation

Severe wear as a result of inadequate oil clearance

Corrosion

Microscopic detail of corrosion

Corrosion is an acid attack on the bearing lining generally caused by inadequate maintenance, extremely hot or cold operation, or inferior oils or fuels

Microscopic detail of cavitation

Example of cavitation - a surface erosion caused by pressure changes in the oil film

Damage from excessive thrust or insufficient axial clearance

Bearing affected by oil dilution caused by excessive blow-by or a rich mixture

22 Use a piston ring installation tool and make sure the identification mark is facing the top of the piston, then slip the ring into the middle groove on the piston (see illustration). Don't expand the ring any more than necessary to slide it over the piston.

23 Install the number one (top) ring in the same manner. Make sure the mark is facing up. Be careful not to confuse the number one and number two rings.

24 Repeat the procedure for the remaining pistons and rings.

INSTALLATION

25 Before installing the piston/connecting rod assemblies, the cylinder walls must be perfectly clean, the top edge of each cylinder bore must be chamfered, and the crankshaft must be in place.

26 Remove the cap from the end of the number one connecting rod (refer to the marks made during removal). Remove the original bearing inserts and wipe the bearing surfaces of the connecting rod and cap with a clean, lint-free cloth. They must be kept spotlessly clean.

9.22 Use a piston ring installation tool to install the number 2 and the number 1 (top) rings - be sure the directional mark on the piston ring(s) is facing toward the top of the piston

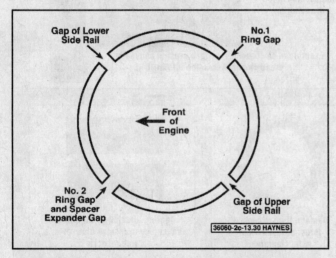

9.30 Position the piston ring end gaps as shown here before installing the piston/connecting rod assemblies into the engine

Connecting rod bearing oil clearance check

▶ **Refer to illustrations 9.30, 9.35, 9.37 and 9.41**

27 Clean the back side of the new upper bearing insert, then lay it in place in the connecting rod.

28 Make sure the tab on the bearing fits into the recess in the rod. Don't hammer the bearing insert into place and be very careful not to nick or gouge the bearing face. Don't lubricate the bearing at this time.

29 Clean the back side of the other bearing insert and install it in the rod cap. Again, make sure the tab on the bearing fits into the recess in the cap, and don't apply any lubricant. It's critically important that the mating surfaces of the bearing and connecting rod are perfectly clean and oil free when they're assembled.

30 Position the piston ring gaps at the specified intervals around the piston as shown (see illustration).

31 Lubricate the piston and rings with clean engine oil and attach a piston ring compressor to the piston. Leave the skirt protruding about 1/4-inch to guide the piston into the cylinder. The rings must be compressed until they're flush with the piston.

32 Rotate the crankshaft until the number one connecting rod journal is at BDC (bottom dead center) and apply a liberal coat of engine oil to the cylinder walls.

33 With the arrow on top of the piston facing the front (timing belt end or timing chain) of the engine, gently insert the piston/connecting rod assembly into the number one cylinder bore and rest the bottom edge of the ring compressor on the engine block. Install the pistons with the cavity mark(s) or arrow facing toward the timing belt or timing chain end of the engine.

34 Tap the top edge of the ring compressor to make sure it's contacting the block around its entire circumference.

35 Gently tap on the top of the piston with the end of a wooden or plastic hammer handle (see illustration) while guiding the end of the connecting rod into place on the crankshaft journal (a pair of wooden dowels would be helpful for this). The piston rings may try to pop out of the ring compressor just before entering the cylinder bore, so keep some downward pressure on the ring compressor. Work slowly, and if any resistance is felt as the piston enters the cylinder, stop immediately. Find out what's hanging up and fix it before proceeding. Do not, for any reason, force the piston into the cylinder - you might break a ring and/or the piston.

9.35 Use a plastic or wooden hammer handle to push the piston into the cylinder

9.37 Place Plastigage on each connecting rod bearing journal parallel to the crankshaft centerline

9.41 Use the scale on the Plastigage package to determine the bearing oil clearance - be sure to measure the widest part of the Plastigage and use the correct scale; it comes with both standard and metric scales

36 Once the piston/connecting rod assembly is installed, the connecting rod bearing oil clearance must be checked before the rod cap is permanently installed.

37 Cut a piece of the appropriate size Plastigage slightly shorter than the width of the connecting rod bearing and lay it in place on the number one connecting rod journal, parallel with the journal axis (see illustration).

38 Clean the connecting rod cap bearing face and install the rod cap. Make sure the mating mark on the cap is on the same side as the mark on the connecting rod (see illustration 9.4).

39 Install the old rod bolts, at this time, and tighten them to the torque listed in this Chapter's Specifications.

➥**Note: Use a thin-wall socket to avoid erroneous torque readings that can result if the socket is wedged between the rod cap and the bolt. If the socket tends to wedge itself between the fastener and the cap, lift up on it slightly until it no longer contacts the cap. DO NOT rotate the crankshaft at any time during this operation.**

40 Remove the fasteners and detach the rod cap, being very careful not to disturb the Plastigage. Discard the cap bolts at this time as they cannot be reused.

➥**Note: The connecting rod bolts must be checked for damaged threads and stretching. The manufacturer specifies that the diameter of a connecting rod bolt must not vary more than 0.004 inch (0.1 mm). Because of the extent of this repair, it is recommended that all connecting rod bolts be replaced with new ones.**

41 Compare the width of the crushed Plastigage to the scale printed on the Plastigage envelope to obtain the oil clearance (see illustration). The connecting rod oil clearance is usually about 0.001 to 0.002 inch. Consult an automotive machine shop for the clearance specified for the rod bearings on your engine.

42 If the clearance is not as specified, the bearing inserts may be the wrong size (which means different ones will be required). Before deciding that different inserts are needed, make sure that no dirt or oil was between the bearing inserts and the connecting rod or cap when the clearance was measured. Also, recheck the journal diameter. If the Plastigage was wider at one end than the other, the journal may be tapered. If the clearance still exceeds the limit specified, the bearing will

have to be replaced with an undersize bearing.

✳✳ CAUTION:

When installing a new crankshaft always use a standard size bearing.

Final installation

43 Carefully scrape all traces of the Plastigage material off the rod journal and/or bearing face. Be very careful not to scratch the bearing - use your fingernail or the edge of a plastic card.

44 Make sure the bearing faces are perfectly clean, then apply a uniform layer of clean moly-base grease or engine assembly lube to both of them. You'll have to push the piston into the cylinder to expose the face of the bearing insert in the connecting rod.

45 Slide the connecting rod back into place on the journal, install the rod cap, install the bolts and tighten them to the torque listed in this Chapter's Specifications.

✳✳ CAUTION:

As stated previously, it is recommended that new bolts be installed.

46 Repeat the entire procedure for the remaining pistons/connecting rods.

47 The important points to remember are:

a) *Keep the back sides of the bearing inserts and the insides of the connecting rods and caps perfectly clean when assembling them.*

b) *Make sure you have the correct piston/rod assembly for each cylinder.*

c) *The arrow or mark on the piston must face the front (timing chain on four-cylinder engines or timing belt on V6 engines) of the engine.*

d) *Lubricate the cylinder walls liberally with clean oil.*

e) *Lubricate the bearing faces when installing the rod caps after the oil clearance has been checked.*

48 After all the piston/connecting rod assemblies have been correctly installed, rotate the crankshaft a number of times by hand to check for any obvious binding.

49 As a final step, check the connecting rod endplay, as described in Step 3. If it was correct before disassembly and the original crankshaft and rods were reinstalled, it should still be correct. If new rods or a new crankshaft were installed, the endplay may be inadequate. If so, the rods will have to be removed and taken to an automotive machine shop for resizing.

---

10 Crankshaft - removal and installation

REMOVAL

▶ **Refer to illustrations 10.1 and 10.3**

➡Note: The crankshaft can be removed only after the engine has been removed from the vehicle. It's assumed that the flywheel or driveplate, crankshaft pulley, timing belt or timing chain, oil pan, oil pump body, oil filter and piston/connecting rod assemblies have already been removed. If equipped with a V6 engine, the rear main oil seal retainer must be unbolted and separated from the block before proceeding with crankshaft removal.

1 Before the crankshaft is removed, measure the endplay. Mount a dial indicator with the indicator in line with the crankshaft and just touching the end of the crankshaft as shown (see illustration).

2 Pry the crankshaft all the way to the rear and zero the dial indicator. Next, pry the crankshaft to the front as far as possible and check the reading on the dial indicator. The distance traveled is the endplay. A typical crankshaft endplay will fall between 0.003 to 0.010 inch (0.076 to 0.254 mm). If it is greater than that, check the crankshaft thrust surfaces for wear after it's removed. If no wear is evident, new main bearings should correct the endplay.

3 If a dial indicator isn't available, feeler gauges can be used. Gently pry the crankshaft all the way to the front of the engine. Slip feeler gauges between the crankshaft and the front face of the thrust bearing or washer to determine the clearance (see illustration).

4 Loosen the main bearing assembly perimeter bolts and the main bearing inner bolts (four-cylinder engines) or the main bearing cap side bolts and the main bolts (V6 engines) 1/4-turn at a time each, until they can be removed by hand. Follow the reverse of the tightening sequence (see illustrations 10.19a, 10.19b and 10.19c).

5 Remove the main bearing assembly (four-cylinder engines) or the main bearing caps (V6 engines). Try not to drop the bearing inserts.

6 Carefully lift the crankshaft out of the engine. It may be a good idea to have an assistant available, since the crankshaft is quite heavy and awkward to handle. With the bearing inserts in place inside the engine block and main bearing bridge, reinstall the bridge or lower crankcase onto the engine block and tighten the bolts finger tight.

INSTALLATION

7 Crankshaft installation is the first step in engine reassembly. It's assumed at this point that the engine block and crankshaft have been cleaned, inspected and repaired or reconditioned.

8 Position the engine block with the bottom facing up.

9 Remove the mounting bolts and lift off the lower crankcase or bearing bridge and main bearing caps.

10 If they're still in place, remove the original bearing inserts from the block and from the main bearing bridge. Wipe the bearing surfaces of the block and main bearing bridge saddle with a clean, lint-free cloth. They must be kept spotlessly clean. This is critical for determining the correct bearing oil clearance.

10.1 Checking crankshaft endplay with a dial indicator

10.3 Checking the crankshaft endplay with feeler gauges at the thrust bearing journal

10.17 Place the Plastigage onto the crankshaft bearing journal as shown

MAIN BEARING OIL CLEARANCE CHECK

▶ Refer to illustrations 10.17, 10.19a, 10.19b, 10.19c and 10.21

11 Without mixing them up, clean the back sides of the new upper main bearing inserts (with grooves and oil holes) and lay one in each main bearing saddle in the engine block. Each upper bearing (engine block) has an oil groove and oil hole in it.

✳✳ CAUTION:

The oil holes in the block must line up with the oil holes in the engine block inserts.

The thrust washer or thrust bearing insert must be installed in the correct location. On the four-cylinder engine the thrust bearing washers are located on the engine block number 4 journal. On the V6 engine they're located on the number 3 journal. Clean the back sides of the lower main bearing inserts and lay them in the corresponding location in the main bearing assembly (four-cylinder engines) or the main bearing caps (V6 engine). Make sure the tab on the bearing insert fits into the recess in the block or main bearing caps.

✳✳ CAUTION:

Do not hammer the bearing insert into place and don't nick or gouge the bearing faces. DO NOT apply any lubrication at this time.

12 Clean the faces of the bearing inserts in the block and the crankshaft main bearing journals with a clean, lint-free cloth.

13 Check or clean the oil holes in the crankshaft, as any dirt here can go only one way - straight through the new bearings.

14 Once you're certain the crankshaft is clean, carefully lay it in position in the cylinder block.

15 Before the crankshaft can be permanently installed, the main bearing oil clearance must be checked.

16 Cut several strips of the appropriate size of Plastigage. They must be slightly shorter than the width of the main bearing journal.

17 Place one piece on each crankshaft main bearing journal, parallel with the journal axis as shown (see illustration).

18 Clean the faces of the bearing inserts in the lower crankcase or main bearing caps. Hold the bearing inserts in place and install the lower crankcase or caps onto the crankshaft and cylinder block. DO NOT disturb the Plastigage.

19 Apply clean engine oil to all bolt threads prior to installation, then install all bolts finger-tight. Tighten the main bearing assembly (four-cylinder engines) (see illustrations) or main bearing caps (V6 engine) in the sequence shown (see illustration) progressing in steps, to the torque listed in this Chapter's Specifications. DO NOT rotate the crankshaft at any time during this operation.

20 Remove the bolts in the reverse order of the tightening sequence and carefully lift the main bearing assembly (four-cylinder engines) or main bearing caps (V6 engines) straight up and off the block. Do not disturb the Plastigage or rotate the crankshaft.

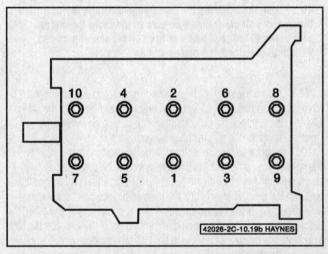

10.19a Main bearing assembly bolt tightening sequence on four-cylinder engines - inner bolts

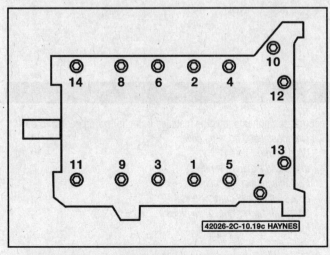

10.19b Main bearing assembly bolt tightening sequence on four-cylinder engines - outer bolts

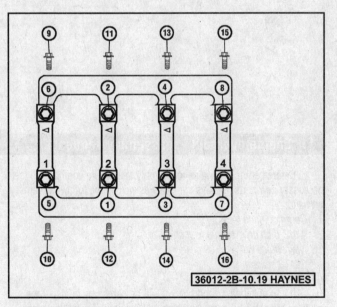

10.19c Main bearing cap bolt tightening sequence on V6 engines

10.21 Use the scale on the Plastigage package to determine the bearing oil clearance - be sure to measure the widest part of the Plastigage and use the correct scale; it comes with both standard and metric scales

21 Compare the width of the crushed Plastigage on each journal to the scale printed on the Plastigage envelope to determine the main bearing oil clearance (see illustration). Check with an automotive machine shop for the oil clearance for your engine.

22 If the clearance is not as specified, the bearing inserts may be the wrong size (which means different ones will be required). Before deciding if different inserts are needed, make sure that no dirt or oil was between the bearing inserts and the caps or block when the clearance was measured. If the Plastigage was wider at one end than the other, the crankshaft journal may be tapered. If the clearance still exceeds the limit specified, the bearing insert(s) will have to be replaced with an under-size bearing insert(s).

✳✳ CAUTION:

When installing a new crankshaft always install a standard bearing insert set.

23 Carefully scrape all traces of the Plastigage material off the main bearing journals and/or the bearing insert faces. Be sure to remove all residue from the oil holes. Use your fingernail or the edge of a plastic card - don't nick or scratch the bearing faces.

FINAL INSTALLATION

24 Carefully lift the crankshaft out of the cylinder block.

25 Clean the bearing insert faces in the cylinder block, then apply a thin, uniform layer of moly-base grease or engine assembly lube to each of the bearing surfaces. Be sure to coat the thrust faces as well as the journal face of the thrust bearing.

26 Make sure the crankshaft journals are clean, then lay the crankshaft back in place in the cylinder block.

27 Clean the bearing insert faces and apply the same lubricant to them. Clean the engine block and the mating surface of the lower crankcase or the bearing caps thoroughly. The surfaces must be free of oil residue. Install the lower main bearing bridge.

28 Prior to installation, apply clean engine oil to all bolt threads, wiping off any excess, then install all bolts finger-tight.

29 Tighten the bolts to the torque listed in this Chapter's Specifications following the correct torque sequence (see illustrations 10.19a, 10.19b and 10.19c).

30 Recheck the crankshaft endplay with a feeler gauge or a dial indicator. The endplay should be correct if the crankshaft thrust faces aren't worn or damaged and if new bearings have been installed.

31 Rotate the crankshaft a number of times by hand to check for any obvious binding. It should rotate with a running torque of 50 in-lbs or less. If the running torque is too high, correct the problem at this time.

32 Install the new rear main oil seal (see Chapter 2A).

11 Engine overhaul - reassembly sequence

1 Before beginning engine reassembly, make sure you have all the necessary new parts, gaskets and seals as well as the following items on hand:

Common hand tools
A 1/2-inch drive torque wrench
New engine oil
Gasket sealant
Thread locking compound

2 If you obtained a short block it will be necessary to install the cylinder head, the oil pump and pick-up tube, the oil pan, the water pump, the timing belt or chain and timing cover, and the valve cover (see Chapter 2A or 2B). In order to save time and avoid problems, the external components must be installed in the following general order:

Thermostat and housing cover
Water pump
Intake and exhaust manifolds
Fuel injection components
Emission control components
Spark plug wires and spark plugs
Ignition coils or coil packs
Oil filter
Engine mounts and mount brackets
Clutch and flywheel (manual transaxle)
Driveplate (automatic transaxle)

12 Initial start-up and break-in after overhaul

✳✳ WARNING:

Have a fire extinguisher handy when starting the engine for the first time.

1   Once the engine has been installed in the vehicle, double-check the engine oil and coolant levels.

2   With the spark plugs out of the engine and the ignition system and fuel pump disabled (see Chapter 4), crank the engine until oil pressure registers on the gauge or the light goes out.

3   Install the spark plugs, hook up the plug wires and restore the ignition system and fuel pump functions.

4   Start the engine. It may take a few moments for the fuel system to build up pressure, but the engine should start without a great deal of effort.

5   After the engine starts, it should be allowed to warm up to normal operating temperature. While the engine is warming up, make a thorough check for fuel, oil and coolant leaks.

6   Shut the engine off and recheck the engine oil and coolant levels.

7   Drive the vehicle to an area with minimum traffic, accelerate from 30 to 50 mph, then allow the vehicle to slow to 30 mph with the throttle closed. Repeat the procedure 10 or 12 times. This will load the piston rings and cause them to seat properly against the cylinder walls. Check again for oil and coolant leaks.

8   Drive the vehicle gently for the first 500 miles (no sustained high speeds) and keep a constant check on the oil level. It is not unusual for an engine to use oil during the break-in period.

9   At approximately 500 to 600 miles, change the oil and filter.

10 For the next few hundred miles, drive the vehicle normally. Do not pamper it or abuse it.

11 After 2,000 miles, change the oil and filter again and consider the engine broken in.

GLOSSARY

B

Backlash - The amount of play between two parts. Usually refers to how much one gear can be moved back and forth without moving the gear with which it's meshed.

Bearing Caps - The caps held in place by nuts or bolts which, in turn, hold the bearing surface. This space is for lubricating oil to enter.

Bearing clearance - The amount of space left between shaft and bearing surface. This space is for lubricating oil to enter.

Bearing crush - The additional height which is purposely manufactured into each bearing half to ensure complete contact of the bearing back with the housing bore when the engine is assembled.

Bearing knock - The noise created by movement of a part in a loose or worn bearing.

Blueprinting - Dismantling an engine and reassembling it to EXACT specifications.

Bore - An engine cylinder, or any cylindrical hole; also used to describe the process of enlarging or accurately refinishing a hole with a cutting tool, as to bore an engine cylinder. The bore size is the diameter of the hole.

Boring - Renewing the cylinders by cutting them out to a specified size. A boring bar is used to make the cut.

Bottom end - A term which refers collectively to the engine block, crankshaft, main bearings and the big ends of the connecting rods.

Break-in - The period of operation between installation of new or rebuilt parts and time in which parts are worn to the correct fit. Driving at reduced and varying speed for a specified mileage to permit parts to wear to the correct fit.

Bushing - A one-piece sleeve placed in a bore to serve as a bearing surface for shaft, piston pin, etc. Usually replaceable.

C

Camshaft - The shaft in the engine, on which a series of lobes are located for operating the valve mechanisms. The camshaft is driven by gears or sprockets and a timing chain. Usually referred to simply as the cam.

Carbon - Hard, or soft, black deposits found in combustion chamber, on plugs, under rings, on and under valve heads.

Cast iron - An alloy of iron and more than two percent carbon, used for engine blocks and heads because it's relatively inexpensive and easy to mold into complex shapes.

Chamfer - To bevel across (or a bevel on) the sharp edge of an object.

Chase - To repair damaged threads with a tap or die.

Combustion chamber - The space between the piston and the cylinder head, with the piston at top dead center, in which air-fuel mixture is burned.

Compression ratio - The relationship between cylinder volume (clearance volume) when the piston is at top dead center and cylinder volume when the piston is at bottom dead center.

Connecting rod - The rod that connects the crank on the crankshaft with the piston. Sometimes called a con rod.

Connecting rod cap - The part of the connecting rod assembly that attaches the rod to the crankpin.

Core plug - Soft metal plug used to plug the casting holes for the coolant passages in the block.

Crankcase - The lower part of the engine in which the crankshaft rotates; includes the lower section of the cylinder block and the oil pan.

Crank kit - A reground or reconditioned crankshaft and new main and connecting rod bearings.

Crankpin - The part of a crankshaft to which a connecting rod is attached.

Crankshaft - The main rotating member, or shaft, running the length of the crankcase, with offset throws to which the connecting rods are attached; changes the reciprocating motion of the pistons into rotating motion.

Cylinder sleeve - A replaceable sleeve, or liner, pressed into the cylinder block to form the cylinder bore.

D

Deburring - Removing the burrs (rough edges or areas) from a bearing.

Deglazer - A tool, rotated by an electric motor, used to remove glaze from cylinder walls so a new set of rings will seat.

E

Endplay - The amount of lengthwise movement between two parts. As applied to a crankshaft, the distance that the crankshaft can move forward and back in the cylinder block.

F

Face - A machinist's term that refers to removing metal from the end of a shaft or the face of a larger part, such as a flywheel.

Fatigue - A breakdown of material through a large number of loading and unloading cycles. The first signs are cracks followed shortly by breaks.

Feeler gauge - A thin strip of hardened steel, ground to an exact thickness, used to check clearances between parts.

Free height - The unloaded length or height of a spring.

Freeplay - The looseness in a linkage, or an assembly of parts, between the initial application of force and actual movement. Usually perceived as slop or slight delay.

Freeze plug - See Core plug.

G

Gallery - A large passage in the block that forms a reservoir for engine oil pressure.

Glaze - The very smooth, glassy finish that develops on cylinder walls while an engine is in service.

H

Heli-Coil - A rethreading device used when threads are worn or damaged. The device is installed in a retapped hole to reduce the thread size to the original size.

I

Installed height - The spring's measured length or height, as installed on the cylinder head. Installed height is measured from the spring seat to the underside of the spring retainer.

J

Journal - The surface of a rotating shaft which turns in a bearing.

K

Keeper - The split lock that holds the valve spring retainer in position on the valve stem.

Key - A small piece of metal inserted into matching grooves machined into two parts fitted together - such as a gear pressed onto a shaft - which prevents slippage between the two parts.

Knock - The heavy metallic engine sound, produced in the combustion chamber as a result of abnormal combustion - usually detonation. Knock is usually caused by a loose or worn bearing. Also referred to as detonation, pinging and spark knock. Connecting rod or main bearing knocks are created by too much oil clearance or insufficient lubrication.

L

Lands - The portions of metal between the piston ring grooves.

Lapping the valves - Grinding a valve face and its seat together with lapping compound.

Lash - The amount of free motion in a gear train, between gears, or in a mechanical assembly, that occurs before movement can begin. Usually refers to the lash in a valve train.

Lifter - The part that rides against the cam to transfer motion to the rest of the valve train.

M

Machining - The process of using a machine to remove metal from a metal part.

Main bearings - The plain, or babbitt, bearings that support the crankshaft.

Main bearing caps - The cast iron caps, bolted to the bottom of the block, that support the main bearings.

O

O.D. - Outside diameter.

Oil gallery - A pipe or drilled passageway in the engine used to carry engine oil from one area to another.

Oil ring - The lower ring, or rings, of a piston; designed to prevent excessive amounts of oil from working up the cylinder walls and into the combustion chamber. Also called an oil-control ring.

Oil seal - A seal which keeps oil from leaking out of a compartment. Usually refers to a dynamic seal around a rotating shaft or other moving part.

O-ring - A type of sealing ring made of a special rubberlike material; in use, the O-ring is compressed into a groove to provide the sealing action.

Overhaul - To completely disassemble a unit, clean and inspect all parts, reassemble it with the original or new parts and make all adjustments necessary for proper operation.

P

Pilot bearing - A small bearing installed in the center of the flywheel (or the rear end of the crankshaft) to support the front end of the input shaft of the transmission.

Pip mark - A little dot or indentation which indicates the top side of a compression ring.

Piston - The cylindrical part, attached to the connecting rod, that moves up and down in the cylinder as the crankshaft rotates. When the fuel charge is fired, the piston transfers the force of the explosion to the connecting rod, then to the crankshaft.

Piston pin (or wrist pin) - The cylindrical and usually hollow steel pin that passes through the piston. The piston pin fastens the piston to the upper end of the connecting rod.

Piston ring - The split ring fitted to the groove in a piston. The ring contacts the sides of the ring groove and also rubs against the cylinder wall, thus sealing space between piston and wall. There are two types of rings: Compression rings seal the compression pressure in the combustion chamber; oil rings scrape excessive oil off the cylinder wall.

Piston ring groove - The slots or grooves cut in piston heads to hold piston rings in position.

Piston skirt - The portion of the piston below the rings and the piston pin hole.

Plastigage - A thin strip of plastic thread, available in different sizes, used for measuring clearances. For example, a strip of plastigage is laid across a bearing journal and mashed as parts are assembled. Then parts are disassembled and the width of the strip is measured to determine clearance between journal and bearing. Commonly used to measure crankshaft main-bearing and connecting rod bearing clearances.

Press-fit - A tight fit between two parts that requires pressure to force the parts together. Also referred to as drive, or force, fit.

Prussian blue - A blue pigment; in solution, useful in determining the area of contact between two surfaces. Prussian blue is commonly used to determine the width and location of the contact area between the valve face and the valve seat.

R

Race (bearing) - The inner or outer ring that provides a contact surface for balls or rollers in bearing.

Ream - To size, enlarge or smooth a hole by using a round cutting tool with fluted edges.

Ring job - The process of reconditioning the cylinders and installing new rings.

Runout - Wobble. The amount a shaft rotates out-of-true.

S

Saddle - The upper main bearing seat.

Scored - Scratched or grooved, as a cylinder wall may be scored by abrasive particles moved up and down by the piston rings.

Scuffing - A type of wear in which there's a transfer of material between parts moving against each other; shows up as pits or grooves in the mating surfaces.

Seat - The surface upon which another part rests or seats. For example, the valve seat is the matched surface upon which the valve face rests. Also used to refer to wearing into a good fit; for example, piston rings seat after a few miles of driving.

Short block - An engine block complete with crankshaft and piston and, usually, camshaft assemblies.

Static balance - The balance of an object while it's stationary.

Step - The wear on the lower portion of a ring land caused by excessive side and back-clearance. The height of the step indicates the ring's extra side clearance and the length of the step projecting from the back wall of the groove represents the ring's back clearance.

Stroke - The distance the piston moves when traveling from top dead center to bottom dead center, or from bottom dead center to top dead center.

Stud - A metal rod with threads on both ends.

T

Tang - A lip on the end of a plain bearing used to align the bearing during assembly.

Tap - To cut threads in a hole. Also refers to the fluted tool used to cut threads.

Taper - A gradual reduction in the width of a shaft or hole; in an engine cylinder, taper usually takes the form of uneven wear, more pronounced at the top than at the bottom.

Throws - The offset portions of the crankshaft to which the connecting rods are affixed.

Thrust bearing - The main bearing that has thrust faces to prevent excessive endplay, or forward and backward movement of the crankshaft.

Thrust washer - A bronze or hardened steel washer placed between two moving parts. The washer prevents longitudinal movement and provides a bearing surface for thrust surfaces of parts.

Tolerance - The amount of variation permitted from an exact size of measurement. Actual amount from smallest acceptable dimension to largest acceptable dimension.

U

Umbrella - An oil deflector placed near the valve tip to throw oil from the valve stem area.

Undercut - A machined groove below the normal surface.

Undersize bearings - Smaller diameter bearings used with re-ground crankshaft journals.

V

Valve grinding - Refacing a valve in a valve-refacing machine.

Valve train - The valve-operating mechanism of an engine; includes all components from the camshaft to the valve.

Vibration damper - A cylindrical weight attached to the front of the crankshaft to minimize torsional vibration (the twist-untwist actions of the crankshaft caused by the cylinder firing impulses). Also called a harmonic balancer.

W

Water jacket - The spaces around the cylinders, between the inner and outer shells of the cylinder block or head, through which coolant circulates.

Web - A supporting structure across a cavity.

Woodruff key - A key with a radiused backside (viewed from the side).

Specifications

General

Displacement	
Four-cylinder models	144 cubic inches (2.4 liters)
V6 models	
2007 and earlier	183 cubic inches (3.0 liters)
2008 and later models	212 cubic inches (3.5 liters)
Bore and stroke	
Four-cylinder models	3.43 x 3.90 inches (87.0 x 99.0 mm)
V6 models	
2007 and earlier	3.39 x 3.39 inches (86.0 x 86.0 mm)
2008 and later	3.50 x 3.66 inches (89.0 x 93.0 mm)
Cylinder compression	
Minimum	135 psi (930 kPa)
Maximum variation between cylinders	28 psi (200 kPa)
Oil pressure (engine at operating temperature)	
Four-cylinder models	
Idle speed	10 psi (70 kPa)
3,000 rpm	44 psi (300 kPa)
V6 models	
Idle speed	10 psi (70 kPa)
3,000 rpm	71 psi (490 kPa)

Torque specifications	Ft-lbs (unless otherwise indicated)	Nm

➡**Note: One foot-pound (ft-lb) of torque is equivalent to 12 inch-pounds (in-lbs) of torque. Torque values below approximately 15 foot-pounds are expressed in inch-pounds, because most foot-pound torque wrenches are not accurate at these smaller values.**

Subframe mounting bolts	See Chapter 10	
Connecting rod bolts*		
Four-cylinder models		
2007 and earlier models		
Step 1	15	20
Step 2	Tighten an additional 90 degrees	
2008 and later models		
Step 1	30	41
Step 2	Tighten an additional 120 degrees	
V6 models		
Step 1	15	20
Step 2	Tighten an additional 90 degrees	
Main bearing assembly/cap bolts		
Four-cylinder models		
Main bolts (see illustration 10.19a)		
Step 1	22	29
Step 2		
2007 and earlier models	Tighten an additional 56 degrees	
2008 and later models	Tighten an additional 48 degrees	
Perimeter bolts (see illustration 10.19b)	16	22

Use new bolts.

Torque specifications	Ft-lbs (unless otherwise indicated)	Nm
V6 models (see illustration 10.19c)		
Main bolts	54	74
Side bolts	36	49
Transaxle-to-engine mounting bolts		
Four-cylinder and V6 automatic		
transaxle models	47	64
V6 manual transaxle models	54	74

Notes

3

COOLING, HEATING AND AIR CONDITIONING SYSTEMS

1   General information

ENGINE COOLING SYSTEM

♦ **Refer to illustrations 1.1a, 1.1b and 1.2**

All vehicles covered by this manual employ a pressurized engine cooling system with thermostatically controlled coolant circulation (see illustrations). An impeller-type water pump mounted on the engine block pumps coolant through the engine. The coolant flows around each cylinder and toward the rear of the engine. Cast-in coolant passages direct coolant around the intake and exhaust ports, near the spark plug areas and in close proximity to the exhaust valve guides.

A wax-pellet type thermostat controls engine coolant temperature. During warm up, the closed thermostat prevents coolant from circulating through the radiator. As the engine nears normal operating temperature, the thermostat opens and allows hot coolant to travel through the radiator, where it's cooled before returning to the engine (see illustration).

The cooling system is sealed by a pressure-type radiator cap, which raises the boiling point of the coolant and increases the cooling efficiency of the radiator. If the system pressure exceeds the cap pressure relief value, the excess pressure in the system forces the spring-loaded valve inside the cap off its seat and allows the coolant to escape through the overflow tube into a coolant reservoir. When the system cools the excess coolant is automatically drawn from the reservoir back into the radiator.

The coolant reservoir serves as both the point at which fresh coolant is added to the cooling system to maintain the proper fluid level and as a holding tank for overheated coolant.

This type of cooling system is known as a closed design because coolant that escapes past the pressure cap is saved and reused.

1.1a Underhood cooling and air conditioning components - four-cylinder model

1	Air conditioning line service port (high side)	3	Radiator
2	Air conditioning line service port (low side)	4	Radiator cap
		5	Coolant reservoir

6	Thermostat (under intake manifold)
7	Fuse and relay box
8	Radiator cover

1.1b Underhood cooling and air conditioning components - V6 model

1	Air conditioning line service port (high side)	
2	Air conditioning line service port (low side)	
3	Radiator	
4	Radiator cap	
5	Coolant reservoir	
6	Thermostat	
7	Fuse and relay box	
8	Radiator cover	

ENGINE COOLING FANS

All vehicles covered by this manual are equipped with two electric cooling fans: a radiator fan and a condenser fan. The fans are controlled electronically. The radiator and condenser fan relays are located in the fuse and relay boxes found in the engine compartment or under the dash. A fan switch is used only on 2003 and 2004 four-cylinder engines and is mounted in the bottom of the radiator. All other years and models (covered in this manual) utilize ECT sensors and work with the onboard computer to control the cooling fans.

HEATING SYSTEM

The heating system consists of a blower fan and heater core located in the heater box, the hoses connecting the heater core to the engine cooling system and the heater/air conditioning control head on the dashboard. Hot engine coolant is circulated through the heater core. When the heater mode is activated, a flap door opens to expose the heater box to the passenger compartment. A fan switch on the control head activates the blower motor, which forces air through the core, heating the air.

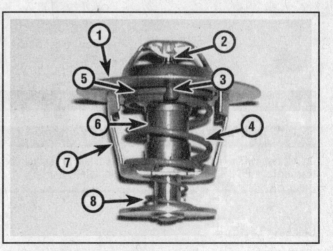

1.2 Typical thermostat (V6 models)

1	Flange	5	Valve seat
2	Piston	6	Valve
3	Jiggle valve	7	Frame
4	Main coil spring	8	Secondary coil spring

AIR CONDITIONING SYSTEM

The air conditioning system consists of a condenser mounted in front of the radiator, an evaporator mounted adjacent to the heater core, a compressor mounted on the engine, a receiver-drier next to the con-denser and the plumbing connecting all of the above components.

A blower fan forces the warmer air of the passenger compartment through the evaporator core (sort of a radiator-in-reverse), transferring the heat from the air to the refrigerant. The liquid refrigerant boils off into low pressure vapor, taking the heat with it when it leaves the evaporator.

2   Antifreeze - general information

▶ **Refer to illustration 2.4**

❈❈ WARNING:

Do not allow antifreeze to come in contact with your skin or painted surfaces of the vehicle. Rinse off spills immediately with plenty of water. Antifreeze is highly toxic if ingested. Never leave antifreeze lying around in an open container or in puddles on the floor; children and pets are attracted by its sweet smell and may drink it. Check with local authorities about disposing of used antifreeze. Many communities have collection centers which will see that antifreeze is disposed of safely. Never dump used antifreeze on the ground or pour it into drains.

The cooling system should be filled with a water/ethylene glycol based antifreeze solution, which will prevent freezing down to at least -20-degrees F (even lower in cold climates). It also provides protection against corrosion and increases the coolant boiling point. The engines in these vehicles have aluminum heads and blocks. The manufacturer recommends that the correct type of coolant be used and strongly urges that coolant types not be mixed (see the Chapter 1 Specifications).

Drain, flush and refill the cooling system at least every other year (see Chapter 1). The use of antifreeze solutions for periods of longer than two years is likely to cause damage and encourage the formation of rust and scale in the system.

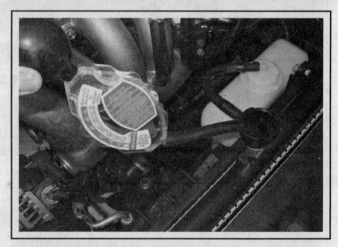

2.4 Use an automotive hydrometer (available at most auto parts stores) to test the condition of your coolant

Before adding antifreeze to the system, inspect all hose connections. Antifreeze can leak through very minute openings.

Hydrometers are available at most auto parts stores to test the coolant (see illustration). Use antifreeze that meets factory specifications (see Chapter 1).

3   Thermostat - check and replacement

❈❈ WARNING:

Do not remove the radiator cap, drain the coolant or replace the thermostat until the engine has cooled completely.

CHECK

1   Before assuming the thermostat is to blame for a cooling system problem, check the coolant level, drivebelt tension (four-cylinder engines only, see Chapter 1) and temperature gauge operation.

2   If the engine seems to be taking a long time to warm up, based on heater output or temperature gauge operation, the thermostat is probably stuck open. Replace the thermostat with a new one.

3   If the engine runs hot, use your hand to check the temperature of the lower radiator hose. If the hose isn't hot, but the engine is, the thermostat is probably stuck closed, preventing the coolant inside the engine from escaping to the radiator. Replace the thermostat.

❈❈ CAUTION:

Don't drive the vehicle without a thermostat. The computer may stay in open loop and emissions and fuel economy will suffer.

4   If the lower radiator hose is hot, it means that the coolant is flowing and the thermostat is open. Consult the *Troubleshooting* Section at the front of this manual for cooling system diagnosis.

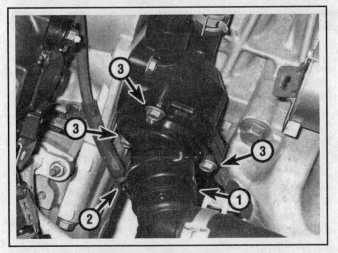

3.9 Thermostat mounting bolts and quick connect fitting details (four-cylinder model)

1   Quick connect fitting
2   Quick connect spring lock
3   Thermostat/cover mounting bolts

3.14 Install a new rubber seal over the thermostat (V6 models)

REPLACEMENT

♦ **Refer to illustrations 3.9 and 3.14**

5   Disconnect the cable from the negative battery terminal (see Chapter 5, Section 1).

6   On V6 engines, remove the battery.

7   Drain the cooling system (see Chapter 1). If the coolant is relatively new or in good condition, save it and reuse it. Read the **Warning** in Section 2.

8   Follow the lower radiator hose to the engine to locate the thermostat housing cover.

9   On four-cylinder engines, remove the quick connect fitting by pulling the spring-lock out and pull the quick connect fitting away from the thermostat by wiggling it free (see illustration).

10   On V6 engines, loosen the hose clamp, then detach the hose from the fitting. If it's stuck, grasp it near the end with a pair of adjustable pliers and twist it to break the seal, then pull it off. If the hose is old or deteriorated, cut it off and install a new one.

➡**Note: If the outer surface of the large fitting that mates with the hose is deteriorated (corroded, pitted, etc.), it may be damaged further by hose removal. If it is, the thermostat housing cover will have to be replaced.**

11   Remove the thermostat housing cover bolts and cover.

➡**Note: On four-cylinder engines, the thermostat and cover are removed and replaced as a single unit (see illustration 3.9).**

If the cover is stuck, tap it with a soft-face hammer to jar it loose. Be prepared for some coolant to spill as the seal is broken.

12   Take note of how the thermostat is installed and the orientation of the jiggle pin and then remove it.

13   Remove all traces of the old seal from the mating surfaces.

14   On V6 models, install a new seal over the thermostat (see illustration). Make sure the cutout is aligned correctly with the jiggle valve.

➡**Note: On four-cylinder engines, install a new O-ring on the thermostat (cover) before installation.**

15   On V6 models, install the new thermostat in the housing without using sealant. Make sure the jiggle pin is positioned correctly and the spring end is directed into the engine.

➡**Note: On four-cylinder engines, the thermostat is positioned in the cover correctly by the manufacturer.**

Make sure the mating surfaces on the thermostat housing are perfectly clean to insure a tight seal before installing the thermostat assembly.

16   Install the thermostat housing cover, tightening the bolts to the torque listed in this Chapter's Specifications.

17   Reattach the hose and tighten the hose clamp securely. Install all components that were previously removed.

18   On four-cylinder models, install the quick connect fitting and hose by pushing the spring-lock fully into position, apply coolant to the fitting contact area and then press the hose on until it clicks.

➡**Note: The factory recommends replacing the O-ring seal inside the quick connect fitting before reinstalling it.**

19   Refill the cooling system (see Chapter 1).

20   Reconnect the battery (see Chapter 5, Section 1).

21   Start the engine and allow it to reach normal operating temperature, then check for leaks and proper thermostat operation (as described in Steps 2 through 4).

4   Engine cooling fans and switch - check and replacement

WARNING:

To avoid possible injury or damage, DO NOT operate the engine with a damaged fan. Do not attempt to repair fan blades - replace a damaged fan with a new one.

➡Note: All air-conditioned models have two fans.

CHECK

♦ Refer to illustrations 4.1, 4.3 and 4.5

1   If the engine is overheating and the cooling fan is not coming on when the engine temperature rises to an excessive level, unplug the fan motor electrical connector (see illustration) and then connect the motor directly to the battery with a fused jumper cable on terminal B. Use another jumper wire to ground terminal A. If the fan motor doesn't come on, replace the motor. These models are equipped with two fans. If the radiator fan motor checks out okay, be sure to test the condenser fan motor as well.

CAUTION:

Do not apply battery power to the harness side of the connector.

2   If the radiator fan motor is okay, but it isn't coming on when the engine gets hot, the fan relay(s) might be defective.
3   Locate the fan relays in the engine compartment fuse/relay box (see illustration).

➡Note: V6 models have an additional fan control relay in a small relay box adjacent to the engine compartment fuse/relay box.

4   Test the relay(s) (see Chapter 12).

5   If the relays are okay, test the radiator fan switch (see illustration).
➡Note: The 2003 and 2004 model years with four-cylinder engines are the only models that utilize a fan switch. On 2005 four-cylinder engines, an ECT sensor replaces the fan switch at the same location, but it is entirely different (see Chapter 6).

The radiator fan switch controls the operation of the fans based on temperature. The fan switch is located in the bottom of the radiator. The switch can be tested with an ohmmeter. When the temperature is below 199-degrees, the switch should be open (no continuity across the switch terminals). When the temperature is above 199-degrees, the switch should be closed (continuity exists across the switch terminals).

6   If the relay(s) and the fan switch are okay, check all wiring and connections to the fan motors. Any further checking should be directed to a qualified repair facility.

REPLACEMENT

Cooling fans

WARNING:

Wait until the engine is completely cool before beginning this procedure.

7   Disconnect the cable from the negative battery terminal (see Chapter 5, Section 1).
8   Set the parking brake and block the rear wheels to prevent the vehicle from rolling. Raise the front of the vehicle and support it securely on jackstands. Remove the lower splash shield from under the radiator (see Chapter 2A).
9   Drain the cooling system (see Chapter 1). If the coolant is relatively new or in good condition, save it and reuse it. Read the **Warning** in Section 2.
10   Remove the coolant reservoir (see Section 5).

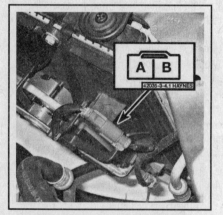

4.1 To test either fan motor, disconnect the electrical connector and use jumper wires to connect the fan directly to the battery (B) and ground (A) - if the fan still doesn't work, replace the motor

4.3 Location of the radiator fan relay (A) and the condenser fan relay (B) (four-cylinder model shown, V6 similar)

4.5 Location of the radiator fan switch (2003 and 2004 four-cylinder models only)

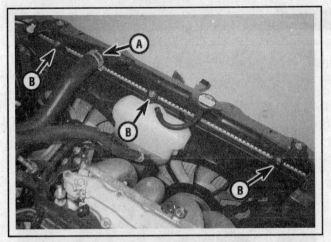

4.13 Use pliers to expand the upper radiator hose clamp (A) and slide it back on the hose, then remove the radiator fan assembly mounting bolts (B) (four-cylinder shown, V6 similar)

4.16 To remove the fan, unscrew the nut in the center, then pull the fan blade from the motor shaft

Four-cylinder models

▶ **Refer to illustrations 4.13, 4.16, and 4.17**

11 Disconnect the fan connectors and fan switch or ECT sensor connector from the radiator (see illustrations 4.1 and 4.5).

12 Remove any wiring harness clamps or anything else connected to the fan shroud assembly.

13 Remove the upper radiator hose from the radiator and move it aside (see illustration).

14 Unbolt the engine cooling fan assembly from the top of the radiator.

15 Carefully lift the fan shroud assembly out of the engine compartment.

➡**Note: It may be necessary to remove the fresh air intake duct cover to get enough clearance to remove the fan assembly (see Chapter 5).**

16 To detach the fan from the motor, remove the motor shaft nut (see illustration).

17 To detach the fan motor from the shroud, remove the mounting screws (see illustration).

V6 models

18 Remove the radiator cover by removing the plastic pushpins (see illustrations 6.4a, 6.4b and 6.4c).

➡**Note: Push-pins that have a Phillips slot in the center can be carefully backed out with a Phillips screwdriver. With the center removed, pull the whole fastener out.**

19 Remove the upper radiator hose.

20 Disconnect the fan electrical connectors that are mounted on each fan shroud.

21 Remove the top radiator brackets.

22 Unbolt each fan shroud assembly from the radiator, detach any wiring harnesses or other parts that attach them to the radiator or engine compartment.

23 Tilt the radiator forward and carefully remove each fan shroud assembly.

All Models

24 Installation is the reverse of removal.

25 Refill the cooling system (see Chapter 1).

4.17 Fan motor mounting screws

26 Reconnect the battery (see Chapter 5, Section 1).

Cooling fan switch (2003 and 2004 four-cylinder models only)

✳✳ WARNING:

Wait until the engine is completely cool before beginning this procedure.

27 Drain the cooling system (see Chapter 1).

28 Raise the front of the vehicle and support it securely on jackstands. Remove the lower splash shield from under the radiator (see Chapter 2A).

29 Disconnect the electrical connector, then unscrew the switch from the radiator (see illustration 4.5).

30 Installation is the reverse of removal, noting the following points:

a) *Use a new sealing ring when installing the switch.*

b) *Refill the cooling system (see Chapter 1).*

c) *Start the engine and allow it to reach normal operating temperature, then verify proper fan operation.*

5 Coolant reservoir - removal and installation

♦ Refer to illustration 5.2

❋❋ WARNING:

Wait until the engine is completely cool before beginning this procedure.

1 Disconnect the reservoir hose from the radiator filler neck. Plug the hose to prevent leakage.
2 Remove the mounting bolt (see illustration).
3 Lift the reservoir out of the engine compartment.
4 Clean out the tank with soapy water and a brush to remove any deposits inside. Inspect the reservoir carefully for cracks. If you find a crack, replace the reservoir.
5 Installation is the reverse of removal.

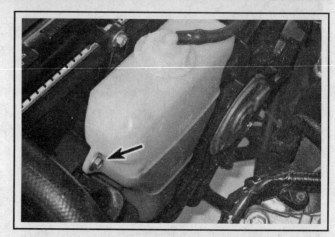

5.2 Location of the coolant reservoir mounting bolt (four-cylinder model shown, V6 similar)

6 Radiator - removal and installation

❋❋ WARNING:

Wait until the engine is completely cool before beginning this procedure.

REMOVAL

♦ Refer to illustrations 6.4a, 6.4b, 6.4c, 6.5, 6.6 and 6.10

1 Disconnect the cable from the negative battery terminal (see Chapter 5, Section 1).

2 Set the parking brake and block the rear wheels. Raise the front of the vehicle and support it securely on jackstands. Remove the splash shield beneath the radiator.
3 Drain the cooling system (see Chapter 1). If the coolant is relatively new or in good condition, save it and reuse it. Read the **Warning** in Section 2.
4 Remove the radiator cover (see illustrations) and the engine cooling fans (see Section 4).
5 Disconnect the lower radiator hose and the transaxle fluid cooling lines (if equipped) from the radiator (see illustration).

➡Note: **Plug the ends of the transaxle cooling lines to minimize fluid loss and contamination.**

6.4a Radiator cover mounting fasteners (four-cylinder model shown, V6 similar)

6.4b Lift up on the center release pin . . .

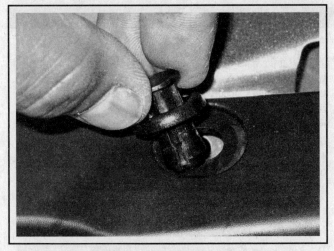

6.4c . . . and remove the entire push-pin

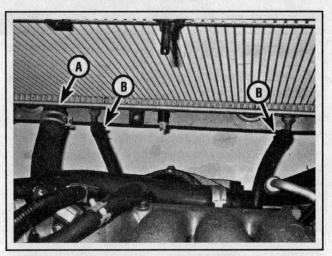

6.5 The lower radiator hose (A) and transaxle cooling lines (B)

6.6 Location of the radiator mounting bracket bolts

6.10 Radiator (A) and condenser (B) lower rubber mounts

6   Remove the radiator brackets (see illustration).

7   Carefully lift out the radiator. Don't spill coolant on the vehicle or scratch the paint.

8   Inspect the radiator for leaks and damage. If it needs repair, have a radiator shop or dealer service department perform the work as special techniques are required.

9   Bugs and dirt can be removed from the radiator by spraying with a garden hose nozzle from the back side. The radiator should be flushed out with a garden hose before reinstallation.

10 Check the radiator mounts (see illustration) for deterioration and replace if necessary.

INSTALLATION

11 Installation is the reverse of the removal procedure. Guide the radiator into the mounts until it seats completely.

12 Tighten the radiator bracket bolts to the torque listed in this Chapter's Specifications.

13 After installation, fill the cooling system with the proper coolant (see Chapter 1).

14 Reconnect the battery (see Chapter 5, Section 1).

15 Start the engine and check for leaks. Allow the engine to reach normal operating temperature, indicated by the upper radiator hose becoming hot. Recheck the coolant level and add more if required.

16 Check and add transaxle fluid as needed.

7 Water pump - check

▶ **Refer to illustrations 7.2 and 7.3**

1   A failure in the water pump can cause serious engine damage due to overheating.

2   If a failure occurs in the pump seal, coolant will leak from under the engine timing belt cover (V6 models) or from the weep hole(s) on the water pump (four-cylinder models) (see illustration).

➡Note: On V6 models, the water pump is mounted behind the engine mount bracket, behind the timing belt covers. On four-cylinder models, it is externally mounted to a water passage just below the alternator.

3   These water pumps are equipped with weep or vent holes. It is possible to check the water pump weep holes using a flashlight. If a failure occurs in the pump seal, coolant will leak from the one (or both) of the holes. Use a flashlight to find the vent holes on the water pump and check for leaks.

➡Note: Because the water pump on V6 models is mounted behind the engine mount bracket and timing belt covers, you'll need to look for coolant leaks on the top of the water pump and towards the bottom of the lower timing belt cover or with the timing belt cover removed (see illustration).

4   If the water pump shaft bearings fail, there may be a howling sound near the water pump while it's running. With the engine off, shaft wear can be felt if the water pump pulley is rocked up-and-down. Don't mistake drivebelt slippage, which causes a squealing sound, for water pump bearing failure.

➡Note For V6 models, it will not be possible to check the water pump shaft and/or pulley without removing the timing belt.

5   A quick water pump performance check can be done by doing the following:

   a) *Make certain that the coolant level in the system is full.*
   b) *Start the vehicle and warm it up fully.*
   c) *Turn the heater on in the passenger compartment.*
   d) *Check for little or no heat output. If this is the case, the water pump may be failing because coolant flow does not appear to be going through the heater core.*

6   A water pump may still be due for replacement even if it's not leaking or making any noise. The only sure way to tell if replacement is necessary is to remove the pump and examine it closely. A loose or corroded impeller, a leaking shaft seal or a worn shaft bearing are all causes for replacement.

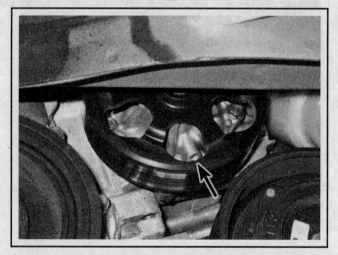

7.2 The water pump weep hole on a four-cylinder engine

7.3 The weep hole (V6 engine) is beneath the pump pulley facing downward - you'll need a flashlight and a small mirror to inspect it (with the timing belt cover removed)

8 Water pump - replacement

❋❋ WARNING:

Wait until the engine is completely cool before beginning this procedure.

1   Disconnect the cable from the negative battery terminal (see Chapter 5, Section 1).

2   Drain the cooling system (see Chapter 1). If the coolant is relatively new or in good condition, save it and reuse it. Read the **Warning** in Section 2.

3   Remove the drivebelt (see Chapter 1).

V6 MODELS

▶ **Refer to illustration 8.5**

4   Remove the timing belt and the timing belt tensioner (see Chapter 2B).

5   Remove the water pump mounting bolts and detach it from the engine (see illustration). Check the impeller on the backside for evidence of corrosion or missing fins.

8.5 Water pump mounting bolts (V6 engine) - one bottom bolt isn't visible in this photo

8.7 Water pump mounting bolts (four-cylinder engine) - one bottom bolt isn't visible in this photo

FOUR-CYLINDER MODELS

♦ **Refer to illustration 8.7**

6   Remove the drivebelt tensioner (see Chapter 1).

7   Remove the water pump mounting bolts and detach it from the engine (see illustration).

➥**Note: Access to some of the mounting bolts may be easier through the wheel well; You'll need to remove the inner fender splash shield (see Chapter 11).**

Check the impeller on the backside of the pump for evidence of corrosion or missing fins.

ALL MODELS

8   Make sure the bolt threads and the threaded holes in the engine are clear of corrosion.

9   Compare the new pump to the old one to make sure they're identical.

10   Remove all traces of the O-ring from the engine mounting surface.

11   Make sure that the mounting surfaces on the engine and water pump are clean.

12   Place a new O-ring into the groove of the new pump

13   Carefully attach the pump to the engine and thread the mounting bolts finger tight. Make sure that the dowel pin(s) are in their original locations (if equipped).

14   Tighten the bolts to the torque listed in this Chapter's Specifications in 1/4-turn increments. Don't overtighten the bolts or the pump may become distorted and leak.

15   Reinstall all parts removed for access to the pump.

16   Refill the cooling system and check the drivebelt tension (see Chapter 1).

17   Reconnect the battery (see Chapter 5, Section 1). Run the engine and check for leaks.

9   Coolant temperature sending unit

All models covered in this manual utilize a variety of electronic sensors and an onboard computer to monitor various engine parameters, engine temperature being one of them. The Powertrain Control Module (PCM) controls the temperature gauge on the instrument cluster. An individual sending unit for the temperature gauge is not necessary with the use of this technology.

10 Blower motor power transistor and blower motor - replacement

❄❄ WARNING:

The models covered by this manual are equipped with Supplemental Restraint systems (SRS), more commonly known as airbags. Always disable the airbag system before working in the vicinity of any airbag system component to avoid the possibility of accidental deployment of the airbag, which could cause personal injury (see Chapter 12).

BLOWER MOTOR POWER TRANSISTOR

❖ **Refer to illustration 10.1**

1   Working in the passenger compartment under the glove box, disconnect the electrical connector from the blower motor power transistor (see illustration).

➡**Note: On 2004 and 2005 models, remove the lower dash panel to gain access to the blower motor transistor. Do this by pulling down on the edge of the panel near the glove box until all retaining clip and pins have been separated.**

2   Remove the blower motor power transistor mounting screws and remove the transistor.

3   Installation is the reverse of removal.

4   Reconnect the battery (see Chapter 5, Section 1).

BLOWER MOTOR

5   Disconnect the electrical connector from the blower motor (see illustration 10.1).

➡**Note: On 2004 and 2005 models, remove the lower dash panel to gain access to the blower motor. Do this by pulling down on**

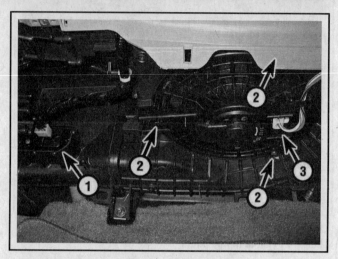

10.1   Blower motor and power transistor details (2003 model shown)

1   Power transistor
2   Blower motor mounting screws
3   Blower motor electrical connector

the edge of the panel near the glove box until all retaining clips and pins have been separated.

6   Remove the blower motor mounting screws and then remove the blower motor assembly.

7   Remove the circlip from the blower motor shaft to release the fan from the motor.

8   Installation is the reverse of removal.

9   Reconnect the battery (see Chapter 5, Section 1).

11 Climate control assembly - removal and installation

❖ **Refer to illustrations 11.3a, 11.3b and 11.4**

❄❄ WARNING:

The models covered by this manual are equipped with Supplemental Restraint systems (SRS), more commonly known as airbags. Always disable the airbag system before working in the vicinity of any airbag system component to avoid the possibility of accidental deployment of the airbag, which could cause personal injury (see Chapter 12).

➡**Note: The radio, navigation unit (if equipped) and climate control head are mounted together and removed as a unit.**

1   Disconnect the cable from the negative battery terminal (see Chapter 5, Section 1).

2   Remove the dashboard upper panel and center pocket (see Chapter 11).

3   Remove the mounting fasteners for the audio and climate control assembly (see illustrations).

4   Disconnect the all electrical connectors and remove the unit (see illustration).

5   The climate control head can now be separated from the assembly by removing the mounting screws.

6   Installation is the reverse of removal.

7   Reconnect the battery (see Chapter 5, Section 1).

11.3a The control assembly upper fasteners

11.3b The control assembly lower fasteners

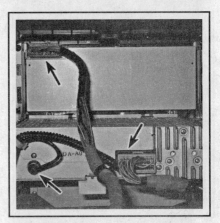

11.4 Electrical connectors on the back of the control assembly (non-navigation unit shown - units with navigation are similar)

12 Heater core - replacement

▶ Refer to illustrations 12.4, 12.5, 12.6, 12.7, 12.9, 12.10, 12.11, 12.13 and 12.16

➥Note: A four-cylinder sedan was used to illustrate this procedure. Coupe and V6 models are configured similarly but not exactly the same.

❈❈ WARNING:

The models covered by this manual are equipped with Supplemental Restraint systems (SRS), more commonly known as airbags. Always disable the airbag system before working in the vicinity of any airbag system component to avoid the possibility of accidental deployment of the airbag, which could cause personal injury (see Chapter 12).

❈❈ WARNING:

The air conditioning system is under high pressure. DO NOT loosen any fittings or remove any components until after the system has been discharged. Air conditioning refrigerant must be properly discharged into an EPA-approved container at a dealer service department or an automotive air conditioning repair facility. Always wear eye protection when disconnecting air conditioning system fittings.

❈❈ WARNING:

Wait until the engine is completely cool before beginning this procedure.

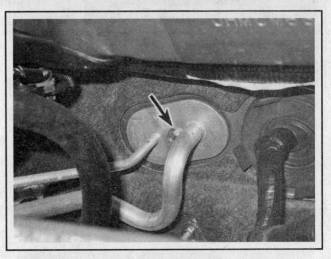

12.4 Remove this bolt to disconnect the air conditioning lines at the firewall

1   If so equipped, have the air conditioning system refrigerant discharged and recovered by an air conditioning technician.
2   Disconnect the cable from the negative battery terminal (see Chapter 5, Section 1).
3   Drain the cooling system (see Chapter 1).
4   Disconnect the air conditioning evaporator lines at the firewall (see illustration).

12.5 Mark the heater valve control cable before removal (upper arrow), then release the clip from the bottom (lower arrow)

12.6 Disconnect the heater hoses from the heater core at the firewall

12.7 One mounting nut for the heater/ air conditioning unit is behind the heater control valve and some brake lines in the engine compartment

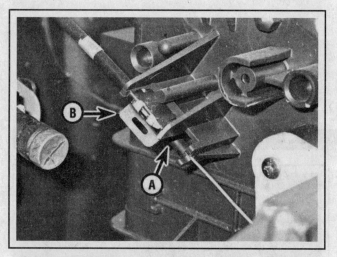

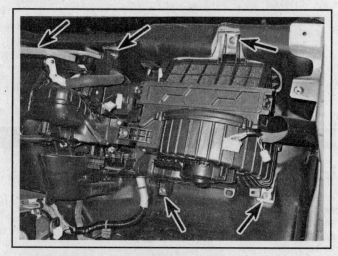

12.9 Mark the heater control cable (A) and lift the tab (B) to release it from the bracket and then remove the cable end from the unit

12.10 Heater/air conditioning unit fastener locations

5   Mark the heater control valve cable at the retaining clip so that it can be reinstalled in the same position. Release the clip and detach the cable (see illustration).

➡**Note: Turn the heater valve arm counterclockwise to the fully open position after the cable has been disconnected.**

6   Disconnect the heater hoses from the heater core at the firewall (see illustration).

7   Remove the heater/air conditioning unit mounting nut from the firewall within the engine compartment (see illustration).

➡**Note: Be careful not to damage any of the lines that are in front of the mounting nut.**

8   Remove the instrument panel (see Chapter 11).

9   Disconnect any electrical connectors to the unit and the heater valve control cable that is located on the left side (see illustration).

10 Remove the mounting fasteners and then lift the heater/air conditioning unit out of the vehicle (see illustration).

11 Remove the mounting screws for the upper duct and then pull it directly up to remove it (see illustration).

➡**Note: Be careful not to damage the evaporator temperature sensor while removing the upper duct. It is a small thin part that will come out along with the duct.**

12 Remove the mounting screws for the lower duct, pull the A/C evaporator up about an inch and then remove the lower duct (see illustration 12.11).

➡**Note: The upper and lower duct cover the A/C evaporator and also secure the lines for the heater core.**

13 Disconnect the electrical connectors and harness fasteners on the unit (see illustration).

14 Remove the mounting screws for the heater outlet duct and then remove it.

15 Remove the mounting screws for the heater core cover and then remove it.

16 Remove the heater core (see illustration).

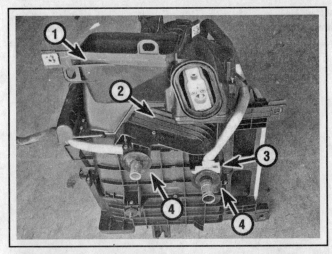

12.11 Heater/air conditioning unit details for heater core removal (mounted-side view)

1	Top duct	3	Line retainer
2	Lower duct	4	Sealing grommets

12.13 Heater/air conditioning unit details for heater core removal (cab-side view)

1	Harness	3	Heater core cover
2	Heater-outlet duct		

17 Installation is the reverse of removal, noting the following points:

a) *When reinstalling the heater/air conditioning unit, make certain that the evaporator drain tube is placed correctly through the port that leads outside.*

b) *Be sure to connect all electrical connectors on the heater/air conditioning unit before reinstalling the instrument panel*

c) *Make sure that the heater control valve cable is placed back in the same position. If cable adjustment is necessary, see step 21.*

d) *Reconnect the heater hoses within the engine compartment.*

18 Reconnect the battery (see Chapter 5, Section 1).

19 Refill the cooling system (see Chapter 1).

20 If equipped with A/C, have the system evacuated, recharged and leak tested by the shop that discharged it.

21 To adjust the heater control valve cable, perform the following steps:

a) *From under the dash, detach the cable from the air mix control (see illustration 12.9).*

b) *Set the temperature control dial to MAX COOL with the blower on LO and the ignition key ON.*

c) *Reattach the cable to the air mix control making sure the cable housing is against the cable stop and secured by the retaining clip.*

d) *In the engine compartment, move the heater control valve to the fully open (extreme clockwise) position and hold it. Attach the cable to the valve control arm, lightly pull on the cable housing to take up any slack and then place the cable housing into the retaining clip and secure it (see illustration 12.5).*

e) *Start the vehicle and operate the climate controls and confirm correct operation.*

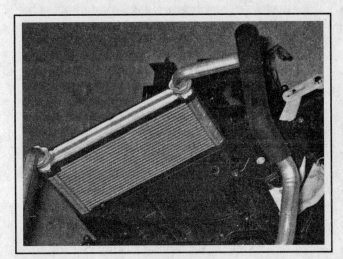

12.16 With the covers removed, the heater core can be pulled out of the unit

13 Air conditioning and heating system - check and maintenance

♦ Refer to illustration 13.1

✸✸ WARNING:

The air conditioning system is under high pressure. DO NOT loosen any fittings or remove any components until after the system has been discharged. Air conditioning refrigerant must be properly discharged into an EPA-approved container at a dealer service department or an automotive air conditioning repair facility. Always wear eye protection when disconnecting air conditioning system fittings.

1   The following maintenance checks should be performed on a regular basis to ensure the air conditioner continues to operate at peak efficiency.

   a) *Check the compressor drivebelt. If it's worn or deteriorated, replace it (see Chapter 1).*
   b) *Check the drivebelt tension and, if necessary, adjust it (see Chapter 1).*
   c) *Check the system hoses. Look for cracks, bubbles, hard spots and deterioration. Inspect the hoses and all fittings for oil bubbles and seepage. If there's any evidence of wear, damage or leaks, replace the hose(s).*
   d) *Inspect the condenser fins for leaves, bugs and other debris. Use a fin comb or compressed air to clean the condenser.*
   e) *Make sure the system has the correct refrigerant charge.*
   f) *Check the evaporator housing drain tube (see illustration) for blockage.*

2   It's a good idea to operate the system for about 10 minutes at least once a month, particularly during the winter. Long term non-use can cause hardening, and subsequent failure, of the seals.

3   Because of the complexity of the air conditioning system and the special equipment necessary to service it, in-depth troubleshooting and repairs are not included in this manual. However, simple checks and component replacement procedures are provided in this Chapter.

4   The most common cause of poor cooling is simply a low system refrigerant charge. If a noticeable drop in cool air output occurs, the following quick check will help you determine if the refrigerant level is low.

CHECKING THE REFRIGERANT CHARGE

5   Warm the engine up to normal operating temperature.

6   Place the air conditioning temperature selector at the coldest setting and the blower at the highest setting. Open the vehicle doors (to make sure the air conditioning system doesn't cycle off as soon as it cools the passenger compartment).

7   With the compressor engaged - the clutch will make an audible click and the center of the clutch will rotate - feel the evaporator inlet and outlet lines at the firewall. The inlet (small diameter) line should feel somewhat warm and the outlet (large diameter) line should feel cold. If so, the system charge is probably adequate.

8   Place a thermometer in the dashboard vent nearest the evaporator and operate the system until the indicated temperature is around 40 to 45 degrees F. If the ambient (outside) air temperature is very high, say 110 degrees F, the duct air temperature may be as high as 60 degrees F, but generally the air conditioning is 30-40 degrees F cooler than the ambient air.

13.1 The end of the evaporator drain hose is located under the vehicle

➡Note: Humidity of the ambient air also affects the cooling capacity of the system. Higher ambient humidity lowers the effectiveness of the air conditioning system.

ADDING REFRIGERANT

♦ Refer to illustrations 13.9, 13.12a, 13.12b and 13.15

9   Buy an automotive charging kit at an auto parts store (see illustration). A charging kit includes a 14-ounce can of refrigerant, a tap valve and a short section of hose that can be attached between the tap valve and the system low side service valve.

✸✸ CAUTION:

Although the system will hold more than one can of refrigerant, don't add more than one can (you could overfill the system).

✸✸ CAUTION:

There are two types of refrigerant used in automotive systems; R-12, which has been widely used on earlier models, and the more environmentally-friendly R-134a used in all models covered by this manual. These two refrigerants (and their appropriate refrigerant oils) are not compatible and must never be mixed or components will be damaged. Use only R-134a refrigerant in the models covered by this manual.

10 Hook up the charging kit by following the manufacturer's instructions.

✸✸ WARNING:

DO NOT hook the charging kit hose to the system high side! The fittings on the charging kit are designed to fit only on the low side of the system.

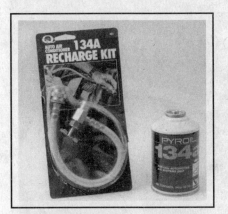

13.9 A basic charging kit for R-134a systems is available at most auto parts stores - it must say R-134a (not R-12) and so should the can of refrigerant

13.12a Cans of R-134a refrigerant (available at auto parts stores) can be added to the 'low side' of the air conditioning system with a simple recharging kit

13.12b Location of the low side (suction) service port (A) and the high side (discharge) service port (B) on a four-cylinder model (V6 models are similar)

11 Back off the valve handle on the charging kit and screw the kit onto the refrigerant can, making sure first that the O-ring or rubber seal inside the threaded portion of the kit is in place.

✳✳ WARNING:

Wear protective eyewear when dealing with pressurized refrigerant cans.

12 Remove the dust cap from the low-side charging connection and attach the quick-connect fitting on the kit hose (see illustrations).

13 Warm up the engine and turn on the air conditioner. Keep the charging kit hose away from the fan and other moving parts.

➡**Note: The charging process requires the compressor to be running. Your compressor may cycle off if the pressure is low due to a low charge. If the clutch cycles off, you can pull the low-pressure cycling switch plug (located at the lower right corner of the condenser) (see illustration 17.2) and attach a jumper wire across the terminals of the electrical connector (on the harness side). This will keep the compressor ON.**

14 Turn the valve handle on the kit until the stem pierces the can, then back the handle out to release the refrigerant. You should be able to hear the rush of gas. Add refrigerant to the low side of the system until the temperature of the evaporator inlet and outlet lines is as described in Step 7. Allow stabilization time between each addition.

15 If you have an accurate thermometer, place it in the center air conditioning vent (see illustration) and note the temperature of the air coming out of the vent. A fully-charged system which is working correctly should cool down to about 40 degrees F. Generally, an air conditioning system will put out air that is 30 to 40 degrees F cooler than the ambient air. For example, if the ambient (outside) air temperature is very high (over 100 degrees F), the temperature of air coming out of the registers should be 60 to 70 degrees F.

16 When the can is empty, turn the valve handle to the closed position and release the connection from the low-side port. Replace the dust cap.

17 Remove the charging kit from the can and store the kit for future use with the piercing valve in the UP position, to prevent inadvertently piercing the can on the next use.

HEATING SYSTEMS

18 If the carpet under the heater core is damp, or if antifreeze vapor or steam is coming through the vents, the heater core is leaking. Remove it (see Section 12) and install a new unit (most radiator shops will not repair a leaking heater core).

19 If the air coming out of the heater vents isn't hot, the problem could stem from any of the following causes:

a) *The thermostat is stuck open, preventing the engine coolant from warming up enough to carry heat to the heater core. Replace the thermostat (see Section 3).*

b) *There is a blockage in the system, preventing the flow of coolant through the heater core. Feel both heater hoses at the firewall. They should be hot. If one of them is cold, there is an obstruction in one of the hoses or in the heater core, or the heater control valve is shut. Detach the hoses and back flush the heater core with a water hose. If the heater core is clear but circulation is impeded, remove the two hoses and flush them out with a water hose.*

c) *If flushing fails to remove the blockage from the heater core, the core must be replaced (see Section 12).*

13.15 Insert a thermometer in the center vent, turn on the air conditioning system and wait for it to cool down; depending on the humidity, the output air should be 30 to 40 degrees cooler than the ambient air temperature

ELIMINATING AIR CONDITIONING ODORS

◆ **Refer to illustration 13.23**

20 Unpleasant odors that often develop in air conditioning systems are caused by the growth of a fungus, usually on the surface of the evaporator core. The warm, humid environment there is a perfect breeding ground for mildew to develop.

21 The evaporator core on most vehicles is difficult to access, and factory dealerships have a lengthy, expensive process for eliminating the fungus by opening up the evaporator case and using a powerful disinfectant and rinse on the core until the fungus is gone. You can service your own system at home, but it takes something much stronger than basic household germ-killers or deodorizers.

22 Aerosol disinfectants for automotive air conditioning systems are available in most auto parts stores, but remember when shopping for them that the most effective treatments are also the most expensive. The basic procedure for using these sprays is to start by running the system in the RECIRC mode for ten minutes with the blower on its highest speed. Use the highest heat mode to dry out the system and keep the compressor from engaging by disconnecting the wiring connector at the compressor (see Section 14).

23 Make sure that the disinfectant can comes with a long spray hose. Point the nozzle through the cabin filter door so that it protrudes inside the evaporator housing (see illustration), and then spray according to the manufacturer's recommendations. Try to cover the whole surface of the evaporator core, by aiming the spray up, down and sideways. Fol-

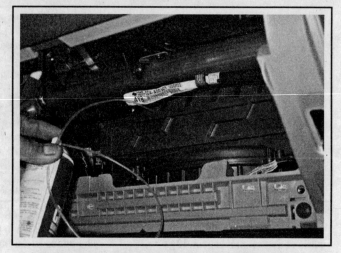

13.23 Remove the glove box (see Chapter 11) and then insert the nozzle of the disinfectant can into the evaporator housing by shoving it through the interior ventilation filter door

low the manufacturer's recommendations for the length of spray and waiting time between applications.

24 Once the evaporator has been cleaned, the best way to prevent the mildew from coming back again is to make sure your evaporator housing drain tube is clear (see illustration 13.1).

14 Air conditioning compressor - removal and installation

❊❊ WARNING:

The air conditioning system is under high pressure. Do not loosen any hose fittings or remove any components until after the system has been discharged. Air conditioning refrigerant must be properly discharged into an EPA-approved recovery/recycling unit at a dealer service department or an automotive air conditioning repair facility. Always wear eye protection when disconnecting air conditioning system fittings.

❊❊ CAUTION:

When replacing entire components, additional refrigerant oil should be added equal to the amount that is removed with the component being replaced. Be sure to read the can before adding any oil to the system, to make sure it is compatible with the R-134a system.

➡**Note: The receiver-drier should be replaced whenever the compressor is replaced.**

REMOVAL

◆ **Refer to illustrations 14.9 and 14.10**

1 Have the air conditioning system refrigerant discharged and

recovered by an air conditioning technician.

2 Disconnect the cable from the negative battery terminal (see Chapter 5, Section 1).

3 Set the parking brake, block the rear wheels and raise the front of the vehicle, supporting it securely on jackstands.

4 Remove the drivebelt (see Chapter 1).

5 Remove the alternator (see Chapter 5).

6 On V6 models, remove the ignition coil cover (see Chapter 5).

7 On V6 models, remove the condenser fan (see Section 4).

8 Remove the splash shield from under the engine compartment (see Chapter 2A).

9 Disconnect the compressor clutch electrical connector (see illustration).

10 Disconnect the refrigerant lines from the compressor. Plug the open fittings immediately to prevent entry of dirt and moisture (see illustration).

11 Remove the compressor mounting bolts (see illustration 14.10).

12 Carefully guide the compressor out of the engine compartment.

➡**Note: On V6 models, be careful not to damage the radiator fins during removal.**

INSTALLATION

13 The clutch may have to be transferred from the old compressor to the new unit.

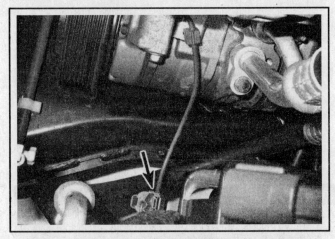

14.9 The location of the compressor clutch electrical connector (four-cylinder model shown, V6 similar)

14.10 Compressor details (four-cylinder model shown, V6 similar)

1   Low side line fitting and fastener
2   High side line fitting and fastener
3   Mounting bolt locations (not all are visible in this photo)

14 Adjust the amount of refrigerant oil in the new compressor using the following calculations:

   a) Drain the refrigerant oil from the old compressor through the suction fitting and measure it in ounces.
   b) Subtract this number from 5-1/3 ounces.
   c) The difference between these two figures is equal to the amount you should drain from the new compressor.

✳✳ CAUTION:

Even if no oil came out of the old compressor, don't drain more than 1-2/3 ounces from the new one.

15 Installation is the reverse of removal, using new O-rings where the line fittings attach to the compressor.

➡**Note: Only use O-rings that are designed specifically for A/C system applications.**

16 Have the system evacuated, recharged and leak tested by an air conditioning technician.

17 Reconnect the battery (see Chapter 5, Section 1).

15 Air conditioning receiver-drier - removal and installation

▶ **Refer to illustration 15.3**

✳✳ WARNING:

The air conditioning system is under high pressure. Do not loosen any hose fittings or remove any components until after the system has been discharged. Air conditioning refrigerant must be properly discharged into an EPA-approved recovery/recycling unit at a dealer service department or an automotive air conditioning repair facility. Always wear eye protection when disconnecting air conditioning system fittings.

✳✳ CAUTION:

When replacing entire components, additional refrigerant oil should be added equal to the amount that is removed with the component being replaced. Be sure to read the can before adding any oil to the system, to make sure it is compatible with the R-134a system.

1   Have the refrigerant discharged and recovered by an air conditioning technician.

2   Remove the condenser (see Section 16).

3   Remove the bracket bolt that mounts the receiver-drier to the condenser (see illustration).

15.3 Air conditioning receiver-drier details

1   Receiver drier
2   Bracket bolt
3   Separate the receiver-drier from the condenser fitting at this point

4   Carefully separate the receiver-drier from the condenser (see illustration 15.3).

5   Installation is the reverse of removal. Be sure to install new O-rings onto the receiver-drier fittings and lightly coat them with refrigerant oil.

➡**Note: Only use O-rings that are designed specifically for A/C system applications.**

If you are replacing the receiver-drier, add 1/3-ounce of refrigerant oil to the new replacement.

6   Reconnect the battery. Refer to Chapter 5, Section 1.

7   Have the system evacuated, charged and leak tested by the shop that discharged it.

16 Air conditioning condenser - removal and installation

❊❊ WARNING:

The air conditioning system is under high pressure. Do not loosen any hose fittings or remove any components until after the system has been discharged. Air conditioning refrigerant must be properly discharged into an EPA-approved recovery/recycling unit at a dealer service department or an automotive air conditioning repair facility. Always wear eye protection when disconnecting air conditioning system fittings.

❊❊ CAUTION:

When replacing entire components, additional refrigerant oil should be added equal to the amount that is removed with the component being replaced. Be sure to read the can before adding any oil to the system, to make sure it is compatible with the R-134a system.

REMOVAL

◗ **Refer to illustrations 16.8 and 16.9**

1   Have the refrigerant discharged and recovered by an air conditioning technician.

2   Disconnect the cable from the negative battery terminal (see Chapter 5, Section 1).

3   On V6 models, remove the battery and battery tray (see Chapter 5).

4   Remove the radiator cover (see illustration 4.18a).

5   Remove the fresh air intake duct cover and tube (see Chapter 4).

6   On V6 models, remove the condenser fan (see Section 4).

7   Remove the radiator brackets (see illustration 6.6).

8   Disconnect the receiver (lower) line from the condenser (see illustration) and the electrical connector for the air conditioning pressure switch (see illustration 17.2). Cap the condenser and line fittings to prevent entry of dirt or moisture.

9   Remove the condenser mounting bolts (see illustration).

10 Remove the discharge (upper) line from the condenser (see illustration 16.8). Cap the condenser and line fittings to prevent entry of dirt or moisture.

11 Carefully lift the condenser out while separating it from its lower mounts to remove it.

INSTALLATION

12 Installation is the reverse of removal. Assemble all connections with new O-rings, lightly lubricated with R-134a refrigerant oil.

➡**Note: Only use O-rings that are designed specifically for A/C system applications.**

If a new condenser was installed, add 5/6-ounce of fresh refrigerant oil.

13 Reconnect the battery. Refer to Chapter 5, Section 1.

14 Have the system evacuated, charged and leak tested by the shop that discharged it.

16.8 The upper and lower line connections to the condenser

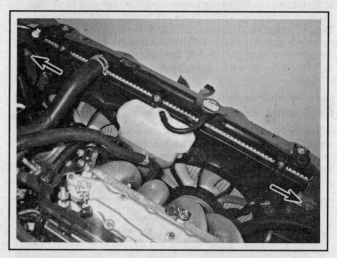

16.9 The location of the condenser mounting bolts

17 Air conditioning pressure switch - replacement

▶ **Refer to illustration 17.2**

✳✳ WARNING:

The air conditioning system is under high pressure. Do not loosen any hose fittings or remove any components until after the system has been discharged. Air conditioning refrigerant must be properly discharged into an EPA-approved recovery/ recycling unit at a dealer service department or an automotive air conditioning repair facility. Always wear eye protection when disconnecting air conditioning system fittings.

➡ **Note: The air conditioning pressure switch detects low and high system pressure and shuts the system off if the pressure exceeds preset values.**

1   Have the refrigerant discharged and recovered by an air conditioning technician.

2   Unplug the electrical connector from the air conditioning pressure switch (see illustration).

➡ **Note: The switch is mounted to the condenser near the lower line fitting.**

3   Unscrew the pressure switch from the condenser.

4   Lubricate the O-ring on the switch with clean refrigerant oil of the correct type.

17.2 The air conditioning pressure switch

5   Screw the new switch in place until hand tight, then tighten it securely.

6   Reconnect the electrical connector.

7   Have the system evacuated, charged and leak tested by the shop that discharged it.

Specifications

General

Radiator cap pressure rating	14 to 18 psi (93 to 123 kPa)
Thermostat rating (opening to fully open temperature range)	169 to 194 degrees F (76 to 90 degrees C)
Cooling system capacity	See Chapter 1
Refrigerant type	R-134a
Refrigerant capacity	Refer to HVAC specification tag

Torque specifications	Ft-lbs (unless otherwise indicated)	Nm

➡**Note: One foot-pound (ft-lb) of torque is equivalent to 12 inch-pounds (in-lbs) of torque. Torque values below approximately 15 ft-lbs are expressed in inch-pounds, since most foot-pound torque wrenches are not accurate at these smaller values.**

Condenser inlet and outlet nuts/bolts	86 in-lbs	10
Condenser bracket bolts	86 in-lbs	10
Radiator bracket bolts	104 in-lbs	12
Thermostat housing cover bolts		
Four-cylinder models	86 in-lbs	10
V6 models	104 in-lbs	12
Water pump bolts	104 in-lbs	12

4

FUEL AND EXHAUST SYSTEMS

Section

Reference to other Chapters

1 General information

AIR INDUCTION SYSTEM

The air induction system consists of the resonator, the air filter assembly, the air intake duct, the throttle body, the intake manifold, the accelerator cable (if equipped) and an array of sensors that monitor the angle of the throttle plate and the amount, temperature and pressure of the incoming air. The resonator is a large plastic reservoir located inside the left front corner of the vehicle, behind the bumper cover and ahead of the inner fender liner, that provides a constant supply of cool ambient air to the air filter housing. The replacement procedures for all of these components - except the intake manifold and the information sensors - are covered in this Chapter. For more information about the intake manifold, refer to Chapter 2. For more information about any information sensors mentioned below, refer to Chapter 6.

2005 and earlier four-cylinder models

The throttle body contains a throttle plate that regulates the amount of air entering the intake manifold. The throttle plate is opened and closed by the accelerator cable. You'll find the procedures for removing, installing and adjusting the accelerator cable and for removing and installing the throttle body in this Chapter. If you ever have to clean, remove, or replace the throttle body, you will be directed to perform the "idle learn procedure" upon completion of this task (see Chapter 5, Section 1).

The Throttle Position (TP) sensor, which is mounted on one end of the throttle plate shaft, is a potentiometer that monitors the opening angle of the throttle plate and sends a proportional voltage signal to the Powertrain Control Module (PCM). The Manifold Absolute Pressure (MAP) sensor, which is located near the throttle body, on the intake manifold, monitors the level of intake manifold vacuum or pressure inside the intake manifold. The Intake Air Temperature (IAT) sensor, which is located on the air intake duct, monitors the temperature of the incoming air. For more information about these sensors, refer to Chapter 6.

An Idle Air Control (IAC) valve is located on the underside of the throttle body. The PCM-controlled IAC valve regulates the amount of air needed to bypass the throttle plate when it's closed during idle conditions. For more information about the IAC valve, refer to Chapter 6.

2006 and later four-cylinder and all V6 models

2006 and later four-cylinder and all V6 models are equipped with an electronic throttle body that does not use a conventional accelerator cable to open and close the throttle plate. Instead, the throttle plate is opened and closed by a PCM-controlled solenoid known as the throttle actuator. There is an "accelerator cable," but it connects the accelerator pedal to the Accelerator Pedal Position (APP) sensor, which is located on the firewall (see Chapter 6 for more information about the APP sensor). The APP sensor (which is actually two sensors - APP sensor "A" and APP sensor "B") monitors the angle of the accelerator pedal and sends a proportional voltage signal to the PCM, which commands the throttle actuator to open or close the throttle plate accordingly. For more information about the APP sensor, refer to Chapter 6.

The Throttle Position (TP) sensor on the electronic throttle body functions much like a conventional TP sensor, except that it's an integral part of the throttle body assembly and thus cannot be serviced separately. The MAP sensor is also located on the throttle body. The MAP sensor is the only component on the throttle body that can be replaced separately from the throttle body. The rest of the throttle body assembly is not serviceable. If anything on the throttle body fails, replace the throttle body. For more information about the APP sensor and the MAP sensor, refer to Chapter 6.

There is no conventional Idle Air Control (IAC) valve on the electronic throttle body. The PCM maintains a steady idle speed by opening and closing the throttle plate in response to factors such as engine load (power steering fluid pressure, air conditioning compressor drag, etc.).

FUEL SYSTEM

The fuel system consists of the fuel tank, the fuel filter, the electric fuel pump, the fuel pressure regulator, the fuel rail, the fuel pulsation damper (four-cylinder models), the fuel injectors and the fuel lines and hoses connecting these components. All models are equipped with Honda's Programmed Fuel Injection (PGM-FI). PGM-FI is a "sequential multiport" system, which means that the fuel injectors deliver fuel directly into the intake ports of the cylinders in firing order sequence. Sequential multiport systems provide much better control of the air/fuel mixture ratio than earlier fuel injection systems, and are therefore able to produce more power, better mileage and lower emissions. For more information about the PGM-FI system, see Section 13. For more information about the PCM and the information sensors, refer to Chapter 6.

Fuel is pumped from the fuel tank to the fuel injection system through a metal line located on the underside of the vehicle, then through a flexible hose that connects the metal line to the fuel rail. All fuel line fittings between the fuel pump and the fuel rail are quick-connect type fittings (see Section 4). The electric fuel pump is located inside the fuel tank and can be accessed through a cover plate in the floor of the vehicle. The fuel pump, fuel pressure regulator, fuel gauge sending unit and fuel filter are integrated into a single assembly. If one of these components must be replaced, you can remove the fuel pump/fuel gauge sending unit, disassemble it and replace the defective part.

The fuel pressure regulator maintains the fuel pressure within the specified operating range. If you ever have to replace the fuel pressure regulator, be sure to take the old unit with you because there are two types of regulators used on these vehicles. On four-cylinder models, one type of regulator is used on non-SULEV models and another type is used on SULEV models. All V6 models use the same pressure regulator as SULEV four-cylinder models.

Four-cylinder models are equipped with a fuel pulsation damper, which is located on the underside of the fuel rail. The pulsation damper mitigates the hydraulic and acoustic "noise" produced by the fuel pump when it's operating. You'll have to remove the fuel rail to remove or replace the pulsation damper.

EXHAUST SYSTEM

The exhaust system consists of the exhaust manifold(s), the catalytic converter(s), the muffler, the tailpipe and the various sections of pipe connecting these components. All four-cylinder and V6 models are equipped with a Three Way Catalytic Converter (TWC), which is located in the exhaust pipe underneath the vehicle. V6 models are also equipped with a pair of Warm Up-Three Way Catalytic Converters (WU-TWCs). The WU-TWCs are bolted directly to the cylinder heads (there are no separate "exhaust manifolds") The main TWC used on all vehicles and the WU-TWCs used on V6 models are all covered in Chapter 6. The information in this Chapter covers maintenance, inspection and service for the rest of the exhaust system, except the exhaust manifold on four-cylinder models, which is in Chapter 2A.

2 Fuel pressure relief procedure

▶ Refer to illustration 2.2

❋❋ WARNING:

Gasoline is extremely flammable, so take extra precautions when you work on any part of the fuel system. Don't smoke or allow open flames or bare light bulbs near the work area, and don't work in a garage where a gas-type appliance (such as a water heater or a clothes dryer) is present. Since gasoline is carcinogenic, wear latex gloves when there's a possibility of being exposed to fuel, and, if you spill any fuel on your skin, rinse it off immediately with soap and water. Mop up any spills immediately and do not store fuel-soaked rags where they could ignite. The fuel system is under constant pressure, so, if any fuel lines are to be disconnected, the fuel pressure in the system must be relieved first. When you perform any kind of work on the fuel system, wear safety glasses and have a Class B type fire extinguisher on hand.

1   Remove the left kick panel (see Chapter 11). (Even though there is a small access door in the kick panel, removing it allows access only to the fuses, not the relays.)

2   Locate the PGM-FI main relay No. 2 (see illustration). Once you have identified the PGM-FI relay No. 2, remove it from the under-dash fuse and relay box.

3   Start the engine. It will cease running immediately. The fuel pressure is now relieved, but there is still fuel in the lines, so be sure to have shop rags handy to mop up any spilled fuel when disconnecting fuel lines.

➡**Note: If the Malfunction Indicator Light (MIL) on the instrument cluster comes on while you're cranking the engine, ignore it. The PCM is simply responding to a lean condition and setting**

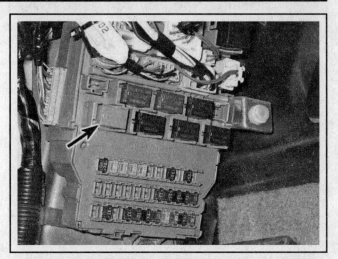

2.2 You'll find PGM-FI main relay No. 2 (fuel pump relay) in the under-dash fuse and relay box

the Diagnostic Trouble Code(s) (DTCs) for lean misfires. The DTCs won't remain in the PCM's memory because they'll be erased when you disconnect the battery.

4   Remove the fuel filler neck cap to relieve the pressure inside the fuel tank.

5   Make sure that you have the anti-theft code for the radio (and navigation system, if equipped) and jot down the frequencies for the radio's station's pre-set buttons. Then disconnect the cable from the negative terminal of the battery (see Chapter 5, Section 1). It's now safe to work on the fuel system.

3 Fuel pump/fuel pressure - check

❋❋ WARNING:

Gasoline is extremely flammable, so take extra precautions when you work on any part of the fuel system. See the Warning in Section 2.

GENERAL CHECKS

1   Verify that there is fuel in the fuel tank.

2   Verify that the fuel pump actually runs. Turn the ignition switch to ON - you should hear a brief whirring noise for about two seconds as the pump comes on and pressurizes the system.

➡**Note: If you can't hear the pump from inside the vehicle, open the fuel filler neck cap, then have an assistant turn the ignition switch to ON while you listen to the pump through the fuel filler neck. If the pump doesn't run, it is either not receiving voltage or it is faulty.**

FUEL PUMP PRESSURE TEST

▶ Refer to illustrations 3.7 and 3.9

3   To measure the fuel pressure, you'll need a fuel pressure gauge capable of reading at least 60 psi (414 kPa). You'll also need some fuel hose for tee-ing into the fuel system at the quick-connect fitting between the fuel supply hose and the fuel rail. And, finally, you'll need an adapter suitable for connecting one end of the gauge hose to the female side of the quick-connect fitting. Fuel pressure gauges and fuel hoses are available at most auto parts stores and automotive retailers. Adapters are sometimes a little more difficult to find. If you can't find the adapter that you need, contact a specialty tool manufacturer.

4   Before getting started, make sure that you have the anti-theft code for the radio and, if equipped, the navigation system. Also write down the radio station presets.

5   Relieve the system fuel pressure (see Section 2).

6   Disconnect the cable from the negative battery terminal (see Chapter 5, Section 1).

3.7 On four-cylinder models, pull off these two plastic covers (A) from the quick-connect fittings that connect this short section of hose (B) to the fuel supply line and to the fuel rail, then disconnect both quick connect fittings (see Section 4) and remove the hose

7   On four-cylinder models, remove the covers from the quick-connect fittings at both ends of the short section of fuel hose that connects the fuel supply line to the fuel rail (see illustration), then disconnect the quick-connect fittings at both ends of the hose (see Section 4).

8   On V6 models, locate the fuel supply line quick-connect fitting at the left end of the rear cylinder head. Remove the cover from the quick-connect fitting and disconnect the quick-connect fitting (see Section 4).

9   Tee your fuel pressure gauge into the fuel system at the point where you just opened it up (see illustration).

10 Reconnect the battery.

11 Make sure that the air conditioning and any other electrical systems are turned off, then turn the ignition switch to ON but don't start the engine yet. The fuel pump should run for about two seconds - pressure should register on the gauge and should hold steady.

12 Start the engine and let it warm up until it's idling at its normal operating temperature.

13 If the fuel pressure is not within specifications, check the following:

3.9 This is what your test rig looks like correctly installed (four-cylinder model shown, V6 models similar)

a) If the pressure is lower than specified, check for a restriction in the fuel system (this includes the fuel line and the inlet strainer at the fuel pump). If no restriction is found, replace the fuel pressure regulator (see Section 7) and the fuel filter (see Section 8), then recheck the fuel pressure. If the fuel pressure is still low, the fuel pump is probably faulty.

b) If the fuel pressure is higher than specified, replace the fuel pressure regulator (see Section 7).

14 If the indicated fuel pressure is outside the operating range listed in this Chapter's Specifications,

15 After the test is complete, relieve the system fuel pressure (see Section 2), then disconnect the cable from the negative battery terminal (see Chapter 5, Section 1).

16 Disconnect your fuel pressure testing rig, then reconnect the fuel supply line quick-connect fitting (see Section 4).

17 Reconnect the cable to the negative battery terminal (see Chapter 5, Section 1).

18 Start the engine and check for fuel leaks.

4   Fuel lines and fittings - general information

▶ Refer to illustrations 4.3a and 4.3b

❋❋ WARNING:

Gasoline is extremely flammable, so take extra precautions when you work on any part of the fuel system. See the Warning in Section 2.

1   Always relieve the fuel pressure before servicing fuel lines or fittings (see Section 2), then disconnect the cable from the negative battery terminal (see Chapter 5, Section 1) before proceeding.

2   The fuel supply lines connect the fuel pump in the fuel tank to the fuel rail on the engine. The Evaporative Emission (EVAP) system vapor lines connect the fuel tank to the EVAP canister and connect the canister to the intake manifold. Whenever you're working under the vehicle, be sure to inspect all fuel and evaporative emission lines for leaks, kinks, dents and other damage. Always replace a damaged fuel or EVAP line immediately. Leaking fuel and EVAP lines will result in loss of fuel and excessive air pollution (the leaking raw fuel emits unburned hydrocarbon vapors into the atmosphere).

Disconnecting Fuel Line Fittings

Two-tab type fitting; depress both tabs with your fingers, then pull the fuel line and the fitting apart

On this type of fitting, depress the two buttons on opposite sides of the fitting, then pull it off the fuel line

Threaded fuel line fitting; hold the stationary portion of the line or component (A) while loosening the tube nut (B) with a flare-nut wrench

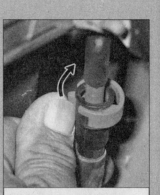

Plastic collar-type fitting; rotate the outer part of the fitting

Metal collar quick-connect fitting; pull the end of the retainer off the fuel line, and disengage the other end from the female side of the fitting . . .

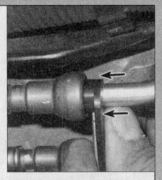

. . . insert a fuel line separator tool into the female side of the fitting, push it into the fitting until it releases the locking tabs inside the fitting, and pull the two halves of the fitting apart

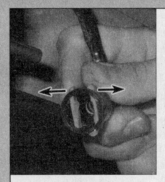

Hairpin-type clip; spread the two legs of the clip apart . . .

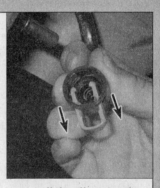

. . . pull the clip out and detach the coupling from the component (fitting detached for clarity)

Spring-lock coupling; remove the safety cover . . .

. . . install a coupling release tool and close the clamshell halves of the tool around the coupling . . .

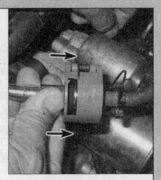

. . . push the tool into the fitting, then pull the two lines apart

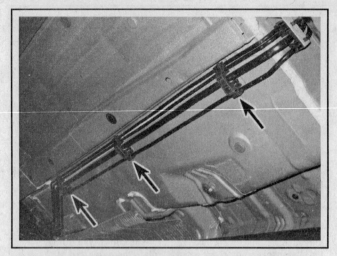

4.3a The fuel and EVAP lines are secured to the underside of the vehicle by several plastic brackets

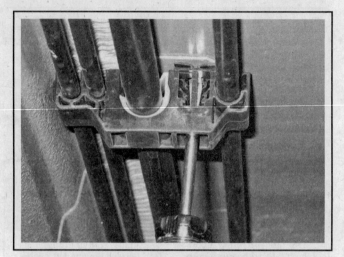

4.3b To release this type of fuel/EVAP line bracket from the underside of the vehicle, insert a screwdriver as shown and spread the teeth apart to release them from the mounting stud, then disengage the bracket from the fuel and EVAP lines

3   All lines are secured to the underbody with small plastic or metal brackets that are attached to the vehicle floorpan (see illustration). Some of these brackets consist of small steel frames with rubber insulators. To detach one of these brackets, simply unbolt it and disassemble it. Other brackets are secured to the pan by two rows of serrated teeth that clamp onto the threads of a fixed stud welded to the underside of the vehicle. To detach one of these plastic brackets from the pan, insert a flat-blade screwdriver into the bracket from directly below (see illustration), then twist the screwdriver to disengage the serrated teeth from the threads of the stud. Once the teeth are disengaged from the stud threads, carefully disengage the clamp from the fuel/EVAP lines. When you remove one of these brackets, it's a good idea to have some new brackets handy, because once you've detached a bracket it might not fit as tightly onto the stud when you install it again. If a bracket feels loose after installation, replace it.

4   If you find signs of dirt in the lines during disassembly, disconnect all lines and blow them out with compressed air. Inspect the fuel strainer on the fuel pump pick-up unit (see Section 6) for damage and deterioration. And inspect the fuel filter, which is an integral component of the fuel pump/fuel gauge sending unit (see Section 8).

STEEL TUBING

5   Because fuel lines used on fuel-injected vehicles are under fairly high pressure, it is critical that they be replaced with lines of equivalent specification. If you have to replace a fuel line, use only steel tubing that meets the manufacturer's specifications. Don't use copper or aluminum tubing to replace steel tubing. These materials cannot withstand normal vehicle vibration.

6   Some steel fuel lines have threaded fittings. When loosening these fittings to service or replace components:

  a) *Always hold the stationary fitting with a wrench while turning the tube nut (this will prevent the line from twisting).*
  b) *If you're going to replace one of these fittings, use original equipment parts or parts that meet original equipment standards.*

PLASTIC TUBING

7   Some fuel lines - between the fuel supply and return pipes of the fuel pump and the front of the fuel tank, for example - are plastic. If you ever have to replace either line, use only the original equipment plastic tubing.

✳✳ CAUTION:

When removing or installing plastic fuel line tubing, be careful not to bend or twist it too much, which can damage it. And damaged fuel lines MUST be replaced! Also, be aware that the plastic fuel tubing is NOT heat resistant, so keep it away from excessive heat. Nor is it acid-proof, so don't wipe it off with a shop rag that has been used to wipe off battery electrolyte. If you accidentally spill or wipe electrolyte on plastic fuel tubing, replace the tubing.

FLEXIBLE HOSES

✳✳ WARNING:

Use only original equipment replacement hoses or their equivalent. Unapproved hoses might fail when subjected to the high operating pressures of the fuel system.

8   Don't route fuel hoses (or metal lines) within four inches of the exhaust system or within ten inches of the catalytic converter. Make sure that no rubber hoses are installed directly against the vehicle, particularly in places where there is any vibration. If allowed to touch some vibrating part of the vehicle, a hose can easily become chafed and it might start leaking. A good rule of thumb is to maintain a minimum of 1/4-inch clearance around a hose (or metal line) to prevent contact with the vehicle underbody.

4.9 Quick-connect fitting color code

Retainer location	Manufacturer	Retainer color	Pipe diameter
Non-SULEV four-cylinder models			
Engine compartment fuel feed hose A, fuel rail side	Tokai	Blue/green	0.3 in (8 mm)
Engine compartment fuel feed hose B, fuel feed hose B side and fuel hose B	Tokai	Green	0.2 in (6.3 mm)
Fuel pump: fuel feed line, fuel pump side	Tokai	Orange	0.4 in (9.5 mm)
Fuel pump: fuel feed line, fuel line side	Tokai	Green	0.2 in (6.3 mm)
EVAP canister, fuel vapor line	Tokai	Orange	0.4 in (9.5 mm)
SULEV four-cylinder models			
Fuel pump: fuel feed neck tube	Tokai	Gray	1.1 in (28.55 mm)
Fuel pump: fuel tank vapor recirculation tube	Tokai	Natural	0.5 in (11.8 mm)
Fuel pump: Fuel feed tank vapor signal tube, fuel tank side	Tokai	Green	0.2 in (6.3 mm)
Fuel pump: Fuel tank vapor signal tube, fuel filler side	Tokai	Blue/green	0.3 in (8 mm)
V6 models			
Engine compartment	Tokai	Blue/green	0.3 in (8 mm)
Fuel pump: fuel feed line, fuel pump side	Tokai	Orange	0.4 in (9.5 mm)
Fuel pump: fuel feed line, fuel line side	Tokai	Green	0.2 in (6.3 mm)
EVAP canister: fuel vapor line	Tokai	Orange	0.4 in (9.5 mm)

DISCONNECTING AND RECONNECTING FUEL SYSTEM FITTINGS

▶ **Refer to illustrations 4.9, 4.11, 4.12, 4.13, 4.14, 4.15 and 4.16**

❋❋ CAUTION:

When disconnecting or reconnecting quick-connect fittings, be careful not to bend or twist them excessively, or they will be damaged and will have to be replaced. Also, be aware that the quick-connect fittings are NOT heat resistant, so keep them away from excessive heat. Nor are they acid-proof, so don't wipe them off with a shop rag that has been used to wipe off battery electrolyte. If you accidentally spill or wipe electrolyte on quick-connect fittings, replace them.

9   There are quick-connect fittings at both ends of the fuel supply line (at the fuel pump and at the fuel rail, and at some EVAP line fittings as well). You MUST replace the quick-connect fitting retainers whenever you disconnect a quick-connect fitting. It is critical that you use the correct replacement retainer, which depends on the manufacturer of the tubing and the end of the tube (fuel pump end or fuel rail end) on which you're installing it, because the retainers are not all the same diameter. To help you identify the retainer(s) you're replacing, Honda color codes them (see illustration).

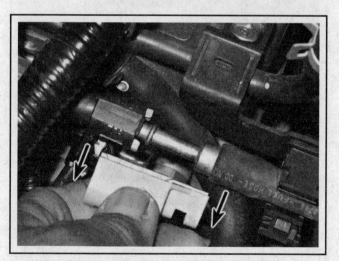

4.11 To remove the protective cover (if equipped) from a quick-connect fitting, simply pull it straight off

10 Relieve the system fuel pressure (see Section 2), then disconnect the cable from the negative battery terminal (see Chapter 5, Section 1).

11 Remove the quick-connect fitting cover (see illustration) if equipped.

12 Holding the black side of the fitting with one hand, squeeze the retainer tabs with a pair of needle nose pliers to release them, then pull

4.12 To disconnect a quick-connect fitting, squeeze the retainer tabs and pull the two halves of the fitting apart until they're separated

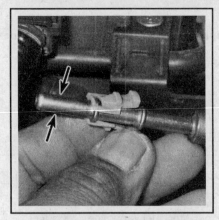

4.13 Spread apart the sides of the old retainer, remove it and discard it, then inspect the contact surface of the fuel line for dirt, damage and rust

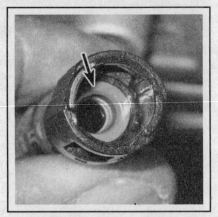

4.14 Whenever you disconnect a quick-connect fitting, be sure to inspect the O-ring inside the fitting. If it's cracked, torn or damaged, replace it

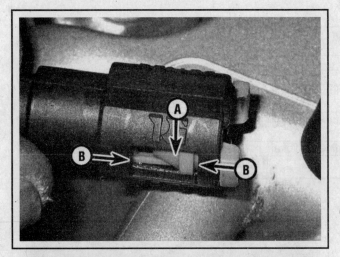

4.15 Insert a new retainer into the female side of the fitting and align the retainer's locking pawls (A) with the windows (B) in the connector

4.16 To reconnect a quick-connect fitting, push the female side of the fitting onto the male side until the locking pawls of the retainer snap into place on the raised ridge on the male pipe

the two halves of the fitting apart (see illustration). Cover the disconnected ends of the fitting with plastic bags to keep out dirt and moisture.

13 Remove the old retainer from the fitting and inspect the contact surface area on the fuel line for dirt and damage (see illustration). If it's dirty, wipe it off with a clean shop rag. If it's rusty, remove and inspect the fuel lines, then remove and inspect the fuel pump (see Section 6), the fuel pressure regulator (see Section 7) and the fuel filter (see Section 8). If any of these components are damaged, replace them (see Sections 6, 7 and 8, respectively).

14 Inspect the old O-ring inside the bore of the fitting (see illustration). If it's cracked, torn or otherwise damaged, replace it.

15 Insert a new retainer into the female side of the fitting (see illus-

tration). Be sure to align the locking pawls of the retainer with the "windows" in the sides of the connector.

16 Press the two halves of the quick-connect fitting together until the locking pawls on the both retainer tabs are locked into place by the ridge on the male end of the fuel pipe (see illustration). You'll hear a clicking sound when the pawls snap into place.

17 Verify that the quick-connect fitting is correctly reconnected by trying to pull the two halves of the connector apart.

18 Install any components that you had to remove to access the fuel line or EVAP line fitting(s).

19 Reconnect the cable to the negative battery terminal (see Chapter 5, Section 1).

20 Start the engine and check for leaks.

5 Fuel pump/fuel gauge sending unit - removal and installation

♦ Refer to illustrations 5.4, 5.5, 5.6, 5.7a, 5.7b, 5.7c, 5.8 and 5.10

✳✳ WARNING:

Gasoline is extremely flammable, so take extra precautions when you work on any part of the fuel system. See the Warning in Section 2.

1   Relieve the fuel system pressure (see Section 2), then remove the fuel filler neck cap to relieve any pressure inside the fuel tank.

2   Disconnect the cable from the negative battery terminal (see Chapter 5, Section 1).

3   Remove the carpeting from the floor of the trunk.

4   Remove the fuel pump access cover screws (see illustration) and remove the fuel pump access cover.

5   Disconnect the electrical connector from the fuel pump/fuel gauge sending unit (see illustration).

6   Disconnect the quick-connect fitting for the fuel supply line (see illustration) and set the supply line aside.

7   On non-SULEV models, remove the fuel pump/fuel gauge sending unit locknut (see illustrations). On SULEV models, remove the six fuel pump retaining nuts (see illustration).

5.4 To detach the fuel pump access cover from the trunk floor, remove these screws

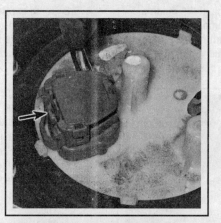

5.5 To disconnect the electrical connector from the fuel pump/fuel gauge sending unit, depress this locking tab and pull the connector straight up

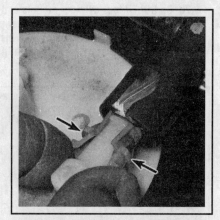

5.6 To disconnect the fuel supply line quick-connect fitting from the fuel pump, depress these two release tabs and pull off the fitting

5.7a This is the special tool for loosening and tightening the fuel pump/fuel gauge sending unit locknut on non-SULEV four-cylinder models. If you're able to obtain one of these tools this is the way to go because it won't damage the plastic locknut

5.7b If you're unable to obtain the special tool, use a large pair of water pump pliers to loosen the locknut on non-SULEV four-cylinder models

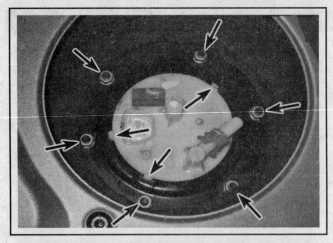

5.7c On SULEV four-cylinder models and on all V6 models, remove these six nuts to detach the fuel pump/fuel gauge sending unit from the fuel tank. When installing the flange, make sure that the three notches are aligned with their corresponding lugs on top of the pump

5.8 Being careful not to damage the fuel gauge sending unit float arm and float, remove the fuel pump/fuel gauge sending unit from the tank. After removing the pump/sending unit, inspect the condition of the seal around the top of the module

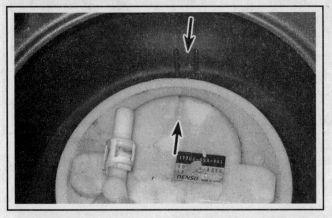

5.10 When installing the fuel pump/fuel gauge sending unit on a non-SULEV model, make sure that the index mark on top of the fuel pump/fuel gauge sending unit is pointing between the two marks on the edge of the hole

8   Remove the fuel pump/fuel gauge sending unit from the tank (see illustration). When removing the pump/fuel gauge sending unit from the

tank, carefully angle it out to protect the float arm and float from damage. After removing the pump/fuel gauge sending unit, inspect the seal for cracks, tears and deterioration. If it's damaged, replace it.

9   Before installing the fuel pump/fuel gauge sending unit in the fuel tank, install a new gasket in the hole first. Don't try to install it with the fuel pump/fuel gauge sending unit, which might cause it to become pinched or distorted.

10   When installing the fuel pump/fuel gauge sending unit on a non-SULEV model, be sure to align the index mark on top of the module between the two marks on the edge of the hole (see illustration).

11   When installing the mounting flange on a SULEV model or on a V6 model, make sure that the three asymmetrically-located notches in the mounting flange are aligned with their corresponding lugs on top of the pump assembly (see illustration 5.7c).

12   Before reconnecting the fuel supply line quick-connect fitting, be sure to replace the O-ring inside the fitting (see Section 4).

13   Installation is otherwise the reverse of removal. On non-SULEV models, be sure to tighten the fuel pump/fuel gauge sending unit locknut securely. When installing the fuel pump/fuel gauge sending unit on an SULEV model, be sure to tighten the retaining nuts to the torque listed in this Chapter's Specifications.

6   Fuel pump/fuel gauge sending unit - replacement

▶ **Refer to illustrations 6.4, 6.5, 6.6, 6.7, 6.8, 6.9 and 6.10**

✳✳ WARNING:

Gasoline is extremely flammable, so take extra precautions when you work on any part of the fuel system. See the Warning in Section 2.

1   Relieve the system fuel pressure (see Section 2), then remove the fuel filler neck cap to relieve any pressure inside the fuel tank.

2   Disconnect the cable from the negative battery terminal (see Chapter 5, Section 1).

3   Remove the fuel pump/fuel gauge sending unit from the fuel tank

(see Section 5) and place it on a clean workbench.

4   Disconnect the electrical connector for the fuel gauge sending unit (see illustration).

5   Remove the fuel gauge sending unit from the fuel pump assembly (see illustration).

6   Disconnect the fuel pump electrical connector and ground wire (see illustration).

7   Remove the fuel pump retainer from the fuel pump housing (see illustration).

8   Remove the rubber insulator from the fuel pump (see illustration).

9   Remove the fuel strainer from the inlet end of the fuel pump (see illustration).

10   Remove the fuel pump from the pump housing (see illustration).

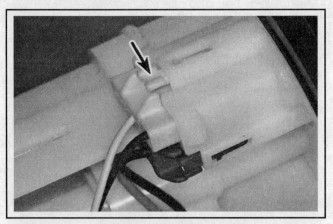

6.4 To disconnect the electrical connector for the fuel gauge sending unit, depress this release tab

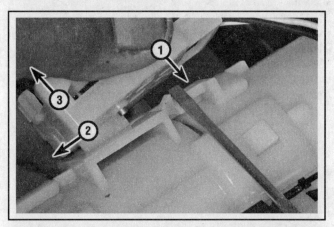

6.5 To detach the fuel gauge sending unit from the fuel pump assembly, depress the lock tab (1), slide the sending unit down (2) so that its mounting tab is in the wider part of its mounting slot, then lift up (3) to disengage the mounting tab from its mounting slot

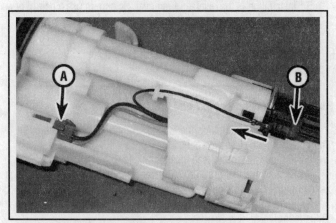

6.6 To disconnect the fuel pump electrical connector, depress the locking tab (A); to disconnect the ground wire, depress the rolled end (B) of the ground wire terminal and slide out the terminal

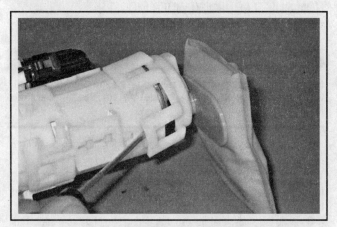

6.7 To disengage the fuel pump retainer from the fuel pump housing, pry the lock tabs off their corresponding lugs, then pull off the retainer

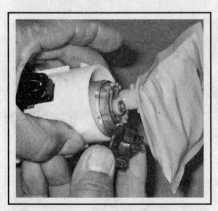

6.8 Remove the rubber insulator from the inlet end of the fuel pump

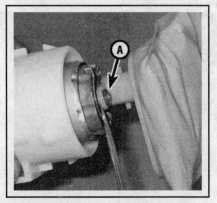

6.9 To detach the fuel strainer from the pump inlet, insert a small screwdriver between the strainer mounting flange and carefully pry it loose until the retaining washer (A) is freed from the stud (a new retaining washer should be used when installing the strainer)

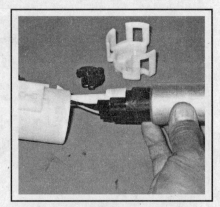

6.10 Pull the fuel pump out of the pump housing. Be careful not to snag the pump power feed wire or the ground wire. If either lead becomes entangled, stop and detangle it. Do NOT use force to pull out either lead

11 If you want to replace the fuel filter, refer to Section 8.

➡Note: Although there is no scheduled maintenance interval for the fuel filter in Chapter 1, you should replace it anytime that the fuel pump pressure drops below the specified minimum.

12 Wash the fuel inlet strainer thoroughly in clean solvent, dry it off and inspect it for tears, cracks, clogging any other damage. If the strainer is damaged or worn, replace it.

13 Be sure to use a new retaining washer when installing the strainer. Installation is otherwise the reverse of removal.

14 Before installing the fuel pump access cover, be sure to connect the cable to the negative battery terminal (see Chapter 5, Section 1), start the engine and check for fuel leaks at the pump fuel line connection. If there are no leaks, install the access cover and the trunk carpet.

7 Fuel pressure regulator - replacement

NON-SULEV FOUR-CYLINDER MODELS

❉❉ WARNING:

Gasoline is extremely flammable, so take extra precautions when you work on any part of the fuel system. See the Warning in Section 2.

1 Remove the fuel pump/fuel gauge sending unit (see Section 5) and place it on a clean workbench.

2 Remove the clip that secures the fuel pressure regulator to the fuel pump/fuel gauge sending unit and pull the regulator out of the fuel pump/fuel gauge sending unit.

3 Note the sleeve that fits over the O-ring end of the regulator. This sleeve must be installed in the correct location for the regulator to fit tightly into the fuel pump/fuel gauge sending unit.

4 Remove and discard the two old fuel pressure regulator O-rings.

5 Installation is the reverse of removal. Be sure to use a pair of new O-rings and don't forget to install the sleeve.

SULEV FOUR-CYLINDER MODELS AND ALL V6 MODELS

▶ **Refer to illustrations 7.7 and 7.8**

6 Remove the fuel pump/fuel gauge sending unit (see Section 5) and place it on a clean workbench.

7 Remove the holder (see illustration).

8 Remove the fuel pressure regulator from the fuel pump/fuel gauge sending unit (see illustration).

9 Remove and discard the old fuel pressure regulator O-ring (see illustration).

10 Installation is the reverse of removal. Be sure to use a new O-ring. Coat the O-ring with a little clean engine oil to protect it from kinking or pinching during installation of the regulator.

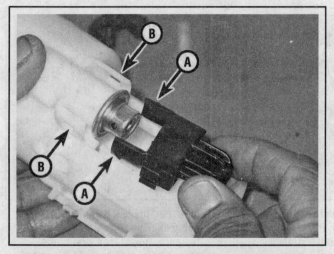

7.7 To detach the fuel pressure regulator holder from the fuel pump, depress these two lugs (A), disengage them from the locking tabs (B) on the pump assembly and pull off the holder (SULEV four-cylinder models and all V6 models)

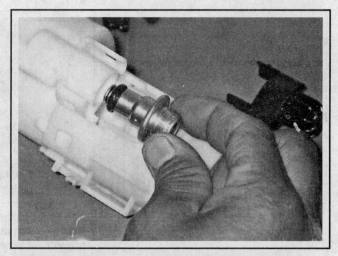

7.8 To remove the fuel pressure regulator from the fuel pump/fuel gauge sending unit, grasp it firmly and pull it straight out (SULEV four-cylinder models and all V6 models)

8 Fuel filter - replacement

▶ **Refer to illustrations 8.4, 8.5 and 8.6**

➡**Note: The fuel filter, which is located in the fuel tank, is an integral part of the fuel pump/fuel gauge sending unit assembly. There is no scheduled maintenance interval for the filter in Chapter 1. But you should replace the filter if the fuel pressure ever drops below the operating pressure listed in this Chapter's Specifications, assuming that the fuel pump and the fuel pressure regulator are okay.**

1   Remove the fuel pump/fuel gauge sending unit (see Section 5).

2   Remove the fuel gauge sending unit and the fuel pump from the fuel filter housing (see Section 6).

3   Remove the fuel pressure regulator from the fuel filter housing (see Section 7).

4   Remove the lower case from the fuel filter housing (see illustration).

5   Remove the fuel pump outlet pipe from the fuel filter housing (see illustration).

6   Remove the gasket from the fuel filter housing (see illustration) if you haven't already done so.

7   Coat the O-rings with clean engine oil only. Use all of the new parts supplied in the replacement kit.

✳✳ CAUTION:

Do not pinch or damage the O-rings during assembly and installation.

8   Installation is the reverse of removal.

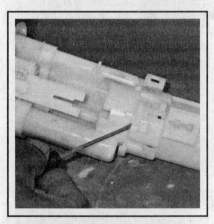

8.4 To detach the lower part of the fuel filter housing, pry the locking tabs loose from their corresponding lugs and pull it off

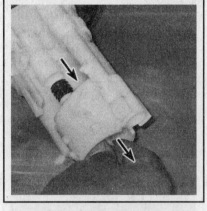

8.5 To remove the fuel pump outlet pipe from the fuel filter housing, pull it straight out

8.6 If you haven't already removed the gasket from the fuel filter housing, do so now

9 Fuel tank - removal and installation

▶ **Refer to illustrations 9.5a, 9.5b, 9.8, 9.9, 9.10, 9.16 and 9.18**

✳✳ WARNING:

Gasoline is extremely flammable, so take extra precautions when you work on any part of the fuel system. See the Warning in Section 2.

1   Relieve the fuel system pressure (see Section 2).

2   The following procedure is much easier to perform if the fuel tank is empty. The tank has no drain plug, so the fuel must be siphoned from the tank with a siphoning kit, which is available at most auto parts stores. Remove the fuel pump/fuel gauge sending unit (see Section 5). Then, using the hole for the fuel pump/fuel gauge sending unit, siphon as much fuel out of the tank as possible.

✳✳ WARNING:

Always siphon fuel into an approved gasoline container. Also, never start the siphoning action by mouth!

3   Make sure that the parking brake lever is in the released position (because you're going to disconnect the parking brake cables).

4   Loosen the rear wheel lug nuts, raise the vehicle and place it securely on jackstands, then remove the rear wheels.

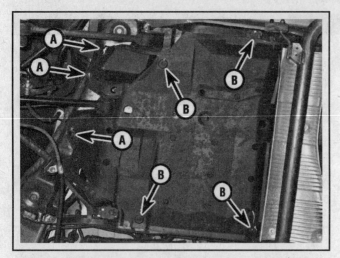

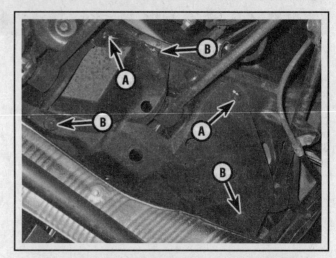

9.5a On SULEV four-cylinder models, remove the left fuel tank cover (2003 model shown, other SULEV four-cylinder models similar, but not identical, in shape and bolt pattern)

A   Push fasteners   B   Bolts

9.5b On SULEV four-cylinder models, remove the right fuel tank cover (2003 model shown, other SULEV four-cylinder models similar, but not identical, in shape and bolt pattern)

A   Push fasteners   B   Bolts

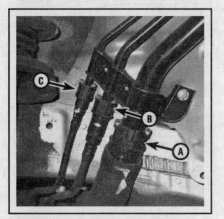

9.8 On SULEV four-cylinder models, disconnect the quick-connect fittings for the fuel filler neck hose (A), the fuel tank vapor recirculation line (B) and the fuel tank vapor signal line (C) (non-SULEV four-cylinder models and V6 models use spring-type hose clamps)

9.9 To disconnect the vapor line fitting (A) from the EVAP canister, depress the two square buttons on the fitting and pull off the fitting

9.10 Disconnect this fuel line quick-connect fitting (A), which is located near the EVAP canister. On SULEV four-cylinder models, also disconnect the EVAP air filter hose (B) (non-SULEV four-cylinder models and V6 models do not have this hose)

5   On SULEV models, remove the fuel tank covers (see illustrations).

6   Disconnect the exhaust system from the rear mounting flange of the catalytic converter (see Chapter 6) all the way back to the muffler. This is a one-piece assembly that hangs from three rubber hangers. While the exhaust system is removed, be sure to inspect the condition of these rubber hangers (see Section 18).

7   On non-SULEV four-cylinder models and on all V6 models, loosen the spring-type hose clamps and disconnect the fuel filler neck hose and the fuel tank vapor hose. Inspect these two hoses for cracks, tears and other deterioration. If either hose is damaged or worn, replace it.

8   On SULEV four-cylinder models, disconnect the quick-connect

fittings for the fuel filler neck, the fuel tank vapor recirculation hose and the fuel tank vapor signal hose (see illustration). (If you're unfamiliar with quick-connect fittings, see Section 4.) Inspect all three hoses for cracks, tears and other deterioration. If a hose is damaged or worn, replace it.

9   Disconnect the vapor line fitting at the EVAP canister (see illustration).

10   Disconnect the quick-connect fitting (next to the EVAP canister) for the fuel line (see illustration).

11   Locate the two rear wheel speed sensors (see Section 2 in Chapter 9), trace each sensor lead up to the electrical connector and disconnect it.

12   On models with rear drum brakes, remove or disconnect the fol-

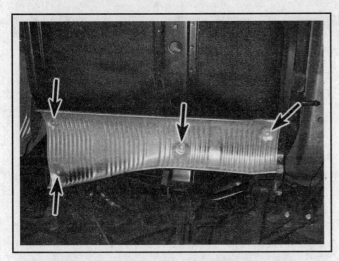

9.16 To detach the exhaust system heat shield, remove these bolts

9.18 Rear suspension subframe mounting bolts

lowing items (refer to Chapter 9 if necessary):

  a) *Disconnect each brake hose from the metal brake line.*
  b) *Remove the bolts that attach the brake backing plates to the rear knuckles.*
  c) *Disconnect the parking brake cables from the rear parking brake levers.*

13 On models with rear disc brakes, remove or disconnect the following items (refer to Chapter 9 if necessary):

  a) *Disconnect the parking brake cables from the rear calipers.*
  b) *Remove the rear brake caliper bolts and remove the calipers from the rear knuckles.*
  c) *Detach the brake hose brackets from the rear knuckles.*
  d) *Using old coat hanger wire or something similar, hang the rear calipers from the coil springs.*

14 Remove the lower shock absorber mounting bolts.
15 Detach the parking brake cable brackets.
16 Remove the exhaust system heat shield (see illustration).
17 Support the suspension subframe with a transmission jack. If you don't have a transmission jack, use a pair of floor jacks.
18 Remove the rear suspension subframe mounting bolts (see illustration). Carefully lower the suspension subframe and fuel tank assembly.
19 Unbolt the four fuel tank retaining strap bolts and carefully lift the fuel tank out of the subframe.
20 Installation is the reverse of removal. Be sure to tighten the fuel tank strap bolts and the rear suspension subframe bolts to the torque listed in this Chapter's Specifications.

10 Fuel tank cleaning and repair - general information

1 Any repairs to the fuel tank or filler neck should be carried out by a professional who has experience in this critical and potentially dangerous work. Even after cleaning and flushing of the fuel system, explosive fumes can remain and ignite during repair of the tank.

2 If the fuel tank is removed from the vehicle, it should not be placed in an area where sparks or open flames could ignite the fumes coming out of the tank. Be especially careful inside garages where a gas-type appliance is located.

11 Air filter housing - removal and installation

AIR INTAKE DUCT

▶ **Refer to illustration 11.1**

1   On non-SULEV 2003 and 2004 four-cylinder models (except LX-P models), disconnect the electrical connector from the IAT sensor, which is located on the air filter housing end of the air intake duct. On 2003 and 2004 SULEV four-cylinder models, LX-P models and all 2005 four-cylinder models, disconnect the electrical connector from the MAF/IAT sensor (see illustration). (This step doesn't apply to V6 models.)

2   Loosen the spring-type hose clamp and disconnect the PCV fresh air intake hose from the air intake duct.

3   On four-cylinder models, disconnect the intake air bypass control thermal valve hose from the air intake duct.

4   On four-cylinder models, detach the wiring harness from the air intake duct.

5   Loosen the hose clamp at the throttle-body-end of the duct.

6   Pull off the upper end of the air intake duct from the air filter housing. (This end of the duct uses a retainer spring instead of a hose clamp to secure it to the air filter housing. It's not necessary to loosen the spring; just pull off the duct.)

7   Remove the air intake duct.

8   Installation is the reverse of removal.

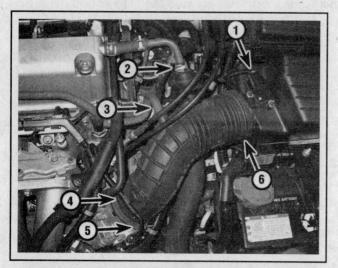

11.1 Air intake duct removal and installation details (four-cylinder models):

1   Disconnect the electrical connector from the MAF/IAT sensor (SULEV model shown; non-SULEV models have an IAT sensor instead, which is located on the air intake duct, near the throttle body)

2   Loosen this spring-type hose clamp and disconnect the PCV fresh air intake hose from the intake duct

3   Disconnect the intake air bypass control thermal valve hose from the intake duct

4   Detach this wiring harness from the air intake duct

5   Loosen this hose clamp screw, then pull off the lower end of the air intake duct from the throttle body

6   The upper end of the air intake duct is secured to the air filter housing by a retaining spring. To disconnect this end of the duct from the air filter housing, simply pull it off

AIR FILTER HOUSING

▶ **Refer to illustration 11.10**

9   Remove the air intake duct (see Steps 1 through 7).

10 Detach the battery cable harness clip (see illustration).

11 Remove the air filter housing mounting bolt.

12 Remove the air filter housing assembly.

13 Installation is the reverse of removal.

RESONATOR

▶ **Refer to illustrations 11.14, 11.15 and 11.17**

➡**Note: The resonator is the large "cold air box" located at the front left corner of the vehicle, in the void between the front bumper cover and the inner fender splash shield. The purpose of the resonator is to provide a large volume of ambient air from which the air induction system can draw intake air. Because it's isolated from the engine compartment, the resonator can provide cooler air to the induction system. And cooler air is denser, which means it has more oxygen in it.**

14 Open the hood and remove the cover from the ambient air intake duct (see illustration).

15 Remove the ambient air intake duct (see illustration).

16 Remove the front bumper cover (see Chapter 11).

17 Remove the resonator mounting bolts (see illustration).

18 Remove the resonator assembly.

19 Installation is the reverse of removal.

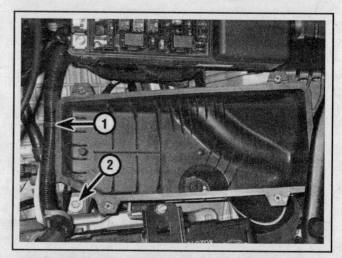

11.10 To remove the air filter housing, detach this clip (1) that secures the battery cable and remove the filter housing mounting bolt (2) (four-cylinder model shown, V6 models similar)

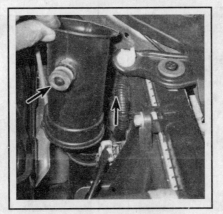

11.14 To detach the cover from the ambient air intake duct, pull out these two push pins (1), then grasp the cover firmly and pull it straight up to disengage it from the cover mounting pin and grommet (2) (four-cylinder model shown, V6 models similar)

11.15 To remove the ambient air intake duct, simply pull it off the resonator inlet tube. Be sure to inspect the condition of the cover mounting grommet. If it's cracked, torn or otherwise deteriorated, replace it (four-cylinder model shown, V6 models similar)

11.17 To detach the resonator, remove these two bolts (four-cylinder resonator shown, V6 models with an automatic transaxle similar, V6 models with a manual transaxle slightly different)

12 Accelerator cable - removal, installation and adjustment

REMOVAL AND INSTALLATION

♦ Refer to illustrations 12.1, 12.2, 12.3, 12.5 and 12.6

➡ Note: Although the photos accompanying this Section depict the accelerator cable on a 2003 through 2005 four-cylinder model, the "accelerator cable" on 2006 and later four-cylinder models and all V6 models is removed, installed and adjusted exactly the same way. The only difference is that the accelerator cable on 2006 and later four-cylinder models and all V6 models terminates at the Accelerator Pedal Position (APP) sensor, which is located on the firewall. The APP sensor has a throttle cam and a cable bracket that are virtually identical to the throttle cam and cable bracket used on a conventional Honda throttle body mounted on the intake manifold.

1 On 2005 and earlier four-cylinder models, remove the engine cover (see illustration). On 2006 and later four-cylinder and all V6 models, remove the two accelerator cable cover bolts and remove the accelerator cable cover from the Accelerator Pedal Position (APP) sensor, which is located on the firewall.

2 Rotate the throttle lever cam on the throttle body or on the APP sensor until the cable is lined up with the slot in the cam, then disengage the cable from the cam (see illustration).

3 Loosen the accelerator cable locknut at the cable bracket (see illustration) and disengage the accelerator cable from its bracket.

➡ Note: If the cable bracket has an "L" shape to it, like the bracket in the accompanying illustration, there is no need to use a back-up wrench to hold the other nut (the adjustment nut) because the kink in the bracket prevents the adjustment nut from turning. If, however, the cable bracket does NOT have an L shape, you will need to use a back-up wrench to prevent the adjustment nut from turning when you loosen the locknut.

12.1 To detach the engine cover from the manifold, remove these two nuts

12.2 To disengage the accelerator cable from the throttle cam, rotate the throttle cam counterclockwise, then thread the cable and the cable end plug out of the slot

12.3 To disengage the accelerator cable from the cable bracket, loosen the cable locknut, then pull the cable housing out of the bracket

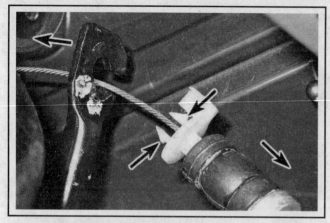

12.5 Disengage the plastic retainer from the accelerator pedal arm by squeezing these two locking tabs together and pulling the cable to the rear, then separate the cable from the pedal arm

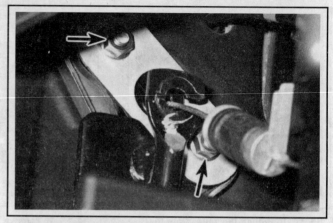

12.6 To detach the accelerator cable housing from the firewall, remove these two nuts (four-cylinder model shown, V6 models similar)

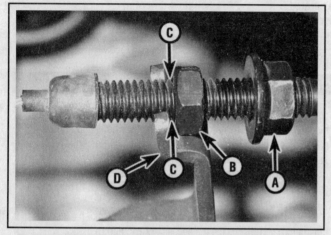

12.9a To adjust the accelerator cable, place the accelerator cable in the cable bracket with the adjusting nut (B) and the locknut (A) on the same side of the bracket (the side facing away from the throttle body), then turn the adjusting nut until there is zero freeplay (C) between the adjusting nut and the cable bracket (D)

12.9b Once the accelerator cable freeplay is correctly adjusted, lift the cable out of the cable bracket (B) and put the adjusting nut (C) on the other side of the cable bracket, then tighten the locknut (A) securely

4   Note the routing of the accelerator cable, then trace the cable from the cable bracket back to the firewall, detaching or disengaging it from any clamps, clips or cable guides.

5   Using a flashlight so that you can see underneath the dash, locate the cable connection at the top of the accelerator pedal, push the upper end of the pedal forward and disengage the cable from the pedal arm (see illustration).

6   To disengage the accelerator cable from the firewall, remove the two retaining nuts that secure the cable mounting flange to the firewall (see illustration), then pull the cable through the firewall into the vehicle.

7   Installation is the reverse of removal. When you're done installing the cable, be sure to adjust it.

ADJUSTMENT

▸ **Refer to illustrations 12.9a and 12.9b**

➡ **Note: The following adjustment procedure applies to both four-cylinder and V6 models. Adjust the cable on a V6 exactly the same way as described here for a four-cylinder engine.**

8   Put the shift lever in Park or Neutral, start the engine, hold it at 3000 rpm until the radiator fan comes on, then allow it to idle.

9   Back off the locknut, then place the accelerator cable in the cable bracket with both the adjusting nut and the locknut on the side of the cable bracket facing away from the throttle body. Then turn the adjusting nut until there is no freeplay between the adjusting nut and the cable bracket (see illustration). When the freeplay is zero, lift up the adjusting nut, place it on the other side of the cable bracket, then tighten the locknut (see illustration).

10 Once the accelerator cable has been installed and adjusted, verify that the throttle valve opens fully when you depress the accelerator pedal and that it returns to its idle position when you release the pedal.

13 Programmed Fuel Injection (PGM-FI) system - general information

The Programmed Fuel Injection (PGM-FI) system is a "sequential multiport" system. This means that there is a fuel injector in each intake port, and that these fuel injectors inject fuel into the intake ports in the cylinder firing order. The injectors are turned on and off by the Powertrain Control Module (PCM). When the engine is running, the PCM constantly monitors engine operating conditions with an array of information sensors, calculates the correct amount of fuel, then varies the interval of time during which the injectors are open. Sequential multiport systems provide much better control of the air/fuel mixture ratio than earlier fuel injection systems, and are therefore able to produce more power, better mileage and lower emissions.

The PGM-FI system uses the PCM and an array of information sensors to determine and deliver the correct air/fuel ratio under all operating conditions. The PGM-FI system consists of three sub-systems: air induction, electronic control and fuel delivery. The PGM-FI system is also closely interrelated with PCM-controlled emission control systems. For additional information about the PCM, the information sensors and the emission control systems, refer to Chapter 6.

AIR INDUCTION SYSTEM

The air induction system consists of the intake air resonator, the air filter assembly, the air intake duct, the throttle body and the intake manifold. The single-barrel, cast aluminum throttle body contains a throttle plate that regulates the amount of air entering the intake manifold. On four-cylinder models, the throttle plate is opened and closed by the accelerator cable.

On V6 models, the throttle plate is opened and closed by a computer-controlled solenoid known as the throttle actuator. There is an accelerator cable on V6 models, but it connects the accelerator pedal to the Accelerator Pedal Position (APP) sensor, which is located at the firewall. The APP sensor is a variable potentiometer (like a throttle position sensor) that outputs an analog voltage signal that's proportional to the angle of the accelerator pedal. This voltage signal is used by the PCM to calculate the correct angle of the throttle plate. The PCM commands the throttle actuator inside the throttle body to open or close to the appropriate angle.

The lower part of the throttle body is heated by engine coolant to prevent icing in cold weather. The throttle body is also the location of the Throttle Position (TP) sensor, a potentiometer that monitors the opening angle of the throttle plate and sends a variable voltage signal to the Powertrain Control Module (PCM). (The throttle body used on V6 models has two TP sensors - TP sensor A and TP sensor B - but both sensors are an integral part of the throttle body, and cannot be serviced separately.)

All models are equipped with a Manifold Absolute Pressure (MAP) sensor. The MAP sensor measures intake manifold pressure and vacuum and generates a variable voltage signal that's proportional to the pressure or vacuum. The PCM uses this data to calculate the load on the engine. On four-cylinder models the MAP sensor is located on the intake manifold, near the throttle body. On V6 models the MAP sensor is located on the throttle body.

All models are also equipped with an Intake Air Temperature (IAT) sensor. The IAT sensor relays a voltage signal to the PCM that varies in accordance with the temperature of the incoming air in the manifold. The PCM uses this data to calculate how rich or lean the air/fuel mixture should be. On 2003 and 2004 four-cylinder models (except SULEV and LX-P models), the IAT sensor is located on the air intake duct.

On 2003 and 2004 four-cylinder SULEV and LX-P models, and on all 2005 four-cylinder models, the IAT sensor is integrated into the Mass Air Flow (MAF) sensor, which is referred to as the MAF/IAT sensor. On V6 models, the IAT sensor is located on the intake manifold, near the throttle body.

All of the air induction components (air filter housing, air intake duct and throttle body) are covered in this Chapter, except for the injector base/intake manifold, which is covered in Chapter 2, and the information sensors, which are covered in Chapter 6.

On four-cylinder models, the Idle Air Control (IAC) system maintains the correct idle speed by regulating the amount of air that bypasses the (closed) throttle plate in response to a command from the Powertrain Control Module (PCM). The IAC system consists of the IAC valve (located on the throttle body), the PCM, and several information sensors, including the Engine Coolant Temperature (ECT) sensor, the Intake Air Temperature (IAT) sensor and the Manifold Absolute Pressure (MAP) sensor. The IAC valve is activated and controlled by the PCM in response to the running conditions of the engine (cold or warm running, power steering pressure high or low, air conditioning system on or off, etc.). As the PCM receives data from the information sensors (vehicle speed, coolant temperature, air conditioning and/or power steering load, etc.) it adjusts the idle according to the demands of the engine and driver.

On V6 models, there is no conventional IAC system. Instead, the idle speed is controlled by the PCM, which controls the angle of the throttle plate inside the throttle body at all engine speed settings.

ELECTRONIC CONTROL SYSTEM

For more information about the electronic control system, i.e. the PCM, its information sensors and output actuators, refer to Chapter 6.

FUEL DELIVERY SYSTEM

The fuel delivery system consists of the fuel pump, the fuel filter, the fuel pressure regulator, the fuel rail and fuel injectors, the fuel pulsation damper (four-cylinder models) and the lines and fittings that carry fuel between all of these components.

The fuel pump is an in-tank design, and it can be removed from the top of the fuel tank without removing the tank. Fuel is drawn through a "sock" (or strainer) at the pump inlet, then pumped out the other end of the pump and through an integral fuel filter. After the pressurized fuel has been filtered, it's pumped through the supply line to the fuel rail in the engine compartment. Another much shorter line is plumbed into the supply line at the pump. This line leads to a fuel pressure regulator - also mounted on the fuel pump assembly - which maintains the fuel pressure within the specified operating range. When the operating pressure exceeds the specified operating range, excess fuel is dumped back into the fuel tank (in other words, there is no fuel "return" line in this system).

The fuel rail, which is bolted to the injector base or intake manifold, functions as a reservoir for pressurized fuel so that there's always enough fuel available for acceleration and high speed operation. The fuel rail also houses the upper end of each fuel injector (the lower end of each injector is inserted into the injector base or intake manifold).

Four-cylinder models are equipped with a fuel pulsation damper, which is located on the underside of the fuel rail. The pulsation damper mitigates the hydraulic and acoustic "noise" produced by the fuel pump when it's operating. You'll have to remove the fuel rail to remove or replace the pulsation damper.

Each fuel injector is a solenoid-actuated, pintle-type design consisting of a solenoid, plunger, needle valve and housing. When the engine is running, there is always voltage on the "hot" side of each injector terminal. The PCM turns the injectors on and off by switching their ground paths on and off. When the ground path for an injector is closed by the PCM, current flows through the solenoid coil, the needle valve raises and pressurized fuel inside the injector housing squirts out the nozzle. The quantity of fuel injected each time an injector opens is determined by the "pulse width," which is the interval of time during which the valve is open.

14 Programmed Fuel Injection (PGM-FI) system - check

♦ **Refer to illustrations 14.7 and 14.9**

⁂ WARNING:

Gasoline is extremely flammable, so take extra precautions when you work on any part of the fuel system. See the Warning in Section 2.

➡ **Note: The following procedure is based on the assumption that the fuel pump is working and the fuel pressure is adequate (see Section 3).**

1   Check all electrical connectors that are related to the system. Check the ground wire connections for tightness. Loose connectors and poor grounds can cause many problems that resemble more serious malfunctions.

2   Verify that the battery is fully charged. The Powertrain Control Module (PCM), information sensors and output actuators (the fuel injectors are output actuators) depend on a stable voltage supply in order to meter fuel correctly.

3   Inspect the air filter element (see Chapter 1). A dirty or partially blocked filter will severely impede performance and economy.

4   Check all fuses related to the fuel system (see Chapter 12). If you find a blown fuse, replace it and see if it blows again. If it does, look for a wire shorted to ground in the circuit(s) protected by that fuse.

5   Check the air induction system between the throttle body and the intake manifold for air leaks, which will cause a lean air/fuel mixture ratio. (When the mixture ratio becomes excessively lean, the engine will misfire.) Also inspect the condition of all vacuum hoses connected to the intake manifold and to the throttle body. A loose or broken vacuum hose will allow false (unmetered) air into the intake manifold. The Manifold Absolute Pressure (MAP) sensor and the PCM can compensate for some false air, but if it's excessive, especially at idle and during other high-intake-manifold-vacuum conditions, the engine will misfire.

6   Remove the air intake duct from the throttle body and look for dirt, carbon, varnish, or other residue in the throttle body, particularly around the throttle plate. If it's dirty, clean it with carb cleaner, a toothbrush and a clean shop towel.

7   With the engine running, place an automotive stethoscope against each injector, one at a time, and listen for a clicking sound that indicates operation (see illustration). If you don't have a stethoscope, touch the tip of a long screwdriver against each injector and listen through the handle.

8   If you can hear the injectors operating, but the engine is misfiring, then the electrical circuits are functioning correctly, but the injectors might be dirty or clogged. Try a commercial injector cleaning product (available at auto parts stores). If cleaning the injectors doesn't help, the injectors probably need to be replaced.

9   If an injector is not operating (it makes no clicking sound), disconnect the injector electrical connector and measure the resistance across the injector terminals with an ohmmeter (see illustration). Compare your measurement with the resistance value listed in this Chapter's Specifications. Replace any injector whose resistance value does not fall within the specifications.

10   If the injector is not operating, but the resistance reading is within specifications, the PCM or the circuit between the PCM and the injector might be faulty.

14.7 Use a stethoscope to listen to each injector. It should make a clicking sound that rises and falls with engine speed

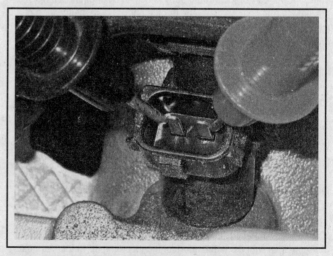

14.9 If an injector isn't working (it's not making a clicking sound), use an ohmmeter to measure the resistance across the two injector terminals

15 Throttle body - removal and installation

✳✳ WARNING:

Wait until the engine is completely cool before beginning this procedure.

FOUR-CYLINDER MODELS

◆ **Refer to illustrations 15.2 and 15.10**

1   Remove the air intake duct (see Section 11).

2   Disconnect the electrical connectors from the throttle body (see illustration).

3   Clamp off the two throttle body coolant hoses and then disconnect them. Be prepared for some coolant spillage.

4   Disconnect all hoses from the throttle body (see illustration 15.2).

5   On 2003 through 2005 four-cylinder models, disconnect the accelerator cable from the throttle cam and the bracket.

6   On 2003 through 2005 four-cylinder models, disconnect the cruise control cable from the throttle cam and the bracket.

➡ **Note: Disconnecting the cruise control cable from the throttle lever cam and cable bracket is the same procedure as disconnecting the accelerator cable (see Section 12).**

7   Detach the wiring harness clip from the small bracket on the throttle body, which is located below the TP sensor (see illustration 15.2).

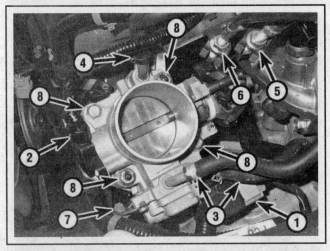

15.2 To remove the throttle body from the intake manifold on a 2003 through 2005 four-cylinder engine, disconnect or remove the following:

1   *Disconnect the Idle Air Control (IAC) valve electrical connector*
2   *Disconnect the Throttle Position (TP) sensor electrical connector*
3   *Disconnect the two coolant hoses*
4   *Disconnect the vacuum hose from the throttle body*
5   *Disconnect the accelerator cable from the throttle cam and bracket (see Section 12)*
6   *Disconnect the cruise control cable (if equipped) from the throttle cam and bracket (see Section 12)*
7   *Detach this wiring harness clip from its bracket*
8   *Remove the throttle body mounting bolts and nuts*

8   Remove the two throttle body mounting bolts and the two mounting nuts (see illustration 15.2) and remove the throttle body.

9   Remove the old throttle body gasket and discard it. Remove all traces of old gasket material from the gasket mating surfaces of the throttle body and the intake manifold.

10   Before installing the throttle body, spray the bore with carburetor cleaner or some other suitable solvent and thoroughly clean the bore, particularly the area below the throttle valve, by wiping off the oily residue, varnish and/or carbon deposits with a clean shop rag (see illustration).

✳✳ CAUTION:

Unless the throttle body that you're cleaning is stripped of all external components (such as the TP sensor or MAP sensor, for example), make sure that you don't spray any of these devices with carb cleaner. Solvent will damage the plastic housings for these units and might even damage the delicate electronics inside them.

11   Installation is the reverse of removal. Be sure to use a new gasket and tighten the throttle body mounting bolts and nuts to the torque listed in this Chapter's Specifications.

12   When you're done, check the coolant level and top it up if necessary (see Chapter 1).

13   Check the accelerator cable adjustment and adjust it if necessary (see Section 12).

14   Perform the PCM idle learn procedure (see Chapter 5, Section 1).

15   Check for air and coolant leaks.

V6 MODELS

16   Disconnect the electrical connector from the MAP sensor.

17   Remove the air intake duct (see Section 11).

18   Disconnect the electrical connector from the throttle body.

19   Disconnect the coolant bypass hoses from the throttle body. Plug

15.10 Spray the bore of the throttle body with carb cleaner or some other suitable solvent, then wipe the bore with a clean shop rag

both hoses to prevent coolant from dripping onto other components.

20 Detach the clip that secures the wiring harness to the bracket on the front side of the throttle body.

21 Remove the throttle body mounting bolts and nut and remove the throttle body.

22 Remove the old throttle body gasket and discard it.

23 Remove all traces of old gasket material from the throttle body and the intake manifold.

24 Installation is the reverse of removal. Be sure to use new gaskets and tighten the throttle body mounting bolts and nut to the torque listed in this Chapter's Specifications.

25 When you're done, check the coolant level and top it up if necessary (see Chapter 1).

26 Perform the PCM idle learn procedure (see Chapter 5, Section 1).

27 Check for air and coolant leaks.

16 Fuel rail and injectors - removal and installation

FOUR-CYLINDER MODELS

▶ **Refer to illustrations 16.5a, 16.5b, 16.7, 16.8a, 16.8b, 16.9, 16.10 and 16.11**

✳✳ WARNING:

Gasoline is extremely flammable, so take extra precautions when you work on any part of the fuel system. See the Warning in Section 2.

1 Relieve the system fuel pressure (see Section 2).

2 Disconnect the cable from the negative battery terminal (see Chapter 5, Section 1).

3 Remove the engine cover (see illustration 12.1).

4 Remove the air intake duct (see Section 11).

5 Disconnect the electrical connectors from the four fuel injectors and from the engine mount control solenoid valve, and remove the injector harness ground cable bolt (see illustrations).

6 Disconnect the quick-connect fitting that connects the fuel supply line to the fuel rail. If you're not yet familiar with the disconnection procedure for this type of fitting, refer to Section 4 for help.

7 Remove the fuel rail mounting nuts (see illustration).

8 Remove the fuel rail and the fuel injectors as a single assembly

(see illustration). If any of the injectors are difficult to extract from their bores, carefully pry them loose by wiggling them from side to side and pulling up at the same time. After removing the fuel rail/injector assembly, remove the two spacers (see illustration).

9 To remove each injector from the fuel rail, remove the retainer clip, then pull the injector out of its bore in the fuel rail (see illustration).

10 Remove and discard the upper and lower O-rings from each injector (see illustration), discard them and install new O-rings. Coat each new O-ring with clean engine oil to make it easier to slide the O-ring into place on the injector. Repeat this procedure for each injector.

➡**Note: Even if you only removed the fuel rail assembly to replace a single injector or a leaking O-ring, it's a good idea to remove all of the injectors from the fuel rail and replace all the O-rings at the same time.**

11 Coat the new upper injector O-rings with clean engine oil, then insert each injector into its corresponding bore in the fuel rail. Make sure that the lug on each injector is centered between the two posts on the end of the fuel rail's injector mounting pipe (see illustration). If you forget to do this, the electrical connector will not be correctly aligned and you might not be able to reconnect the electrical connector.

12 Install the fuel rail spacers on the fuel rail mounting studs.

13 Coat each new lower injector O-ring with clean engine oil and press the injector into its mounting bore in the intake manifold.

14 Once the fuel rail assembly is in place, with all four injectors fully

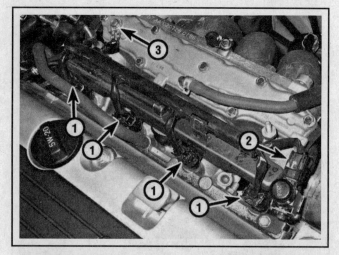

16.5a Disconnect the electrical connectors from the fuel injectors (1) and from the engine mount control solenoid valve (2) and remove the injector harness ground cable bolt (3) (four-cylinder models)

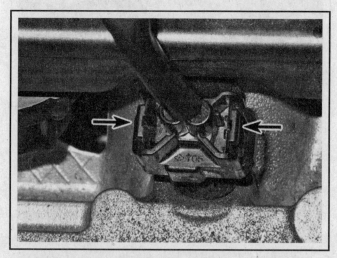

16.5b To disconnect a fuel injector connector, depress these two release tabs and pull off the connector (four-cylinder models)

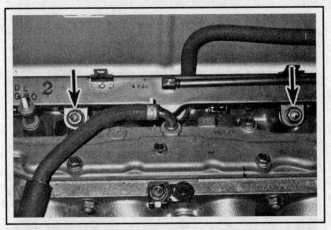

16.7 To detach the fuel rail from the intake manifold, remove these two nuts (four-cylinder models)

16.8a Remove the fuel rail and fuel injectors as a single assembly. If the injectors are difficult to extract from their bores, wiggling the fuel rail from side to side and pulling up at the same time will aid removal

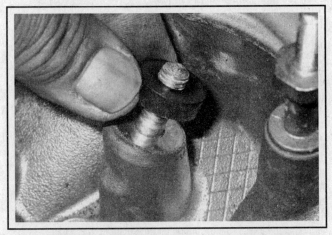

16.8b Remove and inspect the spacers located on the fuel rail mounting studs. If a spacer is cracked or deteriorated, replace it

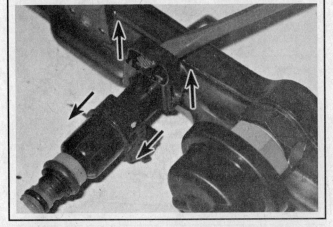

16.9 To remove an injector from the fuel rail, pry up the retainer clip, then pull the injector out of the fuel rail (four-cylinder models)

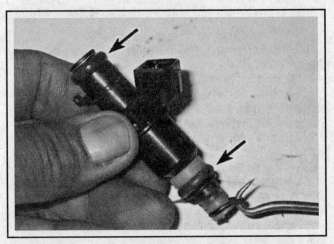

16.10 Be sure to remove and discard all three old injector O-rings. Always install new O-rings before installing the injector (even if you're installing the old injector) (four-cylinder models)

16.11 When installing the injectors into the fuel rail, make sure that the lug (A) on each injector is centered between the two posts (B) on the end of the mounting pipe (so the injector's electrical terminal is oriented correctly) (four-cylinder models)

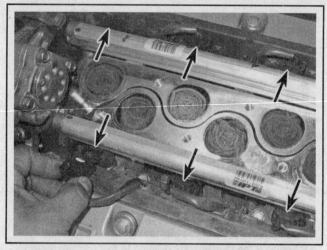

16.23 Disconnect the electrical connectors from the fuel injectors (V6 models)

16.24 To detach the fuel rail from the intake manifold, remove these two bolts from the front fuel rail mounting brackets and two more bolts (not shown) from the rear fuel rail mounting brackets (V6 models)

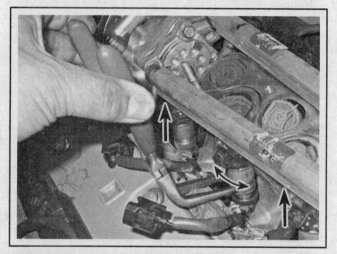

16.25a Remove the fuel rail and fuel injectors as a single assembly (V6 models). If any of the injectors "stick" in their bores, carefully rotate them from side-to-side with a pair of needle-nose pliers while firmly pulling up at the same time

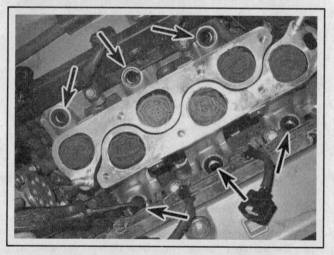

16.25b Carefully pry the sealing ring from each of the six injector bores. Be extremely careful not to damage the injector bores

seated in their respective bores, install the fuel rail mounting nuts and tighten them to the torque listed in this Chapter's Specifications. (Do NOT use the fuel rail mounting nuts to try to force the injectors into their bores.)

15 The remainder of installation is the reverse of removal.

16 When you're done reassembling everything, reconnect the cable to the negative battery terminal (see Chapter 5, Section 1).

17 Turn the ignition switch to ON to activate the fuel pump and build up fuel pressure in the fuel lines and the fuel rail, but DON'T operate the starter yet. Repeat this step two or three times, then check the fuel lines, fuel rails and injectors for fuel leaks.

18 Once you're confident that there are no leaks, start the engine and verify that the injectors are working and there are no fuel leaks.

V6 MODELS

♦ Refer to illustrations 16.23, 16.24, 16.25a, 16.25b and 16.28

19 Relieve the system fuel pressure (see Section 2).

20 Disconnect the cable from the negative battery terminal (see Chapter 5, Section 1).

21 Remove the intake manifold (see Chapter 2B).

22 Disconnect the fuel supply line quick-connect fitting that connects the fuel supply line to the left end of the rear fuel rail. Refer to Section 4 if you don't know how to disconnect this type of fitting.

23 Disconnect the electrical connectors from the fuel injectors (see illustration).

24 Remove the fuel rail mounting bolts (see illustration).

25 Remove the fuel rail and injectors as a single assembly (see illustration). After removing the fuel rail/injector assembly, remove the sealing ring from each injector bore (see illustration) and discard it.

26 Remove the injector retainer clips, then remove the fuel injectors from the fuel rail (see illustration 16.9).

27 Remove the O-rings from each injector (see illustration 16.10), discard them and install new O-rings. Coat each new O-ring with clean engine oil to make it easier to slide the O-ring into place on the injector.

Repeat this procedure for each injector.

➡**Note: Even if you only removed the fuel rail assembly to replace a single injector or a leaking O-ring, it's a good idea to remove all of the injectors from the fuel rail and replace all the O-rings at the same time.**

28 Coat each sealing ring with clean engine oil and press it into an injector bore (see illustration).

29 Coat the new upper injector O-rings with clean engine oil, then insert each injector into its corresponding bore in the fuel rail. Make sure that the lug on each injector is centered between the two posts on the end of the fuel rail's injector mounting pipe (see illustration 16.11). If you forget to do this, the electrical connector will not be correctly aligned and you might not be able to reconnect the electrical connector.

30 Coat each new lower injector O-ring with clean engine oil and press it into that injector's corresponding bore in the intake manifold.

31 Once the fuel rail assembly is in place, with all six injectors fully seated in their respective bores, install the fuel rail mounting bolts and tighten them to the torque listed in this Chapter's Specifications.

32 The remainder of installation is the reverse of removal.

33 When you're done reassembling everything, turn the ignition switch to ON to activate the fuel pump and build up fuel pressure in the fuel lines and the fuel rail, but DON'T operate the starter yet. Repeat this step two or three times, then check the fuel lines, fuel rails and injectors for fuel leaks.

16.28 Coat each new sealing ring with clean engine oil, insert it into the injector bore and push it down until it's fully seated in the bottom of the bore

34 Once you're confident that there are no leaks, start the engine and verify that the injectors are working and there are no fuel leaks.

17 Fuel pulsation damper - removal and installation

♦ **Refer to illustration 17.2**

1 Remove the fuel rail assembly (see Section 16).

2 Unscrew and remove the fuel pulsation damper (see illustration).

3 Remove and discard the old fuel pulsation damper sealing ring.

4 Installation is the reverse of removal. Be sure to use a new sealing ring and to tighten the fuel pulsation damper mounting nut securely.

5 When you're done, start the engine and check for fuel leaks at the fuel pulsation damper.

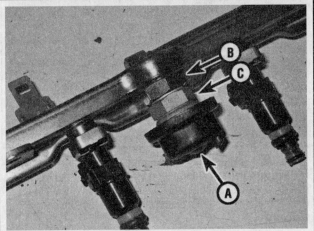

17.2 To remove the fuel pulsation damper (A) from the fuel rail, put a back-up wrench on the welded nut (B) and unscrew the fuel rail nut (C) with another wrench (four-cylinder models)

18 Exhaust system servicing - general information

◆ Refer to illustrations 18.1a, 18.1b, 18.4a and 18.4b

✻✻ WARNING:

Inspect and repair exhaust system components only after enough time has elapsed after driving the vehicle to allow the system components to cool completely. Also, when working under the vehicle, make sure it is securely supported on jackstands.

1   The exhaust system consists of the exhaust manifolds, the catalytic converter, the muffler, the tailpipe and all connecting pipes, flanges and clamps. The exhaust system is isolated from the vehicle body and from chassis components by a series of rubber hangers (see illustrations). Periodically inspect these hangers for cracks, tears and other signs of deterioration. If the hangers are damaged or worn, replace them. These rubber hangers are quite inexpensive, so it's a good idea to keep two or three of them in your toolbox. That way, when you have the vehicle up to inspect or repair something, if you notice that a rubber hanger has broken or is about to break, you'll have a hanger ready to replace it, rather than making a special trip to the dealer to pick up one part.

2   Conduct regular inspections of the exhaust system to keep it safe and quiet. Look for any damaged or bent parts, open seams, holes, loose connections, excessive corrosion or other defects which could allow exhaust fumes to enter the vehicle. Do not repair deteriorated exhaust system components; replace them with new parts.

3   If the exhaust system components are extremely corroded, or rusted together, you'll need welding equipment and a cutting torch to remove them. The convenient strategy at this point is to have a muffler repair shop remove the corroded sections with a cutting torch. If you want to save money by doing it yourself, but you don't have a welding outfit and cutting torch, simply cut off the old components with a hacksaw. If you have compressed air, there are special pneumatic cutting chisels (available from specialty tool manufacturers) that can also be used. If you decide to tackle the job at home, be sure to wear safety goggles to protect your eyes from metal chips and wear work gloves to protect your hands.

4   Here are some simple guidelines to follow when repairing the exhaust system:

   a) *Work from the back to the front when removing exhaust system components.*
   b) *Most exhaust fasteners are subjected to extreme heat, so they can be tough to remove. Exhaust manifold flange and catalytic converter flange fasteners are particularly difficult to loosen because they get hotter than most other parts of the exhaust system. Be sure to apply penetrating oil to these exhaust system fasteners (see illustrations) to make them easier to remove.*
   c) *Use new gaskets, hangers and clamps when installing exhaust systems components.*
   d) *Apply anti-seize compound to the threads of all exhaust system fasteners during reassembly.*
   e) *Be sure to allow sufficient clearance between newly installed parts and all points on the underbody to avoid overheating the floor pan and possibly damaging the interior carpet and insulation. Pay particularly close attention to the catalytic converter and heat shield.*

18.1a Most rubber hangers look something like this one. To replace this type of hanger, pry it off the upper metal hook (which is welded or bolted to the body) and the lower hook (which is welded to the exhaust component that the hanger supports)

18.1b Other rubber hangers are designed more like engine mounts: The rubber insulator is bonded to a metal bracket that's bolted to the vehicle. To replace this type of hanger, remove the mounting bolts and pry the hanger off the pin

18.4a Exhaust manifold flange bolts are particularly difficult to loosen because of the intense heat to which they're subjected, so be sure to apply a liberal dose of penetrant to the bolt threads, then let it do its work for awhile before attempting to loosen the nuts

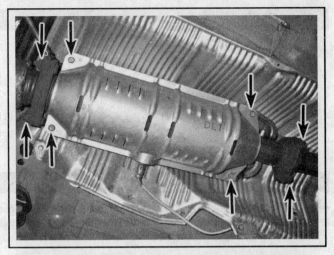

18.4b Catalytic converter flange nuts and heat shield bolts are also difficult to remove because of the high temperatures to which they're exposed, so if they're tough to unscrew, douse them with penetrant, give it time to soak in, then remove them

Specifications

Accelerator cable deflection (all models)	3/8 to 1/2-inch (10 to 12 mm)
Fuel system pressure	
Four-cylinder models	48 to 55 psi (330 to 380 kPa)
V6 models	
2007 and earlier	55 to 63 psi (380 to 430 kPa)
2008 and later	57 to 64 psi (390 to 440 kPa)
Injector resistance	10 to 13 ohms

Torque specifications	Ft-lbs (unless otherwise indicated)	Nm

➡**Note: One foot-pound (ft-lb) of torque is equivalent to 12 inch-pounds (in-lbs) of torque. Torque values below approximately 15 ft-lbs are expressed in inch-pounds, since most foot-pound torque wrenches are not accurate at these smaller values.**

Fuel pump/fuel gauge sending unit retaining nuts (non-SULEV)	36 in-lbs	4
Fuel rail mounting bolts/nuts		
Four-cylinder models (nuts)	16	22
V6 models (bolts)	86 in-lbs	10
Fuel tank strap bolts	28	38
Rear suspension subframe bolts	76	103
Throttle body mounting bolts/nuts (all models)	16	22

5

ENGINE ELECTRICAL SYSTEMS

1   General information, precautions and battery disconnection

The engine electrical systems include all ignition, charging and starting components. Because of their engine-related functions, these components are covered separately from body electrical components such as the lights, the instruments, etc. (which you'll find in Chapter 12).

PRECAUTIONS

Always observe the following precautions when working on the electrical system:

a) *Be extremely careful when servicing engine electrical components. They are easily damaged if checked, connected or handled improperly.*

b) *Never leave the ignition switched on for long periods of time when the engine is not running.*

c) *Never disconnect the battery cables while the engine is running.*

d) *Maintain correct polarity when connecting battery cables from another vehicle during jump starting - see the "Booster battery (jump) starting" Section at the front of this manual.*

e) *Always disconnect the cable from the negative battery terminal before working on the electrical system, but read the following battery disconnection procedure first.*

It's also a good idea to review the safety-related information regarding the engine electrical systems located in the "Safety first!" Section at the front of this manual, before beginning any operation included in this Chapter.

BATTERY DISCONNECTION

Some systems on the vehicle require battery power to be available at all times, either to maintain continuous operation (alarm system, power door locks, etc.), or to maintain control unit memory (radio station presets, Powertrain Control Module and other control units). When the battery is disconnected, the power that maintains these systems is cut. So, before you disconnect the battery, please note the following points to ensure that there are no unforeseen consequences of this action:

a) *Make sure that you have the radio station pre-sets before disconnecting the battery.*

b) *If the radio is equipped with an anti-theft system, make sure that you have the correct anti-theft codes for the radio before disconnecting the battery.*

c) *If the vehicle is equipped with the optional navigation system, make sure that you have the anti-theft codes for it too.*

d) *When the battery, or any of the components listed below, is disconnected, the engine management system's Powertrain Control Module (PCM) will lose some data from its memory regarding the engine idle characteristics. It is imperative that you perform the "PCM idle learn procedure" (see procedure below) after disconnecting any of the components listed below.*

e) *On vehicles with power door locks, it's a wise precaution to remove the key from the ignition and to keep it with you, so that it doesn't get locked inside if the power door locks engage when the battery is reconnected!*

Devices known as "memory-savers" can be used to avoid some of these problems. Precise details vary according to the device used. The typical memory saver is plugged into the cigarette lighter and is con-

nected to a spare battery. Then the vehicle battery can be disconnected from the electrical system. The memory saver will provide sufficient current to maintain audio unit security codes, PCM memory, etc. and will provide power to "always hot" circuits such as the clock and radio memory circuits.

✻✻ WARNING:

Some memory savers deliver a considerable amount of current in order to keep vehicle systems operational after the main battery is disconnected. If you're using a memory saver, make sure that the circuit concerned is actually open before servicing it.

✻✻ WARNING:

If you're going to work near any of the airbag system components, the battery MUST be disconnected and a memory saver must NOT be used. If a memory saver is used, power will be supplied to the airbag, which means that it could accidentally deploy and cause serious personal injury.

To disconnect the battery for service procedures requiring power to be cut from the vehicle, loosen the cable clamp nut and disconnect the cable from the negative battery post. Isolate the cable end to prevent it from coming into accidental contact with the battery post.

THINGS TO DO AFTER RECONNECTING THE BATTERY

After reconnecting the battery, be sure to:

a) *Enter the anti-theft codes for the radio and, if equipped, the navigation system.*

b) *Enter the radio station presets.*

c) *Reset the clock.*

Some procedures in this manual may also require you to reset the power window control unit and/or perform the PCM idle learn procedure after reconnecting the battery. If you're directed to do either or both of these procedures, follow the procedures below.

Resetting the power window control unit

➡**Note: You MUST reset the power window control unit after replacing the power window regulator, the power window motor, the window run channel or the door glass. And you might be directed to reset the control unit after certain other procedures.**

1   Turn the ignition switch to ON.

2   Press the DOWN switch for the left front (driver's) window and lower the window all the way down.

3   Open the driver's door.

➡**Note: Steps 4 through 7 must be performed within five seconds of each other.**

4   Turn the ignition switch to OFF.

5   Press the DOWN switch for the driver's window again and hold it down.

6   Turn the ignition switch to ON.

7   Release the DOWN switch for the driver's window.

8   Repeat Steps 4 through 7 three more times.

9   Wait one second.

10 Verify that AUTO UP and AUTO DOWN don't work. If they do, go back to Step 1 and start over.

11 Move the driver's window all the way down by holding the DOWN switch to the AUTO DOWN position.

12 Pull up and hold the UP switch for the driver's window to the AUTO UP position until the window is fully closed, then continue holding the switch for one more second.

13 Verify that the power window master switch is correctly reset by operating the AUTO UP and AUTO DOWN functions for the driver's window.

14 If the window still doesn't work in AUTO, repeat this procedure several more times. Be sure to pay close attention to the five-second time limit between Steps 4 through 7. If you're unable to reset the power window control unit after this, have it done by a dealer service department or other qualified repair shop.

PCM idle learn procedure

➡Note: You must perform the PCM idle learn procedure after disconnecting or replacing the battery, disconnecting, replacing or resetting the Powertrain Control Module (PCM) or after cleaning or replacing the intake manifold and/or the throttle body. You might be directed to do so after certain other procedures as well.

1 Make sure that all electrical components (air conditioning, rear window defogger, lights, etc.) are turned off.

2 Turn the ignition switch to ON for two seconds.

3 Put the transmission in PARK or NEUTRAL, start the engine, bring the engine speed up to 3000 rpm and hold it there until the radiator fan comes on or until the engine coolant temperature reaches 194-degrees F (90-degrees C).

4 After the radiator fan comes on, allow the engine to idle for at least five minutes with the throttle fully closed. Do not turn on any electrical devices or systems during this five-minute interval.

➡Note: If the radiator fan comes on again, don't count the period during which it's on as part of the five minutes.

2 Battery - emergency jump starting

Refer to the "Booster battery (jump) starting procedure" at the front of this manual.

3 Battery - check and replacement

❊ WARNING:

Always disconnect the cable from the negative battery terminal FIRST and hook it up LAST or the battery may be shorted by the tool being used to loosen the cable clamps.

CHECK

▸ Refer to illustrations 3.1 and 3.3

1 Check the battery state of charge. Visually inspect the indicator eye on the top of the battery; if the indicator eye is black in color charge the battery as described in Chapter 1. Next perform an open voltage circuit test using a digital voltmeter (see illustration).

➡Note: Remove the battery's surface charge before measuring open circuit voltage, or the voltage measurement might be inaccurate. To remove the surface charge, turn on the high beams for ten seconds, then turn them off and let the vehicle stand for two minutes.

With the engine and all accessories Off, touch the negative probe of the voltmeter to the negative terminal of the battery and the positive probe to the positive terminal of the battery. The battery voltage should be 12.6 volts or slightly above. If the battery is less than the specified voltage, charge the battery before proceeding to the next test. Do not proceed with the battery load test unless the battery charge is correct.

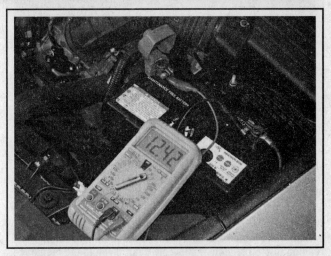

3.1 To test the open circuit voltage of the battery, touch the black probe of the voltmeter to the negative terminal and the red probe to the positive terminal of the battery; a fully charged battery should be at least 12.6 volts

2 Disconnect the negative battery cable, then the positive cable from the battery.

3 Perform a battery load test. An accurate check of the battery condition can only be performed with a load tester (available at most auto parts stores). This test evaluates the ability of the battery to operate the starter and other accessories during periods of high current draw. Hook

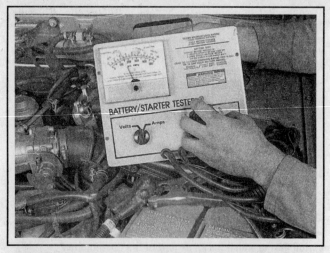

3.3 Some battery load testers (like this one) are equipped with an ammeter that allows you to vary the amount of the load on the battery (less expensive testers only have a load switch that puts the battery under a fixed load)

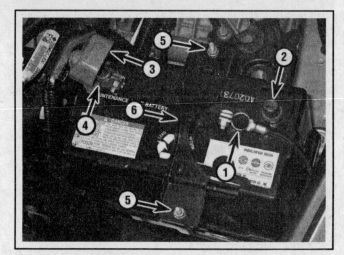

3.4 Battery mounting details

1   Negative cable clamp (always disconnect this one first, and hook it up last)
2   Negative battery terminal
3   Positive terminal cover
4   Positive cable clamp and positive battery terminal
5   Hold-down clamp nuts
6   Hold-down clamp

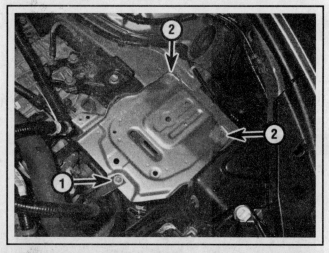

3.8a Remove this bolt (1) to detach the harness bracket from the battery tray. To remove the battery tray, remove these two upper mounting bolts (2) . . .

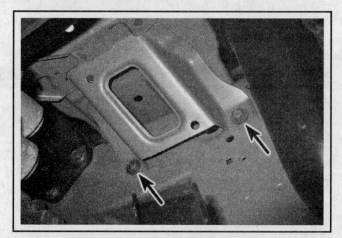

3.8b . . . and loosen these two lower bolts

up a battery load tester to the battery terminals (see illustration). This tool increases the load demand (current draw) on the battery. Maintain the load on the battery for 15 seconds or less and observe that the battery voltage does not drop below 9.6 volts. If the battery condition is weak or defective, the tool will indicate this condition immediately.

➡**Note: Cold temperatures will cause the minimum voltage reading to drop slightly. Follow the chart given in the manufacturer's instructions to compensate for cold climates. Minimum load voltage for freezing temperatures (32-degrees F) should be about 9.1 volts.**

REPLACEMENT

◆ **Refer to illustrations 3.4, 3.8a and 3.8b**

4   Disconnect the cable from the negative battery terminal first, then (and only then!) disconnect the cable from the positive battery terminal (see illustration).

5   Remove the battery hold-down clamp nuts (see illustration 3.4) and remove the hold-down clamp.

6   Lift out the battery. Be careful - it's heavy.

➡**Note: Battery straps and handlers are available at most auto parts stores for a reasonable price. They make it easier to remove and carry the battery.**

7   While the battery is out, inspect the battery tray for corrosion.

8   If there's corrosion on the battery tray, remove the tray's upper mounting bolts, loosen the two lower mounting bolts (see illustrations) and remove the tray from the engine compartment. Clean the deposits from the metal to prevent the battery tray from further corrosion.

9   If you are replacing the battery, make sure you get one that's identical, with the same dimensions, amperage rating, cold cranking rating, etc.

10 Installation is the reverse of removal. Be sure to connect the positive cable first and the negative cable last (see Section 1).

4   Battery cables - check and replacement

♦ **Refer to illustrations 4.4a, 4.4b, 4.4c and 4.4d**

1   Periodically inspect the entire length of each battery cable for damage, cracked or burned insulation and corrosion. Poor battery cable connections can cause starting problems and decreased engine performance.

2   Inspect the cable-to-terminal connections at the ends of the cables for cracks, loose wire strands and corrosion. The presence of white, fluffy deposits under the insulation at the cable terminal connection means that the cable is corroded and should be replaced. Also inspect the battery posts for distortion and corrosion. If they're corroded, clean them up

3   When removing the cables, always disconnect the cable from the negative battery terminal first and hook it up last, or you might accidentally short out the battery with the tool you're using to loosen the cable clamps. Even if you're only replacing the cable for the positive terminal, be sure to disconnect the negative cable from the battery first (see Section 1).

4   Disconnect the old cables from the battery, then trace each cable to its opposite end and disconnect it (see illustrations). Be sure to note the routing of each cable before disconnecting it to ensure correct installation. Starter cable replacement isn't entirely straightforward on the vehicles covered in this manual because the starter cable disappears into a thicket of harnesses and emerges from the other end down at the starter solenoid. What you must do is carefully remove all of the old electrical tape, remove the conduit surrounding each harness, then separate the starter cable from the other wiring. Then, after you've installed the new starter cable, carefully bunch the wiring - including the starter cable - back together again, tape it to hold it together tightly, re-cover it with the conduit, then finish taping all exposed wiring.

5   When purchasing battery cables take the old one(s) with you. It is vitally important that you replace the cables with identical parts.

6   Clean the threads of the solenoid or ground connection with a wire brush to remove rust and corrosion. Apply a light coat of battery terminal corrosion inhibitor or petroleum jelly to the threads to prevent future corrosion.

7   Attach the cable to the solenoid or ground connection and tighten the mounting nut/bolt securely.

8   Before connecting a new cable to the battery make sure that it reaches the battery post without having to be stretched.

9   Connect the cable to the positive battery terminal first, then connect the ground cable to the negative battery terminal (see Section 1).

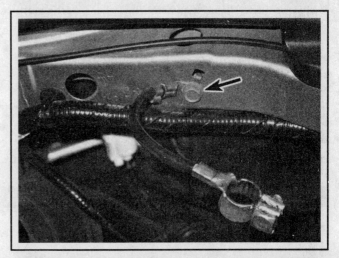

4.4a The battery ground cable is bolted to the left fenderwell

4.4b The battery positive cable harness goes to these two terminals inside the engine compartment fuse and relay box . . .

4.4c . . . to the B+ terminal on the alternator . . .

4.4d . . . and to the terminal on the starter solenoid (four-cylinder model shown, V6 models similar)

5   Ignition system - general information

1   The electronic ignition system consists of the Powertrain Control Module (PCM), the ignition switch, the battery, the ignition coil relay, the ignition coils and the spark plugs. Both four-cylinder and V6 engines are equipped with coil-over-plug-style ignition coils; there are no spark plug wires between the coils and the spark plugs. Each plug has its own coil mounted directly on top of it.

2   The PCM uses data from the Crankshaft Position (CKP) sensor to determine ignition timing during start-ups and to detect misfires when the engine is running. The PCM alters ignition timing in accordance with the data that it receives from the Output Shaft Speed (OSS), the Manifold Absolute Pressure (MAP), the Engine Coolant Temperature (ECT) and the Intake Air Temperature (IAT) sensors that monitor, respectively, engine speed, manifold absolute pressure, coolant temperature and intake air temperature. For more information about the CKP, OSS, MAP, ECT and IAT sensors, refer to Chapter 6.

6   Ignition system - check

▶ Refer to illustration 6.2

1   If a malfunction occurs in the ignition system, check the following items first:

a)   *Make sure that the cable clamps at the battery terminals are clean and tight.*

b)   *Test the condition of the battery (see Section 3). If it doesn't pass all the tests, replace it.*

c)   *Check the ignition coil connections.*

d)   *Check any relevant fuses in the engine compartment fuse and relay box (see Chapter 12). If they're burned, determine the cause and repair the circuit.*

2   If the engine turns over but won't start, disconnect an ignition coil from a spark plug (see Section 7), reconnect the electrical connector to the coil, then attach a spark tester between the ignition coil high-tension terminal and the spark plug (see illustration). Spark testers are available at most auto parts stores. Crank the engine and note whether or not the tester flashes.

3   If the tester flashes during cranking, the coil is delivering sufficient voltage to the spark plug to fire it. Repeat this test for each cylinder to verify that the other coils are OK.

4   If the tester doesn't flash, remove a coil from another cylinder and swap it for the one being tested. If the tester now flashes, you know that the original coil is bad. If the tester still doesn't flash, the PCM or

6.2   To use this type of spark tester, remove a coil (A), insert the tester (B) into the coil, push the boot (C) on the other end of the tester onto the spark plug and crank the engine. If the coil is generating enough voltage to fire the plug, the filament inside the tester housing will flash each time that the plug fires

wiring harness is probably defective. Have the PCM checked out by a dealer service department or other qualified repair shop (testing the PCM is beyond the scope of the do-it-yourselfer because it requires expensive special tools).

5   If the tester flashes during cranking but a misfire code (related to the cylinder being tested) has been stored, the spark plug could be fouled or defective.

7   Ignition coils - replacement

FOUR-CYLINDER MODELS

▶ **Refer to illustrations 7.1, 7.2 and 7.4**

1   Remove the ignition coil cover (see illustration).

2   Disconnect the electrical connector from the ignition coil (see illustration).

3   Remove the ignition coil mounting bolt or stud (see illustration 7.2).

4   Remove the ignition coil from the spark plug (see illustration).

5   Installation is the reverse of removal. Be sure to tighten the ignition coil mounting bolt or stud to the torque listed in this Chapter's Specifications.

V6 MODELS

▶ **Refer to illustrations 7.7 and 7.8**

6   Remove the ignition coil cover.

7   Disconnect the electrical connector from the ignition coil (see illustration).

8   Remove the ignition coil mounting bolt (see illustration).

9   Remove the ignition coil from the spark plug.

10   Installation is the reverse of removal. Be sure to tighten the ignition coil mounting bolt to the torque listed in this Chapter's Specifications.

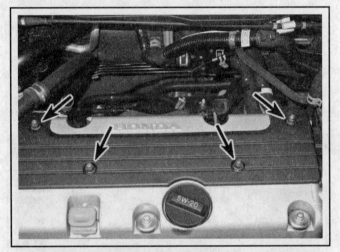

7.1 To access the ignition coils on a four-cylinder engine, remove these four nuts and remove the coil cover

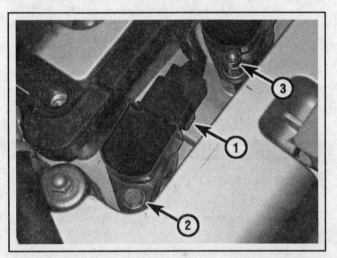

7.2 To remove an ignition coil from a four-cylinder engine, disconnect the electrical connector (1) and remove the mounting bolt (2) or stud (3)

7.4 To disconnect an ignition coil from its spark plug, grasp it firmly and pull straight up

7.7 Disconnect the electrical connector from the ignition coil (V6 models)

7.8 To detach an ignition coil from a V6 model, remove the mounting bolt and pull the coil straight out

8   Charging system - general information and precautions

The charging system includes the alternator (with an integral voltage regulator inside), the battery, an Electrical Load Detector (ELD) unit (in the engine compartment fuse and relay box), a charge indicator light (on the instrument cluster) and the wiring connecting all of these components. The charging system supplies electrical power for the ignition system, the lights, the radio, etc. The alternator is driven by a drivebelt at the right end of the engine. The alternator's voltage output is controlled by an internal voltage regulator, which keeps charging output within a range of about 13.5 to 14.5 volts. The ELD unit sends a variable voltage signal to the Powertrain Control Module (PCM) that varies in accordance with the total power demand imposed on the charging system by the electrical devices and systems in operation. The PCM uses this variable voltage signal to calculate the actual level of charging voltage needed and alters the charging voltage output accordingly.

The charging system doesn't ordinarily require periodic maintenance. However, the drivebelt, battery and wires and connections should be inspected at the intervals outlined in Chapter 1.

The dashboard warning light should come on when the ignition key is turned to ON, but it should go off immediately after the engine is started. If it remains on, there is a malfunction in the charging system (see Section 9).

Be very careful when making electrical circuit connections to a vehicle equipped with an alternator and note the following:

a) *When reconnecting wires to the alternator from the battery, be sure to note the polarity.*

b) *Before using arc-welding equipment to repair any part of the vehicle, disconnect the wires from the alternator and the battery terminals.*

c) *Never start the engine with a battery charger connected.*

d) *Always disconnect both battery leads before using a battery charger.*

e) *The alternator is turned by an engine drivebelt that could cause serious injury if your hands, hair or clothes become entangled in it with the engine running.*

f) *Because the alternator is connected directly to the battery, it could arc or cause a fire if overloaded or shorted out.*

g) *Wrap a plastic bag over the alternator and secure it with rubber bands before steam cleaning the engine.*

9   Charging system - check

▶ **Refer to illustration 9.3**

1   If a malfunction occurs in the charging circuit, do not immediately assume that the alternator is causing the problem. First, check the following items:

a) *Make sure the battery cable clamps, where they connect to the battery, are clean and tight.*

b) *Test the condition of the battery (see Section 3). If it does not pass all the tests, replace it with a new battery.*

c) *Check the external alternator wiring and connections.*

d) *Check the drivebelt condition and tension (see Chapter 1).*

e) *Check the alternator mounting bolts for tightness.*

f) *Run the engine and check the alternator for abnormal noise.*

g) *Check the 120-amp fuse in the engine compartment fuse and relay box (see Chapter 12). If it's burned, determine the cause and repair the circuit.*

h) *Check the charge light on the dash. It should illuminate when the ignition key is turned ON (engine not running). If it doesn't come on, disconnect the electrical connector and the ground wire from the alternator. The charge light should now come on (because by opening the charging circuit, you have eliminated all charging voltage). If the light still doesn't illuminate, check fuse number 21 (7.5 amp), which is located in the left (driver's side) passenger compartment fuse and relay box. If fuse No. 21 is blown, troubleshoot and repair the charge light circuit and then replace the fuse. If the charge light still doesn't come on, check the bulb (see Chapter 12). If it's blown, replace it.*

i) *Make sure that the PCM hasn't stored any diagnostic trouble codes for the Electronic Load Detector (ELD) system (see Chapter 6 for more information about the ELD).*

2   With the ignition key turned to the OFF position, check battery voltage with all electrical accessories (blower fan, radio, cigarette lighter, cooling fan, etc.) turned off. It should be about 12.5 volts (see

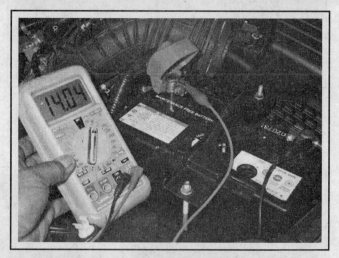

9.3 To check charging voltage, hook up a multimeter to the battery terminals, then start the engine. With the engine running, the voltage should be at least 13.5 volts

illustration 3.1).

3   Check the charging voltage with the engine running. Start the engine, raise the engine rpm to 1500 and check the battery voltage again (see illustration). It should now be at least 13.5 volts.

4   Load the battery and observe the charging voltage. Turn on the high beam headlights, the windshield wipers and the radio, and put the air conditioning blower on HIGH. The voltage should drop and then come back up as each accessory is selected. If the charging system is working correctly, the voltage should stay above 13.5 volts. If the voltage drops below 13 volts, the charging system is defective.

5   Lower the engine rpm back to idle and observe the charging voltage. The charging voltage should not drop below 13 volts with the

decrease in engine rpm. Apply the brakes and observe the charging voltage at idle. It should remain above 13 volts.

6   Turn off all the electrical loads that you turned on in Step 4, run the engine at 1600 rpm and watch the charging voltage rise. It should not rise above 15 volts.

7   If the charging voltage does not exhibit distinct changes when engine rpm increases and accessory loads are added, the voltage regulator is defective. If the charging voltages are low and the drivebelts and battery are all in good condition, the alternator is defective. In this situation, replace the alternator and voltage regulator as a single unit.

10 Alternator - removal and installation

1   Disconnect the cable from the negative battery terminal (see Section 1).

FOUR-CYLINDER MODELS

▶ **Refer to illustrations 10.3, 10.4a and 10.4b**

2   Remove the drivebelt and the drivebelt tensioner (see Chapter 1).
3   Peel back the rubber weather cover, remove the nut that attaches the alternator output cable to the stud on the backside of the alternator, disconnect the alternator output cable and disconnect the electrical connector from the alternator (see illustration). Set the alternator harness aside.
4   Remove the three alternator mounting bolts (see illustrations) and remove the alternator.
5   If you're replacing the alternator, take the old one with you when purchasing the replacement unit. Make sure that the new/rebuilt unit looks identical to the old alternator. Look at the terminals - they should be the same in number, size and location as the terminals on the old alternator. Finally, look at the identification numbers - they will be stamped into the housing or printed on a tag attached to the housing. Make sure the numbers are the same on both alternators.

6   Some new/rebuilt alternators DO NOT have a pulley installed, so you might have to swap the pulley from the old unit to the new/rebuilt one. When buying an alternator, find out the store's policy regarding pulley swaps. Some stores perform this service free of charge. If your local auto parts store doesn't offer this service, you'll have to purchase a puller for removing the pulley and do it yourself.
7   Installation is the reverse of removal. Be sure to tighten the alternator mounting bolts to the torque listed in this Chapter's Specifications. When you're done, go to Step 15.

V6 MODELS

▶ **Refer to illustration 10.11**

8   Disconnect the fan motor and the air conditioning compressor electrical connectors, remove the engine coolant reservoir and remove the fan shroud (see Chapter 3).
9   Remove the drivebelt (see Chapter 1).
10   Peel back the rubber weather cover, remove the nut that attaches the alternator output cable to the stud on the backside of the alternator, disconnect the alternator output cable and disconnect the electrical connector from the alternator (see illustration 10.3).

10.3 Peel back the weather cover (1), remove the nut that connects the battery positive cable to the alternator's output terminal (2), then disconnect the electrical connector (3) from the alternator (four-cylinder model shown, V6 models similar)

10.4a To remove the alternator from its mounting bracket on a four-cylinder engine, remove the upper mounting bolt . . .

10.4b . . . and the two lower mounting bolts

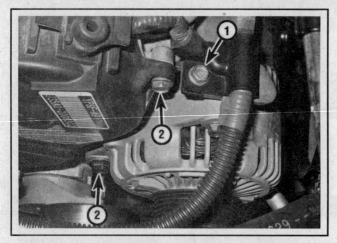

10.11 To detach the alternator wiring harness from the alternator on a V6 engine, remove this bolt (1), then remove the two alternator mounting bolts (2) and remove the alternator

11 Remove the bolt (see illustration) that attaches the alternator wiring harness to the alternator and set the alternator harness aside.

12 Remove the two alternator mounting bolts (see illustration 10.11) and remove the alternator from its mounting bracket.

13 Refer to Steps 5 and 6.

14 Installation is the reverse of removal. Tighten the alternator mounting bolts to the torque listed in this Chapter's Specifications.

ALL MODELS

15 Reconnect the cable to the negative terminal of the battery, then check the charging voltage (see Section 9) to verify that the alternator is operating correctly.

16 Enter the anti-theft codes for the radio and, if equipped, the navigation system. Then enter the radio station presets and reset the clock.

17 Reset the power window control unit (see Section 1).

11 Starting system - general information and precautions

The starting system consists of the battery, a 100-amp fuse, a 50-amp fuse, the ignition switch, the starter cut relay, the clutch start switch (manual transaxle) or transmission range switch (automatics), the starter solenoid and starter motor and the wires connecting all of these components. The solenoid is mounted directly on the starter motor. The starter motor assembly is located in front of the engine block on four-cylinder models and in front of the transaxle on V6 models.

When the ignition key is turned to the START position, the starter solenoid is actuated through the starter control circuit. The starter solenoid then connects the battery to the starter. The battery supplies the electrical energy to the starter motor, which does the actual work of cranking the engine.

On models with a manual transaxle, the starter can only be oper-

ated when the clutch pedal is depressed. On models with an automatic transaxle, the starter can only be operated when the shift lever is in PARK or NEUTRAL.

Always observe the following precautions when working on the starting system:

a) *Excessive cranking of the starter motor can overheat it and cause serious damage. Never operate the starter motor for more than 15 seconds at a time without pausing to allow it to cool for at least two minutes.*

b) *The starter is connected directly to the battery and could arc or cause a fire if mishandled, overloaded or shorted out.*

c) *Always detach the cable from the negative terminal of the battery before working on the starting system.*

12 Starter motor and circuit - check

▶ **Refer to illustrations 12.3 and 12.4**

1 If a malfunction occurs in the starting circuit, do not immediately assume that the starter is causing the problem. First, check the following items:

a) *Make sure the battery cable clamps, where they connect to the battery, are clean and tight.*

b) *Check the condition of the battery cables (see Section 4). Replace any defective battery cables with new ones.*

c) *Test the condition of the battery (see Section 3). If it does not pass all the tests, replace it with a new battery.*

d) *Check the starter solenoid wiring and connections. Refer to the wiring diagrams at the end of Chapter 12.*

e) *Check the starter mounting bolts for tightness.*

f) *Check the fuses in the engine compartment fuse and relay box (see Chapter 12). If they're burned, determine the cause and repair the circuit. Also, check the ignition switch circuit for correct operation (see the wiring diagrams at the end of Chapter 12).*

g) *Check the operation of the gear position switch (automatic transaxle) or clutch start switch circuit (manual transaxle). Make*

sure that the shift lever is in PARK or NEUTRAL (automatic transaxle) or that the clutch pedal is depressed (manual transaxle). Refer to Chapter 7 for the gear position switch check and adjustment procedure. Refer to Chapter 12 wiring diagrams for the necessary circuit checks for the clutch activation system. These systems must operate correctly to provide battery voltage to the starter solenoid.*

h) *Check the operation of the starter cut relay. The starter cut relay is located in the fuse/relay box under the driver's side of the dash. Refer to Chapter 12 for relay testing procedures.*

2 If the starter does not activate when the ignition switch is turned to the start position, check for battery voltage to the solenoid. This will determine if the solenoid is receiving the correct voltage signal from the ignition switch. Connect a voltmeter to the starter solenoid "S" terminal. Then note the indicated voltage when an assistant turns the ignition switch to the START position. It should be about the same as battery voltage. If there's no voltage at the S terminal, refer to the wiring diagrams at the end of Chapter 12 and check the starting system fuses. The two starting system fuses are located inside the engine compartment fuse and relay box. Also check the starter cut relay for correct

12.3 To use an inductive ammeter, simply hold the ammeter over the positive or negative battery cable (whichever cable has better clearance)

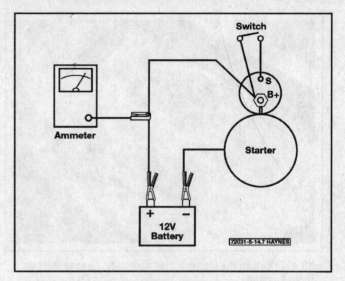

12.4 Starter motor bench testing details

operation. The starter cut relay is located inside the left (driver's side) fuse/relay panel. Refer to Chapter 12 for help with testing relays. If voltage is available but the starter motor doesn't engage and spin the driveplate ring gear, remove the starter from the engine (see Section 13) and bench test the starter (see Step 4).

3   If the starter turns over slowly, check the starter cranking voltage and the current draw from the battery. This test must be performed with the starter assembly on the engine. Crank the engine over (for 10 seconds or less) and observe the battery voltage. It should not drop below 8.5 volts. Also, observe the current draw using an ammeter (see illustration). It should not exceed 380 amps. If the starter motor exceeds these values, replace it. Several conditions might affect the starter's cranking power. The battery must be in good condition and the battery cold-cranking rating must not be under-rated for the application. Be sure to check the battery specifications carefully. The battery terminals and cables must be clean and not corroded. Also, in cases of extremely cold temperatures, make sure the battery and/or engine block is warmed before performing the tests.

4   If the starter is receiving voltage but does not activate, remove and check the starter/solenoid assembly on the bench. Most likely the solenoid is defective. In some rare cases, the engine may be seized, so be sure to try and rotate the crankshaft pulley (see Chapter 2) before proceeding. With the starter/solenoid assembly mounted in a vise on the bench, install one jumper cable from the negative terminal (-) to the body of the starter. Install another jumper cable from the positive terminal (+) on the battery to the B+ terminal on the starter (see illustration). Install a starter switch and apply battery voltage to the solenoid S terminal (for 10 seconds or less) and observe the solenoid plunger, shift lever and overrunning clutch extend and rotate the pinion drive. If the pinion drive extends but does not rotate, the solenoid is operating but the starter motor is defective. If there is no movement but the solenoid clicks, the solenoid and/or the starter motor is defective. If the solenoid plunger extends and rotates the pinion drive, the starter/solenoid assembly is working properly.

13   Starter motor - removal and installation

1   Disconnect the cable from the negative terminal of the battery (see Section 1).

FOUR-CYLINDER MODELS

▸ **Refer to illustrations 13.3, 13.4 and 13.5**

2   Remove the intake manifold (see Chapter 2A).

3   Clearly label, then disconnect, the wires from the terminals on the starter motor solenoid (see illustration). Also disconnect any clips that attach the wiring to the starter assembly.

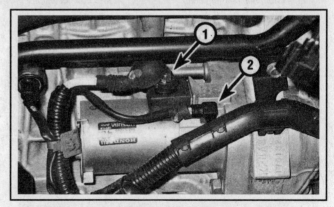

13.3 Starter motor electrical connections (four-cylinder model with an automatic transaxle; starter with manual transaxle has the solenoid on top of the starter, with starter cable and S terminal on the end of solenoid)

1   B+ terminal   *2   S terminal*

13.4 To detach the starter motor assembly, remove the two mounting bolts

13.5 When reconnecting the starter cable to the stud terminal on the solenoid, make sure that the crimped side of the ring terminal faces up on automatics (shown) or forward on manual transaxles (not shown)

13.9 Starter motor details (V6 models)

1	S terminal	3	Starter mounting bolts
2	B terminal (starter cable)		(lower bolt not visible)

4   Remove the starter mounting bolts (see illustration) and detach the starter.

5   Installation is the reverse of removal. If you're installing the starter on an automatic transaxle, make sure that the crimped side of the ring terminal on the starter cable faces up (see illustration). If you're

installing the starter on a manual transaxle, make sure that the crimped side of the ring terminal on the starter cable faces forward, toward the front of the vehicle. On all models, be sure to tighten the starter mounting bolts to the torque listed in this Chapter's Specifications.

6   When you're done, reconnect the cable to the negative terminal of the battery (see Section 1), enter the anti-theft code for the radio and, if equipped, the navigation system, then enter the radio station presets and reset the power window control unit (see Section 1).

V6 MODELS

▶ **Refer to illustration 13.9**

7   Remove the battery (see Section 3).

8   Remove the bolt that attaches the harness bracket and detach the harness bracket.

9   Clearly label, then disconnect the wires from the terminals on the starter motor solenoid (see illustration).

10   Remove the two starter mounting bolts and remove the starter motor.

11   Installation is the reverse of removal. Be sure to tighten the starter mounting bolts to the torque listed in this Chapter's Specifications.

12   When you're done, reconnect the battery, enter the anti-theft code for the radio and, if equipped, the navigation system, then enter the radio station presets and reset the power window control unit (see Section 1).

Specifications

General

Battery voltage
    Engine off   12.6 volts
    Engine running   Approximately 13.5 volts
Firing order
    Four-cylinder models   1-3-4-2
    V6 models   1-4-2-5-3-6

Torque specifications	Ft-lbs (unless otherwise indicated)	Nm

➡**Note: One foot-pound (ft-lb) of torque is equivalent to 12 inch-pounds (in-lbs) of torque. Torque values below approximately 15 ft-lbs are expressed in inch-pounds, since most foot-pound torque wrenches are not accurate at these smaller values.**

	Ft-lbs	Nm
Alternator bolts		
Four-cylinder engines		
2007 and earlier models	16	22
2008 and later models		
8 mm bolt	16	22
10 mm bolt	33	44
V6 engines		
8 mm bolt	16	22
10 mm bolt	33	44
Ignition coil		
Four-cylinder models		
Ignition coil cover bolts	86 in-lbs	10
Ignition coil mounting bolts/studs	104 in-lbs	12
V6 models		
Ignition coil mounting bolts	104 in-lbs	12
Starter mounting bolts		
Four-cylinder models		
Longer bolt	33	44
Shorter bolt	47	64
V6 models		
2007 and earlier		
Longer bolt	47	64
Shorter bolt	33	44
2008 and later		
Manual transaxle models	54	74
Automatic transaxle models	33	44

Notes

6

EMISSIONS AND ENGINE CONTROL SYSTEMS

1 General information

▶ Refer to illustration 1.4

To prevent pollution of the atmosphere from incompletely burned and evaporating gases, and to maintain good driveability and fuel economy, a number of emission control systems are incorporated. They include the:

Catalytic converter(s)
Evaporative Emissions Control (EVAP) system
Exhaust Gas Recirculation (EGR) system
Idle air control system
Intake air bypass control thermal valve (four-cylinder models only)
Intake Manifold Runner Control (IMRC) system (V6 models with manual transaxle only)
On-Board Diagnostic-II (OBD-II) system
Positive Crankcase Ventilation (PCV) system
Programmed Fuel Injection (PGM-FI) system (the electronic engine control system)
intelligent Variable Valve Timing and Lift Electronic Control/Variable Valve Timing Control (i-VTEC/VTC) system (four-cylinder models)
Variable Valve Timing and Lift Electronic Control (VTEC) system (V6 models)

This Chapter includes general descriptions of and component replacement procedures for all of the systems listed above. It also includes replacement procedures for most of the important information sensors used by the Powertrain Control Module (PCM) to monitor engine operating conditions, as well as replacement procedures for most output actuators under PCM control. Replacing certain components, such as the electronic throttle body on V6 models, or the PCM itself on any model, are easy enough to do at home, but you would need a Honda Diagnostic System (HDS) scan tool to do some reprogramming after installing the new component. We will therefore let you know when something is beyond the scope of the home mechanic and recommend instead that you have that particular procedure done by a dealer service department with the special tools needed to restore the engine management system to good working order.

The most frequent cause of emissions problems is simply a loose or broken wire or electrical connector, or a damaged or disconnected vacuum or EVAP hose, so always check all hoses, wiring harnesses and connections first. And before assuming that an emissions control system is malfunctioning, always be sure to inspect the fuel and ignition systems carefully. A symptom that initially appears to be caused by a defective emissions system or device often disappears when the engine is simply tuned up! Of course, the diagnosis of some emission control devices requires specialized tools, equipment and training. If a

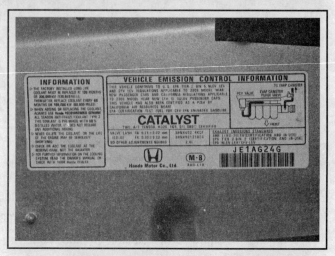

1.4 The Vehicle Emission Control Information (VECI) label specifies the emission-control systems on your vehicle, and includes important tune-up specifications and a vacuum hose routing diagram

procedure is beyond your ability, consult a dealer service department.

➡Note: Because of a Federally mandated extended warranty which covers the emissions control system components, check with your dealer about warranty coverage before working on any emissions-related systems. Once the warranty has expired, you may wish to perform some of the component checks and/or replacement procedures in this Chapter to save money.

Pay close attention to any special precautions outlined in this Chapter. It should be noted that the illustrations of the various systems might not exactly match the system installed on your vehicle because of annual changes made by the manufacturer during production and because of running changes made during a model year.

A Vehicle Emissions Control Information (VECI) label (see illustration) is located in the engine compartment, either on the underside of the hood or attached to the radiator support or one of the strut towers. This label specifies the important emissions systems on the vehicle and it provides the important specifications for tune-ups. Part of the VECI label, the Vacuum Hose Routing Diagram, provides a vacuum hose schematic with emissions components identified. When servicing the engine or emissions systems, the VECI label and the vacuum hose routing diagram should always be checked for up-to-date information.

2 On Board Diagnostic (OBD) system and trouble codes

SCAN TOOL INFORMATION

▶ Refer to illustration 2.1

1 Hand-held scanners are the most powerful and versatile tools for analyzing engine management systems used on later model vehicles (see illustration). Early model scanners handle codes and some diagnostics for many systems. Each brand scan tool must be examined carefully to match the year, make and model of the vehicle you are

working on. Often, interchangeable cartridges are available to access the particular manufacturer (Chrysler, Ford, GM, Honda, Toyota etc.). Some manufacturers will specify by continent (Asia, Europe, USA, etc.).

➡Note: An aftermarket generic scanner should work with any model covered by this manual. Before purchasing a generic scan tool, contact the manufacturer of the scanner you're planning to buy and verify that it will work properly with the OBD-II system you want to scan. If necessary, of course, you can always have the codes extracted by a dealer service department or an independent repair shop with a professional scan tool.

OBD SYSTEM GENERAL DESCRIPTION

2   All models are equipped with the second generation OBD-II system. This system consists of an on-board computer known as the Powertrain Control Module (PCM), and information sensors, which monitor various functions of the engine and send data to the PCM. This system incorporates a series of diagnostic monitors that detect and identify fuel injection and emissions control systems faults and store the information in the computer memory. This updated system also tests sensors and output actuators, diagnoses drive cycles, freezes data and clears codes.

3   This powerful diagnostic computer must be accessed using an OBD-II scan tool and 16-pin Data Link Connector (DLC) located under the driver's dash area. The PCM is located below the center of the instrument panel, mounted to the firewall. The PCM is the brain of the electronically controlled fuel and emissions system. It receives data from a number of sensors and other electronic components (switches, relays, etc.). Based on the information it receives, the PCM generates output signals to control various relays, solenoids (fuel injectors) and other actuators. The PCM is specifically calibrated to optimize the emissions, fuel economy and driveability of the vehicle.

4   It isn't a good idea to attempt diagnosis or replacement of the PCM or emission control components at home while the vehicle is under warranty. Because of a Federally mandated warranty which covers the emissions system components and because any owner-induced damage to the PCM, the sensors and/or the control devices may void this warranty, take the vehicle to a dealer service department if the PCM or a system component malfunctions.

INFORMATION SENSORS

5   **Accelerator Pedal Position (APP) sensor** - The APP sensor, which is part of the electronic throttle control system on V6 models, is located at the right rear corner of the engine compartment. On V6 models, the throttle plate inside the throttle body is electronically controlled by the PCM. As you press the accelerator pedal, the APP sensor alters its voltage signal to the PCM in proportion to the angle of the pedal.

6   **Brake Pedal Position (BPP) switch** - The BPP switch is located at the top of the brake pedal. It's a normally open switch that closes when the brake pedal is applied and sends a signal to the PCM, which interprets this signal as its cue to disengage the torque converter clutch. The BPP switch is also used to disengage the brake shift interlock. For information regarding the replacement and adjustment of the BPP switch, refer to Chapter 9.

7   **Camshaft Position (CMP) sensor** - On four-cylinder models, there are two CMP sensors: CMP sensor A and CMP sensor B. CMP sensor A is located at the left front corner of the cylinder head (opposite end from the timing chain), near the left end of the intake camshaft. CMP sensor B is also located at the left end of the cylinder head, near the left end of the exhaust camshaft. CMP sensor A monitors the position of the camshaft for the Variable Valve Timing and Lift Electronic Control (VTEC) system. CMP sensor B produces a signal that the PCM uses to identify the number 1 cylinder and to time the firing sequence of the fuel injectors. (For more information about the VTEC system, refer to Section 25.) On V6 models, the CMP sensor is located at the right (timing belt) end of the front cylinder head, near the right end of the intake camshaft. The CMP sensor on a V6 produces a signal that the PCM uses to identify the number 1 cylinder and to time the firing sequence of the fuel injectors.

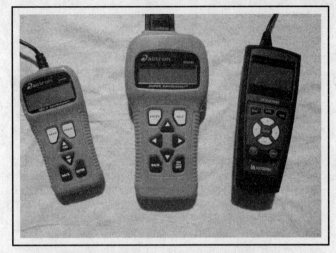

2.1 Scanners like these from Actron and AutoXray are powerful diagnostic aids - they can tell you just about anything you want to know about your engine management system

8   **Crankshaft Position (CKP) sensor** - The CKP sensor produces a signal that the PCM uses to determine crankshaft speed. The PCM uses this information to determine ignition timing, to time the injectors and to detect misfires. On four-cylinder models, the CKP sensor is located on the timing chain cover, at about 7 o'clock in relation to the crankshaft timing chain sprocket. On V6 models, the CKP sensor is located at the timing belt end of the engine, at about 3 o'clock in relation to the crankshaft timing belt sprocket.

9   **Electrical Load Detector (ELD)** - The ELD monitors the electrical load on the system and keeps the PCM informed. The PCM controls the voltage output of the alternator in response to the data conveyed by this signal. The ELD unit is located in, and is an integral component of, the engine compartment fuse and relay box. If the ELD fails, you must replace the fuse and relay box (see Section 6).

10   **Engine Coolant Temperature (ECT) sensor** - The ECT sensor is a thermistor (temperature-sensitive variable resistor) that sends a voltage signal to the PCM, which uses this data to determine the temperature of the engine coolant. The ECT sensor helps the PCM control the air/fuel mixture ratio and ignition timing, and it also helps the PCM determine when to turn the Exhaust Gas Recirculation (EGR) system on and off. On 2003 and 2004 four-cylinder models, the ECT sensor is located at the left end of the cylinder head, right behind the EGR purge valve. On 2005 and later four-cylinder models, this ECT sensor is referred to as "ECT sensor No. 1" because there are two ECT sensors on these models. The second ECT sensor, which is located on the lower backside of the radiator, is referred to as "ECT sensor No. 2." On 2003 and 2004 V6 models, the ECT sensor is located at the left end of the engine, near the throttle body. On 2005 and later models, this ECT sensor is referred to as "ECT sensor No. 1" because there two ECT sensors on these models. The second ECT sensor, which is located under the throttle body, is referred to as "ECT sensor No. 2."

11   **Fuel tank pressure sensor** - The fuel tank pressure sensor measures the fuel tank pressure when the PCM tests the EVAP system, and it's also used to control fuel tank pressure by signaling the EVAP system to purge the tank when the pressure becomes excessive. The fuel tank pressure sensor is located on top of the EVAP canister.

12   **Input shaft (mainshaft) speed sensor** - The input shaft (or mainshaft) speed sensor is a magnetic pick-up coil located on the

automatic transaxle. The PCM compares the signal from the input shaft (mainshaft) speed sensor with the signal from the output shaft (countershaft) speed sensor to calculate whether slippage (wear) is occurring inside the transaxle. On four-cylinder models with an automatic transaxle, the input shaft speed sensor is located on the upper backside of the transaxle. On V6 models with a manual transaxle, the input shaft speed sensor is located on the front side of the transaxle, to the left of the starter motor and above the output shaft speed sensor. On V6 models with an automatic transaxle, the input shaft speed sensor is located at the left front corner of the transaxle.

13 **Intake Air Temperature (IAT) sensor** - The IAT sensor monitors the temperature of the air entering the engine and sends a signal to the PCM. On 2003 and 2004 four-cylinder models (except SULEV and LX-P models), the IAT sensor is located on the air intake duct. On 2003 and 2004 four-cylinder SULEV and LX-P models, and on all 2005 and later four-cylinder models, the IAT sensor is integrated into the Mass Air Flow (MAF) sensor, which is referred to as the MAF/IAT sensor. On V6 models, the IAT sensor is located on the intake manifold, near the throttle body.

14 **Knock sensor** - The knock sensor is a piezoelectric crystal that oscillates in proportion to engine vibration. (The term piezoelectric refers to the property of certain crystals that produce a voltage when subjected to a mechanical stress.) The oscillation of the piezoelectric crystal produces a voltage output that is monitored by the PCM, which retards the ignition timing when the oscillation exceeds a certain threshold. When the engine is operating normally, the knock sensor oscillates consistently and its voltage signal is steady. When detonation occurs, engine vibration increases, and the oscillation of the knock sensor exceeds a design threshold. (Detonation is an uncontrolled explosion, after the spark occurs at the spark plug, which spontaneously combusts the remaining air/fuel mixture, resulting in a pinging or slapping sound.) If allowed to continue, the engine can be damaged. On four-cylinder models, the knock sensor is located on the front side of the block, behind the intake manifold. On V6 models, the knock sensor is located on top of the engine block, under the intake manifold.

15 **Manifold Absolute Pressure (MAP) sensor** - The MAP sensor monitors the pressure or vacuum downstream from the throttle plate, inside the intake manifold. The MAP sensor measures intake manifold pressure and vacuum on the absolute scale, i.e. from zero instead of from sea-level atmospheric pressure (14.7 psi). The MAP sensor converts the absolute pressure into a variable voltage signal that changes with the pressure. The PCM uses this data to determine engine load so that it can alter the ignition advance and fuel enrichment. On four-cylinder models, the MAP sensor is located on the intake manifold, near the throttle body. On V6 models, the MAP sensor is located on the throttle body itself.

16 **Mass Air Flow/Intake Air Temperature (MAF/IAT) sensor** - 2003 and 2004 SULEV four-cylinder models and all 2005 and later four-cylinder models are equipped with a MAF/IAT sensor, which is located on the air filter housing adjacent to the air intake duct. The MAF sensor is the means by which the PCM measures the amount of intake air drawn into the engine. It uses a hot-wire sensing element to measure the amount of air entering the engine. The wire is constantly maintained at a specified temperature above the ambient temperature of the incoming air by electrical current. As intake air passes through the MAF sensor and over the hot wire, it cools the wire, and the control system immediately corrects the temperature back to its constant value. The current required to maintain the constant value is used by the PCM to determine the amount of air flowing through the MAF sensor. The MAF sensor also includes an integral Intake Air Temperature (IAT) sensor. The two components cannot be serviced separately; if either sensor

is defective, replace the MAF/IAT sensor.

17 **Output shaft (countershaft) speed sensor** - The output shaft (or countershaft) speed sensor is a magnetic pick-up coil, which is located on the front of both automatic and manual transaxles. The output shaft speed sensor provides the Powertrain Control Module (PCM) with information about the rotational speed of the output shaft in the transmission. On vehicles with an automatic transaxle, the PCM uses this information to control the torque converter and to calculate speed scheduling and the correct operating pressure for the transaxle. On automatics, the PCM also compares the signal from the input shaft (mainshaft) speed sensor with the signal from the output shaft (countershaft) speed sensor to calculate whether slippage (wear) is occurring inside the transaxle. On vehicles with a manual transaxle, the output shaft speed sensor is simply a vehicle speed sensor for the PCM. On four-cylinder models with a manual transaxle, the output shaft speed sensor is located on the front of the transaxle. On four-cylinder models with an automatic transaxle, the output shaft speed sensor is located on the upper backside of the engine, next to the input shaft speed sensor (the output shaft speed sensor is the one closer to the engine). On V6 models with a manual transaxle, the output shaft speed sensor is located on the front of the motor, to the left of the starter motor and below the input shaft speed sensor. On V6 models with an automatic transaxle, the output shaft speed sensor is located on top of the transaxle, near the backside of the transaxle housing.

18 **Oxygen sensors** - An oxygen sensor is a galvanic battery that generates a small variable voltage signal in proportion to the difference between the oxygen content in the exhaust stream and the oxygen content in the ambient air. The PCM uses the voltage signal from the upstream oxygen sensor to maintain a stoichiometric air/fuel ratio of 14.7:1 by constantly adjusting the pulse width (on-time) of the fuel injectors. There are two oxygen sensors on four-cylinder models: one upstream sensor (ahead of the catalytic converter) and a downstream oxygen sensor, which is located on the catalyst. On V6 models, there are four oxygen sensors. V6 models are equipped with a pair of Warm Up Three-Way Catalytic Converters (WU-TWCs), each of which is an integral part of the exhaust manifold. The upstream oxygen sensor is located at the upper end of the catalyst and the downstream sensor is located at the lower end. (For more information about the WU-TWCs, refer to Section 21).

19 **Power Steering Pressure (PSP) switch** - The PSP switch monitors the pressure inside the power steering system. When the pressure exceeds a certain threshold at idle or during low speed maneuvers, the switch sends a voltage signal to the PCM, which raises the idle slightly to compensate for the extra load on the engine. The PSP switch is located on the power steering pump outlet (pressure) line, right above the dust boot for the steering rack assembly's right tie-rod.

20 **Throttle Position (TP) sensor** - The TP sensor is a potentiometer that receives a constant voltage input from the PCM and sends back a voltage signal that varies in relation to the opening angle of the throttle plate inside the throttle body. This voltage signal tells the PCM when the throttle is closed, half-open, wide open or anywhere in between. The PCM uses this data, along with information from other sensors, to calculate injector pulse width (the interval of time during which an injector solenoid is energized by the PCM). The TP sensor is located on the throttle body, on the end of the throttle plate shaft. The TP sensor is not removable on any model. If it's defective, replace the throttle body.

21 **Transmission range switch** - The transmission range switch, which is used only on automatics, functions like a conventional Park/Neutral Position (PNP) switch. It prevents the engine from starting in any gear other than Park or Neutral, and it closes the circuit for the back-up

lights when the shift lever is moved to Reverse. The PCM also sends a voltage signal to the transmission range switch, which uses a series of step-down resistors that act as a voltage divider. The PCM monitors the voltage output signal from the switch, which corresponds to the position of the manual lever. Thus the PCM is able to determine the gear selected and is able to determine the correct pressure for the electronic pressure control system of the transaxle. The transmission range switch is located on the left end of the transaxle, under a small cover.

OUTPUT ACTUATORS

22 **EVAP canister purge valve** - The EVAP canister purge valve is located at the left rear corner of the engine on all models. The purge valve is normally closed. But when ordered to do so by the PCM, it allows the fuel vapors that are stored in the EVAP canister to be drawn into the intake manifold, where they're mixed with intake air, then burned along with the normal air/fuel mixture, under certain operating conditions.

23 **EVAP canister vent shut valve** - The EVAP canister vent shut valve is located on the EVAP canister, which is located underneath the vehicle. The canister vent shut valve is normally open, but it closes and seals off the EVAP system for inspection and maintenance tests and for OBD-II leak and pressure tests.

24 **Exhaust Gas Recirculation (EGR) valve** - When the engine is put under a load (hard acceleration, passing, going up a steep hill, pulling a trailer, etc.), combustion chamber temperature increases. When combustion chamber temperature exceeds 2500 degrees, excessive amounts of oxides of nitrogen (NOx) are produced. NOx is a precursor of photochemical smog. When combined with hydrocarbons (HC), other reactive organic compounds (ROCs) and sunlight, it forms ozone, nitrogen dioxide and nitrogen nitrate and other nasty stuff. The PCM-controlled EGR valve allows exhaust gases to be recirculated back to the intake manifold where they dilute the incoming air/fuel mixture, which lowers the combustion chamber temperature and decreases the amount of NOx produced during high-load conditions. On four-cylinder models, the EGR valve is located at the left end of the cylinder head, where it's bolted to an external coolant passage known as the water outlet. On V6 models, the EGR valve is located at the left end of the front cylinder head.

25 **Fuel injectors** - The fuel injectors, which spray a fine mist of fuel into the intake ports, where it is mixed with incoming air, are inductive coils under PCM control. For more information about the injectors, see Chapter 4.

26 **Idle Air Control (IAC) valve** - The IAC valve, which is used only four-cylinder models, controls the amount of air allowed to bypass the throttle plate when the throttle plate is at its (nearly closed) idle position. The IAC valve is controlled by the PCM. When the engine is placed under an additional load at idle (high power steering pressure or running the air conditioning compressor during low-speed maneuvers, for example), the engine can run roughly, stumble and even stall. To prevent this from happening, the PCM opens the IAC valve to increase the idle speed enough to overcome the extra load imposed on the engine. The IAC valve is mounted on the underside of the throttle body. (On V6 models, which are equipped with PCM-controlled electronic throttle bodies, the PCM regulates idle air by opening and closing the throttle plate with a solenoid.)

27 **Ignition coils** - There is one ignition coil per spark plug. The coils are located directly on top of the valve cover, directly over the spark plugs. The ignition coils are under the control of the Powertrain Control Module (PCM). There is no separate ignition control module. Instead, "coil drivers" inside the PCM turn the primary side of the coils

on and off. For more information about the ignition coils, see Chapter 5.

28 **Intake Manifold Tuning (IMT) actuator** - V6 models with a manual transaxle are equipped with an Intake Manifold Runner Control (IMRC) system. The PCM-controlled IMT actuator is a component of IMRC-equipped models. The PCM improves torque at low speeds by commanding the IMT actuator to close the actuator valve inside the intake manifold, and improves torque at high speeds by commanding the IMT actuator to open the actuator valve. The IMT actuator replacement procedure is in Section 20. For more information about the special intake manifold used on these models, refer to Chapter 2B.

29 **Throttle actuator** - The throttle actuator is an electric motor, located inside the throttle body, that controls the angle of the throttle plate. On V6 models, which are equipped with an electronic throttle control system, there is no accelerator cable. (There is a cable, but it connects the accelerator pedal only to the Accelerator Pedal Position (APP) sensor - see Step 5). The APP sensor monitors the angle of the accelerator pedal, then delivers an analog voltage signal that's proportional to the pedal angle to the PCM. The PCM uses the analog voltage signal from the APP sensor to control the angle of the throttle plate.

30 **Variable Valve Timing and Lift Electronic Control (VTEC) solenoid valve** - The VTEC system changes valve lift and timing by using more than one cam lobe profile. It changes cam profiles by altering the hydraulic pressure in a special circuit that circulates through the rocker arms. The VTEC solenoid valve is the device that the VTEC system uses to control the oil pressure that locks and unlocks each adjacent pair of intake rocker arms in response to engine speed. On four-cylinder engines, the VTEC solenoid valve is located at the right rear corner of the cylinder head. On V6 engines, the VTEC solenoid valve is located at the right end of the engine. For more information about the VTEC system and the VTEC solenoid valve, see Section 25.

31 **Variable Valve Timing Control (VTC) oil control solenoid valve** - Four-cylinder engines are equipped with the latest version of VTEC, known as intelligent Variable Valve Timing and Lift Electronic Control (i-VTEC). Besides the usual VTEC components, these models are also equipped with Variable Valve Timing Control (VTC), which changes the phase of the intake camshaft. The VTC actuator is an integral part of the intake camshaft timing chain sprocket (see Chapter 2A for more information about the VTC actuator). The VTC oil control solenoid valve is the PCM-controlled device that controls the oil pressure to the actuator. For more information about the i-VTEC system and the VTC oil control solenoid valve, refer to Section 25.

OBTAINING AND CLEARING DIAGNOSTIC TROUBLE CODES (DTCS)

32 All models covered by this manual are equipped with on-board diagnostics. When the PCM recognizes a malfunction in a monitored emission control system, component or circuit, it turns on the Malfunction Indicator Light (MIL) on the dash. The PCM will continue to display the MIL until the problem is fixed and the Diagnostic Trouble Code (DTC) is cleared from the PCM's memory. You'll need a scan tool to access any DTCs stored in the PCM.

33 Before outputting any DTCs stored in the PCM, thoroughly inspect ALL electrical connectors and hoses. Make sure that all electrical connections are tight, clean and free of corrosion. And make sure that all hoses are correctly connected, fit tightly and are in good condition (no cracks or tears). Also, make sure that the engine is tuned up. A poorly running engine is probably one of the biggest causes of emission-related malfunctions. Often, simply giving the engine a good tune-up will correct the problem.

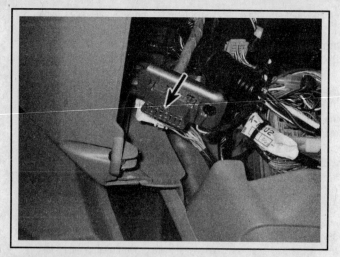

2.34 The Data Link Connector (DLC) is located under the far left end of the dash

Accessing the DTCs

Refer to illustration 2.34

34 On these models, all of which are equipped with On-Board Diagnostic II (OBD-II) systems, the Diagnostic Trouble Codes (DTCs) can only be accessed with a scan tool. Professional scan tools are expensive, but relatively inexpensive generic scan tools (see illustration 2.1) are available at most auto parts stores. Simply plug the connector of the scan tool into the diagnostic connector (see illustration), which is located under the lower edge of the dash, just to the right of the steering column. Then follow the instructions included with the scan tool to extract the DTCs.

35 Once you have outputted all of the stored DTCs, look them up on the accompanying DTC chart.

36 After troubleshooting the source of each DTC make any necessary repairs or replace the defective component(s).

Clearing the DTCs

37 Clear the DTCs with the scan tool in accordance with the instructions provided by the scan tool's manufacturer.

DIAGNOSTIC TROUBLE CODES

38 The accompanying tables are a list of the Diagnostic Trouble Codes (DTCs) that can be accessed by a do-it-yourselfer working at home (there are many, many more DTCs available to professional mechanics with proprietary scan tools and software, but those codes cannot be accessed by a generic scan tool). If, after you have checked and repaired the connectors, wire harness and vacuum hoses (if applicable) for an emission-related system, component or circuit, the problem persists, have the vehicle checked by a dealer service department or other qualified repair shop.

OBD-II TROUBLE CODES

➡ **Note: Not all trouble codes apply to all models.**

Code	Probable cause
P0010	Variable Valve Timing Control (VTC) oil control solenoid valve malfunction
P0011	Variable Valve Timing Control (VTC) system malfunction
P0101	Mass Air Flow (MAF) sensor range or performance problem
P0102	Mass Air Flow (MAF) sensor circuit, low voltage
P0103	Mass Air Flow (MAF) sensor circuit, high voltage
P0107	Manifold Absolute Pressure (MAP) sensor circuit, low voltage
P0108	Manifold Absolute Pressure (MAP) sensor circuit, high voltage
P0111	Intake Air Temperature (IAT) sensor circuit, range or performance problem
P0112	Intake Air Temperature (IAT) sensor circuit, low voltage
P0113	Intake Air Temperature (IAT) sensor circuit, high voltage
P0116	Engine Coolant Temperature (ECT) sensor range or performance problem
P0117	Engine Coolant Temperature (ECT) sensor circuit, low voltage
P0118	Engine Coolant Temperature (ECT) sensor circuit, high voltage
P0122	Throttle Position (TP) sensor circuit, low voltage
P0123	Throttle Position (TP) sensor circuit, high voltage
P0125	Engine Coolant Temperature (ECT) sensor, malfunction or slow response
P0128	Cooling system malfunction
P0133	Upstream oxygen sensor circuit, response malfunction
P0133	Rear upstream oxygen sensor circuit, slow response (V6)
P0134	Upstream oxygen sensor, heater system malfunction
P0134	Rear upstream oxygen sensor, heater system malfunction (V6)
P0135	Upstream oxygen sensor, heater circuit malfunction

OBD-II TROUBLE CODES (CONTINUED)

➡**Note: Not all trouble codes apply to all models.**

Code	Probable cause
P0135	Rear upstream oxygen sensor, heater circuit malfunction (V6)
P0137	Downstream oxygen sensor circuit, low voltage
P0137	Rear downstream oxygen sensor circuit, low voltage (V6)
P0138	Downstream oxygen sensor circuit, high voltage
P0138	Rear downstream oxygen sensor circuit, high voltage (V6)
P0139	Downstream oxygen sensor circuit, slow response
P0139	Rear downstream oxygen sensor circuit, slow response (V6)
P0141	Downstream oxygen sensor, heater circuit malfunction
P0141	Rear downstream oxygen sensor, heater circuit malfunction (V6)
P0153	Front upstream oxygen sensor circuit, slow response (V6)
P0154	Front upstream oxygen sensor, heater system malfunction (V6)
P0155	Front upstream oxygen sensor, heater circuit malfunction (V6)
P0157	Front downstream oxygen sensor circuit, low voltage (V6)
P0158	Front downstream oxygen sensor circuit, high voltage (V6)
P0159	Front downstream oxygen sensor circuit, slow response (V6)
P0161	Front downstream oxygen sensor, heater circuit malfunction (V6)
P0171	Fuel system too lean
P0171	Rear cylinder bank, fuel system too lean (V6)
P0172	Fuel system too rich
P0172	Rear cylinder bank, fuel system too rich (V6)
P0174	Front cylinder bank, fuel system too lean (V6)
P0175	Front cylinder bank, fuel system too rich (V6)

Code	Probable cause
P0222	Throttle Position (TP) sensor B circuit, low voltage
P0223	Throttle Position (TP) sensor B circuit, high voltage
P0300	Random misfire detected
P0301	Cylinder no. 1 misfire detected
P0302	Cylinder no. 2 misfire detected
P0303	Cylinder no. 3 misfire detected
P0304	Cylinder no. 4 misfire detected
P0305	Cylinder No. 5 misfire detected
P0306	Cylinder No. 6 misfire detected
P0325	Knock sensor circuit malfunction
P0335	Crankshaft Position (CKP) sensor circuit, no signal
P0339	Crankshaft Position (CKP) sensor circuit, intermittent interruption
P0340	Camshaft Position (CMP) sensor A, no signal
P0341	CMP sensor and CKP sensor, incorrect phase detected
P0344	Camshaft Position (CMP) sensor A, intermittent interruption
P0351	No. 1 cylinder ignition coil circuit malfunction
P0352	No. 2 cylinder ignition coil circuit malfunction
P0353	No. 3 cylinder ignition coil circuit malfunction
P0354	No. 4 cylinder ignition coil circuit malfunction
P0365	Camshaft Position (CMP) sensor B, no signal
P0369	Camshaft Position (CMP) sensor B, intermittent interruption
P0385	Crankshaft Position (CKP) sensor B, no signal
P0389	Crankshaft Position (CKP) sensor B, intermittent interruption

OBD-II TROUBLE CODES (CONTINUED)

→Note: Not all trouble codes apply to all models.

Code	Probable cause
P0401	Exhaust Gas Recirculation (EGR) system, insufficient flow
P0404	Exhaust Gas Recirculation (EGR) valve circuit, range or performance problem
P0404	Exhaust Gas Recirculation (EGR) control circuit, range or performance problem (V6)
P0406	Exhaust Gas Recirculation (EGR) valve position sensor circuit, high voltage
P0420	Catalyst system efficiency below threshold
P0420	Rear bank catalyst system efficiency below threshold (V6)
P0430	Front bank catalyst system efficiency below threshold (V6)
P0442	Evaporative Emission (EVAP) system, small leak detected
P0443	Evaporative Emission (EVAP) system, canister purge valve circuit malfunction
P0451	Fuel tank pressure sensor, range or performance problem
P0452	Fuel tank pressure sensor circuit, low voltage
P0453	Fuel tank pressure sensor circuit, high voltage
P0455	Evaporative Emission (EVAP) system, large leak detected
P0455	Evaporative Emission (EVAP) system, very small leak detected (V6)
P0456	Evaporative Emission (EVAP) system, very small leak detected
P0457	Evaporative Emission (EVAP) system, leak detected or fuel cap loose or missing
P0461	Fuel level sensor circuit, range or performance problem
P0462	Fuel level sensor circuit, low voltage
P0463	Fuel level sensor circuit, high voltage
P0496	Evaporative Emission (EVAP) system, high purge flow
P0497	Evaporative Emission (EVAP) system, low purge flow

Code	Probable cause
P0498	Evaporative Emission (EVAP) canister vent shut valve circuit, low voltage
P0499	Evaporative Emission (EVAP) canister vent shut valve circuit, high voltage
P050A	Cold start idle air control system performance problem
P050B	Cold start ignition timing control system performance problem
P0506	Idle air control system, rpm lower than expected
P0507	Idle air control system, rpm higher than expected
P0511	Idle Air Control (IAC) valve, circuit malfunction
P0532	Air conditioning pressure sensor circuit low voltage
P0533	Air conditioning pressure sensor circuit high voltage
P0562	Charging system, low voltage
P0563	Powertrain Control Module (PCM) power source circuit, unexpected voltage
P060A	Powertrain Control Module (PCM) (A/T) internal control module malfunction
P0602	Powertrain Control Module (PCM) programming error
P0603	Powertrain Control Module (PCM) internal control module Keep Alive Memory (KAM) error
P0606	Powertrain Control Module (PCM) processor malfunction
P062F	Engine Control Module (ECM)/Powertrain Control Module (PCM) internal control module Keep Alive Memory (KAM) error
P0630	Vehicle Identification Number (VIN) not programmed or mismatched
P0641	Sensor reference voltage A malfunction
P0685	Powertrain Control Module (PCM) power control circuit malfunction
P0700	Automatic transaxle system malfunction
P0715	Input shaft (mainshaft) speed sensor circuit malfunction
P0720	Output shaft (countershaft) speed sensor circuit malfunction

OBD-II TROUBLE CODES (CONTINUED)

➡Note: Not all trouble codes apply to all models.

Automatic transaxle diagnostic trouble codes

Code	Probable cause
P0705	Transaxle Range (TR) switch, multiple shift position input
P0706	Transaxle Range (TR) switch, open circuit
P0711	ATF temperature sensor, range or performance problem
P0712	ATF temperature sensor, short circuit
P0713	ATF temperature sensor, open circuit
P0716	Input shaft (mainshaft) speed sensor, range or performance problem
P0717	Input shaft (mainshaft) speed sensor, no signal input
P0718	Input shaft (mainshaft) speed sensor, intermittent failure
P0721	Output shaft (countershaft) speed sensor, range or performance problem
P0722	Output shaft (countershaft) speed sensor, no signal input
P0723	Output shaft (countershaft) speed sensor, intermittent failure
P0731	First gear, incorrect ratio
P0732	Second gear, incorrect ratio
P0733	Third gear, incorrect ratio
P0734	Fourth gear, incorrect ratio
P0735	Fifth gear, incorrect ratio
P0741	Torque converter clutch circuit performance, or stuck in OFF position
P0746	Automatic transaxle clutch pressure control solenoid valve A stuck in OFF position
P0747	Automatic transaxle clutch pressure control solenoid valve A stuck in ON position
P0751	Shift solenoid valve A stuck in OFF position
P0752	Shift solenoid valve A stuck in ON position

Code	Probable cause
P0756	Shift solenoid valve B stuck in OFF position
P0757	Shift solenoid valve B stuck in ON position
P0761	Shift solenoid valve C stuck in OFF position
P0762	Shift solenoid valve C stuck in ON position
P0771	Shift solenoid valve E stuck in OFF position
P0776	Automatic transaxle clutch pressure control solenoid valve B stuck in OFF position
P0777	Automatic transaxle clutch pressure control solenoid valve B stuck in ON position
P0780	Shift control system
P0796	Automatic transaxle clutch pressure control solenoid valve C stuck in OFF position
P0797	Automatic transaxle clutch pressure control solenoid valve C stuck in ON position
P0812	Transaxle range switch ATP RVS switch
P0842	N position
P0843	Second clutch transaxle fluid pressure switch open or stuck in OFF position
P0847	Third clutch transaxle fluid pressure switch shorted or stuck in ON position
P0848	Third clutch transaxle fluid pressure switch open or stuck in OFF position
P0872	Fourth clutch transaxle fluid pressure switch shorted or stuck in ON position
P0873	Fourth clutch transaxle fluid pressure switch open or stuck in OFF position
P0962	Automatic transaxle clutch pressure control solenoid valve A, open or short circuit
P0963	Automatic transaxle clutch pressure control solenoid valve A
P0966	Automatic transaxle clutch pressure control solenoid valve B, open or short circuit
P0967	Automatic transaxle clutch pressure control solenoid valve B
P0970	Automatic transaxle clutch pressure control solenoid valve C, open or short circuit
P0971	Automatic transaxle clutch pressure control solenoid valve C
P0973	Shift solenoid valve A, short circuit

OBD-II TROUBLE CODES (CONTINUED)

➡Note: Not all trouble codes apply to all models.

Automatic transaxle diagnostic trouble codes

Code	Probable cause
P0974	Shift solenoid valve A, open circuit
P0976	Shift solenoid valve B, short circuit
P0977	Shift solenoid valve B, open circuit
P0979	Shift solenoid valve C, short circuit
P0980	Shift solenoid valve C, open circuit
P0982	Shift solenoid valve D, short circuit
P0983	Shift solenoid valve D, open circuit
P0985	Shift solenoid valve E, short circuit
P0986	Shift solenoid valve E, open circuit
P1009	Variable valve Timing Control (VTC) advance malfunction
P1109	Barometric pressure (BARO) sensor circuit out of range (high)

3 Accelerator Pedal Position (APP) sensor - replacement

→Note: The APP sensor is located on the firewall, at the upper end of the short accelerator cable that connects the accelerator pedal to the APP sensor.

1 Disconnect the accelerator cable from the APP sensor.
2 Disconnect the electrical connector from the APP sensor.

3 Remove the APP sensor mounting bolts and remove the sensor from the firewall.
4 Installation is the reverse of removal.
5 When you're done, adjust the accelerator cable (see Section 12 in Chapter 4).

4 Camshaft Position (CMP) sensor - replacement

FOUR-CYLINDER MODELS

CMP sensor A

♦ Refer to illustrations 4.3 and 4.5

→Note: CMP sensor A, which is located at the left end of the cylinder head near the intake camshaft, is an information sensor for the Variable Valve Timing and Lift Electronic Control (VTEC) system (for more information about the VTEC system, see Section 25).

1 Remove the air filter housing (see Chapter 4).
2 Remove the EGR valve (see Section 23).
3 Disconnect the electrical connector from the CMP sensor (see illustration).
4 Remove the CMP sensor mounting bolt.
5 Remove the CMP sensor (see illustration) and remove the old sensor O-ring and discard it.
6 Installation is the reverse of removal. Be sure to use a new O-ring and tighten the CMP sensor mounting bolt securely.

CMP sensor B

♦ Refer to illustration 4.9

→Note: CMP sensor B, which is located at the left end of the cylinder head, near the exhaust camshaft, is an information sensor the PGM-FI system.

7 Remove the air filter housing (see Chapter 4).
8 Remove the EVAP canister purge valve (see Section 22).
9 Disconnect the electrical connector from the CMP sensor (see illustration).
10 Remove the CMP sensor mounting bolt and remove the CMP sensor.
11 Remove the CMP sensor O-ring and discard it.
12 Installation is the reverse of removal. Be sure to use a new O-ring and tighten the CMP sensor mounting bolt securely.

V6 MODELS

♦ Refer to illustrations 4.19 and 4.20

→Note: The CMP sensor is bolted to the backside of the timing belt rear cover, which is located between the front camshaft sprocket and the right end of the front cylinder head.

13 Put the piston in the No. 1 cylinder at Top Dead Center (see Chapter 2B).
14 Remove the upper timing belt covers (see Chapter 2B).
15 Lock the timing belt adjuster in position by screwing one of the battery hold-down clamp bolts into the boss for the adjuster (see Chapter 2B).
16 Loosen the idler pulley bolt about five or six turns, then remove the timing belt from the front camshaft sprocket (see Chapter 2B).
17 Remove the front camshaft sprocket (see Chapter 2B).

4.3 To remove CMP sensor A from a four-cylinder engine, depress the release tab (1) and disconnect the electrical connector, then remove the sensor mounting bolt (2)

4.5 To remove CMP sensor A from the cylinder head, pull it straight out, then remove and discard the old O-ring (even if you plan to reuse the old sensor, be sure to install a new O-ring)

4.9 To remove CMP sensor B from a four-cylinder engine, depress the release tab (1) and disconnect the electrical connector, then remove the sensor mounting bolt (2)

4.19 To detach the back timing belt cover from the front cylinder head on a V6 model, remove these two bolts

4.20 To detach the CMP sensor from the backside of the back timing belt cover on a V6 model, remove this bolt

18 Disconnect the electrical connector from the CMP sensor.
19 Remove the timing belt rear cover (see illustration).
20 Remove the CMP sensor mounting bolt (see illustration) and

remove the CMP sensor from the timing belt rear cover.
21 Installation is the reverse of removal. Be sure to tighten the CMP sensor mounting bolt securely.

5   Crankshaft Position (CKP) sensor - replacement

FOUR-CYLINDER MODELS

▶ Refer to illustrations 5.2 and 5.4

➡Note: The CKP sensor is located on the timing chain cover, near the crankshaft pulley.

1   Raise the front of the vehicle and support it securely on jackstands.

2   Disconnect the electrical connector from the CKP sensor (see illustration).
3   Remove the CKP sensor mounting bolt and remove the CKP sensor.
4   If you're installing the old CKP sensor, install a new O-ring on the sensor (see illustration).
5   Installation is the reverse of removal. Be sure to tighten the CKP sensor mounting bolt securely.

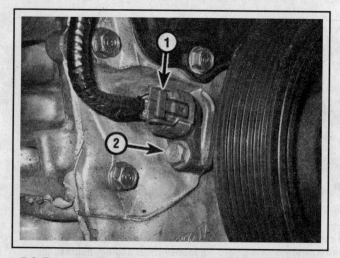

5.2 To remove the CKP sensor from a four-cylinder engine, depress the release tab (1) and disconnect the electrical connector, then remove the sensor mounting bolt (2) and pull the sensor straight out

5.4 Be sure to replace the CKP sensor O-ring if you're reinstalling the old sensor

V6 MODELS

→Note: The CKP sensor is located at the timing belt end of the engine, near the crankshaft timing belt sprocket.

6 Remove the accessory drivebelt (see Chapter 1).

7 Remove the crankshaft pulley and the upper and lower timing belt covers (see Chapter 2B).

8 Remove the CKP sensor mounting bolts and remove the sensor.

9 Disconnect the electrical connector from the CKP sensor.

10 Installation is the reverse of removal. Be sure to tighten the CKP sensor mounting bolts securely.

11 When you're done, drive the vehicle to a Honda dealer immediately and have the service department perform the "CKP Pattern Clear/ CKP Pattern Learn" procedure.

6 Electrical Load Detector (ELD) unit - replacement

♦ Refer to illustrations 6.3, 6.4 and 6.5

→Note: The ELD unit is located in, and is an integral part of, the engine compartment fuse and relay box. The ELD is not separately serviceable and no replacement ELD is available. If the ELD is defective, you must replace the fuse and relay box.

1 Disconnect the cable from the negative battery terminal (see Chapter 5, Section 1).

2 Remove the cover from the engine compartment fuse and relay box.

3 Remove the fuse and relay box mounting bolts and the bolts securing the battery cables (see illustration).

4 Remove the bottom half of the fuse and relay box assembly (see illustration).

5 Disconnect all electrical connectors from the fuse and relay box (see illustration) and remove the fuse and relay box.

6 Installation is the reverse of removal.

7 When you're done, enter the anti-theft codes for the radio and navigation system and enter the radio station presets, then perform the PCM idle learn procedure and reset the power window control unit (see Chapter 5, Section 1).

6.3 To remove the engine compartment fuse and relay box, disconnect the two bolts (1) that connect the battery positive cables and remove the two mounting bolts (2) . . .

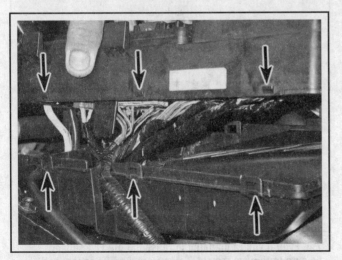

6.4 . . . disengage these three release tabs (and the three tabs on the backside of the box, not shown) from their corresponding lock tabs . . .

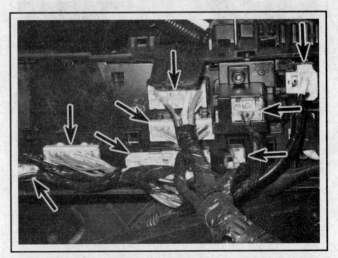

6.5 . . . then flip the fuse and relay box over and disconnect all electrical connectors

7 Engine Coolant Temperature (ECT) sensor - replacement

FOUR-CYLINDER MODELS

※ WARNING:

Wait until the engine has cooled completely before beginning this procedure.

➡Note: On 2003 and 2004 models, the ECT sensor is located at the left end of the cylinder head, behind the EGR valve. On 2005 and later models there are two ECT sensors. The unit on the left end of the cylinder head (same as the unit on 2003 and 2004 models) is referred to as "ECT sensor No. 1." The other ECT sensor, which is located on the lower backside of the radiator (in the same spot as the radiator fan switch on earlier models) is referred to as "ECT sensor No. 2."

1 Drain the engine coolant (see Chapter 1). (If you don't drain the coolant, coolant will flow out when you remove the ECT sensor.)

ECT sensor (2003 and 2004 models)/ECT sensor No. 1 (2005 and later models)

▸ Refer to illustrations 7.4 and 7.6

2 Remove the air filter housing (see Chapter 4).
3 Remove the EVAP canister purge valve (see Section 22).
4 Disconnect the electrical connector from the ECT sensor (see illustration).
5 Unscrew and remove the ECT sensor.

※ CAUTION:

If you're planning to reuse the old ECT sensor, handle it with care. Damage to the ECT sensor will adversely affect the operation of the PGM-FI system.

6 Remove and discard the old ECT sensor O-ring (see illustration). Whether you're planning to reuse the old ECT sensor or install a new unit, be sure to use a new O-ring.
7 Installation is the reverse of removal. Be sure to tighten the ECT sensor to the torque listed in this Chapter's Specifications.
8 Refill the cooling system (see Chapter 1).

ECT sensor No. 2 (2005 and later models)

9 Raise the front end of the vehicle and support it securely on jackstands.
10 Remove the under-vehicle splash shield (see illustration 6.8 in Chapter 2A).
11 Disconnect the electrical connector from the ECT sensor (see illustration 4.5 in Chapter 3).

➡Note: The referenced illustration in Chapter 3 depicts a cooling fan switch, but the procedures for replacing the fan switch and ECT sensor No. 2 are virtually identical.

12 Unscrew and remove the ECT sensor from the radiator.
13 Remove and discard the old ECT sensor O-ring (see illustration 7.6). Whether you're planning to reuse the old ECT sensor or install a new unit, be sure to use a new O-ring.
14 Installation is the reverse of removal. Be sure to tighten the ECT sensor to the torque listed in this Chapter's Specifications.
15 Refill the cooling system (see Chapter 1).

V6 MODELS

➡Note: On 2003 and 2004 models, the ECT sensor is located at the left end of the engine, near the throttle body. On 2005 and later models there are two ECT sensors. The unit near the throttle body is referred to as "ECT sensor No. 1" and the other ECT sensor, which is located under the throttle body, is referred to as "ECT sensor No. 2."

16 Drain the engine coolant (see Chapter 1). (If you don't drain the coolant, some coolant will run out when you remove the ECT sensor.)

7.4 To remove the ECT sensor from the cylinder head on a four-cylinder model, depress the release tab on the underside of the electrical connector (1) and disconnect the connector, then unscrew the sensor (2)

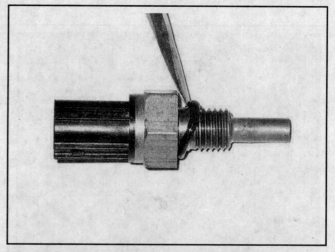

7.6 Even if you're planning to reuse the old ECT sensor, be sure to remove the old O-ring from the ECT sensor and discard it. Always use a new O-ring when installing the ECT sensor

ECT sensor (2003 and 2004 models)/ECT sensor No. 1 (2005 and later models)

17 Remove the air filter housing (see Chapter 4).

18 Disconnect the electrical connector from the ECT sensor.

19 Unscrew and remove the ECT sensor.

20 Remove the old ECT sensor O-ring (see illustration 7.6). Whether you're planning to reuse the old ECT sensor or install a new unit, be sure to use a new O-ring.

21 Installation is the reverse of removal. Be sure to tighten the ECT sensor to the torque listed in this Chapter's Specifications.

22 Refill the cooling system (see Chapter 1).

ECT sensor No. 2 (2005 and later models)

23 Remove the throttle body (see Chapter 4).

24 Disconnect the electrical connector from the ECT sensor.

25 Unscrew and remove the ECT sensor.

26 Remove the old ECT sensor O-ring (see illustration 7.6). Whether you're planning to reuse the old ECT sensor or install a new unit, be sure to use a new O-ring.

27 Installation is the reverse of removal. Be sure to tighten the ECT sensor to the torque listed in this Chapter's Specifications.

28 Refill the cooling system (see Chapter 1).

---

8 Input shaft (mainshaft) and output shaft (countershaft) speed sensors - replacement

FOUR-CYLINDER MODELS

Manual transaxle (output shaft speed sensor only)

➡Note: The output shaft (countershaft) speed sensor is located on the front of the transaxle. There is no input shaft (mainshaft) speed sensor.

1 Remove the air filter housing (see Chapter 4).

2 Disconnect the electrical connector from the output shaft speed sensor.

3 Remove the output shaft speed sensor mounting bolt and remove the sensor.

4 Remove and discard the old sensor O-ring (see illustration 8.9).

5 Installation is the reverse of removal. Be sure to use a new O-ring and tighten the output shaft speed sensor mounting bolt securely.

Automatic transaxle

♦ Refer to illustration 8.6

➡Note: The input shaft (mainshaft) and output shaft (countershaft) speed sensors are both located side-by-side on the upper backside of the transaxle. (The output shaft speed sensor is the one closer to the engine.)

6 Because of their location on the upper backside of the transaxle (see illustration), the input and output speed sensors are equally difficult to access from above or from below. It's a little easier to remove and install either of these sensors from above, which will require removal of the air intake duct and the air filter housing (see Chapter 4) and, if you need even more room to work, remove the engine compartment fuse and relay box (see Section 6). If you decide to work from below, there's no need to remove anything, just raise the front of the vehicle and support it securely on jackstands. However, because of the limited clearance, the sensor electrical connectors are a little more difficult to unplug from below than from above.

Input shaft (mainshaft) speed sensor

♦ Refer to illustration 8.9

7 Disconnect the electrical connector from the input shaft speed sensor (see illustration 8.6).

8 Remove the input shaft speed sensor mounting bolt and remove the sensor.

9 Remove the old input shaft speed sensor O-ring (see illustration) and discard it.

10 Installation is the reverse of removal. Be sure to use a new O-ring and tighten the sensor mounting bolt securely.

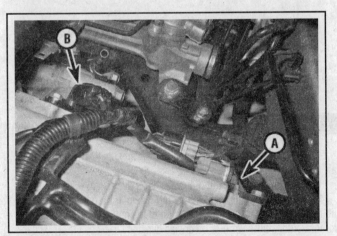

8.6 On four-cylinder models with an automatic transaxle, the input shaft (mainshaft) speed sensor (A) and the output shaft (countershaft) speed sensor (B) are located on the upper backside of the transaxle (fuse and relay box removed for clarity)

8.9 Even if you're installing the old input or output shaft speed sensor, be sure to remove the old O-ring from the speed sensor and replace it with a new O-ring

Output shaft (countershaft) speed sensor

11 Disconnect the electrical connector from the output shaft speed sensor (see illustration 8.6).

12 Remove the input shaft speed sensor mounting bolt and remove the sensor.

13 Remove the old input shaft speed sensor O-ring (see illustration 8.9) and discard it.

14 Installation is the reverse of removal. Be sure to use a new O-ring and tighten the sensor mounting bolt securely.

V6 MODELS

Manual transaxle

→Note: The input shaft (mainshaft) and output shaft (countershaft) speed sensors are located on the front of the transaxle, to the left of the starter motor. The input shaft speed sensor is the upper unit and the output shaft speed sensor is the lower unit.

15 Remove the air intake duct (see Chapter 4).

Input shaft (mainshaft) speed sensor

16 Disconnect the electrical connector from the input shaft speed sensor.

17 Remove the input shaft speed sensor mounting bolt and remove the sensor.

18 Remove the old input shaft speed sensor O-ring (see illustration 8.9) and discard it.

19 Installation is the reverse of removal. Be sure to use a new O-ring and tighten the sensor mounting bolt securely.

Output shaft (countershaft) speed sensor

20 Disconnect the electrical connector from the output shaft speed sensor.

21 Remove the output shaft speed sensor mounting bolt and remove the sensor.

22 Remove the old output shaft speed sensor O-ring (see illustration 8.9) and discard it.

23 Installation is the reverse of removal. Be sure to use a new O-ring and tighten the sensor mounting bolt securely.

Automatic transaxle

→Note: The input shaft (mainshaft) speed sensor is located at the left front corner of the transaxle. The output shaft (countershaft) speed sensor is located on top of the transaxle, near the backside of the transaxle housing.

Input shaft (mainshaft) speed sensor

24 Disconnect the battery cables (see Chapter 5, Section 1), then remove the battery and the battery tray (see Chapter 5, Section 3).

25 Disconnect the electrical connector from the input shaft speed sensor.

26 Remove the input shaft speed sensor mounting bolt and remove the sensor.

27 Remove the old input shaft speed sensor O-ring (see illustration 8.9) and discard it.

28 Installation is the reverse of removal. Be sure to use a new O-ring and tighten the sensor mounting bolt securely.

29 When you're done, enter the anti-theft code for the radio and, if equipped, the navigation system. Enter the radio station presets and reset the clock. Then reset the power window control unit (see Chapter 5, Section 1).

Output shaft (countershaft) speed sensor

30 Disconnect the battery cables (see Chapter 5, Section 1), then remove the battery and the battery tray (see Chapter 5, Section 3).

31 Disconnect the electrical connector from the output shaft speed sensor.

32 Remove the output shaft speed sensor mounting bolt and remove the sensor.

33 Remove the old output shaft speed sensor O-ring (see illustration 8.9) and discard it.

34 Installation is the reverse of removal. Be sure to use a new O-ring and tighten the sensor mounting bolt securely.

35 When you're done, enter the anti-theft code for the radio and, if equipped, the navigation system. Enter the radio station presets and reset the clock. Then reset the power window control unit (see Chapter 5, Section 1).

9 Intake Air Temperature (IAT) sensor - replacement

FOUR-CYLINDER MODELS

2003 and 2004 models (except SULEV and LX-P models)

→Note: The IAT sensor is located on the air intake duct, near the throttle body.

1 Disconnect the electrical connector from the IAT sensor.

2 Remove the spring-type clamp that secures the IAT sensor to the air intake duct.

3 Pull the IAT sensor out of the air intake duct.

4 Inspect the condition of the spring clamp. If it's not still a tight fit, replace it. Also inspect the condition of the mounting hole in the air intake duct. If it's worn or otherwise damaged, replace the air intake duct.

5 Installation is the reverse of removal.

2003 and 2004 SULEV and LX-P models and all 2005 and later models

➡Note: On these models, the IAT sensor is an integral part of the Mass Air Flow (MAF) sensor. Refer to Section 12.

V6 MODELS

➡Note: The IAT sensor is located on the front side of the intake manifold, right next to the throttle body.

6   Disconnect the electrical connector from the IAT sensor.
7   Unscrew the IAT sensor from the intake manifold.
8   Remove and discard the old IAT sensor O-ring.
9   Installation is the reverse of removal. Be sure to use a new sensor O-ring and tighten the IAT sensor securely.

10 Knock sensor - replacement

FOUR-CYLINDER MODELS

▶ **Refer to illustration 10.2**

➡Note: The knock sensor is located on the front side of the engine block, behind the air intake manifold runners.

1   Remove the intake manifold (see Chapter 2A).
2   Disconnect the electrical connector from the knock sensor (see illustration).
3   Unscrew the knock sensor.
4   Installation is the reverse of removal. Be sure to tighten the knock sensor to the torque listed in this Chapter's Specifications.

V6 MODELS

▶ **Refer to illustrations 10.7 and 10.8**

➡Note: The knock sensor is located on top of the engine block, underneath the intake manifold assembly.

5   Remove the upper intake manifold (see Chapter 2B).
6   Remove the fuel rail and injector assembly (see Chapter 4).
7   Disconnect the electrical connector from the knock sensor (see illustration).
8   Unscrew the knock sensor from the engine block (see illustration).
9   Installation is the reverse of removal. Be sure to tighten the knock sensor to the torque listed in this Chapter's Specifications.

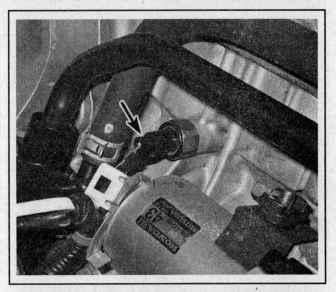

10.2 On four-cylinder models, the knock sensor is located on the front of the block, behind the intake manifold. To remove the knock sensor, disconnect the electrical connector, then unscrew the knock sensor with an appropriate deep socket or wrench

10.7 Disconnect the electrical connector from the knock sensor (V6 models)

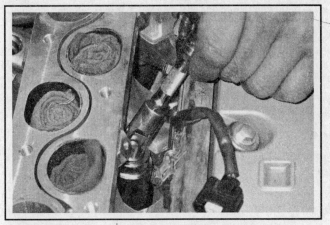

10.8 Use a deep socket to remove the knock sensor from a V6 engine

11 Manifold Absolute Pressure (MAP) sensor - replacement

FOUR-CYLINDER MODELS

♦ **Refer to illustrations 11.1 and 11.3**

➡**Note: The MAP sensor is located on the intake manifold, near the throttle body.**

1   Disconnect the electrical connector from the MAP sensor (see illustration).

2   Remove the MAP sensor retaining screw (see illustration 11.1) and remove the MAP sensor.

3   Remove the old MAP sensor O-ring (see illustration) and discard it.

4   Installation is the reverse of removal. Be sure to use a new O-ring.

V6 MODELS

➡**Note: The MAP sensor is located on top of the throttle body.**

5   Disconnect the electrical connector from the MAP sensor.

6   Remove the MAP sensor retaining screw and remove the sensor.

7   Remove the old MAP sensor O-ring and discard it.

8   Installation is the reverse of removal. Be sure to use a new O-ring.

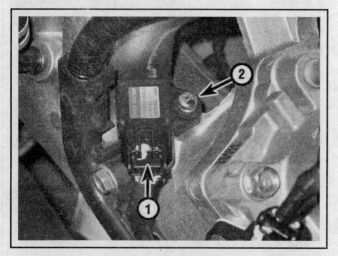

11.1 To remove the MAP sensor from the intake manifold on a four-cylinder engine, depress the release tab (1) and disconnect the electrical connector, then remove the sensor retaining screw (2)

11.3 Be sure to remove and discard the old MAP sensor O-ring. Always use a new O-ring when installing the MAP sensor whether you're installing the old sensor or a new unit

12 Mass Air Flow/Intake Air Temperature (MAF/IAT) sensor - replacement

♦ **Refer to illustration 12.1**

➡**Note: 2003 and 2004 SULEV and LX-P four-cylinder models and all 2005 and later four-cylinder models are equipped with an MAF/IAT sensor, which combines the functions of the MAF and IAT sensors into one unit. The MAF/IAT sensor is located on the air filter housing. The MAF/IAT sensor is not used on any V6 models.**

1   Disconnect the electrical connector from the MAF/IAT sensor (see illustration).

2   Remove the MAF/IAT sensor retaining screws and remove the sensor.

3   Installation is the reverse of removal.

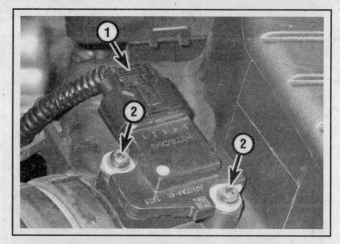

12.1 To remove the MAF/IAT sensor from the air filter housing, depress the release tab (1) and disconnect the electrical connector, then remove the sensor retaining screws (2)

13 Oxygen sensors - replacement

➡️**Note: Because it is installed in the exhaust manifold or pipe, both of which contract when cool, an oxygen sensor might be very difficult to loosen when the engine is cold. Rather than risk damage to the sensor or its mounting threads, start and run the engine for a minute or two, then shut it off. Be careful not to burn yourself during the following procedure.**

1   Remove the key from the ignition key lock cylinder. Raise the vehicle and support it securely on jackstands.

2   Special care must be taken whenever a sensor is serviced.

   a) *Oxygen sensors have a permanently attached pigtail and an electrical connector that cannot be removed. Damaging or removing the pigtail or electrical connector will render the sensor useless.*

   b) *Keep grease, dirt and other contaminants away from the electrical connector and the louvered end of the sensor.*

   c) *Do not use cleaning solvents of any kind on an oxygen sensor.*

   d) *Oxygen sensors are extremely delicate. Do not drop a sensor, throw it around or handle it roughly.*

   e) *Make sure the silicone boot on the sensor is installed in the correct position. Otherwise, the boot might melt and it might prevent the sensor from operating correctly.*

3   On four-cylinder models, the upstream oxygen sensor (Honda calls it the "air fuel ratio sensor" or "A/F sensor") is located at the upper end of the catalyst pipe, right below the exhaust manifold flange. The downstream oxygen sensor is located on the catalyst itself.

4   On V6 models, there are two upstream oxygen sensors, one for each cylinder head. Each upstream oxygen sensor (also referred to by Honda as "air fuel ratio sensors" or "A/F sensors") is located at the upper end of a Warm Up-Three Way Catalytic Converter (WU-TWC). (There are no "exhaust manifolds" on V6 models. Each exhaust manifold is integrated with a WU-TWC into a one-piece assembly.) There are also two downstream oxygen sensors. The downstream oxygen sensors are located at the lower ends of the WU-TWCs, right above the lower flange for each WU-TWC. There is a third Three Way Catalytic Converter (TWC) underneath the vehicle, but it's not equipped with oxygen sensors.

FOUR-CYLINDER MODELS

Upstream oxygen sensor

▶ **Refer to illustrations 13.5 and 13.7**

5   Open the hood and locate the upstream oxygen sensor's electrical connector (see illustration) behind the cylinder head, just to the left of the rear engine mount bracket. Disconnect the upstream oxygen sensor electrical connector.

6   Raise the vehicle and place it securely on jackstands.

7   Unscrew the upstream oxygen sensor with an oxygen sensor socket (see illustration).

8   If you're going to install the old sensor, apply anti-seize compound to the threads of the sensor to facilitate future removal. If you're going to install a new oxygen sensor, it's not necessary to apply anti-seize compound to the threads. The threads on new sensors already have anti-seize compound on them.

9   Installation is the reverse of removal. Be sure to tighten the upstream oxygen sensor to the torque listed in this Chapter's Specifications.

Downstream oxygen sensor

▶ **Refer to illustration 13.10**

10   Slide the front passenger seat all the way forward, then open the right rear door, reach under the seat and peel back the carpet flap that conceals the wiring harness for the downstream oxygen sensor (see illustration). Disconnect the electrical connector for the downstream oxygen sensor, then work the grommet loose where the electrical lead goes through the floorpan and thread the lead through the hole in the floorpan.

11   Raise the vehicle and place it securely on jackstands.

12   Unscrew the downstream oxygen sensor with an oxygen sensor socket (see illustration 13.7).

13.5 On four-cylinder models, you'll find the electrical connector for the upstream oxygen sensor behind the cylinder head, just to the left of the rear engine mount bracket. To disconnect it, simply depress the release tab

13.7 Unscrew the upstream oxygen sensor with an oxygen sensor socket (four-cylinder models)

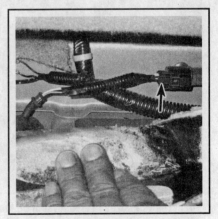

13.10 To access the electrical connector for the downstream oxygen sensor on a four-cylinder models, peel back the carpet from the floor rail underneath the forward edge of the front passenger seat. To disconnect the electrical connector, depress the release tab

13 If you're going to install the old sensor, apply anti-seize compound to the threads of the sensor to facilitate future removal. If you're going to install a new oxygen sensor, it's not necessary to apply anti-seize compound to the threads. The threads on new sensors already have anti-seize compound on them.

14 Installation is the reverse of removal. Be sure to tighten the oxygen sensor to the torque listed in this Chapter's Specifications. Also make sure the grommet seats properly in the floorpan.

V6 MODELS

Upstream oxygen sensors

→Note: The upstream oxygen sensors are located at the upper ends of the Warm Up-Three Way Catalytic Converters (WU-TWCs), which are an integral part of the exhaust manifold assemblies. This procedure applies to the front or rear upstream oxygen sensor.

15 Disconnect the electrical connector from the upstream oxygen sensor.

16 Unscrew the upstream oxygen sensor with an oxygen sensor socket.

17 If you're going to install the old sensor, apply anti-seize compound to the threads of the sensor to facilitate future removal. If you're

going to install a new oxygen sensor, it's not necessary to apply anti-seize compound to the threads. The threads on new sensors already have anti-seize compound on them.

18 Installation is the reverse of removal. Be sure to tighten the oxygen sensor to the torque listed in this Chapter's Specifications.

Downstream oxygen sensor

→Note: The downstream oxygen sensors are located at the lower ends of the Warm Up-Three Way Catalytic Converters (WU-TWCs), which are an integral part of the exhaust manifold assemblies. This procedure applies to the front or rear downstream oxygen sensor.

19 Raise the vehicle and place it securely on jackstands.

20 Disconnect the electrical connector from the downstream oxygen sensor.

21 Unscrew the downstream oxygen sensor with an oxygen sensor socket.

22 If you're going to install the old sensor, apply anti-seize compound to the threads of the sensor to facilitate future removal. If you're going to install a new oxygen sensor, it's not necessary to apply anti-seize compound to the threads. The threads on new sensors already have anti-seize compound on them.

23 Installation is the reverse of removal. Be sure to tighten the oxygen sensor to the torque listed in this Chapter's Specifications.

14 Power Steering Pressure (PSP) switch - replacement

◆ Refer to illustrations 14.1 and 14.3

→Note: The PSP switch is located on the power steering pump outlet (pressure) line, above the right (passenger-side) tie-rod boot, which is located at the right end of the steering rack assembly.

1 Open the hood and locate the power steering pressure switch (see

illustration) in the lower right rear corner of the engine compartment.

2 Disconnect the electrical connector from the PSP switch.

3 Using a back-up wrench, unscrew the PSP switch (see illustration). Be prepared for a little fluid spillage.

4 Installation is the reverse of removal.

5 When you're done lower the vehicle and check the power steering fluid level, adding fluid of the proper type if necessary (see Chapter 1).

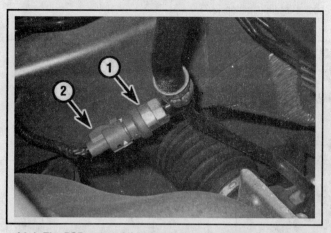

14.1 The PSP switch (1) is located on the pressure line between the power steering pump and the steering gear. To disconnect the electrical connector, depress the release tab (2) and pull off the connector

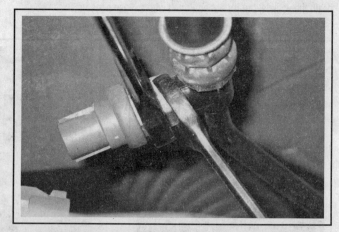

14.3 When unscrewing the PSP switch with a wrench, be sure to use a back-up wrench on the lug that's part of the power steering pressure line so that you don't accidentally kink the metal pressure line

15 Throttle Position (TP) sensor - replacement

On four-cylinder models, the TP sensor is not available as a separate component. If it's defective, replace the throttle body (see Chapter 4). On V6 models, the TP sensor is an integral part of the electronic throttle body. If it's defective, replace the throttle body (see Chapter 4).

6 Transmission range switch - replacement and adjustment

♦ **Refer to illustrations 16.3, 16.4, 16.5 and 16.7**

➡ **Note:** The transmission range switch is located on the left end of the transaxle under a small cover. The photos that accompany this Section depict the transmission range switch on a five-speed automatic transaxle coupled to a four-cylinder engine, but the procedure for V6 models with an automatic transaxle is virtually identical.

1   Put the shift lever inside the vehicle in the Neutral position.

2   Loosen the lug nuts on the left front wheel, raise the vehicle and support it securely on jackstands. Remove the left front wheel.

3   Remove the cover from the transmission range switch (see illustration).

4   Disconnect the electrical connector from the transmission range switch (see illustration).

5   Remove the transmission range switch mounting bolts (see illustration 16.4) and remove the switch.

✢ CAUTION:

While the transmission range switch is removed, do NOT rotate the control shaft on the transaxle.

➡ **Note:** Visualize the slot in the selector control shaft as the shaft for the hour and minute hands on a clock. When you remove the transmission range switch on a four-cylinder model, the upper end of the slot in the selector control shaft should be pointing toward 11 o'clock and the lower end of the slot should be pointing toward 5 o'clock (see illustration). When you remove the transmission range switch on a V6 model, the upper end of the slot in the selector control shaft should be pointing toward 12 o'clock and the lower end of the slot should be pointing toward 6 o'clock.

6   Before installing the transmission range switch, make sure that the switch is in the Neutral position. (You'll hear/feel a click when you put the switch into Neutral.) Also make sure that the selector control shaft is still in the Neutral position (see illustration 16.5) before install-ing the transmission range switch. To put the selector control shaft back in the Neutral position (if it has been moved), insert a screwdriver into the slot and rotate the shaft in a clockwise direction until it stops. As you rotate the shaft, it clicks into each gear position. When you can't rotate the shaft any further, rotate it counterclockwise to the third position (third click), which is Neutral.

7   Install the transmission range switch. Make sure that the flats inside the rotary frame are aligned with the flats on the control shaft, then loosely install the switch mounting bolts. Then use an appropriate diameter drill bit or metal rod to align the rotary frame with the alignment tabs on the edge of the switch (see illustration). This locks the rotary frame in place until you have tightened the range switch mounting bolts.

8   Tighten the transmission range switch mounting bolts securely.

✳✳ CAUTION:

Be careful not to move the transmission range switch while tightening the switch mounting bolts.

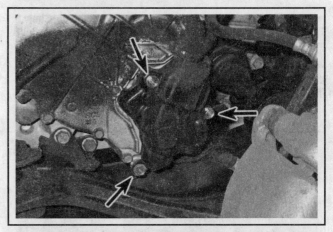

16.3 To detach the transmission range switch cover from the transaxle on a four-cylinder model, remove these three bolts

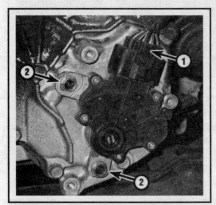

16.4 To disconnect the electrical connector from the transmission range switch on a four-cylinder model, depress this release tab (1), then unplug the connector. To detach the switch from the transaxle, remove the two mounting bolts (2)

16.5 Once the transmission range switch is removed, do NOT move the selector shaft from the Neutral position. When installing the switch, the flats (A) on the switch's rotary frame must be aligned with these flats

16.7 To install the transmission range switch, align the cutouts in the rotary with the two tabs on the edge of the switch housing, then push a drill bit into the rotary frame cutouts and between the tabs to hold the rotary frame in the correct position

9   The remainder of installation is the reverse of removal.

10   When you're done, turn the ignition switch to ON, move the shift lever through all the gears and verify that the transmission range switch is correctly synchronized with the gear position indicator on the instrument cluster. Then verify that the engine will NOT start in any gear position other than Park or Neutral, and that the back-up lights come on when the shift lever is in the Reverse position. If the vehicle fails to meet any of these criteria, readjust the transmission range switch.

17 Powertrain Control Module (PCM) - removal and installation

The PCM is located under the dash, on top of the tunnel, ahead of the center console. It's not difficult to remove, but we don't recommend doing so because there is no reason to remove the PCM unless it's defective and you need to replace it. Unfortunately, if the PCM requires replacement, the new unit must be reprogrammed with a Honda Diag-nostic System (HDS) scan tool. So if you were to remove the old PCM and install a new unit you would be unable to program it at home (or even drive the vehicle to a dealer to have it programmed). The money you would save by installing your own PCM would be more than offset by the cost of having the vehicle towed to a dealer.

18 Idle Air Control (IAC) valve - replacement

♦ Refer to illustrations 18.2 and 18.3

➡ Note 1: This procedure applies to four-cylinder models only. There is no IAC valve on the electronic throttle body used on V6 models.

➡ Note 2: The IAC valve is located on the underside of the throttle body. You must remove the throttle body to replace the IAC valve.

1   Remove the throttle body (see Chapter 4).

2   Remove the IAC valve mounting screws (see illustration) and remove the IAC valve.

3   Remove the old IAC valve gasket (see illustration) and discard it.

4   When installing the IAC valve, be sure to use a new gasket and tighten the IAC valve mounting screws securely.

5   Installation is otherwise the reverse of removal.

6   Check the coolant level and add some, if necessary, to bring it to the appropriate level (see Chapter 1).

18.2 To detach the IAC valve from the throttle body on a four-cylinder model, remove these screws

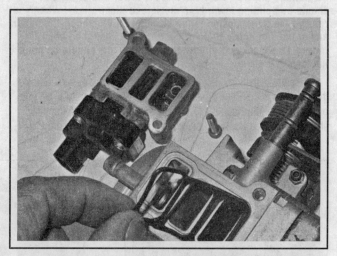

18.3 Be sure to remove and discard the old IAC valve O-ring type gasket. Always use a new gasket when installing the IAC valve whether you're installing the old valve or a new unit

19 Intake air bypass control thermal valve - replacement

♦ Refer to illustrations 19.3

➡ Note: The intake air bypass control thermal valve is located at the left end of the intake manifold. This device is used only on four-cylinder models.

1   Remove the intake manifold cover (see illustration 12.1 in Chapter 4).

2   Remove the air intake duct (see "Air filter housing - removal and installation" in Chapter 4).

3 Disconnect the hoses from the intake air bypass control thermal valve (see illustration).
4 Unscrew the intake air bypass control thermal valve.
5 Installation is the reverse of removal. Be sure to tighten the intake air bypass control thermal valve securely.

19.3 To remove the intake air bypass control thermal valve, disconnect the intake air hose (A) and the air bypass hose (B), then unscrew the valve (C)

20 Intake Manifold Runner Control (IMRC) system - description and component replacement

DESCRIPTION

1 The Intake Manifold Runner Control (IMRC) system, which is used only on V6 models with a manual transaxle, produces improved torque at all engine speeds. It achieves this by rotating a barrel-shaped valve located inside the intake manifold assembly. When the valve is closed, the intake manifold runners are lengthened and there is more torque at low engine speeds. When the valve is open, the runners are shortened and there is more torque at high engine speeds. Here's why: When intake air is drawn into the cylinders at idle or at low engine speeds, less air is needed because the cylinders don't need to be filled so often or so quickly. So at idle and at low engine speeds, the air drawn into an engine with longer intake runners will have a higher velocity than one with shorter intake runners. However, at higher engine speeds, longer intake runners would prevent the cylinders from filling quickly enough and would therefore limit power. Most intake manifold designs are a compromise between the conflicting demands of low and high engine speeds.
2 The Intake Manifold Runner Control (IMRC) system helps to maintain a uniformly higher intake air velocity throughout the engine's operating range. Higher intake air velocity promotes better vaporization of the fuel sprayed into the stream of incoming air by the fuel injectors, which means more complete combustion, more power, better fuel economy and less emissions.
3 The IMRC system consists of the PCM, a PCM-controlled actuator and a specially designed intake manifold. Honda refers to the actuator as the Intake Manifold Tuning (IMT) actuator. Inside the manifold are a pair of long, rectangular-shaped valves mounted on a shaft that is controlled by the actuator. When the engine is idling or operating below a specified rpm, the two valves inside the manifold direct incoming air through a longer path. Directing incoming air through a longer intake path at low engine speeds promotes higher intake air velocities because the incoming air can move more quickly through the intake manifold to fill the cylinders. When engine speed reaches the specified rpm, the PCM energizes the actuator, which turns the shaft and the two valves, altering the intake pathway through the intake manifold. When the valves turn, they send the incoming air through a shorter intake path designed to handle a larger volume of air. At that point, the volume of air drawn into the cylinders is sufficient to promote good velocity even through the shorter intake path. And the shorter intake path enhances performance during heavy acceleration or high cruising speeds.

COMPONENT REPLACEMENT

IMT (IMRC) actuator

4 Remove the intake manifold cover (see "Intake manifold - removal and installation" in Chapter 2B).
5 Disconnect the electrical connector from the IMT (IMRC) actuator.
6 Remove the two IMT (IMRC) actuator mounting bolts and remove the actuator.
7 Remove and discard the old actuator O-ring.
8 Installation is otherwise the reverse of removal. Be sure to use a new O-ring and tighten the IMT (IMRC) actuator mounting bolts to the torque listed in this Chapter's Specifications.

Intake manifold

9 Refer to Chapter 2B.

21 Catalytic converter - general description, check and replacement

➡**Note: Because of a Federally mandated extended warranty which covers emissions-related components like the catalytic converter, check with a dealer service department before replacing the converter at your own expense.**

GENERAL DESCRIPTION

1 A catalytic converter (or catalyst) is an emission control device in the exhaust system that reduces certain pollutants in the exhaust gas stream. There are two types of converters: oxidation converters and reduction converters.
2 Oxidation converters contain a "monolithic substrate" (a ceramic honeycomb) coated with the semi-precious metals platinum and palladium. An oxidation catalyst reduces unburned hydrocarbons (HC) and carbon monoxide (CO) by adding oxygen to the exhaust stream as it passes through the substrate, which in the presence of high temperature and the catalyst materials converts the HC and CO to water vapor (H_2O) and carbon dioxide (CO_2).

3   Reduction converters contain a monolithic substrate coated with platinum and rhodium. A reduction catalyst reduces oxides of nitrogen (NOx) by removing oxygen, which in the presence of high temperature and the catalyst material produces nitrogen (N) and carbon dioxide (CO2).

4   Catalytic converters that combine both types of catalysts in one assembly are known as "three-way catalysts" or TWCs. A TWC can reduce all three pollutants. All catalysts used by the vehicles covered in this manual are equipped with three-way catalysts.

5   Four-cylinder models have a single Three Way Catalytic Converter (TWC) underneath the vehicle. The forward (inlet) flange of the TWC is bolted to the elbow pipe that connects its to the exhaust manifold and the rear (outlet) flange of the TWC is bolted to the rest of the exhaust system.

6   On V6 models, there are three catalysts. The two Warm Up-Three Way Catalytic Converters (WU-TWCs) are integral components of the exhaust manifolds for the front and rear cylinder heads. (On V6 models, you must replace a WU-TWC in order to replace an exhaust manifold, and vice versa.) The third catalyst on V6 models is a Three Way Catalytic Converter (TWC) underneath the vehicle. This TWC is similar in appearance and location to the single TWC used on four-cylinder models. Its forward flange is bolted to the exhaust pipe that's connected to the two exhaust manifold/WU-TWCs, and its rear flange is bolted to the rest of the exhaust system.

CHECK

7   The test equipment for a catalytic converter (a loaded-mode dynamometer and a five-gas analyzer) is expensive. If you suspect that the converter on your vehicle is malfunctioning, take it to a dealer or authorized emission inspection facility for diagnosis and repair.

8   Whenever you raise the vehicle to service underbody components, inspect the converter assembly for leaks, corrosion, dents and other damage. Carefully inspect the welds and/or flange bolts and nuts that attach the front and rear ends of the converter to the exhaust system. If you note any damage, replace the converter.

9   Although catalytic converters don't break too often, they can become clogged or even plugged up. The easiest way to check for a restricted converter is to use a vacuum gauge to diagnose the effect of a blocked exhaust on intake vacuum.

a) Connect a vacuum gauge to any intake manifold vacuum source (any pipe on the intake manifold with a vacuum hose connected to it will provide the necessary intake manifold vacuum).

b) Warm the engine to operating temperature, place the transaxle in Park (automatic models) or Neutral (manual models) and apply the parking brake.

c) Note the vacuum reading at idle and jot it down.

d) Quickly open the throttle to near its wide-open position and then quickly get off the throttle and allow it to close. Note the vacuum reading and jot it down.

e) Do this test three more times, recording your measurement after each test.

f) If your fourth reading is more than one in-Hg lower than the reading that you noted at idle, the exhaust system might be restricted (the catalytic converter could be plugged, OR an exhaust pipe or muffler could be restricted).

REPLACEMENT

Four-cylinder models

▶ Refer to illustration 21.12

10 Raise the vehicle and place it securely on jackstands.

11 Remove the upstream and downstream oxygen sensors (see Section 13).

12 Remove the heat shield bolts (see illustration) and remove the heat shield.

13 Remove the nuts that attach the forward flange of the catalytic converter to the elbow pipe.

14 Remove the nuts that attach the rear flange of the catalytic converter to the rest of the exhaust system (see illustration 21.12).

15 Installation is the reverse of removal. Be sure to tighten the nuts at both flanges securely.

V6 models

Warm Up-Three Way Catalytic Converter (WU-TWC)

16 If you're removing the front WU-TWC, remove the condenser fan and shroud (see "Engine cooling fans and switch - check and replacement" in Chapter 3). If you're removing the rear WU-TWC, remove the intermediate shaft (see Chapter 8).

17 Disconnect the electrical connectors from the upstream and downstream oxygen sensors (see Section 13). (It's a good idea to also remove the upstream and downstream oxygen sensors so that they won't be damaged in the event that you accidentally drop the WU-TWC.)

18 Remove the four heat shield bolts and remove the two heat shields from the WU-TWC.

19 Remove the three lower flange nuts and separate the exhaust pipe flange from the WU-TWC's lower mounting flange.

20 Remove the four upper flange nuts and remove the front WU-TWC.

21 Remove and discard the old gasket.

22 Installation is the reverse of removal. Be sure to use a new gasket and tighten the flange nuts securely.

Under-vehicle Three-Way Catalytic Converter (TWC)

23 Removing and installing the under-vehicle TWC is essentially the same procedure as doing so on a four-cylinder model. Refer to Steps 10 through 15.

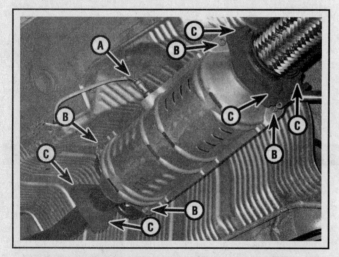

21.12 To remove the under-vehicle catalytic converter, unscrew the oxygen sensor (A), remove the heat shield bolts (B), then remove the mounting flange nuts (C) (one forward flange nut not shown)

22 Evaporative Emissions Control (EVAP) system - general description and component replacement

GENERAL DESCRIPTION

1 The Evaporative Emissions Control (EVAP) system prevents fuel system vapors (which contain unburned hydrocarbons) from escaping into the atmosphere. On warm days, vapors trapped inside the fuel tank expand until the pressure reaches a certain threshold. Then the fuel vapors are routed from the fuel tank through the EVAP two-way valve to the EVAP canister, where they're stored temporarily until the next time the vehicle is operated. When the conditions are right (engine warmed up, vehicle up to speed, moderate or heavy load on the engine, etc.), the PCM opens the canister purge valve, which allows fuel vapors to be drawn from the canister into the intake manifold. Once in the intake manifold, the fuel vapors mix with incoming air before being drawn through the intake ports into the combustion chambers where they're burned up with the rest of the air/fuel mixture. The EVAP system is complex and virtually impossible to troubleshoot without the right tools and training. However, the following description should give you a good idea of how it works:

2 The EVAP canister is located under the vehicle, in front of the fuel tank. The canister, which contains activated carbon, is a repository for storing fuel vapors. You'll have to raise the vehicle to inspect or replace the canister, or any other part of the EVAP system, except for the canister purge valve (which is located in the engine compartment). But the canister is designed to be maintenance-free and should last the life of the vehicle. There are two other important components located on the canister: the canister vent shut valve and the fuel tank pressure sensor.

3 The canister vent shut valve is located on the EVAP canister. The canister vent shut valve is normally closed, but it opens to allow fresh air from the filter to enter the EVAP canister when the canister is being purged.

4 The fuel tank pressure sensor is also located on the EVAP canister. The fuel tank pressure sensor monitors the pressure inside the fuel tank, converts fuel tank absolute pressure into a variable voltage signal and transmits this data to the PCM.

5 The EVAP canister purge valve, which is under the control of the Powertrain Control Module (PCM), regulates the flow of vapors being purged from the EVAP canister into the intake manifold. The canister purge valve is always closed when engine coolant temperature is below 147-degrees F (64-degrees C), which cuts off intake manifold vacuum to the EVAP canister. Above that threshold the PCM opens or closes the purge valve in accordance with data from various information sensor inputs. The interval of time during which the purge valve is opened by the PCM is known as its "duty cycle." On four-cylinder engines, the canister purge valve is attached to a small bracket that is bolted to the left end of the cylinder head. On V6 engines, it's attached to a small bracket that's bolted to the left rear corner of the intake manifold, right behind the throttle body.

GENERAL SYSTEM CHECKS

6 The most common symptom of a faulty EVAP system is a strong fuel odor (particularly during hot weather). If you smell fuel while driving or (more likely) right after you park the vehicle and turn off the engine, check the fuel filler cap first. Make sure that it's screwed onto the fuel filler neck all the way. If the odor persists, inspect all EVAP hose connections, both in the engine compartment and under the vehicle. You'll have to raise the vehicle and place it securely on jackstands to inspect most of the EVAP system, since it's located under the vehicle. Be sure to inspect each hose attached to the canister for damage and leakage along its entire length. Repair or replace as necessary. Inspect the canister for damage and look for fuel leaking from the bottom. If fuel is leaking or the canister is otherwise damaged, replace it.

7 Poor idle, stalling, and poor driveability can be caused by a defective fuel vapor vent valve or canister purge valve, a damaged canister, cracked hoses, or hoses connected to the wrong tubes. Fuel loss or fuel odor can be caused by fuel leaking from fuel lines or hoses, a cracked or damaged canister, or a defective vapor valve.

8 To check for excessive fuel vapor pressure in the fuel tank, remove the gas cap and listen for the sound of pressure release. If the fuel tank emits a "whooshing" sound when you open the filler cap, fuel tank vapor pressure is excessive. Inspect the canister vapor hoses and the canister inlet port for blockage or collapsed hoses. Also inspect the vapor vent valve. A complete test can only be done with a Honda Diagnostic System (HDS) scan tool (see Section 2), which will run a series of checks using the fuel tank pressure sensor and other output actuators to detect excessive pressure. You'll have to take the vehicle to a dealer service department or other qualified repair shop to have the EVAP system professionally diagnosed.

COMPONENT REPLACEMENT

EVAP canister purge valve

Four-cylinder models

◆ **Refer to illustrations 22.9 and 22.10**

➡**Note: The EVAP canister purge valve is mounted on a small bracket located at the left rear corner of the cylinder head.**

9 Remove the two bolts that attach the purge valve's mounting bracket to the cylinder head (see illustration) and pull the purge valve and its mounting bracket forward so that you can access the electrical connector and the EVAP hoses.

22.9 To detach the EVAP canister purge valve mounting bracket from the cylinder head on a four-cylinder model, remove these two bolts

22.10 To remove the EVAP canister purge valve, disconnect the electrical connector (1), loosen the hose clamps (2) and disconnect both EVAP hoses, then remove the three mounting screws (3) (four-cylinder models)

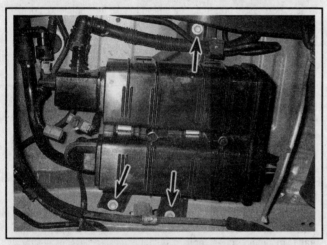

22.20 To detach the EVAP canister assembly from the underside of the vehicle, remove these three mounting bracket bolts, then lower the canister and disconnect the remaining hose and electrical connector

10 Disconnect the electrical connector from the EVAP canister purge valve (see illustration).

11 Clearly label the two EVAP hoses connected to the canister purge valve, then loosen the spring-type hose clamps and disconnect both hoses (see illustration 22.10).

12 To separate the purge valve from its mounting bracket, remove the three purge valve mounting screws (see illustration 22.10).

13 Installation is the reverse of removal.

V6 models

➡**Note: The EVAP canister purge valve is mounted on a small bracket located at the left rear corner of the intake manifold, right behind the throttle body.**

14 Disconnect the electrical connector from the EVAP canister purge valve.

15 Clearly label the vacuum hoses connected to the canister purge valve, then disconnect them from the purge valve.

16 Remove the purge valve mounting screws and remove the valve from its mounting bracket.

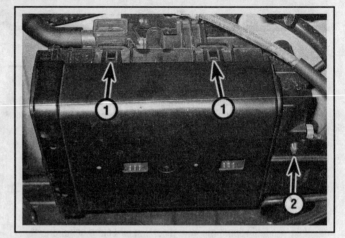

22.19 To remove the EVAP canister cover, disengage the tabs on both sides (1), squeeze the pin (2) for the canister vent shut valve connector (SULEV models only), then pull off the cover

17 Installation is the reverse of removal.

EVAP canister

▶ **Refer to illustrations 22.19 and 22.20**

18 Raise the vehicle and place it securely on jackstands.

19 Remove the EVAP canister cover (see illustration).

20 Disconnect all hoses and electrical connectors that are accessible with the canister in place, then remove the canister mounting bolts (see illustration). Lower the canister and its mounting bracket as a single assembly, then disconnect the EVAP hose and electrical connector from the vent shut valve (SULEV models) and/or from the fuel tank pressure sensor.

21 Remove the two nuts that attach the EVAP canister to its mounting bracket and separate the canister from the mounting bracket.

22 If you're planning to replace the EVAP canister, remove the fuel tank pressure sensor and the vent shut valve from the old canister (see below) and install them on the new canister.

23 Installation is the reverse of removal.

Fuel Tank Pressure (FTP) sensor

▶ **Refer to illustration 22.25**

24 Remove the EVAP canister (see Steps 18 through 21).

25 Remove the FTP sensor retaining clip and pull the sensor straight up (see illustration).

26 Remove the old FTP sensor O-ring and discard it.

27 Installation is the reverse of removal. Be sure to use a new FTP sensor O-ring.

EVAP canister vent shut valve

▶ **Refer to illustrations 22.29 and 22.30**

28 Remove the EVAP canister (see Steps 18 through 21).

29 Using a small screwdriver, pry loose the lock tabs on the cap (see illustration) and remove the cap.

✷✷ CAUTION:

Be careful not to damage the lock tabs. If you break them, you'll have to replace the cap.

22.25 To release the FTP sensor from the EVAP canister, pull out this retainer clip, then pull the sensor straight up

22.29 To remove the vent shut valve cap, carefully pry open these three locking tabs and pull off the cap. Make sure that you don't damage any of the locking tabs, or you'll have to replace the cap

22.30 To remove the vent shut valve, simply pull it out of the canister. Be sure to remove and discard the old shut valve O-ring. Always use a new O-ring when installing the shut valve

30 To remove the vent shut valve from the EVAP canister, simply pull it out (see illustration).

31 Remove and discard the old vent shut valve O-ring.

32 Installation is the reverse of removal. Be sure to use a new O-ring, but don't coat the O-ring with engine oil.

23 Exhaust Gas Recirculation (EGR) system - general description and component replacement

GENERAL DESCRIPTION

1 Oxides of nitrogen (or simply NOx) is a compound that is formed in the combustion chambers when the oxygen and nitrogen in the incoming air mix together. NOx is a natural by-product of high combustion chamber temperatures. When NOx is emitted from the tailpipe, it mixes with reactive organic compounds (ROCs), hydrocarbons (HC) and sunlight to form ozone and photochemical smog. The Exhaust Gas Recirculation (EGR) system reduces oxides of nitrogen by recirculating exhaust gases from the exhaust manifold, through the EGR valve and intake manifold, then back to the combustion chambers, where it mixes with the incoming air/fuel mixture before being consumed. These recirculated exhaust gases "dilute" the incoming air/fuel mixture, which cools the combustion chambers, thereby reducing NOx emissions.

2 All models are equipped with an EGR system. The EGR system consists of the Powertrain Control Module (PCM), the EGR valve, the EGR valve position sensor (an integral part of the EGR valve) and various other information sensors that the PCM uses to determine when to open the EGR valve. On four-cylinder models, the EGR valve is located at the left end of the cylinder head. On V6 models, the EGR valve is located at the left end of the front cylinder head.

3 The degree to which the EGR valve is opened is referred to as "EGR valve lift." The PCM is programmed to produce the ideal EGR valve lift for varying operating conditions. The EGR valve position sensor, which is an integral part of the EGR valve, detects the amount of EGR valve lift and sends this information to the PCM. The PCM then compares it with the appropriate EGR valve lift for the operating conditions. The PCM increases current flow to the EGR valve to increase valve lift and reduces the current to reduce the amount of lift. If EGR flow is inappropriate to the operating conditions (idle, cold engine, etc.) the PCM simply cuts the current to the EGR valve and the valve closes.

EGR VALVE REPLACEMENT

Four-cylinder models

▶ Refer to illustration 23.5

➡Note: The EGR valve is located at the left end of the cylinder head.

4 Remove the air intake duct and, if you need even more room, remove the air filter housing (see Chapter 4).

5 Disconnect the electrical connector from the EGR valve (see illustration).

23.5 To remove the EGR valve from a four-cylinder model, disconnect the electrical connector (1) and remove the mounting nuts (2)

23.9 EGR valve mounting nuts (V6 models)

6 Remove the EGR valve mounting nuts and remove the EGR valve.

7 Remove and discard the old EGR valve gasket. Be careful not to scratch or gouge the gasket mounting surfaces of the EGR valve or the water outlet casting to which the EGR valve is bolted.

8 Installation is the reverse of removal. Be sure to use a new EGR valve gasket, and tighten the EGR valve mounting nuts to the torque listed in this Chapter's Specifications.

V6 MODELS

▶ Refer to illustration 23.9

➥Note: The EGR valve is located at the left end of the front cylinder head, where it is bolted to the water passage.

9 Disconnect the electrical connector from the EGR valve, then remove the EGR valve mounting nuts (see illustration) and remove the EGR valve from the water passage.

10 Remove and discard the old EGR valve gasket.

11 Installation is the reverse of removal. Be sure to use a new EGR valve gasket and tighten the EGR valve mounting nuts to the torque listed in this Chapter's Specifications.

24 Positive Crankcase Ventilation (PCV) system - general description, check and component replacement

GENERAL DESCRIPTION

▶ Refer to illustration 24.1

1 The Positive Crankcase Ventilation (PCV) system (see illustration) reduces hydrocarbon emissions by scavenging crankcase vapors.

24.1 Positive Crankcase Ventilation (PCV) system on a four-cylinder engine:

A *Fresh air inlet hose (connects the air intake duct to the valve cover)*
B *PCV valve (screwed into the water passage)*
C *PCV hose (connects the PCV valve to the intake manifold)*

It does this by circulating fresh air from the air intake duct into and through the crankcase, where it mixes with blow-by gases before being drawn by intake manifold vacuum through a PCV valve to the intake manifold. To maintain idle quality, the PCV valve restricts the flow of crankcase vapors into the intake manifold when intake manifold vacuum is high, and allows full flow when intake manifold decreases. The main components of the PCV system are the PCV valve and a pair of hoses, the fresh air inlet hose and the crankcase ventilation hose (also known as the PCV hose).

2 The fresh air inlet hose draws fresh air from the air intake duct to the valve cover, where it's drawn into the crankcase and mixes with blow-by gases. This mixture of fresh air and crankcase vapors is drawn into the intake manifold by intake manifold vacuum through the PCV valve and the crankcase ventilation hose, which connects the crankcase to the intake manifold.

3 On four-cylinder models, the fresh air inlet hose connects the air intake duct to the left end of the valve cover. The crankcase ventilation hose (PCV hose) connects the crankcase to the intake manifold. But the PCV valve isn't actually bolted to or screwed into the crankcase itself. Instead, it's screwed into a large casting known as the "water passage." (The water passage, which is bolted to the front of the block, next to the timing chain cover, also houses the thermostat and the water pump.)

4 On V6 models, the fresh air inlet hose connects the air intake duct to the left end of the valve cover for the rear cylinder head. The crankcase ventilation hose connects the crankcase to the intake manifold. But the PCV valve isn't actually bolted to or screwed into the crankcase. Instead, it's screwed into the right end of the front side of the valve cover for the front cylinder head.

24.5a Inspect the fresh air inlet hose for cracks, tears and deterioration. If it's damaged or worn, replace it. To remove the hose, simply loosen the hose clamps and pull it off

24.5b Inspect the PCV hose for cracks, tears and deterioration. If it's damaged, replace it. To remove the hose, loosen the clamps and pull it off

24.6 To check the PCV valve, pinch off the crankcase ventilation hose with the engine idling and verify that the PCV valve makes a clicking sound

CHECK

▶ **Refer to illustrations 24.5a, 24.5b and 24.6**

5 Inspect the fresh air inlet hose (see illustration) and the PCV valve and crankcase ventilation hose (see illustration). Inspect the two PCV system hoses for cracks, tears and deterioration. If either hose is damaged or worn, replace it.

6 Start the engine and allow it to warm up. With the engine idling, pinch off the crankcase ventilation hose (see illustration) and verify that the PCV valve makes a clicking sound. If there is no clicking sound, the crankcase ventilation hose might be clogged or punctured. Remove the crankcase ventilation hose, blow it out with compressed air, then inspect it for damage.

7 If the hose is damaged or clogged, replace it, then retest the PCV valve. If the valve still doesn't click, replace it.

COMPONENT REPLACEMENT

Four-cylinder models

Fresh air inlet hose

8 Loosen the hose clamps at both ends of the fresh air inlet hose (see illustration 24.5a), slide them back and disconnect the hose from the air intake duct and from the pipe on the valve cover.

9 Installation is the reverse of removal. Make sure that both hose clamps are in good shape. If either one is loose, replace it.

Crankcase ventilation hose

10 Loosen the hose clamps at both ends of the crankcase ventilation hose (see illustration 24.5b), then disconnect the hose from the PCV valve and from the intake manifold.

11 Installation is the reverse of removal. Make sure that both hose clamps are in good shape. If either one is loose, replace it.

PCV valve

▶ **Refer to illustration 24.13**

12 Disconnect the crankcase ventilation hose (see illustration 24.5b).
13 Unscrew the PCV valve (see illustration).
14 Remove and discard the PCV valve washer.

15 Installation is the reverse of removal. Be sure to use a new PCV valve washer and tighten the PCV valve securely.

V6 models

Fresh air inlet hose

16 Simply loosen the hose clamps at both ends of the fresh air inlet hose, slide them back and disconnect the hose from the air intake duct and from the pipe on the valve cover.

17 Installation is the reverse of removal. Make sure that both hose clamps are in good shape. If either one is loose, replace it.

Crankcase ventilation hose

18 Loosen the hose clamps at both ends of the crankcase ventilation hose, then disconnect the hose from the PCV valve and from the intake manifold.

19 Installation is the reverse of removal. Make sure that both hose clamps are in good shape. If either one is loose, replace it.

PCV valve

20 Disconnect the crankcase ventilation hose.
21 Remove the PCV valve retaining bolt and remove the PCV valve.
22 Remove and discard the old PCV valve O-rings.
23 Installation is the reverse of removal. Be sure to use new O-rings.

24.13 To remove the PCV valve, unscrew it from the water passage (four-cylinder models)

25 Variable Valve Timing and Lift Electronic Control (VTEC) systems - description and component replacement

DESCRIPTION

1 A low-lift, short-duration camshaft intake lobe produces good torque, quick response, good fuel economy and low emissions at lower engine speeds, but can't deliver sufficient air/fuel mixture to the combustion chamber at higher engine speeds. A high-lift, long-duration intake cam lobe produces good power at high engine speeds, but produces a lumpy idle and poor driveability, wastes fuel and produces unacceptable emissions at lower engine speeds. That's why camshaft intake lobe profiles are always a compromise between economy and performance. But Honda's Variable Valve Timing and Lift Electronic Control (VTEC) system allows an engine to operate economically and make good power at the same time.

2 The VTEC system is used on all models covered in this manual. The principal differences between VTEC and non-VTEC engines are in the cylinder head, the camshaft(s) and the rocker arms. The block, the lubrication and cooling systems and most other components are identical on VTEC and non-VTEC engines. For more information about the cylinder head, the camshaft(s) and the rocker arms, see Chapter 2. This Section is intended to familiarize you with how VTEC works and to show you how to replace the PCM-controlled components such as the VTEC solenoid valve and the VTC oil control solenoid valve.

VTEC system (V6 models)

3 There are two cam lobes for each pair of intake valves on the SOHC V6 engine. These primary and secondary lobe profiles differ in lift and duration: the secondary lobe has lower lift and less duration (it opens later and closes sooner), while the primary lobe has higher lift and more duration (opens sooner and closes later). Each lobe operates its own rocker arm, which in turn pushes on its own valve. At low speeds, the secondary camshaft lobe operates one intake valve and the primary cam lobe operates the other valve. The low-lift, short-duration lobe produces good low-end torque and responsiveness.

4 When more power is needed at higher engine speeds, the PCM activates the VTEC solenoid valve, which allows higher oil pressure to a hydraulically-operated, spring-loaded pin inside the primary rocker arm. When hydraulic pressure overcomes spring pressure the pin slides sideways and locks the secondary rocker arm to the primary rocker arm. The two rocker arms are both activated by the primary cam lobe; the secondary rocker arm no longer contacts its own camshaft lobe again until the system is disengaged. So both valves are now opened by the primary camshaft lobe with its higher lift and longer duration, increasing performance.

5 The PCM turns the VTEC solenoid on and off in accordance with engine rpm, vehicle speed, throttle opening angle, engine load and coolant temperature. Although diagnosis of the VTEC system is beyond the scope of the home mechanic, it's not difficult to replace the VTEC solenoid valve or to clean the filter for the system, both of which are outlined below.

Intelligent Variable Valve Timing and Lift Electronic Control (i-VTEC) system (four-cylinder models)

6 The intelligent VTEC (i-VTEC) system used on the DOHC four-cylinder engine is similar in operation to the SOHC VTEC system used on V6 models, except that they also employ Variable Valve Timing Control (VTC).

Variable Valve Timing Control (VTC) (four-cylinder models)

7 The VTEC system changes the valve lift and duration of the intake camshaft by using two different cam profiles. The VTC system, which is employed only on i-VTEC systems, changes the phase of the intake camshaft, which is another way of saying that it changes the cam timing, except that it does so continuously, not just when engine speed exceeds a certain threshold, as with the VTEC system. The VTC system, which is also operated by hydraulic (oil) pressure, improves fuel efficiency even more than VTEC alone, and it reduces exhaust emissions at all combinations of engine speed, vehicle speed and engine load.

8 When the engine is under a light load, the VTC control actuator (located inside the intake cam timing chain sprocket) is at its base position. The angle of the intake cam lobes is retarded to reduce the entry of exhaust gases into the intake ports and to achieve stable fuel consumption during lean burn.

9 When the engine is under a medium-to-high load, the VTC control actuator is at its advance control position. Cam angle is advanced slightly to reduce the effect of a diluted charge when the EGR system is operating by reducing the accompanying pumping loss. The intake valve is closed quickly to help reduce the entry of air/fuel mixture into the intake port and to improve the charging effect.

10 When the engine is operating at higher speeds, the VTC control actuator is at its advance-base position. The cam phase angle is controlled for maximum valve timing and maximum engine power.

COMPONENT REPLACEMENT

Four-cylinder models (i-VTEC/VTC)

VTC oil control solenoid valve

▶ **Refer to illustrations 25.11 and 25.13**

➡**Note: The VTC oil control solenoid valve is located at the right end of the engine, in a recess in the timing chain cover, right below the valve cover.**

11 Disconnect the electrical connector from the VTC oil control solenoid valve (see illustration).

12 Remove the VTC oil control solenoid mounting bolt and remove the solenoid valve.

13 Remove and discard the old VTC oil control solenoid valve O-ring (see illustration).

14 Inspect the VTC oil control solenoid valve for clogging. If the oil control solenoid valve is clogged, replace it.

15 Installation is the reverse of removal. Be sure to use a new O-ring and tighten the solenoid valve mounting bolt to the torque listed in this Chapter's Specifications.

i-VTEC solenoid valve

▶ **Refer to illustrations 25.16, 25.18, 25.19 and 25.20**

➡**Note: The i-VTEC solenoid valve is located on the backside of the cylinder head, at the far right end.**

16 Disconnect the electrical connectors from the i-VTEC solenoid valve and from the i-VTEC oil pressure switch (see illustration).

17 Raise the front of the vehicle and place it securely on jackstands.

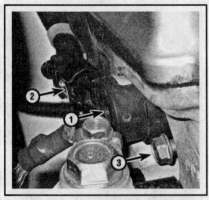

25.11 To remove the VTC oil control solenoid valve (1) from the timing chain cover, depress the release tab (2), unplug the electrical connector, then remove the valve mounting bolt (3)

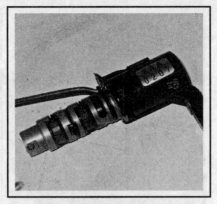

25.13 Be sure to remove the old O-ring from the VTC oil control solenoid valve and discard it. Always use a new O-ring when installing the oil control solenoid valve

25.16 Disconnect the electrical connectors from the i-VTEC solenoid valve (A) and from the i-VTEC oil pressure switch (B)

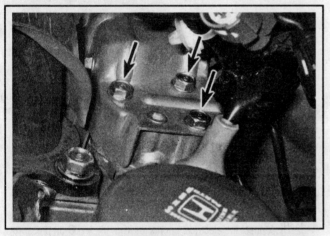

25.18 To detach the i-VTEC solenoid valve mounting bracket from the cylinder head, remove the solenoid valve mounting bracket bolts and remove the solenoid valve and mounting bracket as a single assembly

25.19 To separate the i-VTEC solenoid valve from its mounting bracket, remove this bolt

18 Remove the i-VTEC solenoid valve mounting bracket bolts (see illustration) and remove the i-VTEC solenoid and mounting bracket from the cylinder head as a single assembly.

19 Remove the bolt that attaches the mounting bracket to the i-VTEC solenoid valve (see illustration) and separate the valve from the bracket.

20 Remove and discard the i-VTEC solenoid valve O-ring/oil filter screen (see illustration).

21 Installation is the reverse of removal. Be sure to use a new O-ring/oil filter screen and tighten the i-VTEC solenoid valve mounting bolts to the torque listed in this Chapter's Specifications.

i-VTEC oil pressure switch

♦ **Refer to illustrations 25.23 and 25.24**

➡ **Note:** The i-VTEC oil pressure switch is located on the back-side of the cylinder head, at the far right end. It's screwed into the i-VTEC solenoid valve.

22 Remove the i-VTEC solenoid valve assembly (see Steps 16 through 18) and separate the i-VTEC solenoid valve from its mounting bracket.

25.20 Remove and discard the old O-ring/oil filter from the i-VTEC solenoid

25.23 Unscrew the i-VTEC oil pressure switch from the i-VTEC solenoid valve

25.24 Remove and discard the old i-VTEC oil pressure switch O-ring

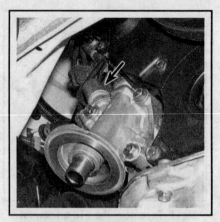

25.27 On V6 engines, the VTEC solenoid valve is located on top of the oil filter housing. To disconnect the electrical connector, trace the electrical lead from the solenoid valve up to the connector and unplug it

23 Unscrew the i-VTEC oil pressure switch from the i-VTEC solenoid valve (see illustration).

24 Remove and discard the old oil pressure switch O-ring (see illustration).

25 Installation is the reverse of removal. Be sure to use a new O-ring and tighten the i-VTEC oil pressure switch to the torque listed in this Chapter's Specifications.

V6 models (VTEC)

VTEC solenoid valve

♦ Refer to illustration 25.27

➥Note: The VTEC solenoid valve is located at the right end of the engine, on top of the oil filter housing, next to the VTEC oil pressure switch.

26 Raise the front of the vehicle and place it securely on jackstands.

27 Locate the VTEC solenoid valve (see illustration), then trace the electrical lead up to the electrical connector and disconnect it.

28 Remove the two VTEC solenoid valve mounting bolts and remove the solenoid valve.

29 Remove and discard the VTEC solenoid valve O-ring.

30 Installation is the reverse of removal. Be sure to use a new O-ring and tighten the VTEC solenoid valve mounting bolts to the torque listed in this Chapter's Specifications.

VTEC oil pressure switch

➥Note: The VTEC oil pressure switch is located at the right end of the engine, on top of the oil filter housing, next to the VTEC solenoid valve.

31 Raise the front of the vehicle and place it securely on jackstands.

32 Disconnect the electrical connector from the VTEC oil pressure switch.

33 Unscrew and remove the VTEC oil pressure switch.

34 Remove and discard the old VTEC oil pressure switch O-ring.

35 Installation is the reverse of removal. Be sure to use a new O-ring and tighten the oil pressure switch to the torque listed in this Chapter's Specifications.

Torque specifications	Ft-lbs (unless otherwise indicated)	Nm

→**Note:** One foot-pound (ft-lb) of torque is equivalent to 12 inch-pounds (in-lbs) of torque. Torque values below approximately 15 ft-lbs are expressed in inch-pounds, since most foot-pound torque wrenches are not accurate at these smaller values.

Engine Coolant Temperature (ECT) sensor		
Four-cylinder models	104 in-lbs	12
V6 models	156 in-lbs	18
Exhaust Gas Recirculation (EGR) valve		
mounting nuts (all models)	16	22
Intake Manifold Tuning (IMT) actuator		
mounting bolts (V6 models)	86 in-lbs	9.8
Knock sensor (all models)	23	31
Oxygen sensors	33	44
intelligent Variable Valve Timing and Lift Electronic Control/Variable Valve Timing Control		
(i-VTEC/VTC) system (four cylinder models)		
VTC oil control solenoid valve mounting bolt	104 in-lbs	12
i-VTEC solenoid valve mounting bolts	86 in-lbs	9.8
Mounting bracket-to-i-VTEC solenoid valve bolt	104 in-lbs	12
i-VTEC oil pressure switch	16	22
Variable Valve Timing and Lift Electronic Control (VTEC) system (V6 models)		
VTEC solenoid valve mounting bolts	16	22
VTEC oil pressure switch	16	22
Transmission range switch control shaft		
locknut (2008 and later V6 models)	104 in-lbs	12

Notes

7A
MANUAL TRANSAXLE

Section

Reference to other Chapters

1   General information

Vehicles covered by this manual are equipped with either a five-speed (four cylinder models) or six-speed (V6 models) manual transaxle or a five-speed automatic transaxle.

All information on the manual transaxle is included in this Part of Chapter 7. Service procedures for the five-speed automatic transaxle can be found in Chapter 7, Part B. You'll also find certain procedures common to both transaxles - such as oil seal replacement - in this Chapter.

Depending on the expense involved in having a transaxle over-hauled, it might be a better idea to consider replacing it with either a new or rebuilt unit. Your local dealer or transaxle shop should be able to supply information concerning cost, availability and exchange policy. Regardless of how you decide to remedy a transaxle problem, you can still save a lot of money by removing and installing the unit yourself.

2   Driveaxle oil seals - replacement

▶ **Refer to illustrations 2.4 and 2.6**

1   Oil leaks frequently occur due to wear of the driveaxle oil seals. Replacement of these seals is relatively easy, since the repair can usually be performed without removing the transaxle from the vehicle.

2   Driveaxle oil seals are located at the sides of the transaxle, where the driveaxles are attached. If leakage at the seal is suspected, raise the vehicle and support it securely on jackstands. If the seal is leaking, lubricant will be found on the sides of the transaxle, below the seals.

3   Refer to Chapter 8 and remove the driveaxles.

4   Use a screwdriver or prybar to carefully pry the oil seal out of the transaxle bore (see illustration).

5   If the oil seal cannot be removed with a screwdriver or prybar, a special oil seal removal tool (available at auto parts stores) will be required.

6   Using a seal driver or a large deep socket (slightly smaller than the outside diameter of the seal) as a drift, install the new oil seal (see illustration). Drive it into the bore squarely and make sure it's completely seated. Coat the seal lip with transaxle lubricant.

7   Install the driveaxle(s). Be careful not to damage the lip of the new seal.

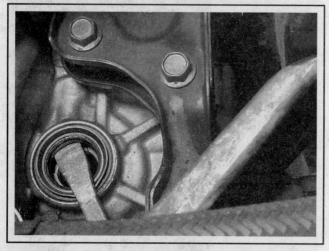

2.4 Insert the tip of a large screwdriver or prybar behind the oil seal and very carefully pry it out

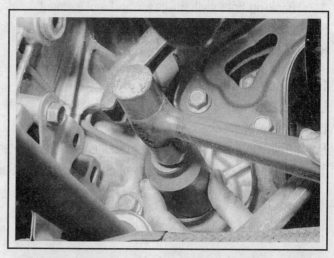

2.6 Using a large socket or a section of pipe, drive the new seal squarely into the bore

3   Shift cables - removal and installation

▶ **Refer to illustration 3.7**

1   Remove the center console (see Chapter 11).

2   Remove the cotter pins and detach the cable ends from the lock pins on the shift lever.

3   Pry off the spring clips and detach the cables from the shift lever housing. Rotate the cables until the squared edge aligns with the slot in the shift lever housing cutout.

4   Pull back the carpet and dislodge the grommet from the floorpan.

5   Raise the front of the vehicle and support it securely on jackstands.

6   Unscrew the nut and detach the cable bracket from the floorpan.

7 Remove the cotter pins and washers and detach the cables from the shift levers on the transaxle (see illustration).

8 Pry off the spring clip(s) and detach the cable(s) from the bracket on the transaxle.

9 Guide the cable(s) through the floorpan.

10 Installation is the reverse of removal

3.7 Remove the cotter pins and washers and disconnect the select cable from the select lever (lower right arrow) and the shift cable from the shift lever (upper right arrow), then pry off the retaining clips from the brackets

4 Back-up light switch - check and replacement

CHECK

▶ **Refer to illustration 4.4**

1 Before testing the back-up light switch, check the fuse in the engine compartment fuse/relay box. Refer to the wiring diagrams at the end of Chapter 12.

2 Put the shift lever in Reverse and turn the ignition switch to the On position. The back-up lights should go on. Turn off the ignition switch.

3 If the back-up lights don't go on, check the back-up light bulbs in the tail light assembly.

4 If the fuse and bulbs are both okay, locate the back-up light switch on top of the transaxle (see illustration), trace the leads back to the electrical connector, unplug the connector and hook up an ohmmeter or continuity tester across the terminals of the back-up light switch.

5 With the shift lever in Reverse, there should be continuity; with the shifter in any other gear, there should be no continuity.

6 If the switch fails this test, replace it (see below).

7 If the switch is OK, but the back-up lights aren't coming on, check for power to the switch. If voltage is not available, trace the circuit between the switch and the fuse block. If power is present, trace the circuit between the switch and the back-up lights for an open circuit condition.

4.4 The back-up light switch on the manual transaxle is located near the starter

REPLACEMENT

8 Unplug the back-up light switch electrical connector.

9 Unscrew the back-up light switch.

10 Discard the old washer.

11 Using a new washer, install the new switch.

12 Plug in the connector.

5 Manual transaxle - removal and installation

REMOVAL

1 Remove the air intake duct and the air filter housing (see Chapter 4).

2 Remove the battery and the battery tray (see Chapter 5).

3 Remove the clutch release cylinder and hydraulic line, without disconnecting any fittings. Support the cylinder out of the way with a

length of wire or rope.

❋❋ **CAUTION:**

Don't depress the clutch pedal while the release cylinder is removed.

4   Remove the starter (see Chapter 5).

5   Clearly label and disconnect all vacuum lines, emissions hoses, electrical connectors and wiring harness clamps/brackets that may interfere with transaxle removal. Masking tape and/or a touch up paint applicator work well for marking items. Take instant photos or sketch the locations of components and brackets.

6   Support the engine with an engine support fixture or an engine hoist (an engine support fixture is recommended, as it doesn't have legs that extend under the vehicle that would get in the way). Connect the sling or chain to the left end (driver's side) of the engine, not to the lifting eye on the transaxle. Use the threaded hole(s) in the left end (driver's side) of the cylinder head(s) to attach the sling or chain.

7   Loosen the front wheel lug nuts, then raise the vehicle and support it securely on jackstands. Remove the wheels.

8   Remove the engine splash shield (see Chapter 2) and the inner fender splash shields (see Chapter 11). Cover the fenders and cowl using special pads. An old bedspread or blanket will also work.

9   Drain the transaxle fluid (see Chapter 1).

10 Remove the front section of the exhaust pipe, between the exhaust manifold(s) and the downstream catalytic converter.

11 Remove the driveaxles and the intermediate shaft (see Chapter 8).

12 Disconnect the shift cables from the transaxle (see Section 3).

13 Remove all of the powertrain mounts except the right side (drive-belt end) mount (see Chapter 2).

14 Remove the subframe (see Chapter 10).

15 Support the transaxle with a jack, preferably one made for this purpose. Secure the transaxle to the jack with straps or chains.

16 Remove the transaxle-to-engine bolts.

17 Move the transaxle away from the engine to disengage the transaxle input shaft from the clutch disc, and far enough to clear the pressure plate. Lower the transaxle from the vehicle.

➡Note: It may be necessary to slowly lower the engine a slight amount while the jack supporting the transaxle is being lowered. This will provide more clearance between the transaxle and the body.

INSTALLATION

18 If removed, install the clutch components (see Chapter 8).

19 Make sure the two dowel pins are installed. With the transaxle secured to the jack with a chain, raise it into position behind the engine, then carefully slide it forward, engaging the two dowel pins on the transaxle with the corresponding holes in the block and the input shaft with the clutch plate hub splines. Do not use excessive force to install the transaxle - if the input shaft does not slide into place, readjust the angle of the transaxle so it is level and/or turn the input shaft so the splines engage properly with the clutch plate hub.

20 Install the transaxle-to-engine bolts and tighten them to the torque listed in this Chapter's Specifications.

21 The remainder of installation is the reverse of removal, noting the following points:

a) Refill the transaxle with the specified type of lubricant (see Chapter 1).

b) Tighten the driveaxle/hub nuts to the torque listed in the Chapter 8 Specifications.

c) Tighten the wheel lug nuts to the torque listed in the Chapter 1 Specifications.

d) Road test the vehicle for proper operation and check for leaks.

6   Manual transaxle overhaul - general information

1   Overhauling a manual transaxle is a difficult job for the do-it-yourselfer. It involves the disassembly and reassembly of many small parts. Numerous clearances must be precisely measured and, if necessary, changed with select fit spacers and snap-rings. As a result, if transaxle problems arise, it can be removed and installed by a competent do-it-yourselfer, but overhaul should be left to a transaxle repair shop. Rebuilt transaxles may be available - check with your dealer parts department and auto parts stores. At any rate, the time and money involved in an overhaul is almost sure to exceed the cost of a rebuilt unit.

2   Nevertheless, it's not impossible for an inexperienced mechanic to rebuild a transaxle if the special tools are available and the job is done in a deliberate step-by-step manner so nothing is overlooked.

3   The tools necessary for an overhaul include internal and external snap-ring pliers, a bearing puller, a slide hammer, a set of pin punches, a dial indicator and possibly a hydraulic press. In addition, a large, sturdy workbench and a vise or transaxle stand will be required.

4   During disassembly of the transaxle, make careful notes of how each piece comes off, where it fits in relation to other pieces and what holds it in place. Noting how the parts are installed when you remove them will make it much easier to get the transaxle back together.

5   Before taking the transaxle apart for repair, it will help if you have some idea what area of the transaxle is malfunctioning. Certain problems can be closely tied to specific areas in the transaxle, which can make component examination and replacement easier. Refer to the *Troubleshooting* Section at the front of this manual for information regarding possible sources of trouble.

Torque specifications	Ft-lbs	Nm
Transaxle-to-engine mounting bolts		
Four cylinder models	47	64
V6 models	54	74
Starter bolts	See Chapter 5	

7B

AUTOMATIC TRANSAXLE

Section

Reference to other Chapters

1   General information

The automatic transaxle is an electronically controlled, 5-speed unit. The automatic transaxles are designated MCLA or BCLA (four-cylinder models) and BAYA or MAYA (V6 models). The transaxle model number is stamped onto a plate on the transaxle. Refer to *Vehicle identification numbers* at the front of this manual for the location of the plate.

Due to the complexity of the clutches and the hydraulic control system, and because of the special tools and expertise required to perform an automatic transaxle overhaul, it should not be undertaken by the home mechanic. Therefore, the procedures in this Chapter are limited to general diagnosis, shift cable adjustment, certain component replacement procedures and transaxle removal and installation.

If the transaxle requires major repair work, it should be left to a dealer service department or an automotive or transaxle repair shop. You can, however, remove and install the transaxle yourself and save the expense, even if the repair work is done by a transaxle shop (but be sure a proper diagnosis has been made before removing the transaxle).

2   Diagnosis - general

➡ **Note: Automatic transaxle malfunctions may be caused by five general conditions: poor engine performance, improper adjustments, hydraulic malfunctions, mechanical malfunctions or malfunctions in the computer or its signal network. Diagnosis of these problems should always begin with a check of the easily repaired items: fluid level and condition (see Chapter 1), shift cable adjustment and transmission range switch adjustment. Next, perform a road test to determine if the problem has been corrected or if more diagnosis is necessary. If the problem persists after the preliminary tests and corrections are completed, additional diagnosis should be done by a dealer service department or transaxle repair shop. Refer to the Troubleshooting section at the front of this manual for information on symptoms of transaxle problems.**

PRELIMINARY CHECKS

1   Drive the vehicle to warm the transaxle to normal operating temperature.

2   Check the fluid level as described in Chapter 1:

   a) *If the fluid level is unusually low, add enough fluid to bring the level within the designated area of the dipstick, then check for external leaks (see below).*

   b) *If the fluid level is abnormally high, drain off the excess, then check the drained fluid for contamination by coolant. The presence of engine coolant in the automatic transaxle fluid indicates that a failure has occurred in the internal radiator walls that separate the coolant from the transaxle fluid (see Chapter 3).*

   c) *If the fluid is foaming, drain it and refill the transaxle, then check for coolant in the fluid, or a high fluid level.*

3   Check for any stored trouble codes (see Chapter 6).

➡ **Note: If the engine is malfunctioning, do not proceed with the preliminary checks until it has been repaired and runs normally.**

4   Check the throttle control cable for freedom of movement (see Chapter 4).

5   Inspect the shift cable linkage (see Section 3). Make sure that it's properly adjusted and that it operates smoothly.

FLUID LEAK DIAGNOSIS

6   Most fluid leaks are easy to locate visually. Repair usually consists of replacing a seal or gasket. If a leak is difficult to find, the following procedure may help.

7   Identify the fluid. Make sure it's transaxle fluid and not engine oil or brake fluid (automatic transaxle fluid is a deep red color).

8   Try to pinpoint the source of the leak. Drive the vehicle several miles, then park it over a large sheet of cardboard. After a minute or two, you should be able to locate the leak by determining the source of the fluid dripping onto the cardboard.

9   Make a careful visual inspection of the suspected component and the area immediately around it. Pay particular attention to gasket mating surfaces. A mirror is often helpful for finding leaks in areas that are hard to see.

10   If the leak still cannot be found, clean the suspected area thoroughly with a degreaser or solvent, then dry the area.

11   Drive the vehicle for several miles at normal operating temperature and varying speeds. After driving the vehicle, visually inspect the suspected component again.

12   Once the leak has been located, the cause must be determined before it can be properly repaired. If a gasket is replaced but the sealing flange is bent, the new gasket will not stop the leak. The bent flange must be straightened.

13   Before attempting to repair a leak, check to make sure that the following conditions are corrected or they may cause another leak.

➡ **Note: Some of the following conditions cannot be fixed without highly specialized tools and expertise. Such problems must be referred to a transaxle shop or a dealer service department.**

Gasket leaks

14   Check the right side cover periodically. Make sure the bolts are tight, no bolts are missing, the gasket is in good condition and the cover is not damaged.

15   If the leak is from the right side cover area, the bolts may be too tight, the sealing surface of the transaxle housing may be damaged, the gasket may be damaged or the transaxle casting may be cracked or porous. If sealant instead of gasket material has been used to form a seal between the cover and the transaxle housing, it may be the wrong sealant.

Seal leaks

16   If a transaxle seal is leaking, the fluid level or pressure may be too high, the vent may be plugged, the seal bore may be damaged, the seal itself may be damaged or improperly installed, the surface of the shaft protruding through the seal may be damaged or a loose bearing may be causing excessive shaft movement.

17   Make sure the dipstick tube seal is in good condition and the tube is properly seated. Periodically check the area around the speedometer gear or sensor for leakage. If transaxle fluid is evident, check the O-ring for damage.

Case leaks

18 If the case itself appears to be leaking, the casting is porous and will have to be repaired or replaced.

19 Make sure the oil cooler hose fittings are tight and in good condition.

Fluid comes out vent pipe or fill tube

20 If this condition occurs, the transaxle is overfilled, there is coolant in the fluid, the case is porous, the dipstick is incorrect, the vent is plugged or the drain-back holes are plugged.

---

3   Shift cable - removal, installation and adjustment

✳✳ WARNING:

The models covered by this manual are equipped with Supplemental Restraint systems (SRS), more commonly known as airbags. Always disable the airbag system before working in the vicinity of any airbag system component to avoid the possibility of accidental deployment of the airbag, which could cause personal injury (see Chapter 12). Do not use a memory saving device to preserve the PCM's memory when working on or near airbag system components.

REMOVAL

◆ **Refer to illustrations 3.2, 3.3, 3.6, 3.7, 3.8 and 3.9**

1   Remove the center console (see Chapter 11).

2   Position the shift lever in R. Remove the locking nut from the pin on the shift lever (see illustration).

3   Press the holder lock release mechanism and pull the socket holder from the shift lever bracket base (see illustration).

4   Raise the vehicle and support it securely on jackstands.

5   Remove the exhaust pipe (see Chapter 4) and the heat shield.

6   Working under the vehicle near the console, remove the shift

cable guide bracket and grommet from the body (see illustration).

7   Remove the bolts from the shift cable holder (see illustration).

➡ Note: To prevent damage to the control lever joint, remove the shift cable holder first, and then the shift cable cover.

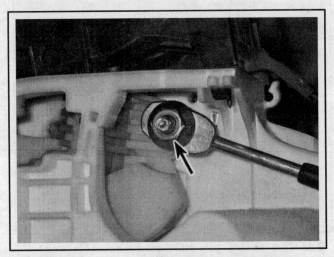

3.2 Remove the locking nut from the shift lever pin

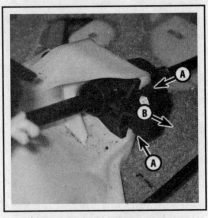

3.3 Press the holder lock release mechanism tabs (A) and pull the socket holder (B) away from the shift lever bracket base

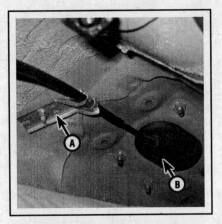

3.6 Remove the shift cable guide bracket (A) and grommet (B) from the floorpan

3.7 Remove the bolts from the shift cable holder

3.8 Remove the bolts from the shift cable cover

3.9 Remove the spring clip (A) and the control pin (B) from the control lever (four cylinder models; V6 models have a lock bolt)

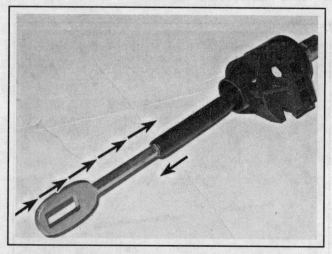

3.13 Push the shift cable until it stops and then back one click into the Reverse position

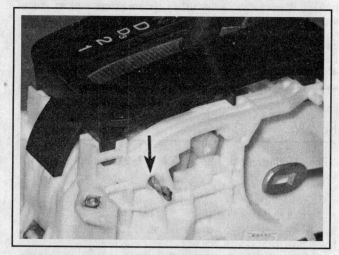

3.14 Install a 0.24 inch (6 mm) pin (here a 15/64-inch drill bit is being used) into the alignment hole on the shift lever bracket base and into the alignment hole in the shift lever

8   Remove the bolts from the shift control cover (see illustration) and separate it from the transaxle.

9   Remove the spring clip and the control pin (four-cylinder models) (see illustration) or lock bolt (V6 models) from the control lever on the transaxle.

10   Remove the shift cable assembly.

INSTALLATION AND ADJUSTMENT

♦ **Refer to illustrations 3.13 and 3.14**

11   Installation is the reverse of the removal procedure, however, don't connect the cable to the shift lever bracket or lever inside the vehicle yet.

12   Make sure the shift lever is still in the Reverse position.

13   Push the shift cable all the way in until it stops and then back one click into the reverse position (see illustration).

14   Install a 0.24 inch pin (6 mm) into the positioning hole on the shift lever bracket base and into the alignment hole on the shift lever (see illustration). A drill bit with the correct diameter will also work.

➡**Note: On some models the alignment hole is located towards the rear of the shifter. On others it's near the front.**

15   Align the socket holder on the shift cable with the slot on the bracket base (see illustration 3.3). Slide the holder onto the bracket base until it snaps into place.

16   Install the shift cable end onto the shift lever pin, making sure it fits over the square shank on the pin (see illustration).

17   Install the nut on the shift lever pin and tighten it securely.

18   Remove the alignment pin or drill bit from the alignment hole.

19   Turn the ignition key to On (don't start the engine), move the shift lever to each gear position and verify that the gear position indicator light comes on in each position. Make sure the engine only starts in Park and Neutral.

20   The remainder of installation is the reverse of removal.

4 Shift lever assembly - removal and installation

▶ Refer to illustration 4.4

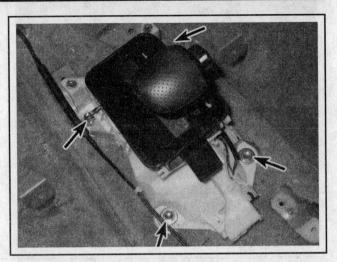

4.4 Shift lever assembly mounting bolts

※※ WARNING:

The models covered by this manual are equipped with Supplemental Restraint systems (SRS), more commonly known as airbags. Always disable the airbag system before working in the vicinity of any airbag system component to avoid the possibility of accidental deployment of the airbag, which could cause personal injury (see Chapter 12). Do not use a memory saving device to preserve the PCM's memory when working on or near airbag system components.

1 Remove the center console (see Chapter 11).
2 Disconnect the shift cable from the shift lever assembly (see Section 3).
3 Disconnect the shift interlock solenoid connector and the park pin switch connector (see Section 5).
4 Remove the four mounting bolts from the shift lever bracket base (see illustration).
5 Installation is the reverse of removal. Be sure to adjust the shift cable (see Section 3).

5 Shift Interlock system - description and solenoid replacement

※※ WARNING:

The models covered by this manual are equipped with Supplemental Restraint systems (SRS), more commonly known as airbags. Always disable the airbag system before working in the vicinity of any airbag system component to avoid the possibility of accidental deployment of the airbag, which could cause personal injury (see Chapter 12). Do not use a memory saving device to preserve the PCM's memory when working on or near airbag system components.

DESCRIPTION

1 Vehicles equipped with an automatic transaxle have an interlock system to prevent the shifter from being moved out of the Park position unless the brake is applied. It also prevents the key from being removed from the ignition lock cylinder unless the shifter is placed in the Park position. The interlock system consists of two subsystems: a shift lock system and a key interlock system.

Key interlock system

2 The key interlock system prevents the ignition key from being removed from the ignition switch unless the shift lever is in the Park position.

Shift lock system

3 The shift lock system prevents the shift lever from moving from the Park position unless the brake pedal is depressed. Nor can the shift lever be shifted when the brake pedal and the accelerator pedal are depressed at the same time. In the event of a system malfunction, you can release the shift lever by inserting the ignition key or a screwdriver into the release slot near the shift lever.

SOLENOID REPLACEMENT

➡Note 1: **The following procedure pertains only to the shift lock solenoid. For information on how to replace the key interlock solenoid, refer to the "Ignition switch/key lock cylinder replacement" Section in Chapter 12. The key interlock solenoid isn't available separately.**

➡Note 2: **There are two types of shift lever assemblies used on these vehicles; Type A and Type B. The Type B shifter has the alignment hole (as used for cable adjustment) near the rear of the shifter body (see illustration 3.14). The Type A shifter has the alignment hole near the front.**

Type A system

4 Remove the shift lever assembly (see Section 4).
5 Disconnect the shift lock solenoid electrical connector.
6 Turn the shifter assembly upside down. Pry the plastic lock tab to free the solenoid, then slide the solenoid out of the shifter assembly.
7 Install the plunger and plunger spring into the new shift lock solenoid (see illustration 5.15).
8 Engage the hole in the end of the plunger with the post of the shift lock stop.
9 Connect the shift lock solenoid electrical connector.
10 The remainder of installation is the reverse of removal.

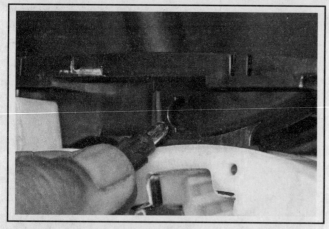

5.13 Turn the bulb holder counterclockwise to unlock it and remove it from the gear indicator panel

Type B system

▶ **Refer to illustrations 5.13, 5.14, 5.15 and 5.16**

11 Remove the center console (see Chapter 11).

12 Disconnect the shift lock solenoid electrical connector.

13 Remove the light bulb socket from the gear indicator panel (see illustration).

14 Pry the lock tab and release the shift lock solenoid (see illustration). Remove the shift lock solenoid from the shift lever assembly.

15 Install the plunger and plunger spring into the new shift lock solenoid (see illustration).

16 Engage the hole in the end of the plunger with the post of the shift lock stop (see illustration).

17 The remainder of installation is the reverse of removal.

5.14 Pry up the lock tab to release the shift lock solenoid

5.15 Install the plunger and plunger spring into the new shift lock solenoid

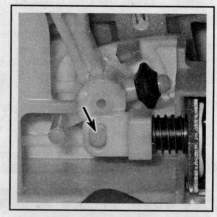

5.16 Engage the hole in the end of the plunger with the post of the shift lock stop

6 Automatic transaxle - removal and installation

▶ **Refer to illustrations 6.13 and 6.15**

✱✱ WARNING:

The models covered by this manual are equipped with Supplemental Restraint systems (SRS), more commonly known as airbags. Always disable the airbag system before working in the vicinity of any airbag system component to avoid the possibility of accidental deployment of the airbag, which could cause personal injury (see Chapter 12). Do not use a memory saving device to preserve the PCM's memory when working on or near airbag system components.

REMOVAL

1 Open the hood and cover the fenders and cowl using special pads. An old bedspread or blanket will also work. Remove the air intake duct and the air filter housing (see Chapter 4).

2 Remove the battery and the battery tray (see Chapter 5).

3 Remove the starter (see Chapter 5).

4 Clearly label and disconnect all vacuum lines, emissions hoses, electrical connectors and wiring harness clamps/brackets that may interfere with transaxle removal. Masking tape and/or a touch up paint applicator work well for marking items. Take instant photos or sketch the locations of components and brackets.

5 Disconnect the automatic transaxle fluid cooler lines from the transaxle. Be sure to position a pan to catch excess fluid. Plug the lines to prevent leakage.

6 Support the engine with an engine support fixture or an engine hoist (an engine support fixture is recommended, as it doesn't have legs that extend under the vehicle that would get in the way). Connect the sling or chain to the left end (driver's side) of the engine, not to the lifting eye on the transaxle. Use the threaded hole(s) in the left end (driver's side) of the cylinder head(s) to attach the sling or chain.

7 Loosen the front wheel lug nuts, then raise the vehicle and support it securely on jackstands. Remove the wheels.

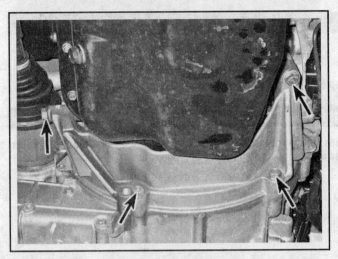

6.13 Location of the transaxle brace mounting bolts

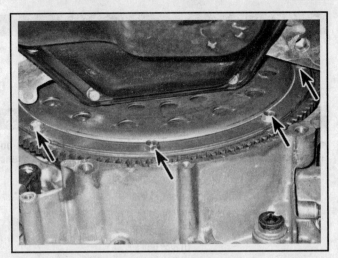

6.15 Rotate the driveplate to gain access to all the torque converter bolts

8   Remove the engine splash shield (see Chapter 2A) and the inner fender splash shields (see Chapter 11).

9   Disconnect the shift control cable from the transaxle (see Section 3).

10   Drain the transaxle fluid (see Chapter 1). Be sure to use a new sealing washer when you reinstall the drain plug.

11   Remove the front section of the exhaust pipe, between the exhaust manifold(s) and the downstream catalytic converter.

12   Remove the driveaxles and the intermediate shaft (see Chapter 8).

13   Remove the transaxle brace (see illustration) and the torque converter cover.

14   Mark the relationship of the torque converter to the driveplate so that they can be reinstalled in the same relationship to one another.

15   Remove the torque converter-to-driveplate bolts (see illustration) one at a time by rotating the crankshaft pulley for access to each bolt.

16   Remove all of the powertrain mounts except the right side (drive-belt end) mount (see Chapter 2A).

17   Remove the subframe (see Chapter 10).

18   Support the transaxle with a jack, preferably one made for this purpose. Secure the transaxle to the jack with straps or chains.

19   Remove the transaxle-to-engine bolts.

20   Move the transaxle back to disengage it from the engine block dowel pins and make sure the torque converter is detached from the driveplate. Secure the torque converter to the transaxle so it will not fall out during removal. Lower the transaxle from the vehicle.

➡Note: It may be necessary to slowly lower the engine a slight amount while the jack supporting the transaxle is being lowered. This will provide more clearance between the transaxle and the body.

INSTALLATION

21   Honda recommends flushing the transaxle cooler and the cooler hoses and lines with solvent whenever the transaxle is removed from the vehicle. Flush the lines and fluid cooler thoroughly and make sure no solvent remains in the lines or cooler after flushing. It's a good idea to repeat the flushing procedure with clean automatic transaxle fluid to ensure that no solvent remains in the lines or cooler.

22   Prior to installation, make sure that the torque converter hub is securely engaged in the transaxle pump. With the transaxle secured to the jack, raise it into position. Be sure to keep it level so the torque converter does not slide out.

23   Line-up the marks you made on the torque converter and driveplate.

24   Make sure the dowel pins are still installed, then move the transaxle forward carefully until the dowel pins are engaged with the holes in the engine block.

25   Install the transaxle-to-engine bolts and tighten them to the torque listed in this Chapter's Specifications.

✶✶ CAUTION:

Don't use the bolts to force the transaxle and engine together. If the transaxle doesn't slide easily up against the engine, find out why before you tighten the bolts

26   The remainder of installation is the reverse of the removal procedure, noting the following points:

 a) Install all of the driveplate bolts before tightening any of them. Tighten the driveplate bolts to the torque listed in this Chapter's Specifications.

 b) Tighten the driveaxle/hub nuts to the torque listed in the Chapter 8 Specifications.

 c) Tighten the wheel lug nuts to the torque listed in the Chapter 1 Specifications.

 d) Refill the transaxle with the specified type and amount of lubricant (see Chapter 1). Note that the transaxle may require more fluid than in a normal fluid and filter change, since the torque converter may be empty (the converter is not drained during a fluid change).

 e) Start the engine, set the parking brake and shift the transaxle through all gears three times. Make sure the shift cable is adjusted properly (see Section 4).

 f) Allow the engine to reach its proper operating temperature with the transaxle in Park or Neutral, then turn it off and check the fluid level again.

 g) Road test the vehicle and check for fluid leaks.

Specifications

General

Fluid type and capacity .... See Chapter 1

Torque specifications	Ft-lbs (unless otherwise indicated)	Nm

➡ **Note: One foot-pound (ft-lb) of torque is equivalent to 12 inch-pounds (in-lbs) of torque. Torque values below approximately 15 ft-lbs are expressed in inch-pounds, since most foot-pound torque wrenches are not accurate at these smaller values.**

	Ft-lbs	Nm
Transaxle-to-engine mounting bolts		
2007 and earlier models	47	64
2008 and later models		
Four-cylinder engines		
10 mm bolts	33	44
12 mm bolts	47	64
V6 engines	47	64
Torque converter-to-driveplate bolts	104 in-lbs	12
Torque converter cover bolts	104 in-lbs	12

8

CLUTCH AND DRIVELINE

1 General information

The information in this Chapter deals with the components from the rear of the engine to the front wheels, except for the transaxle, which is dealt with in the previous Chapter. For the purposes of this Chapter, these components are grouped into two categories - clutch and driveaxles. Separate Sections within this Chapter offer general descriptions and checking procedures for components in each of the two groups.

Since nearly all the procedures covered in this Chapter involve working under the vehicle, make sure it's securely supported on sturdy jackstands or on a hoist where the vehicle can be easily raised and lowered.

2 Clutch - description and check

1　All vehicles with a manual transaxle use a single dry-plate, diaphragm-spring type clutch. The clutch disc has a splined hub which allows it to slide along the splines of the transaxle input shaft. The clutch and pressure plate are held in contact by spring pressure exerted by the diaphragm in the pressure plate.

2　The clutch release system is operated by hydraulic pressure. The hydraulic release system consists of the clutch pedal, a master cylinder and fluid reservoir, the hydraulic line, a release (or slave) cylinder which actuates the clutch release lever and the clutch release (or throwout) bearing.

3　When pressure is applied to the clutch pedal to release the clutch, hydraulic pressure is exerted against the outer end of the clutch release lever. As the lever pivots the shaft fingers push against the release bearing. The bearing pushes against the fingers of the diaphragm spring of the pressure plate assembly, which in turn releases the clutch plate.

4　Terminology can be a problem when discussing the clutch components because common names are in some cases different from those used by the manufacturer. For example, the driven plate is also called the clutch plate or disc, the clutch release bearing is sometimes called a throwout bearing, the release cylinder is sometimes called the operating or slave cylinder.

5　Other than to replace components with obvious damage, some preliminary checks should be performed to diagnose clutch problems. These checks assume that the transaxle is in good working condition.

a)　The first check should be of the fluid level in the clutch master cylinder (see Chapter 1). If the fluid level is low, add fluid as necessary and inspect the hydraulic system for leaks. If the master cylinder reservoir has run dry, bleed the system as described in Section 5 and retest the clutch operation.

b)　To check clutch spin-down time, run the engine at normal idle speed with the transaxle in Neutral (clutch pedal up - engaged). Disengage the clutch (pedal down), wait several seconds and shift the transaxle into Reverse. No grinding noise should be heard. A grinding noise would most likely indicate a problem in the pressure plate or the clutch disc.

c)　To check for complete clutch release, run the engine (with the parking brake applied to prevent movement) and hold the clutch pedal approximately 1/2-inch from the floor. Shift the transaxle between 1st gear and Reverse several times. If the shift is rough, component failure is indicated. Check the release cylinder pushrod travel. With the clutch pedal depressed completely, the release cylinder pushrod should extend substantially. If it doesn't, check the fluid level in the clutch master cylinder.

d)　Visually inspect the pivot bushing at the top of the clutch pedal to make sure there is no binding or excessive play.

e)　Crawl under the vehicle and make sure the clutch release lever is solidly mounted on the ballstud.

3 Clutch master cylinder - removal and installation

1　Remove the air filter housing (see Chapter 4).

2　Remove the battery and battery tray (see Chapter 5).

3　Disconnect the hydraulic line mounting bracket.

4　Clamp a pair of locking pliers onto the clutch fluid feed hose, a couple of inches downstream of the reservoir. The pliers should be just tight enough to prevent fluid flow when the hose is disconnected.

5　Disconnect the hydraulic line at the cylinder. Loosen the fluid feed hose clamp and detach the hose from the cylinder. Have rags handy as some fluid will be lost as the line is removed. Cap or plug the ends of the lines (and/or hose) to prevent fluid leakage and the entry of contaminants.

6　Working under the dashboard, remove the cotter pin or spring clip from the master cylinder pushrod clevis. Pull out the clevis pin to disconnect the pushrod from the pedal. Unscrew the two clutch master cylinder retaining nuts and remove the cylinder.

7　Installation is the reverse of removal, noting the following points:

a)　Use new gasket between the master cylinder and the firewall. Tighten the master cylinder mounting nuts to the torque listed in this Chapter's Specifications.

b)　Install a new O-ring seal on the hydraulic line fitting at the master cylinder.

c)　Fill the clutch master cylinder reservoir with brake fluid conforming to DOT 3 specifications and bleed the clutch system as outlined in Section 5.

❊❊❊ CAUTION:

Don't allow brake fluid to come into contact with the paint as it will damage the finish.

Clutch release cylinder - removal and installation

REMOVAL

1 Remove the battery and battery tray (see Chapter 5). Disconnect the hydraulic line mounting bracket.

2 Remove the roll pins securing the hydraulic line to the release cylinder, then disconnect the line. Have a small can and rags handy - some fluid will be spilled as the line is removed. Plug the line to prevent excessive fluid loss.

3 Remove the two release cylinder mounting bolts and remove the release cylinder.

INSTALLATION

4 Lightly lubricate the release cylinder pushrod and the release fork pocket with high temperature grease. Install the release cylinder on the clutch housing. Make sure the pushrod is seated in the release fork pocket, then tighten the mounting bolts to the torque listed in this Chapter's Specifications.

5 Install a new O-ring on the hydraulic line, then connect the hydraulic line to the release cylinder and install the roll pins.

6 The remainder of installation is the reverse of removal, noting the following points:

   a) Fill the clutch master cylinder with brake fluid conforming to DOT 3 specifications.

   b) Bleed the system as described in Section 5.

Clutch hydraulic system - bleeding

1 Bleed the hydraulic system whenever any part of the system has been removed or the fluid level has fallen so low that air has been drawn into the master cylinder. The bleeding procedure is very similar to bleeding a brake system.

2 Fill the master cylinder with new brake fluid conforming to DOT 3 specifications.

✳ CAUTION:

Do not re-use any of the fluid coming from the system during the bleeding operation or use fluid which has been inside an open container for an extended period of time.

3 Remove the dust cap which fits over the bleeder valve and push a length of plastic hose over the valve. Place the other end of the hose into a clear container with about two inches of brake fluid. The hose end must be in the fluid at the bottom of the container.

4 Have an assistant depress the clutch pedal and hold it. Open the bleeder valve on the release cylinder, allowing fluid to flow through the hose. Close the bleeder valve when the flow of fluid (and bubbles) ceases. Once closed, have your assistant release the pedal.

5 Continue this process until all air is evacuated from the system, indicated by a solid stream of fluid being ejected from the bleeder valve each time with no air bubbles in the hose or container. Keep a close watch on the fluid level inside the clutch master cylinder reservoir - if the level drops too far, air will get into the system and you'll have to start all over again.

6 Check carefully for proper operation before placing the vehicle into normal service.

Clutch components - removal, inspection and installation

✳ WARNING:

Dust produced by clutch wear is hazardous to your health. DO NOT blow it out with compressed air and DO NOT inhale it. DO NOT use gasoline or petroleum-based solvents to remove the dust. Brake system cleaner should be used to flush the dust into a drain pan. After the clutch components are wiped clean with a rag, dispose of the contaminated rags and cleaner in a covered, marked container.

➡ Note: On V6 models, a special tool is required to compress the clutch pressure plate during clutch removal and installation.

REMOVAL

♦ Refer to illustrations 6.5 and 6.6

1 Access to the clutch components is normally accomplished by removing the transaxle, leaving the engine in the vehicle. If the engine is being removed for major overhaul, check the clutch for wear and replace worn components as necessary. However, the relatively low cost of the clutch components compared to the time and trouble spent gaining access to them warrants their replacement anytime the engine or transaxle is removed, unless they are new or in near-perfect condition. The following procedures are based on the assumption the engine will stay in place.

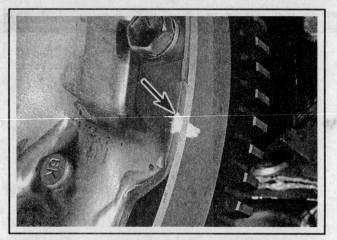

6.5 Mark the relationship of the pressure plate to the flywheel (if you're planning to re-use the old pressure plate)

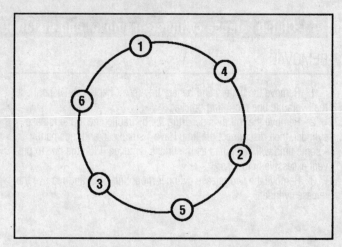

6.6 Pressure plate mounting bolt loosening sequence

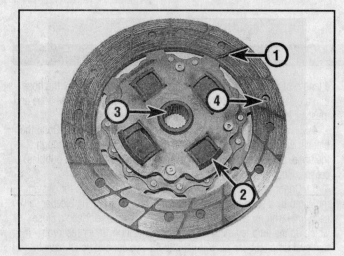

6.10 The clutch disc

1   *Lining* - this will wear down in use
2   *Springs or dampers* - check for cracking and deformation
3   *Splined hub* - the splines must not be worn and should slide smoothly on the transaxle input shaft splines
4   *Rivets* - these secure the lining and will damage the flywheel or pressure plate if allowed to contact the surfaces

2   Remove the transaxle from the vehicle (see Chapter 7, Part A). Support the engine while the transaxle is out. Preferably, an engine support fixture or a hoist should be used to support it from above.

3   The clutch fork and release bearing can remain attached to the transaxle housing for the time being.

4   On a four-cylinder model, to support the clutch disc during removal, install a clutch alignment tool through the clutch disc hub.

5   Carefully inspect the flywheel and pressure plate for indexing marks. The marks are usually an X, an O or a white letter. If they cannot be found, scribe or paint marks yourself so the pressure plate and the flywheel will be in the same alignment during installation (see illustration).

6   If you're working on a V6 model, install the special factory tool or equivalent according to the manufacturer instructions. Then loosen the

pressure plate-to-flywheel bolts in the pattern shown (see illustration).

CAUTION:

The use of this tool is necessary to remove and install the pressure plate without damaging it. The tool compresses the diaphragm spring and takes the pressure off of the clutch cover while the bolts are removed and installed. It also incorporates an alignment tool to center the clutch disc in the pressure plate.

7   On four-cylinder models, turning each bolt a little at a time, loosen the pressure plate-to-flywheel bolts. Work in a criss-cross pattern until all spring pressure is relieved. Then hold the pressure plate securely and completely remove the bolts, followed by the pressure plate and clutch disc.

INSPECTION

► Refer to illustrations 6.10, 6.12a and 6.12b

8   Ordinarily, when a problem occurs in the clutch, it can be attributed to wear of the clutch driven plate assembly (clutch disc). However, all components should be inspected at this time.

9   Inspect the flywheel for cracks, heat checking, grooves and other obvious defects. If the imperfections are slight, a machine shop can machine the surface flat and smooth, which is highly recommended regardless of the surface appearance. Refer to Chapter 2 for the flywheel removal and installation procedure.

10   Inspect the lining on the clutch disc. There should be at least 1/16-inch of lining above the rivet heads. Check for loose rivets, distortion, cracks, broken springs and other obvious damage (see illustration). As mentioned above, ordinarily the clutch disc is routinely replaced, so if in doubt about the condition, replace it with a new one.

11   The release bearing should also be replaced along with the clutch disc (see Section 7).

12   Check the machined surfaces and the diaphragm spring fingers of the pressure plate (see illustrations). If the surface is grooved or otherwise damaged, replace the pressure plate. Also check for obvious damage, distortion, cracking, etc. Light glazing can be removed with emery cloth or sandpaper. If a new pressure plate is required, new and re-manufactured units are available.

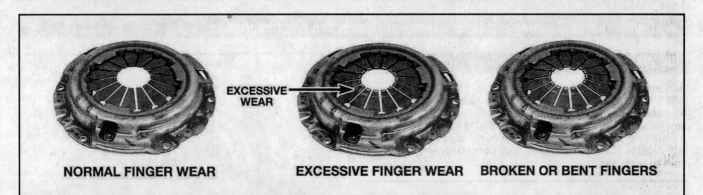

6.12a Replace the pressure plate if excessive wear or damage are noted

6.12b Inspect the pressure plate surface for excessive score marks, cracks and signs of overheating

6.14 Center the clutch disc in the pressure plate with a clutch alignment tool

INSTALLATION

▶ **Refer to illustration 6.14**

13 Before installation, clean the flywheel and pressure plate machined surfaces with brake cleaner, lacquer thinner or acetone. It's important that no oil or grease is on these surfaces or the lining of the clutch disc. Handle the parts only with clean hands.

14 Position the clutch disc and pressure plate against the flywheel with the clutch held in place with an alignment tool (see illustration). Make sure the disc is installed properly (most replacement clutch discs will be marked "flywheel side" or something similar - if not marked, install the clutch disc with the damper springs toward the transaxle).

15 Tighten the pressure plate-to-flywheel bolts only finger tight, working around the pressure plate.

16 If you're working on a four-cylinder model, center the clutch disc by ensuring the alignment tool extends through the splined hub and into the pilot bearing in the crankshaft. Wiggle the tool up, down or side-to-side as needed to center the disc. Tighten the pressure plate-to-flywheel bolts a little at a time, working in a criss-cross pattern to prevent distorting the cover. After all of the bolts are snug, tighten them to the torque listed in this Chapter's Specifications. Remove the alignment tool.

17 If you're working on a V6 model, install the special factory tool or equivalent according to the manufacturer instructions. Use the tool to apply pressure to the diaphragm spring, then tighten the pressure plate-to-flywheel bolts in the pattern shown in illustration 6.6. Tighten the pressure plate-to-flywheel bolts a little at a time, working in a criss-cross pattern to prevent distorting the cover.

18 Using high-temperature grease, lubricate the inner groove of the release bearing (see Section 7). Also place a small amount of grease on the release lever contact areas and the transaxle input shaft bearing retainer.

19 Install the clutch release bearing (see Section 7).

20 Install the transaxle and all components removed previously.

7 Clutch release bearing and lever - removal, inspection and installation

✻✻ WARNING:

Dust produced by clutch wear is hazardous to your health. DO NOT blow it out with compressed air and DO NOT inhale it. DO NOT use gasoline or petroleum-based solvents to remove the dust. Brake system cleaner should be used to flush the dust into a drain pan. After the clutch components are wiped clean with a rag, dispose of the contaminated rags and cleaner in a covered, marked container.

REMOVAL

1   Remove the transaxle (see Chapter 7A).
2   Pull the clutch release fork off the ballstud and slide the release bearing off the input shaft along with the release fork.

INSPECTION

▶ **Refer to illustration 7.4**

3   Wipe off the bearing with a clean rag and inspect it for damage, wear and cracks. Don't immerse the bearing in solvent - it's sealed for life and immersion in solvent will ruin it.
4   Hold the center of the bearing and rotate the outer portion while applying pressure (see illustration). If the bearing doesn't turn smoothly or if it's noisy or rough, replace it.
➡**Note: Considering the difficulty involved with replacing the release bearing, we recommend replacing the release bearing whenever the clutch components are replaced.**

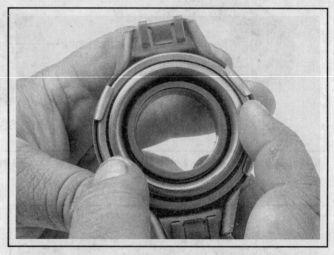

7.4 Hold the bearing by the outer race and rotate the inner race while applying pressure - if the bearing doesn't turn smoothly or if it's noisy, replace the bearing

INSTALLATION

5   Lightly lubricate the friction surfaces of the release bearing, ballstud and the sleeve of the input shaft bearing retainer with high-temperature grease.
6   Install the release lever and bearing onto the input shaft.
7   The remainder of installation is the reverse of removal.

8 Clutch pedal adjustment

PEDAL HEIGHT

▶ **Refer to illustration 8.1**

1   The height of the clutch pedal is the distance the pedal sits off the floor with the carpet pulled back (see illustration). If the pedal height is not within the specified range, it must be adjusted.
2   To adjust the clutch pedal, loosen the locknut on the clutch start switch or adjusting bolt and back the switch out until it no longer touches the pedal, then loosen the locknut on the clutch pushrod. Turn the pushrod to adjust the pedal height, then tighten the locknut.
3   Turn the switch or bolt clockwise until it just contacts the pedal arm, then turn it in an additional 3/4 to 1 turn. Tighten the locknut.
4   Adjust the clutch start switch as described in Section 9.

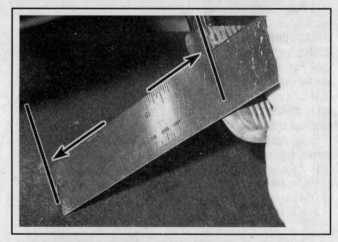

8.1 Pedal height is the distance between the pedal and the floor (with the carpet pulled back)

PEDAL FREEPLAY

▶ **Refer to illustration 8.5**

5   The freeplay is the pedal slack, or the distance the pedal can be depressed before it begins to have any effect on the clutch system (see illustration). If the pedal freeplay is not within the specified range, it must be adjusted.

6   To adjust the pedal freeplay, loosen the locknut on the clutch pushrod. Then back off the pushrod to adjust the pedal freeplay to the specified range and retighten the locknut.

7   Check and, if necessary, adjust the clutch start switch (see Section 9).

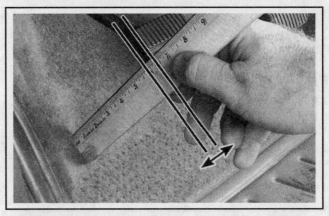

8.5 Pedal freeplay is the distance the pedal travels before resistance is felt

Clutch start switch - check and replacement

CHECK

1   Verify that the engine will not start when the clutch pedal is released.

2   Verify that the engine will start when the clutch pedal is depressed all the way.

3   If the engine won't start with the pedal depressed, or starts with the pedal released, unplug the electrical connector to the switch. The clutch start switch is located near the top of the clutch pedal. Check continuity between the connector terminals with the clutch pedal depressed.

4   If there's continuity between the terminals with the pedal depressed, the switch is okay; if there's no continuity between the ter-

minals with the pedal depressed, replace the switch. If there's continuity between the terminals when the clutch pedal is released, replace the switch.

REPLACEMENT

5   Unplug the switch electrical connector, if you haven't already done so.

6   Loosen the locknut and unscrew the switch from the clutch pedal bracket.

7   Installation is the reverse of removal. To adjust the switch, loosen the locknut and turn the switch in or out, as necessary, to provide continuity through the switch when the clutch pedal is depressed.

Driveaxle - removal and installation

REMOVAL

▶ **Refer to illustrations 10.2, 10.3, 10.6a and 10.6b**

1   Loosen the front wheel lug nuts, raise the vehicle and support it securely on jackstands. Remove the wheel.

2   Unstake the driveaxle/hub nut with a punch or chisel (see illustration).

3   Loosen the driveaxle/hub nut with a large socket and breaker bar (see illustration), then remove the driveaxle/hub nut from the axle and discard it.

4   Remove the damper fork-to-lower control arm bolt, then separate

10.2 Use a punch or chisel and unstake the driveaxle/hub nut

10.3 To prevent the hub from turning while you're loosening the driveaxle/hub nut, wedge a prybar between two of the wheel studs

10.6a Use a large screwdriver or prybar to pop the inner end of the driveaxle from the transaxle, or . . .

10.6b . . . if you're removing a driveaxle from a vehicle equipped with an intermediate shaft, insert the prybar between the intermediate shaft bearing and the driveaxle to pop it loose

10.7a Pry the old spring clip from the inner end of the driveaxle with a small screwdriver or awl

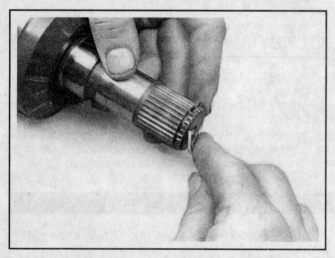

10.7b To install the new spring clip, start one end in the groove and work the clip over the shaft end, into the groove

the lower control arm from the steering knuckle (see Chapter 10).

5   Swing the knuckle/hub assembly out (away from the vehicle) until the end of the driveaxle is free of the hub.

➡**Note: If the driveaxle splines stick in the hub, tap on the end of the driveaxle with a plastic hammer. Support the outer end of the driveaxle with a piece of wire to avoid unnecessary strain on the inner CV joint.**

6   Pry the inner CV joint out of the transaxle - or, on models so equipped, the intermediate shaft, using a large screwdriver or prybar (see illustrations). Support the CV joints and carefully remove the driveaxle from the vehicle. To prevent damage to the intermediate shaft seal or the differential seal, hold the inner CV joint horizontal until the

driveaxle is clear of the intermediate shaft or transaxle.

INSTALLATION

▶ **Refer to illustrations 10.7a and 10.7b**

7   Pry the old spring clip from the inner end of the driveaxle and install a new one (see illustrations). Lubricate the differential or intermediate shaft seal with multi-purpose grease and raise the driveaxle into position while supporting the CV joints.

8   Insert the splined end of the inner CV joint into the differential side gear or intermediate shaft and make sure the spring clip locks in its groove.

9   Apply a light coat of multi-purpose grease to the outer CV joint splines, pull out on the strut/steering knuckle assembly and install the stub axle into the hub.

10 Insert the stud of the steering knuckle balljoint into the lower control arm and tighten the nut (see the torque specifications in Chapter 10). Be sure to use a new cotter pin. Install the damper fork (see Chapter 10).

11 Install the driveaxle/hub nut. Tighten the hub nut securely, but don't try to tighten it to the actual torque specification until you've lowered the vehicle to the ground.

12 Grasp the inner CV joint housing (not the driveaxle) and pull out to make sure the driveaxle has seated securely in the transaxle.

13 Install the wheel and lug nuts, then lower the vehicle. Tighten the lug nuts to the torque listed in the Chapter 1 Specifications.

14 Tighten the driveaxle/hub nut to the torque listed in this Chapter's Specifications, then, using a hammer and a punch, stake the collar of the nut into the slot in the driveaxle. Install the wheel cover or hub cap.

15 Check the differential lubricant, adding as necessary to bring it to the appropriate level (see Chapter 1).

11 Intermediate shaft - removal and installation

REMOVAL

1   Remove the right driveaxle (see Section 10).

2   Remove the three bearing support-to-engine block bolts and slide the intermediate shaft out of the transaxle. Be careful not to damage the differential seal when pulling the shaft out.

3   Check the support bearing for smooth operation by turning the shaft while holding the bearing. If it feels rough or sticky it should be replaced. Take it to a dealer service department or other repair shop, as special tools are needed to perform this job.

INSTALLATION

4   Lubricate the lips of the transaxle seal with multi-purpose grease. Carefully guide the intermediate shaft into the transaxle side gear, then install the mounting bolts through the bearing support. Tighten the bolts to the torque listed in this Chapter's Specifications.

5   Install a new spring clip on the inner CV joint and seat the drive-axle into the intermediate shaft splines.

6   Reinstall the driveaxle (see Section 10).

12 Driveaxle boot - replacement

➡Note 1: If the CV joints are worn, indicating the need for an **overhaul (usually due to torn boots), explore all options before beginning the job. Complete rebuilt driveaxles are available on an exchange basis, which eliminates much time and work. If you decide to rebuild a CV joint, check on the cost and availability of parts before disassembling the driveaxle.**

➡Note 2: Some auto parts stores carry split-type replacement **boots, which can be installed without removing the driveaxle from the vehicle. This is a convenient alternative; however, the driveaxle should be removed and the CV joint disassembled and cleaned to ensure the joint is free from contaminants such as moisture and dirt which will accelerate CV joint wear.**

INNER CV JOINT

1   Remove the driveaxle (see Section 10).

2   Mount the driveaxle in a vise with wood-lined jaws, to prevent damage to the axleshaft. Check the CV joints for excessive play in the radial direction, which indicates worn parts. Check for smooth operation throughout the full range of motion for each CV joint. If a boot is torn,

the recommended procedure is to disassemble the joint, clean the components and inspect for damage due to loss of lubrication and possible contamination by foreign matter. If the CV joint is in good condition, lubricate it with CV joint grease and install a new boot.

Disassembly

▶ **Refer to illustrations 12.4a, 12.4b, 12.5, 12.6 and 12.7**

3   Cut the boot clamps with side-cutters, then remove and discard them.

4   Using a screwdriver, carefully pry up on the edge of the CV boot, pull it off the CV joint housing and slide it down the axleshaft, exposing the tri-pod assembly. Mark the relationship of the joint housing to the tri-pod (see illustration). To separate the axleshaft and tri-pod assembly from the inner joint housing, simply pull the housing straight off (see illustration).

➡Note: When removing the housing, hold the rollers in place on **the tri-pod to prevent the rollers and the needle bearings from falling free.**

5   Remove the tri-pod assembly snap-ring with a pair of snap-ring pliers (see illustration).

12.4a Mark the relationship of the tri-pod to the housing

12.4b Remove the boot from the inner CV joint and slide the joint housing from the tri-pod

12.5 Remove the snap-ring with a pair of snap-ring pliers

12.6 Make marks on the tri-pod and the driveaxle to ensure that they are reassembled properly

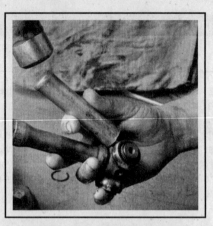

12.7 Drive the tri-pod joint from the driveaxle with a brass punch and hammer (be careful not to damage the bearing surfaces or the splines on the shaft)

12.10a Install the tri-pod with the recessed portion of the splines facing the axleshaft

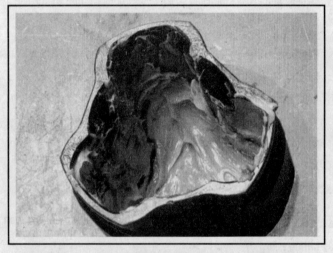

12.10b Place grease at the bottom of the CV joint housing

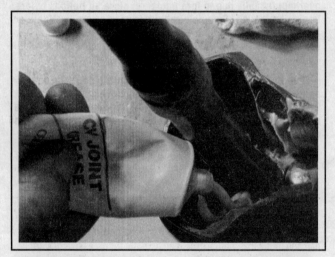

12.10c Install the boot and clamps onto the axleshaft, then insert the tri-pod into the housing, followed by the rest of the grease

6   Mark the tri-pod to the axleshaft to ensure that they are reassembled properly (see illustration).

7   Use a hammer and a brass drift to drive the tri-pod assembly from the axleshaft (see illustration).

8   Slide the boot off the shaft.

Inspection

9   Thoroughly clean all components with solvent until the old CV joint grease is completely removed. Inspect the bearing surfaces of the tri-pod and housing for cracks, pitting, scoring and other signs of wear. If any part of the inner CV joint is worn, you must replace the entire joint. Depending on the availability of parts, you may even have to purchase a complete driveaxle assembly.

➡**Note: If you're working on a right-side driveaxle on a manual transaxle model, check the center bearing for smooth operation. If it feels rough or is noisy when rotated, take the intermediate shaft to an automotive machine shop to have the old bearing pressed out and a new one pressed in.**

Reassembly

▸ **Refer to illustrations 12.10a, 12.10b, 12.10c, 12.12, 12.13, 12.15a, 12.15b, 12.15c, 12.15d and 12.15e**

10   Wrap the splines on the inner end of the axleshaft with electrical or duct tape to protect the boots from the sharp edges of the splines and slide the clamps and boot onto the axleshaft (see illustration 12.18g). Remove the tape and place the tri-pod on the axleshaft with the recessed portion of the splines toward the shaft (see illustration). Tap the tri-pod onto the shaft with a brass drift until it's seated and install the snap-ring. Apply grease to the tri-pod assembly and inside the housing (see illustration). Insert the tri-pod into the housing and pack the remainder of the grease around the tri-pod (see illustration).

11   Slide the boot into place, making sure the raised bead on the inside of the seal boot is positioned in the groove on the interconnecting shaft. If the driveaxle has multiple locating grooves on the shaft, position the boot so only one of the grooves (the thinnest) is exposed. Position the sealing boot into the groove on the housing retaining groove.

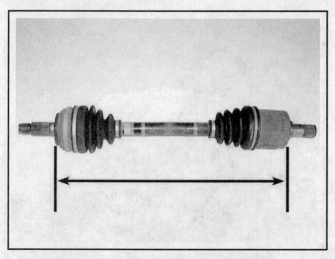

12.12 Adjust the driveaxle to the length listed in this Chapter's Specifications (this dimension is critical for maintaining the correct pressure inside sliding CV joints)

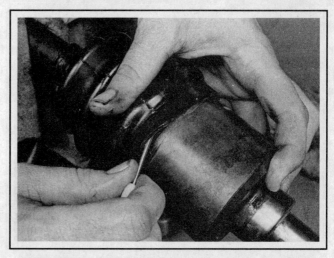

12.13 With the driveaxle set to the proper length, equalize the pressure inside the boot by inserting a small, dull screwdriver between the boot and the outer race

12.15a You'll need a special tightening tool to install band-type boot clamps: install the band with its end pointing in the direction of axle rotation and tighten it securely . . .

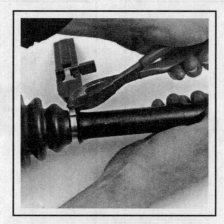

12.15b . . . then bend down the end of the clamp back and cut off the excess

12.15c If you're installing crimp-type boot clamps, you'll need a pair of special crimping pliers (available at most auto parts stores)

12 Adjust the length of the driveaxle (see illustration). Refer to the Specifications listed in this Chapter for the correct driveaxle length.

13 Equalize the pressure inside the boot by inserting a small, dull, flat screwdriver tip between the boot and the CV joint housing (see illustration).

14 Make sure each end of the boot is seated properly, and the boot is not distorted.

15 Install the boot clamps. There are three types of clamps you're likely to encounter: the band type, which requires a special tightening tool, the crimp type (which also requires a special tool), or the fold-over type (see illustrations).

16 The driveaxle is now ready for installation (see Section 10).

12.15d To install fold-over type boot clamps, bend the tang down . . .

12.15e . . . then tap the tabs over to hold it in place

12.18a Cut off the band retaining the boot to the shaft, then slide the boot toward the center of the shaft

12.18b Clean all grease off the axleshaft and paint a mark on the shaft, then measure the distance from your mark to the face of the inner race and record this measurement; the inner race must be installed on the axleshaft in exactly the same position in which it was installed prior to removal

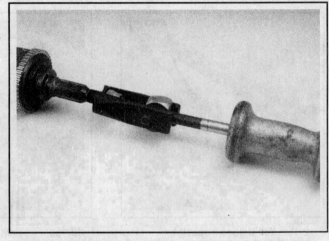

12.18c Outer CV joints can be removed with a slide hammer; you'll need an adapter and a slide hammer setup such as the one shown here

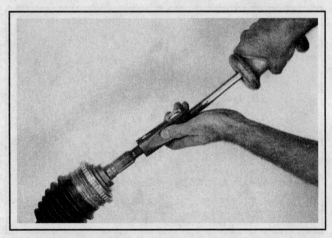

12.18d With the axleshaft firmly clamped down in a bench vise and the adapter gripping the driveaxle/hub nut, carefully extract the outer CV joint from the axleshaft

OUTER CV JOINT

▶ **Refer to illustrations 12.18a through 12.18l**

17 Remove the driveaxle (see Section 10).

18 Refer to the accompanying illustrations and perform the outer CV joint boot replacement procedure (see illustrations 12.18a through 12.18l).

12.18e After the old grease has been rinsed away, move the inner race through its full range of motion and inspect the bearing surfaces for wear or damage

12.18f Apply CV joint grease through the splined hole, then insert a wooden dowel (slightly smaller in diameter than the hole) into the hole and push down - the dowel will force the grease into the joint. Repeat this until the joint is packed

12.18g Wrap the splined area of the axleshaft with tape to prevent damage to the boot when installing it

12.18h Install the small clamp and the boot on the driveaxle and apply grease to the inside of the axle boot until . . .

12.18i . . . the level is up to the end of axle

12.18j Install a new circlip into the groove at the end of the driveaxle. Position the CV joint assembly on the driveaxle, aligning the splines . . .

12.18k . . . then use a hammer and brass punch to carefully drive the joint onto the driveaxle to the same spot it was in before disassembly (see illustration 12.18b)

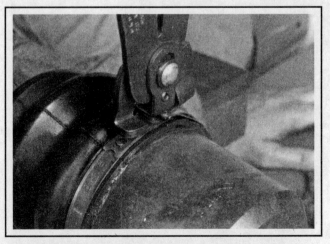

12.18l Seat the inner end of the boot in the groove and install the retaining clamp, then do the same on the other end of the boot - tighten boot clamps with the special tool

Specifications

General

Clutch fluid type	See Chapter 1

Clutch

Clutch pedal	
Height	7.52 inches (191 mm)
Freeplay	0.39 to 0.71 inch (10 to 18 mm)

Driveaxles

Driveaxle length	
Four-cylinder engine	
Manual transaxle	
Left axle	21.42 to 21.61 inches (544 to 549 mm)
Right axle	18.62 to 18.82 inches (473 to 478 mm)
Automatic transaxle	
Left axle	21.61 to 21.81 inches (549 to 554 mm)
Right axle	33.43 to 33.62 inches (849 to 854 mm)
V6 engine	
Manual transaxle	
Left axle	21.81 to 22.01 inches (554 to 559 mm)
Right axle	20.16 to 20.35 inches (512 to 5.17 mm)
Automatic transaxle	
Left axle	21.81 to 22.01 inches (554 to 559 mm)
Right axle	20.16 to 20.35 inches (512 to 517 mm)

Torque specifications	Ft-lbs (unless otherwise indicated)	Nm

➡ **Note: One foot-pound (ft-lb) of torque is equivalent to 12 inch-pounds (in-lbs) of torque. Torque values below approximately 15 ft-lbs are expressed in inch-pounds, since most foot-pound torque wrenches are not accurate at these smaller values.**

Clutch master cylinder mounting nuts		
2007 and earlier models	112 in-lbs	13
2008 and later models	16	22
Clutch pressure plate-to-flywheel bolts	19	25
Clutch release cylinder mounting fasteners	16	22
Driveaxle hub/nut		
Four-cylinder engine		
Automatic transaxle	134	181
Manual transaxle	181	245
V6 engine	181	245
Intermediate shaft bearing support mounting bolts	29	39
Wheel lug nuts	See Chapter 1	

9

BRAKES

Section

1 General information

The vehicles covered by this manual are equipped with hydraulically operated front and rear brake systems. The front brakes are disc type and the rear brakes are either disc or drum type. Both the front and rear brakes are self adjusting. The disc brakes automatically compensate for pad wear, while the drum brakes incorporate an adjustment mechanism which is activated as the parking brake is applied.

HYDRAULIC SYSTEM

The hydraulic system consists of two separate circuits. The master cylinder has separate reservoir chambers for the two circuits, and, in the event of a leak or failure in one hydraulic circuit, the other circuit will remain operative. A dual proportioning valve on the firewall provides brake balance between the front and rear brakes.

POWER BRAKE BOOSTER

The power brake booster - which utilizes engine manifold vacuum and atmospheric pressure to provide assistance to the hydraulically operated brakes - is mounted on the firewall in the engine compartment.

PARKING BRAKE

The parking brake operates the rear brakes only, through cable actuation. It's activated by a lever mounted in the center console.

SERVICE

After completing any operation involving disassembly of any part of the brake system, always test drive the vehicle to check for proper braking performance before resuming normal driving. When testing the brakes, perform the tests on a clean, dry, flat surface. Conditions other than these can lead to inaccurate test results.

Test the brakes at various speeds with both light and heavy pedal pressure. The vehicle should stop evenly without pulling to one side or the other. Avoid locking the brakes, because this slides the tires and diminishes braking efficiency and control of the vehicle.

Tires, vehicle load and wheel alignment are factors which also affect braking performance.

PRECAUTIONS

There are some general cautions and warnings involving the brake system on this vehicle:

a) *Use only brake fluid conforming to DOT 3 specifications.*

b) *The brake pads and linings contain fibers which are hazardous to your health if inhaled. Whenever you work on brake system components, clean all parts with brake system cleaner. Do not allow the fine dust to become airborne. Also, wear an approved filtering mask.*

c) *When working with brake fluid, wear appropriate hand protection such as latex or vinyl gloves. Protect any painted surface from contact with brake fluid. Remove any spilled brake fluid with shop or paper towels and discard properly.*

d) *Safety should be paramount whenever any servicing of the brake components is performed. Do not use parts or fasteners which are not in perfect condition, and be sure that all clearances and torque specifications are adhered to. If you are at all unsure about a certain procedure, seek professional advice. Upon completion of any brake system work, test the brakes carefully in a controlled area before putting the vehicle into normal service. If a problem is suspected in the brake system, don't drive the vehicle until it's fixed.*

e) *Used brake fluid is considered a hazardous waste and it must be disposed of in accordance with federal, state and local laws.* **DO NOT pour it down the sink, into septic tanks or storm drains, or on the ground.**

f) *Clean up any spilled brake fluid immediately and then wash the area with large amounts of water. This is especially true for any finished or painted surfaces.*

2 Anti-lock brake (ABS), traction control (TCS) and vehicle stability assist (VSA) systems - general information

GENERAL INFORMATION

1 The anti-lock brake system (used on four-cylinder models only), the traction control system (used along with ABS on 2003 through 2005 V6 models) and the vehicle stability assist system (used on 2006 and later V6 models) are all variations on the same principle and share similar components. They all are designed to maintain steerability, directional stability and optimum deceleration under severe conditions. They do so by monitoring the rotational speed of each wheel and controlling the brake fluid pressure to each wheel. The VSA also has a yaw rate sensor that measures any sideways movement of the vehicle.

2 The systems have several components - the wheel speed sensors, the electronic control unit (ECU), the hydraulic unit and, in the case of the VSA system, the yaw rate sensor. A wheel speed sensor at each wheel sends a variable voltage to the ECU that monitors these signals, compares them to its program and determines if a wheel is about to lock up or is adversely affecting the vehicle's handling. The ECU signals the hydraulic unit to reduce hydraulic pressure at one or more of the brake calipers. Electrically operated solenoid valves handle pressure modulation.

3 If a problem develops in the system, a warning light will glow on the instrument panel. Sometimes a visual inspection of the system will help locate the problem. Carefully inspect all wiring harnesses, especially where they are vulnerable near the wheels. Look for signs of chafing caused by incorrectly routed wires. If a wheel sensor harness is damaged, then the sensor must be replaced.

✳✳ WARNING:

Do NOT try to repair a wiring harness. These systems are sensitive to even the smallest changes in resistance. Repairing the harness could change the resistance and cause the system to malfunction. If the wiring harness is damaged in any way, it must be replaced.

2.9a The front wheel speed sensors are located on the steering knuckles

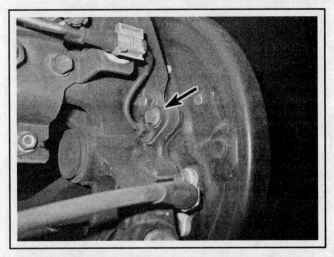

2.9b The rear wheel speed sensors are located on the rear wheel knuckles

❋❋ CAUTION:

Make sure that the ignition is turned off before unplugging or reattaching any electrical connections.

DIAGNOSIS AND REPAIR

4   If a dashboard warning light comes on and stays on while the vehicle is in operation, the ABS, TCS or VSA system needs attention. Although special diagnostic tools are necessary to properly diagnose the system, you can perform a few preliminary checks before taking the vehicle to a dealer service department or other qualified repair shop.

  a) Check the brake fluid level in the reservoir.
  b) Verify that all electrical connectors are securely snapped together.
  c) Check the electrical connectors at the hydraulic control unit. It's located at the right front fender.
  d) Check the fuses.
  e) Follow the wiring harness to each wheel and verify that all connections are secure and that the wiring is undamaged.

5   If the above preliminary checks do not rectify the problem, the vehicle should be diagnosed by a dealer service department or other qualified repair shop. Due to the complex nature of this system, all actual repair work must be done by a qualified automotive technician.

WHEEL SPEED SENSOR - REMOVAL AND INSTALLATION

▶ Refer to illustrations 2.9a and 2.9b

6   Loosen the wheel lug nuts, raise the vehicle and support it securely on jackstands. Remove the wheel.

7   Make sure the ignition key is turned to the Off position.

8   Trace the wiring back from the sensor, detaching all brackets and clips while noting its correct routing, then disconnect the electrical connector.

9   Remove the mounting bolt and carefully pull the sensor out from the knuckle (see illustrations).

10 Installation is the reverse of the removal procedure. Tighten the mounting bolt to the torque listed in this Chapter's Specifications.

11 Install the wheel and lug nuts, tightening them securely. Lower the vehicle and tighten the lug nuts to the torque listed in the Chapter 1 Specifications.

3   Disc brake pads - replacement

❋❋ WARNING:

Disc brake pads must be replaced on both front and rear wheels at the same time - never replace the pads on only one side. Also, the dust created by the brake system is harmful to your health. Never blow it out with compressed air and don't inhale any of it. An approved filtering mask should be worn when working on the brakes. Do not, under any circumstances, use petroleum-based solvents to clean brake parts. Use brake system cleaner only!

➡Note: This procedure applies to front and rear disc brakes.

1   Remove the cap from the brake fluid reservoir.

2   Loosen the wheel lug nuts, raise the front, or rear, of the vehicle and support it securely on jackstands.

3   Remove the front, or rear, wheels. Work on one brake assembly at a time, using the assembled brake for reference if necessary.

4   Inspect the brake disc carefully as outlined in Section 5. If machining is necessary, follow the information in that Section to remove the disc, at which time the calipers and pads can be removed as well.

3.5 Using a large C-clamp, push the piston back into the caliper - note that one end of the clamp is on the back side of the caliper and the other end (screw end) is pressing on the outer brake pad

3.6a Before removing anything, spray the assembly with brake system cleaner to remove the dust produced by brake pad wear - DO NOT blow the dust off with compressed air!

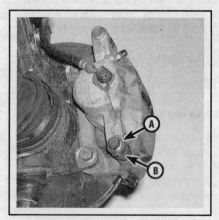

3.6b Unscrew the lower caliper mounting bolt (A) (note the flats on the caliper pin [B]; when installing the caliper, make sure one of the flats rests against the projection on the caliper) . . .

3.6c . . . then swing the caliper up . . .

3.6d . . . and secure it to the strut with a piece of wire

3.6e Remove the outer brake pad and shim

FRONT PADS

Refer to illustrations 3.5 and 3.6a through 3.6n

5 Push the piston back into the bore to provide room for the new brake pads. A C-clamp can be used to accomplish this (see illustration). As the piston is depressed to the bottom of the caliper bore, the fluid in the master cylinder will rise. Make sure it doesn't overflow. If necessary, siphon off some of the fluid.

6 Follow the accompanying illustrations, beginning with illustration 3.6a, for the actual pad replacement procedure. Be sure to stay in order and read the caption under each illustration. Once you have installed the new pads, proceed to Step 19.

3.6f Remove the inner brake pad and shim(s)

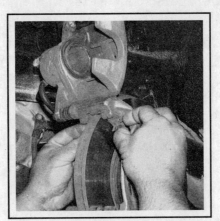

3.6g Remove and inspect the upper and lower brake pad retainer clips

3.6h The pad retainer clips should fit snugly into their respective grooves in the caliper mounting bracket; if they don't, replace them

3.6i Apply anti-squeal compound to the back of the pads, then install the shim(s)

3.6j Install the new inner pad; make sure the "ears" on the upper and lower ends of the pad are fully engaged with their respective grooves and the pad retainer clips

3.6k Install the new outer pad and shim (if the new pad has no shim, take the old shim off the old pad and install it on the new outer pad)

3.6l Before installing the caliper, remove the caliper pin dust boots and inspect them for tears and cracks; if they're damaged, replace them

3.6m Clean off the caliper sliding pins and coat them with high-temperature grease

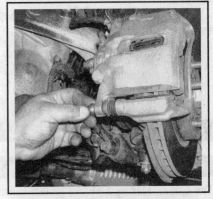

3.6n Swing the caliper down over the disc and new pads (if the piston hits the inner pad, depress the piston further into the caliper bore with your C-clamp), then install the lower bolt and tighten it to the torque listed in this Chapter's Specifications (be sure to hold the pin with a wrench)

3.9 Remove the outer pad and shim

3.10 Remove the inner pad and shim

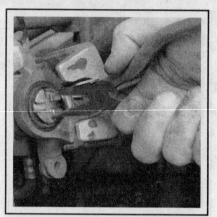

3.17 To provide clearance for the new brake pads, back the piston into the caliper bore by rotating it with a pair of needle-nose pliers (if the piston is difficult to turn, special caliper piston tools are available at auto parts stores)

REAR PADS

♦ **Refer to illustrations 3.9, 3.10 and 3.17**

7 Wash the brake assembly with brake system cleaner (see illustration 3.6a).

8 Remove the caliper mounting bolts while holding the caliper pins with a second wrench, then remove the caliper from its mounting bracket and hang the caliper out of the way with a piece of wire. Don't let the caliper hang by the brake hose.

9 Remove the outer brake pad and shim (see illustration).

10 Remove the inner brake pad and shim(s) (see illustration).

11 Remove and inspect the upper and lower pad retainer clips.

12 Install the pad retainer clips. They should fit snugly in the caliper mounting bracket; if they don't, replace them. Apply a thin film of high-temperature grease to the retainer.

13 Apply a small amount of high-temperature grease to both sides of the shims.

14 Install the new inner pad and shim(s). Make sure the "ears" on the upper and lower ends of the pad are fully engaged with their respective grooves and the pad retainer clips

15 Install the new outer pad and shim.

16 Before installing the caliper, remove the caliper pin dust boots

and inspect them for tears and cracks; if they're damaged, replace them.

17 Retract the piston by engaging the tips of a pair of needle-nose pliers with two of the grooves in the face of the piston and turning it until it bottoms in the bore (see illustration). Now, rotate the piston out until one of its grooves is aligned with the tab on the inner brake pad when you install the caliper. You may have to adjust the piston position by turning it back and forth to fit the tab in the groove. If the piston dust boot becomes distorted when the piston is turned, turn the piston in the opposite direction to restore the shape of the boot, but make sure the groove is aligned properly.

18 Install the caliper mounting bolts while holding the caliper pins with a second wrench. Tighten them to the torque listed in this Chapter's Specifications.

FRONT OR REAR PADS

19 Install the wheel and lug nuts, lower the vehicle and tighten the lug nuts to the torque listed in the Chapter 1 Specifications.

20 Apply and release the brake pedal several times to bring the pads into contact with the brake discs.

21 Check the brake fluid level and add fluid, if necessary (see Chapter 1). Check the operation of the brakes in an isolated area before driving the vehicle in traffic.

4 Disc brake caliper - removal and installation

❊ WARNING:

The dust created by the brake system is harmful to your health. Never blow it out with compressed air and don't inhale any of it. An approved filtering mask should be worn when working on the brakes. Do not, under any circumstances, use petroleum-based solvents to clean brake parts. Use brake system cleaner only!

➡**Note: Always replace the calipers in pairs (front/front, rear/rear) - never replace just one of them.**

FRONT

Removal

♦ **Refer to illustrations 4.2a and 4.2b**

1 Loosen - but don't remove - the lug nuts on the front wheels. Raise the front of the vehicle and place it securely on jackstands. Remove the front wheels.

2 Disconnect the brake line from the caliper and plug it to keep contaminants out of the brake system and to prevent losing any more

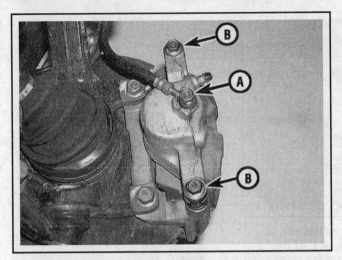

4.2a Remove the brake hose banjo bolt (A), then unscrew the caliper mounting bolts (B)

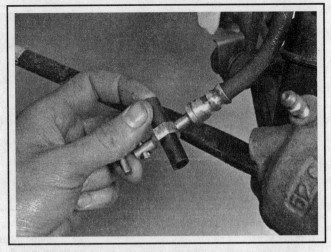

4.2b Using a short piece of rubber hose of the appropriate diameter, plug the brake line banjo fitting

brake fluid than is necessary (see illustrations).

➡**Note: If you're simply removing the caliper for access to other components, don't disconnect the hose.**

3   Remove the caliper mounting bolts.
4   Detach the caliper from its mounting bracket.

Installation

5   Install the caliper by reversing the removal procedure. Remember to replace the sealing washers on either side of the brake line fitting with new ones. Tighten the caliper mounting bolts and the banjo bolt to the torque listed in this Chapter's Specifications.
6   Bleed the brake system (see Section 10).
7   Install the wheels and lug nuts and lower the vehicle. Tighten the wheel lug nuts to the torque listed in the Chapter 1 Specifications.

REAR

Removal

8   Loosen - but don't remove - the lug nuts on the rear wheels. Raise the rear of the vehicle and place it securely on jackstands.

Remove the rear wheels.

9   Unscrew the banjo bolt and detach the brake line from the caliper. Plug the fitting to prevent fluid loss and contamination (see illustration 4.2b).

➡**Note: If you're simply removing the caliper for access to other components, don't disconnect the hose.**

10 Remove the caliper mounting bolts while holding the caliper pins with a second wrench.
11 Remove the clip securing the parking brake cable to the caliper's parking brake lever, then separate the cable from the caliper.
12 Detach the caliper from its mounting bracket.

Installation

13 Install the caliper by reversing the removal procedure. Remember to replace the sealing washers on either side of the brake line fitting with new ones. Tighten the caliper mounting bolts and the banjo bolt to the torque listed in this Chapter's Specifications.
14 Bleed the brake system (see Section 10).
15 Install the wheels and lug nuts. Lower the vehicle and tighten the lug nuts to the torque listed in the Chapter 1 Specifications.

5   Brake disc - inspection, removal and installation

❋❋ **WARNING:**

The dust created by the brake system is harmful to your health. Never blow it out with compressed air and don't inhale any of it. An approved filtering mask should be worn when working on the brakes. Do not, under any circumstances, use petroleum-based solvents to clean brake parts. Use brake system cleaner only!

INSPECTION

▶ **Refer to illustrations 5.2, 5.3, 5.4a, 5.4b and 5.5**

1   Loosen the wheel lug nuts, raise the vehicle and support it securely on jackstands. Remove the wheel and install the lug nuts to hold the disc in place against the hub flange.

➡**Note: If the lug nuts don't contact the disc when screwed on all the way, install washers under them. If you're checking the rear disc, release the parking brake.**

5.2 Caliper mounting bracket-to-knuckle bolts

5.3 The brake pads on this vehicle were obviously neglected, as they wore down completely and cut deep grooves into the disc - wear this severe means the disc must be replaced

5.4a To check disc runout, mount a dial indicator as shown and rotate the disc

5.4b Using a swirling motion, remove the glaze from the disc surface with sandpaper or emery cloth

5.5 Use a micrometer to measure disc thickness

5.6a If the disc retaining screws are stuck, use an impact screwdriver to loosen them

2   Remove the brake caliper as outlined in Section 4. It isn't necessary to disconnect the brake hose. After removing the caliper bolts, suspend the caliper out of the way with a piece of wire. Remove the two caliper mounting bracket-to-steering knuckle bolts (see illustration) or, on rear calipers, the bracket-to-knuckle bolts and remove the mounting bracket.

3   Visually inspect the disc surface for score marks and other damage. Light scratches and shallow grooves are normal after use and may not always be detrimental to brake operation, but deep scoring requires disc removal and refinishing by an automotive machine shop. Be sure to check both sides of the disc (see illustration). If pulsating has been noticed during application of the brakes, suspect disc runout.

4   To check disc runout, place a dial indicator at a point about 1/2-inch from the outer edge of the disc (see illustration). Set the indicator to zero and turn the disc. The indicator reading should not exceed the specified allowable runout limit. If it does, the disc should be refinished by an automotive machine shop.

➡**Note: The discs should be resurfaced regardless of the dial indicator reading, as this will impart a smooth finish and ensure a perfectly flat surface, eliminating any brake pedal pulsation or other undesirable symptoms related to questionable discs. At the very least, if you elect not to have the discs resurfaced, remove the glaze from the surface with emery cloth or sandpaper, using a swirling motion (see illustration).**

5   It's absolutely critical that the disc not be machined to a thickness under the specified minimum thickness. The minimum (or discard) thickness is cast or stamped into the disc. The disc thickness can be checked with a micrometer (see illustration).

REMOVAL

♦ **Refer to illustrations 5.6a and 5.6b**

6   Remove the lug nuts which were installed to hold the disc in place, or remove the two disc retaining screws (see illustration) and

remove the disc from the hub. If the disc is stuck to the hub and won't come off, thread two bolts into the holes provided (see illustration) and tighten them. Alternate between the bolts, turning them a couple of turns at a time, until the disc is free. Remove the disc from the hub.

INSTALLATION

7   Place the disc in position over the threaded studs. Install the disc retaining screws and tighten them securely.

8   Install the caliper mounting bracket and caliper, tightening the bolts to the torque values listed in this Chapter's Specifications.

9   Install the wheel, then lower the vehicle to the ground. Tighten the lug nuts to the torque listed in the Chapter 1 Specifications. Depress the brake pedal a few times to bring the brake pads into contact with the disc. Bleeding won't be necessary unless the brake hose was disconnected from the caliper. Check the operation of the brakes carefully before driving the vehicle.

5.6b If the disc is stuck, thread two 8 mm bolts into the threaded holes in the disc and tighten them to force the disc off the hub

6   Drum brake shoes - replacement

▶ **Refer to illustrations 6.2, 6.4a through 6.4p and 6.5**

❋❋ WARNING:

Drum brake shoes must be replaced on both wheels at the same time - never replace the shoes on only one wheel. Also, the dust created by the brake system is harmful to your health. Never blow it out with compressed air and don't inhale any of it. An approved filtering mask should be worn when working on the brakes. Do not, under any circumstances, use petroleum-based solvents to clean brake parts. Use brake system cleaner only!

❋❋ CAUTION:

Whenever the brake shoes are replaced, the return and hold-down springs should also be replaced. Due to the continuous heating/cooling cycle the springs are subjected to, they can lose tension over a period of time and may allow the shoes to drag on the drum and wear at a much faster rate than normal.

1   Loosen the wheel lug nuts, raise the rear of the vehicle and support it securely on jackstands. Block the front wheels to keep the vehicle from rolling. Remove the rear wheels. Release the parking brake.

2   Remove the brake drum. It should simply pull straight off the hub. If the drum won't come off, tap it carefully with a soft-faced mallet, or screw a couple of 8.0 mm bolts into the tapped holes (see illustration). If it still won't budge, the shoes have probably carved wear grooves into

6.2 If the drum is hard to pull off, thread a pair of 8 mm bolts into the holes provided to force the drum off

the drum. To get the drum off, you'll have to retract them. Remove the rubber plug in the backing plate. Use one screwdriver inserted through the hole in the backing plate to hold the self-adjuster lever away from the adjuster star wheel, then use another screwdriver to rotate the star wheel until the drum can be removed.

6.4a Details of the rear drum brake assembly

1 Self-adjuster lever	6 Self-adjuster spring
2 Adjuster assembly	7 Lower return spring
3 Wheel cylinder	8 Parking brake cable
4 Upper return spring	9 Parking brake lever
5 Retainer spring	

6.4b Before removing anything, clean the brake assembly with brake cleaner and allow it to dry - position a drain pan under the brake assembly to catch the residue - DO NOT USE COMPRESSED AIR TO BLOW BRAKE DUST OFF THE PARTS!

6.4c Push down on the retainer spring with a screwdriver, then turn the pin to align its blade with the slot (repeat this on the other spring)

6.4d Pull the upper return spring back while supporting the brake shoe and unhook the spring from the shoe (a pair of diagonal cutting pliers are being used here because they grip the spring well, but care must be taken so as not to damage the spring)

6.4e Remove the adjuster/spring assembly from the leading brake shoe

3   Replacing the shoes is a lot easier if you remove the rear wheel bearing cap, spindle nut and washer, and slide off the hub unit (see Chapter 10).

4   Follow illustrations 6.4a through 6.4p for the inspection and replacement of the brake shoes. Be sure to stay in order and read the caption under each illustration. All four rear brake shoes must be replaced at the same time, but to avoid mixing up parts, work on only one brake assembly at a time.

5   Before reinstalling the drum it should be checked for cracks, score marks, deep scratches and hard spots, which will appear as small discolored areas. If the hard spots cannot be removed with fine emery cloth or if any of the other conditions listed above exist, the drum must

6.4f Detach the lower return spring . . .

6.4g . . . and remove the self-adjuster lever and spring

6.4h Remove the parking brake lever retaining clip; be careful not to lose the wave washer that is under the clip

6.4i Lubricate the brake shoe contact areas on the backing plate with high-temperature grease

6.4j Clean the adjuster bolt and clevis, then lubricate the threads and ends with high-temperature grease

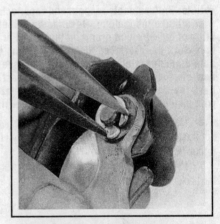

6.4k Put the new trailing shoe on the lever, place the wave washer over the pin, then install the retaining clip; crimp the ends of the clip together with a pair of needle-nose pliers

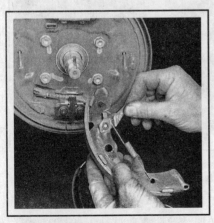

6.4l Install the adjusting lever and spring on the new leading shoe

6.4m Install the lower return spring

6.4n Install the adjuster assembly . . .

6.4o . . . and connect the upper return spring

6.4p Install both retainer springs

6.5 The maximum allowable diameter is cast into the drum (typical)

be taken to an automotive machine shop to have it machined.

➡Note: Professionals recommend resurfacing the drums whenever a brake job is done. Resurfacing will eliminate the possibility of out-of-round drums. If the drums are worn so much that they can't be resurfaced without exceeding the maximum allowable diameter (stamped into the drum) (see illustration), then new ones will be required. At the very least, if you elect not to have the drums resurfaced, remove the glazing from the surface with sandpaper or emery cloth using a swirling motion.

6   Install the hub and bearing unit, the washer and a new spindle nut if removed previously (see Chapter 10). Tighten the nut to the torque listed in the Chapter 10 Specifications.

7   Install the brake drum. Insert a screwdriver through the hole in the backing plate and turn the star wheel on the adjuster until the brake shoes drag on the drum, then turn the adjuster in the opposite direction until they don't drag as the drum is turned (this is a preliminary adjustment).

8   Mount the wheel, install the lug nuts, then lower the vehicle. Tighten the lug nuts to the torque listed in the Chapter 1 Specifications.

9   Depress the brake pedal several times, which will bring the shoes into the proper adjustment.

10 Check brake operation before driving the vehicle in traffic.

❊❊ WARNING:

Do not operate the vehicle if you are in doubt about the effectiveness of the brake system.

7   Wheel cylinder - removal and installation

❊❊ WARNING:

The dust created by the brake system is harmful to your health. Never blow it out with compressed air and don't inhale any of it. An approved filtering mask should be worn when working on the brakes. Do not, under any circumstances, use petroleum-based solvents to clean brake parts. Use brake system cleaner only!

➡Note: If replacement is indicated (usually because of fluid leakage or sticky operation), it is recommended that the wheel cylinders be replaced, not overhauled. Always replace the wheel cylinders in pairs - never replace just one of them.

REMOVAL

◗ Refer to illustration 7.4

1   Raise the rear of the vehicle and support it securely on jackstands. Block the front wheels to keep the vehicle from rolling.

2   Remove the brake shoe assembly (see Section 6).

3   Remove all dirt and foreign material from around the wheel cylinder.

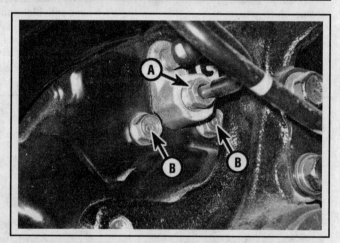

7.4 Disconnect the brake line (A), then remove the wheel cylinder mounting bolts (B)

4   Disconnect the brake line (see illustration). Don't pull the brake line away from the wheel cylinder.

5   Remove the wheel cylinder mounting bolts.

6 Detach the wheel cylinder from the brake backing plate and immediately plug the brake line to prevent fluid loss and contamination.

INSTALLATION

7 Apply a small amount of RTV sealant between the backing plate and wheel cylinder, then place the wheel cylinder in position and install the bolts finger tight. Connect the brake line to the cylinder, being careful not to cross thread the fitting. Tighten the wheel cylinder mounting bolts to the torque listed in this Chapter's Specifications. Now tighten the brake line fitting securely.

8 Install the brake shoe assembly (see Section 6).
9 Bleed the brakes (see Section 10).
10 Check the operation of the brakes carefully before driving the vehicle.

---

8 Master cylinder - removal and installation

REMOVAL

♦ **Refer to illustrations 8.2a, 8.2b and 8.5**

1 The master cylinder is located in the engine compartment, mounted to the power brake booster.
2 Remove the cable clamp and the left strut brace (see illustrations).
3 Using a large syringe or equivalent, siphon the brake fluid from the master cylinder reservoir and dispose of it properly.

✳✳ CAUTION:

Brake fluid will damage paint. Cover all painted surfaces and avoid spilling fluid during this procedure.

4 Disconnect the electrical connector from the fluid level warning switch.
5 Place rags under the fluid fittings and prepare caps or plastic bags to cover the ends of the lines once they are disconnected. Loosen the fittings at the ends of the brake lines where they enter the master cylinder (see illustration). To prevent rounding off the corners on these nuts, the use of a flare-nut wrench, which wraps around the nut, is preferred. Pull the brake lines slightly away from the master cylinder and plug the ends to prevent contamination.

6 Remove the nuts attaching the master cylinder to the power booster. Pull the master cylinder off the studs and out of the engine compartment. Again, be careful not to spill the fluid as this is done.
7 If a new master cylinder is being installed, remove the reservoir from the master cylinder and transfer it to the new master cylinder. Be sure to install new seals when transferring the reservoir.

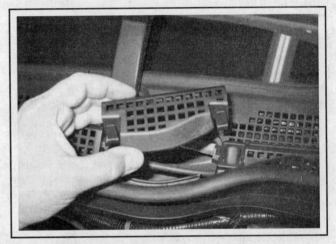

8.2a Remove the access cover for the strut brace mounting bolts

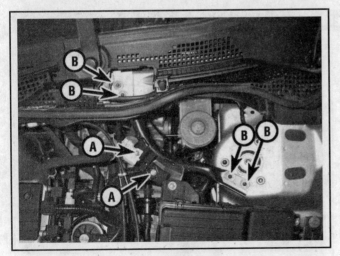

8.2b Remove the mounting bolts for the cable clamp (A) and the strut brace (B)

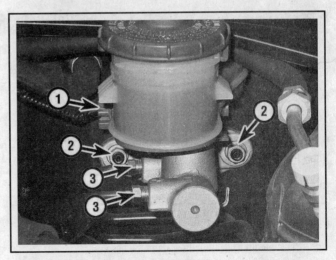

8.5 Master cylinder mounting details

1 *Electrical connector*
2 *Mounting nuts*
3 *Brake line fittings*

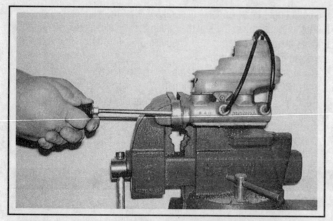

8.9 The best way to bleed air from the master cylinder before installing it on the vehicle is with a pair of bleeder tubes that direct brake fluid into the reservoir during bleeding

INSTALLATION

◆ Refer to illustration 8.9

8 Bench bleed the new master cylinder before installing it. Mount the master cylinder in a vise, with the jaws of the vise clamping on the mounting flange.

9 Attach a pair of master cylinder bleeder tubes to the outlet ports of the master cylinder (see illustration).

10 Fill the reservoir with brake fluid of the recommended type (see Chapter 1).

11 Slowly push the pistons into the master cylinder (a large Phillips screwdriver can be used for this) - air will be expelled from the pressure chambers and into the reservoir. Because the tubes are submerged in fluid, air can't be drawn back into the master cylinder when you release the pistons.

12 Repeat the procedure until no more air bubbles are present.

13 Remove the bleed tubes, one at a time, and install plugs in the open ports to prevent fluid leakage and air from entering. Install the reservoir cap.

14 Install the master cylinder over the studs on the power brake booster and tighten the attaching nuts only finger tight at this time.

➡**Note: Be sure to install a new rod seal on the master cylinder.**

15 Thread the brake line fittings into the master cylinder. Since the master cylinder is still a bit loose, it can be moved slightly in order for the fittings to thread in easily. Do not strip the threads as the fittings are tightened.

16 Fully tighten the mounting nuts, then the brake line fittings. Tighten the nuts to the torque listed in this Chapter's Specifications.

17 Fill the master cylinder reservoir with fluid, then bleed the master cylinder and the brake system as described in Section 10. To bleed the cylinder on the vehicle, have an assistant depress the brake pedal and hold the pedal to the floor. Loosen the fitting to allow air and fluid to escape. Repeat this procedure on both fittings until the fluid is clear of air bubbles.

✲✲ CAUTION:

Have plenty of rags on hand to catch the fluid - brake fluid will ruin painted surfaces. After the bleeding procedure is completed, rinse the area under the master cylinder with clean water.

18 The remainder of installation is the reverse of removal. Test the operation of the brake system carefully before placing the vehicle into normal service.

✲✲ WARNING:

Do not operate the vehicle if you are in doubt about the effectiveness of the brake system. On models equipped with ABS, it is possible for air to become trapped in the anti-lock brake system hydraulic control unit, so, if the pedal continues to feel spongy after repeated bleedings or the BRAKE or ANTI-LOCK light stays on, have the vehicle towed to a dealer service department or other qualified shop to be bled with the aid of a scan tool.

9 Brake hoses and lines - inspection and replacement

1 About every six months, with the vehicle raised and placed securely on jackstands, the flexible hoses which connect the steel brake lines with the front and rear brake assemblies should be inspected for cracks, chafing of the outer cover, leaks, blisters and other damage. These are important and vulnerable parts of the brake system and inspection should be complete. A light and mirror will be needed for a thorough check. If a hose exhibits any of the above defects, replace it with a new one.

FLEXIBLE HOSES

◆ Refer to illustration 9.3

2 Clean all dirt away from the ends of the hose.

3 To disconnect a brake hose from the brake line, unscrew the metal tube nut with a flare nut wrench, then remove the U-clip from the female fitting at the bracket and remove the hose from the bracket (see illustration).

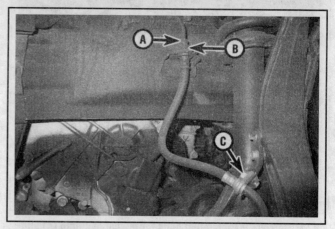

9.3 Unscrew the brake line threaded fitting with a flare-nut wrench to protect the fitting corners from being rounded off (A), then pull off the U-clip (B) with a pair of pliers and remove the brake line mounting bolt (C)

4   Disconnect the hose from the caliper, discarding the sealing washers on either side of the fitting.

5   Using new sealing washers, attach the new brake hose to the caliper. Tighten the brake hose banjo bolt to the torque listed in this Chapter's Specifications.

6   To reattach a brake hose to the metal line, insert the end of the hose through the frame bracket, make sure the hose isn't twisted, then attach the metal line by tightening the tube nut fitting securely. Install the U-clip at the frame bracket.

7   Carefully check to make sure the suspension or steering components don't make contact with the hose. Have an assistant push down on the vehicle and also turn the steering wheel lock-to-lock during inspection.

8   Bleed the brake system (see Section 10).

METAL BRAKE LINES

9   When replacing brake lines, be sure to use the correct parts. Don't use copper tubing for any brake system components. Purchase steel brake lines from a dealer parts department or auto parts store.

10 Prefabricated brake line, with the tube ends already flared and fittings installed, is available at auto parts stores and dealer parts departments. These lines can be bent to the proper shapes using a tubing bender.

11 When installing the new line make sure it's well supported in the brackets and has plenty of clearance between moving or hot components.

12 After installation, check the master cylinder fluid level and add fluid as necessary. Bleed the brake system as outlined in Section 10 and test the brakes carefully before placing the vehicle into normal operation.

10 Brake hydraulic system - bleeding

▶ Refer to illustration 10.8

WARNING:

If air has found its way into the hydraulic control unit on models with ABS, the system must be bled with the use of a scan tool. If the brake pedal feels "spongy" even after bleeding the brakes, or the ABS light on the instrument panel does not go off, or if you have any doubts whatsoever about the effectiveness of the brake system, have the vehicle towed to a dealer service department or other repair shop equipped with the necessary tools for bleeding the system.

WARNING:

Wear eye protection when bleeding the brake system. If the fluid comes in contact with your eyes, immediately rinse them with water and seek medical attention.

➡Note: Bleeding the brake system is necessary to remove any air that's trapped in the system when it's opened during removal and installation of a hose, line, caliper, wheel cylinder or master cylinder.

1   It will probably be necessary to bleed the system at all four brakes if air has entered the system due to low fluid level, or if the brake lines have been disconnected at the master cylinder.

2   If a brake line was disconnected only at a wheel, then only that caliper or wheel cylinder must be bled.

3   If a brake line is disconnected at a fitting located between the master cylinder and any of the brakes, that part of the system served by the disconnected line must be bled.

4   Remove any residual vacuum (or hydraulic pressure) from the brake power booster by applying the brake several times with the engine off.

5   Remove the master cylinder reservoir cap and fill the reservoir with brake fluid. Reinstall the cap.

➡Note: Check the fluid level often during the bleeding operation and add fluid as necessary to prevent the fluid level from falling low enough to allow air bubbles into the master cylinder.

10.8 When bleeding the brakes, a hose is connected to the bleed screw at the caliper and submerged in brake fluid - air will be seen as bubbles in the tube and container (all air must be expelled before moving to the next wheel)

6   Have an assistant on hand, as well as a supply of new brake fluid, an empty clear plastic container, a length of plastic, rubber or vinyl tubing to fit over the bleeder valve and a wrench to open and close the bleeder valve.

7   Beginning at the front left wheel, loosen the bleeder screw slightly, then tighten it to a point where it's snug but can still be loosened quickly and easily.

8   Place one end of the tubing over the bleeder screw fitting and submerge the other end in brake fluid in the container (see illustration).

9   Have the assistant slowly depress the brake pedal and hold it in the depressed position.

10 While the pedal is held depressed, open the bleeder screw just enough to allow a flow of fluid to leave the valve. Watch for air bubbles to exit the submerged end of the tube. When the fluid flow slows after a couple of seconds, tighten the screw and have your assistant release the pedal.

11 Repeat Steps 9 and 10 until no more air is seen leaving the tube,

then tighten the bleeder screw and proceed to the right front wheel, the right rear wheel and the left rear wheel, in that order, and perform the same procedure. Be sure to check the fluid in the master cylinder reservoir frequently.

12 Never use old brake fluid. It contains moisture which can boil, rendering the brake system inoperative.

13 Refill the master cylinder with fluid at the end of the operation.

14 Check the operation of the brakes. The pedal should feel solid when depressed, with no sponginess. If necessary, repeat the entire process.

⁂ WARNING:

Do not operate the vehicle if you are in doubt about the effectiveness of the brake system. On models equipped with ABS, it's possible for air to become trapped in the anti-lock brake system hydraulic control unit, so, if the pedal continues to feel spongy after repeated bleedings or the BRAKE or ANTI-LOCK light stays on, have the vehicle towed to a dealer service department or other qualified shop to be bled with the aid of a scan tool.

11 Power brake booster - removal and installation

OPERATING CHECK

1 Depress the brake pedal several times with the engine off and make sure there is no change in the pedal reserve distance.

2 Depress the pedal and start the engine. If the pedal goes down slightly, operation is normal.

AIRTIGHTNESS CHECK

3 Start the engine and turn it off after one or two minutes. Depress the brake pedal several times slowly. If the pedal goes down farther the first time but gradually rises after the second or third depression, the booster is airtight.

4 Depress the brake pedal while the engine is running, then stop the engine with the pedal depressed. If there is no change in the pedal reserve travel after holding the pedal for 30 seconds, the booster is airtight.

REMOVAL

▸ **Refer to illustrations 11.11 and 11.12**

5 Power brake booster units should not be disassembled. They require special tools not normally found in most automotive repair stations or shops. They are fairly complex and because of their critical relationship to brake performance it is best to replace a defective booster unit with a new or rebuilt one.

6 To remove the booster, first remove the brake master cylinder as described in Section 8.

7 Disconnect the hose leading from the engine to the booster. Be careful not to damage the hose when removing it from the booster fitting.

8 Remove and set aside the engine compartment fuse/relay box (see Chapter 12).

9 Unclip the brake lines from the firewall.

10 Remove the air filter housing (see Chapter 4).

11 Working inside the vehicle, locate the pushrod clevis pin connecting the booster to the brake pedal (see illustration). Remove the clevis pin retaining clip with pliers and pull out the pin.

12 Remove the four nuts (see illustration) holding the brake booster to the firewall.

13 Slide the booster straight out from the firewall until the studs clear the holes and pull the booster, brackets and gaskets from the engine compartment area.

INSTALLATION

14 Installation procedures are the reverse of those for removal. Tighten the booster mounting nuts to the torque listed in this Chapter's Specifications. Also, be sure to use a new cotter pin on the clevis pin.

15 After the final installation of the master cylinder and brake hoses and lines, bleed the brakes as described in Section 10.

11.11 Remove the retaining clip and clevis pin to disconnect the pushrod from the pedal

11.12 Remove the four booster mounting nuts

12 Parking brake - adjustment

▶ **Refer to illustration 12.3**

1   Remove the center console (see Chapter 11).

2   Block the front wheels, raise the rear of the vehicle and support it securely on jackstands. Apply the parking brake lever until you hear one click.

3   Tighten the adjusting nut on the equalizer while rotating the rear wheels (see illustration). Stop turning the nut when the brakes just start to drag on the rear wheels.

4   Release the parking brake lever and check to see that the brakes don't drag when the rear wheels are turned. The travel on the parking brake lever should be as listed in the Chapter 1 Specifications when properly adjusted.

5   Lower the vehicle and reinstall the center console.

12.3 The parking brake adjusting nut is on the equalizer assembly

13 Brake light switch/Brake Pedal Position switch - replacement

▶ **Refer to illustration 13.1**

1   Disconnect the electrical connector from the brake light switch (see illustration).

2   Rotate the switch counterclockwise slightly, so it unlocks from its holder, then pull it out of the holder.

3   To install the switch, insert it into its holder (canted slightly counterclockwise as during removal) and push it in until the switch body contacts the bracket on the brake pedal. Rotate the switch 45-degrees clockwise to lock it into place.

4   Plug the electrical connector into the switch.

13.1 Brake light switch electrical connector

14 Brake pedal - adjustment

BRAKE PEDAL HEIGHT

▶ **Refer to illustration 14.2**

1   Disconnect the brake light switch electrical connector, then remove the brake light switch (see Section 13).

2   Pull the carpet back and find the insulator cutout, then with the brake pedal fully released, measure the distance from the top of the pad to the floor (see illustration).

3   If the height is not as listed in this Chapter's Specifications, it must be adjusted.

4   Loosen the locknut just in front of the clevis on the power brake booster pushrod.

5   Turn the booster pushrod until the pedal height is correct.

6   Tighten the locknut.

7   After adjusting the pedal height, check the freeplay, then install the brake light switch (see Section 13).

BRAKE PEDAL FREEPLAY

▶ **Refer to illustration 14.8**

8   Press down lightly on the brake pedal and measure the distance that it moves freely before resistance is felt (see illustration). The freeplay should be within the specified limits. If it isn't, check the clevis, clevis pin and the hole in the brake pedal arm for excessive wear.

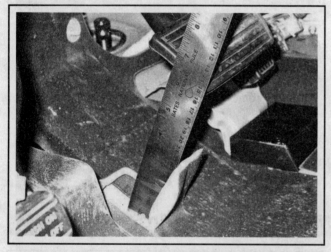

14.2 With the brake pedal fully released, measure the distance from the top of the pedal pad to the floor

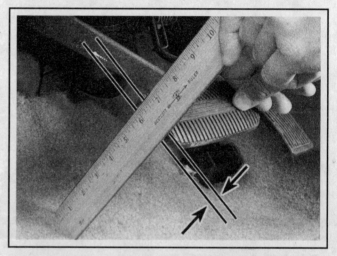

14.8 To measure brake pedal freeplay, press down lightly on the pedal and measure the distance that it moves freely before resistance is felt

Specifications

General

Brake fluid type	See Chapter 1
Brake pedal	
Height (with carpet removed)	
Manual transaxle models	
2007 and earlier models	6-9/16 inches (167 mm)
2008 and later models	6-9/64 inches (156 mm)
Automatic transaxle models	
2004 through 2007 models	6-3/4 inches (171 mm)
2008 and later models	6-3/32 inches (155 mm)
Freeplay	1/16 to 3/16 inch (1 to 5 mm)

Disc brakes

Brake pad minimum thickness	See Chapter 1
Disc lateral runout limit	0.004 inch (0.10 mm)
Disc minimum thickness	Cast into disc
Parallelism (thickness variation) limit	0.0006 inch (0.015 mm)

Drum brakes

Maximum drum diameter	Cast into drum
Shoe lining minimum thickness	See Chapter 1

Torque specifications	Ft-lbs (unless otherwise indicated)	Nm

➡**Note: One foot-pound (ft-lb) of torque is equivalent to 12 inch-pounds (in-lbs) of torque. Torque values below approximately 15 ft-lbs are expressed in inch-pounds, since most foot-pound torque wrenches are not accurate at these smaller values.**

Brake hose banjo fitting bolt	25	34
Caliper mounting bracket bolts		
Front	80	108
Rear		
2007 and earlier models	41	55
2008 and later models	80	108
Caliper mounting guide pins/bolts		
Front		
2007 and earlier models		
Four-cylinder models	26	35
V6 models	37	50
2008 and later models)		
Nissin calipers (10 mm bolt)	37	50
Akebono calipers (8 mm bolt)	25	34
Rear	17	23
Master cylinder mounting nuts		
2007 and earlier models	132 in-lbs	15
2008 and later models	17	23
Power brake booster mounting nuts	115 in-lbs	13
Wheel cylinder mounting bolts	84 in-lbs	9
Wheel speed sensor mounting bolt	86 in-lbs	10
Wheel lug nuts	See Chapter 1	

*Use new bolts

Notes

Section

Reference to other Chapters

10

SUSPENSION AND STEERING SYSTEMS

1 General information

♦ **Refer to illustrations 1.1 and 1.2**

The front suspension is a fully independent design with upper and lower control arms, shock absorber/coil spring assemblies and a stabilizer bar (see illustration).

Each side of the rear suspension uses a trailing arm, a leading arm, two unequal length lower control arms (one is called a lower arm, the other is called the control arm), an upper control arm and a shock absorber/coil spring unit (see illustration). A stabilizer bar connects the suspension on each side, to reduce body roll.

All models use a power-assisted rack-and-pinion steering gear. The power steering system employs an engine-driven pump connected by hoses to the steering gear.

Frequently, when working on the suspension or steering system components, you may come across fasteners which seem impossible to loosen. These fasteners on the underside of the vehicle are continually subjected to water, road grime, mud, etc., and can become rusted or frozen, making them extremely difficult to remove. In order to unscrew these stubborn fasteners without damaging them (or other components), be sure to use lots of penetrating oil and allow it to soak in for a while. Using a wire brush to clean exposed threads will also ease removal of the nut or bolt and prevent damage to the threads. Sometimes a sharp blow with a hammer and punch is effective in breaking the bond between a nut and bolt threads, but care must be taken to prevent the punch from slipping off the fastener and ruining the threads. Heating the stuck fastener and surrounding area with a torch sometimes helps too,

1.1 Front suspension components

1	Stabilizer bar	4	Lower control arm
2	Subframe	5	Lower balljoint
3	Strut/coil spring assembly	6	Damper fork
		7	Tie-rod end

but isn't recommended because of the obvious dangers associated with fire. Long breaker bars and extension, or cheater, pipes will increase leverage, but never use an extension pipe on a ratchet - the ratcheting mechanism could be damaged. Sometimes, turning the nut or bolt in the tightening (clockwise) direction first will help to break it loose. Fasteners that require drastic measures to unscrew should always be replaced with new ones.

Since most of the procedures that are dealt with in this Chapter involve jacking up the vehicle and working underneath it, a good pair of jackstands will be needed. A hydraulic floor jack is the preferred type of jack to lift the vehicle, and it can also be used to support certain components during various operations.

※ WARNING:

Never, under any circumstances, rely on a jack to support the vehicle while working on it. Whenever any of the suspension or steering fasteners are loosened or removed they must be inspected and, if necessary, be replaced with new ones of the same part number or of original equipment quality and design. Torque specifications must be followed for proper reassembly and component retention. Never attempt to heat or straighten any suspension or steering component. Instead, replace any bent or damaged part with a new one.

1.2 Rear suspension components

1	Stabilizer bar	4	Rear knuckle (hub and bearing)	7	Upper arm
2	Shock absorber/coil spring assembly	5	Trailing arm	8	Control arm
3	Leading arm	6	Lower arm		

2 Shock absorber/coil spring assembly (front) - removal and installation

REMOVAL

▶ **Refer to illustrations 2.3 and 2.5**

1 Loosen the wheel lug nuts, raise the vehicle and support it securely on jackstands. Remove the wheel.
2 Place a floor jack under the lower control arm to support it.
3 Remove the damper fork-to-shock pinch bolt (see illustration).
4 Remove the damper fork-to-lower control arm bolt and remove the fork. It may be necessary to tap the fork from the shock absorber.
5 Support the shock absorber and coil spring assembly and remove the five upper mounting nuts (see illustration). Carefully remove the unit from the fenderwell.

INSTALLATION

6 Guide the shock absorber assembly up into the fenderwell and insert the five upper mounting studs through the holes in the body. Once the studs protrude from the holes, install the nuts so the assembly

won't fall back through, but don't tighten the nuts completely yet. The shock absorber is heavy and awkward, so get an assistant to help you, if possible.
7 Insert the lower end of the shock absorber into the damper fork.

✳✳ CAUTION:

Make sure the aligning tab on the back of the shock body enters the slot in the damper fork.

8 Connect the damper fork to the lower control arm, using a new nut on the damper fork bolt. Raise the lower control arm with a floor jack to simulate normal ride height, then tighten the damper fork pinch bolt and damper fork-to-lower control arm bolt/nut to the torque listed in this Chapter's Specifications.
9 Install the wheel and lug nuts, lower the vehicle and tighten the lug nuts to the torque listed in the Chapter 1 Specifications.
10 Tighten the upper mounting nuts to the torque listed in this Chapter's Specifications.

2.3 Damper fork fasteners

2.5 Front shock absorber mounting nuts

1 10 x 1.25 nuts   *2 8 x 1.25 nuts*

3 Shock absorber or coil spring - component replacement

▶ **Refer to illustrations 3.3, 3.4a and 3.4b**

➡**Note:** If the shocks or coil springs exhibit the telltale signs of wear (leaking fluid, loss of damping capability, chipped, sagging or cracked coil springs) explore all options before beginning any work. The shock absorbers or coil springs are not serviceable individually and must be replaced if a problem develops. However, complete assemblies may be available on an exchange basis, which eliminates much time and work. Whichever route you choose to take, check on the cost and availability of parts before disassembling your vehicle.

✳✳ WARNING:

Disassembling a shock/coil spring is potentially dangerous and utmost attention must be directed to the job, or serious injury may result. Use only a high-quality spring compressor and carefully follow the manufacturer's instructions furnished with the tool. After removing the coil spring from the shock assembly, set it aside in a safe, isolated area.

1 Remove the shock absorber/coil spring assembly (see Section 2 or 10).

2 Mount the shock/coil spring assembly in a vise. Line the vise jaws with wood or rags to prevent damage to the unit and don't tighten the vise excessively.

3 Following the tool manufacturer's instructions, install the spring compressor (which can be obtained at most auto parts stores or equipment yards on a daily rental basis) on the spring and compress it sufficiently to relieve all pressure from the upper spring seat. This can be verified by wiggling the spring (see illustration).

➥Note: Note the orientation of the upper mount in relation to the lower mounting eye (when reassembling the unit the mount will have to be in the same position). Make a sketch or some matchmarks to help you get the mount positioned properly when reinstalling it.

4 Hold the shock damper rod with an Allen wrench, and unscrew the retaining nut with a box-end wrench (see illustrations).

3.3 Install the spring compressor following the tool manufacturer's instructions; compress the spring until all pressure is relieved from the upper spring seat (you can verify that the spring is loose by wiggling it)

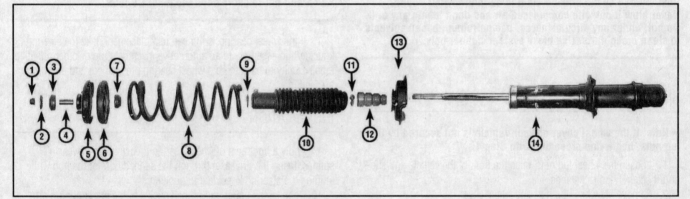

3.4a Exploded view of a front shock absorber/coil spring assembly

1 Self-locking nut	6 Damper mounting rubber	11 Bump stop plate
2 Damper mounting washer	7 Spring mounting rubber	12 Bump stop
3 Damper mounting rubber	8 Spring	13 Dust cover lower mounting
4 Damper mounting collar	9 Dust cover plate	14 Damper unit
5 Damper mounting base	10 Dust cover	

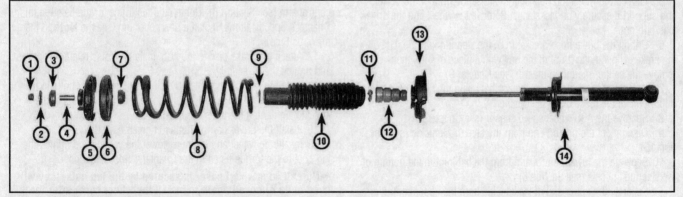

3.4b Exploded view of a rear shock absorber/coil spring assembly

1 Self-locking nut	6 Damper mounting rubber	11 Bump stop plate
2 Damper mounting washer	7 Spring mounting rubber	12 Bump stop
3 Damper mounting rubber	8 Spring	13 Dust cover lower mounting
4 Damper mounting collar	9 Dust cover plate	14 Damper unit
5 Damper mounting base	10 Dust cover	

5 Disassemble the parts from the damper, taking care to lay the parts out in the exact order in which they are removed.

⁂ WARNING:

When removing the compressed spring, lift it off carefully and set it in a safe place. Keep the ends of the spring away from your body.

6 Reassembly is the reverse of removal, noting the following points:

a) *Carefully place the spring onto the shock absorber body, with the end of the spring resting in the lowest part of the seat.*
b) *Use a new self-locking nut, then tighten the nut to the torque listed in this Chapter's Specifications.*
c) *Before releasing the spring compressor, make sure the upper mount is oriented as it was before removal in Step 3.*

7 After removing the spring compressor tool, the unit is ready for installation (see Section 2 or 10).

4 Steering knuckle and hub - removal and installation

⁂ WARNING:

Dust created by the brake system is harmful to your health. Never blow it out with compressed air and don't inhale any of it. Do not, under any circumstances, use petroleum-based solvents to clean brake parts. Use brake system cleaner only.

REMOVAL

➡**Note: If the wheel cover on your vehicle is not secured by the lug nuts, begin this procedure with Step 4.**

1 Loosen the wheel lug nuts, raise the front of the vehicle and support it securely on jackstands.
2 Remove the wheel lug nuts and wheel cover.
3 Using a punch, unstake the front axle nut (see Chapter 8). Install the wheel and lug nuts, excluding the wheel cover, then lower the vehicle.
4 Using a breaker bar and socket, loosen the driveaxle/hub nut (see Chapter 8).

➡**Note: Be sure to unstake the driveaxle/hub nut before attempting to remove it.**

5 Loosen the wheel lug nuts slightly, raise the front of the vehicle and support it securely on jackstands. Remove the wheel and the drive-axle/hub nut.
6 Unbolt the brake hose bracket from the steering knuckle. Unbolt the brake caliper, hang it out of the way with a piece of wire, then remove the caliper mounting bracket (see Chapter 9).
7 Remove the two mounting screws that retain the brake disc to the hub. Remove the brake disc (see Chapter 9).
8 Remove the ABS wheel speed sensor (see Chapter 9).
9 Disconnect the tie-rod end from the steering knuckle (see Section 15).
10 Separate the lower control arm from the balljoint in the bottom of the steering knuckle (see Section 8).
11 Separate the upper end of the knuckle from the upper control arm balljoint (see Section 9).
12 Carefully pull the knuckle and hub assembly off of the driveaxle. If necessary, tap on the end of the driveaxle with a soft-face hammer. Support the driveaxle with a piece of wire to prevent damage to the inner CV joint.

⁂ CAUTION:

Be careful not to overextend the inner CV joint.

13 If the wheel bearing is in need of replacement, take the steering knuckle/hub assembly to an automotive machine shop or other qualified repair facility to have the old wheel bearing pressed out and a new one pressed in.

INSTALLATION

14 Apply a light coat of wheel bearing grease to the driveaxle splines. Insert the driveaxle through the splined bore of the hub while guiding the steering knuckle into position.
15 Connect the upper end of the knuckle to the upper control arm balljoint (see Section 9). Tighten the balljoint stud nut to the torque listed in this Chapter's Specifications. Install a new cotter pin.

➡**Note: Tighten the nut to the lower torque value given in the Specifications, then, if necessary, tighten it an additional amount to line up the slots in the nut with the hole in the balljoint stud to allow cotter pin insertion. Insert the pin from front to rear.**

16 Connect the balljoint on the bottom of the knuckle to the lower control arm (see Section 8). Tighten the nut to the torque listed in this Chapter's Specifications. Install a new cotter pin (see the **Note** in the previous Step).
17 Attach the brake disc to the hub, install the disc retaining screws and tighten them securely.
18 Install the caliper mount and caliper, tightening the bolts to the proper torque (see Chapter 9). Attach the brake hose bracket to the knuckle, tightening the bolts securely.
19 Install the driveaxle/hub nut and tighten it securely.
20 Install the wheel and lug nuts, lower the vehicle and tighten the lug nuts to the torque listed in the Chapter 1 Specifications.

➡**Note: If your wheel cover is secured by the lug nuts, they will need to be removed again to install the wheel cover after the next step has been completed.**

21 Tighten the driveaxle/hub nut to the torque listed in the Chapter 8 Specifications and then re-stake it with a blunt chisel.
22 Loosen the lugs nuts, raise the vehicle and support it securely. Remove the lug nuts and install the wheel cover (if equipped).
23 Install the lug nuts, lower the vehicle and tighten the lug nuts to the torque listed in the Chapter 1 Specifications.

5 Hub and wheel bearing assembly (front) - removal and installation

Due to the special tools and expertise required to press the hub and bearing from the steering knuckle, this job should be left to a professional mechanic. However, the steering knuckle and hub may be removed and the assembly taken to an automotive machine shop or other qualified repair facility equipped with the necessary tools. See Section 4 for the steering knuckle and hub removal procedure.

6 Stabilizer bar and bushings (front) - removal, inspection and installation

REMOVAL

▶ **Refer to illustrations 6.2 and 6.3**

1 Lower the front subframe (see Section 24).

➡**Note: It's important to mention that the need to remove the stabilizer bar from the vehicle is usually due to damage from an accident. If this is the case, it is highly likely that other major components (such as the subframe itself) have also been damaged. We recommend having the vehicle inspected by a qualified body repair shop before replacing the stabilizer bar.**

2 Remove the link nuts to separate the stabilizer bar link assemblies from the stabilizer (see illustration).

➡**Note: Use an Allen wrench to prevent the ballstud from turning when removing the attaching link nut.**

3 Remove the stabilizer bar bushing bracket bolts (see illustration).

➡**Note: Access the bushing brackets through the wheelwells.**

4 Remove the stabilizer bar from the vehicle.

INSPECTION

5 Inspect for cracked, torn, or distorted stabilizer bar bushings, bushing brackets, and worn or damaged stabilizer bar links.

6 To replace damaged stabilizer bar bushings, remove the bracket, open the bushing slit and peel the bushing from the stabilizer bar.

✳✳ CAUTION:

Install the new bushings with the slits facing the same way that the original bushing slits faced.

INSTALLATION

7 Guide the stabilizer bar into position. Install the brackets and bolts, tightening them to the torque listed in this Chapter's Specifications.

8 Connect the stabilizer bar to the links. Tighten the nuts to the torque listed in this Chapter's Specifications.

➡**Note: Use new self-locking nuts to attach the stabilizer bar links.**

9 Install the wheels and lug nuts. Lower the vehicle and tighten the lug nuts to the torque listed in the Chapter 1 Specifications.

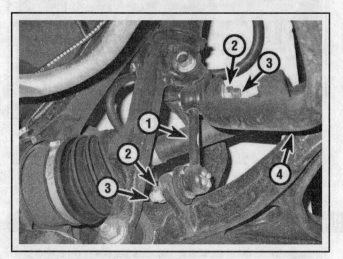

6.2 Remove the upper or lower link nut; if you're replacing the link, remove both nuts

1   *Stabilizer bar link*
2   *Link nut*
3   *Ballstud (hold with Allen wrench)*
4   *Front stabilizer bar*

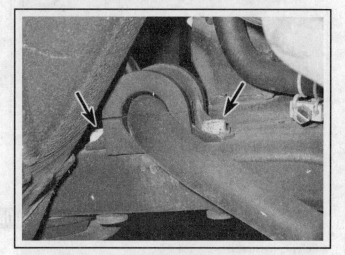

6.3 Stabilizer bar bushing retainer and bolts

7 Balljoints - replacement

The front suspension uses two balljoints; the upper balljoint is mounted in the upper control arm, and the lower balljoint is mounted in the steering knuckle. The rear suspension uses one balljoint, on the outer end of the upper arm. The balljoints are not serviceable separately and require replacement of the upper control arm or the steering knuckle in the event of balljoint failure. Check with your local auto parts store or a dealer parts department on the availability of parts before disassembling your vehicle.

The balljoint boots, however, are replaceable. They are secured by a wire set ring and are easily replaced after the components have been separated.

8 Lower control arm (front) - removal and installation

▶ **Refer to illustrations 8.4 and 8.5**

1   Loosen the front wheel lug nuts, raise the vehicle, place it securely on jackstands and remove the wheel.

2   Remove the through-bolt and detach the damper fork from the lower control arm (see Section 2).

3   Detach the stabilizer bar link from the lower control arm (see Section 6).

4   Remove the cotter pin from the castle nut on the lower balljoint stud. Loosen the nut, but don't remove it yet (this will prevent the components from separating violently). Using a two-jaw puller, separate the lower control arm from the balljoint in the steering knuckle (see illustration). Remove the nut.

5   Remove the pivot and front bolts from the inner end of the lower control arm (see illustration) and then remove the arm.

6   Installation is the reverse of removal, noting the following points:

  a) Raise the outer end of the control arm with a floor jack to simulate normal ride height before tightening the pivot bolt and inner front bolt.

  b) Be sure to install a new cotter pin (and read the **Note** in Section 4, Step 15).

  c) Tighten the wheel lug nuts to the torque listed in the Chapter 1 Specifications.

8.4 The lower control arm with two-jaw puller installed

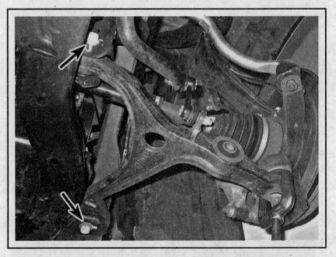

8.5 The lower control arm mounting and pivot bolt locations

9 Upper control arm (front) - removal and installation

▶ **Refer to illustrations 9.3 and 9.6**

➡**Note: A 6mm x 300mm rod will be needed for upper control arm installation.**

1   Loosen the front wheel lug nuts, raise the vehicle, place it securely on jackstands and remove the wheel. Support the lower control arm with a floor jack.

2   Remove the shock absorber/coil spring assembly (see Section 2).

Remove the ABS wheel speed sensor bracket from the upper control arm.

3   Remove the cotter pin, then loosen, but do not remove, the castle nut from the upper balljoint stud (see illustration). The nut will prevent the upper control arm and the steering knuckle from separating violently in the next step.

4   Separate the upper control arm from the steering knuckle with a two-jaw puller, then remove the nut. Don't let the top of the steering knuckle fall outward. If necessary, secure it with a piece of wire.

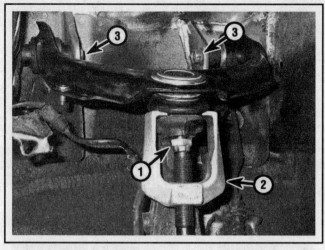

9.3 Use a two-jaw puller to separate the balljoint from the steering knuckle

1	Castle nut (loosened)
2	Two-jaw puller
3	Upper control arm pivot bolts

5   Remove the upper control arm pivot bolts (see illustration 9.3) and the upper control arm.

6   Installation is the reverse of removal, noting the following points:

a) Fabricate a tool (6mm x 300mm rod) and place it in the holes provided in the frame to position the upper control arm (see illustration).

9.6 A special tool is placed for installation of the upper control arm

b) With the tool in place, install the control arm pivot bolts and tighten them to the torque values listed in this Chapter's Specifications.

c) Be sure to tighten all other fasteners securely and use the torque values listed in this Chapter's Specifications. Install a new cotter pin (and read the **Note** in Section 4, Step 15).

10 Shock absorber/coil spring assembly (rear) - removal and installation

♦ Refer to illustrations 10.2, 10.4 and 10.6

1   Loosen the rear wheel lug nuts, raise the vehicle, place it securely on jackstands and remove the rear wheels.

2   Remove the rear package shelf trim cover (see illustration). Refer to Chapter 11 for additional details.

➡Note: Step 3 applies to sedans only.

3   Remove the seat back side trim panel (see Chapter 11).

4   Remove the shock absorber upper mounting nuts (see illustration).

5   Remove the nut from the upper end of the stabilizer link (see Section 13).

6   Remove the shock absorber lower mounting bolt (see illustration).

10.2 Remove the rear seat trim panel for access to the shock absorber upper mount

10.4 Remove the nuts from the shock absorber studs

10.6 Rear shock absorber lower mounting bolt

7 Pull the rear knuckle down and remove the shock absorber/coil spring assembly.

8 To inspect or replace the shock absorber or coil spring, see Section 3.

9 Installation is the reverse of removal, noting the following points:

a) *Raise the rear knuckle with a floor jack to simulate normal ride height before tightening the shock absorber lower mounting bolt to the torque listed in this Chapter's Specifications.*

b) *Tighten the upper mounting nuts to the torque listed in this Chapter's Specifications.*

c) *Tighten the wheel lug nuts to the torque listed in the Chapter 1 Specifications.*

11 Rear knuckle - removal and installation

REMOVAL

1 Loosen the rear wheel lug nuts, raise the rear of the vehicle and support it securely on jackstands. Remove the wheel.

Disc brake models

2 Unbolt the brake hose bracket from the knuckle. Unbolt the brake caliper, hang it out of the way with a piece of wire, then remove the caliper mounting bracket (see Chapter 9).

3 Remove the two mounting screws that retain the brake disc to the hub. Remove the brake disc (see Chapter 9).

4 Remove the hub and bearing assembly from the knuckle (see Section 12).

5 Remove the brake disc splash guard.

Drum brake models

6 Disconnect the brake line from the wheel cylinder and plug or cap each end (see Chapter 9).

7 Remove the hub and bearing assembly from the knuckle (see Section 12).

8 Remove the bolts that mount the backing plate to the knuckle.

All models

9 Detach the upper end of the stabilizer bar link from its mount (see Section 13).

10 Detach the lower end of the shock absorber assembly from the knuckle (see Section 10).

11 Unbolt the suspension arms from the knuckle (see Section 14).

12 Remove the knuckle from the suspension arms.

13 If the wheel bearing is in need of replacement, replace the hub and bearing assembly as a single unit.

INSTALLATION

14 Connect the suspension arms to the knuckle, but don't tighten the fasteners yet (see Section 14).

15 Connect the lower end of the shock absorber to the knuckle, but don't tighten the bolt yet (see Section 10).

16 Attach the stabilizer bar link to its bracket on the knuckle (see Section 13).

17 Install the hub and bearing assembly (see Section 12).

18 Install the brake components (see Chapter 9).

➡**Note: Models with drum brakes require brake system bleeding after the brake line is reattached to the wheel cylinder.**

19 Raise the rear suspension with a floor jack to simulate normal ride height, then tighten the fasteners to the torque listed in this Chapter's Specifications.

20 Install the wheel and lug nuts, lower the vehicle and tighten the lug nuts to the torque listed in the Chapter 1 Specifications.

12 Hub and wheel bearing assembly (rear) - removal and installation

☀ WARNING:

Dust created by the brake system is harmful to your health. Never blow it out with compressed air and don't inhale any of it. Do not, under any circumstances, use petroleum-based solvents to clean brake parts. Use brake system cleaner only.

➡**Note: The rear hub and bearing are combined into a single assembly. The bearing is sealed for life and requires no lubrication or attention. If the bearing is worn or damaged, replace the entire hub and bearing assembly.**

2007 AND EARLIER MODELS

▶ **Refer to illustrations 12.3a, 12.3b and 12.5**

1 Loosen the rear wheel lug nuts, raise the rear of the vehicle, support it securely on jackstands. Block the front wheels to prevent the vehicle from rolling. Remove the wheels.

2 Remove the brake drum or disc (see Chapter 9).

3 Remove the dust cover then unstake and remove the hub retaining nut (see illustrations).

4 Remove the hub and bearing assembly from the spindle.

5 Installation is the reverse of removal, noting the following points:

a) *Install a new hub retaining nut and tighten it to the torque listed in this Chapter's Specifications. Stake the new hub nut in place (see illustration).*

➡**Note: Apply a little clean engine oil to the seating surface of the hub retaining nut before installing it.**

b) *Install the dust cover by tapping lightly around the edge until it is seated.*

c) *On models with rear disc brakes, tighten all the caliper bolts to the torque listed in the Chapter 9 Specifications.*

d) *Install the wheel and lug nuts. Lower the vehicle and tighten the lug nuts to the torque listed in the Chapter 1 Specifications.*

12.3a Using a hammer and chisel, remove the dust cover

12.3b Unstake the hub nut

12.5 Stake the new hub nut in place

2008 AND LATER MODELS

6   Loosen the rear wheel lug nuts. Raise the rear of the vehicle and support it securely on jackstands.

7   Remove the brake disc (see Chapter 9).

8   Remove the hub assembly mounting bolts from the back side.

9   Remove the hub and bearing assembly from the trailing arm.

10 Installation is the reverse of removal. Tighten all fasteners to the proper torque specifications.

13 Stabilizer bar and bushings (rear) - removal and installation

♦ **Refer to illustrations 13.2 and 13.3**

1   Loosen the rear wheel lug nuts, raise the rear of the vehicle, place it securely on jackstands and remove the rear wheels.

2   Remove the stabilizer bar-to-link nuts (see illustration).

➡ **Note: Use an Allen wrench to prevent the ballstud from turning when removing the attaching link nut.**

3   Unbolt the bushing bracket from each side of the stabilizer bar

(see illustration) and then remove the bar.

4   Pull the retainers off the bar and inspect the bushings for cracks, breaks and other signs of deterioration (see Section 6). If the bushings are damaged, replace them. Also check the stabilizer bar links for loose balljoints and other damage, replacing them if necessary.

5   Installation is the reverse of removal.

➡ **Note: Use new self-locking nuts to attach the stabilizer bar links.**

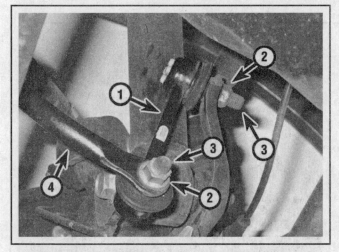

13.2 Remove the upper or lower link nut; if you're replacing the link, remove both nuts

1	Stabilizer bar link	3	Ballstud (hold with
2	Link nut		Allen wrench)
		4	Rear stabilizer bar

13.3 Stabilizer bar bracket bolts

14 Rear suspension arms - removal and installation

※ WARNING:

When loading the suspension with a floor jack, be extremely careful not to lift the vehicle from the jackstands or make the vehicle unstable.

➡ **Note 1: When installing any of the following components, it is recommended that new self-locking nuts are used.**

➡ **Note 2: The following components should be installed by lightly tightening the fasteners. Once installed, load the suspension with the vehicle's weight and torque the fasteners to specification. Loading the suspension can be accomplished by placing a floor jack securely under the knuckle and raising it just enough to simulate normal ride height.**

1   Loosen the rear wheel lug nuts, raise the vehicle, place it securely on jackstands and remove the wheel.

UPPER ARM

▶ **Refer to illustration 14.5**

2   To disconnect the upper arm balljoint from the knuckle, remove the lock pin and loosen the castle nut on the ballstud. Install a small two-jaw puller to unseat the ballstud from the knuckle (see illustration 9.3). Once the ballstud is loose, remove the castle nut and separate the arm from the knuckle entirely.

※ CAUTION:

Take note of the direction of the castle nut lock pin; It is critical for proper installation.

3   Remove the brake hose bracket bolts and swing the hose/hydraulic line to the side.

4   If the vehicle is equipped with ABS, remove the wheel speed sensor to prevent damage to the wiring harness.

5   Remove the pivot bolt that attaches the inner end of the upper arm to the chassis (see illustration).

6   Remove the upper arm. Inspect the bushing for cracks and deterioration and the balljoint for looseness and other signs of wear. If any undesirable conditions exist, replace the arm.

7   Installation is the reverse of removal. Be sure to tighten all fasteners to the torque values listed in this Chapter's Specifications after raising the rear knuckle with a floor jack to simulate normal ride height. Install a new lock pin on the castle nut.

➡ **Note 1: Although the position of the lock pin may vary a little, install it with the closed end of the pin pointed towards the front of the vehicle.**

➡ **Note: See the Warning and Notes at the beginning of this Section.**

LOWER ARM

▶ **Refer to illustration 14.8**

8   Remove the nut and bolt that attaches the lower arm to the knuckle (see illustration).

9   Remove the pivot bolt that attaches the inner end of the lower arm to the chassis.

10   Remove the lower arm.

11   Inspect the lower arm bushings for cracks and deterioration. If either of them are worn, replace the arm.

12   Installation is the reverse of removal. Be sure to tighten all fasteners to the torque values listed in this Chapter's Specifications after raising the rear knuckle with a floor jack to simulate normal ride height.

➡ **Note: See the Warning and Notes at the beginning of this Section.**

14.5   The upper arm pivot bolt is behind the brake line bracket in this illustration

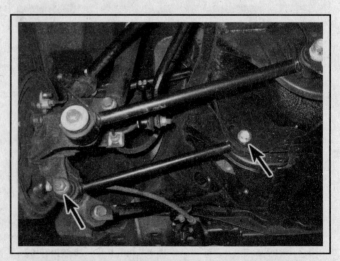

14.8   Remove the nut and bolt from the lower arm at the knuckle (left arrow) and the bolt at the inner end of the arm (right arrow)

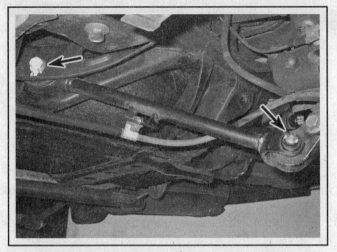

14.14 Trailing arm bolt locations (right arrow - bolt head on opposite side)

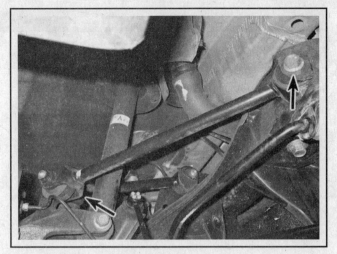

14.19 Leading arm bolt locations

TRAILING ARM

♦ **Refer to illustration 14.14**

13 Disconnect the parking brake cable bracket from the trailing arm.

14 Remove the bolt that attaches the trailing arm to the knuckle (see illustration).

15 Remove the bolt that attaches the trailing arm to the chassis.

16 Remove the trailing arm.

17 Inspect the bushing at the forward end of the arm. If it's cracked or deteriorated, replace the arm.

18 Installation is the reverse of removal. Be sure to tighten all fasteners to the torque values listed in this Chapter's Specifications after raising the rear knuckle with a floor jack to simulate normal ride height.

➡**Note: See the Warning and Notes at the beginning of this Section.**

LEADING ARM

♦ **Refer to illustration 14.19**

19 Remove the bolt that attaches the leading arm to the knuckle (see illustration).

20 Remove the bolt that attaches the leading arm to the chassis.

21 Remove the leading arm.

22 Inspect the bushing at the inner end of the arm. If it's cracked or deteriorated, replace the arm.

23 Installation is the reverse of removal. Be sure to tighten all fasteners to the torque values listed in this Chapter's Specifications after raising the rear knuckle with a floor jack to simulate normal ride height.

➡**Note: See the Warning and Notes at the beginning of this Section.**

CONTROL ARM

♦ **Refer to illustration 14.24**

24 Remove the nut that attaches the control arm to the knuckle (see illustration).

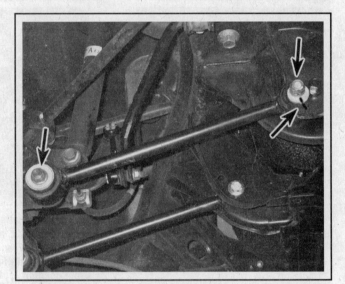

14.24 Control arm bolt locations with a mark on the adjusting cam

25 Mark the relationship of the adjustment cam to the subframe at the inner end of the arm (see illustration 14.24). Remove the nut and bolt that attaches the inner end of the control arm to the chassis.

26 Remove the control arm.

27 Inspect the control arm bushings for cracks and deterioration. If either of them are worn, replace the arm.

28 Installation is the reverse of removal. Be sure to tighten all fasteners to the torque values listed in this Chapter's Specifications after raising the rear knuckle with a floor jack to simulate normal ride height. Also, be sure to align the marks you made on the adjustment cam and subframe.

➡**Note: See the Warning and Notes at the beginning of this Section.**

15 Tie-rod ends - removal and installation

REMOVAL

▶ **Refer to illustrations 15.2, 15.3 and 15.4**

1   Loosen the wheel lug nuts, raise the front of the vehicle and support it securely on jackstands. Apply the parking brake and block the rear wheels to keep the vehicle from rolling off the jackstands. Remove the wheel.

2   Loosen the tie-rod end jam nut (see illustration).

3   Mark the relationship of the tie-rod end to the threaded portion of the tie-rod. This will ensure that the toe-in setting is restored upon reassembly (see illustration).

4   Remove the cotter pin and loosen the nut from the tie-rod end ballstud a few turns. Disconnect the tie-rod end ballstud from the steering arm with a puller (see illustration).

5   Remove the nut from the ballstud, separate the tie-rod end from the steering knuckle, and then unscrew the tie-rod end from the tie-rod.

INSTALLATION

6   Thread the tie-rod end onto the tie-rod to the marked position and connect the tie-rod end to the steering arm. Install the nut onto the ballstud and tighten it to the torque listed in this Chapter's Specifications. Install a new cotter pin.

➡ **Note: If necessary, tighten the nut a little more to allow insertion of the cotter pin. Never loosen the nut to align the cotter pin holes.**

7   Tighten the jam nut securely and install the wheel. Lower the vehicle and tighten the lug nuts to the torque listed in the Chapter 1 Specifications.

8   Have the front end alignment checked and, if necessary, adjusted.

15.2 Using a back-up wrench to prevent the tie-rod end from turning, loosen the jam nut

15.3 Make an alignment mark on the exposed threads, along the edge of the tie-rod end, so the new tie-rod end will be installed in the exact same position

15.4 Use a two-jaw puller to separate the tie-rod end from the steering knuckle arm

16 Steering wheel - removal and installation

❈❈ WARNING:

These models are equipped with a Supplemental Restraint System (SRS), more commonly known as airbags. Always disable the airbag system before working in the vicinity of any airbag system component to avoid the possibility of accidental deployment of the airbag(s), which could cause personal injury (see Chapter 12).

❈❈ WARNING:

Do not use a memory saving device to preserve the PCM or radio memory when working on or near airbag system components.

REMOVAL

▶ **Refer to illustrations 16.2, 16.3a, 16.3b, 16.4, 16.6, 16.8 and 16.10**

1   Make sure the front wheels are pointed straight ahead, then disconnect the cable from the negative terminal of the battery (see Chapter 5, Section 1). Wait at least three minutes before proceeding.

2   Remove the access panel from the bottom of the steering wheel for the airbag module and horn connectors (see illustration).

3   Pull the connectors from their brackets and unplug them (see illustrations).

4   Remove the airbag module fasteners from each side of the steering wheel (see illustration).

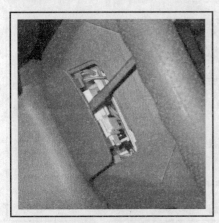

16.2 Remove the connector access panel from the underside of the steering wheel

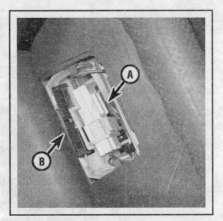

16.3a Remove and disconnect the electrical connectors for the airbag module (A) and the horn (B)

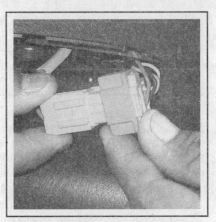

16.3b The airbag module connector has a sliding spring lock that must be moved to separate the connector

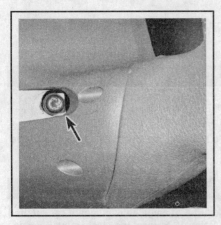

16.4 Remove the airbag fasteners from each side of the steering wheel

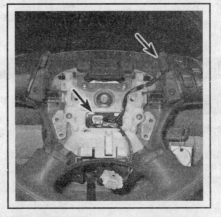

16.6 Disconnect the cruise control switch at either of these connectors

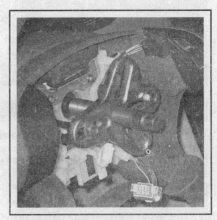

16.8 Use a steering wheel puller to remove the steering wheel

5   Pull the airbag module out and carefully set it in a safe location.

❋❋ WARNING:

Carry the airbag module with the trim side facing away from you, and set the airbag module down with the trim side facing up. Don't place anything on top of the airbag module.

6   Disconnect the cruise control switch (if equipped) (see illustration).

➡ **Note: Disconnect audio control, navigation guide or any other switches if so equipped.**

7   Loosen the steering wheel retaining bolt until about 1/2-inch of the threads are showing between the bolt head and the steering wheel.

8   Remove the steering wheel using a steering wheel puller (see illustration). The puller screw must be contacting the steering wheel bolt or shaft.

❋❋ CAUTION:

Don't thread the bolts of the puller into the steering wheel more than five turns, as they could contact the airbag clockspring and damage it.

❋❋ CAUTION:

While the steering wheel is removed, DO NOT turn the steering shaft. If you do so, the airbag clockspring could be damaged.

Once the steering wheel has been released from the shaft, remove the puller and retaining bolt, make a mark indicating the relationship of the steering wheel hub to the steering shaft, then pull the steering wheel off the shaft.

9   If it is necessary to remove the clockspring, remove the steering column covers (see Chapter 11).

10 Unplug the clockspring electrical connectors and then carefully release the locking tabs and detach it from the combination switch assembly (see illustration).

INSTALLATION

11 With the front wheels pointed straight ahead, make sure that the airbag clockspring is centered with the arrow on the clockspring pointing up. This shouldn't be a problem as long as you have not turned the steering shaft while the wheel was removed. If for some reason the shaft was turned, center the clockspring as follows:

a) Rotate the clockspring clockwise until it stops.
b) Rotate the clockspring counterclockwise about 3 full turns until the arrow on the clockspring points straight up.

12 Be sure to align the index mark on the steering wheel hub with the mark on the shaft when you slip the wheel onto the shaft. Make sure the locating pins on the clockspring engage the holes in the backside of the steering wheel, and the notches in the steering wheel hub engage the tabs on the turn signal canceling cam. Install a NEW steering wheel bolt and tighten it to the torque listed in this Chapter's Specifications.

13 Connect the cruise control switch connector and any other switch connectors that may have been removed.

16.10 Release the clockspring lock tabs for removal

14 Reattach the airbag module using NEW fasteners and tighten them to the torque listed in this Chapter's Specifications.

15 Reconnect and secure the electrical connectors for the airbag module and the horn.

16 Reconnect the negative battery cable (see Chapter 5, Section 1).

17 Steering column - removal and installation

✳✳ WARNING:

These models are equipped with a Supplemental Restraint System (SRS), more commonly known as airbags. Always disable the airbag system before working in the vicinity of any airbag system component to avoid the possibility of accidental deployment of the airbag(s), which could cause personal injury (see Chapter 12).

✳✳ WARNING:

Do not use a memory saving device to preserve the PCM or radio memory when working on or near airbag system components.

REMOVAL

▶ Refer to illustrations 17.5, 17.6, 17.7a, 17.7b, 17.8a and 17.8b

1 Park the vehicle with the wheels pointing straight ahead. Disconnect the cable from the negative terminal of the battery (see Chapter 5, Section 1).

2 Adjust the steering wheel so that it's tilted to its uppermost position and fully extended telescopically.

3 Remove the steering wheel (see Section 16).

✳✳ CAUTION:

Do not rotate the steering shaft or clockspring. Also, do not change the angle of the front wheels without the steering wheel installed. If either of these things occur, the steering wheel could be installed incorrectly resulting in damage to the airbag clockspring.

4 Remove the steering column covers (see Chapter 11).

5 Remove the combination switch assembly (see illustration).

➡Note: Make sure to disconnect the electrical connectors to the assembly.

✳✳ CAUTION:

Do not rotate the clockspring; it could be damaged if re-installed incorrectly. Refer to Section 16 to reset the clockspring if necessary.

6 From inside the vehicle under the dashboard, remove the steering universal joint cover (see illustration).

7 Mark the relationship of both parts of the slider shaft to each other. Also, mark the relationship of the universal joint and the steering input shaft. Remove the pinch bolt from the universal joint and then separate it from the input shaft (see illustrations).

➡Note: The slider shaft will separate if it is not held together.

8 Remove the steering column mounting fasteners, lower the column and pull it to the rear, making sure nothing is still connected, then remove the column (see illustrations).

INSTALLATION

9 Guide the steering column into position, then install the steering column mounting fasteners and tighten them to the torque listed in this Chapter's Specifications.

10 Connect the steering universal joint to the input shaft from the steering gear. Install the pinch bolt making certain that it fits in the groove in the input shaft and then tighten it to the torque listed in this Chapter's Specifications.

11 The remainder of installation is the reverse of removal. Reconnect the negative battery cable (see Chapter 5, Section 1).

17.5 Mounting screw locations for the combination switch assembly

17.6 Pull up on the cover's edges near the fasteners to remove it

17.7a Mark the relationship of both sections of the slider shaft just in case they become separated during removal

17.7b Mark the relationship of the U-joint to the steering gear input shaft (A) then remove the U-joint pinch bolt (B)

17.8a Steering column fasteners - left side

17.8b Steering column fasteners - right side

18 Steering gear boots - replacement

▶ Refer to illustration 18.3

1 Loosen the lug nuts, raise the front of the vehicle and support it securely on jackstands. Remove the wheel.

2 Remove the tie-rod end and jam nut (see Section 15).

3 Remove the steering gear boot clamps (see illustration) and slide off the boot.

4 Before installing the new boot, wrap the threads on the end of the tie-rod with a layer of tape so the small end of the new boot isn't damaged when putting it on.

5 Slide the new boot into position on the steering gear until each end seats in its groove, then install and tighten the new clamps.

6 Remove the tape and install the tie-rod end (see Section 15).

7 Install the wheel and lug nuts. Lower the vehicle and tighten the lug nuts to the torque listed in the Chapter 1 Specifications.

18.3 Steering gear boot clamp locations. The outer clamp can be loosened like a hose clamp, but the inner one must be cut off

19 Steering gear - removal and installation

※※ WARNING:

Make sure the steering shaft is not turned while the steering gear is removed or you could damage the airbag system. To prevent the shaft from turning, place the ignition key in the LOCK position or thread the seat belt through the steering wheel and clip it into place.

➡**Note: This procedure requires lowering the rear part of the subframe 1-3/16 inches (30mm).**

REMOVAL

▶ **Refer to illustrations 19.6, 19.8, 19.9, 19.10, 19.13a, 19.13b and 19.16**

1   Disconnect the cable from the negative battery terminal (see Chapter 5, Section 1).

19.6 Fastener locations for the lower U-joint cover

2   Drain the power steering fluid from the reservoir. This can be accomplished with a suction tool or large syringe, or by disconnecting the fluid hose and draining the fluid into a container.
3   Loosen the front wheel lug nuts, raise the vehicle and support it securely on jackstands. Remove both front wheels.

➡**Note: The jackstands must be behind the front suspension subframe, not supporting the vehicle by the subframe.**

4   From inside the vehicle under the dashboard, remove the steering universal joint cover (see illustration 17.6).
5   Mark the relationship of the universal joint to the steering input shaft and the slider shaft. Remove the pinch bolt from the universal joint and then separate it from the input shaft (see illustration 17.7).

➡**Note: To keep the slider shaft from separating, loop wire through the universal joints on each end and tighten it to hold the two parts of the shaft together.**

6   Remove the lower universal joint cover and seal (see illustration).
7   Detach the tie-rod ends from the steering knuckles (see Section 15).
8   Remove the heat shield (see illustration).
9   Remove the return hose and feed line anchors from the subframe and steering gear bracket (see illustration).
10 Using a flare nut wrench, remove the return and feed lines from the steering gear (see illustration). Cap or plug all open connections.

➡**Note: Placing shop towels under the line connections will help protect surrounding parts from spilled fluid.**

11 Remove the middle mounts on each side of the subframe (see illustration 24.7).
12 Remove the mounting bolts on the left side of the steering gear along with the small stiffener plate (see illustration 19.10).
13 Note the alignment marks on the rear of the subframe (see illustrations).
14 Using two floor jacks, support the subframe. Position one jack on each side of the subframe, midway between the front and rear corners (see illustration 24.15).
15 Loosen all of the subframe rear mounting bolts 1-3/16 inches (30 mm). Do not remove the subframe bolts.

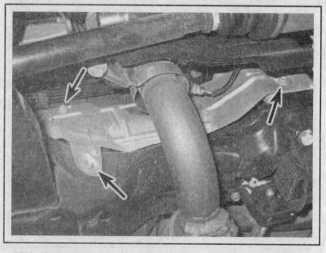

19.8 Heat shield and mounting bolt locations (four-cylinder model shown, V6 model similar)

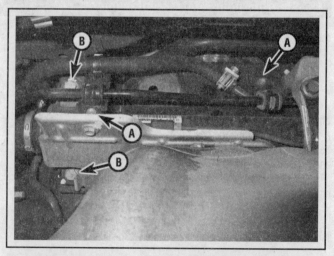

19.9 The hose and line anchors for the steering gear (A) and the right side steering gear mounting bracket (B) (four-cylinder model shown, V6 model similar)

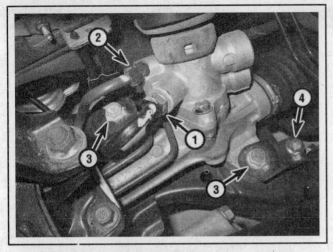

19.10 Steering gear mounting details

1 Pressure line	3 Mounting bolts
2 Return line	4 Stiffener plate bolt

19.13a Subframe, bracket and chassis details

1 Subframe alignment marks
2 Bracket alignment edge
3 Alignment tool holes

19.13b Both rear corners of the subframe must be aligned like the one is this illustration

19.16 The subframe is lowered down to the loosened bolts (the floor jacks must continue to support the subframe - do not rely on these bolts to support the subframe)

16 Carefully lower the jacks until the subframe contacts the loosened bolts (see illustration).

➡**Note: Do not remove the jacks.**

17 Remove the two mounting bolts and bracket on the right side of the steering gear (illustration 19.9).

18 Carefully move the steering gear forward and remove the rubber grommet around the steering input shaft.

➡**Note: Note the locating lug on the steering gear which fits into a slot on the grommet.**

19 Apply tape around the input shaft to protect it (and other components) during removal.

20 Guide the steering gear assembly through the left wheel opening and remove it from the vehicle.

INSTALLATION

21 Installation is the reverse of removal, noting the following points:

a) Tighten the steering gear mounting bolts to the torque listed in Chapter's Specifications.

b) With the jacks supporting the subframe, replace the loosened subframe bolts with new ones. Align the reference marks on the subframe (see illustrations 19.13a and 19.13b), then tighten the subframe mounting bolts to the torque listed in this Chapter's Specifications.

c) Fill the power steering pump with the recommended fluid (see Chapter 1) and bleed the system (see Section 21). Check for leaks and recheck the fluid level.

d) Run the engine and check for proper operation and leaks. Shut off the engine and recheck the fluid level.

e) Reconnect the negative battery cable (see Chapter 5, Section 1).

f) Have the front end alignment checked and, if necessary, adjusted.

20 Power steering pump - removal and installation

◆ Refer to illustration 20.3

➡ Note: Use shop towels to protect engine components from spilled fluid during this procedure. Clean any spilled fluid immediately.

1 On V6 models, remove the engine mount bracket on the right side of the engine (see Chapter 2B).

2 Remove the drivebelt (see Chapter 1).

3 Place a clamp on the power steering feed hose to minimize fluid loss when the hose is disconnected, then disconnect the fluid hoses at the pump (see illustration). Note the difference between the pressure and the return (feed) hoses; the return hose is held to the pump with a spring type clamp, and the pressure line has two bolts holding it to the pump body. Cap or plug both hoses to prevent leakage or contamination. Install a new O-ring on the end of the pressure line.

4 Remove the pump mounting bolts and then remove the pump from the engine.

5 Installation is the reverse of removal. Be sure to bleed the power steering system (see Section 21).

20.3 Power steering pump details

1 Pressure line
2 Feed (return) line
3 Mounting bolt locations - right arrow indicates mounting bolt that is out of view in this illustration

21 Power steering system - bleeding

1 Following any operation in which the power steering fluid lines have been disconnected, the power steering system must be bled to remove all air and obtain proper steering performance.

2 With the front wheels in the straight ahead position, check the power steering fluid level (see Chapter 1). If it's low, add fluid until it reaches the lower mark on the reservoir.

3 Start the engine and allow it to run at fast idle. Recheck the fluid level and add more if necessary to reach the lower mark on the reservoir.

4 Bleed the system by turning the wheels from side-to-side, without hitting the stops. This will work the air out of the system. Keep the reservoir full of fluid as this is done.

5 When the air is worked out of the system, return the wheels to the straight ahead position and leave the vehicle running for several more minutes before shutting it off.

6 Road test the vehicle to be sure the steering system is functioning normally and noise free.

7 Recheck the fluid level to be sure it is up to the upper mark on the reservoir while the engine is at normal operating temperature. Add fluid if necessary (see Chapter 1).

22 Wheels and tires - general information

◆ Refer to illustration 22.1

1 All vehicles covered by this manual are equipped with metric-sized fiberglass or steel belted radial tires (see illustration). Use of other size or type of tires may affect the ride and handling of the vehicle. Don't mix different types of tires, such as radials and bias belted, on the same vehicle as handling may be seriously affected. It's recommended that tires be replaced in pairs on the same axle, but if only one tire is being replaced, be sure it's the same size, structure and tread design as the other.

2 Because tire pressure has a substantial effect on handling and wear, the pressure on all tires should be checked at least once a month or before any extended trips (see Chapter 1).

3   Wheels must be replaced if they are bent, dented, leak air, have elongated bolt holes, are heavily rusted, out of vertical symmetry or if the lug nuts won't stay tight. Wheel repairs that use welding or peening are not recommended.

4   Tire and wheel balance is important to the overall handling, braking and performance of the vehicle. Unbalanced wheels can adversely affect handling and ride characteristics as well as tire life. Whenever a tire is installed on a wheel, the tire and wheel should be balanced by a shop with the proper equipment.

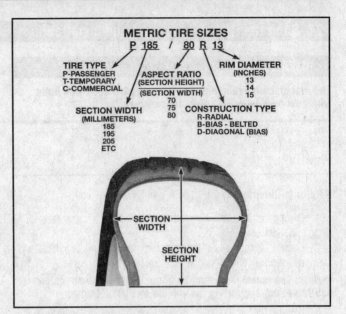

22.1 Metric tire size codes

23 Wheel alignment - general information

▶ **Refer to illustration 23.1**

1   A wheel alignment refers to the adjustments made to the wheels so they are in proper angular relationship to the suspension and the ground. Wheels that are out of proper alignment not only affect steering control, but also increase tire wear. Toe-in can be adjusted on the front and rear wheels. The front and rear camber angles and front caster angles should be checked to determine if any of the suspension components are worn out, bent or damaged (see illustration).

2   Getting the proper wheel alignment is a very exacting process, one in which complicated and expensive machines are necessary to perform the job properly. Because of this, you should have a technician with the proper equipment perform these tasks. We will, however, use this space to give you a basic idea of what is involved with wheel alignment so you can better understand the process and deal intelligently with the shop that does the work.

3   Toe-in is the turning in of the wheels. The purpose of a toe specification is to ensure parallel rolling of the wheels. In a vehicle with zero toe-in, the distance between the front edges of the wheels will be the same as the distance between the rear edges of the wheels. The actual amount of toe-in is normally only a fraction of an inch. At the front end, toe-in is controlled by the tie-rod end position on the tie-rod. At the rear it is adjusted by turning an adjusting cam bolt on the inner end of the rear control arm. Incorrect toe-in will cause the tires to wear improperly by making them scrub against the road surface.

4   Camber is the tilting of the wheels from the vertical when viewed from the front or rear of the vehicle. When the wheels tilt out at the top, the camber is said to be positive (+). When the wheels tilt in at the top the camber is negative (-). The amount of tilt is measured in degrees from vertical and this measurement is called the camber angle. This angle affects the amount of tire tread which contacts the road and compensates for changes in the suspension geometry when the vehicle is cornering or traveling over an undulating surface. Camber isn't adjustable on these vehicles.

5   Caster is the tilting of the top of the steering axis from the vertical. A tilt toward the rear is positive caster and a tilt toward the front is negative caster. Caster isn't adjustable on these vehicles.

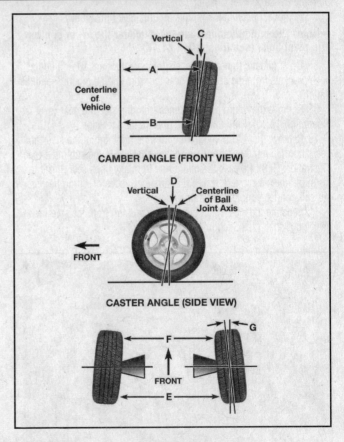

23.1 Camber, caster and toe-in angles

A minus B = C (degrees camber)
D = degrees caster
E minus F = toe-in (measured in inches)
G = toe-in (expressed in degrees)

24 Subframe (front) - removal and installation

❊❊ WARNING:

The manufacturer recommends replacing the subframe bolts with new ones whenever they are removed.

REMOVAL

▶ **Refer to illustrations 24.7, 24.8 and 24.15**

1 Disconnect the cable from the negative battery terminal (see Chapter 5, Section 1).

2 Loosen the front wheel lug nuts, raise the front of the vehicle and support it securely on jackstands. Remove both front wheels.

➡**Note: The jackstands must be behind the front suspension subframe, not supporting the vehicle by the subframe.**

3 Remove the engine splash shield (see Chapter 2A, Section 16).

4 Remove the front section of the exhaust pipe, between the exhaust manifold(s) and the downstream catalytic converter.

5 Remove the lower control arms (see Section 8).

6 On automatic transaxle models, disconnect the shift control cable from the transaxle (see Chapter 7B).

7 Remove the subframe middle mounts (see illustration).

➡**Note: The middle mounts are located near the lower control arm pivot bolts (see illustration 24.15).**

8 On automatic transaxle models, remove the transaxle oil cooler hose brackets from the subframe near the front engine mount (see illustration).

9 Remove the return and feed lines from the steering gear (see illustration 19.10). Plug the lines to prevent fluid leakage.

10 Remove the return line from under the right end of the steering gear and then remove it from the anchor attached to the subframe (see illustration 19.9). Release the return line from any clips securing it to the subframe. Also check to see that no other hoses or wiring harnesses are still connected to the subframe.

11 Separate the steering column universal joint from the steering gear input shaft (see Section 19).

12 Using two floor jacks, support the subframe. Position one jack on each side of the subframe, midway between the front and rear corners (see illustration 24.15).

13 Support the engine with an engine support fixture or an engine hoist (an engine support fixture is recommended, as it doesn't have legs that extend under the vehicle that would get in the way). Connect the sling or chain to the left end (driver's side) of the engine, not to the lifting eye on the transaxle. Use the threaded hole(s) in the left end (driver's side) of the cylinder head(s) to attach the sling or chain. Place a washer between the bolt head(s) and the chain, and tighten the bolt securely. Take up the slack in the chain, but don't lift the engine.

❊❊ WARNING:

DO NOT place any part of your body under the engine when it's supported only by a hoist or other lifting/support device.

14 Remove all of the powertrain mounts except the right side (drive-belt end) mount (see Chapter 2A).

15 With the jacks sufficiently supporting the subframe, remove all subframe-to-chassis mounting bolts (see illustration).

16 Carefully lower the jacks until the subframe is resting on the ground.

➡**Note: The steering gear and stabilizer bar will still be attached to the subframe when it's lowered.**

INSTALLATION

17 Installation is the reverse of removal, noting the following points:

a) *Replace the subframe bolts with new ones. Align the reference marks on the subframe then tighten the subframe mounting bolts to the torque listed in this Chapter's Specifications.*

➡**Note: Use a long drift tool (or equivalent) in the alignment holes in the rear corners of the subframe, subframe brackets and chassis to aid alignment. Refer to Section 19 for the index marks on the rear corners of the subframe (see illustrations 19.13a and 19.13b).**

24.7 Mounting bolts for the subframe middle mount (one on each side)

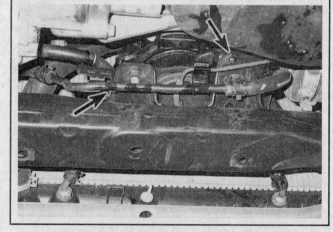

24.8 Remove the transaxle cooler line brackets from the subframe - four-cylinder shown, V6 is similar

b) Check the power steering fluid and automatic transaxle (if equipped) fluid levels, adding as necessary (see Chapter 1).

c) Tighten the all other suspension and steering fasteners to the torque listed in this Chapter's Specifications.

d) Reconnect the negative battery cable (see Chapter 5, Section 1).

e) Have the front end alignment checked and, if necessary, adjusted.

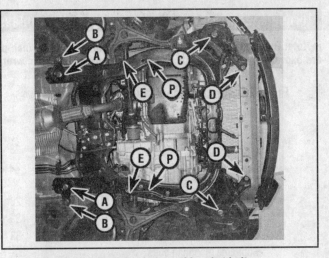

24.15 Subframe mounting bolts and bracket bolt designations - (E) is the location for the middle mount upper and side bolts and (P) is for the floor jack pad locations (see this Chapter's Specifications)

Specifications

General

Power steering fluid type	See Chapter 1

Torque specifications	Ft-lbs (unless otherwise indicated)	Nm

➡ **Note: One foot-pound (ft-lb) of torque is equivalent to 12 inch-pounds (in-lbs) of torque. Torque values below approximately 15 ft-lbs are expressed in inch-pounds, since most foot-pound torque wrenches are not accurate at these smaller values.**

Front suspension

	Ft-lbs	Nm
Damper fork pinch bolt*		
2007 and earlier models	32	43
2008 and later models	36	49
Damper fork-to-lower control arm		
through-bolt/nut*	47	64
Lower control arm inner pivot bolt*	47	64
Lower control arm inner bolt (front)*		
2007 and earlier models	61	83
2008 and later models	65	88
Shock absorber-to-body mounting nuts*		
8 x 1.25	16	22
10 x 1.25		
2007 and earlier models	37	50
2008 and later models	41	55
Damper shaft nut*	22	29

*Use new fasteners

Torque specifications	Ft-lbs (unless otherwise indicated)	Nm

➡ **Note:** One foot-pound (ft-lb) of torque is equivalent to 12 inch-pounds (in-lbs) of torque. Torque values below approximately 15 ft-lbs are expressed in inch-pounds, since most foot-pound torque wrenches are not accurate at these smaller values.

Front suspension (continued)

	Ft-lbs	Nm
Stabilizer bar link nut*		
2007 and earlier models		
Upper	28	38
Lower	22	29
2008 and later models		
Upper	28	38
Loewr	29	39
Stabilizer bar bracket bolts*	33	44
Subframe mounting bolts		
Rear mounting bolt and bracket bolt (see illustration 24.15)		
Bolt A	76	103
Bolt B	69	94
Front mounting bolt and bracket bolt (see illustration 24.15)		
Bolt C	76	103
Bolt D	40	54
Middle mount upper and side bolts (see illustration 24.7)		
Bolt 1	33	45
Bolts 2	36	49
Lower balljoint nut*	58 to 65	78 to 88
Upper balljoint nut*		
2007 and earlier models	29 to 35	39 to 47
2008 and later models*	33 to 38	44 to 52
Upper control arm pivot bolts*	23	31
Wheel speed sensor bracket nut	86 in-lbs	10

Rear suspension

	Ft-lbs	Nm
Lower arm inner pivot bolt*	43	59
Lower arm-to-knuckle bolt/nut*	43	59
Control arm inner pivot bolt/nut*	42	57
Control arm-to-knuckle nut*	43	59
Trailing arm-to-chassis bolt*	43	59
Trailing arm-to-knuckle bolt*	43	59
Leading arm inner pivot bolt*	43	59
Leading arm-to-knuckle bolt*	43	59
Upper arm inner pivot bolt*	43	59
Upper arm-to-knuckle castle nut*		
2007 and earlier models	36 to 43	49 to 59
2008 and later models*	51 to 58	69 to 78
Hub nut (2007 and earlier models)*	134	181
Hub and bearing assembly-to-knuckle bolts		
(2008 and later models)	72	98

*Use new fasteners

Torque specifications	Ft-lbs (unless otherwise indicated)	Nm
Stabilizer bar link nut*		
Upper		
2007 and earlier models	29	39
2008 and later models*	33	44
Lower	28	38
Stabilizer bar bracket bolts*	16	22
Shock absorber-to-knuckle bolt*		
2007 and earlier models	43	59
2008 and later models	47	64
Shock absorber upper mounting nuts*		
2007 and earlier models	37	50
2008 and later models	41	55
Damper shaft nut*	22	29
Airbag system		
Airbag module Torx bolts	86 in-lbs	10

Steering system

Power steering pump mounting bolts	16	22
Power steering line bolts	96 in-lbs	11
Slider shaft pinch bolt*	21	28
Steering column fasteners*	144 in-lbs	16
Steering gear mounting bolts (left side)*		
2007 and earlier models	43	59
2008 and later models	54	74
Steering gear mounting clamp bolts (right side)*	28	38
Steering wheel bolt	29	39
Tie-rod end-to-steering knuckle nut		
2007 and earlier models	33	44
2008 and later models	40	54

*Use new fasteners

Notes

11

BODY

Section

1 General information

These models feature a unibody layout, using a floor pan with front and rear frame side rails which support the body components, and front and rear subframes which support suspension systems and other mechanical components.

Certain components are particularly vulnerable to accident damage and can be unbolted and repaired or replaced. Among these parts are the body moldings, bumpers, front fenders, the hood and trunk lid and all glass.

Only general body maintenance practices and body panel repair procedures within the scope of the do-it-yourselfer are included in this Chapter.

2 Body - maintenance

1 The condition of your vehicle's body is very important, because the resale value depends a great deal on it. It's much more difficult to repair a neglected or damaged body than it is to repair mechanical components. The hidden areas of the body, such as the wheel wells, the frame and the engine compartment, are equally important, although they don't require as frequent attention as the rest of the body.

2 Once a year, or every 12,000 miles, it's a good idea to have the underside of the body steam cleaned. All traces of dirt and oil will be removed and the area can then be inspected carefully for rust, damaged brake lines, frayed electrical wires, damaged cables and other problems.

3 At the same time, clean the engine and the engine compartment with a steam cleaner or water soluble degreaser.

4 The wheel wells should be given close attention, since undercoating can peel away and stones and dirt thrown up by the tires can cause the paint to chip and flake, allowing rust to set in. If rust is found, clean down to the bare metal and apply an anti-rust paint.

5 The body should be washed about once a week. Wet the vehicle thoroughly to soften the dirt, then wash it down with a soft sponge and plenty of clean soapy water. If the surplus dirt is not washed off very carefully, it can wear down the paint.

6 Spots of tar or asphalt thrown up from the road should be removed with a cloth soaked in solvent.

7 Once every six months, wax the body and chrome trim. If a chrome cleaner is used to remove rust from any of the vehicle's plated parts, remember that the cleaner also removes part of the chrome, so use it sparingly.

3 Vinyl trim - maintenance

Don't clean vinyl trim with detergents, caustic soap or petroleum based cleaners. Plain soap and water works just fine, with a soft brush to clean dirt that may be ingrained. Wash the vinyl as frequently as the rest of the vehicle.

After cleaning, application of a high quality rubber and vinyl protectant will help prevent oxidation and cracks. The protectant can also be applied to weather-stripping, vacuum lines and rubber hoses, which often fail as a result of chemical degradation, and to the tires.

4 Upholstery and carpets - maintenance

1 Every three months remove the carpets or mats and clean the interior of the vehicle (more frequently if necessary). Vacuum the upholstery and carpets to remove loose dirt and dust.

2 Leather upholstery requires special care. Stains should be removed with warm water and a very mild soap solution. Use a clean, damp cloth to remove the soap, then wipe again with a dry cloth. Never use alcohol, gasoline, nail polish remover or thinner to clean leather upholstery.

3 After cleaning, regularly treat leather upholstery with a leather wax. Never use car wax on leather upholstery.

4 In areas where the interior of the vehicle is subject to bright sunlight, cover leather seats with a sheet if the vehicle is to be left out for any length of time.

5 Body repair - minor damage

PLASTIC BODY PANELS

The following repair procedures are for minor scratches and gouges. Repair of more serious damage should be left to a dealer service department or qualified auto body shop. Below is a list of the equipment and materials necessary to perform the following repair procedures on plastic body panels. Although a specific brand of material may be mentioned, it should be noted that equivalent products from other manufacturers may be used instead.

Wax, grease and silicone removing solvent
Cloth-backed body tape
Sanding discs
Drill motor with three-inch disc holder
Hand sanding block
Rubber squeegees
Sandpaper
Non-porous mixing palette
Wood paddle or putty knife
Curved tooth body file
Flexible parts repair material

Flexible panels (front and rear bumper fascia)

1 Remove the damaged panel, if necessary or desirable. In most cases, repairs can be carried out with the panel installed.

2 Clean the area(s) to be repaired with a wax, grease and silicone removing solvent applied with a water-dampened cloth.

3 If the damage is structural, that is, if it extends through the panel, clean the backside of the panel area to be repaired as well. Wipe dry.

4 Sand the rear surface about 1-1/2 inches beyond the break.

5 Cut two pieces of fiberglass cloth large enough to overlap the break by about 1-1/2 inches. Cut only to the required length.

6 Mix the adhesive from the repair kit according to the instructions included with the kit, and apply a layer of the mixture approximately 1/8-inch thick on the backside of the panel. Overlap the break by at least 1-1/2 inches.

7 Apply one piece of fiberglass cloth to the adhesive and cover the cloth with additional adhesive. Apply a second piece of fiberglass cloth to the adhesive and immediately cover the cloth with additional adhesive in sufficient quantity to fill the weave.

8 Allow the repair to cure for 20 to 30 minutes at 60-degrees to 80-degrees F.

9 If necessary, trim the excess repair material at the edge.

10 Remove all of the paint film over and around the area(s) to be repaired. The repair material should not overlap the painted surface.

11 With a drill motor and a sanding disc (or a rotary file), cut a "V" along the break line approximately 1/2-inch wide. Remove all dust and loose particles from the repair area.

12 Mix and apply the repair material. Apply a light coat first over the damaged area; then continue applying material until it reaches a level slightly higher than the surrounding finish.

13 Cure the mixture for 20 to 30 minutes at 60-degrees to 80-degrees F.

14 Roughly establish the contour of the area being repaired with a body file. If low areas or pits remain, mix and apply additional adhesive.

15 Block sand the damaged area with sandpaper to establish the actual contour of the surrounding surface.

16 If desired, the repaired area can be temporarily protected with several light coats of primer. Because of the special paints and techniques required for flexible body panels, it is recommended that the vehicle be taken to a paint shop for completion of the body repair.

STEEL BODY PANELS

▶ **See photo sequence**

Repair of minor scratches

17 If the scratch is superficial and does not penetrate to the metal of the body, repair is very simple. Lightly rub the scratched area with a fine rubbing compound to remove loose paint and built-up wax. Rinse the area with clean water.

18 Apply touch-up paint to the scratch, using a small brush. Continue to apply thin layers of paint until the surface of the paint in the scratch is level with the surrounding paint. Allow the new paint at least two weeks to harden, then blend it into the surrounding paint by rubbing with a very fine rubbing compound. Finally, apply a coat of wax to the scratch area.

19 If the scratch has penetrated the paint and exposed the metal of the body, causing the metal to rust, a different repair technique is required. Remove all loose rust from the bottom of the scratch with a pocket knife, then apply rust inhibiting paint to prevent the formation of rust in the future. Using a rubber or nylon applicator, coat the scratched area with glaze-type filler. If required, the filler can be mixed with thinner to provide a very thin paste, which is ideal for filling narrow scratches. Before the glaze filler in the scratch hardens, wrap a piece of smooth cotton cloth around the tip of a finger. Dip the cloth in thinner and then quickly wipe it along the surface of the scratch. This will ensure that the surface of the filler is slightly hollow. The scratch can now be painted over as described earlier in this section.

Repair of dents

20 When repairing dents, the first job is to pull the dent out until the affected area is as close as possible to its original shape. There is no point in trying to restore the original shape completely as the metal in the damaged area will have stretched on impact and cannot be restored to its original contours. It is better to bring the level of the dent up to a point which is about 1/8-inch below the level of the surrounding metal. In cases where the dent is very shallow, it is not worth trying to pull it out at all.

21 If the back side of the dent is accessible, it can be hammered out gently from behind using a soft-face hammer. While doing this, hold a block of wood firmly against the opposite side of the metal to absorb the hammer blows and prevent the metal from being stretched.

22 If the dent is in a section of the body which has double layers, or some other factor makes it inaccessible from behind, a different technique is required. Drill several small holes through the metal inside the damaged area, particularly in the deeper sections. Screw long, self-tapping screws into the holes just enough for them to get a good grip in the metal. Now the dent can be pulled out by pulling on the protruding heads of the screws with locking pliers.

23 The next stage of repair is the removal of paint from the damaged area and from an inch or so of the surrounding metal. This is done with a wire brush or sanding disk in a drill motor, although it can be done just as effectively by hand with sandpaper. To complete the preparation for filling, score the surface of the bare metal with a screwdriver or the tang of a file, or drill small holes in the affected area. This will provide a good grip for the filler material. To complete the repair, see the subsection on filling and painting later in this Section.

Repair of rust holes or gashes

24 Remove all paint from the affected area and from an inch or so of the surrounding metal using a sanding disk or wire brush mounted in a drill motor. If these are not available, a few sheets of sandpaper will do the job just as effectively.

25 With the paint removed, you will be able to determine the severity of the corrosion and decide whether to replace the whole panel, if possible, or repair the affected area. New body panels are not as expensive as most people think and it is often quicker to install a new panel than to repair large areas of rust.

26 Remove all trim pieces from the affected area except those which will act as a guide to the original shape of the damaged body, such as headlight shells, etc. Using metal snips or a hacksaw blade, remove all loose metal and any other metal that is badly affected by rust. Hammer the edges of the hole in to create a slight depression for the filler material.

27 Wire brush the affected area to remove the powdery rust from the surface of the metal. If the back of the rusted area is accessible, treat it with rust inhibiting paint.

28 Before filling is done, block the hole in some way. This can be done with sheet metal riveted or screwed into place, or by stuffing the hole with wire mesh.

29 Once the hole is blocked off, the affected area can be filled and painted. See the following subsection on filling and painting.

These photos illustrate a method of repairing simple dents. They are intended to supplement Body repair - minor damage in this Chapter and should not be used as the sole instructions for body repair on these vehicles.

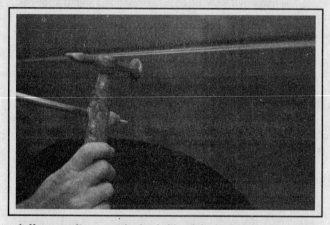

1 If you can't access the backside of the body panel to hammer out the dent, pull it out with a slide-hammer-type dent puller. Tap with a hammer near the edge of the dent to help 'pop' the metal back to its original shape, about 1/8-inch below the surface of the surrounding metal

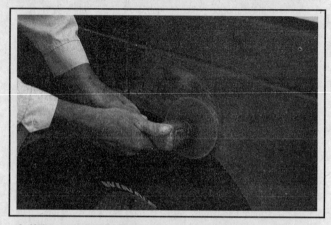

2 Using coarse-grit sandpaper, remove the paint down to the bare metal. Clean the repair area with wax/silicone remover.

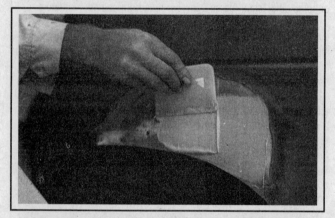

3 Following label instructions, mix up a batch of plastic filler and hardener, then quickly press it into the metal with a plastic applicator. Work the filler until it matches the original contour and is slightly above the surrounding metal

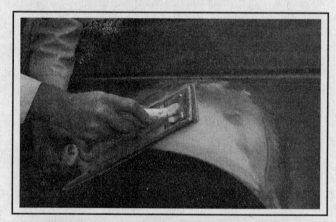

4 Let the filler harden until you can just dent it with your fingernail. File, then sand the filler down until it's smooth and even. Work down to finer grits of sandpaper - always using a board or block - ending up with 360 or 400 grit

5 When the area is smooth to the touch, clean the area and mask around it. Apply several layers of primer to the area. A professional-type spray gun is being used here, but aerosol spray primer works fine

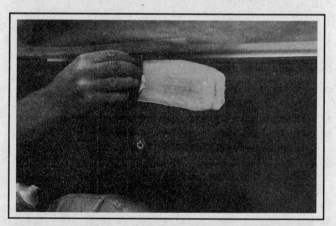

6 Fill imperfections or scratches with glazing compound. Sand with 360 or 400-grit and re-spray. Finish sand the primer with 600 grit, clean thoroughly, then apply the finish coat. Don't attempt to rub out or wax the repair area until the paint has dried completely (at least two weeks)

Filling and painting

30 Many types of body fillers are available, but generally speaking, body repair kits which contain filler paste and a tube of resin hardener are best for this type of repair work. A wide, flexible plastic or nylon applicator will be necessary for imparting a smooth and contoured finish to the surface of the filler material. Mix up a small amount of filler on a clean piece of wood or cardboard (use the hardener sparingly). Follow the manufacturer's instructions on the package, otherwise the filler will set incorrectly.

31 Using the applicator, apply the filler paste to the prepared area. Draw the applicator across the surface of the filler to achieve the desired contour and to level the filler surface. As soon as a contour that approximates the original one is achieved, stop working the paste. If you continue, the paste will begin to stick to the applicator. Continue to add thin layers of paste at 20-minute intervals until the level of the filler is just above the surrounding metal.

32 Once the filler has hardened, the excess can be removed with a body file. From then on, progressively finer grades of sandpaper should be used, starting with a 180-grit paper and finishing with 600-grit wet-or-dry paper. Always wrap the sandpaper around a flat rubber or wooden block, otherwise the surface of the filler will not be completely flat. During the sanding of the filler surface, the wet-or-dry paper should be periodically rinsed in water. This will ensure that a very smooth finish is produced in the final stage.

33 At this point, the repair area should be surrounded by a ring of bare metal, which in turn should be encircled by the finely feathered edge of good paint. Rinse the repair area with clean water until all of the dust produced by the sanding operation is gone.

34 Spray the entire area with a light coat of primer. This will reveal any imperfections in the surface of the filler. Repair the imperfections with fresh filler paste or glaze filler and once more smooth the surface with sandpaper. Repeat this spray-and-repair procedure until you are satisfied that the surface of the filler and the feathered edge of the paint are perfect. Rinse the area with clean water and allow it to dry completely.

35 The repair area is now ready for painting. Spray painting must be carried out in a warm, dry, windless and dust free atmosphere. These conditions can be created if you have access to a large indoor work area, but if you are forced to work in the open, you will have to pick the day very carefully. If you are working indoors, dousing the floor in the work area with water will help settle the dust, which would otherwise be in the air. If the repair area is confined to one body panel, mask off the surrounding panels. This will help minimize the effects of a slight mismatch in paint color. Trim pieces such as chrome strips, door handles, etc., will also need to be masked off or removed. Use masking tape and several thickness of newspaper for the masking operations.

36 Before spraying, shake the paint can thoroughly, then spray a test area until the spray painting technique is mastered. Cover the repair area with a thick coat of primer. The thickness should be built up using several thin layers of primer rather than one thick one. Using 600-grit wet-or-dry sandpaper, rub down the surface of the primer until it is very smooth. While doing this, the work area should be thoroughly rinsed with water and the wet-or-dry sandpaper periodically rinsed as well. Allow the primer to dry before spraying additional coats.

37 Spray on the top coat, again building up the thickness by using several thin layers of paint. Begin spraying in the center of the repair area and then, using a circular motion, work out until the whole repair area and about two inches of the surrounding original paint is covered. Remove all masking material 10 to 15 minutes after spraying on the final coat of paint. Allow the new paint at least two weeks to harden, then use a very fine rubbing compound to blend the edges of the new paint into the existing paint. Finally, apply a coat of wax.

6   Body repair - major damage

1   Major damage must be repaired by an auto body shop specifically equipped to perform unibody repairs. These shops have the specialized equipment required to do the job properly.

2   If the damage is extensive, the body must be checked for proper alignment or the vehicle's handling characteristics may be adversely affected and other components may wear at an accelerated rate.

3   Due to the fact that all of the major body components (hood, fenders, etc.) are separate and replaceable units, any seriously damaged components should be replaced rather than repaired. Sometimes the components can be found in a wrecking yard that specializes in used vehicle components, often at considerable savings over the cost of new parts.

7   Hinges and locks - maintenance

Once every 3000 miles, or every three months, the hinges and latch assemblies on the doors, hood and trunk should be given a few drops of light oil or lock lubricant. The door latch strikers should also be lubricated with a thin coat of grease to reduce wear and ensure free movement. Lubricate the door and trunk locks with spray-on graphite lubricant.

8   Windshield and fixed glass - replacement

Replacement of the windshield and fixed glass requires the use of special fast-setting adhesive/caulk materials and some specialized tools and techniques. These operations should be left to a dealer service department or a shop specializing in glass work.

9 Hood - removal, installation and adjustment

REMOVAL AND INSTALLATION

▸ **Refer to illustrations 9.2 and 9.4**

➡**Note: The hood is heavy and somewhat awkward to remove and install - at least two people should perform this procedure.**

1 Use blankets or pads to cover the fenders and cowl areas. This will protect the body and paint as the hood is lifted off.

2 Scribe or draw alignment marks around the bolt heads to ensure proper alignment during installation (see illustration).

3 Disconnect any cables or wire harnesses which will interfere with removal. On V6 models, unbolt the hood support strut from the hood.

➡**Note: On 2006 and later V6 models, the hood support strut can be disconnected from the lower pivot by using a small screwdriver to pull out the metal clip and then pulling the bottom of the strut from the pivot ball.**

4 Have an assistant help you support the weight of the hood. Remove the hinge-to-hood bolts (see illustration).

5 Lift off the hood.

6 Installation is the reverse of removal. If you position the hood so that the hinges fit within the scribe marks you made before loosening the bolts, in the same location they were in prior to removal, then the hood should still be aligned. Of course, if you're installing a new hood, or forgot to scribe the hinge positions, then you'll need to readjust the hood position.

ADJUSTMENT

▸ **Refer to illustration 9.11**

7 You can adjust the hood fore-and-aft and right-and-left by means of the elongated holes in the hinges.

8 Scribe a line around the entire hinge plate so you can judge the amount of movement.

9 Loosen the bolts and move the hood into correct alignment. Move it only a little at a time. Tighten the hinge bolts or nuts and carefully lower the hood to check the alignment.

10 If necessary after installation, the entire hood latch assembly can be adjusted up-and-down as well as from side-to-side on the upper radiator support so the hood closes securely and is flush with the fenders (see illustration 10.3b). To do this, scribe a line around the hood latch mounting bolts to provide a reference point. Then loosen the bolts and reposition the latch assembly as necessary. Following adjustment, retighten the mounting bolts.

11 Adjust the vertical height of the leading edge of the hood by screwing the edge cushions in or out so that the hood, when closed, is flush with the fenders (see illustration).

12 The hood latch assembly, as well as the hinges, should be periodically lubricated with white lithium-base grease to prevent sticking and wear.

9.2 Scribe or draw alignment marks around the hood hinges to ensure proper alignment of the hood when it's reinstalled

9.4 With the help of an assistant, remove the four hinge bolts then lift off the hood

9.11 To adjust the vertical height of the leading edge of the hood so it's flush with the fenders, turn each edge cushion clockwise (to lower the hood) or counterclockwise (to raise the hood)

10 Hood release latch and cable - removal and installation

LATCH

▸ **Refer to illustrations 10.2, 10.3a, 10.3b and 10.4**

1 If you're working on a coupe model, remove the front bumper cover (see Section 11).

2 If you're working on a sedan model, remove the radiator cover (see illustration).

3 Remove the hood latch cover (see illustration), then scribe a line around the latch to aid alignment when installing, detach the latch retaining bolts from the radiator support (see illustration) and remove the latch.

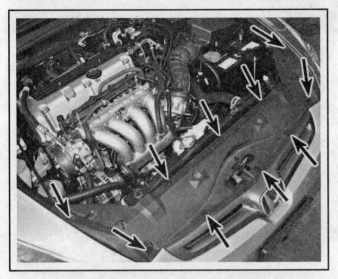

10.2 Remove the fasteners securing the radiator cover

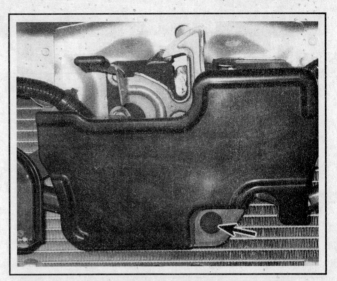

10.3a Remove the fastener securing the hood latch cover

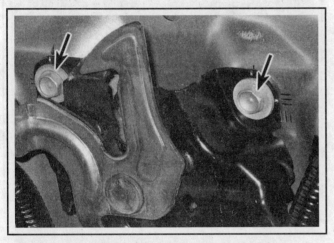

10.3b Remove the two bolts securing the hood latch

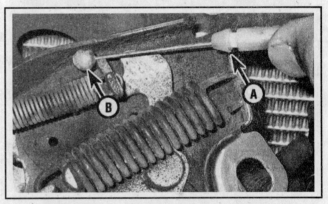

10.4 Detach the cable (A) then unhook the end from the latch (B)

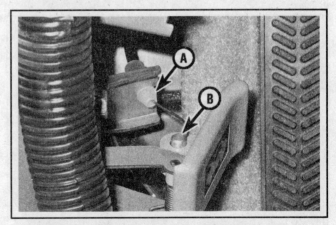

10.8 Detach the cable (A) then unhook the end from the latch (B)

4   Disconnect the hood release cable by disengaging the cable from the latch assembly (see illustration).

5   Installation is reverse of the removal.

➡ Note: Adjust the latch so the hood engages securely when closed and the hood bumpers are slightly compressed.

CABLE

▶ **Refer to illustration 10.8**

6   Disconnect the hood release cable from the latch assembly (see illustration 10.4), then detach the cable from any retaining clips securing it to the radiator support.

7   Attach a piece of wire or string to the latch end of the cable.

8   Working in the passenger's compartment, remove the driver's side kick panel. Detach the cable from the hood release lever (see illustration).

9   Remove the radiator upper support bracket, then detach the cable from the retaining clip.

10 Pull the cable into the passenger compartment. Ensure that the new cable has a grommet attached, then remove the old cable from the wire and replace it with the new cable.

11 Pull the wire back through the body.

12 Installation is the reverse of the removal.

➡ Note: Push on the grommet to seat it in the body completely.

11 Bumper covers - removal and installation

FRONT

▶ **Refer to illustrations 11.2**

1 Raise the vehicle and support it securely on jackstands.

2 Working under the vehicle, detach the bolts or screws securing the lower edges of the bumper cover (see illustration).

3 Working in the front wheel opening, remove the retaining screw securing the bumper cover to the fenderwell.

4 Remove the fasteners securing the radiator cover, then remove the cover (see illustration 10.2).

5 Pull the bumper cover out and away from the vehicle.

6 Installation is the reverse of removal.

REAR

▶ **Refer to illustrations 11.8, 11.9 and 11.10**

7 Raise the vehicle and support it securely on jackstands.

8 Working under the vehicle, detach the plastic clips and screws securing the lower edge of the bumper cover (see illustration).

9 Remove the screws securing the bumper cover in the rear wheel openings (see illustration).

10 Open the trunk and remove the screws and clips securing the upper edge of the bumper cover (see illustration). Pull the bumper cover out and away from the vehicle.

11 Installation is the reverse of removal.

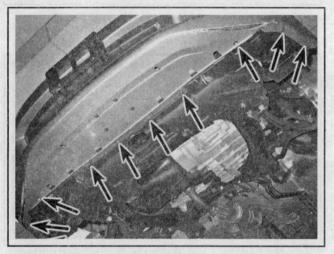

11.2 Bumper cover lower fasteners

11.8 Remove the bumper cover lower mounting fasteners

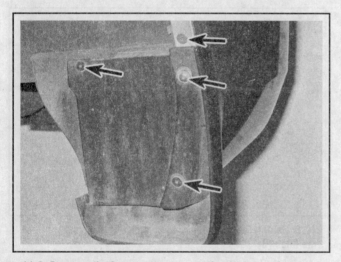

11.9 Remove the bumper cover mounting fasteners from the rear wheel openings

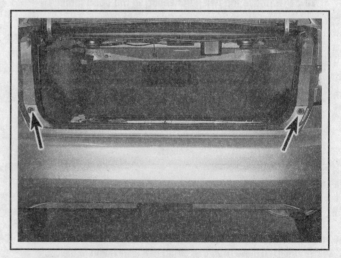

11.10 Remove the fasteners along the upper edge of the bumper cover

12 Front fender - removal and installation

◗ **Refer to illustrations 12.3, 12.4, 12.5a, 12.5b, 12.5c, 12.5d and 12.5e**

1 Loosen the wheel lug nuts, raise the front of the vehicle and support it securely on jackstands. Remove the wheel.

2 Remove the front bumper cover (see Section 11). Remove the headlight housing (see Chapter 12).

3 Remove the fasteners securing the inner fender splash shield and detach the shield (see illustration).

4 Remove the front fender hood seal (see illustration).

5 Remove the fender mounting bolts (see illustrations).

6 Detach the fender. It's a good idea to have an assistant support the fender while it's being moved away from the vehicle to prevent damage to the surrounding body panels.

7 Installation is the reverse of removal.

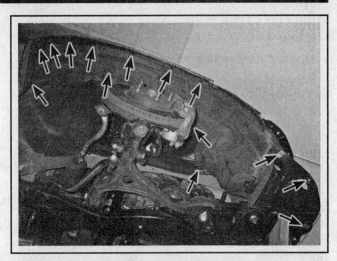

12.3 Remove the fasteners retaining the inner fender splash shield

12.4 The front fender hood seal is secured by two fasteners

12.5a Remove the bolt and detach the bracket behind the headlight

12.5b The lower rear corner of the fender is retained by a bolt

12.5c The upper rear corner of the fender is retained to the A-pillar with a bolt

12.5d Remove the bolts . . .

12.5e . . . along the top of the fender

13 Trunk lid latch and lock cylinder - removal and installation

TRUNK LID LATCH

▶ **Refer to illustration 13.3**

1   Open the trunk and scribe a line around the trunk lid latch assembly for a reference point to aid the installation procedure.

2   If you're working on a vehicle equipped with a power latch, disconnect the electrical connector.

3   Detach the two retaining bolts and remove the latch (see illustration).

4   Remove the end of the latch release cable from the latch.

5   Installation is the reverse of removal.

13.3 Trunk lid latch retaining bolts

TRUNK LOCK CYLINDER

▶ **Refer to illustration 13.6**

6   Open the trunk and look upward through the trunk lid access hole behind the right taillight. Remove the lock cylinder rod from its clip and remove the lock's mounting bolt (see illustration). On models so equipped, disconnect the electrical connector from the lock.

7   Twist the lock about 45 degrees and remove it from the trunk.

8   Installation is the reverse of removal.

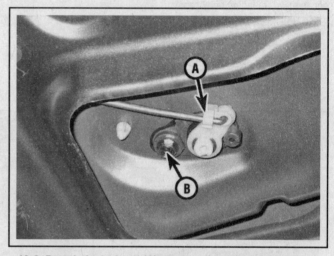

13.6 Detach the lock rod (A), then remove the bolt (B)

14 Trunk lid - removal and installation

➡ **Note: The trunk lid is heavy and somewhat awkward to remove and install - at least two people should perform this procedure.**

REMOVAL AND INSTALLATION

▶ **Refer to illustrations 14.3 and 14.4**

1   Open the trunk lid and cover the edges of the trunk compartment with pads or cloths to protect the painted surfaces when the lid is removed.

2   Unplug the electrical connectors for the license plate lights, brake lights, and trunk lock actuator, and remove the wire harness and actuator cable from the trunk lid (see Section 15). Tie string or wire to the cables before withdrawing them from the trunk lid so they can be pulled back into the trunk lid when it's reinstalled.

3   Scribe or draw alignment marks around the trunk hinges (see illustration).

4   Remove the hinge-to-trunk lid bolts from both sides and lift off the trunk lid (see illustration).

5   Installation is the reverse of removal. Be sure to align the hinge flanges with the marks made on the trunk lid during removal.

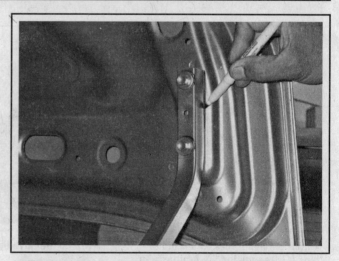

14.3 Draw around the hinge with a marking pen before loosening the bolts to ensure proper alignment of the trunk lid when it's reinstalled

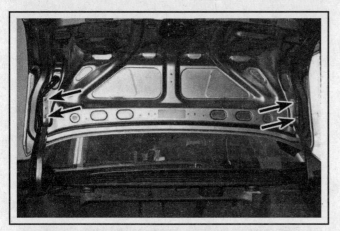

14.4 With an assistant helping you support the trunk lid, remove the four trunk lid retaining bolts

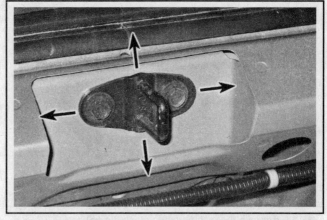

14.7 To adjust the trunk lid striker, loosen the bolts and move the striker as necessary

ADJUSTMENT

♦ Refer to illustration 14.7

6   After installation, close the lid and see if it's in proper alignment with the adjacent body surfaces. Fore-and-aft and side-to-side adjustments of the lid are controlled by the position of the hinge bolts in the slots. To adjust it, loosen the hinge bolts, reposition the lid and retighten the bolts.

7   The height of the rear of the lid in relation to the surrounding body panels when closed can be adjusted by loosening the lock striker bolts, moving the striker up/down or left/right, then re-tightening the bolts (see illustration).

➡**Note: Make a reference mark around the striker before making adjustments.**

8   Finally, you can fine-tune the height of the trailing edge of the trunk lid by turning the trunk lid edge cushions (round rubber bumpers, one on each side) in or out to lower or raise the trunk as necessary.

15 Trunk release and fuel door cable - removal and installation

RELEASE LEVER

♦ Refer to illustrations 15.1a, 15.1b, 15.1c and 15.1d

1   Detach the lower trim panel for access to the release cable and lever, then remove the lever retaining bolt (see illustrations). Detach the cable from the release assembly.

2   Installation is the reverse of removal.

CABLES

♦ Refer to illustration 15.4

3   Working in the trunk, remove the plastic clips securing the driver's side and rear inside finishing panels to allow access to the fuel door assembly.

15.1a Pry off the plastic trim cover . . .

15.1b . . . then remove the fastener . . .

15.1c . . . and detach the lower trim panel

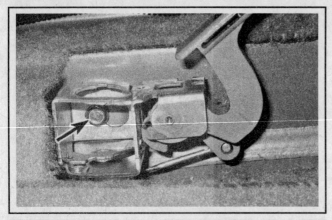

15.1d Remove the fastener and detach the release lever assembly

15.4 From inside the trunk, rotate the fuel door release cable 90-degrees so the tabs line up with the slots in the body, then withdraw it

4   Twist the cable 90-degrees to align the tabs on the striker assembly with the slots in the body and withdraw it into the rear compartment (see illustration). Detach the trunk release cable from the trunk lid latch (see Section 13).

5   Remove the left door sill plate, the rear seat and the left rear quar-ter trim panel. Pull the carpet back and detach all the cable retaining clips.

6   Working in the trunk, pull the cable towards the rear of the vehicle.

7   Installation is the reverse of removal.

16 Door trim panels - removal and installation

FRONT DOORS

▸ **Refer to illustrations 16.1, 16.2, 16.3a, 16.3b, 16.4 and 16.6**

1   Remove the inside door handle trim cover, then remove the mounting screws (see illustration).

2   Remove the pull handle trim cover, then remove the mounting screw (see illustration).

3   Remove the power window switch, then disconnect the electrical connectors from the power window switch (see illustrations).

4   Remove the door trim panel using a door panel removal tool (see illustration). Start from the bottom of the trim panel and work around the perimeter until all the fasteners have been released from the door.

5   Lift the trim panel up to disengage the panel from the upper door ridge, unplug any electrical connectors, disconnect the inner handle cable, and remove the panel.

6   For access to the door outside handle or the door window regulator inside the door, raise the window fully, then carefully peel back the plastic watershield (see illustration).

7   Installation is the reverse of removal.

REAR DOORS

8   Remove the inside door handle trim cover. Remove the mounting screws (see illustration 16.1).

9   Remove the power window switch, then disconnect the electrical connector from the power window switch.

16.1 Remove the door handle trim cover then remove the screw from the inside pull handle area

16.2 Pry up the door handle trim cover then remove the screw from the inside pull handle area

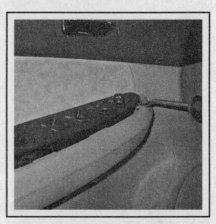

16.3a Carefully pry the switch assembly out of the pull handle . . .

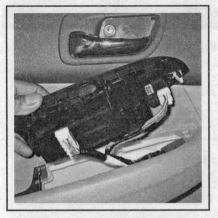

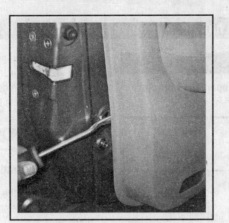

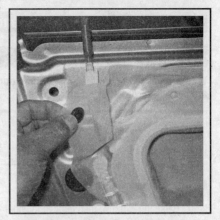

16.3b . . . and disconnect the electrical connectors from the switch assembly

16.4 Carefully pry the clips free so the door trim panel can be removed

16.6 Peel back the plastic water shield to gain access to the outside handle or window regulator

10 Remove the pull handle trim cover, then remove the pull handle retaining screw.

11 Remove the door trim panel using a door panel removal tool. Start from the bottom of the trim panel and work around the perimeter until all the fasteners have been released from the door.

12 Lift the trim panel up to disengage the panel from the upper door ridge, unplug any electrical connectors, disconnect the inner handle cable, and remove the panel.

13 For access to the door outside handle or the door window regulator inside the door, raise the window fully, then carefully peel back the plastic watershield.

17 Door - removal and installation

➡Note: The door is heavy and somewhat awkward to remove and install - at least two people should perform this procedure.

REMOVAL AND INSTALLATION

♦ Refer to illustrations 17.6 and 17.8

1 Lower the window completely in the door, then disconnect the cable from the negative battery terminal (see Chapter 5, Section 1).

2 Open the door all the way and support it on jacks or blocks covered with rags to prevent damaging the paint.

3 Remove the door trim panel and water deflector as described in Section 16.

4 Disconnect all electrical connections, ground wires and harness retaining clips from the door.

➡Note: It is a good idea to label all connections to aid the reassembly process.

5 From the door side, detach the rubber conduit between the body and the door. Then pull the wiring harness through the conduit hole and remove it from the door.

6 Remove the door stop strut (see illustration).

7 Mark around the door hinges with a pen or a scribe to facilitate realignment during reassembly.

8 With an assistant holding the door, remove the hinge-to-door bolts (see illustration) and lift the door off.

9 Installation is the reverse of removal.

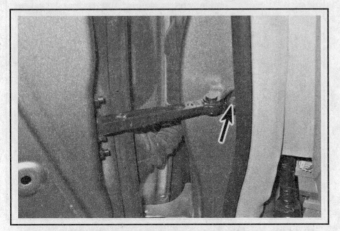

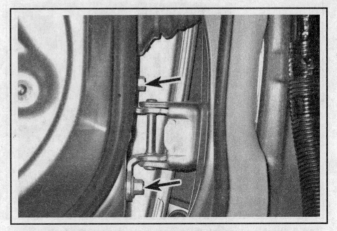

17.6 Remove the door strut retaining bolt

17.8 Remove the door hinge bolts

18 Door latch, lock cylinder and handles - removal and installation

✳✳ CAUTION:

Wear gloves when working inside the door openings to protect against cuts from sharp metal edges.

DOOR LATCH

♦ **Refer to illustrations 18.3 and 18.4**

1 Raise the window, then remove the door trim panel and watershield (see Section 16).
2 Working through the large access hole, remove the glass run channel.
3 Disconnect the lock knob from the door (see illustration).
4 Remove the screws securing the latch to the door (see illustration).
5 Disengage the outside door handle-to-latch rod and the outside door lock-to-latch rod. All door lock rods are attached by plastic clips. The plastic clips can be removed by unsnapping the portion engaging

the connecting rod and then pulling the rod out of its locating hole. Disconnect the electrical connectors at the latch. Remove the latch assembly from the door.
6 Installation is the reverse of removal.

OUTSIDE HANDLE AND DOOR LOCK CYLINDER

♦ **Refer to illustrations 18.8, 18.9 and 18.11**

7 To remove the outside handle and lock cylinder assembly, raise the window and remove the door trim panel and watershield (see Section 16).
8 Working through the access holes, disengage the plastic clips that secure the outside handle-to-latch rod and the outside door lock-to-latch rod (see illustration).
9 Loosen the lock cylinder protector screw (see illustration).
10 Remove the bolts securing the lock cylinder, protector and lock cylinder switch, then remove it as an assembly.
11 Remove the outside handle retaining bolt and spacer (see illustration), then remove the handle from the vehicle.
12 Installation is the reverse of removal.

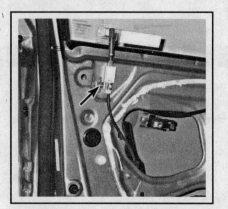

18.3 Remove the bolt securing the lock knob

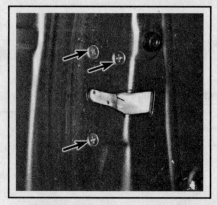

18.4 Remove the latch screws from the end of the door

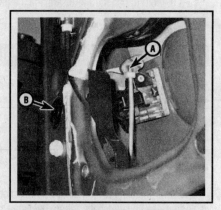

18.8 Detach the handle-to-latch rod (A) then remove the access plug to disconnect the lock actuating rod (B)

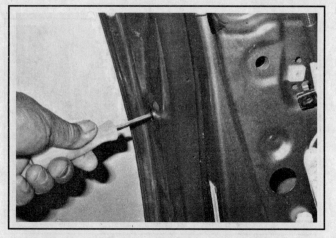

18.9 Working through the access hole, loosen the lock cylinder protector screw

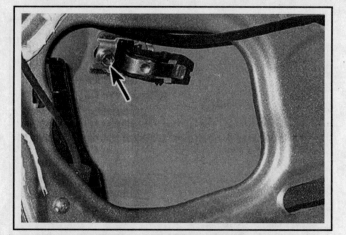

18.11 Remove the fastener and spacer securing the outside handle

19 Door window glass - removal and installation

▶ Refer to illustration 19.2

✳✳ CAUTION:

Wear gloves when working inside the door openings to protect against cuts from sharp metal edges.

    1   Remove the door trim panel and the plastic watershield (see Section 16).
    2   Raise the window glass just enough to access the window retaining bolts through the holes in the door frame (see illustration).
    3   Place a rag over the glass to help prevent scratching the glass and remove the two glass mounting bolts.
    4   Remove the glass by tilting it slightly, pulling it up and out.
    5   Installation is the reverse of removal.

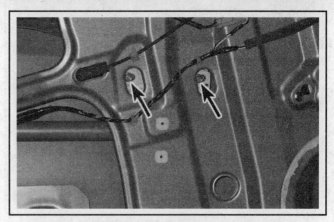

19.2 Raise the window just enough to access the glass retaining bolts through the holes in the door fram, then remove the bolts securing the glass to the equalizer arm

20 Door window glass regulator - removal and installation

▶ Refer to illustration 20.4

✳✳ CAUTION:

Wear gloves when working inside the door openings to protect against cuts from sharp metal edges.

    1   Remove the door trim panel and the plastic watershield (see Section 16).
    2   Remove the window glass assembly (see Section 19).
    3   Disconnect the electrical connector from the window regulator motor.
    4   Remove the regulator mounting bolts (see illustration), then slide the regulator assembly out of the service hole in the door frame to remove it.
    5   Installation is the reverse of removal.

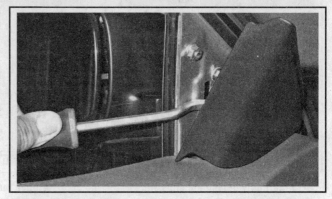

20.4 Regulator mounting bolt locations

21 Mirrors - removal and installation

OUTSIDE MIRRORS

▶ Refer to illustrations 21.1 and 21.3

    1   Lower the window, then pry off the mirror trim cover (see illustration).
    2   Disconnect the electrical connector from the mirror (if equipped).

21.1 Use a small screwdriver or trim removal tool to pry off the mirror cover

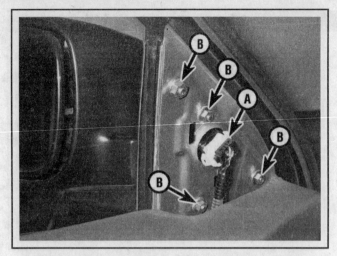

21.3 Unplug the electrical connector (A) and remove these four nuts (B)

3 Remove the mirror retaining nuts and detach the mirror from the vehicle (see illustration).
4 Installation is the reverse of removal.

INSIDE MIRROR

5 Turn the mirror base 90-degrees.
6 Slide the mirror down towards the bottom of the windshield and detach it from the mounting bracket.
7 If the support base for the mirror has come off the windshield, it can be reattached with a special mirror adhesive kit available at auto parts stores. Clean the glass and support the base thoroughly and follow the directions on the adhesive package.
8 Installation is the reverse of removal.

22 Center console - removal and installation

♦ Refer to illustrations 22.3, 22.4, 22.5a, 22.5b, 22.6, 22.7 and 22.8

✳ WARNING:

Models covered by this manual are equipped with a Supplemental Restraint System (SRS), more commonly known as airbags. Always disable the airbag system before working in the vicinity of any airbag system component to avoid the possibility of accidental deployment of the airbag, which could cause personal injury (see Chapter 12).

1 Disconnect the cable from the negative terminal of the battery (see Chapter 5, Section 1).

2 On manual transaxle models, unscrew the shift lever knob.
3 Pry off the gear selector trim bezel (see illustration) and disconnect the electrical connector, if equipped with heated seats.
4 Remove the screws securing the front of the console (see illustration).
5 Remove the console pocket (see illustrations).
6 Remove the center holder (see illustration).
7 Remove the center console center mounting screws (see illustration).
8 Remove the console rear retaining screws (see illustration).
9 Disconnect any electrical connections and remove the console from the vehicle.
10 Installation is the reverse of removal.

22.3 Carefully detach the clips and remove the trim ring from around the shifter

22.4 Remove the console front mounting fasteners

22.5a Pry out the console pocket tray . . .

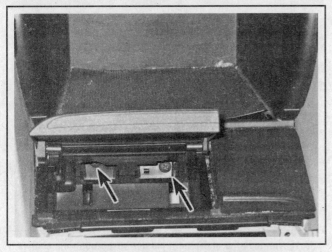
22.5b . . . then remove the two screws securing the pocket

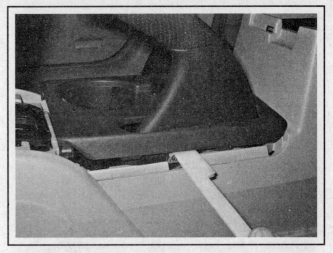
22.6 Carefully detach the clips with a trim stick and remove the center holder

22.7 Remove the console's center mounting screws

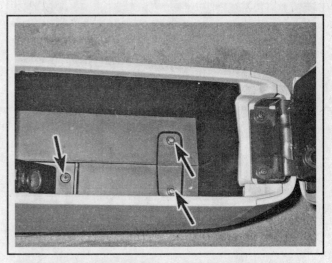
22.8 Open the center console box lid and pull out the mat, then remove the screws

23 Dashboard trim panels - removal and installation

⁜ WARNING:

Models covered by this manual are equipped with a Supplemental Restraint System (SRS), more commonly known as airbags. Always disable the airbag system before working in the vicinity of any airbag system component to avoid the possibility of accidental deployment of the airbag, which could cause personal injury (see Chapter 12).

1 Disconnect the cable from the negative battery terminal (see Chapter 5, Section 1).

PASSENGER'S DASHBOARD UNDER COVER

2 Pull the edge of the panel down nearest the glove box until the clips are disengaged and remove the panel.

3 Installation is the reverse of removal.

DRIVER'S DASHBOARD UNDER COVER

4 Pull the edge of the panel down until the clips are disengaged and remove the panel.

5 Installation is the reverse of removal.

DRIVER'S DASHBOARD LOWER COVER

▶ **Refer to illustration 23.7**

6 Tilt the steering wheel up to the highest position.

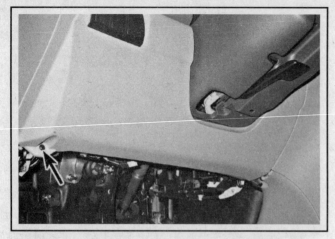

23.7 Remove this screw, then pull the bottom edge back to release the lower clips

23.15 Remove the instrument cluster bezel mounting screws

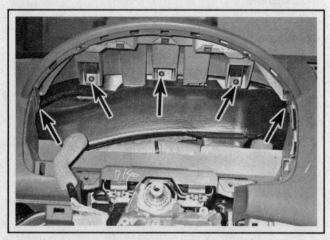

23.19 Instrument cluster visor mounting screws

23.20 Use a small taped screwdriver and release the center clip, then using a hooked tool, release the clips securing both sides of the upper panel. Using a trim tool, release the remaining clips and remove the panel

7 Remove the screw (see illustration), then pull the bottom edge of the panel back until the bottom clips are disengaged.

8 Grasp the upper edge of the panel and carefully pull back the panel to release the upper clips and remove the panel.

9 Installation is the reverse of removal.

GLOVE BOX

10 Open the glove box door and detach the glove box damper from the door.

11 At the bottom of the glove box, remove the screws from the hinges.

12 Push in on the sides of the glove box to release the glove box stops, then remove the glove box.

13 Installation is the reverse of removal.

INSTRUMENT CLUSTER BEZEL

▶ Refer to illustration 23.15

14 Tilt the steering wheel down to the lowest position.

15 Remove the screws (see illustration), then grasp the bezel securely and pull back to detach the clips from the instrument panel.

16 Installation is the reverse of removal.

INSTRUMENT CLUSTER VISOR

▶ Refer to illustration 23.19

17 Remove the instrument cluster bezel (see Steps 14 and 15).

18 Remove the instrument cluster (see Chapter 12).

19 Remove the screws (see illustration), then remove the visor from the dashboard.

UPPER PANEL

▶ Refer to illustration 23.20

20 Release the center clip, then grasp the sides of the panel and gently pull back to remove the panel (see illustration).

21 Disconnect the electrical connectors.

22 Installation is the reverse of removal.

CENTER POCKET

▶ **Refer to illustration 23.24**

23 Remove the center console pocket (see illustrations 22.5a and 22.5b).

24 Remove the screws securing the bottom of the center pocket (see illustration).

25 Open the center pocket and grasp the pocket, carefully pull it out to detach the upper clips, then remove the pocket.

23.24 Center pocket mounting screws

---

24 Steering column covers - removal and installation

▶ **Refer to illustration 24.3**

❄ **WARNING:**

Models covered by this manual are equipped with a Supplemental Restraint System (SRS), more commonly known as airbags. Always disable the airbag system before working in the vicinity of any airbag system component to avoid the possibility of accidental deployment of the airbag, which could cause personal injury (see Chapter 12).

1 Disconnect the cable from the negative battery terminal (see Chapter 5, Section 1).

2 Move the column to the lowest position.

3 Remove the retaining screws, then separate the halves and remove the covers (see illustration).

4 Installation is the reverse of the removal procedure.

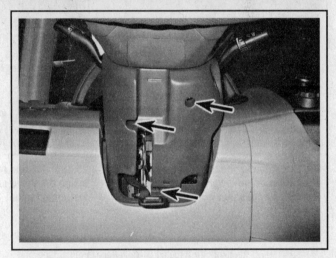

24.3 Steering column cover retaining screws

---

25 Instrument panel - removal and installation

▶ **Refer to illustrations 25.5, 25.7, 25.8, 25.13a, 25.13b, 25.14a, 25.14b and 25.14c**

❄❄ **WARNING:**

Models covered by this manual are equipped with a Supplemental Restraint System (SRS), more commonly known as airbags. Always disable the airbag system before working in the vicinity of any airbag system component to avoid the possibility of accidental deployment of the airbag, which could cause personal injury (see Chapter 12).

➡**Note 1:** This is a difficult procedure for the home mechanic. There are many hidden fasteners, difficult angles to work in and many electrical connectors to tag and disconnect/connect. We recommend that this procedure be done only by an experienced do-it-yourselfer.

➡**Note 2:** During removal of the instrument panel, make careful notes of how each piece comes off, where it fits in relation to other pieces and what holds it in place. If you note how each part is installed before removing it, getting the instrument panel back together again will be much easier.

➡**Note 3:** It is not necessary, but it is suggested to remove both front seats to allow additional working space and lessen the chance of damage to the seats during this procedure.

25.5 Remove the front pillar trim by carefully releasing the clips

25.7 Carefully pull the side kick panels to release the clips

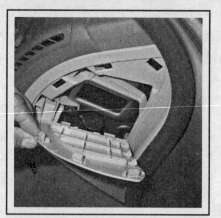

25.8 Carefully pry off the right dashboard side cover

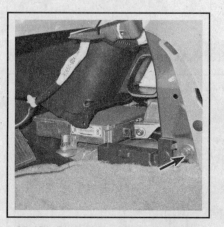

25.13a Remove the lower bolts from both sides of the lower center part of the instrument panel . . .

25.13b . . . and the four bolts inside the lower center part of the instrument panel

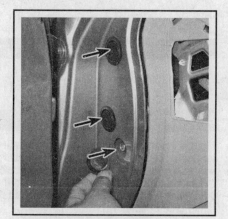

25.14a Remove the bolts securing the instrument panel from the left support structure . . .

1 Disconnect the cable from the negative battery terminal (see Chapter 5, Section 1).

2 Remove the steering wheel (see Chapter 10).

3 Remove the center floor console (see Section 22).

4 Remove all of the dashboard trim panels described in Section 23.

5 Remove the front pillar trim (see illustration).

6 Disconnect the steering intermediate shaft from the steering gear input shaft (see Chapter 10).

7 Remove the side kick panels (see illustration).

8 Remove the right dashboard side cover (see illustration).

9 Remove the glove box (see Section 23).

10 Remove the radio and the heater control assembly (see Chapter 3).

11 Remove the rear vent ducts.

12 Disconnect the instrument panel electrical connectors.

➡**Note: A number of electrical connectors must be disconnected in order to remove the instrument panel. Most are designed so that they will only fit on the matching connector (male or female), but if there is any doubt, mark the connectors with masking tape and a marking pen before disconnecting them.**

13 Remove the fasteners securing the lower center part of the instrument panel (see illustrations).

14 Remove the fasteners securing the rest of the instrument panel (see illustrations).

15 Pull the instrument panel towards the rear of the vehicle and detach any electrical connectors interfering with removal.

16 Once all the electrical connectors are detached, lift the instrument panel then pull it away from the windshield and take it out through the driver's door opening.

➡**Note: This is a two-person job.**

17 Installation is the reverse of removal.

18 Reconnect the battery. Refer to Chapter 5, Section 1.

25.14b . . . right support structure . . .

25.14c . . . and from under the driver's side of the instrument panel

26 Cowl cover - removal and installation

▶ **Refer to illustrations 26.2a and 26.2b**

1   Remove the windshield wiper arms (see Chapter 12).

2   Remove the hood seal and the push-pin fasteners securing the cowl covers (see illustrations).
3   Installation is the reverse of removal.

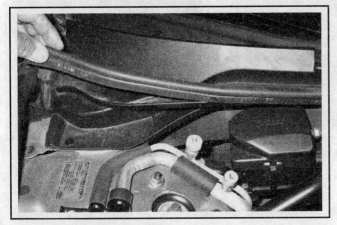

26.2a Remove the hood seal . . .

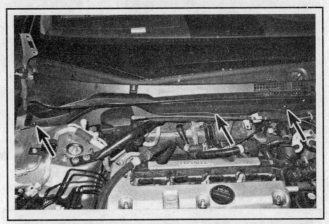

26.2b . . . then detach the plastic fasteners and remove the cowl covers

27 Seats - removal and installation

✳✳ WARNING:

The front seat belts are equipped with pre-tensioners, which are pyrotechnic (explosive) devices designed to retract the seat belts in the event of a collision. On models equipped with pre-tensioners, do not remove the front seat belt retractor assemblies, and do not disconnect the electrical connectors leading to the assemblies. Problems with the pre-tensioners will turn on the SRS (airbag) warning light on the dash. If any pre-tensioner problems are suspected, take the vehicle to a dealer service department.

✳✳ WARNING:

On models with side-impact airbags, be sure to disarm the airbag system before beginning this procedure (see Chapter 12).

FRONT SEAT

▶ **Refer to illustrations 27.2a and 27.2b**

1   Disconnect the cable from the negative battery terminal (see Chapter 5, Section 1).

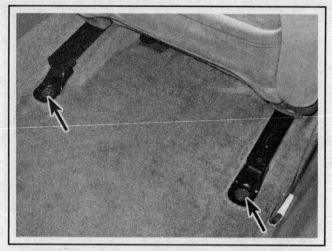

27.2a Move the front seat all the way forward to access the rear retaining bolts . . .

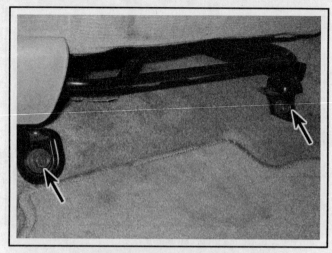

27.2b . . . then move the seat all the way to the rear to access the front retaining bolts

27.6 Pull back on the latches to release the front of the seat cushion

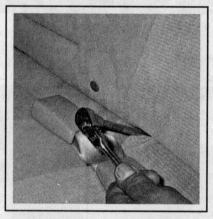

27.7 Remove the rear seat cushion retaining bolt

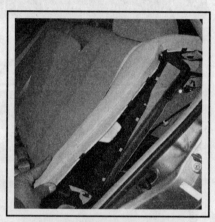

27.8a With the seat cushion removed, remove the fastener securing the seat side bolster . . .

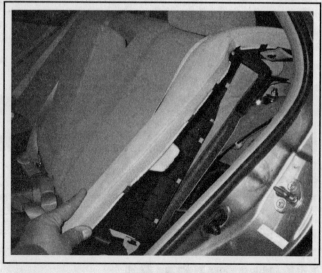

27.8b . . . then gently release the clips and remove the bolster

2   Position the seat all the way forward, then all the way to the rear to access the seat retaining bolts (see illustrations). Detach any bolt trim covers and remove the retaining bolts.

3   If you're working on a 2004 and later model, unlock the lower seatbelt anchor by inserting the tip of a small screwdriver into the lower anchor cover to detach the seatbelt from the anchor.

4   Tilt the seat upward to access the underneath, then disconnect any electrical connectors and lift the seat from the vehicle.

5   Installation is the reverse of removal.

REAR SEAT

Sedan models

▶ Refer to illustrations 27.6, 27.7, 27.8a, 27.8b and 27.9

6   Release the two latches at the front of the seat cushion (see illustration).

7   Remove the seat cushion bolt and remove the cushion (see illustration).

8   Remove the bolt securing the seat side bolsters, then remove the side bolsters (see illustrations).

9   Pull the seat back forward, then remove the fasteners securing the seat hinge and remove the seat backs (see illustration).

Coupe models

10   Release the two latches at the front of the seat cushion (see illustration 27.6).

11   Remove the seat cushion bolt and remove the cushion (see illustration 27.7).

12   Pull the seat back forward, then remove the fasteners securing the seat pivot brackets and remove the seat backs.

27.9 Remove the fasteners securing the seat pivot bracket

NOTES

12

CHASSIS ELECTRICAL SYSTEM

1 General information

The electrical system is a 12-volt, negative ground type. Power for the lights and all electrical accessories is supplied by a lead/acid-type battery, which is charged by the alternator.

This Chapter covers repair and service procedures for the various electrical components not associated with the engine. Information on the battery, ignition system, alternator and starter motor can be found in Chapter 5.

It should be noted that when portions of the electrical system are serviced, the negative battery cable should be disconnected from the battery to prevent electrical shorts and/or fires.

2 Electrical troubleshooting - general information

♦ **Refer to illustrations 2.5a and 2.5b**

1 A typical electrical circuit consists of an electrical component, any switches, relays, motors, fuses, fusible links or circuit breakers related to that component and the wiring and connectors that link the component to both the battery and the chassis. Wiring diagrams are included at the end of this Chapter to help you pinpoint an electrical circuit problem.

2 Before tackling any troublesome electrical circuit, study the appropriate wiring diagrams to get a complete understanding of what makes up that individual circuit. Noting if other components related to the circuit are operating correctly, for instance, can often narrow trouble spots, down. If several components or circuits fail at one time, chances are the problem is in a fuse or ground connection, because several circuits are often routed through the same fuse and ground connections.

3 Electrical problems usually stem from simple causes, such as loose or corroded connections, a blown fuse, a melted fusible link or a failed relay. Visually inspect the condition of all fuses, wires and connections in a problem circuit before troubleshooting the circuit.

4 If test equipment and instruments are going to be utilized, use the diagrams to plan ahead of time where you will make the necessary connections in order to accurately pinpoint the trouble spot.

5 Basic electrical troubleshooting tools include a circuit tester, test light or voltmeter, a continuity tester, a set of test leads and a jumper wire (preferably with a circuit breaker), which can be used to bypass electrical components (see illustrations). Before attempting to locate a problem with test instruments, use the wiring diagram(s) to decide where to make the connections.

VOLTAGE CHECKS

♦ **Refer to illustration 2.6**

6 Voltage checks should be performed if a circuit is not functioning correctly. Connect one lead of a circuit tester to either the negative battery terminal or a known good ground. Connect the other lead to a connector in the circuit being tested, preferably nearest to the battery or fuse (see illustration). If the bulb of the tester lights, voltage is present, which means that the part of the circuit between the connector and the battery is problem free. Continue checking the rest of the circuit in the same fashion. When you reach a point at which no voltage is present, the problem lies between that point and the last test point with voltage. Most of the time the problem can be traced to a loose connection.

➡**Note: Keep in mind that some circuits receive voltage only when the ignition key is in the ACC or ON position.**

FINDING A SHORT

7 One method of finding shorts in a live circuit is to remove the fuse and connect a test light in place of the fuse terminals (fabricate two jumper wires with small spade terminals, plug the jumper wires into the fuse box and connect the test light). There should be no voltage present in the circuit. Move the suspected wiring harness from side-to-side while watching the test light. If the bulb goes on, there is a short to ground somewhere in that area, probably where the insulation has rubbed through.

GROUND CHECK

8 Perform a ground test to check whether a component is correctly grounded. Disconnect the battery and connect one lead of a continuity tester or multimeter (set to the ohm scale), to a known good ground. Connect the other lead to the wire or ground connection being tested. If the resistance is low (less than 5 ohms), the ground is good. If the bulb on a self-powered test light does not go on, the ground is not good.

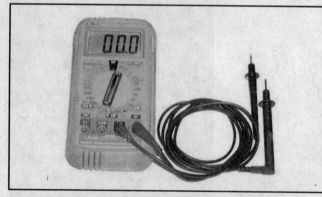

2.5a The most useful tool for electrical troubleshooting is a digital multimeter that can check volts, amps, and test continuity

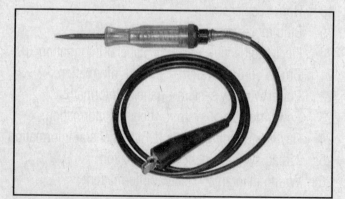

2.5b A simple test light is a very handy tool used for testing voltage

CONTINUITY CHECK

▶ **Refer to illustration 2.9**

9 Do a continuity check to verify that there are no opens in a circuit. With the circuit off (no power in the circuit), a self-powered continuity tester or multimeter can be used to check the circuit. Connect the test leads to both ends of the circuit (or to the power end and a good ground), and if the test light comes on the circuit is passing current correctly (see illustration). If the resistance is low (less than 5 ohms), there is continuity; if the reading is 10,000 ohms or higher, there is a break somewhere in the circuit. The same procedure can be used to test a switch, by connecting the continuity tester to the switch terminals. With the switch turned to ON, the test light should come on (or low resistance should be indicated on a meter).

FINDING AN OPEN CIRCUIT

10 When diagnosing for possible open circuits, it is often difficult to locate them by sight because the connectors hide oxidation or terminal misalignment. Merely wiggling a connector on a sensor or in the wiring harness may correct the open circuit condition. Remember this when an open circuit is indicated when troubleshooting a circuit. Intermittent problems may also be caused by oxidized or loose connections.

11 Electrical troubleshooting is simple if you keep in mind that all electrical circuits are basically electricity running from the battery, through the wires, switches, relays, fuses and fusible links to each electrical component (light bulb, motor, etc.) and to ground, from which it is passed back to the battery. Any electrical problem is an interruption in the flow of electricity to and from the battery.

CONNECTORS

▶ **Refer to illustration 2.15**

12 Most electrical connections on these vehicles consist of multiple-terminal plastic connectors. The two halves of most connectors are locked together by tabs molded into the plastic connector shells. So always look for the release tab(s) or locking tab(s) on a connector and release it/them before trying to disconnect the connector. If the connector is too dirty to find the release or locking tab(s), wipe it off. If a connector is in a dark area, use a flashlight. You might have to look closely (very closely!) at some connectors before you figure out how to separate the two halves, because the locking or release tabs are engaged in a way that is not immediately clear. And many connectors have not one but two sets of release or locking tabs.

13 Connectors are usually locked together by release tabs that you simply depress to release, or by locking tabs that you spread apart or pry loose from some projection on the other half of the connector. Once you have figured out how to release a connector with locking or release tabs, carefully depress the release tabs or pry the locking tabs apart with a small screwdriver, then separate the connector halves. Pull only on the connector halves. Never pull on the wires or the wiring harness, because you might damage the wires and terminals inside the connector.

14 Each pair of connector terminals has a male half and a female half. This is particularly important to remember when you look at a connector terminal guide in a wiring diagram or wiring schematic, because you need to know whether you're looking at the wiring harness side or the component side of the connector. Connector halves are mirror images of each other, and a terminal that is shown on the right side end-view of one half will be on the left side end view of the other half. In other words, the terminal locations - and terminal numbering, if applicable - will be flipped).

15 It is often necessary to take circuit voltage measurements with a connector connected. Whenever possible, carefully insert a small straight pin (not your meter probe) into the rear of the connector shell to contact the terminal inside, then clip your meter lead to the pin. This kind of connection is called backprobing (see illustration). When inserting a test probe into a male terminal, be careful not to distort the terminal opening. Doing so can lead to a poor connection and corrosion at that terminal later. Using the small straight pin instead of a meter probe results in less chance of deforming the terminal connector.

2.6 In use, a basic test light's lead is clipped to a known good ground, then the pointed probe can test connectors, wires or electrical sockets - if the bulb lights, battery voltage is present at the test point

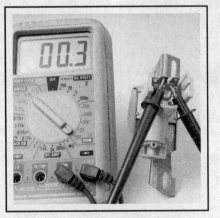

2.9 With a multimeter set to the ohm scale, resistance can be checked across two terminals - when checking for continuity, a low reading indicates continuity, a very high or infinite reading indicates lack of continuity

2.15 To backprobe a connector, insert a small, sharp probe (such as a straight-pin) into the back of the connector alongside the desired wire until it contacts the metal terminal inside; connect your meter leads to the probes - this allows you to test a functioning circuit

3 Fuses - general information

FUSES

▶ **Refer to illustrations 3.1a, 3.1b and 3.2**

The electrical circuits of the vehicle are protected by a combination of fuses, circuit breakers and relays (for more information about circuit breakers, refer to Section 4; for more information about relays, refer to Section 5). Fuse and relay boxes are located in the engine compartment and underneath the left end of the dashboard (see illustrations). A wide array of mini and maxi-style fuses is used to protect various circuits. These fuses, which employ a blade terminal design, can be removed and installed without special tools. Each fuse protects a specific circuit or circuits, and the protected circuits are identified on the fuse panel cover. If the fuse panel cover is difficult to read, or missing, you can also refer to your owner's manual, which includes a complete guide to all fuses and relays in all three fuse/relay boxes.

If an electrical component fails, always check the fuse first. The best way to check a fuse is with a test light. Check for power at the exposed terminal tips of each fuse. If power is present on one side of the fuse but not the other, the fuse is blown. A blown fuse can also be confirmed by visually inspecting it (see illustration).

Be sure to replace blown fuses with the correct type. Fuses of different ratings are physically interchangeable, but only fuses of the correct rating should be used. Replacing a fuse with one of a higher or lower value than specified is not recommended. Each electrical circuit needs a specific amount of protection. The amperage value of each fuse is molded into the fuse body.

If the replacement fuse immediately fails, don't replace it again until the cause of the problem is isolated and corrected. In most cases, this will be a short circuit in the wiring caused by a broken or deteriorated wire.

3.1a The engine compartment fuse and relay box is located in the left side of the engine compartment, behind the air filter housing. To locate a fuse or relay, open the lid and refer to the fuse and relay guide imprinted on the underside of the lid (this information is also available in your owner's manual)

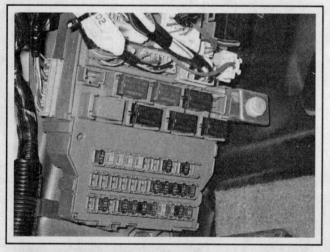

3.1b The under-dash fuse and relay box is located in the left kick panel. (Kick panel removed for clarity. With it installed, you can only access the fuses. For kick panel removal, see Chapter 11, Section 25)

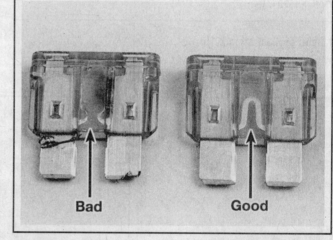

Bad   Good

3.2 When a fuse blows, the element between the terminals melts. The fuse on the left is blown, while the one on the right is good

4 Circuit breakers - general information

Circuit breakers protect certain circuits, such as the power windows or heated seats. The number of circuit breakers employed on your vehicle depends on its electrical accessories. Some circuit breakers are located in a fuse/relay box; others are located as stand-alone units under the dash and in other locations throughout the vehicle.

Because a circuit breaker resets automatically, a temporary or intermittent electrical overload in a circuit-breaker-protected system will cause the circuit to open momentarily, then close again. If a circuit-breaker-protected circuit does not close, or constantly opens and closes, check it immediately. There's probably an intermittent short or ground somewhere in the circuit that's causing the current overload, which causes the circuit breaker to cycle the circuit on and off.

For a basic check, pull the circuit breaker up out of its socket on the fuse panel, but just far enough to probe with a voltmeter. The breaker should still contact the sockets.

With the voltmeter negative lead on a good chassis ground, touch each end prong of the circuit breaker with the positive meter probe. There should be battery voltage at each end. If there is battery voltage only at one end, the circuit breaker must be replaced.

Some circuit breakers must be reset manually.

5   Relays - general information and testing

GENERAL INFORMATION

1   Many electrical accessories - the fuel injection system, horns, starter, and fog lamps, for example - use relays to control current to components. A relay allows a low-current circuit (the control circuit) to be used to open and close a high-current circuit (the power circuit). If a relay is defective, the component(s) powered by the high-current circuit controlled by the relay will not operate. Relays are located in the engine compartment fuse/relay box and in or near the under-dash fuse and relay box (see illustrations 3.1a and 3.1b). If a relay is suspect, test it using the procedure below, or have it tested by a dealer service department or a repair shop. If a relay is defective, replace it. Relays cannot be repaired.

➡Note: To access the relays located at the under-dash fuse and relay box, you'll have to remove the left kick panel (see Chapter 11, Section 25).

TESTING

2   There are two basic types of relays used in these vehicles: the normally-open type and the five-terminal type. Five-terminal relays have different internal circuitry and one more external spade terminal than the normally-open type relays. To test a relay, remove it from the vehicle and use an ohmmeter to check for continuity.

Normally-open type relays

♦ Refer to illustration 5.4

3   Normally-open type relays are used for:

Accessory power socket relay
Air conditioning compressor clutch relay
Air conditioning condenser fan relay
Blower motor relay
Ignition coil relay
PGM-FI main relay No. 1
PGM-FI main relay No. 2
Power window relay
Radiator fan relay
Rear window defogger relay
Starter cut relay
Upstream oxygen sensor relay

4   Normally-open type relays (see illustration) have four external spade terminals: two horizontal terminals, one on top of the other, with two vertical terminals, side-by-side, below them. In other words, the two horizontal terminals are perpendicular to the two vertical terminals. So an easy way to determine whether you're dealing with a normally-open

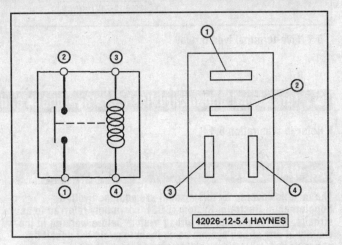

5.4 Normally-open type relay

type relay is to place the relay you want to test on a table top or workbench, with the spade terminals facing toward you. Then position it so that its two horizontal terminals are on top and its two vertical terminals are on the bottom. If that's what it looks like, it's a normally-open type relay. Some normally-open type relays have numbered terminals (1, 2, 3, 4, etc.) and some don't. If the normally-open type relay that you want to test doesn't have numbered terminals, how do you know which terminal is No. 1, which is No. 2, etc.? Here's a simple way to determine terminal numbering: All normally-open type relays are numbered from top-to-bottom and from left-to-right, so once you have your relay positioned with the two horizontal terminals at the top, those are terminal Nos. 1 and 2, respectively. And the two vertical terminals below them are numbered from left to right, so those two lower terminals are Nos. 3 and 4.

5   To test a normally-open type relay, verify that there is no continuity between terminal No. 1 and No. 2 when the power is disconnected. Then verify that there is continuity between terminal No. 1 and No. 2 when the No. 3 and No. 4 terminals are connected to power and ground, respectively.

Five-terminal type B relays

♦ Refer to illustration 5.7

6   Five-terminal type B relays are used for:

Daytime running lights relay (Canadian models)
Moonroof-closing relay
Moonroof-opening relay
Seat heater relay

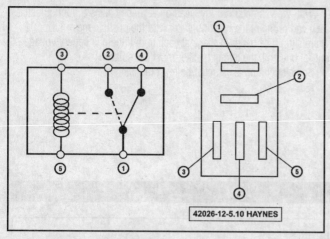

5.7 Five-terminal type B relay

7   Five-terminal type B relays are easy to identify because they have five terminals (see illustration) instead of four. To determine the terminal numbering, place a five-terminal relay with its two terminals at the top and parallel to the table top, and with the other three vertical terminals underneath the two upper horizontal ones. The top terminal is No. 1, the one below it is No. 2 and the three terminals below No. 2 are, from left to right, Nos. 3, 4 and 5.

8   To test a five-terminal relay verify that there is continuity between terminal No. 1 and No. 4 when the power is disconnected. Then verify that there is continuity between terminal No. 1 and No. 2 when power and ground are connected to the No. 3 and No. 5 terminals.

6   Turn signal and hazard flasher relay - check and replacement

▶ **Refer to illustration 6.1**

⁕⁕ **WARNING:**

The models covered by this manual are equipped with a Supplemental Restraint System (SRS), commonly referred to as airbags. Always disable the airbag system before working in the vicinity of any airbag system component to avoid the possibility of accidental deployment of the airbag, which could cause personal injury (see Section 25).

1   The turn signal and hazard flashers are controlled by the turn signal and hazard flasher relay, which is located above the under-dash fuse and relay box, which is located at the left kick panel (see illustration).

2   To access the turn signal and hazard flasher relay, remove the left kick panel (see Chapter 11, Section 25).

3   If the flasher unit is functioning correctly, you'll hear an audible click when it's operating. If one of the turn signal indicator lights on the instrument cluster flashes more rapidly than normal, a turn signal bulb for that side has a blown filament.

4   If neither turn signal indicator blinks, the problem might be a blown fuse, a faulty turn signal and hazard flasher relay, a broken switch or a loose or open connection. If the left or right turn signal fuse has blown, check the wiring for a short before installing a new fuse.

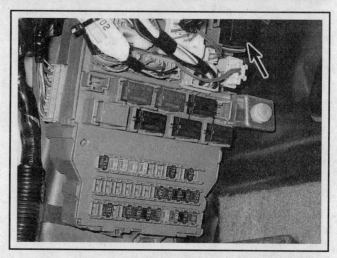

6.1 The turn signal and hazard flasher relay is located above the under-dash fuse and relay box (left kick panel removed)

5   If the turn signal and hazard flasher relay is bad, take it with you when buying a replacement unit. Make sure that the replacement unit is identical to the original.

7   Steering column switches - replacement

⁕⁕ **WARNING:**

The models covered by this manual are equipped with a Supplemental Restraint System (SRS), more commonly known as airbags. Always disable the airbag system before working in the vicinity of any airbag system component to avoid the possibility of accidental deployment of the airbag, which could cause personal injury (see Section 25).

1   Disconnect the cable from the negative battery terminal (see Chapter 5, Section 1), then wait at least three minutes before proceeding.

2   Remove the driver's dashboard lower cover and the steering column covers (see Chapter 11).

7.3 The steering column switches are fed by electrical connector A. The electrical connector for the combination light switch (B) plugs into the windshield wiper/ washer switch

7.4 To detach the combination light switch from the switch housing, remove these screws, then insert an awl through this hole, push down to disengage the tab, then slide the switch out to the left

7.9 To detach the windshield wiper/ washer switch from the switch housing, remove these screws, insert an awl through this hole, push firmly on the switch to disengage it from the combination switch assembly and slide the switch out to the right

COMBINATION LIGHT SWITCH

◆ **Refer to illustrations 7.3 and 7.4**

3   Disconnect the electrical connector from the wiper/washer switch (see illustration).

4   Remove the combination light switch retaining screws (see illustration).

5   To remove the combination light switch from the switch housing, push down on the retaining tab then slide the switch out.

6   Installation is the reverse of removal.

7   After you're done, reconnect the cable to the negative battery terminal (see Chapter 5, Section 1).

WINDSHIELD WIPER/WASHER SWITCH

◆ **Refer to illustration 7.9**

8   Disconnect the electrical connectors from the windshield wiper/ washer switch (see illustration 7.3).

9   Remove the windshield wiper/washer switch retaining screws (see illustration).

10   To remove the windshield wiper/washer switch, slide it out to the right.

11   Installation is the reverse of removal.

12   After you're done, reconnect the cable to the negative battery terminal (see Chapter 5, Section 1).

8   Ignition switch/key lock cylinder assembly- replacement

◆ **Refer to illustrations 8.2 and 8.3**

✳✳ WARNING:

All models covered by this manual are equipped with a Supplemental Restraint System (SRS), more commonly known as airbags. Always disable the airbag system before working in the vicinity of any airbag system component to avoid the possibility of accidental deployment of the airbag, which could cause personal injury (see Section 25).

1   Remove the dashboard lower cover and the steering column covers (see Chapter 11).

2   Disconnect the electrical connector from the ignition switch/key lock cylinder assembly (see illustration).

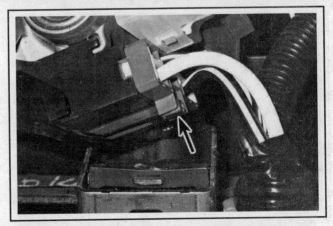

8.2 To release the electrical connector from the ignition switch/key lock cylinder assembly, depress this release tab, then pull out the connector

8.3 To remove the clamp that secures the ignition switch/key lock cylinder assembly to the steering column, center-punch these two shear bolts, then drill them out

3   Center-punch the shear bolts (see illustration) that attach the ignition switch/key lock cylinder assembly clamp to the steering column. Then drill a hole in both bolts, unscrew them with a screw extractor, remove the clamp and remove the ignition switch/key lock cylinder assembly.

4   Install the new ignition switch/key lock cylinder assembly on the steering column without the ignition key inserted. Install the mounting clamp and new shear bolts but don't tighten the bolts yet. Insert the ignition key and verify that the ignition key turns freely and that the steering wheel lock works correctly. Once you've verified that everything is working correctly, tighten the two shear bolts until the hex heads twist off.

5   Installation is otherwise the reverse of removal.

9   Dashboard switches - replacement

✳✳ WARNING:

The models covered by this manual are equipped with a Supplemental Restraint System (SRS), more commonly known as airbags. Always disable the airbag system before working in the vicinity of any airbag system component to avoid the possibility of accidental deployment of the airbag, which could cause personal injury (see Section 25).

MOONROOF SWITCH

1   Push out or carefully pry out the moonroof switch from the dashboard lower cover and disconnect the electrical connector from the switch.
2   Installation is the reverse of removal.

TRACTION CONTROL SWITCH

3   Push out or carefully pry out the switch panel located in the lower left corner of the dashboard and disconnect the electrical connector from the traction control switch

4   Push out or carefully pry out the traction control switch from the switch panel.
5   Installation is the reverse of removal.

HAZARD FLASHER SWITCH

▶ **Refer to illustrations 9.7 and 9.8**

➡**Note: The photos accompanying this procedure depict the hazard flasher switch on a 2003 model. On 2004 and later models, the hazard flasher switch is in the same location, but the passenger's airbag cutoff indicator is integrated into the upper part of the switch housing. However, it's removed and installed exactly the same way as the unit shown here.**

6   Remove the upper dash panel (see Chapter 11).
7   Disconnect the electrical connector from the backside of the hazard flasher switch (see illustration).
8   Depress the release tabs on the top and bottom of the hazard flasher switch housing and pull out the hazard flasher switch from the center panel (see illustration).
9   Installation is the reverse of removal.

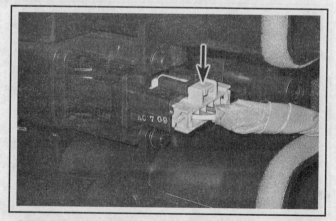

9.7 To release the electrical connector for the hazard flasher switch, depress this tab and pull out the connector

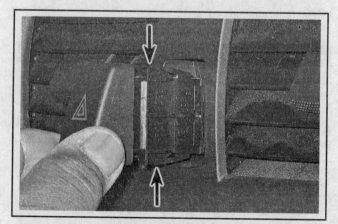

9.8 To remove the hazard flasher switch from the panel, depress the two release tabs on the top and bottom of the switch housing, then pull the switch out

10 Instrument cluster - removal and installation

◆ Refer to illustrations 10.2 and 10.3

❋❋ WARNING:

The models covered by this manual are equipped with a Supplemental Restraint System (SRS), more commonly known as airbags. Always disable the airbag system before working in the vicinity of any airbag system component to avoid the possibility of accidental deployment of the airbag, which could cause personal injury (see Section 25).

1 Remove the instrument cluster bezel (see Chapter 11).
2 Remove the instrument cluster mounting screws (see illustration).
3 Pull out the cluster and disconnect the electrical connector from the backside (see illustration).
4 Installation is the reverse of removal.

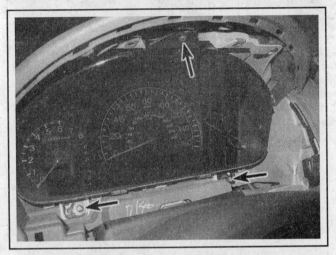

10.2 To detach the instrument cluster from the dash, remove these three screws

10.3 Pull the instrument cluster out of the dash, depress this release tab and disconnect the electrical connector

11 Wiper motor - check and replacement

WIPER MOTOR CIRCUIT CHECK

➡Note: Refer to the wiring diagrams for wire colors in the following checks. When checking for voltage, probe a grounded 12-volt test light to each terminal at a connector until it lights; this verifies voltage (power) at the terminal. If the following checks fail to locate the problem, have the system diagnosed by a dealer service department or other properly equipped repair facility.

1 If the wipers work slowly, make sure that the battery is fully charged and in good condition (see Chapters 1 and 5). If the battery is in good shape, remove the wiper motor (see below) and operate the wiper arms by hand. Check for binding linkage and pivots. Lubricate or repair the linkage or pivots as necessary. Reinstall the wiper motor. If the wipers still operate slowly, check for loose or corroded connections, especially the ground connection. If all connections look OK, replace the motor.

2 If the wipers fail to operate when activated, check the fuse (see Section 3). If the fuse is OK, connect a jumper wire between the wiper motor's ground terminal and ground, then retest. If the motor works now, repair the ground connection. If the motor still doesn't work, turn the wiper switch to the HI position and check for voltage at the motor.

➡Note: Remove the hood seal and cowl covers (see Chapter 11) and disconnect the electrical connector (see Step 8 below).

3 If there's voltage at the connector, remove the motor and check it off the vehicle with fused jumper wires from the battery. If the motor now works, check for binding linkage (see Step 1). If the motor still doesn't work, replace it. If there's no voltage to the motor, check for voltage at the wiper control relays. If there's voltage at the wiper control relays and no voltage at the wiper motor, have the switch tested. If the switch is OK, the wiper control relay is probably bad. See Section 5 for relay testing.

4 If the interval (delay) function is inoperative, check the continuity of all the wiring between the switch and the wiper control module.

5 If the wipers fail to park (if they stop at the position that they're in when the switch is turned off instead of returning to their normal off position), turn the wiper switch to OFF and the ignition switch to ON, then check for voltage at the park feed wire of the wiper motor connector. If no voltage is present, check for an open circuit between the wiper motor and the fuse panel.

11.6a To access the windshield wiper arm retaining nut, pull off the trim cap, then remove the nut

11.6b After removing the windshield wiper arm retaining nut, mark the relationship of the wiper arm to the wiper motor shaft to ensure that the arm is correctly positioned when installing it again later

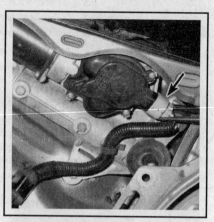

11.8 Disconnect the electrical connector from the windshield wiper motor

11.9 To detach the windshield wiper motor and linkage assembly, remove these four bolts

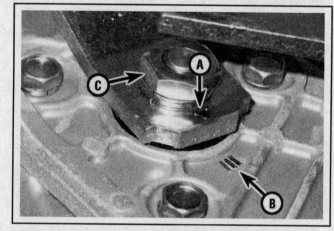

11.10 To disconnect the linkage from the wiper motor shaft, note the relationship of the arrow (A) on the linkage arm to the alignment marks (B) on the wiper motor mounting bracket, then remove the linkage arm-to-wiper motor shaft retaining nut (C)

WIPER MOTOR REPLACEMENT

▶ Refer to illustrations 11.6a, 11.6b, 11.8, 11.9, 11.10 and 11.11

6   Open the hood. Remove the covers from the windshield wiper arm retaining nuts (see illustration), then remove the wiper arm retaining nuts. Mark the position of each wiper arm in relation to its shaft (see illustration), then remove the wiper arms.

7   Remove the hood seals and cowl covers (see Chapter 11).

8   Disconnect the electrical connector from the windshield wiper motor (see illustration).

9   Remove the windshield wiper linkage/motor assembly mounting bolts (see illustration) and remove the windshield wiper motor and wiper linkage as a single assembly.

10   Separate the windshield wiper linkage from the wiper motor (see illustration).

11   Remove the windshield wiper motor mounting bolts (see illustration) and separate the motor from its mounting bracket.

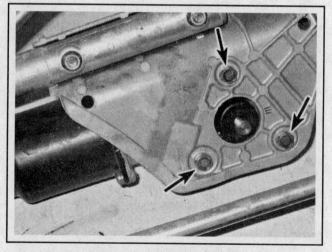

11.11 To detach the wiper motor from its mounting bracket, remove these three bolts

12 Before installing the windshield wiper linkage (especially if you're installing the old linkage), be sure to grease the moving parts.

13 Installation is otherwise the reverse of removal. Be sure to align the marks you made between the linkage arm and the motor mounting bracket and between the windshield wiper arm and the motor shaft.

14 Turn on the windshield wipers and verify that the wiper motor operates correctly in all modes.

12 Radio and speakers - removal and installation

❋❋ WARNING:

The models covered by this manual are equipped with a Supplemental Restraint System (SRS), more commonly known as airbags. Always disable the airbag system before working in the vicinity of any airbag system component to avoid the possibility of accidental deployment of the airbag, which could cause personal injury (see Section 25).

RADIO

▶ **Refer to illustration 12.2**

➡Note: Before beginning this procedure, make sure that you have the anti-theft code for the radio and that you have written down the frequencies for the radio station preset buttons.

1 Remove the climate control assembly (see Chapter 3).
2 Remove the radio mounting bolts (see illustration) and remove the radio from its mounting bracket.
3 Installation is the reverse of removal.

SPEAKERS

Front door speakers

▶ **Refer to illustrations 12.5 and 12.6**

4 Remove the front door trim panel (see Chapter 11).
5 The front door speakers are secured to the door by three clips - one larger clip at the top and two smaller clips at the bottom - that are spaced 120 degrees apart. Working from the top, carefully pry the speaker out of door by pushing down firmly on the larger upper clip (see illustration).
6 Disconnect the electrical connector (see illustration) and remove the speaker from the vehicle.
7 Installation is the reverse of removal.

Tweeters

▶ **Refer to illustrations 12.8a, 12.8b and 12.9**

8 Carefully pry up the tweeter speaker grille with a small screwdriver and disconnect the electrical connector (see illustrations).

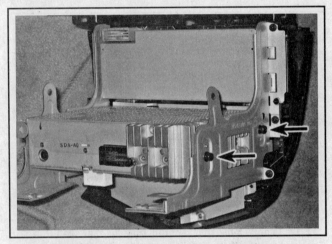

12.2 To detach the radio from the mounting brackets, remove the two screws from each side

12.5 To detach a front door speaker from the door, push down firmly on the clip at the top, pull out the upper part of the speaker, then lift the speaker up to disengage the two clips at the bottom

12.6 Depress the two release tabs on the side of the electrical connector to unplug it

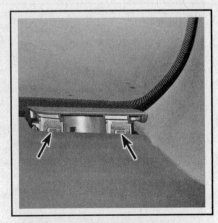

12.8a Carefully insert a small screwdriver into the gap between the tweeter speaker grille and the dashboard, at the spot where each of these two metal spring clips is located, and gently pry up the speaker grille . . .

12.8b . . . then disconnect the electrical connector from the tweeter

12.9 The tweeter is locked to the grille by three small lugs that protrude into three small "windows" in the ring that surrounds the tweeter. To release these lugs, carefully pry each lug loose with a small screwdriver, then pull out the tweeter

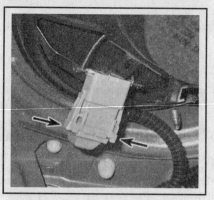

12.11 To disconnect the electrical connector from one of the rear speakers, depress these two release tabs and unplug the connector

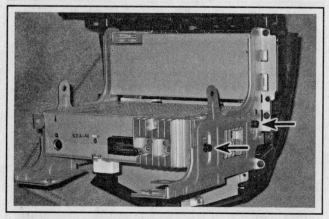

12.12 To detach the speaker grille from the rear shelf trim panel, squeeze each of these four split pins together and push them up through their mounting holes

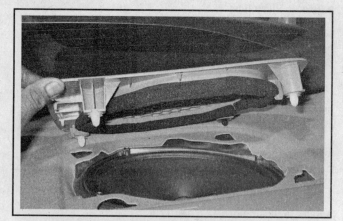

12.13 Once you have released the four split locator pins from the trunk side, simply remove the speaker grille from the rear shelf trim panel

9   Separate the tweeter from the grille (see illustration).

✳✳ CAUTION:

The cylindrical plastic housing that surrounds the tweeter is very thin, so be extremely careful when removing the tweeter. If you damage the housing, you'll have to replace the grille.

10   Installation is the reverse of removal.

Rear speakers

◆ Refer to illustrations 12.11, 12.12 12.13 and 12.14

11   Open the trunk and disconnect the electrical connector from the rear speaker that you want to replace (see illustration).
12   Push up the four split locator pins for the speaker grille (see illustration).
13   From inside the vehicle, remove the speaker grille from the rear shelf trim panel (see illustration).
14   Remove the speaker mounting screws (see illustration) and pull the speaker out of its receptacle in the rear shelf trim panel.
15   Installation is the reverse of removal.

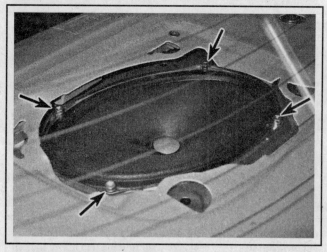

12.14 To detach a rear speaker from the rear shelf trim panel, remove these four screws

13 Antenna - removal and installation

REAR WINDOW ANTENNA GRID

1   All models use a rear window-mounted antenna grid, which is similar to the defogger grid on the rear window. To replace the antenna, you have to replace the rear window. However, you can easily repair the antenna grid as long as the broken part is no more than one inch long. The procedure for repairing the antenna grid is identical to repairing the rear window defogger grid (see Section 14).

REAR WINDOW ANTENNA COIL

⬥ **Refer to illustrations 13.3 and 13.4**

2   Remove the left rear seat bolster (see Chapter 11).
3   Remove the left C (rear) pillar trim (see illustration).
4   Disconnect the antenna coil electrical connectors (see illustration).
5   Remove the antenna coil mounting bolt.
6   Installation is the reverse of removal.

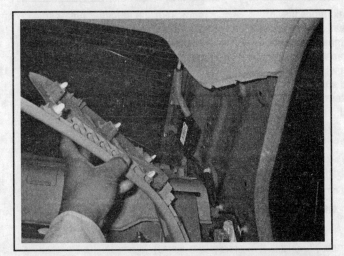

13.3 Using a trim panel removal tool, carefully pry loose the left C (rear) pillar trim panel

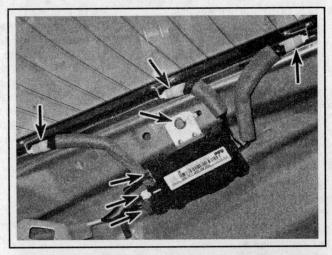

13.4 To remove the window antenna coil, disconnect all six electrical connectors, then remove the coil mounting bolt

14 Rear window defogger - check and repair

1   The rear window defogger consists of a number of horizontal elements baked onto the glass surface.
2   Small breaks in the element can be repaired without removing the rear window.

CHECK

⬥ **Refer to illustrations 14.4, 14.5 and 14.7**

3   Turn the ignition switch and defogger system switches to the ON position. Using a voltmeter, place the positive probe against the defogger grid positive terminal and the negative probe against the ground terminal. If battery voltage is not indicated, check the fuse, defogger switch and related wiring. If voltage is indicated, but all or part of the defogger doesn't heat, proceed with the following tests.
4   When measuring voltage during the next two tests, wrap a piece of aluminum foil around the tip of the voltmeter positive probe and press the foil against the heating element with your finger (see illustration). Place the negative probe on the defogger grid ground terminal.

14.4 When measuring voltage at the rear window defogger grid, wrap a piece of aluminum foil around the positive probe of the voltmeter and press the foil against the wire with your finger

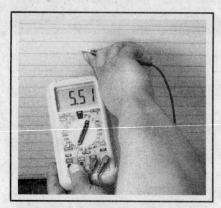

14.5 To determine if a heating element has broken, check the voltage at the center of each element - if the voltage is 6-volts, the element is unbroken

14.7 To find the break, place the voltmeter negative lead against the defogger ground terminal, place the voltmeter positive lead with the foil strip against the heat wire at the positive terminal end and slide it toward the negative terminal end. The point at which the voltmeter deflects from several volts to zero volts is the point at which the wire is broken

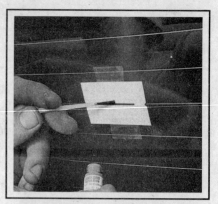

14.13 To use a defogger repair kit, apply masking to the inside of the window at the damaged area, then brush on the special conductive coating

5   Check the voltage at the center of each heating element (see illustration). If the voltage is 5 or 6-volts, the element is okay (there is no break). If the voltage is zero, the element is broken between the center of the element and the positive end. If the voltage is 10 to 12-volts the element is broken between the center of the element and ground. Check each heating element.

6   Connect the negative lead to a good body ground. The reading should stay the same. If it doesn't, the ground connection is bad.

7   To find the break, place the voltmeter negative probe against the defogger ground terminal. Place the voltmeter positive probe with the foil strip against the heating element at the positive terminal end and slide it toward the negative terminal end. The point at which the voltmeter deflects from several volts to zero is the point at which the heating element is broken (see illustration).

REPAIR

▶ **Refer to illustration 14.13**

8   Repair the break in the element using a repair kit for this purpose (available at most auto parts stores). Make sure that the repair kit includes plastic conductive epoxy.

9   Prior to repairing a break, turn off the system and allow it to cool off for a few minutes.

10 Lightly buff the element area with fine steel wool, then clean it thoroughly with rubbing alcohol.

11 Use masking tape to mask off the area being repaired.

12 Thoroughly mix the epoxy, following the instructions provided with the repair kit.

13 Apply the epoxy material to the slit in the masking tape, overlapping the undamaged area about 3/4-inch on either end (see illustration).

14 Allow the repair to cure for 24 hours before removing the tape and using the system.

15 Headlight bulb - replacement

▶ **Refer to illustrations 15.3 and 15.4**

✳✳ WARNING:

Halogen gas filled bulbs are under pressure and can shatter if the surface is scratched or the bulb is dropped. Wear eye protection and handle the bulbs carefully, grasping only the base whenever possible. Do not touch the surface of the bulb with your fingers because the oil from your skin could cause it to overheat and fail prematurely. If you do touch the bulb surface, clean it with rubbing alcohol.

1   If you're going to replace the low-beam headlight bulb, remove the two forward fasteners securing the inner fender splash shield (see Chapter 11), then pull the splash shield back for access to the bulb. If you're replacing the low beam headlight on V6 models with a manual transmission, also remove the air duct, which is accessible through the inner fender panel.

2   If you're going to replace a high-beam bulb on the left (driver's) side, remove the air intake cover from in front of the battery.

3   Disconnect the electrical connector from the headlight (see illustration).

4   Remove the bulb socket from the headlight housing (see illustration).

5   To install a new bulb socket into the headlight housing, align the lugs on the socket with the slots in the periphery of the socket mounting hole, insert the bulb socket into the mounting hole and rotate it clockwise until it stops.

6   Installation is otherwise the reverse of removal.

7   When you're done, verify that the new headlight bulb operates correctly.

15.3 To disconnect an electrical connector from a headlight bulb socket, depress this release lever and pull off the connector

15.4 To remove the bulb socket from the headlight housing, turn it counterclockwise 45-degrees and pull it out

16 Headlights - adjustment

▶ Refer to illustrations 16.1a, 16.1b and 16.3

❋❋ CAUTION:

The headlights must be aimed correctly. If adjusted incorrectly they could blind the driver of an oncoming vehicle and cause a serious accident or seriously reduce your ability to see the road. The headlights should be checked for correct aim every 12 months and any time a new headlight is installed or front end body work is performed. It should be emphasized that the

following procedure is only an interim step that will provide temporary adjustment until a properly equipped shop can adjust the headlights.

1   The vertical adjuster (see illustration) is located on the upper backside of each headlight housing (there are no horizontal adjusters). Use a Phillips screwdriver to turn the adjusters (see illustration).

2   There are several methods for adjusting the headlights. The simplest method requires masking tape, a blank wall and a level floor.

16.1a The headlight vertical adjusters are located in these little holes in the radiator trim cover

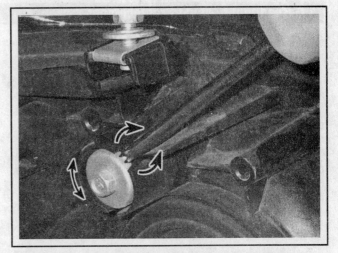

16.1b Insert a Phillips screwdriver through the adjustment hole and engage the teeth of the adjuster wheel as shown (headlight removed for clarity). To lower the headlight, turn the adjuster clockwise; to raise the headlight, turn the adjuster counterclockwise

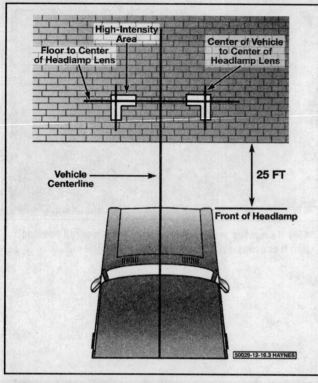

16.3 Headlight adjustment details

3   Position masking tape vertically on the wall in relation to the vehicle centerline and in relation to the centerlines of both headlights (see illustration).

4   Position a horizontal tape line in reference to the centerline of all the headlights.

➡**Note: It might be easier to position the tape on the wall with the vehicle parked only a few inches away.**

5   Adjustment should be made with the vehicle parked 25 feet from the wall, sitting level, the gas tank half-full and no heavy load in the vehicle.

6   With the low beams turned on, position the high intensity zone so it is two inches below the horizontal line.

7   With the high beams on, the high intensity zone should be vertically centered with the exact center just below the horizontal line.

➡**Note: It might not be possible to position the headlight aim exactly for both high and low beams. If a compromise must be made, keep in mind that the low beams are the most used and have the greatest effect on safety.**

8   If you have any difficulty adjusting the headlights, have them adjusted by a dealer service department as soon as possible.

17 Headlight housing - replacement

▶ **Refer to illustrations 17.2a, 17.2b, 17.3 and 17.4**

1   Remove the front bumper cover (see Chapter 11).

2   Remove the headlight housing mounting bolts (see illustrations) and pull the housing out.

3   Disconnect the electrical connectors from the headlight bulb sockets (see illustration 15.2) and remove the front turn signal/side marker light bulb socket (see illustration).

4   If you're replacing the headlight housing, detach the corner bumper beam - the small black metal piece that's attached to the underside of the headlight housing (see illustration) and install it on the new headlight housing.

5   Installation is the reverse of removal.

17.2a To detach the headlight housing from the vehicle, remove these four bolts . . .

17.2b . . . and this bolt

17.3 To remove a front turn signal/ side marker light bulb socket, turn it counterclockwise and pull it out

17.4 To detach the corner bumper beam from the headlight housing, remove this bolt

18 Horn - replacement

♦ Refer to illustration 18.2

➡ Note: The two horns are located in front of the radiator and condenser. You can remove or replace either horn separately from the other horn.

1　Remove the radiator cover (see Chapter 3).

2　Disconnect the electrical connector(s) from the horn(s) (see illustration).

3　Remove the horn mounting bracket bolt(s) and remove the horn(s).

4　Installation is the reverse of removal.

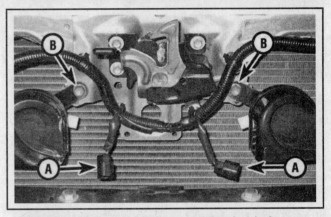

18.2 To detach the horn(s), disconnect the electrical connector(s) (A) and remove the horn mounting bracket bolt(s) (B)

19 Bulb replacement

EXTERIOR LIGHT BULBS

Front turn signal/side marker light bulb

♦ Refer to illustration 19.5

1　Loosen the left or right front wheel lug nuts. Raise the front of the vehicle and place it securely on jackstands. Remove the left or right front wheel.

2　Remove the two forward fasteners securing the inner fender splash shield (see Chapter 11), then pull the splash shield back for access to the bulb.

3　Disconnect the electrical connector from the front turn signal/side marker light bulb socket.

4　Remove the bulb socket (see illustration 17.3) and pull it out of the housing.

5　Remove the turn signal/side marker light bulb from the socket (see illustration). To remove the bulb from the socket, push it into the socket, rotate it counterclockwise, then pull it out of the socket. To

19.5 To remove a front turn signal/side marker light bulb from its socket, turn the bulb counterclockwise and pull it out of the socket

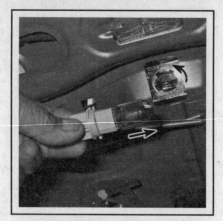

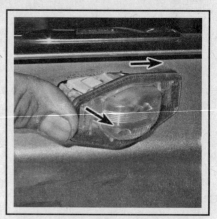

19.7 To disconnect the electrical connector from the high-mount brake light bulb socket, depress this release lever and unplug the connector

19.8 To remove the bulb socket from the high-mount brake light assembly, turn the socket counterclockwise and pull it out. To remove the bulb from the socket, simply pull it straight out of the socket

19.15a To remove the license plate light assembly, push it firmly to the right, pull out the left side . . .

install a new bulb, push it into the socket until it's seated, then give it a clockwise turn to lock it into place in the socket.

6   Installation is otherwise the reverse of removal.

High-mount brake light

2003 through 2005 models

♦ **Refer to illustrations 19.7 and 19.8**

7   Open the trunk and locate the electrical connector for the high-mount brake light, which is located in the underside of the trunk roof, just ahead of the trunk lid light (see illustration). Disconnect the electrical connector from the high-mount brake light bulb socket.

8   To remove the bulb socket from the high-mount brake light assembly rotate the bulb socket counterclockwise and pull it out (see illustration).

9   To remove the old bulb from the bulb socket simply pull it straight out of the holder. To install a new bulb, push it straight into the bulb socket.

10   Installation is the reverse of removal.

2006 and later models

➡**Note: 2006 and later models use LEDs instead of conventional bulbs. This procedure is for replacement of the LED unit.**

11   Remove the plastic pins from the trunk lid inner cover and lower it enough for access to the light assembly.

12   Disconnect the wiring.

13   Remove the four mounting nuts and lift out the light. It must be replaced as a unit. Installation is the reverse of removal.

License plate light

♦ **Refer to illustration 19.15a, 19.15b and 19.16**

14   On coupes, remove the license plate trim. Open the trunk lid, remove the two trim retaining nuts and release the four clips (one in the upper middle, one in the lower middle and one at each end), then remove the license plate trim.

15   Pull out the license plate light assembly and disconnect the electrical connector from the license plate light housing (see illustrations).

16   Separate the lens from the housing (see illustration).

17   Remove the old bulb from the housing by pulling it straight out, then install a new bulb in the housing.

18   Installation is the reverse of removal.

Taillight bulbs

2003 through 2005 models

♦ **Refer to illustrations 19.19, 19.20 and 19.21**

19   Open the trunk lid. To access the outer taillight bulbs (in the vehicle's rear fender), open the access door in the trunk carpeting (see illustration).

20   There are taillight bulbs in the trunk lid and in the rear fender. Each taillight assembly has two bulb holders (see illustration). If you're replacing a bulb in the outer taillight assembly, the upper bulb holder is for the brake/tail/rear side marker light bulb; the lower bulb holder is for the turn signal light bulb. If you're replacing a bulb in the inner taillight assembly, the upper bulb holder is for the brake and taillight bulb and the lower bulb holder is for the turn signal bulb. To remove any of these bulb holders, rotate the holder counterclockwise and pull it out of the taillight assembly.

21   To remove an inner taillight bulb from its holder, pull it straight out (see illustration).

22   To install a bulb in its holder, push it straight into the holder.

23   Installation is the reverse of removal.

2006 and later models

➡**Note: 2006 and later models use LEDs instead of conventional bulbs. This procedure is for replacement of the LED unit.**

24   Remove the rear bumper cover (see Chapter 11).

25   Remove the plastic retainers and lift out the inner trunk side trim panel.

26   Disconnect the wiring from the taillights.

27   Remove the fasteners from the taillight assembly and pull it rearward.

28   Remove the gasket from the taillight housing.

29   Release the wiring harness on two-door models. Be sure to note how it's installed.

19.15b . . . then pull out the assembly far enough to depress the release tab on the electrical connector and unplug the connector

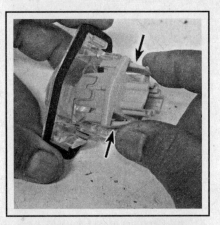

19.16 To separate the housing from the lens, depress these two release tabs and pull off the housing

19.19 To access the outer taillights (in the rear fender), open this access door

19.20 To disconnect a taillight bulb electrical connector, depress the release tab and pull off the connector. To remove the bulb holder, turn it counterclockwise and pull it out of the taillight housing

19.21 To remove a brake light/taillight/side marker light bulb or a rear turn signal bulb from the holder, simply pull it straight out of the holder

19.32 Carefully pry off the ceiling light lens with a small screwdriver

30 Remove the four mounting screws and disconnect the wiring from the LED.

31 Installation is the reverse of removal.

INTERIOR LIGHTS

Ceiling light

▶ Refer to illustrations 19.32 and 19.33

32 Using a fingernail file or a small screwdriver, pry off the lens (see illustration). Be careful not to damage the plastic trim around the edge of the lens.

33 Remove the old bulb from the two metal clips (see illustration).

34 Install the new bulb. Make sure that it's fully seated between the two metal clips.

35 Install the lens. Make sure that it snaps back into place.

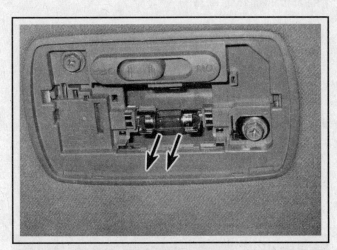

19.33 To remove the ceiling light bulb, simply pull it straight down. When installing a new bulb, make sure that it snaps into place between the metal clips at each end

19.36 Carefully pry off the front individual map light lens with a small screwdriver

19.40 Carefully pry off the lens covering the light bulb for the vanity mirror

19.41 To remove the old light bulb from the vanity mirror, carefully pry it loose with a small screwdriver.

19.45 To remove an illumination bulb from the hazard flasher switch (or from any other dashboard switches with this type of bulb), simply rotate the bulb holder counterclockwise and pull it out of the switch

19.47 To remove the trunk light assembly, pop it out and pull it down. To remove the bulb, simply pull it straight out

Front individual map light

▶ Refer to illustration 19.36

36 Carefully pry off the lens with a fingernail file or with a small screwdriver (see illustration).
37 Remove the old bulb from the two metal clips.
38 Insert the new bulb into its receptacle and push it straight up until it stops.
39 Install the lens. Make sure that it snaps into place.

Vanity mirror light bulbs

▶ Refer to illustrations 19.40 and 19.41

40 Open the cover for the vanity mirror and carefully pry off the lens (see illustration).
41 Remove the old light bulb from the vanity mirror housing (see illustration).

❋❋ WARNING:

Pry only on the metal ends, not the glass.

42 Insert a new light bulb into the two metal clips until it snaps into place.
43 Install the lens. Make sure that it snaps into place.

Hazard flasher switch bulb

▶ Refer to illustration 19.45

44 Remove the hazard flasher switch (see Section 9).
45 Unscrew and remove the light bulb from the left side of the hazard flasher switch (see illustration).
46 Installation is the reverse of removal.

Trunk light bulb

▶ Refer to illustration 19.47

47 Open the trunk and locate the trunk light, which is located just ahead of the trunk lid. Remove the trunk light lens (see illustration).
48 To remove the old bulb pull it straight out.
49 Installation is the reverse of removal.

20 Electric side view mirrors - general information

1   Most electric rear view mirrors use two motors to move the glass; one for up-and-down adjustments and one for left-right adjustments.

2   During mirror adjustment, the power mirror adjustment switch sends voltage to the left or right side mirror. With the ignition key turned to ON (engine not running), operate the mirror adjustment switch through all of its functions (left-right and up-down) for both the left and right side mirrors.

3   Listen carefully for the sound of the electric motors running in the mirrors.

4   If you can hear the motors but the mirror glass doesn't move, there's a problem with the drive mechanism inside the mirror.

5   If the mirrors do not operate and no sound comes from the mirrors, check the fuse (see Section 3).

6   If the fuse is OK, remove the power mirror adjustment switch (see Chapter 11, Section 16). Have the switch continuity checked by a dealership service department or other qualified automobile repair facility.

7   Inspect the ground connections. Make sure that they're tight and corrosion-free.

8   If the mirror still doesn't work, remove the mirror (see Chapter 11) and check the wires at the mirror for voltage.

9   If there is no voltage in any switch position, check the circuit between the mirror and the adjustment switch for opens and shorts.

10 If there's voltage, remove the mirror and test it off the vehicle with jumper wires. If the mirror fails this test, replace it.

21 Cruise control system - general information

FOUR-CYLINDER MODELS

1   The cruise control system maintains the vehicle speed that you select until you depress the brake pedal, depress the clutch pedal (on models with a manual transaxle), shift the transaxle (models with an automatic transaxle), or turn the system off. The cruise control system consists of the following components:

Cruise control combination switch (on the steering wheel)
Cruise main and cruise control indicators(LEDs on the instrument cluster that light up when cruise control system is on)
Cruise control unit (the computer that controls the cruise control actuator)
Cruise control actuator (the electric motor that controls the actuator cable)
Actuator cable (controls the angle of the throttle plate inside the throttle body)
Brake pedal position switch (located at upper end of brake pedal; deactivates the system when pedal is depressed)
Clutch pedal position switch (located at upper end of clutch pedal; deactivates system when clutch pedal is depressed)
Transmission range switch (located on transaxle; deactivates system when automatic transaxle is downshifted)

2   Here's how it works: When you select the speed that you want to go, the cruise control unit takes control of the throttle plate in the throttle body. It maintains the selected speed with the cruise control actuator, which is connected to the throttle cam on the throttle body by the actuator cable. The system maintains the selected speed until you turn it off, depress the brake or clutch pedal (manual transaxle) or shift the transmission (automatic transaxle).

3   The diagnostic procedures for troubleshooting the cruise control system are beyond the scope of this manual, but the following general procedures will help you identify common problems.

4   Check the fuses (see Section 3). In the engine compartment fuse and relay box, check fuse No. 22 (100 amp) and fuse No. 23 (50 amp). In the under-dash fuse and relay box, check fuse No. 18 (15 amp).

5   Have an assistant operate the brake lights while you check their operation (voltage from the brake light switch deactivates the cruise control).

6   If the brake lights don't come on or stay on all the time, correct the problem and retest the cruise control system.

7   Visually inspect the actuator cable between the cruise control actuator and the throttle cam for freedom of movement. The cable should move freely without binding or sticking. If the cable is kinked or frayed, replace it.

8   Test drive the vehicle to determine if the cruise control is now working. If it isn't, take it to a dealer service department or an automotive electrical specialist for further diagnosis.

V6 MODELS

9   From inside the vehicle, the cruise control system on V6 models seems identical to the system used on four-cylinder models, with the same indicators on the cluster, the same cruise control switch on the steering wheel, same brake and clutch pedal position switches, etc. However, there is no cruise control unit (module) as on four-cylinder models. Instead, the cruise control system is under the direct control of the Powertrain Control Module (PCM). Under the hood, there is no actuator, nor actuator cable, because these models have an electronically-controlled throttle body (no accelerator cable). When you select the speed that you want to maintain, the PCM controls vehicle speed by opening and closing the throttle plate by means of a computer-controlled solenoid (motor) inside the throttle body.

10 The diagnostic procedures for troubleshooting the cruise control system are beyond the scope of this manual, but if the system can't be set, or the set speed doesn't cancel when the brake pedal is depressed, check the fuses. Start with fuse No. 13 (20 amp) in the engine compartment fuse and relay box, then check fuse No. 18 (15 amp) in the under-dash fuse and relay box. If the set speed doesn't cancel when the CANCEL button is depressed, check fuse No. 13 (20 amp).

11 Other than checking the fuses, the diagnostic procedures for troubleshooting the cruise control system on V6 models are beyond the scope of this manual. A dealer service department should handle any further testing.

22　Power window system - general information

1　The power window system operates electric motors, mounted in the doors, which lower and raise the windows. The system consists of the control switches, the motors, regulators, glass mechanisms and associated wiring.

2　The power windows can be lowered and raised from the master control switch by the driver or by remote switches located at the individual windows. Each window has a separate motor, which is reversible. The position of the control switch determines the polarity and therefore the direction of operation.

3　The circuit is protected by a fuse and a circuit breaker. Each motor is also equipped with an internal circuit breaker, this prevents one stuck window from disabling the whole system.

4　The power window system will only operate when the ignition switch is turned to ON. There's also a main switch at the master power window control panel (in the driver's door) which, when activated, disables the switches at the rear windows and the switch at the passenger's window. So if there's a problem with the passenger window or with either of the rear windows, make sure that it's not simply a matter of flipping the main switch before proceeding.

5　The procedures listed below are general in nature, so if you can't find the problem using them, take the vehicle to a dealer service department.

6　If the power windows won't operate, always check the fuses and relays first (see Sections 3 and 5). Also verify that there's voltage to the relay and that the relay is well grounded.

7　If only the rear windows are inoperative, or if the windows only operate from the master control switch, check the main switch for continuity in the unlocked position. Replace it if it doesn't have continuity (see Chapter 11, Section 16).

8　Check the wiring between the switches and the fuse and relay box for continuity. Repair the wiring, if necessary.

9　If only one window is inoperative from the main switch, try the other control switch at the window.

➡**Note: This doesn't apply to the driver's door window.**

10　If the same window works from one switch, but not the other, check the switch for continuity.

11　If the switch tests OK, check for a short or open in the circuit between the affected switch and the window motor.

12　If one window is inoperative from both switches, remove the trim panel from the affected door (see Chapter 11, Section 16) and check for voltage at the switch and at the motor while the switch is operated.

13　If voltage is reaching the motor, disconnect the glass from the regulator (see Chapter 11). Move the window up-and-down by hand while checking for binding and damage. Also check for binding and damage to the regulator. If the regulator is not damaged and the window moves up and down smoothly, replace the motor. If there's binding or damage, lubricate, repair or replace parts, as necessary.

14　If voltage isn't reaching the motor, check the wiring in the circuit for continuity between the switches and motors. You'll need to consult the wiring diagram for the vehicle.

23　Power door lock system - general information

1　A power door lock system operates the door lock actuators mounted in each door. The system consists of the switches, actuators, a control unit and associated wiring. On some models, the power door lock system is part of the security alarm system. On these models, the power door lock system is more complex, and more difficult to diagnose. Therefore, home troubleshooting is limited to simple checks of the wiring connections and actuators for minor faults that can be easily repaired.

2　Power door lock systems are operated by bi-directional solenoids located in the doors. The lock switches have two operating positions: LOCK and UNLOCK. When activated, the switch sends a ground signal to the door lock control unit to lock or unlock the doors. Depending on which way the switch is activated, the control unit reverses polarity to the solenoids, allowing the two sides of the circuit to be used alternately as the feed (positive) and ground side.

3　The following general guidelines should help you quickly identify and repair typical problems. If you're unable to locate the trouble using these guidelines, consult a dealer service department.

4　Always check the fuses first (see Section 3 and your owners' manual).

5　Operate the door lock switches in both directions (LOCK and UNLOCK) with the engine off. Listen for the click of the solenoids operating.

6　Test the switches for continuity. Remove the switches and have them checked by a dealer service department.

7　Check the wiring between the switches, control unit and solenoids for continuity. Repair the wiring if there's no continuity.

8　Check for a bad ground at the switches and at the control unit.

9　If only one lock solenoid doesn't operate, remove the trim panel from the door with the bad solenoid (see Chapter 11, Section 16) and check for voltage at the solenoid while the lock switch is operated. One of the wires should have voltage in the Lock position; the other should have voltage in the Unlock position.

10　If the inoperative solenoid is receiving voltage, replace the solenoid.

11　If the inoperative solenoid isn't receiving voltage, check for an open or short in the wire between the lock solenoid and the control unit.

➡**Note: Wire harnesses typically break between the body and door, because repeatedly opening and closing the door fatigues and eventually breaks the wires.**

24　Daytime Running Lights (DRL) - general information

The Daytime Running Lights (DRL) system illuminates the headlights whenever the engine is running. The only exception is with the engine running and the parking brake engaged. Once the parking brake is released, the lights will remain on as long as the ignition switch is on, even if the parking brake is later applied. The DRL system supplies reduced power to the headlights during daylight operation to prolonging headlight life.

25 Airbag system - general information

GENERAL INFORMATION

1   All models are equipped with a Supplemental Restraint System (SRS), more commonly known as airbags. This system is designed to protect the driver, and the front seat passenger, from serious injury in the event of a head-on or frontal collision. It uses a pair of crash sensors mounted behind the front bumper. The airbag assemblies are mounted on the steering wheel and inside the passenger's end of the dash.

2   Some models are also equipped with side-impact airbags. On two-door models, the side-impact sensors are mounted in the sides of the front seat backs. On four-door models, there are side-impact sensors in the sides of the front seat backs and on the inside of the body, near the trailing edges of the rear doors. Additionally, other models are equipped with side curtain airbags, which are concealed behind the headliner and extend from the front of the interior to the rear.

AIRBAG MODULE

Driver's side airbag

3   The airbag inflator module contains a housing incorporating the airbag and inflator unit, mounted in the center of the steering wheel. The inflator assembly is mounted on the back of the housing over a hole through which gas is expelled, inflating the bag almost instantaneously when an electrical signal is sent from the SRS unit (the system's processor). A clockspring on the steering column under the steering wheel carries this signal to the module. This clockspring assembly can transmit an electrical signal regardless of steering wheel position. The igniter in the airbag converts the electrical signal to heat and ignites the powder, which inflates the bag.

4   For information on how to remove and install the driver's side airbag, refer to Chapter 10, Section 16.

Passenger's side airbag

5   The airbag is mounted in the upper part of the passenger's end of the dashboard, above the glove box. The passenger's side airbag is considerably larger than the steering wheel-mounted unit. The airbag trim cover on top of the dash splits open when the bag is inflated.

SRS CONTROL UNIT

6   This unit supplies the current to the airbag system in the event of the collision, even if battery power is cut off. It checks this system every time the vehicle is started, causing the "SRS" light to go on, then off, if the system is operating correctly. If there is a fault in the system,

the light will go on and stay on, or it will flash, or the dash will make a beeping sound. If this happens, take the vehicle to your dealer immediately for service.

DISARMING THE SYSTEM AND OTHER PRECAUTIONS

✳✳ WARNING:

Failure to follow these precautions could result in accidental deployment of the airbag and personal injury.

7   Whenever working in the vicinity of the steering wheel, the right end of the dashboard or any of the other SRS system components, the system must be disarmed. To disarm the system:

  a) *Point the wheels straight ahead and turn the key to the LOCK position.*
  b) *Disconnect the cable from the negative battery terminal. Refer to Chapter 5, Section 1 for the disconnecting procedure.*
  c) *WAIT AT LEAST THREE MINUTES FOR THE BACK-UP POWER SUPPLY TO BE DEPLETED.*

8   Whenever handling an airbag module, always keep the airbag opening side (the trim, or upholstered side) pointed away from your body. Never place the airbag module on a workbench or other surface with the airbag opening facing the surface. Always place the airbag module in a safe location with the airbag opening facing up.

9   Never measure the resistance of any SRS component or use any electrical test equipment on any of the wiring or components. An ohmmeter has a built-in battery supply that could accidentally deploy the airbag.

10 Never use electrical welding equipment on a vehicle equipped with an airbag without first disconnecting the airbag electrical connectors. The connector for the driver's side airbag is located near the steering column (see Chapter 10, Section 16); the connector for the passenger's side airbag is located inside the dash, near the glove box. These connectors - and all SRS component connectors - are bright yellow for easy identification.

11 Never dispose of a live airbag module or seat belt pre-tensioner. Return it to a dealer service department or other qualified repair shop for safe deployment and disposal.

AIRBAG MODULE REMOVAL AND INSTALLATION

12 Refer to Chapter 10, Section 16, for the driver's side airbag module and clockspring removal and installation procedures.

26 Wiring diagrams - general information

Since it isn't possible to include all wiring diagrams for every year covered by this manual, the following diagrams are those that are typical and most commonly needed.

Prior to troubleshooting any circuits, check the fuses and relays to ensure that they're in good condition. Make sure that the battery is correctly charged and check the cable connections (see Chapters 1 and 5).

When checking a circuit, make sure that all connections are clean and tight, with no broken or loose terminals. If an electrical connector is difficult to disconnect, it's probably because the two halves of the con-

nector are locked together on one or two sides of the connector. So stop and look for the locks, which are usually small plastic tabs that must either be depressed to unlock them, or must be released with a small screwdriver. If you have a problem finding the lock(s), clean off the connector with electronic parts cleaner, then look again. If you're trying to unplug a connector that's located in a dark area, use a flashlight to find the locks. When disconnecting an electrical connector, do NOT pull on the wires; pull on the two halves of the connector itself.

Notes

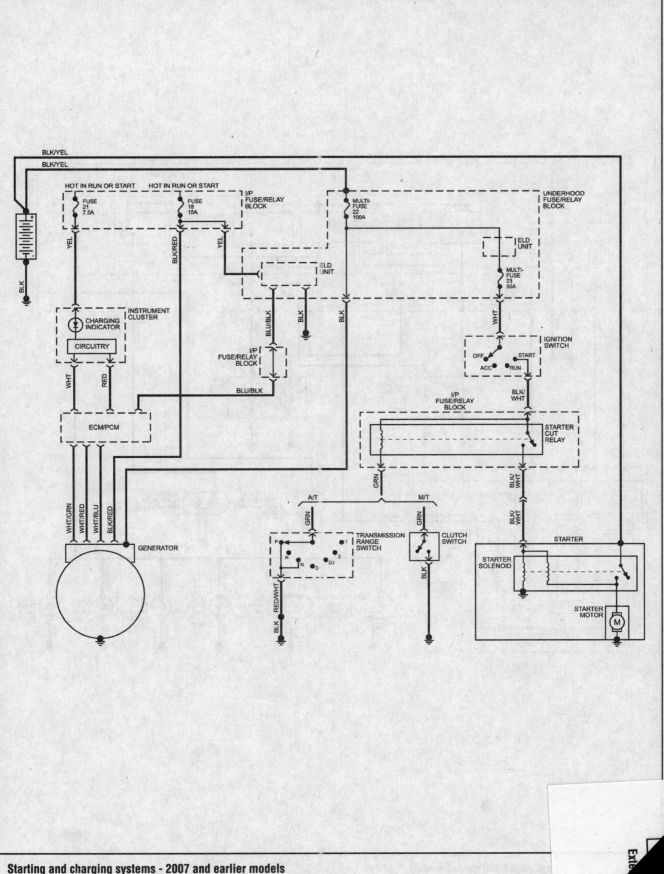

Starting and charging systems - 2007 and earlier models

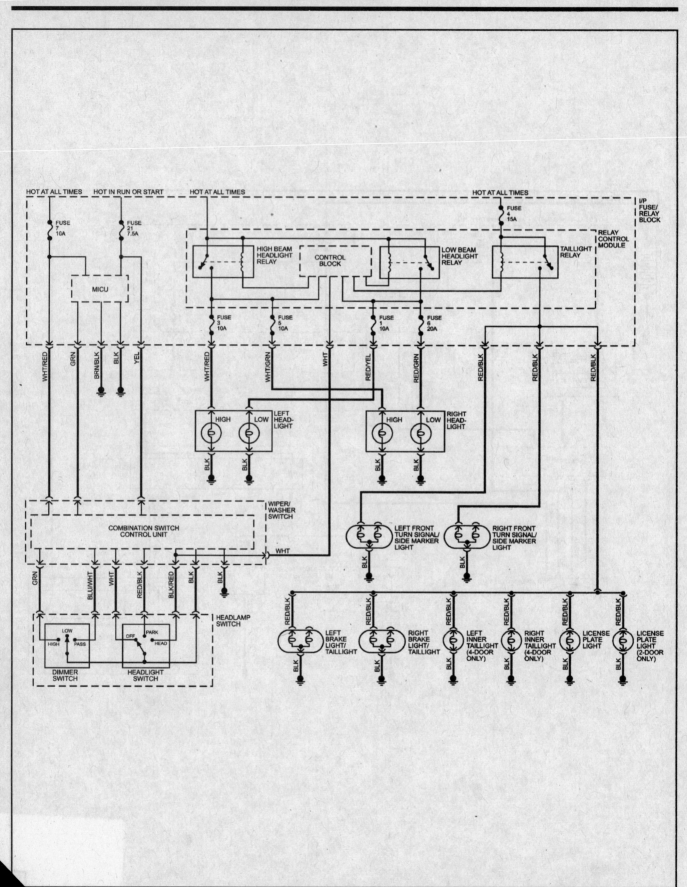

rior lighting system - 2007 and earlier models (1 of 2)

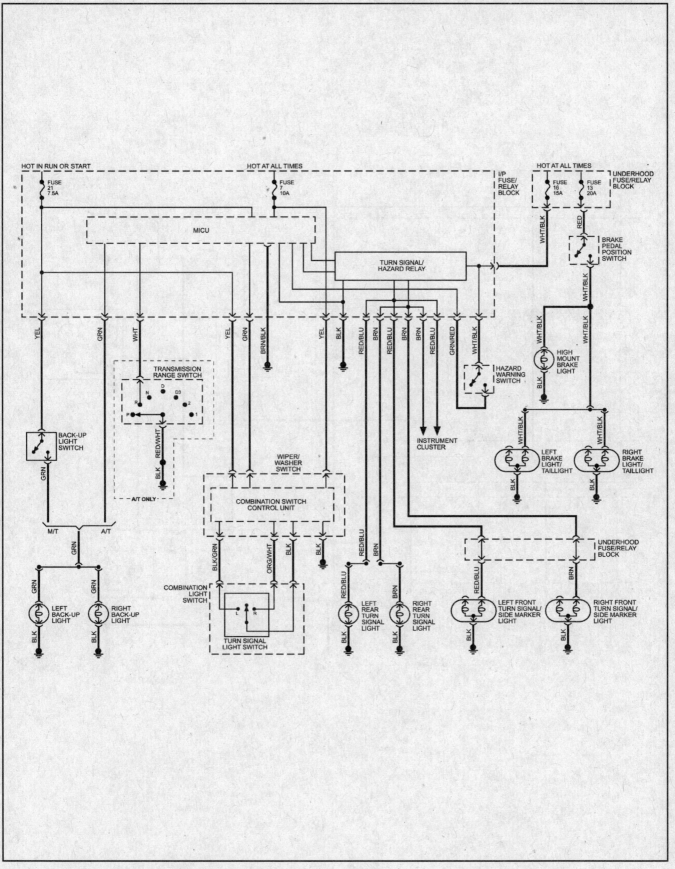

Exterior lighting system - 2007 and earlier models (2 of 2)

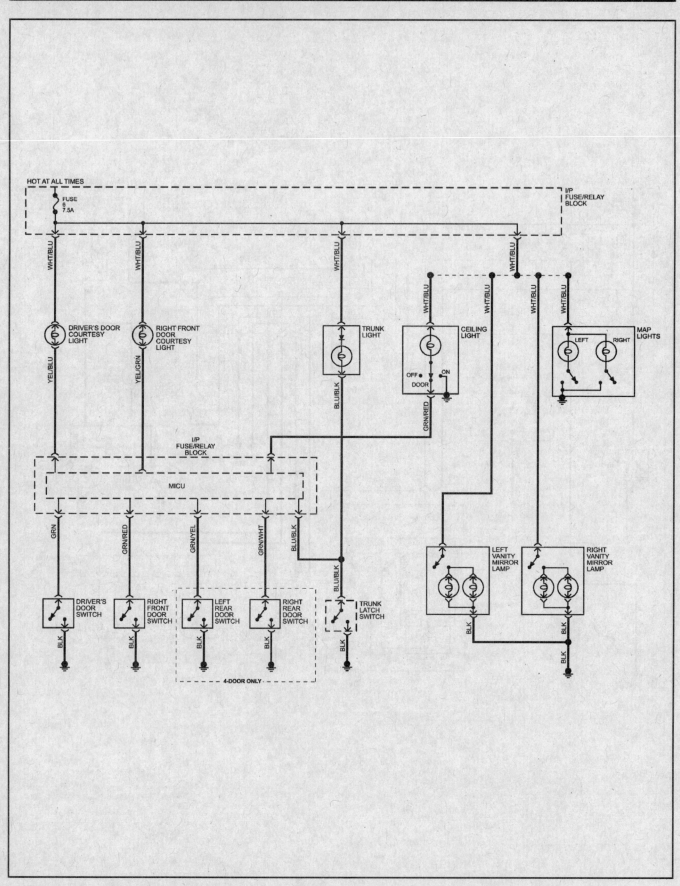

Interior lighting system - 2007 and earlier models

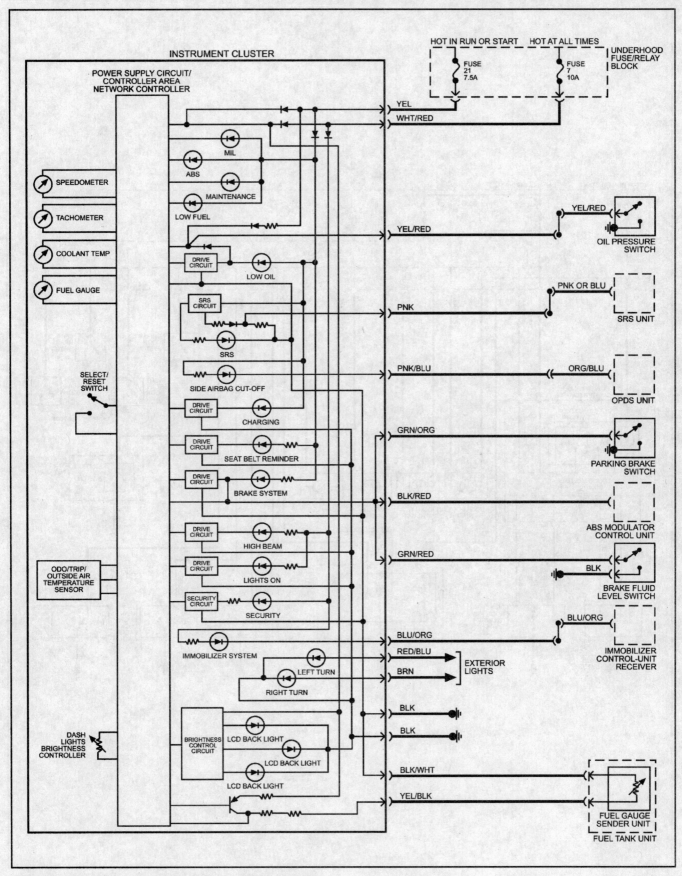

Instrument cluster warning system - 2007 and earlier models

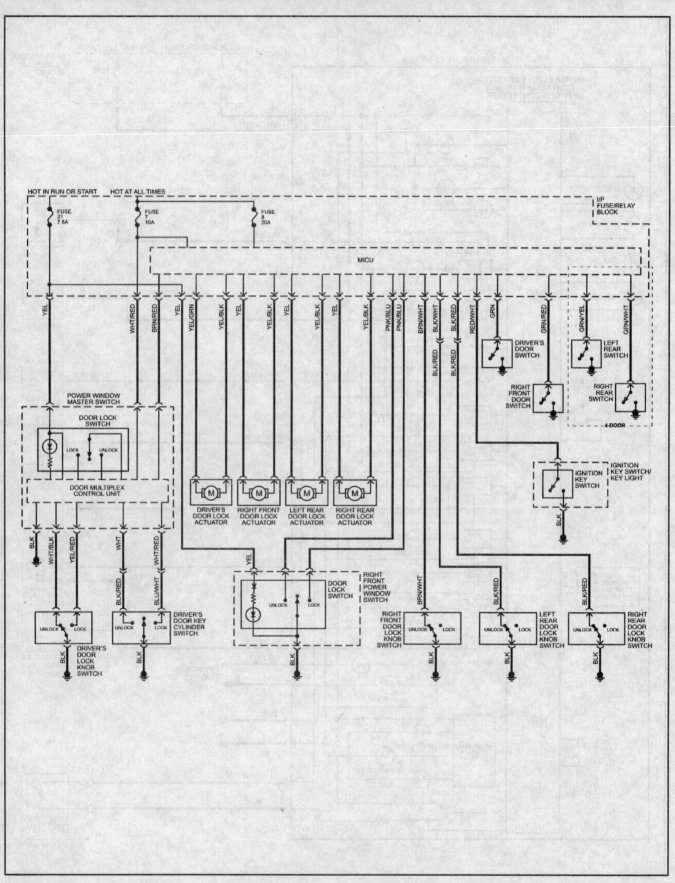

Power door lock system - 2007 and earlier models

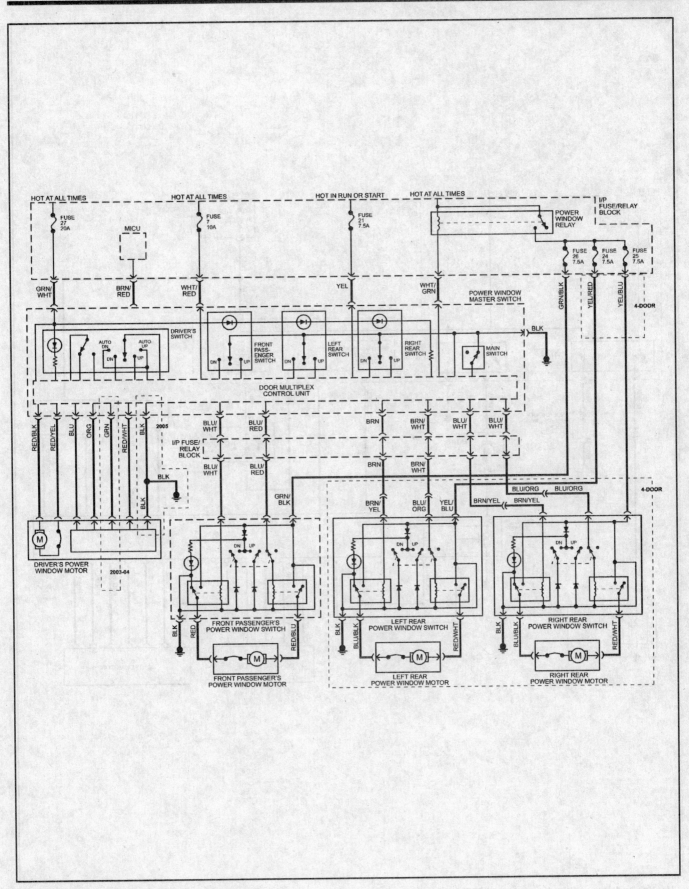

Power window system - 2007 and earlier models

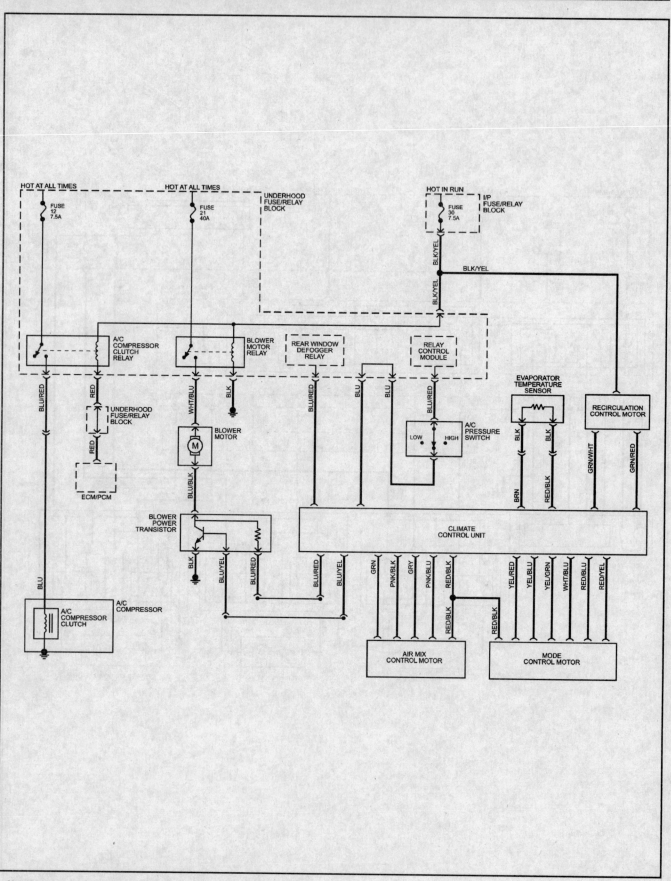

Heating and air conditioning system - 2007 and earlier models

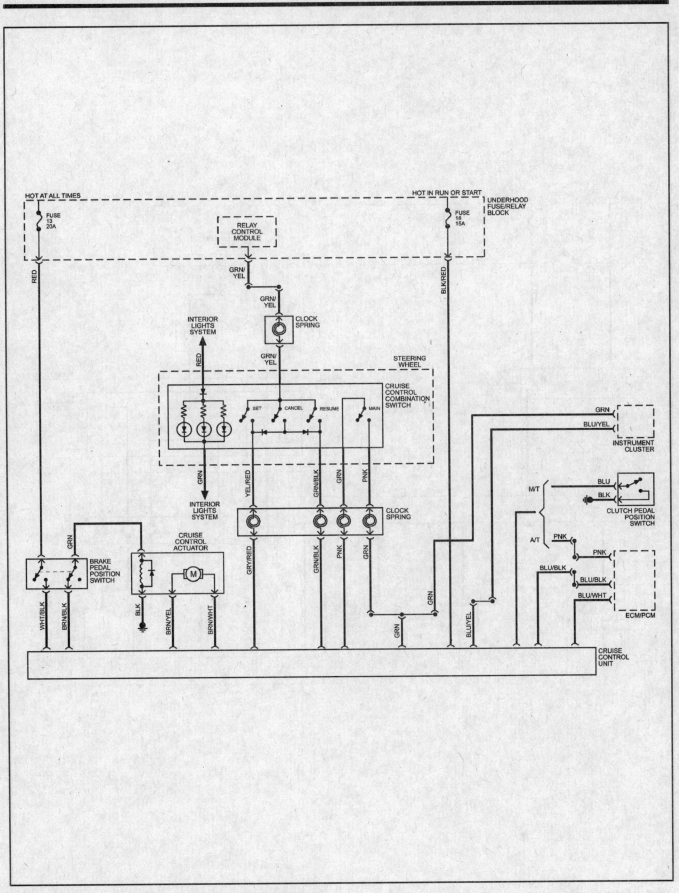

Cruise control system - 2007 and earlier 4-cylinder models

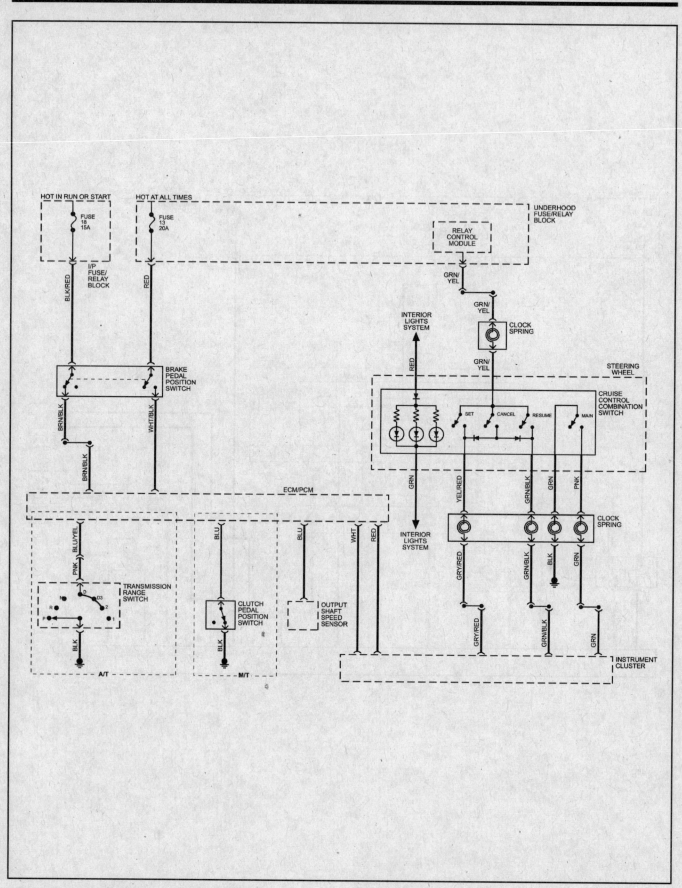

Cruise control system - 2007 and earlier V6 models

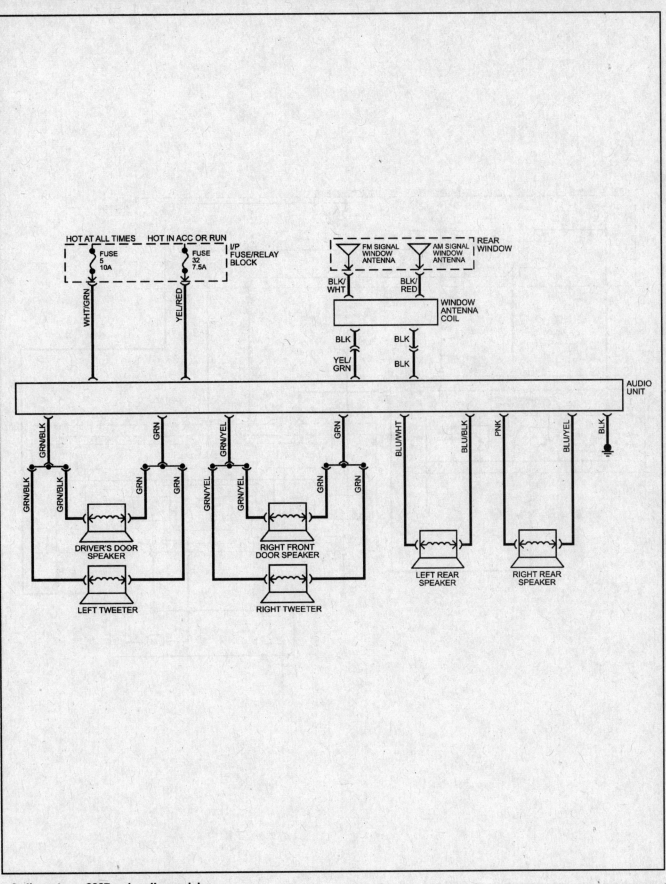

Audio system - 2007 and earlier models

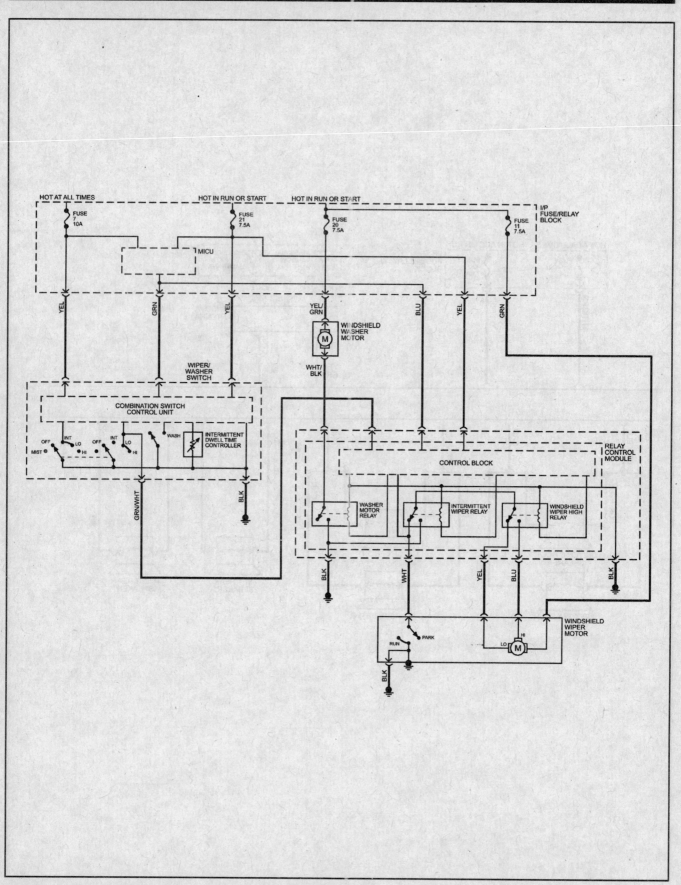

Windshield wiper and washer system - 2007 and earlier models

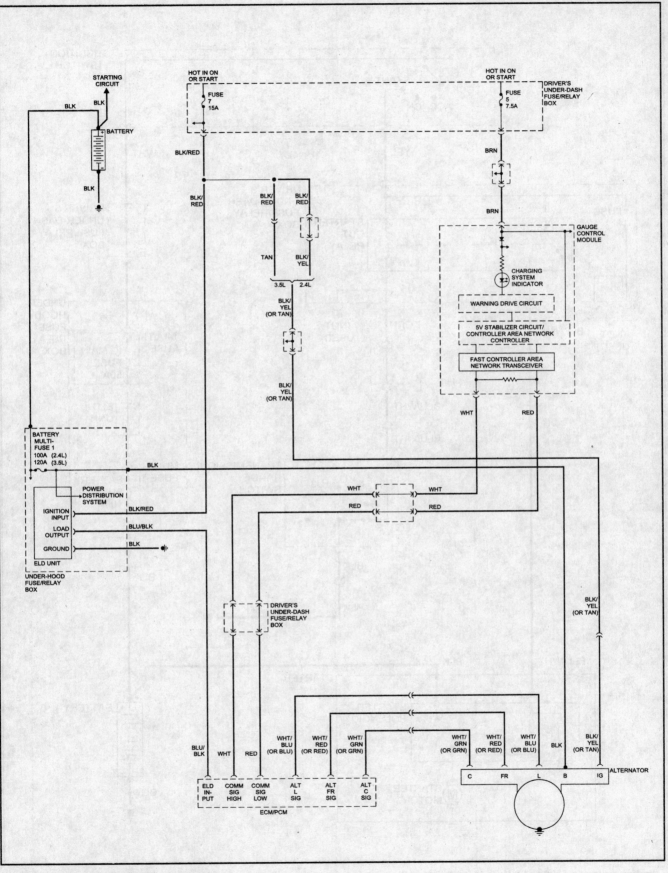

Charging systems - 2008 and later models

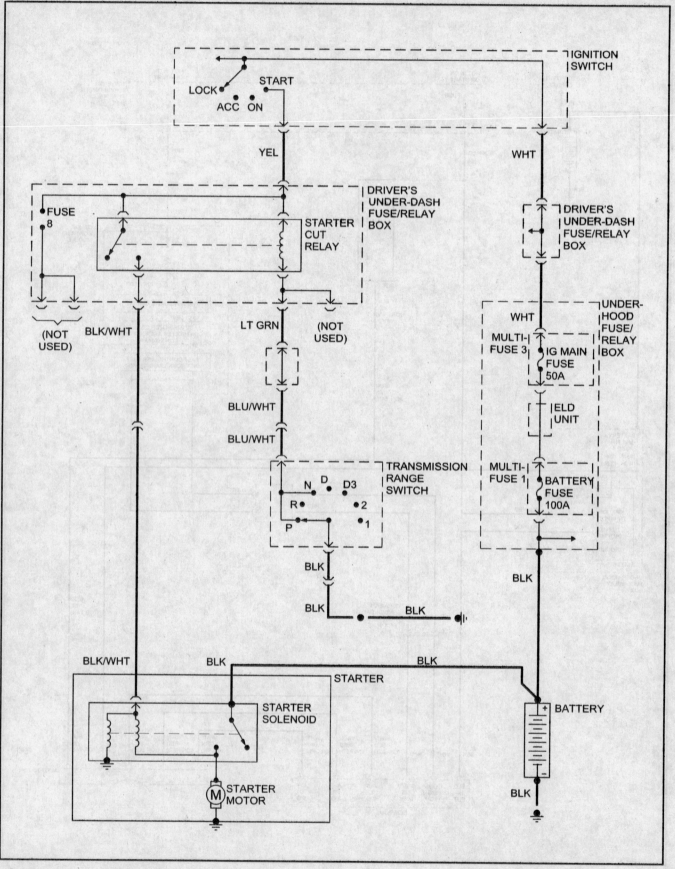

Starting systems - 2008 and later 2.4L models (1 of 2)

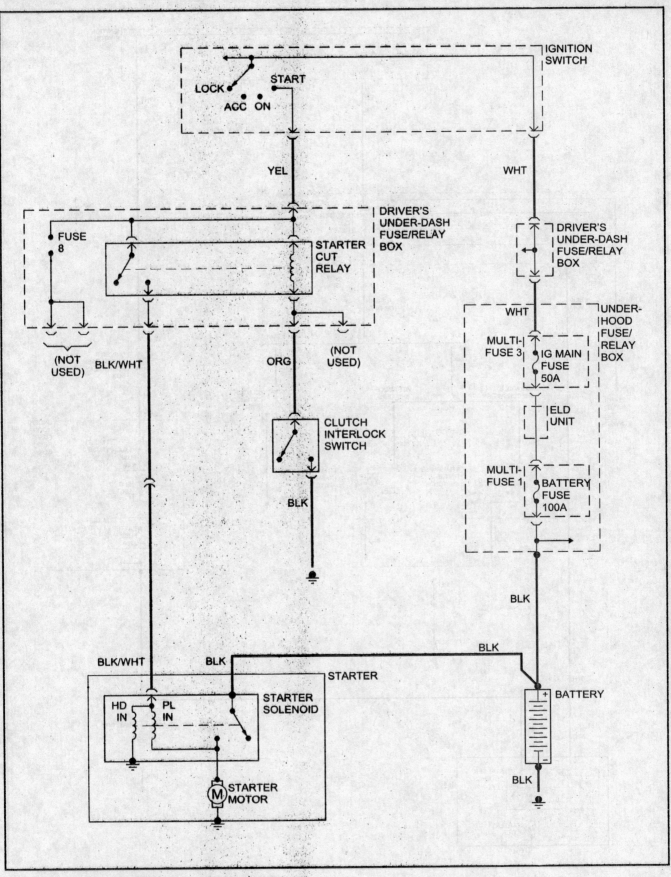

Starting systems - 2008 and later 2.4L models (2 of 2)

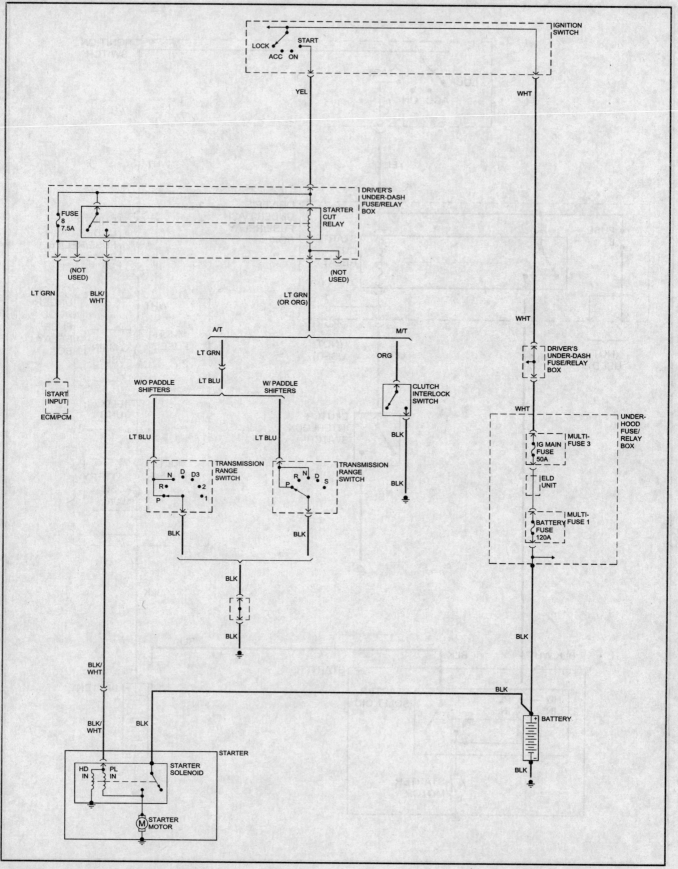

Starting systems - 2008 and later 3.5L models

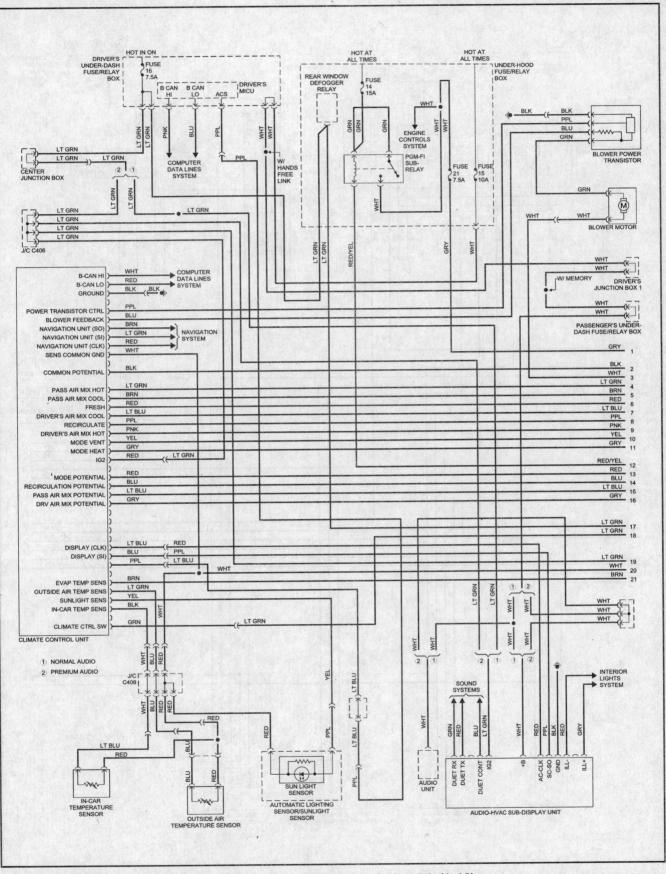

Air conditioning and engine cooling fan system (Auto A/C) - 2008 and later 2.4L models (1 of 3)

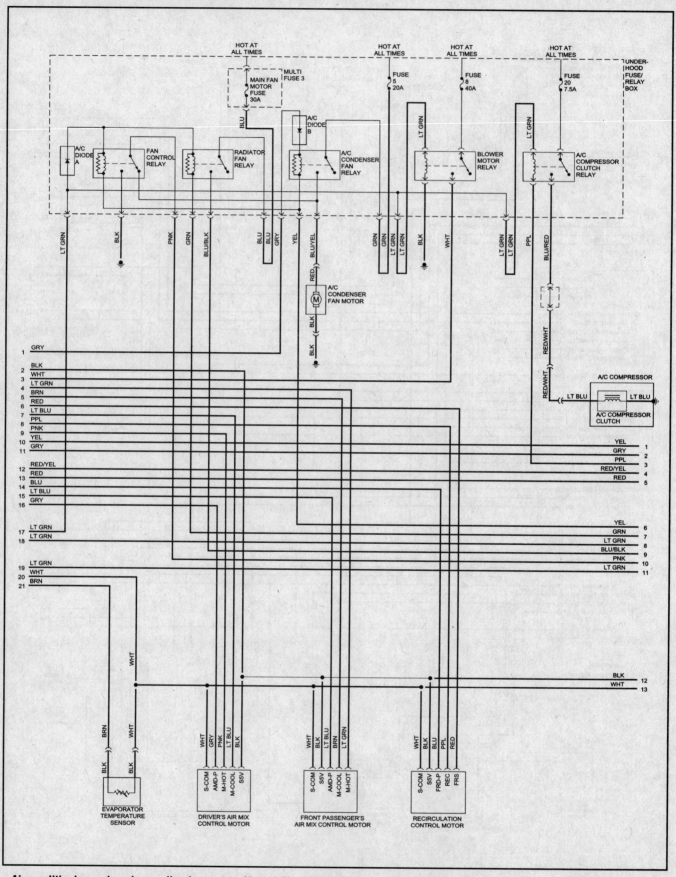

Air conditioning and engine cooling fan system (Auto A/C) - 2008 and later 2.4L models (2 of 3)

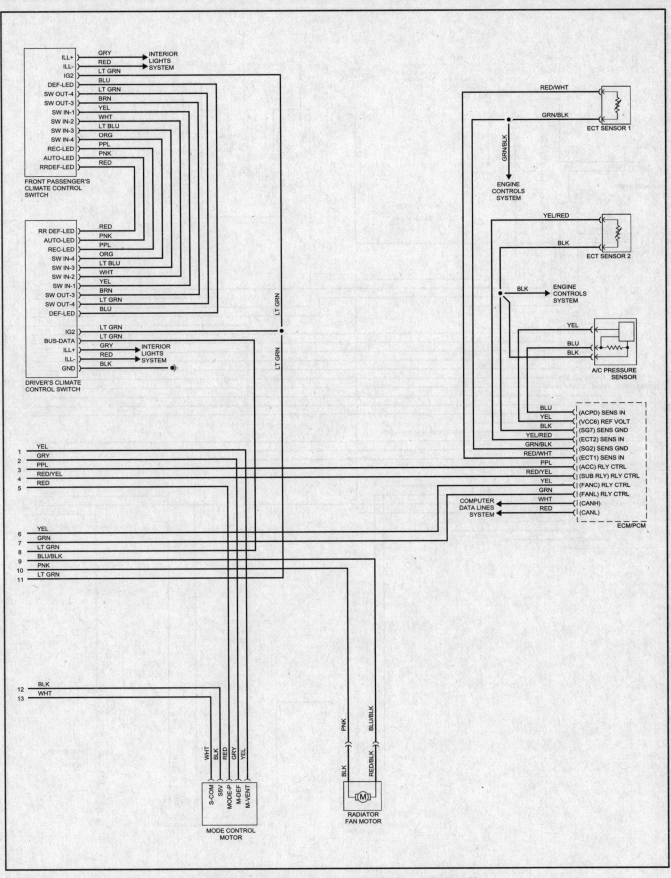

Air conditioning and engine cooling fan system (Auto A/C) - 2008 and later 2.4L models (3 of 3)

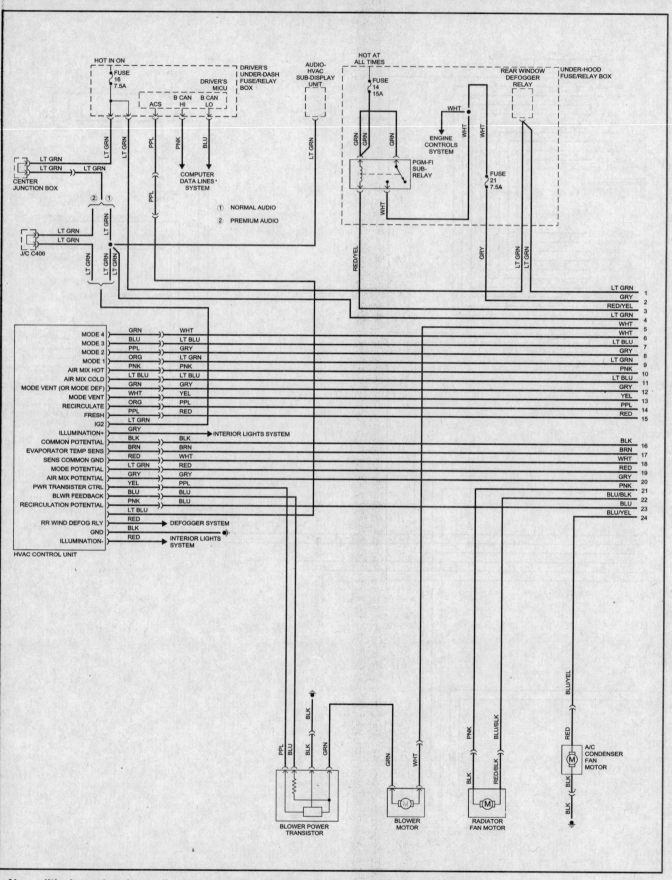

Air conditioning and engine cooling fan system (Manual A/C) - 2008 and later 2.4L models (1 of 2)

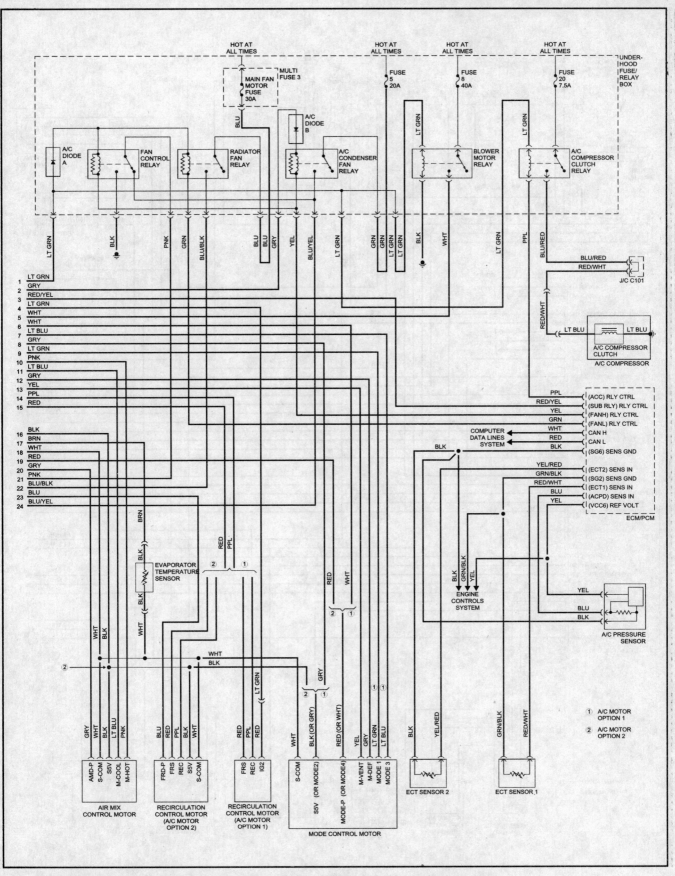

Air conditioning and engine cooling fan system (Manual A/C) - 2008 and later 2.4L models (2 of 2)

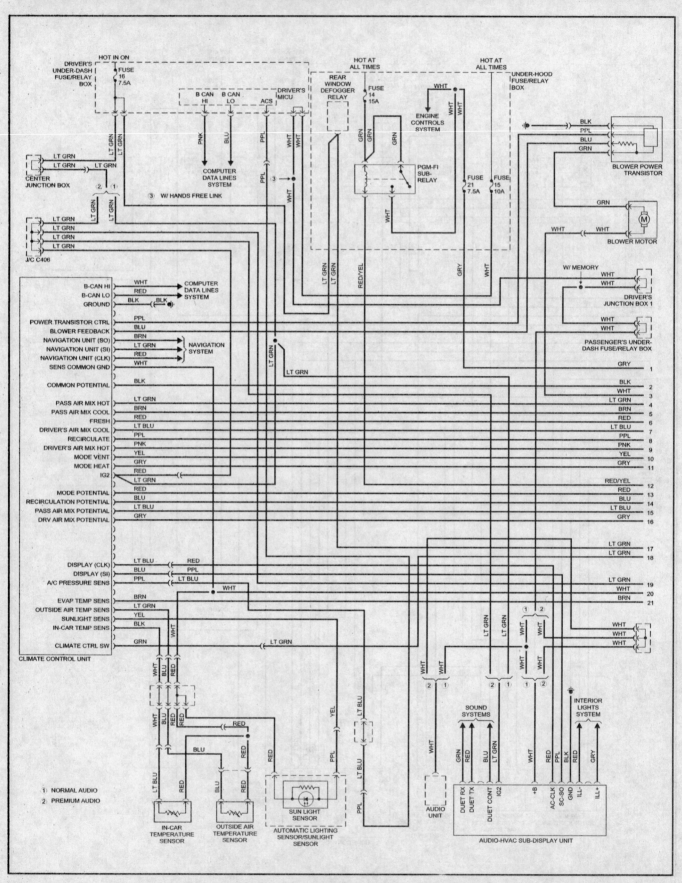

Air conditioning and engine cooling fan system (Auto A/C) - 2008 and later 3.5L models (1 of 3)

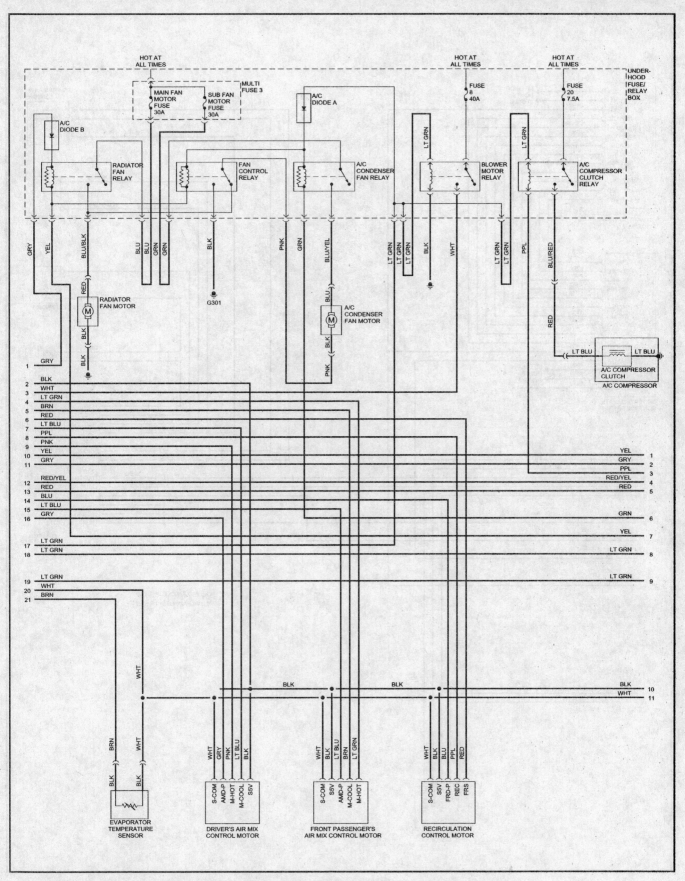

Air conditioning and engine cooling fan system (Auto A/C) - 2008 and later 3.5L models (2 of 3)

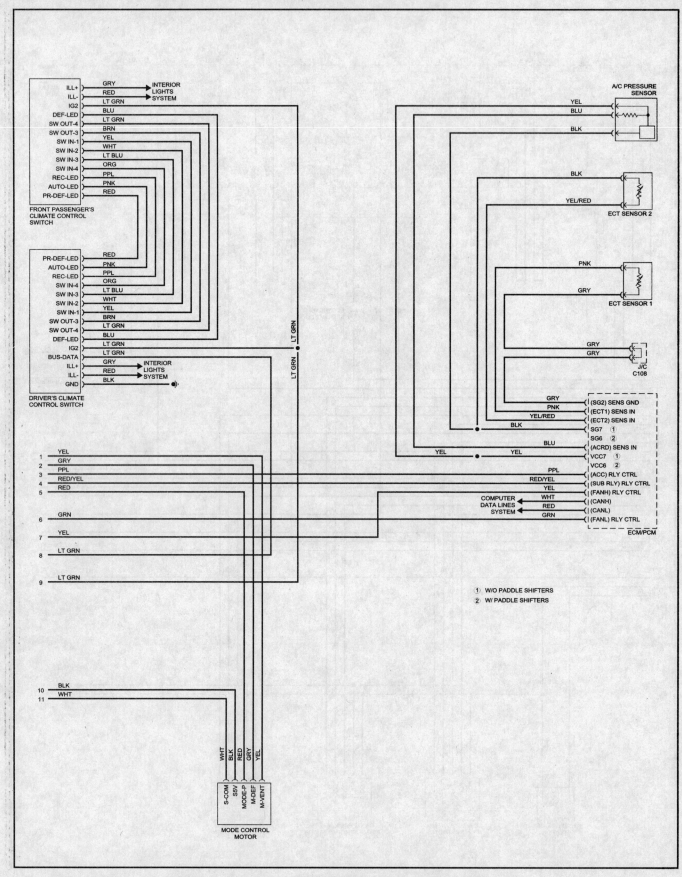

Air conditioning and engine cooling fan system (Auto A/C) - 2008 and later 3.5L models (3 of 3)

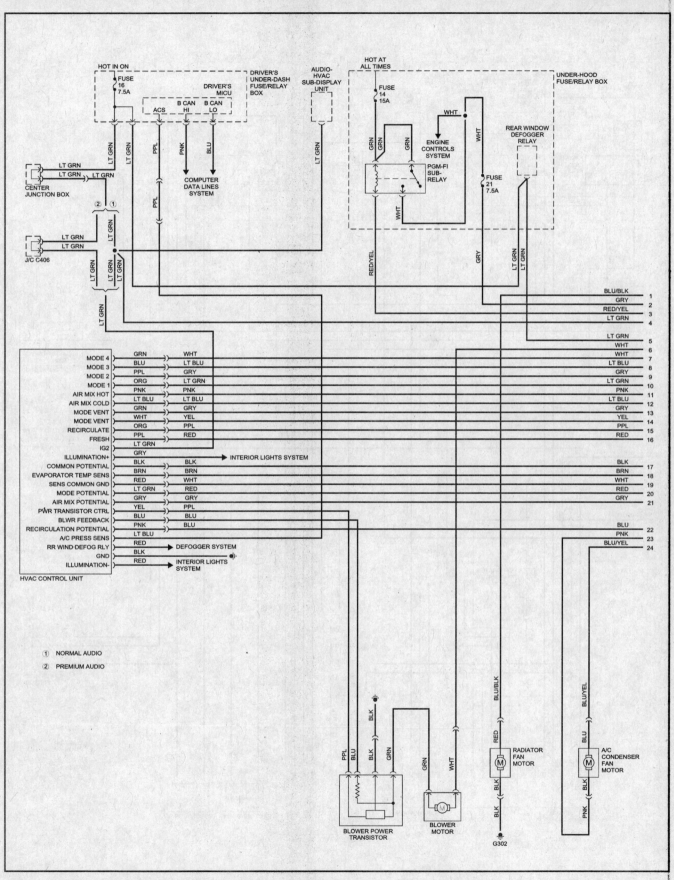

Air conditioning and engine cooling fan system (Manual A/C) - 2008 and later 3.5L models (1 of 2)

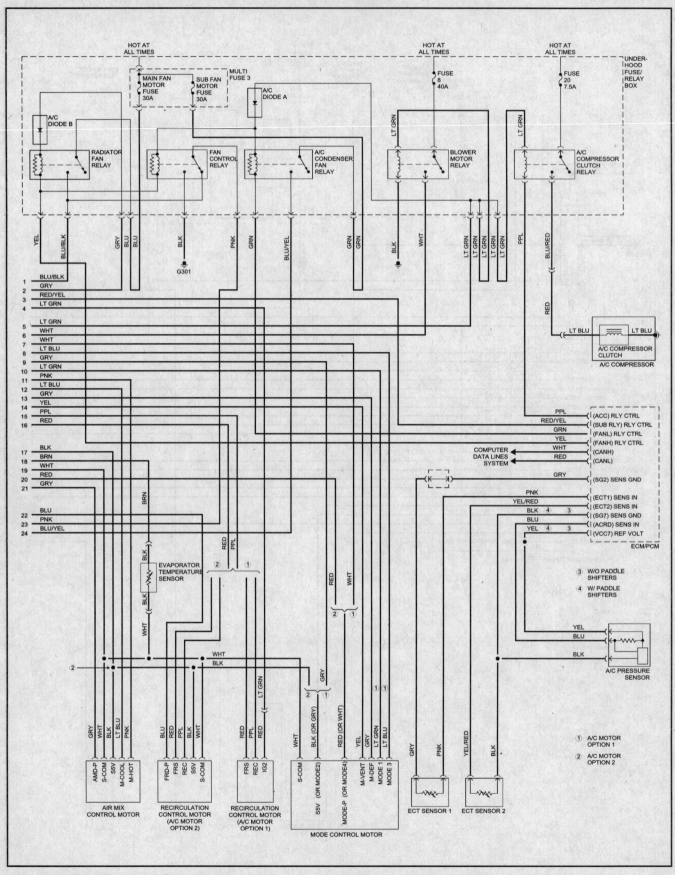

Air conditioning and engine cooling fan system (Manual A/C) - 2008 and later 3.5L models (2 of 2)

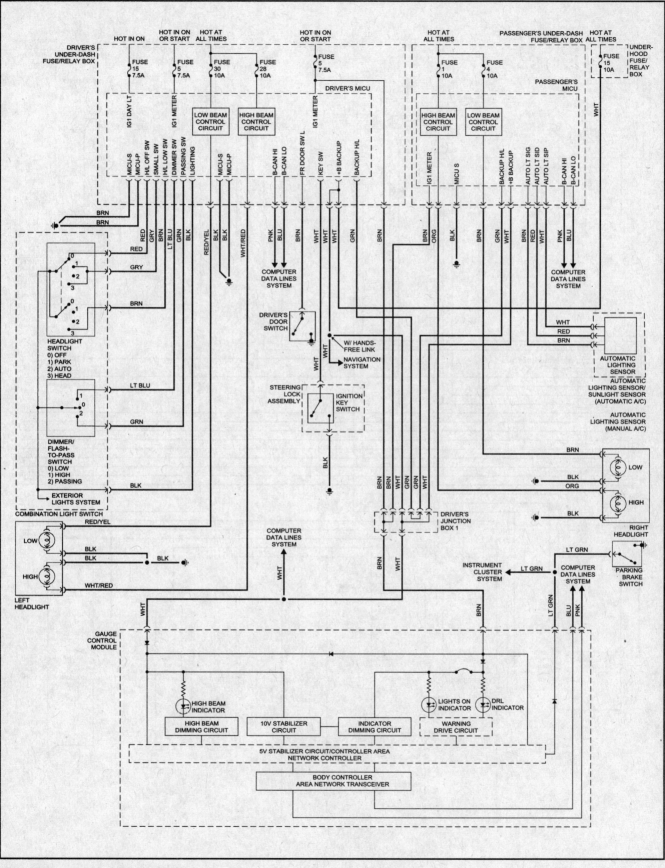

Headlight systems - 2008 and later models

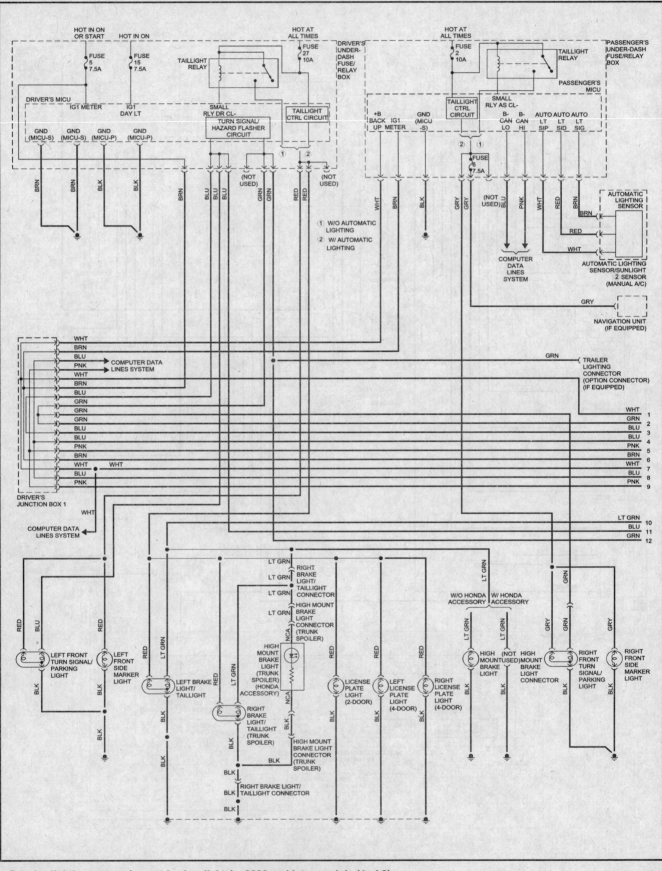

Exterior lighting system (except backup lights) - 2008 and later models (1 of 2)

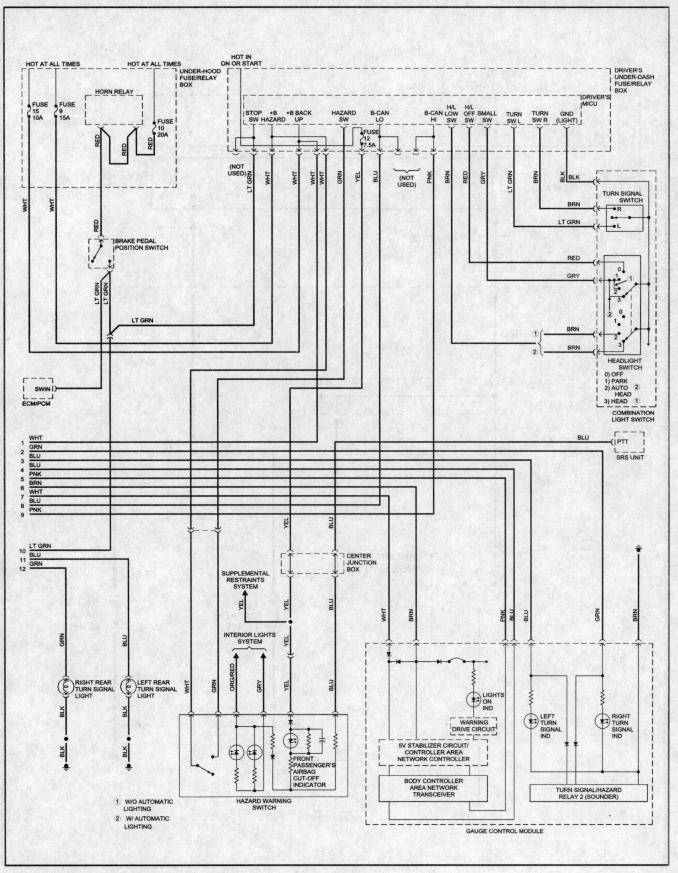

Exterior lighting system (except backup lights) - 2008 and later models (2 of 2)

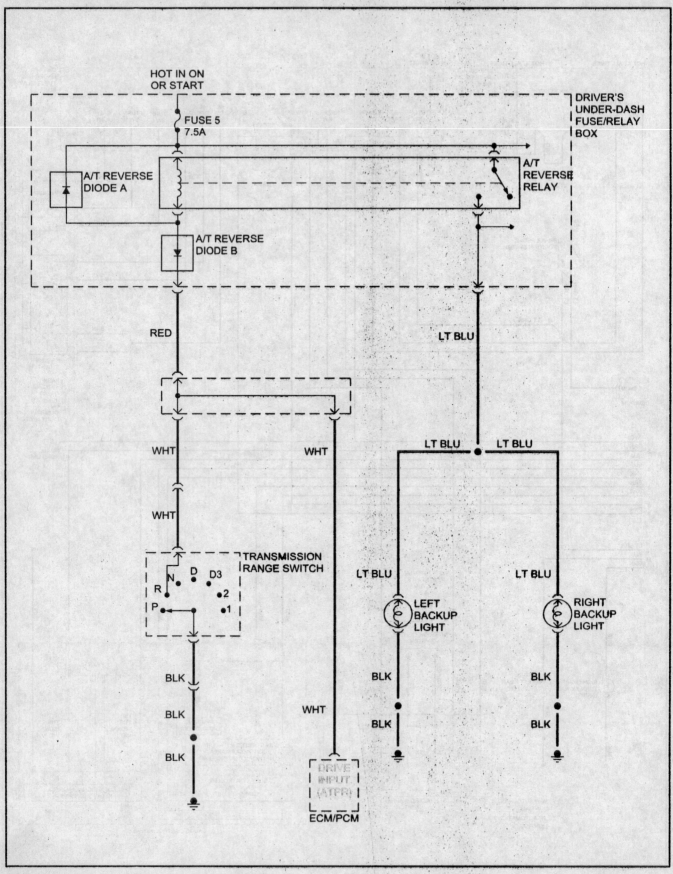

Backup light system - 2008 and later 2.4L models (1 of 2)

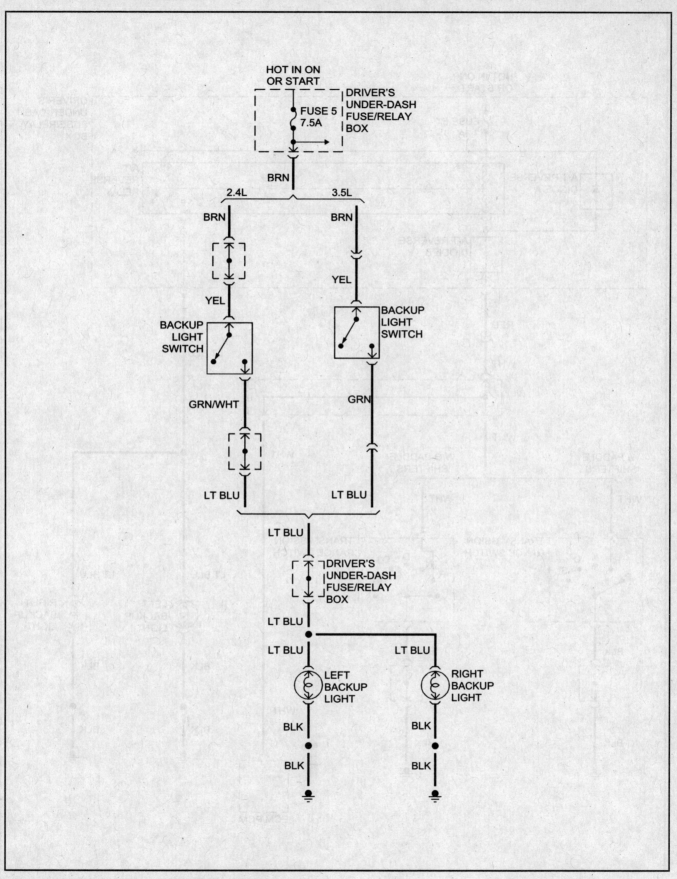

Backup light system - 2008 and later 2.4L models (2 of 2)

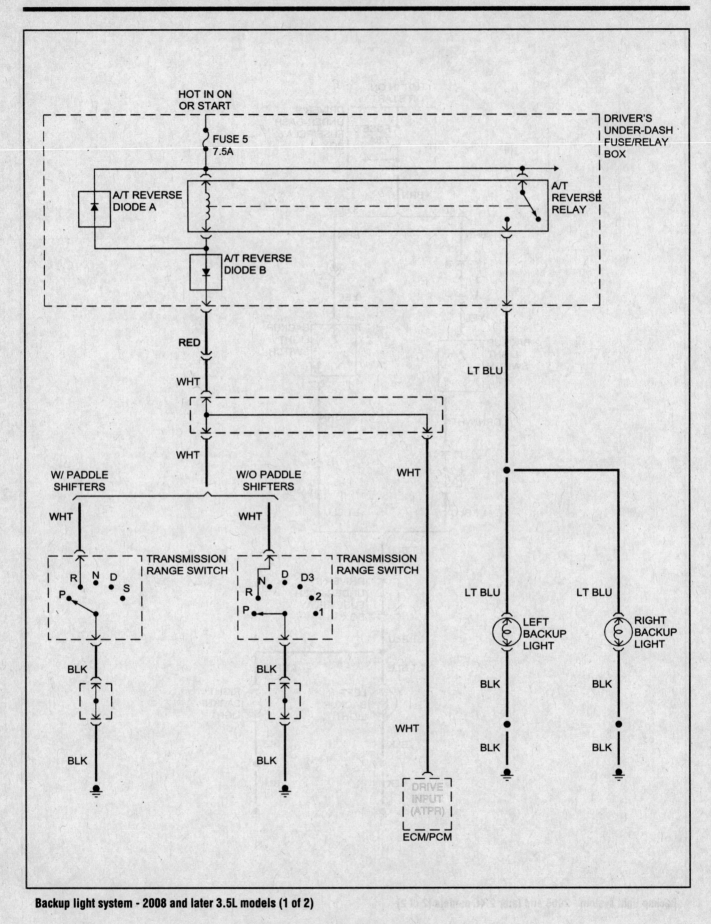

Backup light system - 2008 and later 3.5L models (1 of 2)

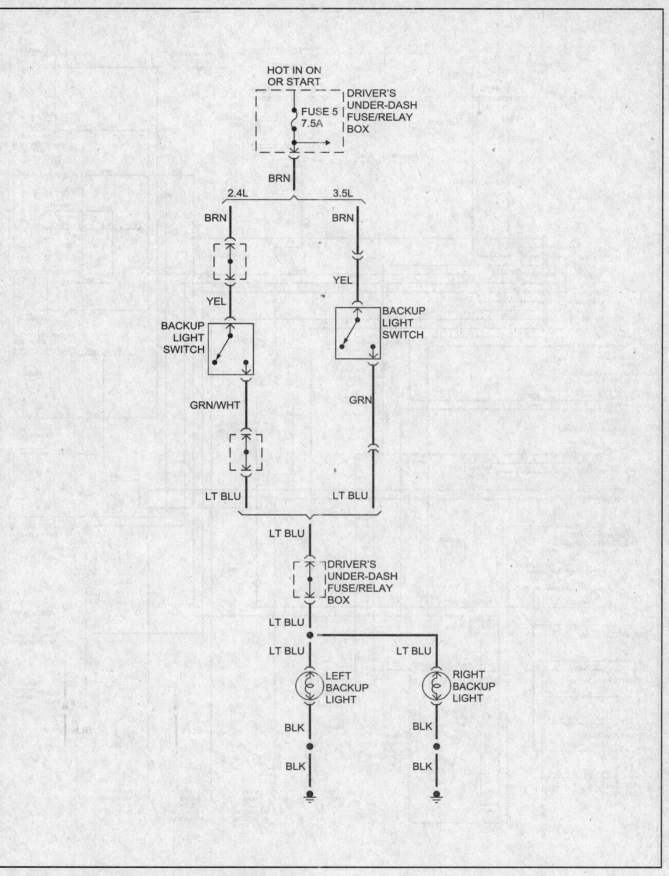

Backup light system - 2008 and later 3.5L models (2 of 2)

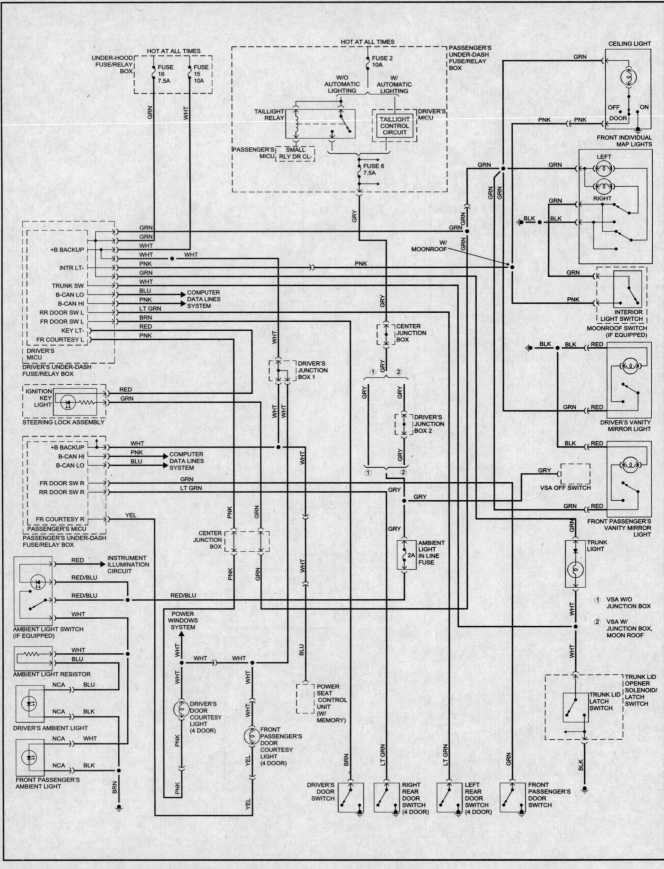

Interior lighting system (courtesy) - 2008 and later models

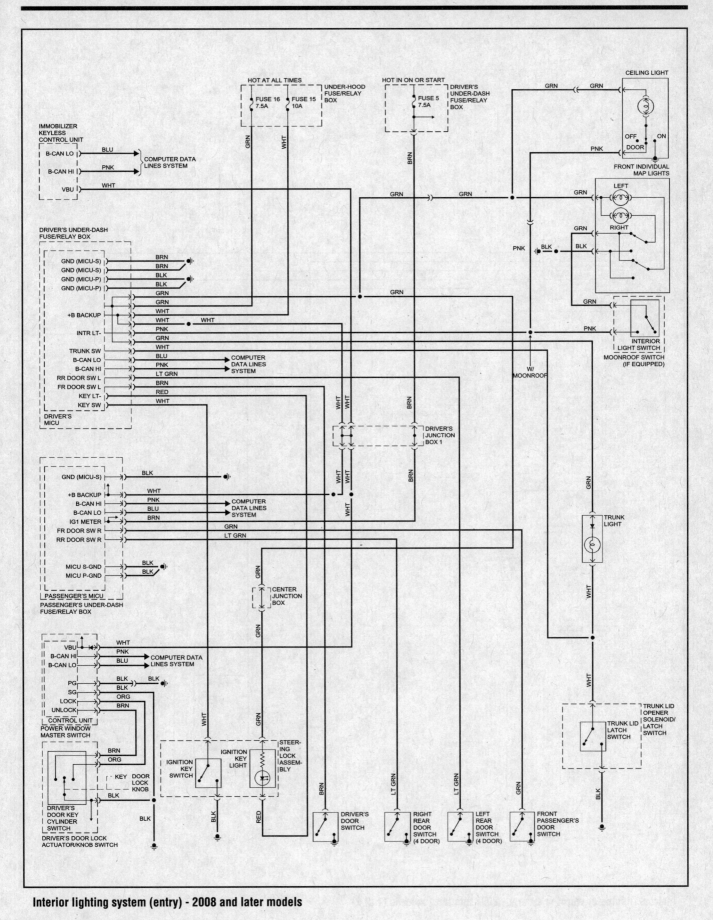

Interior lighting system (entry) - 2008 and later models

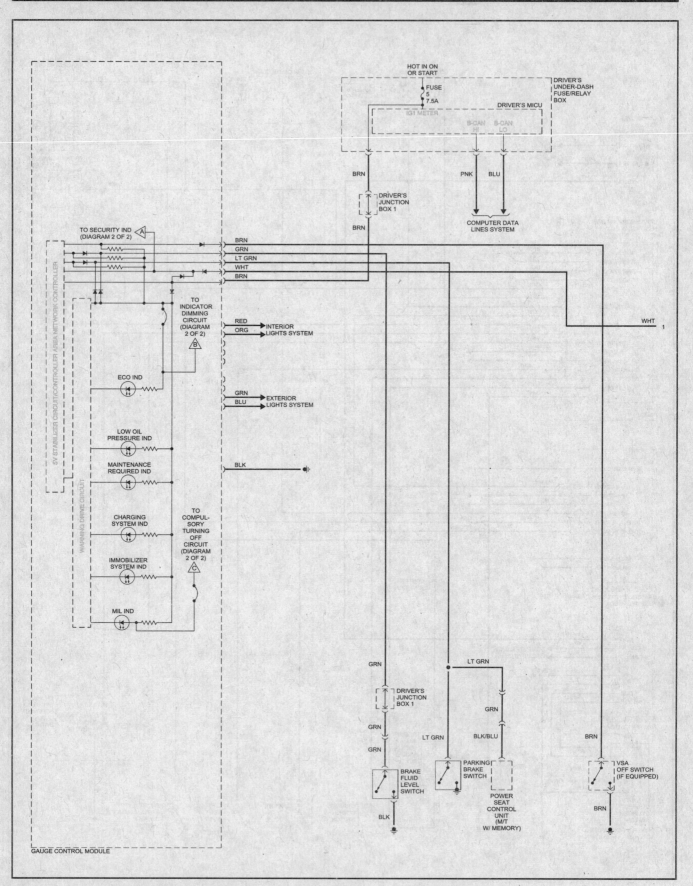

Instrument cluster warning system - 2008 and later models (1 of 2)

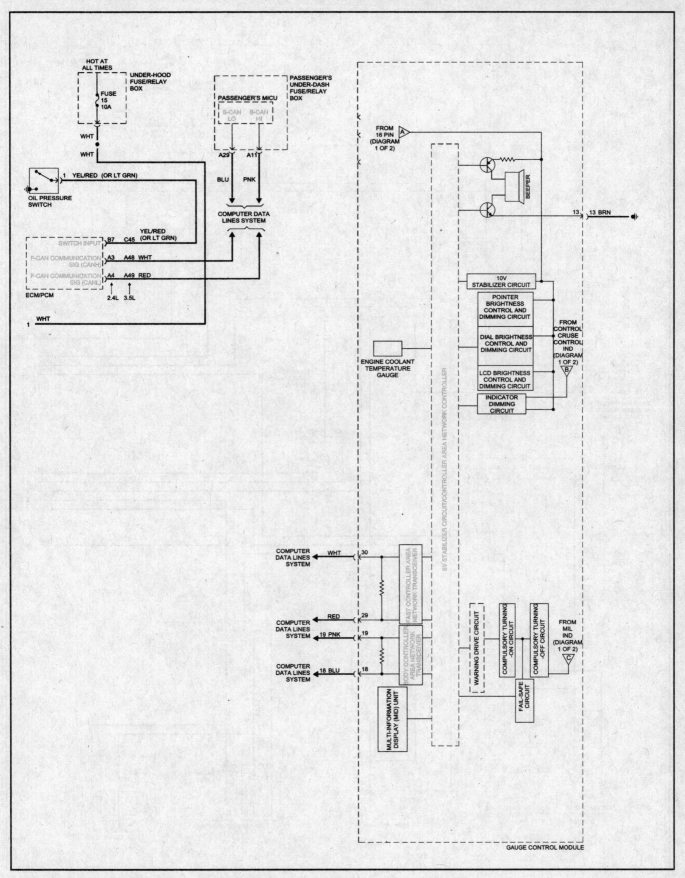

Instrument cluster warning system - 2008 and later models (2 of 2)

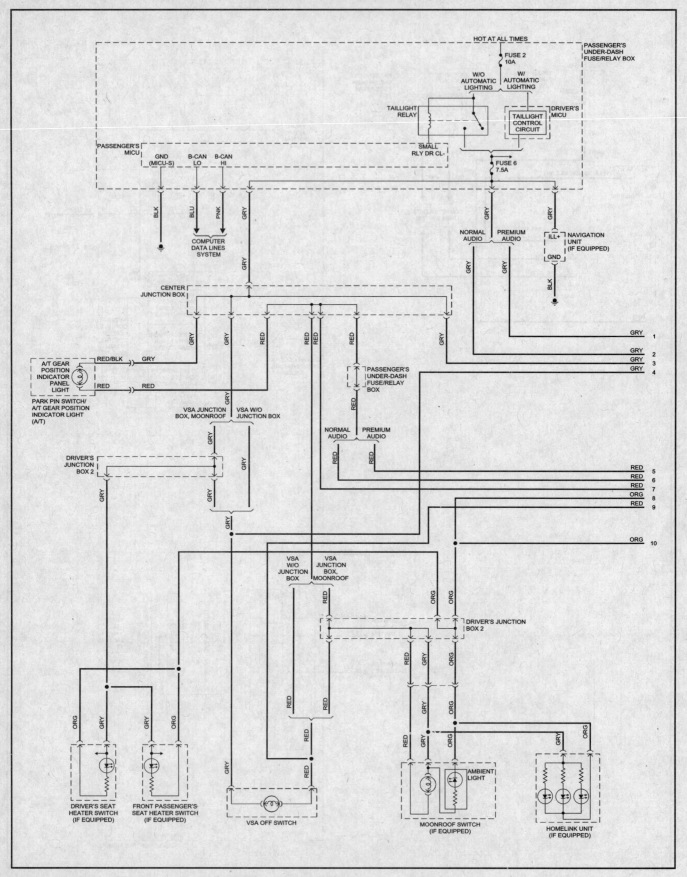

instrument panel and switch illumination - 2008 and later models (1 of 3)

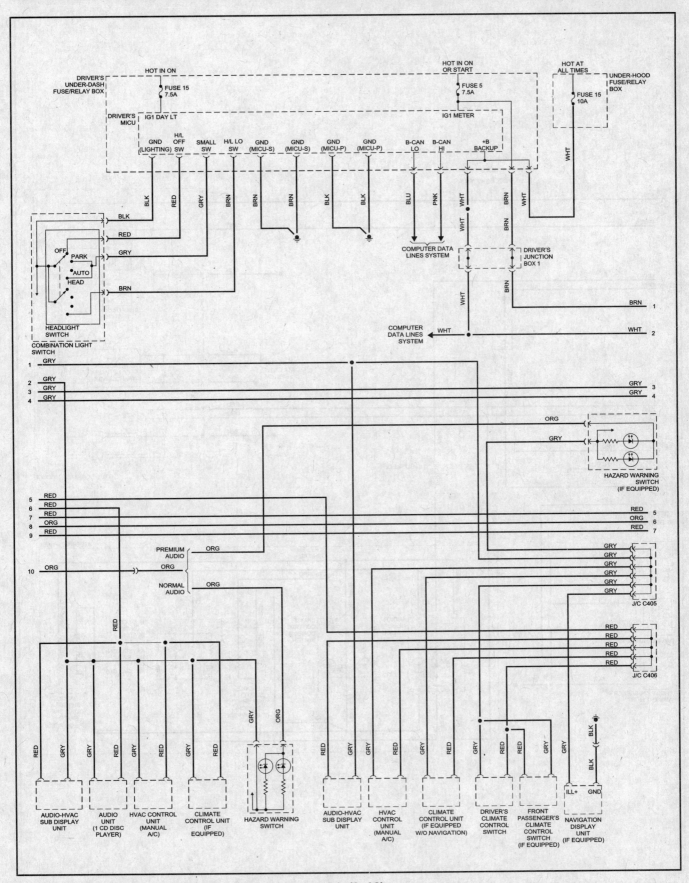

Instrument panel and switch illumination - 2008 and later models (2 of 3)

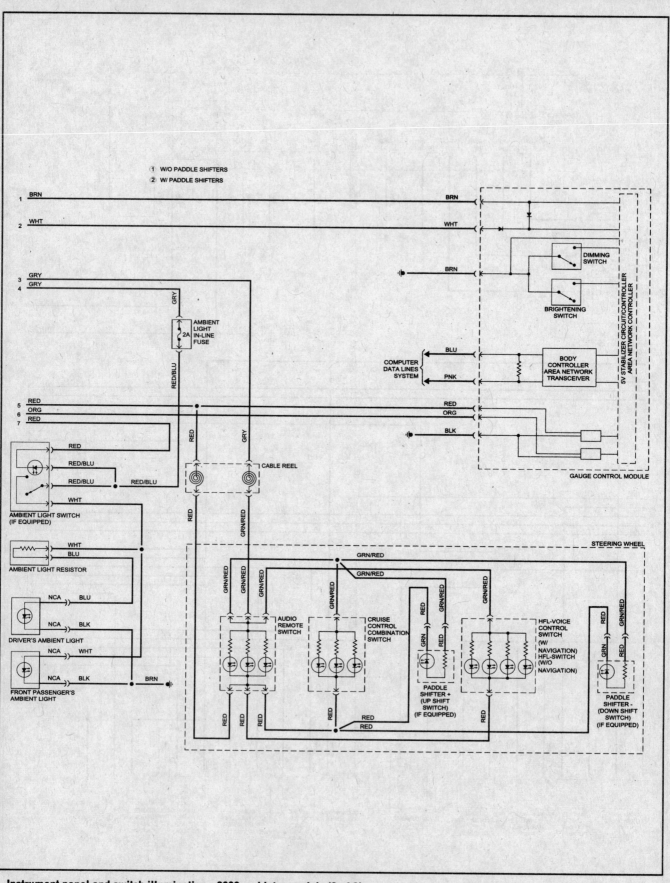

Instrument panel and switch illumination - 2008 and later models (3 of 3)

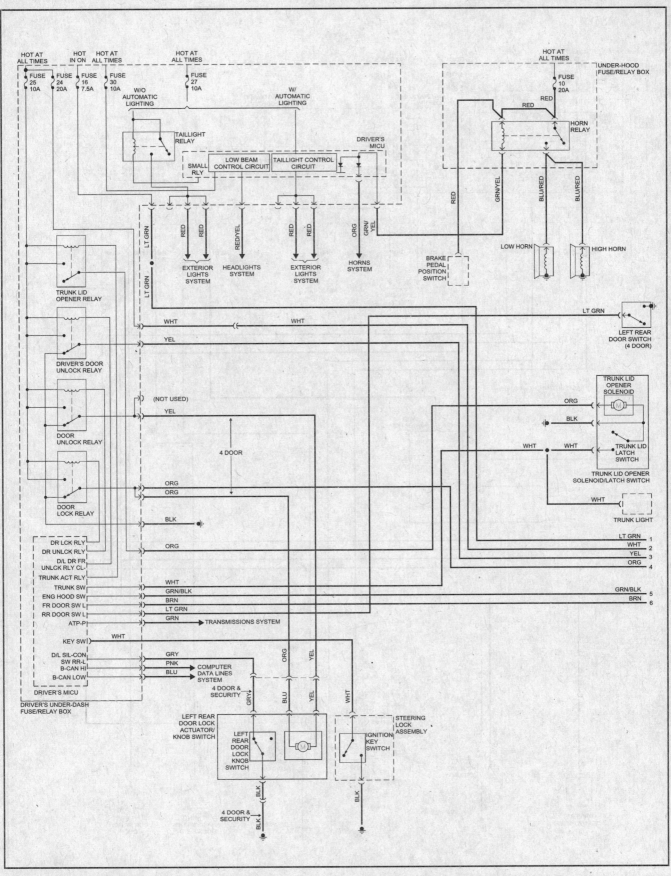

Power door lock system - 2008 and later models (1 of 3)

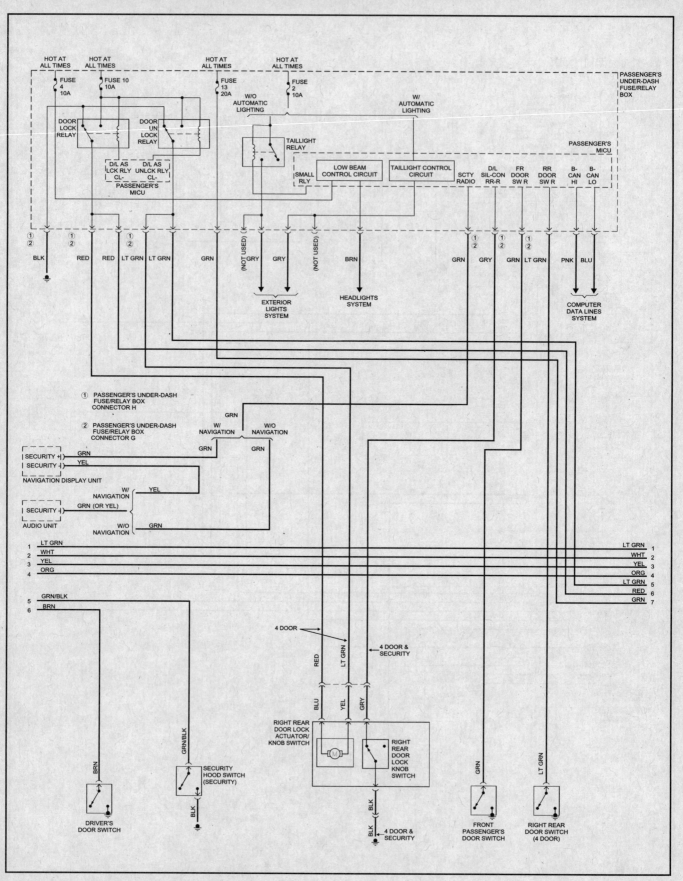

Power door lock system - 2008 and later models (2 of 3)

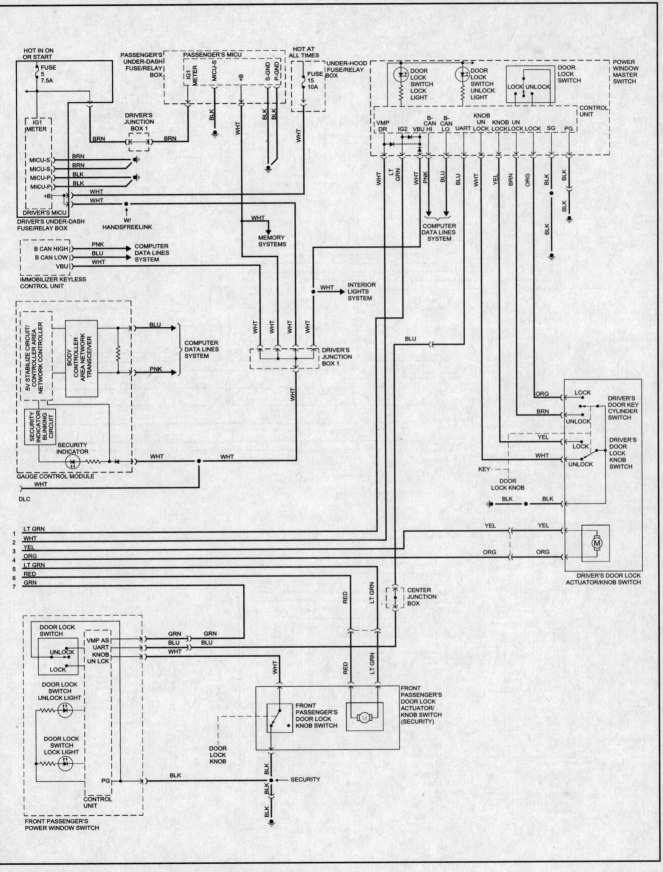

Power door lock system - 2008 and later models (3 of 3)

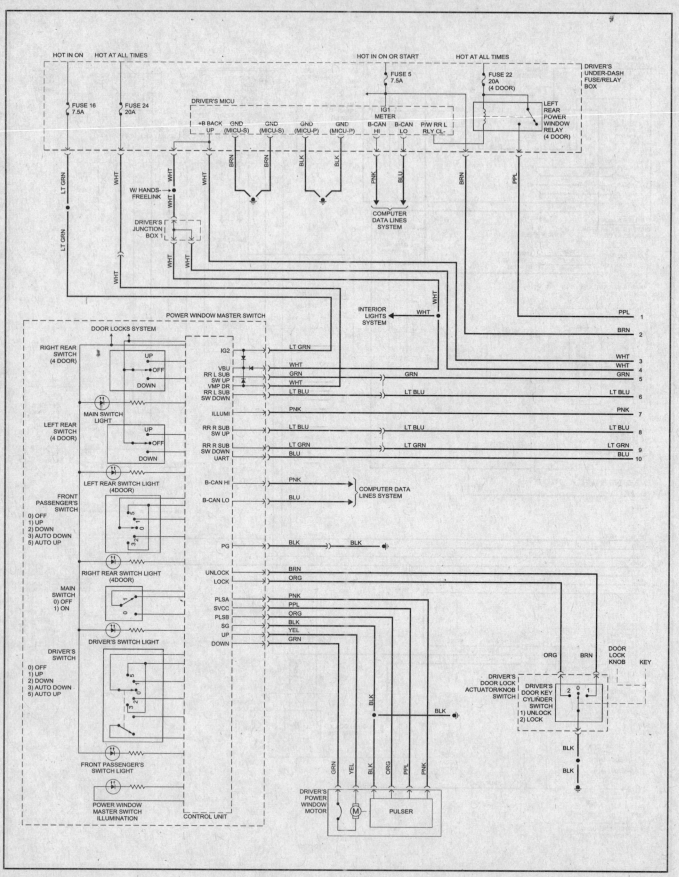

Power window system - 2008 and later models (1 of 3)

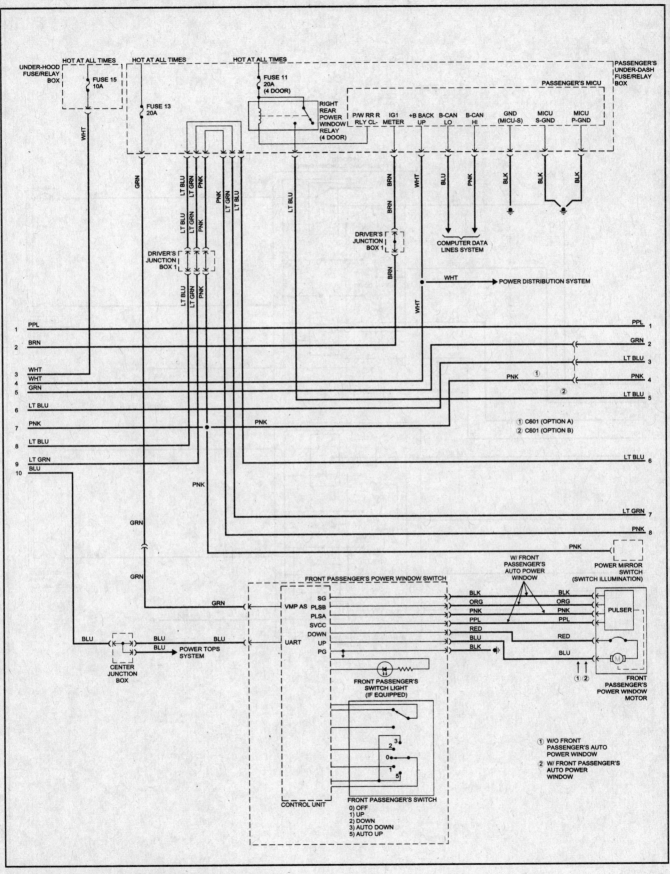

Power window system - 2008 and later models (2 of 3)

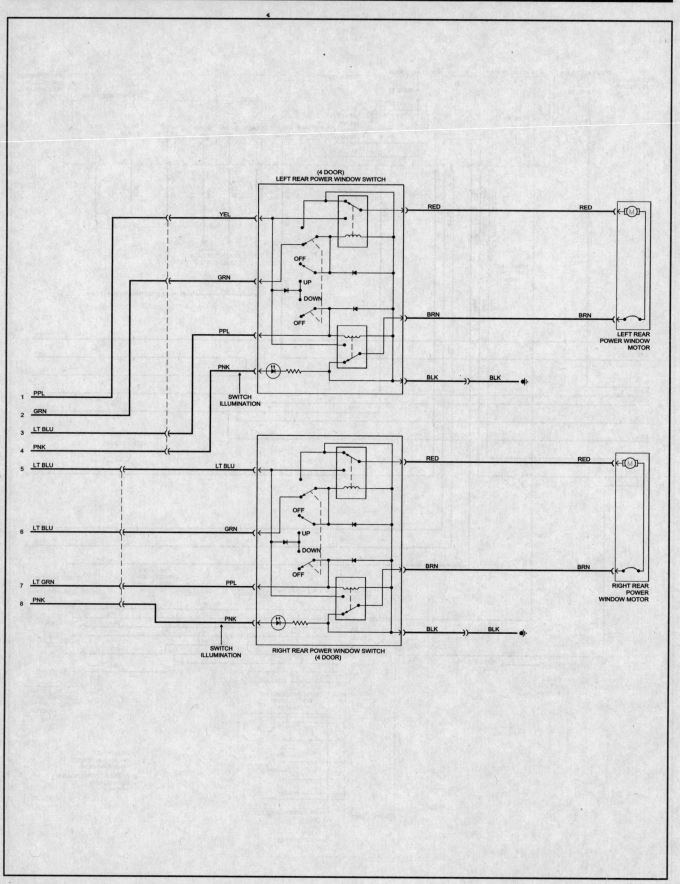

Power window system - 2008 and later models (3 of 3)

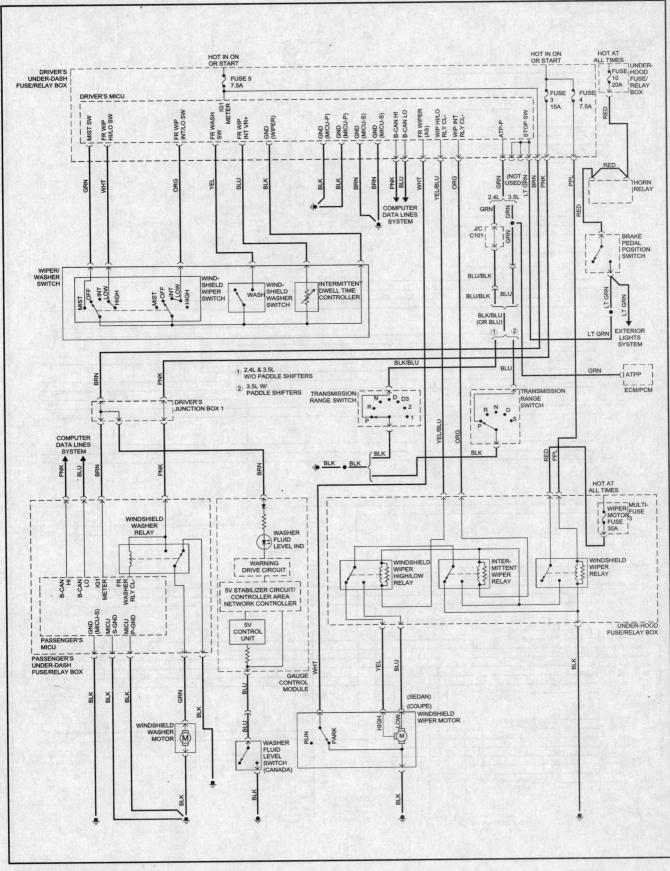

Wiper/washer system - 2008 and later models

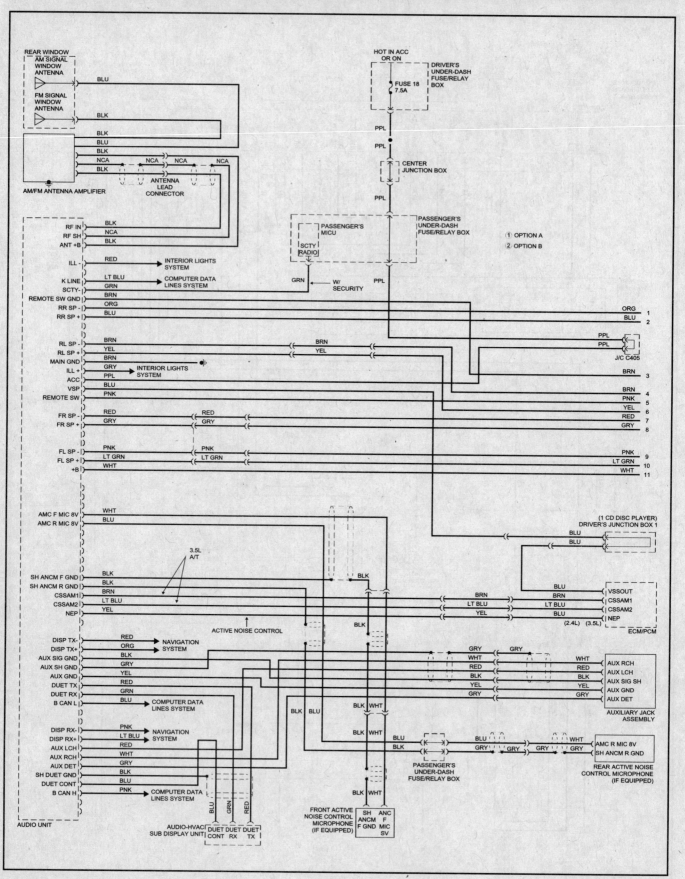

Audio system - 2008 and later models (1 of 3)

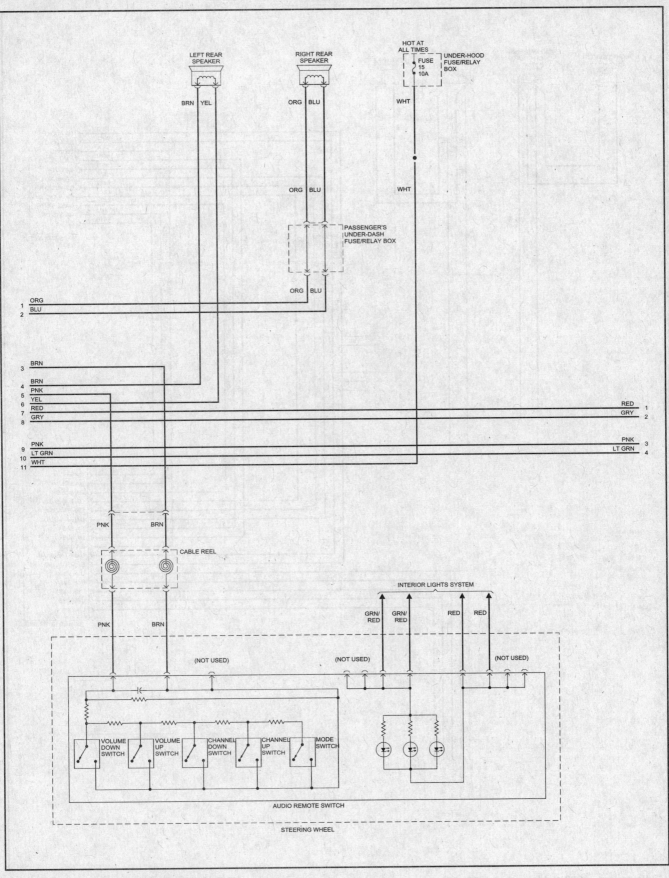

Audio system - 2008 and later models (2 of 3)

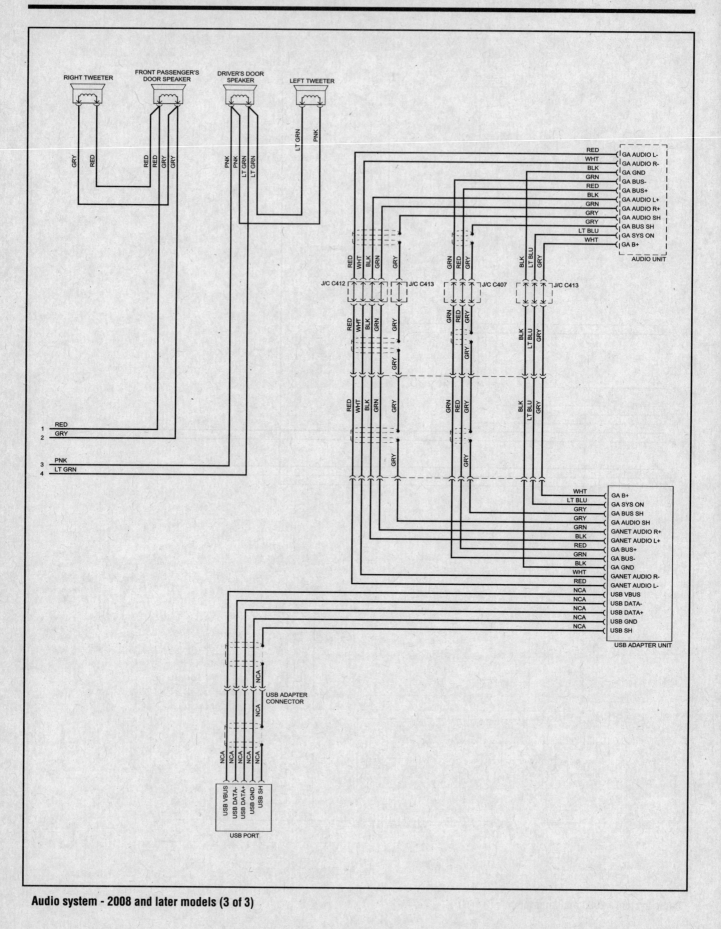

Audio system - 2008 and later models (3 of 3)

GLOSSARY

AIR/FUEL RATIO: The ratio of air-to-gasoline by weight in the fuel mixture drawn into the engine.

AIR INJECTION: One method of reducing harmful exhaust emissions by injecting air into each of the exhaust ports of an engine. The fresh air entering the hot exhaust manifold causes any remaining fuel to be burned before it can exit the tailpipe.

ALTERNATOR: A device used for converting mechanical energy into electrical energy.

AMMETER: An instrument, calibrated in amperes, used to measure the flow of an electrical current in a circuit. Ammeters are always connected in series with the circuit being tested.

AMPERE: The rate of flow of electrical current present when one volt of electrical pressure is applied against one ohm of electrical resistance.

ANALOG COMPUTER: Any microprocessor that uses similar (analogous) electrical signals to make its calculations.

ARMATURE: A laminated, soft iron core wrapped by a wire that converts electrical energy to mechanical energy as in a motor or relay. When rotated in a magnetic field, it changes mechanical energy into electrical energy as in a generator.

ATMOSPHERIC PRESSURE: The pressure on the Earth's surface caused by the weight of the air in the atmosphere. At sea level, this pressure is 14.7 psi at 32°F (101 kPa at 0°C).

ATOMIZATION: The breaking down of a liquid into a fine mist that can be suspended in air.

AXIAL PLAY: Movement parallel to a shaft or bearing bore.

BACKFIRE: The sudden combustion of gases in the intake or exhaust system that results in a loud explosion.

BACKLASH: The clearance or play between two parts, such as meshed gears.

BACKPRESSURE: Restrictions in the exhaust system that slow the exit of exhaust gases from the combustion chamber.

BAKELITE: A heat resistant, plastic insulator material commonly used in printed circuit boards and transistorized components.

BALL BEARING: A bearing made up of hardened inner and outer races between which hardened steel balls roll.

BALLAST RESISTOR: A resistor in the primary ignition circuit that lowers voltage after the engine is started to reduce wear on ignition components.

BEARING: A friction reducing, supportive device usually located between a stationary part and a moving part.

BIMETAL TEMPERATURE SENSOR: Any sensor or switch made of two dissimilar types of metal that bend when heated or cooled due to the different expansion rates of the alloys. These types of sensors usually function as an on/off switch.

BLOWBY: Combustion gases, composed of water vapor and unburned fuel, that leak past the piston rings into the crankcase during normal engine operation. These gases are removed by the PCV system to prevent the buildup of harmful acids in the crankcase.

BRAKE PAD: A brake shoe and lining assembly used with disc brakes.

BRAKE SHOE: The backing for the brake lining. The term is, however, usually applied to the assembly of the brake backing and lining.

BUSHING: A liner, usually removable, for a bearing; an anti-friction liner used in place of a bearing.

CALIPER: A hydraulically activated device in a disc brake system, which is mounted straddling the brake rotor (disc). The caliper contains at least one piston and two brake pads. Hydraulic pressure on the piston(s) forces the pads against the rotor.

CAMSHAFT: A shaft in the engine on which are the lobes (cams) which operate the valves. The camshaft is driven by the crankshaft, via a belt, chain or gears, at one half the crankshaft speed.

CAPACITOR: A device which stores an electrical charge.

CARBON MONOXIDE (CO): A colorless, odorless gas given off as a normal byproduct of combustion. It is poisonous and extremely dangerous in confined areas, building up slowly to toxic levels without warning if adequate ventilation is not available.

CARBURETOR: A device, usually mounted on the intake manifold of an engine, which mixes the air and fuel in the proper proportion to allow even combustion.

CATALYTIC CONVERTER: A device installed in the exhaust system, like a muffler, that converts harmful byproducts of combustion into carbon dioxide and water vapor by means of a heat-producing chemical reaction.

CENTRIFUGAL ADVANCE: A mechanical method of advancing the spark timing by using flyweights in the distributor that react to centrifugal force generated by the distributor shaft rotation.

CHECK VALVE: Any one-way valve installed to permit the flow of air, fuel or vacuum in one direction only.

CHOKE: A device, usually a moveable valve, placed in the intake path of a carburetor to restrict the flow of air.

CIRCUIT: Any unbroken path through which an electrical current can flow. Also used to describe fuel flow in some instances.

CIRCUIT BREAKER: A switch which protects an electrical circuit from overload by opening the circuit when the current flow exceeds a predetermined level. Some circuit breakers must be reset manually, while most reset automatically.

COIL (IGNITION): A transformer in the ignition circuit which steps up the voltage provided to the spark plugs.

COMBINATION MANIFOLD: An assembly which includes both the intake and exhaust manifolds in one casting.

COMBINATION VALVE: A device used in some fuel systems that routes fuel vapors to a charcoal storage canister instead of venting them into the atmosphere. The valve relieves fuel tank pressure and allows fresh air into the tank as the fuel level drops to prevent a vapor lock situation.

COMPRESSION RATIO: The comparison of the total volume of the cylinder and combustion chamber with the piston at BDC and the piston at TDC.

CONDENSER: 1. An electrical device which acts to store an electrical charge, preventing voltage surges. 2. A radiator-like device in the air conditioning system in which refrigerant gas condenses into a liquid, giving off heat.

CONDUCTOR: Any material through which an electrical current can be transmitted easily.

CONTINUITY: Continuous or complete circuit. Can be checked with an ohmmeter.

COUNTERSHAFT: An intermediate shaft which is rotated by a mainshaft and transmits, in turn, that rotation to a working part.

CRANKCASE: The lower part of an engine in which the crankshaft and related parts operate.

CRANKSHAFT: The main driving shaft of an engine which receives reciprocating motion from the pistons and converts it to rotary motion.

CYLINDER: In an engine, the round hole in the engine block in which the piston(s) ride.

CYLINDER BLOCK: The main structural member of an engine in which is found the cylinders, crankshaft and other principal parts.

CYLINDER HEAD: The detachable portion of the engine, usually fastened to the top of the cylinder block and containing all or most of the combustion chambers. On overhead valve engines, it contains the valves and their operating parts. On overhead cam engines, it contains the camshaft as well.

DEAD CENTER: The extreme top or bottom of the piston stroke.

DETONATION: An unwanted explosion of the air/fuel mixture in the combustion chamber caused by excess heat and compression, advanced timing, or an overly lean mixture. Also referred to as "ping".

DIAPHRAGM: A thin, flexible wall separating two cavities, such as in a vacuum advance unit.

DIESELING: A condition in which hot spots in the combustion chamber cause the engine to run on after the key is turned off.

DIFFERENTIAL: A geared assembly which allows the transmission of motion between drive axles, giving one axle the ability to turn faster than the other.

DIODE: An electrical device that will allow current to flow in one direction only.

DISC BRAKE: A hydraulic braking assembly consisting of a brake disc, or rotor, mounted on an axle, and a caliper assembly containing, usually two brake pads which are activated by hydraulic pressure. The pads are forced against the sides of the disc, creating friction which slows the vehicle.

DISTRIBUTOR: A mechanically driven device on an engine which is responsible for electrically firing the spark plug at a predetermined point of the piston stroke.

DOWEL PIN: A pin, inserted in mating holes in two different parts allowing those parts to maintain a fixed relationship.

DRUM BRAKE: A braking system which consists of two brake shoes and one or two wheel cylinders, mounted on a fixed backing plate, and a brake drum, mounted on an axle, which revolves around the assembly.

DWELL: The rate, measured in degrees of shaft rotation, at which an electrical circuit cycles on and off.

ELECTRONIC CONTROL UNIT (ECU): Ignition module, module, amplifier or igniter. See Module for definition.

ELECTRONIC IGNITION: A system in which the timing and firing of the spark plugs is controlled by an electronic control unit, usually called a module. These systems have no points or condenser.

END-PLAY: The measured amount of axial movement in a shaft.

ENGINE: A device that converts heat into mechanical energy.

EXHAUST MANIFOLD: A set of cast passages or pipes which conduct exhaust gases from the engine.

FEELER GAUGE: A blade, usually metal, or precisely predetermined thickness, used to measure the clearance between two parts.

FIRING ORDER: The order in which combustion occurs in the cylinders of an engine. Also the order in which spark is distributed to the plugs by the distributor.

FLOODING: The presence of too much fuel in the intake manifold and combustion chamber which prevents the air/fuel mixture from firing, thereby causing a no-start situation.

FLYWHEEL: A disc shaped part bolted to the rear end of the crankshaft. Around the outer perimeter is affixed the ring gear. The starter drive engages the ring gear, turning the flywheel, which rotates the crankshaft, imparting the initial starting motion to the engine.

FOOT POUND (ft. lbs. or sometimes, ft.lb.): The amount of energy or work needed to raise an item weighing one pound, a distance of one foot.

FUSE: A protective device in a circuit which prevents circuit overload by breaking the circuit when a specific amperage is present. The device is constructed around a strip or wire of a lower amperage rating than the circuit it is designed to protect. When an amperage higher than that stamped on the fuse is present in the circuit, the strip or wire melts, opening the circuit.

GEAR RATIO: The ratio between the number of teeth on meshing gears.

GENERATOR: A device which converts mechanical energy into electrical energy.

HEAT RANGE: The measure of a spark plug's ability to dissipate heat from its firing end. The higher the heat range, the hotter the plug fires.

HUB: The center part of a wheel or gear.

HYDROCARBON (HC): Any chemical compound made up of hydrogen and carbon. A major pollutant formed by the engine as a byproduct of combustion.

HYDROMETER: An instrument used to measure the specific gravity of a solution.

INCH POUND (inch lbs.; sometimes in.lb. or in. lbs.): One twelfth of a foot pound.

INDUCTION: A means of transferring electrical energy in the form of a magnetic field. Principle used in the ignition coil to increase voltage.

INJECTOR: A device which receives metered fuel under relatively low pressure and is activated to inject the fuel into the engine under relatively high pressure at a predetermined time.

INPUT SHAFT: The shaft to which torque is applied, usually carrying the driving gear or gears.

INTAKE MANIFOLD: A casting of passages or pipes used to conduct air or a fuel/air mixture to the cylinders.

JOURNAL: The bearing surface within which a shaft operates.

KEY: A small block usually fitted in a notch between a shaft and a hub to prevent slippage of the two parts.

MANIFOLD: A casting of passages or set of pipes which connect the cylinders to an inlet or outlet source.

MANIFOLD VACUUM: Low pressure in an engine intake manifold formed just below the throttle plates. Manifold vacuum is highest at idle and drops under acceleration.

MASTER CYLINDER: The primary fluid pressurizing device in a hydraulic system. In automotive use, it is found in brake and hydraulic clutch systems and is pedal activated, either directly or, in a power brake system, through the power booster.

MODULE: Electronic control unit, amplifier or igniter of solid state or integrated design which controls the current flow in the ignition primary circuit based on input from the pick-up coil. When the module opens the primary circuit, high secondary voltage is induced in the coil.

NEEDLE BEARING: A bearing which consists of a number (usually a large number) of long, thin rollers.

OHM: (Ω) The unit used to measure the resistance of conductor-to-electrical flow. One ohm is the amount of resistance that limits current flow to one ampere in a circuit with one volt of pressure.

OHMMETER: An instrument used for measuring the resistance, in ohms, in an electrical circuit.

OUTPUT SHAFT: The shaft which transmits torque from a device, such as a transmission.

OVERDRIVE: A gear assembly which produces more shaft revolutions than that transmitted to it.

OVERHEAD CAMSHAFT (OHC): An engine configuration in which the camshaft is mounted on top of the cylinder head and operates the valve either directly or by means of rocker arms.

OVERHEAD VALVE (OHV): An engine configuration in which all of the valves are located in the cylinder head and the camshaft is located in the cylinder block. The camshaft operates the valves via lifters and pushrods.

OXIDES OF NITROGEN (NOx): Chemical compounds of nitrogen produced as a byproduct of combustion. They combine with hydrocarbons to produce smog.

OXYGEN SENSOR: Use with the feedback system to sense the presence of oxygen in the exhaust gas and signal the computer which can reference the voltage signal to an air/fuel ratio.

PINION: The smaller of two meshing gears.

PISTON RING: An open-ended ring with fits into a groove on the outer diameter of the piston. Its chief function is to form a seal between the piston and cylinder wall. Most automotive pistons have three rings: two for compression sealing; one for oil sealing.

PRELOAD: A predetermined load placed on a bearing during assembly or by adjustment.

PRIMARY CIRCUIT: the low voltage side of the ignition system which consists of the ignition switch, ballast resistor or resistance wire, bypass, coil, electronic control unit and pick-up coil as well as the connecting wires and harnesses.

PRESS FIT: The mating of two parts under pressure, due to the inner diameter of one being smaller than the outer diameter of the other, or vice versa; an interference fit.

RACE: The surface on the inner or outer ring of a bearing on which the balls, needles or rollers move.

REGULATOR: A device which maintains the amperage and/or voltage levels of a circuit at predetermined values.

RELAY: A switch which automatically opens and/or closes a circuit.

RESISTANCE: The opposition to the flow of current through a circuit or electrical device, and is measured in ohms. Resistance is equal to the voltage divided by the amperage.

RESISTOR: A device, usually made of wire, which offers a preset amount of resistance in an electrical circuit.

RING GEAR: The name given to a ring-shaped gear attached to a differential case, or affixed to a flywheel or as part of a planetary gear set.

ROLLER BEARING: A bearing made up of hardened inner and outer races between which hardened steel rollers move.

ROTOR: 1. The disc-shaped part of a disc brake assembly, upon which the brake pads bear; also called, brake disc. 2. The device mounted atop the distributor shaft, which passes current to the distributor cap tower contacts.

SECONDARY CIRCUIT: The high voltage side of the ignition system, usually above 20,000 volts. The secondary includes the ignition coil, coil wire, distributor cap and rotor, spark plug wires and spark plugs.

SENDING UNIT: A mechanical, electrical, hydraulic or electro-magnetic device which transmits information to a gauge.

SENSOR: Any device designed to measure engine operating conditions or ambient pressures and temperatures. Usually electronic in nature and designed to send a voltage signal to an on-board computer, some sensors may operate as a simple on/off switch or they may provide a variable voltage signal (like a potentiometer) as conditions or measured parameters change.

SHIM: Spacers of precise, predetermined thickness used between parts to establish a proper working relationship.

SLAVE CYLINDER: In automotive use, a device in the hydraulic clutch system which is activated by hydraulic force, disengaging the clutch.

SOLENOID: A coil used to produce a magnetic field, the effect of which is to produce work.

SPARK PLUG: A device screwed into the combustion chamber of a spark ignition engine. The basic construction is a conductive core inside of a ceramic insulator, mounted in an outer conductive base. An electrical charge from the spark plug wire travels along the conductive core and jumps a preset air gap to a grounding point or points at the end of the conductive base. The resultant spark ignites the fuel/air mixture in the combustion chamber.

SPLINES: Ridges machined or cast onto the outer diameter of a shaft or inner diameter of a bore to enable parts to mate without rotation.

TACHOMETER: A device used to measure the rotary speed of an engine, shaft, gear, etc., usually in rotations per minute.

THERMOSTAT: A valve, located in the cooling system of an engine, which is closed when cold and opens gradually in response to engine heating, controlling the temperature of the coolant and rate of coolant flow.

TOP DEAD CENTER (TDC): The point at which the piston reaches the top of its travel on the compression stroke.

TORQUE: The twisting force applied to an object.

TORQUE CONVERTER: A turbine used to transmit power from a driving member to a driven member via hydraulic action, providing changes in drive ratio and torque. In automotive use, it links the driveplate at the rear of the engine to the automatic transmission.

TRANSDUCER: A device used to change a force into an electrical signal.

TRANSISTOR: A semi-conductor component which can be actuated by a small voltage to perform an electrical switching function.

TUNE-UP: A regular maintenance function, usually associated with the replacement and adjustment of parts and components in the electrical and fuel systems of a vehicle for the purpose of attaining optimum performance.

TURBOCHARGER: An exhaust driven pump which compresses intake air and forces it into the combustion chambers at higher than atmospheric pressures. The increased air pressure allows more fuel to be burned and results in increased horsepower being produced.

VACUUM ADVANCE: A device which advances the ignition timing in response to increased engine vacuum.

VACUUM GAUGE: An instrument used to measure the presence of vacuum in a chamber.

VALVE: A device which control the pressure, direction of flow or rate of flow of a liquid or gas.

VALVE CLEARANCE: The measured gap between the end of the valve stem and the rocker arm, cam lobe or follower that activates the valve.

VISCOSITY: The rating of a liquid's internal resistance to flow.

VOLTMETER: An instrument used for measuring electrical force in units called volts. Voltmeters are always connected parallel with the circuit being tested.

WHEEL CYLINDER: Found in the automotive drum brake assembly, it is a device, actuated by hydraulic pressure, which, through internal pistons, pushes the brake shoes outward against the drums.

MASTER INDEX

D

DASHBOARD
switches, replacement, 12-8
trim panels, removal and installation, 11-17
DAYTIME RUNNING LIGHTS (DRL), GENERAL INFORMATION, 12-22
DEFOGGER, REAR WINDOW, CHECK AND REPAIR, 12-13
DIAGNOSIS, 0-23
DIAGNOSTIC TROUBLE CODES, ACCESSING, 6-2
DISC BRAKE
caliper, removal and installation, 9-6
disc, inspection, removal and installation, 9-7
pads, replacement, 9-3
DISCONNECTING FUEL LINE FITTINGS, 4-5
DOOR
latch, lock cylinder and handles, removal and installation, 11-14
removal and installation, 11-13
trim panels, removal and installation, 11-12
window glass regulator, removal and installation, 11-15
window glass, removal and installation, 11-15
DRIVEAXLE
boot
check, 1-20
replacement, 8-9
intermediate shaft, removal and installation, 8-9
oil seals, replacement, 7A-2
removal and installation, 8-7
DRIVEBELT
check and replacement, 1-24
tensioner, replacement, 1-25
DRUM BRAKE SHOES, REPLACEMENT, 9-9

E

ELECTRIC SIDE VIEW MIRRORS, GENERAL INFORMATION, 12-21
ELECTRICAL LOAD DETECTOR (ELD) UNIT, REPLACEMENT, 6-17
ELECTRICAL TROUBLESHOOTING, GENERAL INFORMATION, 12-2
EMISSIONS AND ENGINE CONTROL SYSTEMS, 6-1
ENGINE COOLANT TEMPERATURE (ECT) SENSOR, REPLACEMENT, 6-18
ENGINE COOLANT, LEVEL CHECK, 1-8
ENGINE COOLING FANS AND SWITCH, CHECK AND REPLACEMENT, 3-6
ENGINE ELECTRICAL SYSTEMS, 5-1
ENGINE FRONT COVER, FOUR-CYLINDER ENGINE, REMOVAL AND INSTALLATION, 2A-7

ENGINE, GENERAL OVERHAUL PROCEDURES, 2C-1
crankshaft, removal and installation, 2C-18
cylinder compression check, 2C-4
engine overhaul
disassembly sequence, 2C-11
reassembly sequence, 2C-20
engine rebuilding alternatives, 2C-7
engine removal, methods and precautions, 2C-7
engine, removal and installation, 2C-8
general information, 2C-2
initial start-up and break-in after overhaul, 2C-21
oil pressure check, 2C-4
pistons and connecting rods, removal and installation, 2C-12
vacuum gauge diagnostic checks, 2C-5
ENGINE, IN-VEHICLE REPAIR PROCEDURES
Four-cylinder engine, 2A-1
balance shaft assembly and balance shafts, removal, inspection and installation, 2A-14
camshafts and rocker arms, removal, inspection and installation, 2A-10
crankshaft pulley and front oil seal, removal and installation, 2A-8
cylinder head, removal and installation, 2A-11
engine front cover, removal and installation, 2A-7
Engine Mount Control System, description and check, 2A-18
exhaust manifold, removal and installation, 2A-6
flywheel/driveplate, removal and installation, 2A-15
intake manifold and injector base, removal and installation, 2A-4
i-VTEC system, description and component checks, 2A-9
oil pan, removal and installation, 2A-12
oil pump, removal, inspection and installation, 2A-13
powertrain mounts, check and replacement, 2A-16
rear main oil seal, replacement, 2A-15
repair operations possible with the engine in the vehicle, 2A-2
timing chain and sprockets, removal, inspection and installation, 2A-7
Top Dead Center (TDC) for number 1 piston, locating, 2A-2
valve clearance check and adjustment, 2A-3
valve cover, removal and installation, 2A-3
water passage, removal and installation, 2A-16
V6 engine, 2B-1
camshafts, removal, inspection and installation, 2B-14
crankshaft front oil seal, replacement, 2B-10
cylinder heads, removal and installation, 2B-16
Engine Mount Control System, description and check, 2B-20
exhaust manifold, removal and installation, 2B-7
flywheel/driveplate, removal and installation, 2B-19
intake manifold, removal and installation, 2B-5
oil pan, removal and installation, 2B-17
oil pump, removal, inspection and installation, 2B-18
powertrain mounts, check and replacement, 2B-20
rear main oil seal, replacement, 2B-20